INQUISI
EYES

Slade Painters in Edwardian Wessex

INQUISITIVE EYES

Gwen Yarker

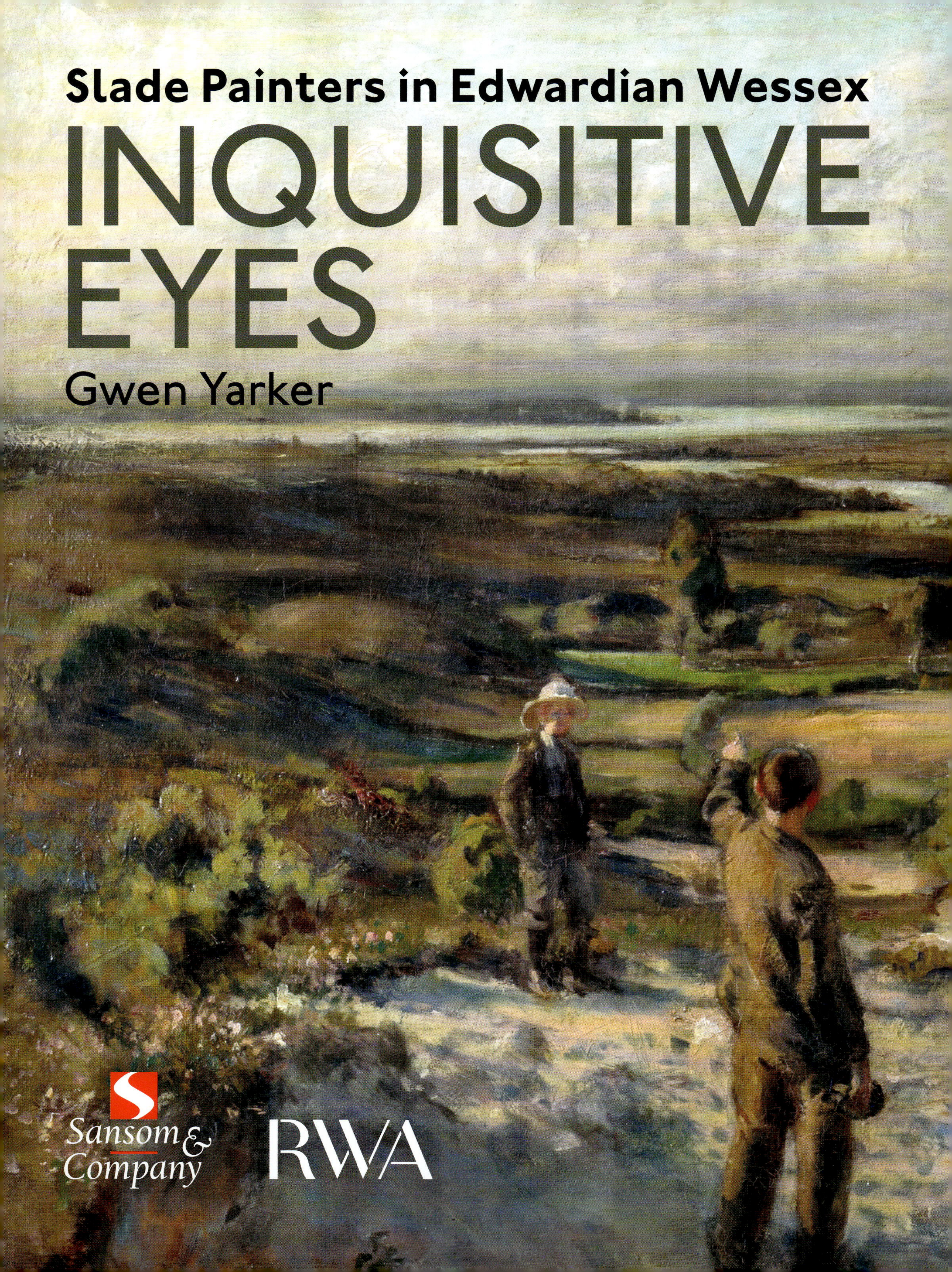

Sansom & Company

RWA

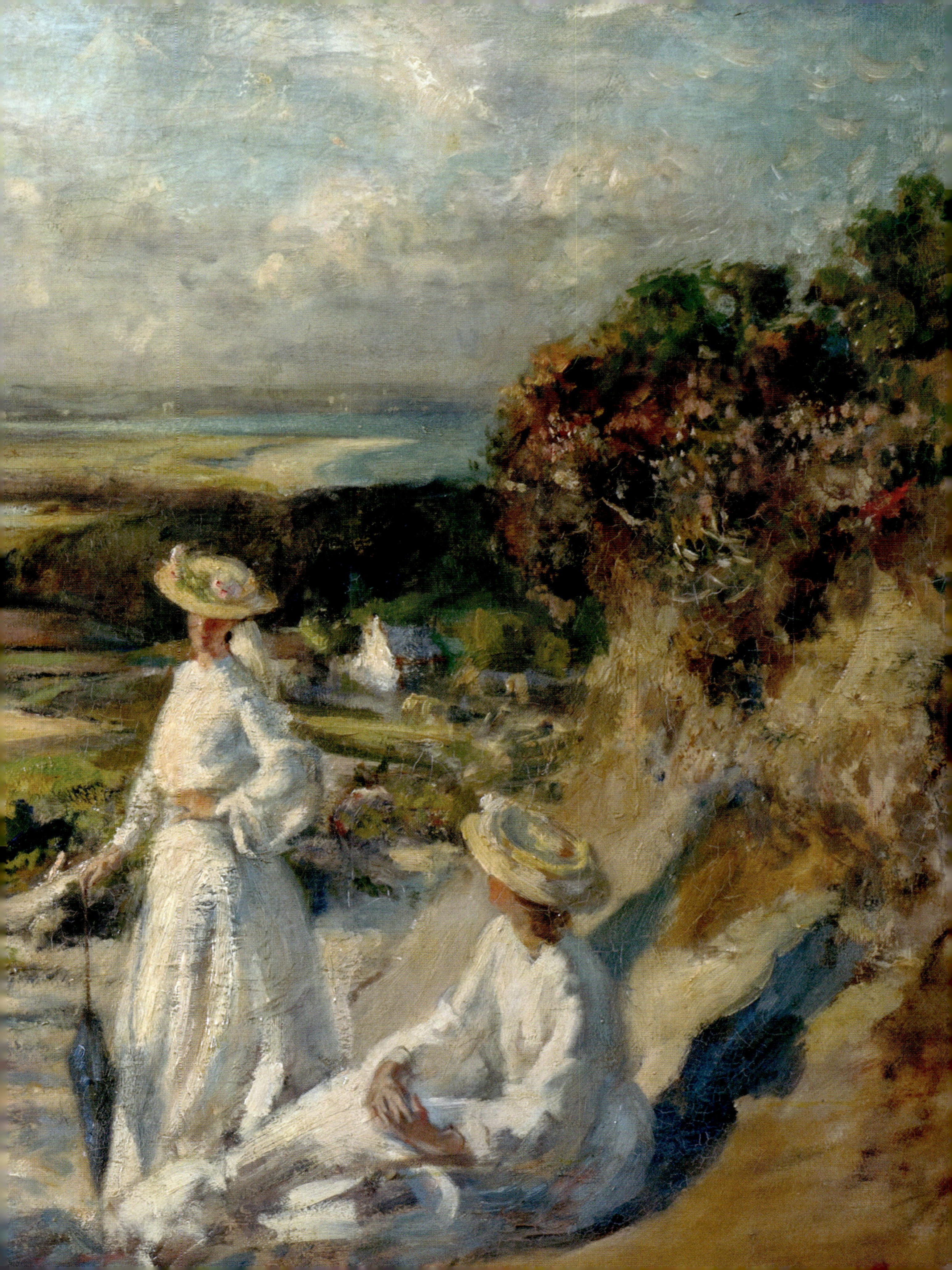

First published in 2016 by Sansom & Co
a publishing imprint of Redcliffe Press Ltd.,
81G Pembroke Road, Bristol BS8 3EA

info@sansomandcompany.co.uk
www.sansomandcompany.co.uk

Published in conjunction with the exhibition at the
Royal West of England Academy, Bristol BS8 1PX,
6 February–12 June 2016

Delivered in partnership with the National Maritime Museum, part
of Royal Museums Greenwich, and supported by The Foyle Foundation
and the Paul Mellon Centre for Studies in British Art.

NATIONAL MARITIME MUSEUM FOYLE FOUNDATION PAUL MELLON CENTRE for Studies in British Art

ISBN 978-1-908326-85-0

British Library Cataloguing-in-Publication Data
A catalogue record for this book is available from the British Library

Design and typesetting by E&P Design
Printed and bound by Cambrian Printers Ltd

Front cover: Augustus John, *The Blue Pool* (detail), 1911, oil on panel
© estate of Augustus John/Aberdeen Art Gallery and Museum, Scotland/Bridgeman Images
Frontispiece: Henry Tonks, *The Lost Path* (detail), 1905, oil on canvas
private collection

CONTENTS

INTRODUCTION

> The whole country was like a Steer and so was the day. I expected to see many Sladites perched on the surrounding hills like myself, but luckily the season was too late for them and all have disappeared.
> VANESSA BELL, 1910[1]

Inquisitive Eyes: Slade Painters in Edwardian Wessex looks at the specific moment between 1880 and 1914 when landscapes produced in Dorset were at the forefront of modern British art, from the Impressionism of Philip Wilson Steer and Henry Tonks, to the work of Augustus John and Bloomsbury painters Vanessa Bell and Roger Fry. By 1910 the Dorset landscape had become so intrinsically associated with Steer and the 'Sladites' that Vanessa Bell saw the 'Isle' of Purbeck, not just as Thomas Hardy's Wessex, but through the lens of Steer. The purpose of this book, and associated exhibition, is to examine how this happened and to recover the important role that the landscape of Wessex played in the development of British art in the decades before the First World War. Building on the work of art historians Lisa Tickner, Ysanne Holt, Kenneth McConkey and Tim Barringer, this book looks at the key paintings produced in Purbeck during the period.[2] This account also includes the recovery of female Slade painters, such as Evelyn Cheston, Katherine Everett and Helen McNicoll.

Two main themes run through my narrative. The first charts the evolution of British approaches to landscape in the first decades of the twentieth century, through the recognition of Dorset as a location that attracted a diverse range of painters. Massive artistic activity over the period saw almost 300 painters working in Purbeck, frequently exhibiting these Dorset views in London.[3] This volume of work suggested the possibility of examining the material with a geographical rather than stylistic focus. This approach has clear parallels with recent studies into artists at St Ives, Newyln and Staithes and raises the prospect of reading Dorset as another such artists' colony.[4] It is important, however, to make the qualified distinction that, unlike Newlyn and St Ives, Dorset was not home to any 'schools' of art, so that painters were not visiting to study, but to paint the landscape *en plein air* for exhibiting in London. Whilst other writers have adopted a geographic approach to artists in Dorset, for example James Wilkes, who has also highlighted the complexity of reading the Purbeck landscape through the Studland paintings of Vanessa Bell, and Ilay Cooper's

1. Letter from Vanessa Bell to Virginia Woolf, 3 October 1910, Berg Collection, NYPL (New York Public Library), cited in Lisa Tickner, *Modern Life and Modern Subjects: British Art in the Early Twentieth Century*, New Haven and London: Yale University Press, 2000, p.133, fn.60.
2. Tickner; Ysanne Holt, *British Artists and the Modernist Landscape*, Surrey: Ashgate, 2003; Kenneth McConkey, *The New English: A History of the New English Art Club*, London: Royal Academy of Arts, 2006, p.98, fn.6; Tim Barringer, '"There's the Life for a Man Like Me": Rural Life and Labour in Edwardian Art and Music', Angus Trumble and Andrea Wolk Rager, eds, *Edwardian Opulence: British Art at the Dawn of the Twentieth Century*, New Haven and London: Yale University Press, 2013.
3. I am indebted to Bob Field, whose research is revealing the huge number of artists working in Purbeck.
4. Writing on the burgeoning artistic colony at St Ives, Marion Whybrow and David Tovey have taken a similar geographic approach to painters visiting and settling there from the 1880s. See Marion Whybrow, *St Ives, 1893–1993: Portrait of an Art Colony*, Suffolk: ACC Art Books, 1994, and David Tovey, *Pioneers of St Ives Art at Home and Abroad, 1889–1914*, Tewkesbury: Wilson Books, 2008. For an analysis of artists' colonies, particularly artists working at Staithes over the same period, see Robert Slater, *Artists' Colonies in Staithes and Runswick Bay, c.1880–1914*, unpublished doctoral thesis submitted for the degree of Doctor of Philosophy, University of Leicester, March 2010.

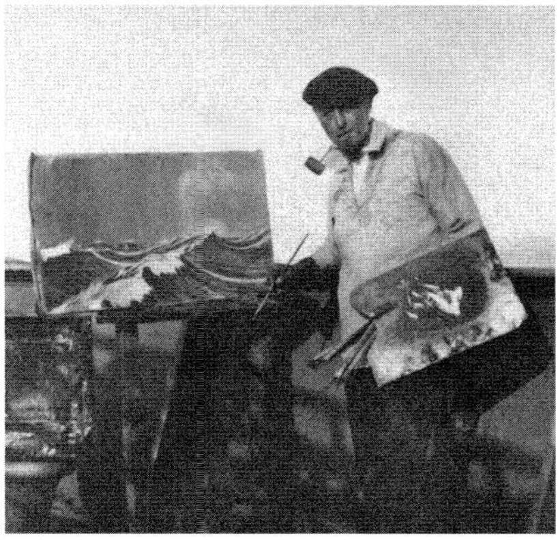

FIG. 1
John Everett painting at sea, c.1902
photograph Katherine Everett; private collection

recent examination of the Spencer Watsons at Purbeck, this study covers a more precise story, presenting the reasons why the artists in question came to this area between 1880 and 1914.[5]

The second theme running through my text relates to the recovery of the personal and artistic networks surrounding the Dorset-born painter John Everett, which drew artists to Dorset in the first two decades of the twentieth century. This throws up critical new detail about the life and work of an important circle of Slade painters, including William Orpen and Augustus John.

Born in Dorset, John Everett (fig. 1) joined the Slade School of Art in London in October 1896, where his tutors were Henry Tonks, Philip Wilson Steer, Frederick (Fred) Brown and Walter Westley Russell. Everett's remarkable group of fellow students included Orpen and John, who both rented rooms in his mother Augusta's house at 21 Fitzroy Street, near Tottenham Court Road, between 1896 and 1901. Nicknamed 'the Newcomes', after Thackeray's novel of the same name, this bohemian salon, with Augusta at its heart and where students Augustus and Gwen John, William Orpen, William Crampton Gore and Grace Westray all rented rooms, resulted in an extraordinarily creative period as Everett's close associates influenced each other at the start of their careers. Talented as a draughtsman and painter, Everett enjoyed a close friendship with John and Orpen at the beginning of their careers, exhibiting with them at the New English Art Club, but it was surely also Everett's misfortune to attend the Slade with such formidable talents. Although in their artistic shadow, a lifelong friendship was forged between John, Orpen and Everett. This is confirmed through a considerable body of largely overlooked illustrated letters from Orpen to Everett, some of which feature in this book, as well as by my rediscovery of Everett's manuscript memoirs in a private collection. The latter was described by John Rothenstein as 'an extremely candid and detailed record', and it places Everett at the centre of the most remarkable group of Slade painters at the outset of their careers.[6] Full of incident, commentary and opinion, his account details the students and tutors who visited him in Dorset up to 1914.

This study demonstrates that Everett was instrumental in persuading artists to visit Purbeck, leading to the realization that Dorset actually played host to major figures such as Philip Wilson Steer, whose most important mature landscapes were made whilst staying close to Everett, and Henry Tonks, whose *The Lost Path* (1905) and *Summer* (1908) both relied on Everett's wife as a model and were painted in Purbeck. Augustus John sought Everett's help in finding him a home in Dorset for his large family and dependants, resulting in their move in 1911 to Alderney Manor, owned by Everett's aunt Lady Wimborne.

This project is the result of new research, originating from a Caird Fellowship at the National Maritime Museum, which enabled me to examine their large Everett collection of over 1,000 oils, 1,000 works on paper and more than 350 sketchbooks. Despite this considerable body of work no one has attempted to research or publish Everett's life and he has largely been regarded as a maritime painter.[7] My research led to the realization that Everett was also a prolific painter of landscapes. Examining the oil

5. See Peter Davies, *Art in Poole and Dorset*, Poole: Poole Historic Trust, 1987; Vivienne Light, *Circles and Tangents: Art in the Shadow of Cranborne Chase*, Frome: Canterton Books, 2011, 2012; and James Wilkes, *A Fractured Landscape of Modernity: Culture and Conflict in the Isle of Purbeck*, Basingstoke: Palgrave Macmillan, 2014.
6. John Everett, *Wicked Devils, Wicked Devils*, unpublished manuscript memoirs, 1945, private collection; John Rothenstein, 'Augustus John', *Modern English Painters: Sickert to Smith*, London: Eyre & Spottiswoode, 1952, p.178.
7. 'Last Will and Testament of Herbert Barnard Everett', 6 Finchley Place, London NW8, 30 September 1946; Everett bequeathed his marine work, 'Every thing [sic] with a ship or boat in it', to the NMM.

sketches resulted in a clearer understanding of his extant Dorset work, while Everett's sketchbooks provided an outline chronology (albeit somewhat confounded by his habit of using up empty pages years later).

As a man of private means, Everett was free from the need to satisfy patrons or dealers and this enabled him to combine his dual passions for painting and sailing, initially in deep-sea sailing ships to Australia and New Zealand and later in steamers across the Atlantic or to the Mediterranean. A lively autobiography, *Bricks and Flowers*, published by Everett's estranged wife Katherine soon after his death, is perhaps more entertaining than accurate.[8] The rediscovered correspondence with Everett from Orpen, Henry Tonks, Charles Conder, William Crampton Gore, John and even Thomas Hardy provides a rich source of anecdote and supports the idea that these artists were linked until the First World War. The drawings and letters from Orpen to Everett illustrate their easy relationship and demonstrate that the former students remained close to their tutor Henry Tonks.

Although many of the paintings in the book are now in public institutions, retrieving others still in private collections formed a key part of this project. This brings to notice works not seen for almost one hundred years, such as Steer's Dorset views and, in the case of Tonks' *The Lost Path,* works hitherto untraced. The group of Orpen watercolours, once owned by Everett, were last shown at an exhibition at the Royal Academy in 1933. Everett's own work is seen for the first time in this book in this Dorset context, together with paintings by artists who trained with him, or exhibited at the New English and Royal Academy, but are now overlooked, such as Evelyn Cheston, Harry van der Weyden, Arthur Friedenson and Helen McNicoll. The retrieval of Everett's life and activities therefore brings new contexts and lost associations to familiar works, redefining the emergence of British landscape painting in the early twentieth century and providing a specific geographical context to a previously diffuse story of stylistic evolution.

Gwen Yarker
February 2016

ABBREVIATIONS USED THROUGHOUT THE BOOK

DNHAS: Dorset Natural History and Archaeological Society (formerly Dorset Field Club)
New English: New English Art Club
NMM: National Maritime Museum, London
RA: Royal Academy, London
RWA: Royal West of England Academy, Bristol
Slade: Slade School of Fine Art, University College, London (UCL)

8. Katherine Everett, *Bricks and Flowers: Memoirs of Katherine Everett*, London: Constable, 1949, reprint 1951. Only Katherine referred to her mother-in-law Augusta Everett as Aurelia; she was otherwise known by her baptized name, Augusta.

ONE

INTRODUCING WESSEX

> The Wessex of romance is gradually becoming the Wessex of the twentieth century. Alas! that it should be so.[1]

The writer David Cecil described Dorset as a 'land of downs and moor and woodlands and beech groves and clumps of yew and steep chalky escarpments', accommodating relatively modest country houses and small agricultural estates.[2] At the turn of the twentieth century rural life in Dorset still marched to the rhythm of the eighteenth. The primary industry, agriculture, was in decline, partly through increased mechanization. The population in 1891 was 194,517, with market towns like Wareham, Sherborne, Sturminster Newton, Shaftesbury, Blandford and Wimborne operating as semi-autonomous areas, with the county town of Dorchester dominating.[3] Writing in the *Art Journal* in 1901, the artist Arthur Tomson described Dorchester as the centre of a 'peculiarly rural population'.[4] Noting that on market day:

> for miles around, on all the roads that lead to Dorchester, the sheep may be seen moving slowly, and in dry weather in dense clouds of dust ... Few people have at hand a greater variety of landscape to enjoy than the inhabitants of Dorchester. Wander where you may, you are sure to find extensive views or pleasant solitudes.[5]

Most populous was the ancient seaport of Poole, whose picturesque quay and quaint narrow streets hinted at its colourful maritime past, and which Augustus John called 'a centre for Breton onion-men'.[6] The tall masts of sailing ships, importing Baltic and Russian timber, and exporting Purbeck stone and clay, created an appealing scenic backdrop for painters. On the waterfront Poole Pottery, using local clay, started in 1873, after Jesse Carter bought a broken-down pottery site and developed a company Roger Fry later worked with. The area around Wareham and Corfe had supplied clay to potteries like Wedgwood for over 150 years, leaving behind landscape features much admired by painters. Portland and Purbeck limestone quarrying had long been an important source of wealth for Dorset, together with chalk quarrying to make lime. But around 1900 all this was about to change as Dorset opened up to new industries and increased tourism.

1. C. Holland, 'The Work of Frederick Whitehead, a Painter of Thomas Hardy's "Wessex"', *The Studio*, 1904, June no. 135, vol. xxxii, pp.105–19. Frederick Whitehead cited p 116. Clive Holland is the pseudonym for Charles James Hankinson.
2. David Cecil, 'Introduction', *Some Dorset Country Houses: A Personal Selection*, Wimborne: The Dovecote Press, 1985, p.2.
3. W. Mate, *Dorsetshire Illustrated 1900*, W. Mate and Sons, Illustrated Guides, Dewsbury: reprint by Chantry Press, 1986, p.4.
4. A. Tomson, 'Dorchester', *The Art Journal*, 1901, pp.231–5.
5. Ibid, p.233, 'The Frome strikes me as an exceedingly impressionable river, full of drama during the winter, but in the summer, especially in the early summer, it moves like a man of leisure and one full of infinite content ... Quaintly placed villages there are plenty, within half-a-dozen miles of Dorchester; some almost in the water-meadows, and some on higher ground, but none built very high up on the downs and hills. Everywhere there are picturesque groups of trees, and everywhere, in water-meadow or on down, a pastoral life is proceeding, that is of much the same interest and importance in the Dorset landscapes, as are the figures and animals in the pictures by Constable and David Cox', p.233.
6. Augustus John, *Chiarascuro: Fragments of Autobiography*, London: Jonathan Cape, 1952, p.104. Although this sounds facetious, Everett's drawing of Poole onion-men confirms John's observation.

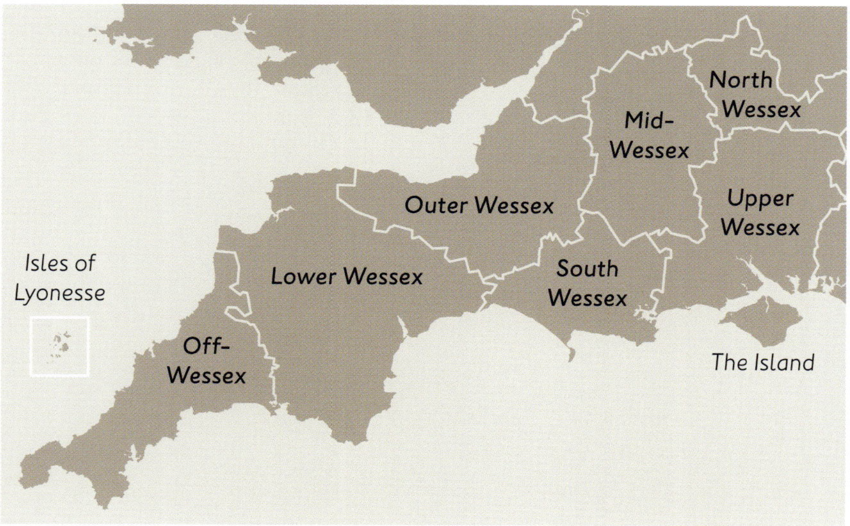

FIG. 2
Thomas Hardy's Wessex

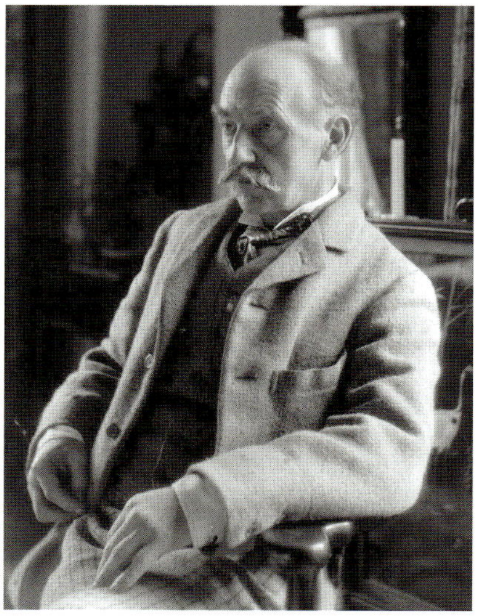

FIG. 3
Thomas Hardy, c.1894
glossy bromide print by Clive Holland; © National Portrait Gallery, London

THE HARDY EFFECT

Towards the end of the nineteenth century, the Dorset countryside seemed almost indistinguishable from the writings of Thomas Hardy (fig. 3). His novels and characters were steeped in the Dorset downs and heath, detailing the rural daily life increasingly perceived through his novels. Dorset became defined as 'Hardy country', emulating 'Shakespeare' or 'Constable' country.[7] Conscious of the explicitly local nature of his work, Hardy evoked the ancient kingdom of Wessex as the territorial definition that offered him a broad context in which to place his work, which was often steeped in folklore, adding to its wildness, mystique and sense of prehistory. The term first appeared in the *Mayor of Casterbridge* in 1886, and was intended by Hardy to provide unity and cohesion of place, with Dorset acknowledged to be South Wessex (fig. 2).[8] Although Hardy's concept constantly evolved, it evoked an ancient world within, belying the modern thrum of cars and railways.[9] The quaintness of the Dorset dialect meticulously recorded by William Barnes and evocatively used by Hardy was seen to link it with ancient Britons. From the late 1880s this Hardy-effect influenced artists painting in the county, whilst Hardy keenly reviewed their interpretations of 'his' landscape through their exhibitions and through work he saw being done in the area.[10] Arguably, his encouragement contributed to the influx of landscape painters working in the county *en plein air*, as the favoured method of capturing the landscape, from the painter Frederick Whitehead onwards.

Whitehead travelled in France, studying at the Académie Julian and working at Barbizon, where he learned to paint *plein air* landscapes in varying light and conditions. In Dorset Whitehead adopted a lifestyle later assumed by Augustus John, spending six months each year living in his caravan, 'The Rambler', with a small portable studio for painting in all weathers (fig. 4). Whitehead's wife Beatrice, who hailed from Dorchester, even dressed as a gypsy and told fortunes. With Hardy's encouragement, Whitehead was in Dorset painting landscapes by 1893, the year he exhibited *Tess of*

7. See Holland. Both Whitehead and Arthur Meade married Dorchester girls.
8. See Sidney Heath, *The Heart of Wessex*, London: Blackie and Son Limited, 1910; Saxleby, F. Outwin, *A Thomas Hardy Dictionary*, London: Kegan Paul, 1911; Clive Holland, *Wessex*, illustrated by Walter Tyndale, London: Adam and Charles Black, 1906.
9. Letter from Thomas Hardy, Hôtel de la Poste, 28 Fossé Aux Loups, Brussels, 28 September 1896 to Bertram Windle, Richard Little Purdy and Michael Millgate, eds, *The Collected Letters of Thomas Hardy*, vol. 2, Oxford: Clarendon Press, 1980, pp.131–3.
10. Whitehead exhibited 50 Dorset and Wiltshire pictures in Dorchester, 4 February 1897.

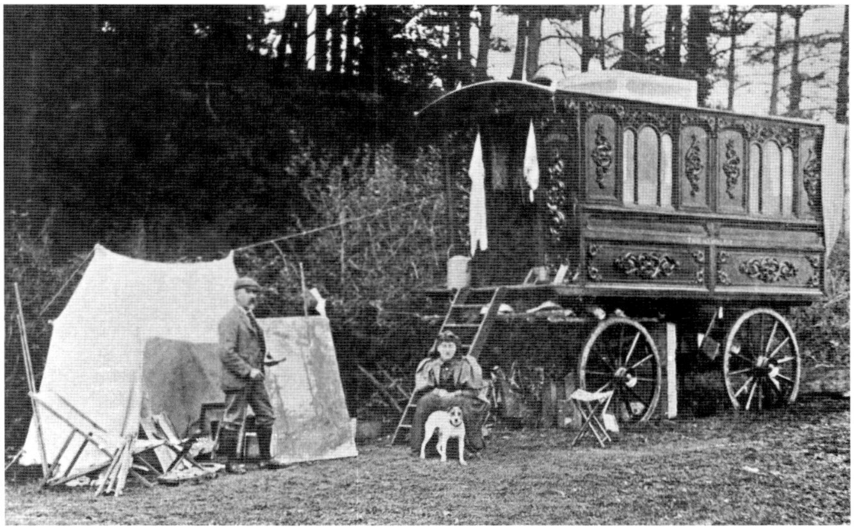

FIG. 4

Frederick and Beatrice Whitehead by their caravan 'Rambler', c.1897

© DNHAS; courtesy Dorset County Museum

the D'Urbervilles' Ancestral Home at the Royal Academy and also married Beatrice. Whitehead considered Hardy's Wessex an atmospheric, 'coy' land of cottages, streams and heath … 'if one wishes to paint Nature one must study her not only under the conditions for which one on any particular occasion seeks, but always and under every fickle change.'[11]

An announcement in the *Dorset County Chronicle* in May 1895 sought artists' work promoting the 'picturesqueness' of Dorset and 'Especially Illustrative of Thomas Hardy's Tales' for an exhibition at Dickenson and Foster's New Bond Street Gallery. Two hundred Wessex views, under a Hardyesque heading, featured in the show, visited by the Princess of Wales and the Crown Prince of Denmark.[12] By the late 1890s Helen Allingham had also exhibited small watercolours of Dorset's rustic countryside, highlighting the cottages and villagers of a fast disappearing way of life.[13] Allingham provided 12 illustrations for the 1874 serialization of Hardy's novel *Far from the Madding Crowd* in the *Cornhill Magazine* before she visited Dorset, leading to generalized illustrations providing a backdrop to the human drama.[14]

There is much evidence to suggest that Hardy actively engaged with artists painting the Dorset countryside, like Whitehead, Arthur Meade and William Wiehe Collins.[15] In correspondence with amateur water-colourist and Dorset chronicler, Henry Joseph Moule, Hardy made explicit references to locations and scenes in his writing that he suggested artists might paint, before concluding that the autonomy of his fictional Wessex should be left intact.[16] Hardy's wife Emma was also interested in Whitehead's paintings, and wrote poetry to accompany his work.[17] Her oil painting *Bulbarrow*, 1897 (DNHAS), is prominently inscribed 'after Whitehead'.[18] Artists were quick to exploit the commercial benefits of a Hardy connection in the Bond Street exhibitions of 1895 and 1896.[19] The writer Holland observed that Dickenson and Foster's Wessex exhibition, 'Thomas Hardy's Country', attracted 'considerable attention outside art circles because of

11. Holland p.108.
12. 'Notices', *Dorset County Chronicle*, 25 July 1895, p.4. The 1895 'Wessex' exhibition exclusively featured Dorset, with an engraving of Whitehead's major painting, *East Stoke Mill*, on the cover. Artists featured were Frederick Whitehead, Henry John Yeend King, Professor Hubert Herkomer, Arthur Meade, C.J. Barraud, Douglas Fox Pitt, Alfred Parsons, Newton Bennett and Camille Vernede.
13. In an email discussion with the author, 12 October 2013, Annabel Watts confirmed that Allingham's watercolours of Dorset subjects date from the late 1890s. 'In the case of Dorset, she painted around the Bridport area in particular. One or two of her exhibited works were garden scenes but most of them are of thatched cottages and farmhouses. Since she and her husband, William, had lived in Surrey in the 1880s they were fully aware of the concern highlighted by the likes of John Ruskin and William Morris about the demolition of ancient buildings, which was a topical subject at the time. Owing to her attention to detail, Helen Allingham's watercolours are a valuable and accurate record of humble, and usually overlooked, rustic homes and their regional variations of building materials' See too Anne Helmreich, 'The Marketing of Helen Allingham: The English Cottage and National Identity', Steven Adams and Anna Gruetzner Robins, eds, *Gendering Landscape Art*, Manchester: Manchester University Press and Rutgers University Press, 2000, pp.45–60.
14. A regular contributor to the *Illustrated London News*, Allingham was commissioned by editor Leslie Stephen, without Hardy's knowledge, to provide full-page plates and vignettes for the serialized version of *Far from the Madding Crowd* (1874), in the *Cornhill Magazine*. Only illustration 11, featured in the November edition, is a recognizable Dorset landscape.
15. F.H. Haines, 'Frederick W.N. Whitehead', *The Dorset Year Book*, Society of Dorset Men, 1938, p.11.
16. See Gwen Yarker, *A Victorian's View of Dorset: The Life and Watercolours of Henry Joseph Moule, 1825–1904*, Dorchester: Henry Ling, 1997. Everett collaborated, with Hardy's knowledge, on a series of oils, drawings and prints based on Hardy Country in 1924, now in the collection of DNHAS.
17. Whitehead's *The River Frome, Moreton, Near Dorchester*, 1901, oil on canvas, 90.30 x 70 cm, was accompanied by Emma Hardy's untitled poem, 'Where the River Stilled Its Depths by the Weir, the Painter Sat Apart' … See Peter Nahum, Leicester Galleries archive.
18. *Bulbarrow*, E.L. Hardy, inscribed 'after Whitehead', oil on canvas, 23 x 38 cm, ART2230, DNHAS Collection.
19. The 1896 Dickenson & Foster show, 'West Country Scenery', included Dorset subjects by Frederick Whitehead, C.J. Barraud, H. Fisher, A. Mansel, Douglas Fox Pitt and Tom Trythall Rowe.

Mr. Hardy's connection with the county'.[20] Authors, too, caught on, with various books published on Hardy's Dorset during the decade, such as C.G. Harper's *The Hardy Country*, 1905.[21] Hardy mourned the passing of rural ways and its impact on 'his' countryside with the word-pictures he created in his writings. This, perhaps, left little room for any artist to attempt social realism focusing on workers in the fields, with the emphasis placed, instead, on location. This is true of the Slade and New English painters in Dorset during the first decade of the century attuned to the Hardyean-Wessex effect. Former Slade students Charles and Evelyn Cheston rented a house at Studland in 1906. Relishing Hardy's descriptions of 'every hamlet of cob and thatch', Cheston wrote of their conscious reading of Hardy's novels in the evening and then painting the landscape during the day. Aiming at spontaneity and a more intuitive response to the landscape, the primary concern became capturing the scene through colour and light, to reflect ever-changing weather or moods of landscape and sea.

In *Howard's End*, published in 1910, E.M. Forster presented the Dorset landscape as a parable for the state of England and its countryside.

> If one wanted to show a foreigner England, perhaps the wisest course would be to take him to the final section of the Purbeck Hills, and stand him on their summit, a few miles to the east of Corfe. Then system after system of our island would roll together under his feet. Beneath him is the valley of the Frome, and all the wild lands that come tossing down from Dorchester, black and gold, to mirror their gorse in the expanses of Poole ... Nor is Suburbia absent. Bournemouth's ignoble coast cowers to the right, heralding the pine-trees that mean, for all their beauty, red houses and the Stock Exchange, and extend to the gates of London itself ...[22]

The county suggested an ancient, timeless world contrasting with the inexorable westerly march of Bournemouth's accreting suburbs. Described by Hardy in 1891 'as a city of detached mansions; a Mediterranean lounging-place on the English Channel', Dorset's close neighbour in Hampshire heralded the new, unfamiliar world order posited by Forster.[23] Bournemouth represented urbanization, with major building projects rapidly changing the face of the region, at odds with the slower pace of rural Dorset, imbued with nostalgic readings of Hardy's novels. With the speculative growth of Bournemouth and Swanage during the late nineteenth century, a housing scheme, Studland Bay Estate, was proposed with villas to be constructed at Studland, supplied by a brickworks established on the heath.[24] Aggressively promoted, in the end only the brickworks ever came to fruition, but this, combined with a possible rail link over the bay during the 1900s, reflected growing pressure for development of the area, which by 1915 convinced the illustrator and author Sidney Heath that Studland's picturesque qualities would soon be a thing of the past.

As the new century dawned, the huge success of Hardy's writing, combined with an influx of motorcars and mass media, was opening up the Dorset countryside. Alive to these rapid changes, writers like Hardy and Forster lamented creeping suburbanization, industrialization and human intervention specifically in Dorset, a conflict impacting on artistic as well as literary evocations of the county.[25] Forster acknowledged the profound influence on the countryside brought about through the burgeoning

20. Holland, p.110. Hardy scholars, Michael Millgate and James Gibson, suggest Holland's enthusiasm was anathema to Hardy.
21. See Bertram C.A. Windle, *The Wessex of Thomas Hardy*, London: John Lane, 1906; Wilkinson Sherren, *The Wessex of Romance*, London: new and revised edition, Francis Griffiths, 1908. Hermann Lea's *Thomas Hardy's Wessex*, London: Macmillan and Co. Ltd, 1913, was published after Lea spent a considerable time in the county, including a visit to the Whiteheads in their caravan.
22. E.M. Forster, *Howard's End*, London: Arnold, 1910. A key theme is the creeping urbanization of southern England. Forster pessimistically regarded the Purbeck Hills as a survivor against the 'red brick tide'. He wrote, 'the reason fails, like a wave on the Swanage beach; the imagination swells, spreads, and deepens, until it becomes geographic and encircles England', p.164.
23. Thomas Hardy, *Tess of the D'Urbervilles: A Pure Woman*, London: James R. Osgood, 1892, p.402.
24. See too Hume Swaine, in *An Artist's Rambles Round About Swanage*, London: Hume Swaine, 1893, Reproduced Weymouth: Gallant Publications,1989, in which the artist actively promoted 'eligible sites for Building' in Swanage: 'the air is pure and bracing and there is perfect drainage to the sea' and 'The Sites and views are all that can be desired', unpaginated.
25. Holland, pp.105–19.

middle class, following the rural decline begun in the 1870s. In her excellent analysis of interpretations of the Edwardian landscape, Ysanne Holt has suggested that by the end of the nineteenth century the countryside was viewed as a national asset, following the work of writers such as Rider Haggard and Charles Masterman in his troubling analysis, *The Condition of England* of 1909. Masterman presented rural Edwardian England as 'hastening to decay', with cottages and farm buildings abandoned and land steadily turned to grass.[26] He argued that rural regions' considered efforts to consolidate the nation's hold on the Empire overseas came at the expense of workers at home. This was the reality of the Dorset countryside that painters faced. Forster saw the threat posed by the motorcar, which opened up the countryside to tourism, a fear shared by painters like Steer.

Throughout Dorset the severe agricultural depression led to low wages and poor housing and an exodus of farm workers forced to leave the land to live in towns. The rush to the city rapidly changed agricultural communities and the way farms were managed, with many broken up. Arfleet Mill, near Corfe Castle, where Everett lived between 1907 and 1910, was abandoned and eventually allowed to fall into neighbouring clay pits.[27] Acknowledging these tensions, Forster presented the Dorset landscape, once comparatively isolated and self-contained, as ageless, standing for values explored by Hardy. Imbued with the Dorset landscape his work confronted social and rural deprivation in parallel with the beauty of nature and the land. For most readers, this countryside probably represented nostalgia and memory rather than actual experience, with Dorset increasingly viewed as a place of recreation.

The influx of outsiders through tourism and new housing was viewed as damaging the old rural and 'unspoilt' world, as visitors became the destroyers, arriving in such numbers that Steer and D.S. MacColl despaired at seeing sites like Corfe Castle engulfed by tourists.[28] Yet there had never been a moment when its countryside was untouched by human intervention. The Purbeck landscape was littered with the evidence of past and recent industrial activity, somewhat at odds with Forster's pastoralism.[29] Its barrows, medieval water meadows, pools in disused clay pits, heathland, chalk and lime pits appealed to the visiting Slade/New English artists for their painterly potential. Situated on a peninsula with water on three sides, an ancient coastline and with remarkable geology and limestone quarries, Purbeck felt cut off from the rest of Dorset. It was this remoteness from encroaching modernity that made it so compelling to the artists. Everett relished this isolation, often living in his boat as a studio, or renting a hut on Worbarrow for three months to paint (figs 85–91).

THE RISE OF TOURISM

During the second half of the nineteenth century Dorset was gradually opened up to tourism. The main-line railway from Southampton to Dorchester via Wareham was opened by 1847, and in 1885 the first train ran from Swanage to Corfe Castle and Wareham. Conscious of competing with neighbouring Bournemouth, in 1900 the London and South Western Railway distributed 50,000 guides to Swanage and the area, actively promoting it as a tourist destination from London.[30] Visitors to discreet, sedate

26. Holt, 'Landscape and Modernity', p.3; Charles F.G. Masterman, *The Condition of England*, London: Methuen & Co., 1909, pp.190 and 203. Henry Rider Haggard, Preface, *Rural England: Being an Account of Agricultural and Social Researches Carried Out in 1901 and 1902*, vol. 1, London: Longmans, Green and Co., 1902, revised version 1906. In 1901 Rider Haggard travelled around Britain commenting on agriculture after the serious decline of the 1870s, defining the land and rural population as the 'backbone of the Empire'.
27. Arfleet clay had supplied Wedgwood since the eighteenth century.
28. Dugald Sutherland MacColl, *Life, Work and Setting of Philip Wilson Steer*, London: Faber, 1945. MacColl described 'coach-loads of grossly fed and apathetic tourists' visiting Corfe, p.168.
29. Wilkes includes a detailed discussion of industrial Purbeck as a 'fundamentally divergent landscape sharp with contradictions', p.131.
30. 'How to Advertise Swanage as a Health Resort', *Dorset County Chronicle*, 22 November 1900, p.7.

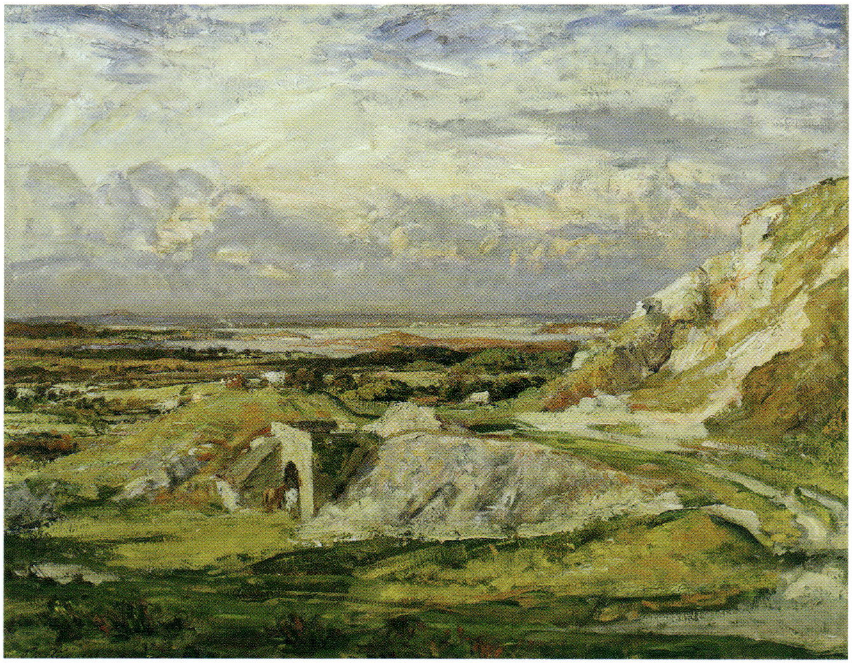

FIG. 5
Philip Wilson Steer / ***The Lime-Kiln near Corfe Castle***
1908 / oil on canvas / 86.3 x 112 cm

nearby Studland enjoyed the beach, but did not venture into the barren hinterland painted by Everett, Collins and others.[31] Dorset residents and tourists took horse-drawn charabanc excursions to its seaside, landmarks and countryside. The coastline and seaside resorts remained the most popular destinations, particularly Lulworth Cove. In the summer paddle steamers and pleasure boats visited from Weymouth, Swanage and Bournemouth. Woodbury Hill Fair (Hardy's Greenhill fair), held every September near Bere Regis, witnessed the countryside 'letting its hair down'. Everett described it as 'the great outing of the year for rustics', and recalled bumping into Slade contemporaries Augustus John and Percy Wyndham Lewis there in 1903, when they were staying close by at East Lulworth.[32] Walking and cycling holidays became popular, with cycling maps such as Pattison's 1900 *Cyclist's Road Map of Dorset, Wilts, Hampshire, etc,* all contributing to an influx of visitors. Artists like Alfred Rich, Arthur Streeton (fig. 80) and Tom Roberts visited Dorset on cycling holidays, to paint.

Touring holidays opened up the countryside to urban visitors, inevitably changing the nature of the county. By 1900 the *Dorset County Chronicle* promoted the benefits of the Benz with its ability to tackle steep Dorset hills.[33] It made the news when the first car passed through West Lulworth on 29 May 1899, and the photographs used in W. Mate's illustrated guidebook of Dorset still show a wholly car-free countryside.[34] Noting the unreliability of the car, Everett confirmed that 'in England in 1900 you hardly ever saw a motor car [sic], the motor cycle must have come in around 1901.'[35] Conscious of this rapid speed of change, in 1900 the Reverend Miles Barnes decided to record the county in photographs and organized

31. Charles Cheston, *Evelyn Cheston Member of the New English Art Club, 1908–1929,* London: Faber & Faber Ltd, 1931, p.25.
32. Everett, *Memoirs,* pp.34, 104. In 1924 Everett produced an oil painting of the fair at Woodbury Hill (DNHAS). There is no surviving work by Wyndham Lewis or John firmly dating to this trip, unless John's etching of Lewis dated 1903 relates.
33. 'The Perfection of Motor-car Riding', *Dorset County Chronicle,* 13 December 1900, p.4.
34. *Dorset County Chronicle,* 1 June 1899, p.5.
35. Everett, *Memoirs,* p.109.

a survey of Dorset under the auspices of the Dorset County Museum. Kept in nine folio volumes, they constituted an important permanent record of Dorset views of towns, villages, mansions, churches, antiquities and the county's social and industrial life, known to artists like Everett, Tomson and Collins, who all belonged to the museum's field club.[36]

Edwardian Dorset was certainly not insulated or immune from world events. But just at the moment when the technological advances of motor-cars and aeroplanes were hurtling the county towards the unknown, Dorset was also celebrating an undefined old-fashioned 'golden' era 'untouched by the modernising spirit which destroys all loveliness'.[37] Sherborne set the national trend with its famous pageant of 1905, seeking to re-enact the glories of its past history. Mate described Dorset as full of 'a people who have borne a brave part in their share of the work of building up a great and powerful England', a reference not only to the past, but acknowledging that maintaining the Empire was costly in human lives and sacrifice.[38]

Ushering in the new century, the bleak editorial of the *Dorset County Chronicle* outlined the grim realities of the war being waged by Britain in South Africa.[39] Most villages experienced its impact, fundraising for the War Fund and dependants whilst receiving the lists of local men injured or killed.[40] Local newspapers were full of rising national and international tensions and by 1908 the possibility of a European conflict was being openly discussed.

In 1909 Studland witnessed the first all-women's medical training camp set up to assist at the scene of battle, organized by Mabel St Clair Stobart. It was also the year in which several of the emergent Bloomsbury group first visited. Political unrest came when suffragettes were ejected from a Liberal-Party fête on 2 August 1909 held at Canford Park, the home of Everett's aunt Lady Wimborne.[41] A hostile crowd turned on two local girls with no connection to the movement, before suffragette Annie Kenney and fellow sympathizers were forcibly evicted for questioning Everett's third cousin, Winston Churchill, on the budget.[42] Kathleen Mansell-Pleydell of Whatcombe, Blandford, confided to John Everett's wife Katherine (née Herbert) that she was sheltering Mrs Pankhurst after her release from prison. Katherine refused to join the crusade on the basis that women were 'more ignorant than men, and they are unlikely to vote with any solidarity as women'.[43] In 1910 Vanessa Bell famously photographed suffragist Marjorie Strachey at Studland, holding up a 'votes for women' pamphlet for the camera.[44]

AN EARLY SKETCHING GROUND

Holt has observed that art magazines *The Studio* and *Art Journal* reviewed guidebooks that advocated counties like Sussex and Dorset as ideal locations to sketch, contributing to the invasion of visitors and artists. At the beginning of the century, the painter and member of the New English, Arthur Tomson, lived in Dorset and contributed several illustrated essays to the *Art Journal* extolling the virtues of Dorchester, Cerne Abbas and Studland.[45] On his retirement, Dorchester-born surgeon Fredrick Treves published *Highways and Byways in Dorset* in 1906 with illustrations by

36. List of members, *Proceedings of the Dorset Natural History and Antiquarian Field Club*, Dorchester: Dorset County Chronicle, vols xix–xxxv, 1898–1914.
37. Louis Napoleon Parker at a meeting of the Society of Arts in December 1905.
38. Mate, p.3.
39. '1899 – A Retrospect', *Dorset County Chronicle*, 4 January 1900, p.1[illegible].
40. *Dorset County Chronicle*, 4 January 1900, p.4.
41. Trumble, 'The Soldier, the King, and the Proconsul: An Edwardian Processional', p.35.
42. See Estelle Sylvia Pankhurst, *The Suffragette: The History of the Women's Militant Suffrage Movement 1905–1910*, New York: Sturgis and Walton, 1911, pp.413–14.
43. Katherine Everett, 1951, p.269.
44. London, Tate archive, TGA 9020/1, Vanessa Bell Photograph Album showing Clive Bell, Desmond MacCarthy, Marjorie Strachey and Molly MacCarthy.
45. Tomson and his first wife, the poet Rosamund, eloped in 1886 and divorced ten years later. Initially admired by Thomas Hardy, Rosamund wrote under the pseudonym of Graham R. Tomson. Arthur secondly married Agnes Mary Hastings, a descendant of Warren Hastings, and they had settled in Dorset by 1900.

Joseph Pennell.[46] By the turn of the twentieth century, the profusion of landscape paintings hanging on the walls of exhibitions revealed their potential as affirmations of national identity. Some were bought for art galleries in the colonies with this in mind. Conscious of Dorset as a tourist attraction, the Slade landscapes, tinged with nostalgia, led to a sense of what the countryside stood for in nationalistic terms. So the county was not only inextricably linked with Hardy, who provided the 'brand', but also with visitors admiring the quaint buildings (many under threat of demolition) the wildness, folklore and ancient history evident in landscape features such as Maiden Castle or Creech Barrow.

By the early twentieth century, improved transport links meant that Dorset was so easily accessible for London art schools, galleries, contacts and patrons that there was no need to establish a colony dictated by distance from the metropolis. Its rich source of subject matter increasingly attracted England's leading artists, and Dorset became a particular focus for Slade tutors and students over the summers of 1908–11. Slade students were encouraged to use their summer breaks to sketch in the countryside, with Walter Westley Russell giving painting classes in Richmond, Yorkshire, in 1902.[47] Others headed further afield to Cornwall's St Ives or Newlyn, or to Staithes in the north-east, to join established colonies of painters. Artists from these groups, such as Arthur Friedenson, Frank Richards and Fred Milner, visited Dorset, but did not promote the rustic naturalism of Newlyn or Staithes, focusing instead on the effects of light, colour and atmosphere in the landscape.[48] Everett observed that fellow artists wintered in St Ives and travelled away in the summer, with some coming to Dorset. Purbeck appeared to offer them a world isolated from the stresses of modern life, in which to maintain a pre-modern existence. Visiting *plein air* painters were alive to Dorset's rapidly changing countryside, with Whitehead and Arthur Meade the first impressionistic painters working directly from nature. Everett later recalled that Hardy sat for Meade for his portrait, now untraced.[49]

The main outlet for exhibiting Dorset work remained the Royal Academy. Increasingly however, the New English offered greater freedom from academic conventions, along with those London galleries like the Goupil, eager to attract the plutocracy to spend their new wealth buying art. Lacking a long tradition of land ownership, these new art patrons were lawyers like Judge Evans, bankers or businessmen like Geoffrey Blackwell, who adopted the houses and lifestyle of a country squire and sought paintings endorsing their perception of the countryside. Blackwell owned a significant number of oils and watercolours of Dorset subjects, painted during this period by Philip Wilson Steer and Charles Conder.[50] The Dorset they encountered and painted was a place of artistic possibility and of escape for incomers, but not one untouched by modernity for those who actually lived there.

46. American artist Joseph Pennell lectured in illustration at the Slade. In Dorset, schools of art included Bridport, established in 1865, Dorchester in 1867, Weymouth in 1877 and Poole by 1880. Henry Joseph Moule organized sketching tours to Swanage and Corfe in the 1890s. In her elliptical book *Fresh Leaves and Green Pastures*, London: Eveleigh Nash, 1909, Jane Panton hinted at a school of landscape painting near Wareham. Panton, married to a Wareham brewer, disguised the identity of people she was writing about, which led to confusion and litigation.
47. Cheston, p.19.
48. The Cornwall Art Index project reveals Richards worked at Lulworth in 1885, Newlyn in 1892 and Wareham in 1902. By 1917 he was at Bournemouth. http://cornwallartists.org/cornwall-artists/frank-richards.
49. Meade studied in Paris under Jean-Léon Gerôme and at Bushey under Hubert Herkomer. Primarily a landscape artist, he also painted portraits, including the untraced Thomas Hardy portrait, and was based in St Ives from 1890. He painted 'Wessex' subjects in Thomas Hardy's Dorset between 1891 and 1904 and 1916 to 1918. In 1898 Meade exhibited his narrative painting, *The Landing of the Danes in Dorset*, 1898, at the RA.
50. Anne Blackwell's personal compilation volume of her father Geoffrey Blackwell's collection at the family house at Norcott Hill, Berkhamsted, 12 July 1938, included paintings by P.W. Steer, G. Philpot, L. Pissarro, H. Tonks, D.Y. Cameron, W.W. Russell, G. Clausen, C.J. Holmes, C. Conder, M. Bone, A. McEvoy, J.S. Sargent, W. Sickert, A. John, D.S. MacColl, A. Sisley, W. Orpen, A. Munnings, W. Gore, G. Chowne, J. Guthrie, F. Dodd, F. Short, J.M. Whistler, C. Monet and J.B. Manson, (private collection).

TWO

PAINTING OUT OF DOORS IN DORSET

Central to the narrative of Slade painters visiting Dorset during the Edwardian decade is the now little-known painter John Everett, chiefly identified through footnotes in fellow painters' biographies. Taught by Henry Tonks and Philip Wilson Steer, Everett was at the Slade with a remarkable group of painters. Although his own career differed from those of his contemporaries, particularly Augustus John and William Orpen, he became a prolific landscape and marine painter and eventually an official war artist. His recently rediscovered, unpublished memoirs give a clear account of his association with many of the most important early twentieth-century British painters. This chapter looks at Everett's initial artistic influences and the significance of the emergence of artists working *en plein air* in Dorset in the generation before the Slade artists visited. Painters such as Arthur Meade and Frederick Whitehead suggest a precedent for a particular kind of *en plein air* naturalism for artists working in the county in the following decades.[1] They were painting out of doors on a large scale, before the arrival of Slade artists like Tonks and Steer, and were travelling around in gypsy caravans before Augustus John famously did so. Everett had spotted Dorset's potential for artists a decade before he became the conduit for his contemporaries and other major London figures visiting the county.

EVERETT'S EARLY ARTISTIC INFLUENCES

Born in Dorchester in 1876, Herbert Barnard Everett (known as John by 1901) was the only child of the Reverend Henry Everett, respected Rector of Holy Trinity Church, Dorchester (fig. 6) and the formidable Augusta Frances Harriet Everett (née Stewart) (fig. 7). Everett was related to the painter John Everett Millais on his father's side and through his mother to countless members of the British and Anglo-Irish aristocracy. It was the larger-than-life Augusta who became an influential figure to a generation of Slade students.[2] Art and travel were powerful influences on Everett's Dorchester childhood, with frequent travel to the Continent, where he was exposed to European art. This pattern continued into his later life, supporting Amy Meyers' identification of ceaseless shuttling across international boundaries as an integral aspect of British art in the opening decade of the twentieth century.[3] Everett bought his first oil paints and

1. Whitehead continued *plein air* painting in Dorset into the 1920s.
2. Augusta Francis Harriet Stewart, daughter of the Reverend Edward Stewart and Louisa Anne Herbert, married the Reverend Henry Everett on 13 October 1875.
3. See Amy Meyers, 'Director's Foreword', *Edwardian Opulence*, p.viii.

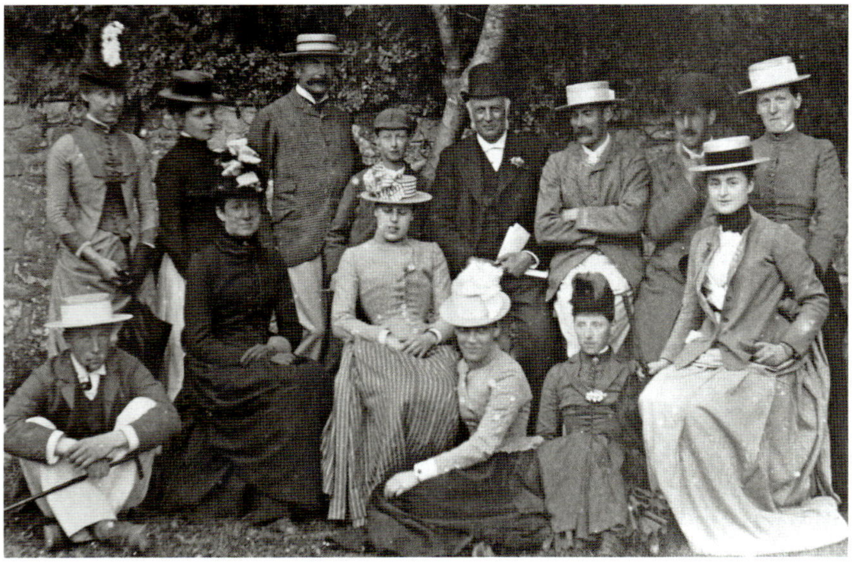

FIG. 6
A picnic outing to Lulworth, 1888; the Reverend Henry Everett in bowler hat (centre) and his son Herbert to his right
© DNHAS; courtesy Dorset County Museum

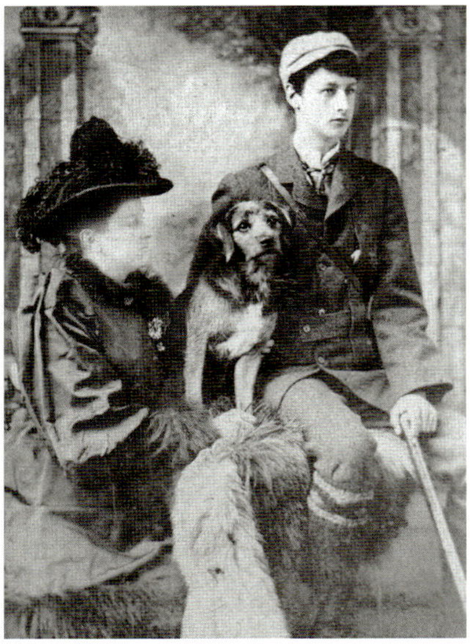

FIG. 7
Newly widowed Augusta Everett with her son John, c.1896
private collection

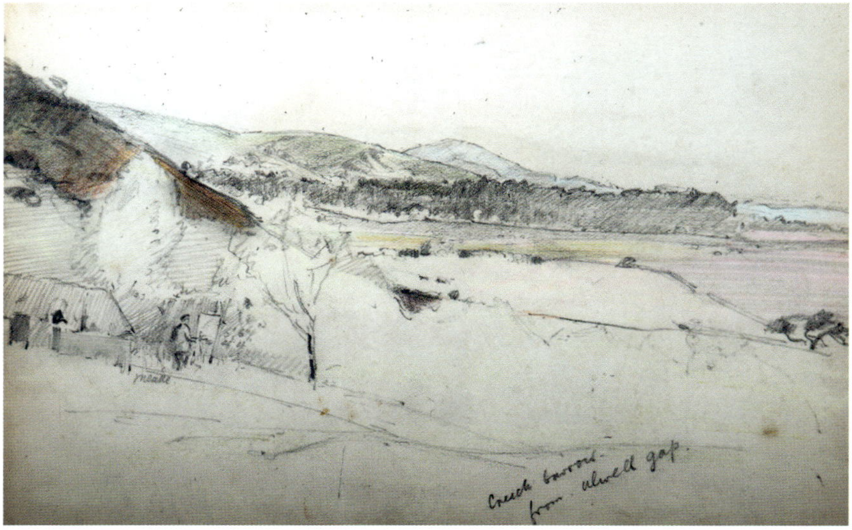

FIG. 8
John Everett / ***Creech Barrow from Ulwell Gap***
1896 / pencil and wash
Arthur Meade is shown working on a large canvas (left) during a trip to Swanage
private collection

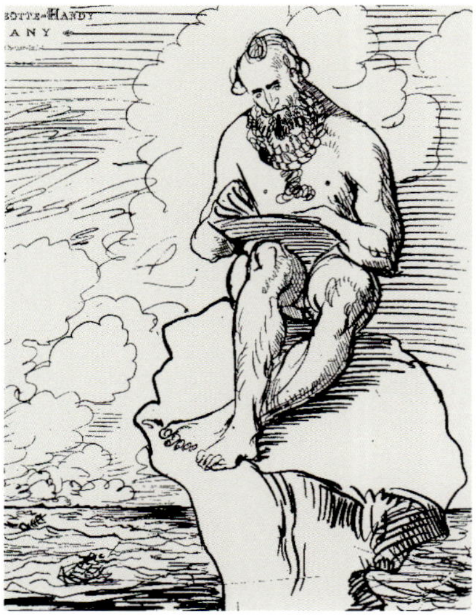

FIG. 9
William Orpen
The Father of the Lizard
1901
Highlighting John Everett's enthusiasm for painting Cornish seascapes
private collection

panels in Munich in 1894 before travelling to Venice and receiving painting lessons from Luigi Lanza.[4] The family wintered in St Moritz while his father Henry was English Chaplain there, returning one spring via Venice and witnessing the opening of the first International Exhibition of Pictures, the forerunner of the Venice Biennale.

Arthur Meade, a painter of land and seascapes, was Everett's formative artistic influence in Dorset, hired by Augusta to tutor her young son in drawing and painting.[5] Augusta also arranged for Meade to study at the Académie Julian in Paris when tutor to her nephew, Alexander Hellier Berens, a keen wildlife artist.[6] In November 1895 Everett stayed with Meade on his first visit to St Ives, remaining in Cornwall until the following March – a trip which consolidated Everett's decision to become a professional painter. His stay coincided with the determining moment when St Ives was evolving into an artists' 'colony' focusing on *plein air* painting.

The completion of the Tamar railway bridge in 1859 had opened up Cornwall to visiting painters, further improved by the arrival of the branch line to St Ives from Penzance in 1877. The St Ives Arts Club was formed by 1890, with an influx of artists trained in Paris and driven by their admiration for the ideas of Jules Bastien-Lepage.[7] They focused on open-air land and seascapes in a free style, which ran parallel to artists settling at Staithes and Runswick Bay.[8] At the time of Everett's visit, Louis Grier and Julius Olsson were establishing their school of marine painting, aimed at capturing the effects of light over the sea and freed from academic convention. Their atmospheric paintings of waves, clouds and sky, and those of Adrian Stokes, who rejected maritime narratives in favour of painting these effects, influenced Everett.[9] He described St Ives as

> [w]onderful … like an Italian place, 600 fishing boats in the harbour, schooners, brigantines on the beach. We had a life class there. There were about 80 painters there. They had turned many of the fishing lofts into studios. We had an artists' club where we all used to meet on Sat.[sic] nights.[10]

For Everett, the value of St Ives came from the companionship of fellow artists in their converted sail lofts, ateliers and schools, and in later years he often returned to Cornwall (fig. 9).[11]

Seeking isolated locations to paint reflected the pan-European desire, first pioneered in France, for an uncomplicated simple life, and was adopted in Dorset by Whitehead, Meade and Everett.[12] By 1894 Everett was painting *en plein air* each summer in Dorset with Meade, sleeping in tents close to Holme Bridge, or renting cottages at Moreton, Dorchester or East Stoke near Wareham. There were practical considerations in attempting to work *en plein air* in the British countryside (fig. 8). The artist Alfred East, writing in 1906, advised painting *en plein air* with a sturdy easel capable of withstanding the vagaries of British weather, but easily taken apart for transportation.[13] Acknowledging the considerable difficulties artists faced painting out of doors in Britain's uncertain and ever-changing climate, East predicted that painting *en plein air* would result in smaller canvases, not least because it made it easier to capture a scene while chasing the transience of nature through light and shadow. But in the 1890s Meade and Whitehead were attempting large-scale works specifically for exhibition, entirely

4. Luigi Lanza mainly painted *vedute* of his native Venice.
5. The son of a Bath shopkeeper, choirboy at Bath Abbey and railway porter, Meade was discovered by Augusta Everett.
6. Everett, *Memoirs* p.16. Augusta funded Berens at the Slade. Everett described him as wild, with a penchant for painting cadavers.
7. Attending the first committee meeting at the home of Louis Grier on 1 August 1890 were Adrian Stokes (President), Eardley Wilmot Blomefield, William Eadie, Charles Greville Morris, Edward Emerson Simmons, William Holt Yates Titcomb and Henry Harewood Robinson (Hon Sec), see Cornwall Artists Index.
8. Slater defined artists' colonies as groups of artists working and living at a particular place over a period of time, drawing inspiration from the people and views. He identified areas of commonality with artists' colonies throughout Britain and further afield, escaping the modernity of urban centres, rejecting industrialization and seeking a return to nature amidst people they considered 'unsullied' by civilization. Yet, as Slater points out, the towns and cities they criticized as dirty and ugly were those they largely depended upon to sell their paintings in an increasingly sophisticated art world, pp.2–3.
9. When by 1897 Olsson and Grier were unable to work together, Talmage joined Olsson instead, Tovey, p.127.
10. Everett, *Memoirs*, p.30, the heyday of painting in St Ives was between 1895 and 1910.
11. Everett listed the St Ives painters who influenced him as being John and Mia Arnesby Brown, Algernon Talmage, Julius Olsson, Fred Milner, John Noble Barlow, Henry Harewood Robinson, Adrian and Marianne Stokes and Edmund Fuller, Everett, *Memoirs*, p.30. Other visitors in the last two decades of the nineteenth century included Walter Sickert, James Abbott McNeill Whistler, Mortimer Mempes and Philip Wilson Steer.
12. In the absence of any unifying manifesto, the determination to paint in the open air and be true to nature was without any reforming zeal. Towards the end of the first decade of the century this was fused with the need to examine some inner truth.
13. See Alfred East, 'Equipment' in *The Art of Landscape Painting in Oil Colour*, Cassell & Co., London, 1906, p.7.

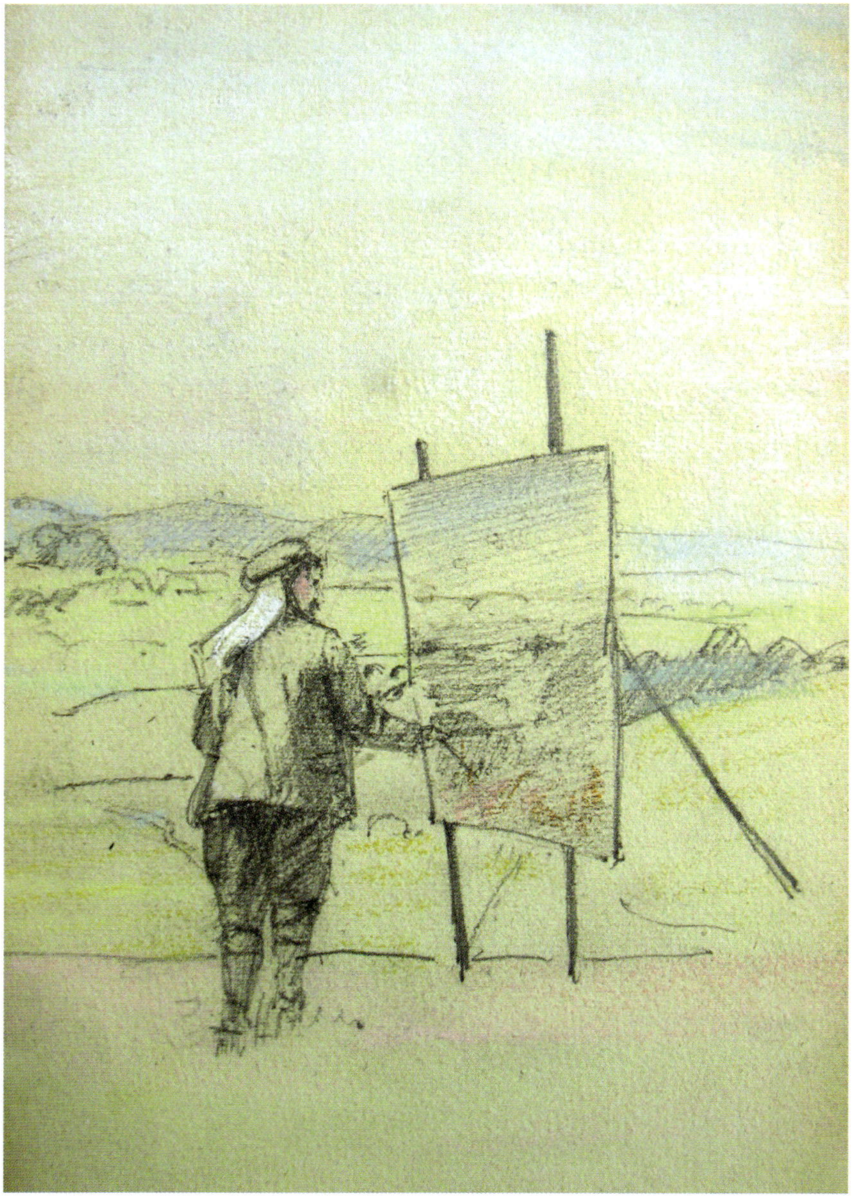

FIG. 10
John Everett
Arthur Meade painting a 6'6" x 4'4" canvas at East Stoke near Wareham
1896 / pencil and pastel

executed out of doors. A sketch Everett made in 1896 depicts Meade working on just such a large landscape, on the heath on the Wareham Road near East Stoke (fig. 10). Meade's favoured canvas size was 6 ft 6 in. x 4 ft 4 in.[14] Working in the decade before 1900, Meade and Whitehead used such large canvases in their attempts at harmonious effects, focusing on atmospheric landscapes and subtleties of light. Whitehead adopted a muted palette to respond to Dorset's discreet landscape, concentrating on the varying conditions of light, atmosphere and broad sweeps of sky. His impressionistic, broad views of heath, river, downland and quarries, often without narrative incident, reflected the tonal qualities and softness he learned in France.[15]

14. Everett, *Memoirs*, p.28.
15. William Pye was another *plein air* painter working in the area from 1894, having settled near Weymouth. He focused chiefly on coastal scenes around Weymouth, Portland and Lulworth.

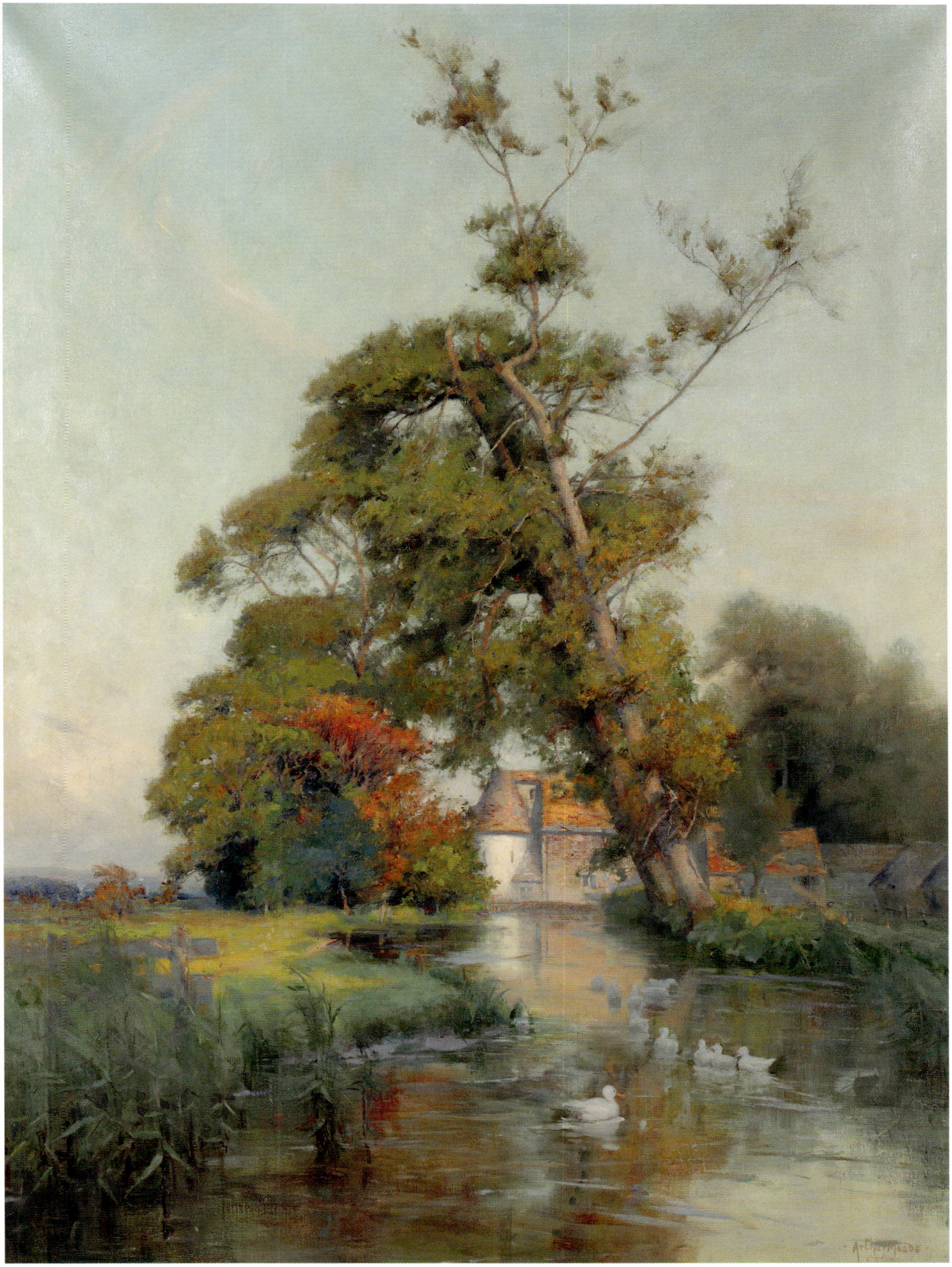

FIG. 11
Arthur Meade / ***Old Mill on the Frome***
c.1895 / oil on canvas / 112 x 86.9 cm

The Whiteheads entered into the spirit of their nomadic existence (fig. 4), and Whitehead depicted the life of the Benham family, true Dorset gypsies, in his painting *The Gypsie's Home* [sic] exhibited at the Royal Academy in 1899. Attracted by the allure of gypsy bohemianism, the Whiteheads' caricature of a gypsy lifestyle was adopted later by John Everett and Augustus John. In February 1902 Katherine and John Everett spent a month in a gypsy caravan at Kingsbury Green, loaned by a distant relative, Lord Dundonald (fig. 13). The Gypsy Lore Society was formed in 1888, and much has been written of the bohemian outdoor lifestyle during the late Victorian period, when it became fashionable for urban gentlemen to hire Romany-style caravans for holidays. The life of the gypsy was even compared with that of landscape painters, through their close physical proximity to the land.[16] This *modus vivendi* was adopted as the rapidly expanding population heralded an uncertain future for rural life. The cultural historian George Behlmer has suggested that gentlemen taking to a caravan kept in touch with rural values and represented the core of Englishness.[17] The appeal of 'roughing it' also applied to the Slade painters in Purbeck during the 1900s, who appropriated abandoned Purbeck cottages formerly inhabited by farm workers forced out by the agricultural depression. There the artists rejoiced at the lack of basic facilities. Everett later described staying in a cottage on the shores of Poole Harbour: 'We led a sort of wild life down there, never saw a soul, used to sail over to Poole for provisions ... We had a jolly nice time.'[18]

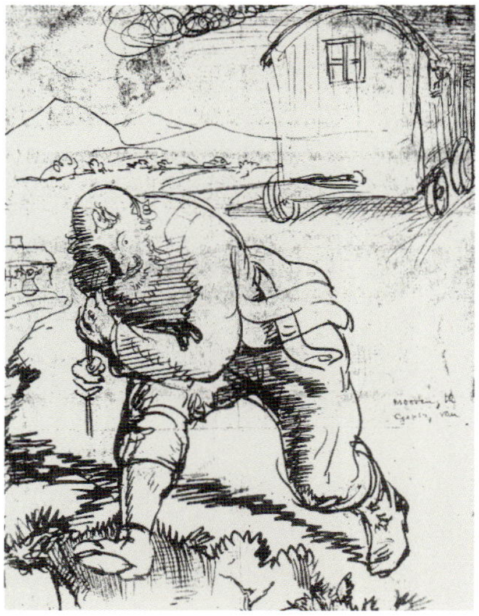

FIG. 13
William Orpen
Moving the Gypsy Van
1902
Everett towing the caravan
private collection

There was an interchange of artists between St Ives and Dorset. Everett recorded that St Ives painters Fred Milner and Henry Harewood Robinson camped close to the mill at East Stoke, where they joined Everett, Meade and Whitehead. They painted side by side, with Whitehead producing *East Stoke Mill* (fig. 14) while Meade's *Old Mill on the Frome* was hung 'on the line' (at a particularly advantageous height) at the Royal Academy in 1896

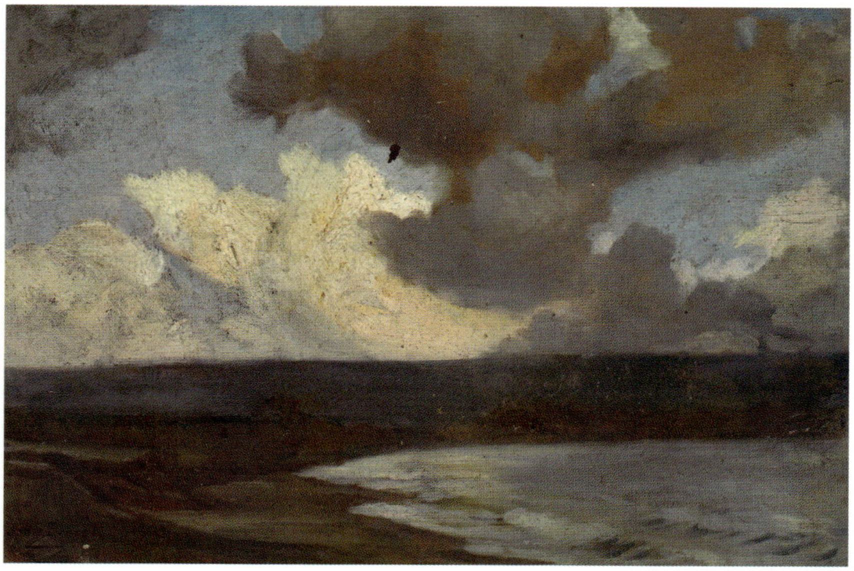

FIG. 12
John Everett / *Swanage*
c.1899 / oil sketch on cardboard / 31 x 47.5 cm

16. Barringer, p.147, refers to the landscape painter Rex Vicat Cole.
17. George K. Behlmer, 'The Gypsy Problem in Victorian England', *Victorian Studies*, vol. 28, no. 2 (Winter, 1985), pp. 231–53, Indiana University Press, p.238.
18. Everett, *Memoirs*, p.109.

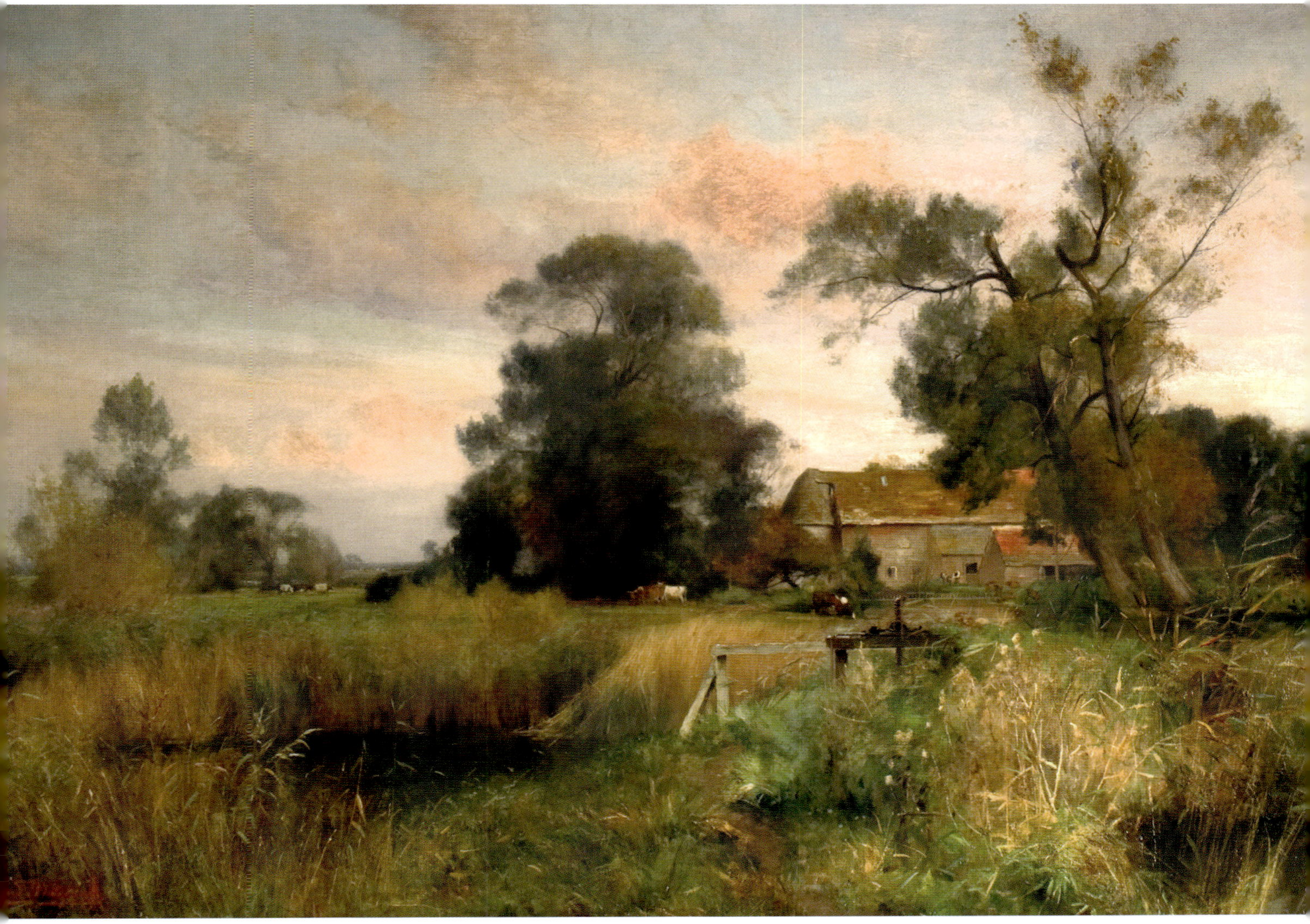

FIG. 14
Frederick Whitehead / ***East Stoke Mill***
1895 / oil on canvas / 107.5 x 160 cm

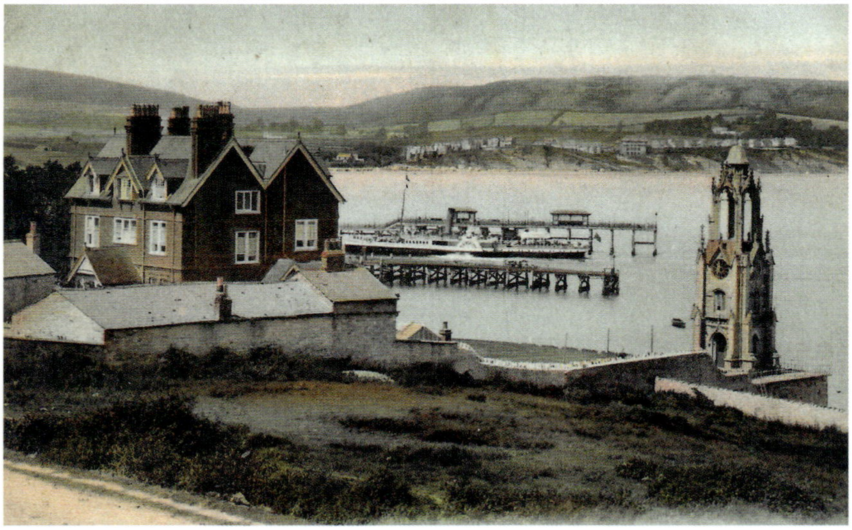

FIG. 15

Swanage Bay showing Peveril Tower, 1900. Augusta Everett's house with cottages is on the left, John Everett's bedroom is in the Wellington Clock Tower on the right

(fig. 11).[19] Their local links, combined with Hardy's encouragement, saw them based to the east of Dorchester around the River Frome, on sites described by Hardy in *Tess* as the 'Vale of the Great Dairies'.

By September 1895, the Everetts had left Dorchester for their new home, Peveril Tower, close to the shore at Swanage. Everett's father Henry died the following spring and was buried in Dorchester, where over 1,000 attended the graveside. John Everett's oil sketch of Swanage (fig. 12) illustrates the view over Swanage Bay, the sandy bay facing east and protected from the major south-westerly storms, towards Ballard Down with the major chalk exposure of Ballard Cliff beneath the down. The painting typifies Everett's muted palette from this period. The intensity of the cloud above the downs, and reflections in the water in the central foreground, hint at his growing awareness of St Ives marine painters like Olsson. Once a fishing and quarrying village, Swanage had become a seaside resort catering for holidaymakers. It still combined old-world quaintness with curious sections of salvaged buildings rescued by Mowlem and Burt, including the Wellington Clock tower, which once stood at one end of London Bridge. This separate tower on the sea wall of the Everetts' home, Peveril Tower, was used by John Everett as his bedroom (fig. 15), and proved the ideal position from which to paint the sea.[20] The Dorset landscape, with its Hardyesque connotations, began attracting artists from the mid-1880s. By the turn of the century it was soon to attract many of the Slade group, who visited through their Everett connections, many at the invitation of Augusta.

19. Meade exhibited Dorset and Wessex paintings at the RA in 1897, 1898, 1900,1904 and 1916–18.
20. See Wilkes for the history of Peveril Tower, p.80.

THREE

'THE GRAND EPOCH OF THE SLADE'[1]

Stimulated by his time painting with Meade in Dorset and Cornwall, in October 1896 Everett joined the Slade School of Fine Art, part of the University of London. Situated in Gower Street, the Slade was then at the height of its success.[2] It had been founded in 1871 for the teaching of professional artists with its main focus the use of the live model. This chapter explores how Everett became a key figure within an important generation of Slade students who included Augustus John, William Orpen, Gwen John and William Crampton Gore; their tutors Fred Brown, Philip Wilson Steer, Henry Tonks and Walter Westley Russell; and established painters such as Charles Conder and Arthur Streeton.[3] Everett's memoirs describe his time there with fellow students, male and female, whom Augustus John thought 'abounded in talent'.[4] Everett's recently widowed mother, Augusta, who joined the Slade with her son, kept a boarding house where many of the students stayed, and this chapter will reveal how it became a bohemian centre for artists and their friends. Augusta also invited many of the painters to her house in Swanage, which for most marked their introduction to Dorset. These painters began to exhibit their work at the New English Art Club, the principal forum for the display of works produced by Slade painters, particularly their paintings produced in Dorset. During Everett's time at the Slade, between 1896 and 1900, the UCL calendars list the remarkable students attending, many of whom remained largely in touch until the outbreak of war.

The Slade School, like St Ives and Newlyn, freely welcomed women artists, and during Everett's time there were more than double the number of female as male students.[5] Reflecting in 1958, Augustus John wrote in *The Times*:

> in what I have called the Grand Epoch of the Slade, the male students cut a poor figure; in fact they can hardly be said to have existed. In talent as well as looks the girls were supreme. But these advantages for the most part came to nought under the burdens of domesticity which loomed ahead for most of them and which even when acceptable could be for some almost too heavy to bear.

The women students included Gwen Salmond, Edna Waugh, Wyn George, Margaret Legge, Ethel Hatch, Ursula Tyrwhitt, Fairlie Harmar, Gwen John and Ida Nettleship. Yet despite their evident ability none, aside from Gwen John, remain household names, leaving female Slade students like Katherine

1. Letter to *The Times* from Augustus John, referring to Gwen Salmond, later Lady Smith's, death. 'Lady Smith. Grand Epoch of the Slade School', 'Obituary', *The Times*, 1 February 1958, p.8.
2. See Stephen Chaplin's typed manuscript, 'Report by Slade School of Art Archivist, 1990–97', *A Slade School Reader, 1868–1975: A Compendium of Documents in UCL, vol. 2, 1868–1930*, Slade archive MSS ADD400 (A623, A631), 19 March 1998. The Slade signing-in books are incomplete and though Everett's signature does not appear before 18 December 1896 (*Fine Arts Book, 1894*, Slade archive), he joined in the October, together with his mother and half cousin Katherine Herbert. This same confusion applies to Orpen's actual start date. Chaplin, section 6:19 notes there is a gap in the Slade records for 1894, 1895, 1897, 1898, 1900–1903, 1905 and 1906, p.120.
3. Founded in 1871 through a bequest from Felix Slade who envisaged a school where fine art would be studied within a university. The heyday of the Slade was between 1893 and 1917. From the outset it offered female students an education on equal terms to men, an affirmation of the independent artistic character of the Slade. Chaplin notes that famous students during the heyday included Augustus and Gwen John, Edna Clark Hall, William Orpen, G.K. Chesterton, Ambrose McEvoy, William Rothenstein, Albert Rothenstein, Ambrose Heal and Constance Gore-Booth (Countess Markievicz).
4. John, *Chiaroscuro*, p.48. See Chaplin 6:8, 'The mythology of a period of exceptional student talent at the Slade', who noted that 'what is remarkable about John's generation is that their innovations were welcomed with unalloyed acclaim by their senior, established teachers.'
5. In Cornwall Everett recalled sitting as a model for Marianne Stokes (née Preindlsberger) in her converted St Ives sail loft, perhaps for *Aucassin et Nicolette*, c.1898, see Sotheby's *19th Century European Painting, Drawings and Sculpture*, New York, 26 May 1994, Lot 97. She also created a series of religious pictures between 1887 and 1899. Her husband Adrian was a pivotal member of the early St Ives colony and first president of the Arts Club. The Slade signing-in books reveal over twice the number of women signed in each day as men. Bruce Arnold, *Orpen: Mirror to an Age*, London: Jonathan Cape, 1981, suggests the ratio was two-thirds women to men, p.44.

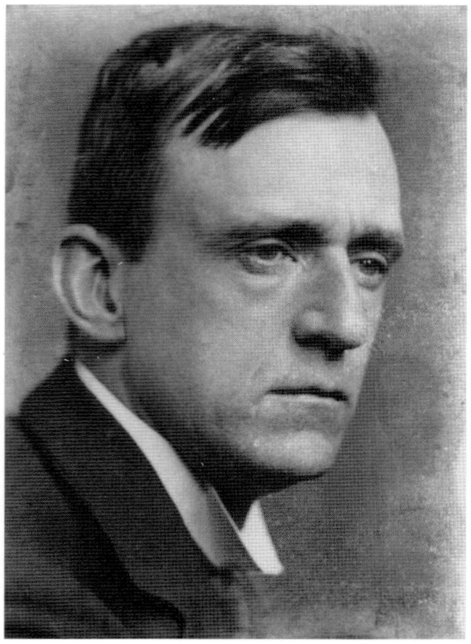

FIG. 16
Henry Tonks, 1902
half-plate glass negative by George Charles Beresford; © National Portrait Gallery, London

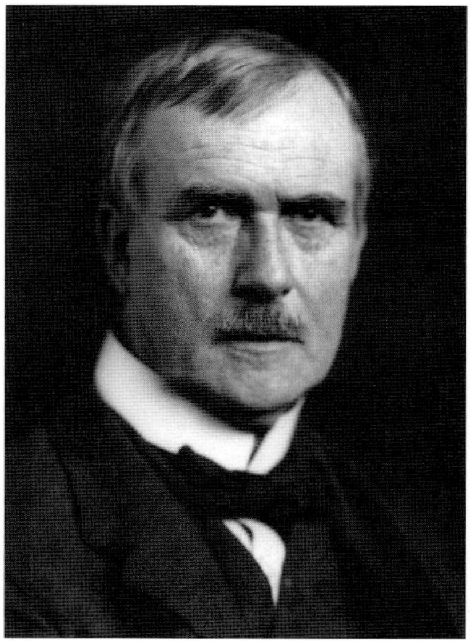

FIG. 17
Philip Wilson Steer, 1922
half-plate glass negative by George Charles Beresford; © National Portrait Gallery, London

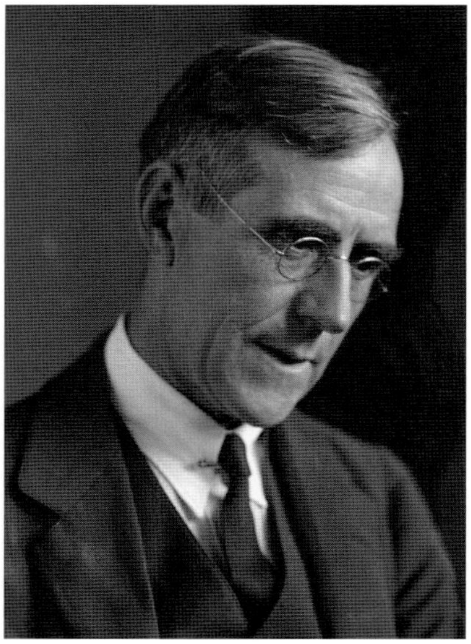

FIG. 18
Sir Walter Westley Russell, 1922
dry-plate glass negative by George Charles Beresford; © National Portrait Gallery, London

Everett resorting to recording their time there in print. Her memoir, *Bricks and Flowers*, includes a lively and important account of her time at the Slade, which has been, for the most part, overlooked. The talented painter Evelyn Cheston (née Davy) is now largely forgotten, and it was left to her husband Charles to publish a posthumous account of her life and work.[6]

THE SLADE TUTORS

Gods of longer standing[7]

Four tutors, Brown (fig. 19) Tonks (fig. 16), Steer (fig. 17) and Russell (fig. 18), did much to shape the Slade and influence several generations of students. The discovery that all four painted in Purbeck over summer vacations sits at the heart of this story.[8] Everett credited Brown with the Slade's significant achievements, bringing around 80 Westminster School of Art students with him in 1892. By 1894 Brown, as Slade Professor, restated the importance of drawing, first introduced by Alphonse Legros.[9] Brown astutely appointed Tonks, Steer and Russell to create a team whose teaching had a major impact on British painting at the beginning of the twentieth century.[10] Steer joined the staff in 1893 and became a close friend of Brown, joining him on summer painting trips to Dorset.[11] Henry Tonks, formerly a pupil of Frederick Treves, was a surgeon and anatomy lecturer at the London Hospital. Already a fine draughtsman, Tonks arrived at the Slade the year after Steer, and used his detailed knowledge of anatomy to emphasize the importance of students' observation of the precise structure of the body. The influential art critic, painter and writer D.S. MacColl described Steer and Tonks as complementary and with a profound respect for each other, with Steer the 'instinctive artist, hater of theory' and Tonks 'the academician "in excelsis"'.[12]

6. Jessica Christian, *Wyn George, Traveller and Artist*, Wimborne Minster: The Dovecote Press, 2013, details some of the female students. Sixteen-year-old Winifred (Wyn) George from Blandford, Dorset, was at the Slade with the Everetts and kept a detailed diary of their first year. Combined with the Everett accounts, they offer the most vivid insight into the Slade students and tutors of that period. George's diary is particularly relevant since the Slade archives are so patchy for this period.
7. Albert Rutherston, 'From Orpen and Gore to the Camden Town Group', *The Burlington Magazine*, vol. 83, no. 485, August 1943, pp.201–5.
8. Brown exhibited Dorset subjects *Poole Harbour* (51) in the 1909 summer exhibition of the New English and *A Dorset Farm* (194) in the summer show of 1910, both untraced.
9. Chaplin, part 2 sections 6:9–6:22, p.112. Chaplin confirms the difficulties gaining a clear picture of Brown in the absence of letters, catalogues, diaries and only a few extant works of art such as his *Self-portrait*, 1932 (Tate).
10. Fothergill indentified a linear progression of draughtsmanship via Legros from Dorset-born artist Alfred Stevens.
11. For a detailed description of these trips see MacColl, p.78.
12. MacColl, 'Teaching the Slade School, 1893–1930', p.131.

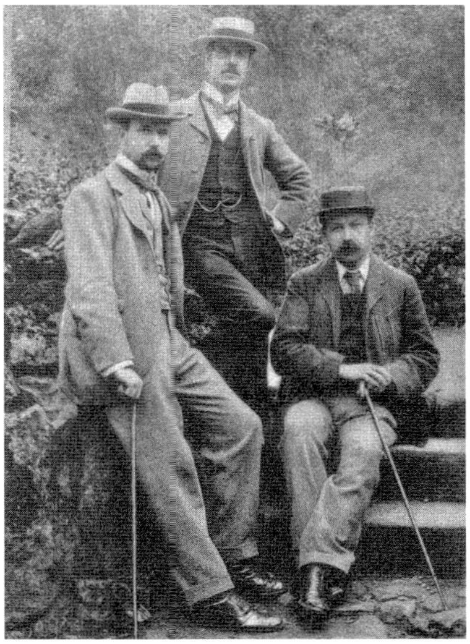

FIG. 19
[l. to r] Frederick Brown, William Coles and Philip Wilson Steer

Together with his contemporary Walter Sickert, Steer was in the vanguard of the progressive British artists who looked to France for inspiration. Steer, who had trained in Paris, developed a consciously modern approach to landscape. Through rigorous personal tuition, he showed students how to gradually build up detail and expression of form, stressing that artistic style came from nature rather than stylists.[13] Tonks was a strict, though kind teacher, occasionally prone to sharp criticism or sarcasm, who succeeded Brown as Professor in 1918. Tonks was dedicated to teaching and encouraging his students, and, with his fellow tutors, discreetly bought their work from exhibitions. The exception was Augusta Everett, who so baffled and exasperated him that he refused to teach her and consigned her permanently to the skeleton room in the basement.[14]

Russell taught at the Slade from 1895 to 1927, having been one of the more talented students studying under Brown at Westminster. Like Tonks and Steer, Russell was at Studland over several summers, staying with the Chestons (see fig. 81). Brown was keen for his students to frequent the National Gallery and other London collections, such as the British Museum print room.[15] Encouraged to study the old masters, they were also attracted by contemporary French painters such as Degas and Monet. Tonks, who admired Watteau and Ingres, was interested in the work of the French Impressionists, but later distrusted the Post-Impressionist emphasis on the distortion of form and the subjective use of colour.

METHOD AT SLADE

The Slade's teaching centred round the fundamental belief in the importance of life drawing, with models in the life room each day.[16] Like all the students, Everett started in the Antique Room to learn balance and proportion by drawing from casts, but soon joined a dozen other men in the Life Room, drawing from the life model in pencil or black chalk.[17] Curator Emma Chambers has observed that life drawing was the most important component of the Slade curriculum: 'Tonks emphasised the importance of close observation of the model, and drawing was seen primarily as a tool for exploring form', as the students were given freedom to experiment in figure composition.[18] The emphasis on daily drawing of live models saw students complain at the consequent lack of painting tuition; as Randolph Schwabe later observed, 'action, construction and proportion' were the most important ingredients, but painting was not as rigorously taught.[19] In his memoirs John Everett remembered that:

> the teaching at the Slade was practically confined to drawing form. If we could have gone to the Slade in the morning and Paris in the afternoon [that] would have been ideal. Tonks never taught painting. He always had great difficulty when he handled a brush. Steer, who was a brilliant painter, was inarticulate. It was only when he took a brush you could understand what he meant. Still, it was something to be taught anything in schools, you learn from your fellow students rather than from the masters. We had a fine lot of draughtsmen at the Slade.[20]

Bruce Arnold's biography of Orpen described the Slade as an art school run by artists for artists.[21] Writing to fellow painter Ronald Gray in 1901, Tonks suggested that during the period of Augustus John's 'Grand Epoch',

13. See Chaplin, chapter six, section 6:52, p.137.
14. See Katherine Everett, p.77.
15. Everett, *Memoirs*, p.41, Everett recalled having a ticket to the British Museum print room.
16. A comparison between the two different teaching systems of the Slade and Royal Academy is discussed by Randolph Schwabe, 'Three Teachers: Brown, Tonks and Steer', *The Burlington Magazine*, vol. 82, (June 1943), pp.141–6.
17. Everett, *Memoirs*, pp.36–7.
18. Emma Chambers, 'Slade School Influences on the Camden Town Group 1896–1910', in Helena Bonett, Ysanne Holt, Jennifer Mundy, eds, *The Camden Town Group in Context*, Tate Research Publications, May 2012, https://www.tate.org.uk/art/research-publications/camden-town-group/emma-chambers-slade-school-influences-on-the-camden-town-group-1896-1910-r1104373, accessed 20 August 2015.
19. See Schwabe, p.142.
20. Everett, *Memoirs*, p.41.
21. Arnold, p.38.

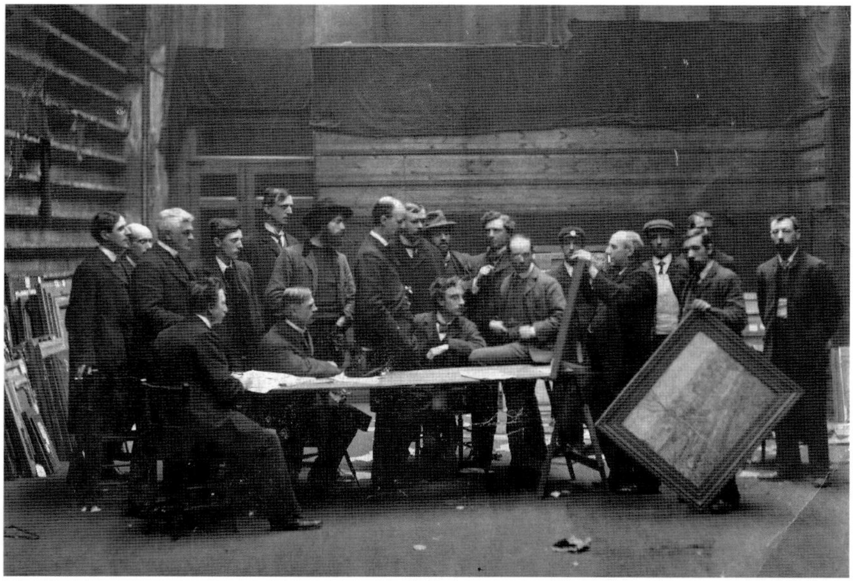

FIG. 20
*Last Jury of the New English Art Club at the Dudley Gallery, 1904**

* Back row (l to r): Walter Russell, David Muirhead, Alfred Rich, Ambrose McEvoy, Henry Tonks, Augustus John, D.S. MacColl, Philip Wilson Steer, Muirhead Bone, H. Francis Bate. Front row (seated): Fred Winter, Fred Brown, Roger Fry and William Rothenstein.

'the Slade continues to produce geniuses, we turn them out every year'.[22] In his memorial address dedicated to Henry Tonks, MacColl confirmed this 'fruit of the Brown-Tonks collaboration; a rare vintage of English draughtsmanship in Augustus John (fig. 23), and a host of others then and later'.[23] Faced with this remarkably talented group of students during the most illustrious period in its history, described by critic William Gaunt as 'individuals, in a sort of interim between a world of tradition and the world of change', tutors proffered instruction whilst allowing students their head, encouraging them to take the initiative in their work.[24] Tonks furthered individuality whilst inviting his students to be critical and questioning, and maintained privately that he learnt more from his pupils than they from him.[25] He formed lifelong friendships with those he admired and considered objectively serious.

THE NEW ENGLISH ART CLUB

In his 1937 memorial to Tonks, MacColl described the Slade as 'a nursery for the New English Art Club'.[26] Brown and Steer played leading roles setting up the New English in 1886, with fellow painters who had trained in Paris ateliers, and felt the Royal Academy denied them adequate opportunities to publicly display their work.[27] MacColl was instrumental in promoting the New English as it effectively came under the control of the Slade tutors. The first exhibition, which took place at the Marlborough Gallery in London, showed work by Steer, John Singer Sargent, George Clausen and Brown and challenged the Royal Academy's dominance and emphasis on history painting and anecdote. From that point the New English became the natural exhibiting space for Slade students and their tutors, with two exhibitions a year held in the summer and winter. Under its influence, works on paper also featured in the exhibitions by 1904.[28]

22. Quoted in Michael Holroyd, *Augustus John*, London: Pimlico, 2011, p.41. John, letter to The *Times*.
23. *Memorial to Tonks*. Chelsea Old Church, Thursday, 14 January 1937. An Address by D.S. MacColl, Exhibition Room, University College, Thursday, 25 November 1937, p.5.
24. William Gaunt, *A Concise History of English Painting*, London: Thames & Hudson, 1976, p.207. 'Nature and Art', *The Times*, 19 May 1933, p.10, includes a letter from Paul Nash, as a riposte to Tonks, in which he uses the phrase 'crisis of brilliance' to describe the students of 1896 to 1901.
25. 'Professor Tonks', *The Times*, 9 January 1937, p. 14; issue 47578.
26. MacColl, p.5.
27. *The Studio*, no.60, 1914, p.301. See too McConkey, pp.23–4. McConkey asserts that Paris in the final decades of the nineteenth century thronged with students of all nationalities and had become the world centre for art production.
28. Chaplin, 6:1–6:21, p.110.

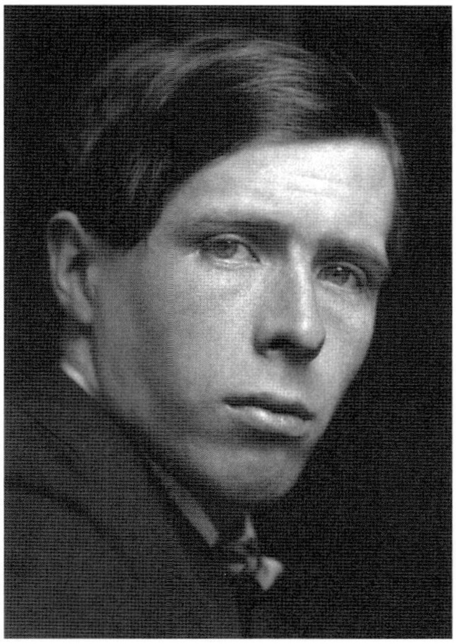

FIG. 21
William Orper, 1903
platinum print by George Charles Beresford; © National Portrait Gallery, London

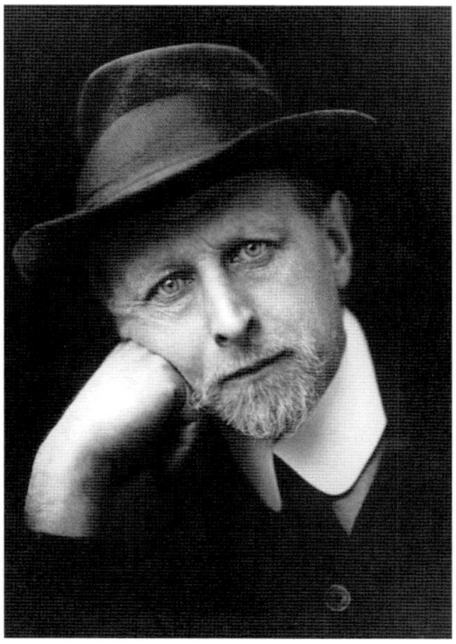

FIG. 22
John Everett, c.1901
photograph by George Charles Beresford; © National Portrait Gallery, London

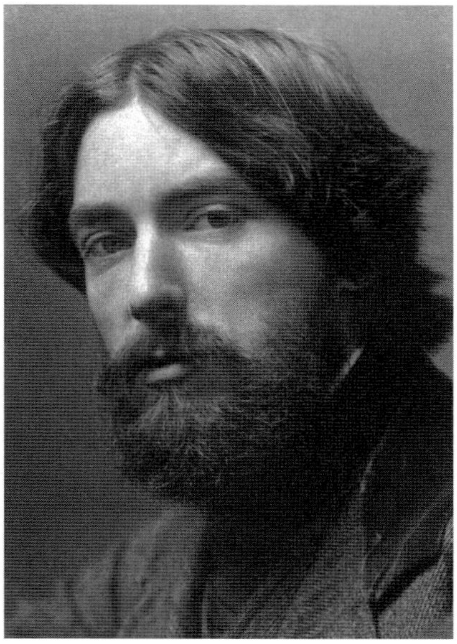

FIG. 23
Augustus John, 1902
sepia platinotype print by George Charles Beresford; © National Portrait Gallery, London

Each work submitted for exhibition was judged on artistic merits, not on academic formulae, with an emphasis on atmosphere, qualities of light, colour, harmony and tonal nuance. Although controlled by Slade tutors, works by the students were not assured acceptance by the Selecting Jury. It is telling that, of the 14 members of the 1904 jury (fig. 20), nine had visited Dorset to paint by 1916. In 1903 Orpen (fig. 21) wrote admiring a landscape by Everett (fig. 22), which had been rejected by the New English, for which Orpen blamed the frame.[29] The success of the New English was partly the result of influential patrons and collectors, who included: Sir Hugh Lane, Sir Michael Sadler, Lord Henry Bentinck, Judge William Evans, Geoffrey Blackwell and Charles Rutherston. Exhibitions provided the opportunity to see new ideas coming over the Channel, such as the Goupil exhibition at Dowdeswell's in 1899.[30] The New English resulted in a fresh wave of foreign influence, with paintings by Monet and Degas loaned to its exhibitions.[31] However, British art scholar McConkey contends that at this date the New English sought a British rather than French rationale for Impressionism, with Steer leading the way with his reappraisal of British artists like Constable and Gainsborough. Certainly Charles Cheston acknowledged that painters were consciously aiming at Constable's easy appearance of nature.[32]

SLADE STUDENTS

The precocious careers of William Orpen and Augustus John saw fellow Slade students sensing that they were witnessing a rare outburst of talent. Annual competitions for prizes, intended to refer to events from the Bible or heroic history, were introduced in 1897. They became a vital part of the Slade year and acted as a form of quality control, with Evelyn Cheston and Augustus John joint second prize-winners for figure painting in 1897–8.

29. Letter from William Orpen, 31 Sandbeck Park, Rotherham, November 1903 to John Everett at Woolbridge Manor (private collection), 'your landscape wanted a heavy floral frame and the design of the picture was big and firm. I know it's very hard to choose the right frame but one always knows one's mistake when one sees other frames and pictures alongside.' Everett exhibited nine paintings at the New English between 1900 and 1910.
30. Chaplin, 6:65c, p.149.
31. Ibid.
32. Cheston, p.27.

This was the year in which Orpen showed the early promise which anticipated his stylized pen-and-wash drawings, known for their freshness and immediacy and incorporating literary and contemporary figures, sometimes in costume.[33]

Everett's close student friends included Augustus John, Ambrose McEvoy, William Crampton Gore, Charles Stabb, Charles Julien Tharp and William Orpen.[34] His time at the Slade was intermittent, perhaps because the outstanding talent of close contemporaries meant highly competent artists like Everett faced an uphill task to stand out. His response was to scorn all forms of self-promotion and to exhibit largely away from London, where he felt more confident. Perhaps this intentional distancing from the competitive side of being an artist explains his year away from the Slade at sea.

In May 1898, aged 22, Everett headed to the London Docks and signed on as an ordinary seaman in the deep-sea sailing ship *Iquique*, bound for Australia, a trip marking the first of his 16 sea voyages.[35] Intending to paint on the voyage, Everett laid in a large supply of artists' oils, watercolours and materials from Percy Young, art supplier to the Slade. He found the voyage exciting, climbed the rigging in bare feet, admired the professionalism of the crew and relished their heady tales of shipwrecks and exotic South Sea islands. Everett regarded the sea as a site of escapism away from the irritations and demands of life ashore. His contemplative oil sketch (fig. 24) shows a lone figure seated on *Iquique*'s deck. He saw parallels between the life of the sailor and that of the painter, noting 'the utterly unconventional life of the artist and the sailor ... both vagabonds and wanderers'. It is a notable measure of his ability and the recognition he had achieved that, in 1907, his wash-and-pen deck scene on the *Iquique* was amongst 37 Slade works included in John Fothergill's *Collection of Drawings and Some Pictures Done by Past and Present Students of the London Slade School of Art, 1893–1907.*[36]

LIFE AT THE NEWCOMES

Augusta Everett's house, 21 Fitzroy Street, became one of the centres of life for a generation of Slade students, who named it 'the Newcomes' after an incident in William Makepeace Thackeray's book of the same name published in 1855. At the heart of the book, set in Fitzroy Square, is a young man, Clive Newcome, who had aspirations of becoming a painter, although the profession was frowned on by his relatives and acquaintances. This was a situation which perhaps resonated for students, such as Orpen, who admired the work of Thackeray. Augusta Everett proved a unifying force for the students, whom she amused and fascinated. Larger than life, loud, eccentrically dressed, charming and well connected, Augusta did not care what people thought of her. Informal and highly sociable, at Fitzroy Street she took the students under her wing, some of whom rented rooms at the Newcomes.

This house would form the setting for some of the most memorable and important images produced by Orpen and others in this early period, which will be discussed further in chapter four. Everett recalled that Augusta kept the top floor with two bedrooms for herself and Everett's

33. *London: The Slade and UCL*, PCF catalogue, London, 2005, p.98. The Slade art collection was started when the awarding of yearly prizes to top students was combined with a collection scheme in 1897 and the Summer Composition Prize and the Figure and Head Painting Prizes were kept by the school. See Chaplin, 6:66, pp.149–51. John's drawing of Evelyn was shown at the New English exhibition in 1962, *The Late Augustus John*, no. 354, loaned by Charles Cundall.

34. These portraits of Slade students and tutors (figs 16–21) were taken by fellow student, George Charles Beresford, the original model for 'M'Turk' in Kipling's *Stalky and Co.*, and for a while a close friend of Orpen. Beresford became an important portrait photographer, and the National Portrait Gallery has hundreds of examples of his work.

35. On the trip Everett developed his practice of keeping a log, with numerous observations of clouds, sea state and sky as well as sketches of shipping and life on deck.

36. John Fothergill, ed., *The Slade: A Collection of Drawings and Some Pictures Done by Past and Present Students of the London Slade School of Art, 1893–1907*, London: Slade School, University College, 1907, plate 79, *Ship's Deck*. Everett's signed drawing, *The Iquique: View Aft from the Forecastle*, 1898, pencil and wash on paper mounted on board, now in NMM collection, PAH4284, inscribed verso *Iquique 98*.

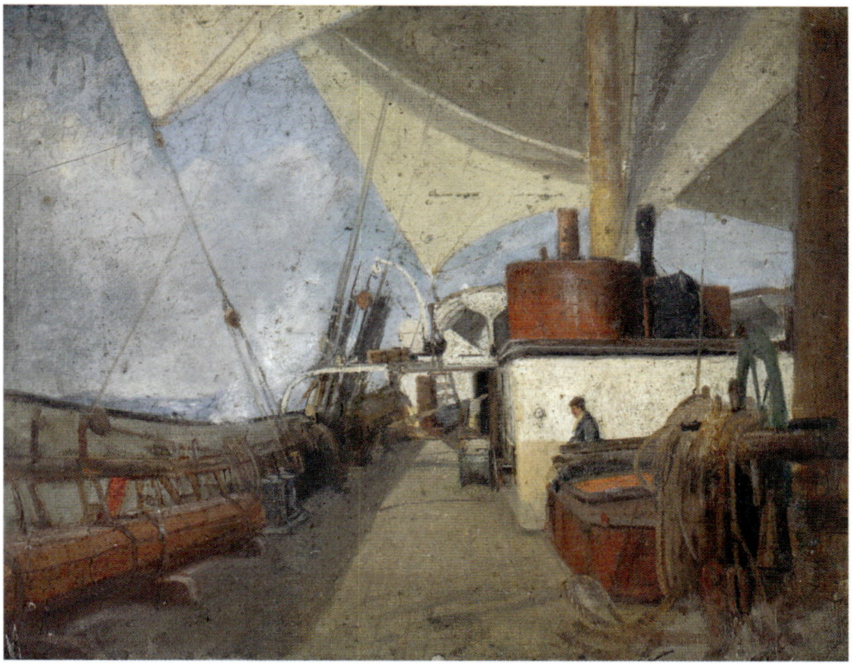

FIG. 24
John Everett / ***Deck Scene on the 'Iquique'***
1899 / oil sketch on board / 24.7 x 32.3 cm

half cousin Katherine Herbert, also at the Slade, and let the rest of the house to other students. She turned a top-lit basement workshop into a drawing room complete with fireplace and pillar supporting the roof. Rothenstein described the Newcomes as 'comfortless quarters' though economical. For several years Augusta's sociable Sunday School afternoons formed a gathering point for the students, who tolerated her hymn singing by smuggling in bottles of spirits, despite her voluble pronouncements on the evils of drink.[37] Inevitably this caused amusement amongst the painters aware of the bibulous reputations of Augustus John and Charles Conder. Yet perhaps the unconventional Augusta provided a haven for Augustus, Gwen and Winifred John, who had lost their mother at a young age.[38] The house also became an important place for artistic experimentation, with the floor often littered with Augustus John's drawings.[39] On his return from Vattetot-sur-Mer in September 1899, Orpen took up residence.[40] He bought furniture from Augusta, including the four-poster bed which features in his portrait of Augustus John now in the National Portrait Gallery (see fig. 48).

The Slade group was extended to include family and former students, making for a rich social life, which involved many excursions and outings. Ethel Hatch recalled a spring picnic in about 1899, when Augusta invited around 18 of them to picnic at the home of her Dorset friends, the Dudley Ryders at Westbrook, Boxmoor in Hertfordshire.[41] Travelling by train they were met by Augusta wearing a sunbonnet and seated in the Dudley Ryders' large yellow farm cart, led by a driver in a smock. The Dudley Ryders provided the picnic tea for Augusta's group, whom they believed to be her Sunday School, and which Everett, Orpen, John and Rothenstein

37. Holroyd, p.80.
38. Gwen John's watercolour sketch shows 21 Fitzroy Street (UCL collection), when they shared rooms over the winter of 1897–8. Rosa Waugh, Gwen's brother Augustus and sister Winifred then studying music, sit with Michel Salaman. Gwen appears outside the window, with her back to the room. The Johns' mother, already incapacitated with chronic rheumatism, died in 1884, precipitating a move for the family from Haverfordwest to Tenby. See Holroyd, pp.5–7,11–13.
39. Everett, *Memoirs*, p.42, and Arnold, p.55.
40. Everett, *Memoirs*, p.75.
41. Interview with Ethel Hatch (1869–1975) for the BBC's Third Programme, 'Out of the Air'. See *The Listener*, 'Partie de Campagne', 'Out of the Air', 23 November 1967, issue 2017, p.669. A photograph of the picnic featured under the heading, 'Fifty Years: The Art World of the Nineties' in *The Times*, 2 March 1932, p.16.

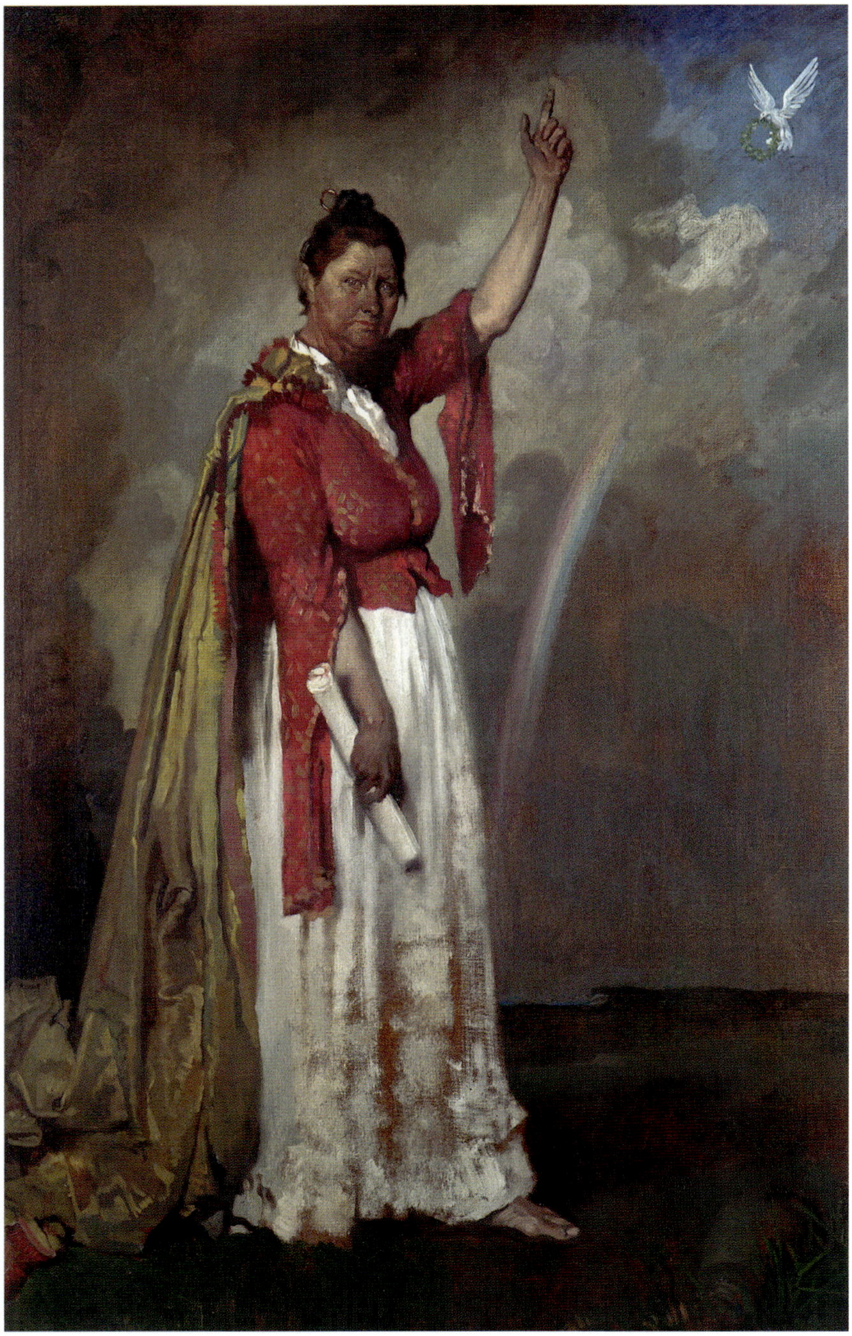

FIG. 25

William Orpen / ***Augusta Everett on the Island of Patmos***

c.1901 / oil on canvas / 91.4 x 63.5 cm

Fascinated by Augusta Everett, Orpen has positioned her in a cave on Patmos, adopting the role of John the Apostle receiving a vision of Jesus. Taken from the Book of Revelation, from which Augusta loudly cited passages in the skeleton room at the Slade, Orpen is celebrating her eccentricity

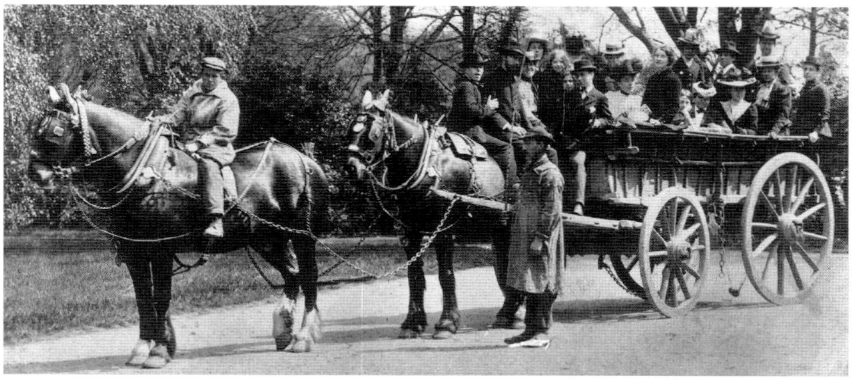

FIG. 26

*Augusta Everett's Slade Picnic at Boxmoor, Hertfordshire, c.1899**

vintage bromide print; © National Portrait Gallery, London

* William Orpen and Augustus John are seated on the horse, with Albert Rothenstein behind. Artists in the cart include Augusta in the centre, William and Alice Rothenstein, John Everett, Ethel Hatch and Edna Clark Hall.

supplemented with bottles of rum, whisky, brandy and gin.[42] Augustus John got spectacularly drunk.[43] A press photograph (fig. 26) of the trip reveals the close-knit group with Augusta in their midst. She particularly fascinated William Orpen, prompting Katherine Everett to write that … 'Billy Orpen with his great sense of fun enjoyed Aurelia [Katherine's name for Augusta]. He painted her and made some comic drawings of her' and also of himself at the Newcomes (fig. 28).[44] Mesmerized by her erratic behaviour, Orpen discovered he had been conned by Augusta over his portrait of her (fig. 25). He wrote to Everett:

> You must see that the picture was stolen from me by that great grand and most wonderful woman I know namely your mother – in fact the portrait of Mrs. Everett all round has been one of the greatest swindles of modern times and I should have things written about it.[45]

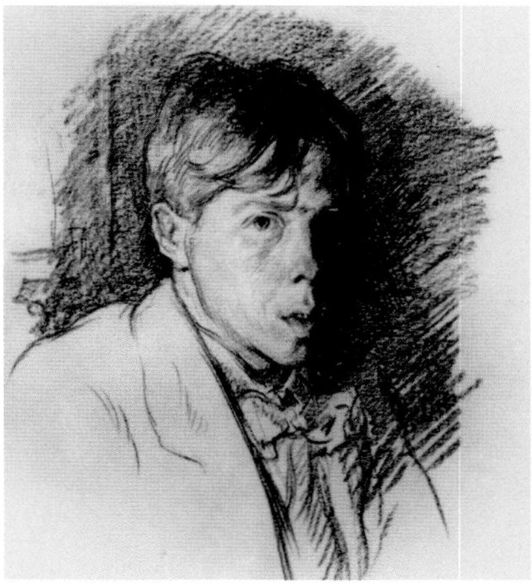

FIG. 27

William Orpen / *Self-Portrait*

c.1898 / pencil / 19.1 x 14.6cm

© National Portrait Gallery, London

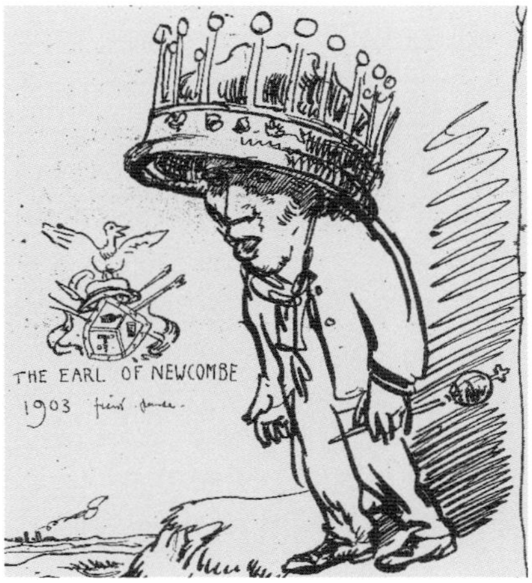

FIG. 28

William Orpen / *Earl of Newcombe*

1903

The coat of arms (a wine bottle, cork-screw and glass, topped with his hat) allude to his enthusiasm for drinking

private collection

42. Lt Col. Dudley Granville Richard Ryder's wife Ada, née Carr Glyn, daughter of Lt-Gen. Sir John Plumptre Carr Glyn, was born in Wimborne and knew Augusta from Dorset days.
43. Everett, *Memoirs*, pp.81–2.
44. Katherine Everett, p.116. A faint set of initials, *A.R.*, lower left on Orpen's self-portrait, led to a suggested attribution of fellow Slade student and friend Albert Rutherston. The drawing was sold as a drawing by Albert Rutherston but by 28 March 1958 was reappraised as a self-portrait when sold at Christie's.
45. Letter from William Orpen, Metropolitan School of Art, Dublin, November 1908, to John Everett, private collection.

EVERETT, JOHN AND FRIENDSHIP

> If you want to become a genius, dive on to a rock.[46]

Augustus John and John Everett were closely linked during their student days in London, and later in Dorset, which will be discussed further in chapter seven. At the Slade from 1894, Augustus was joined by his sister Gwen the following year, and from early in 1897 they shared Augusta's first-floor flat with their sister Winifred and fellow Slade student Grace Westray. Everett's memoirs indicate his close friendship with John, describing him initially as 'a poor physical specimen, never played games … a quiet boy, a great reader, a studious youth producing unexceptional work' (fig. 29).[47] After John sustained a serious head injury on rocks at Tenby, Everett offered an account of the changes this caused, noting that John

> suddenly developed. Physically and mentally. Started doing brilliant drawings, fellows used to watch him draw, and pick up his drawings off the floor. He started to grow a beard, and filled out physically. I was not the only one who noticed it. I, knowing him much better than the others, I was more conscious of it.[48]

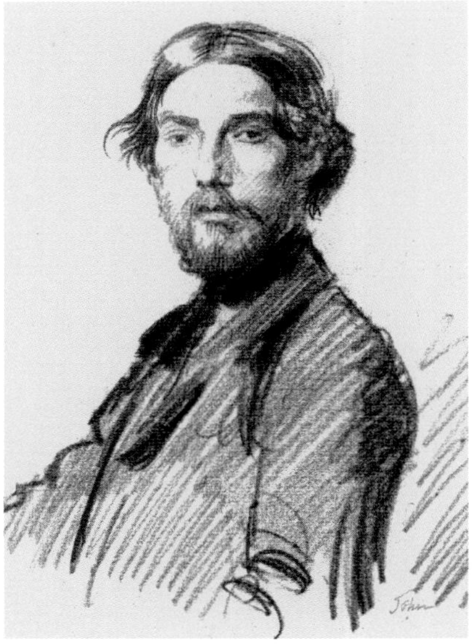

FIG. 29
Augustus John / *Self-Portrait*
c.1901 / chalk / 26 x 17.8 cm
estate of Augustus John/Bridgman Art Library; © National Portrait Gallery

Everett's version of the transformation of John's character from 'poor physical specimen' into a legendary rabble-rouser with a remarkable talent for drawing was accepted by John Rothenstein, leading to Everett's assertion that: 'if you want to become a genius, dive on to a rock.'[49] Everett remained John's stalwart friend, accepting unquestioningly his complicated life and likening him to the *Iquique* sailors he so admired. Everett's memoirs indicate they remained in contact and later experimented with printmaking.[50]

Back from sea in 1899, Everett returned to his Fitzroy Street studio and met up with all his old friends. He joined John, Orpen and Conder in frequenting music halls and theatres, mingling with a wide cross-section of society at the Café Royal and the beer hall of Olde Gambrinus. According to Everett, John was grimily dressed as a Parisian artist of the 1880s, wearing a large black hat and baggy corduroy trousers on which he wiped his brushes.[51] The group was often joined by Arthur Streeton, who later visited Everett in Dorset.

Around this date Orpen was producing a large number of pen-and-wash drawings, many of which were given to Everett, who loaned 15 to the Royal Academy in 1933. This recently rediscovered and important resource throws light on their relationship. The drawings all follow a format characterizing Orpen's early work: a combination of literary and historical themes with contemporary characters, frequently his friends. The history subjects produced for Slade competitions were combined with a feeling that artists should paint the contemporary.[52] In his Summer School composition of 1897 Orpen showed early promise by incorporating historical, literary and contemporary figures.[53] Augustus John set the precedent for future Slade Summer Composition Prizes in 1898 with *Moses and The Brazen Serpent*, a confident demonstration of his understanding of Old Master compositional devices. The following year painter Hubert Wellington wrote that the competition saw Orpen adopting Hogarthian conventions in his conflation of a history painting with contemporary figures in an interior entitled *Play Scene from 'Hamlet'* (Houghton Hall): 'the whole painting has a lurking air

46. Everett, *Memoirs*, p.42.
47. Ibid.
48. Ibid.
49. John Rothenstein, p.178.
50. Everett, *Memoirs*, p.168.
51. Ibid, p.74.
52. Chaplin, 6:66, pp.149–51, and 6.67.
53. 'Bathers', long a favoured subject for painters, was the title chosen for the 1900 Summer Composition Prize at the Slade, jointly won by Everett's associate, Charles Julian Tharp, and Max West, PCF, p.100.

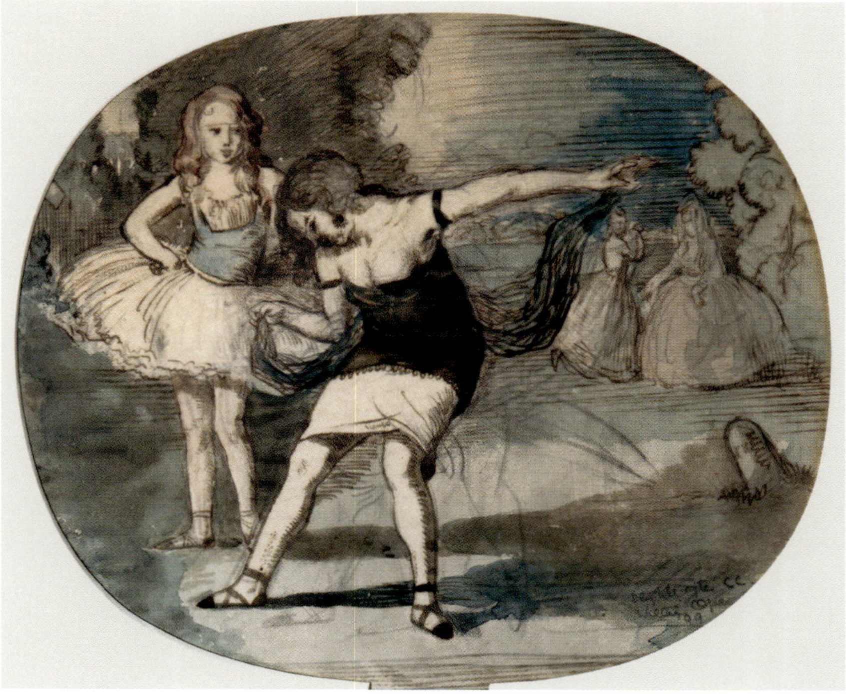

FIG. 30
William Orpen / ***Willi's Dance***
c.1899 / pen and wash / 23 x 27 cm
A frequent visitor to music halls and the theatre, Orpen shows two dancers rehearse as supernatural dancing-girls
private collection

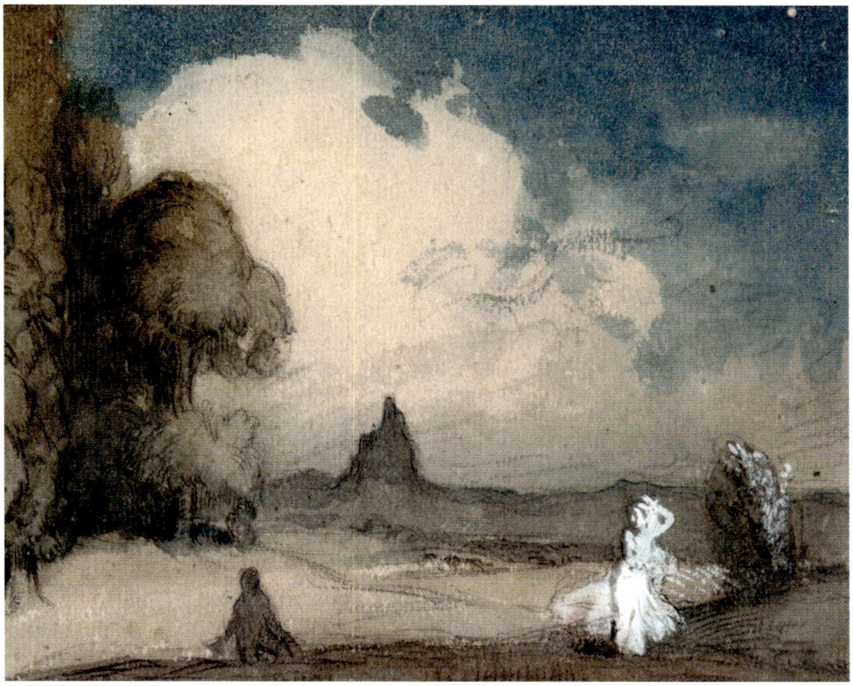

FIG. 31
William Orpen / ***Romance***
1900 / pencil, pen, wash and body colour / 20 x 25.5 cm
private collection

of irony and bravado which comes as rather a shock in a sober competition.'[54] Precisely the combination of literary reference and modern anecdote adopted by Orpen in the drawings he gave Everett.

Orpen's sketches of his fellow students inform the nature of their friendships and are a powerful adjunct to Everett's memoirs. For instance, Orpen gave Everett his drawing of Augustus John wearing a new green corduroy suit, with the caption *John at Sight of a Lady*, Vattetot-sur-Mer, 1899. Orpen presented Everett with a pen-and-wash sketch of dancers, *Willi's Dance* (fig. 30), a reference to Heinrich Heine's 1837 essay on folklore, *Elementargeister*, or *Elemental Spirits*.[55] The willis were supernatural dancing-girls, who rose from their graves and drove the men who jilted them at the altar to death, through their abandoned, wild dancing. Orpen shows two ballet dancers rehearsing on the stage against a sylvan backdrop. The dancer in the centre holds a black veil, implying she represents a willi, contrasting with the relaxed attitude of the blonde ballerina to her right. In the distance, two female figures, dressed in costume, typify the work of Conder, whom Orpen admired. *Le Villi* (*The Willi(s)* or *The Fairies*) was turned into an opera-ballet by Puccini and enjoyed a revival at the beginning of the twentieth century, when Orpen's group, regular visitors to music and concert halls in London, probably saw it.[56] 'Willi' may also be Orpen's play on his name. His *Romance* (fig. 31) is a related sketch; in the dreamy, sylvan setting a female dancer in white – perhaps another willi – performs a dance to a seated male.[57] Orpen and John read Heinrich Heine and were sharing ideas of the supernatural at the time, so that Augustus John incorporated a similar dancing figure in his large oil painting *Walpurgis Night* (private collection), which shows Faust and Mephistopheles witnessing a witches' coven on the summit of the Brocken.[58]

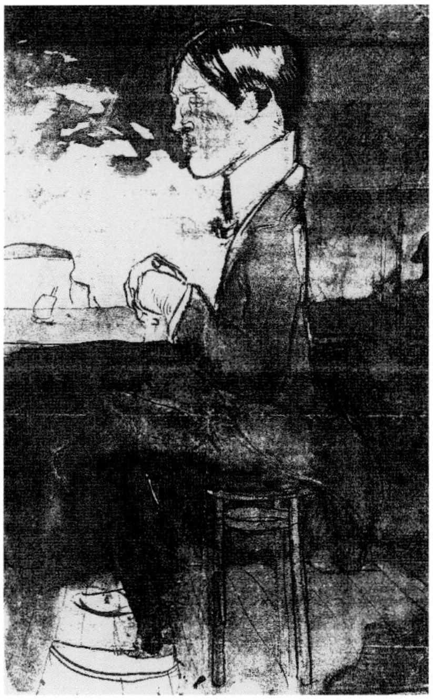

FIG. 32
William Orpen
Mr C. A Portrait by the Sea
1900
private collection

JOHN AND CONDER IN SWANAGE, 1900

> The country here is lovely beyond words[59]

It was on his second Dorset trip to the Everetts in 1900 that John began working on *Walpurgis Night*.[60] The ever-hospitable and eccentric Augusta evidently enjoyed the company of Slade students and their friends, and often invited them to stay during vacations at her Swanage home, Peveril Tower (fig. 15), very close to the sea. Katherine Everett recalled the students bathing, sketching and going for moonlight walks along the cliffs. Gwen and Augustus John stayed in the summer of 1899 and John returned in early summer the following year, with Conder (fig. 32) and Slade students Margaret (Daisy) Legge and Elinor Monsell, whom Conder promptly propositioned.[61] John, with trimmed beard, tailcoat, cap and high collar, wrote to Orpen of Augusta's teetotal regime: 'Conder and I have a cottage to ourselves we drink milk and soda and tea in large quantities tho' I must confess to a pint of beer occasionally on going into the town.'[62] He wrote rhapsodically to William Rothenstein about the Dorset countryside: 'the country here is lovely beyond words. Corfe Castle and the neighbourhood would make you mad with painter's cupidity.'[63]

Older than the other students, Conder was a friend of William Rothenstein. Conder was also much admired by Orpen and was a drinking companion

54. Hubert L.Wellington, 'The Slade School Summer Competition since 1893', ed. John Fothergill, p.25.
55. The name Willi [or Wili] comes from the Slavic description of Vila or sylvan spirits.
56. Composed by Giacomo Puccini to an Italian libretto by Ferdinando Fontana, the original one-act version was first performed at the Teatro Dal Verme, Milan, on 31 May 1884 and modified to form its final version by 1892. Later it was used in the ballet *Giselle*. The two-act romantic French ballet, *Les Wilis* (or *Night Dancers*) on this theme, known as Giselle, was first produced in Paris in1841. The ballet is about a peasant girl named Giselle who dies of a broken heart after discovering her lover is betrothed to another. The willis summon Giselle from her grave and target her lover for death, but Giselle's love frees him from their grasp. *Giselle* fell out of fashion in the late nineteenth century and was not performed in London until 1911 at Covent Garden Royal Opera House.
57. Wilfrid Meynell, 'William Orpen', *The Artist*, August 1901, no. 260, p.182. The drawing featured with the title *Romance* in Meynell's article focusing on the importance of the young William Orpen.
58. A pen-and-wash drawing of the same subject (Tate) shows how this group of artists were collaborating. See too Augustus John, *Finishing Touches*, London: Jonathan Cape, 1966, p.40.
59. Undated letter from Augustus John c/o Mrs Everett, Peveril Tower, Swanage, Dorset, to William Rothenstein, *Men and Memories: A History of the Arts, 1872–1922. Being the Recollections of William Rothenstein*, vol. I, London: Faber and Faber, 1931, p.355.
60. Tate Archive, letter to Augustus John, Fryern Court, Fordingbridge, 5 July 1957 and John's reply.
61. Everett, *Memoirs*, p.84. Margaret Legge and John Everett remained in contact for the rest of their lives. Monsell and Legge are probably the young women featured in Conder's *On the Beach, Swanage*, 1900 (Manchester City Art Gallery).
62. Undated letter from Augustus John c/o Mrs Everett, Peveril Tower, Swanage, Dorset, to William Orpen, 1900, private collection.
63. John to Rothenstein, p.355.

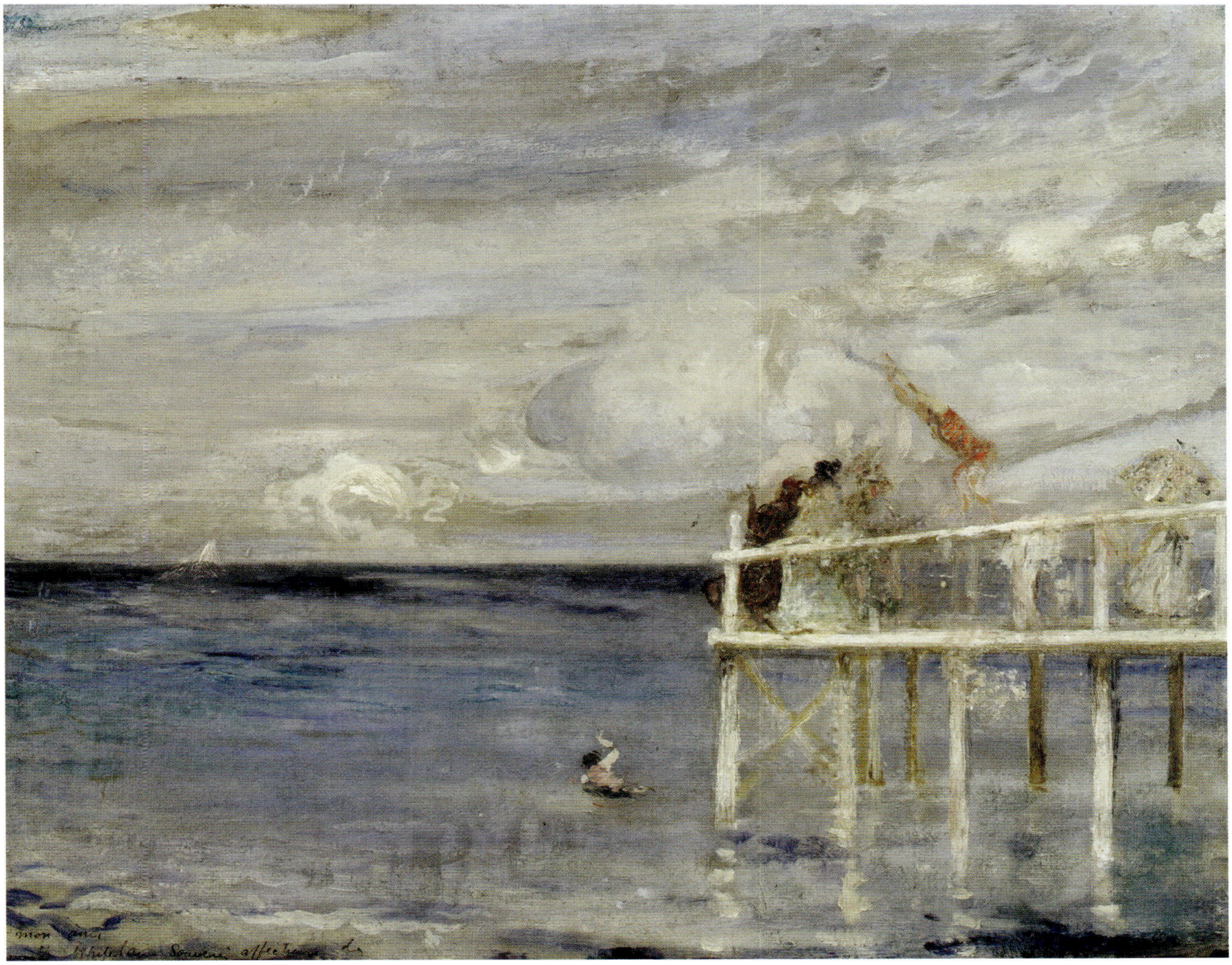

FIG. 33
Charles Conder / ***Swanage***
c.1899–1901 / oil on cardboard / 39.3 x 49.5 cm

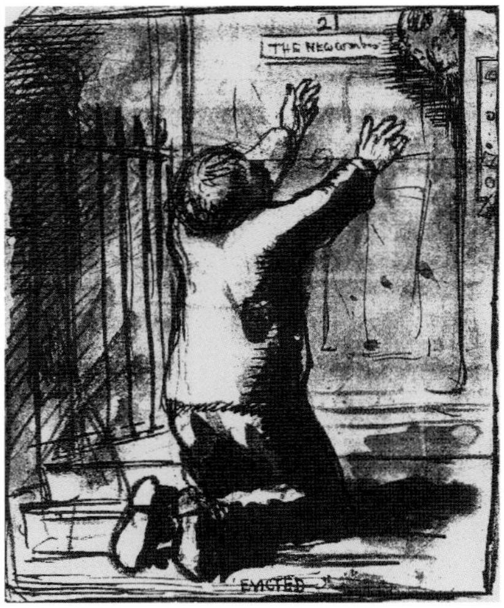

FIG. 34
William Orpen / *Evicted*
c.1901
Orpen pleading with Everett to be allowed back in to the Newcomes
private collection

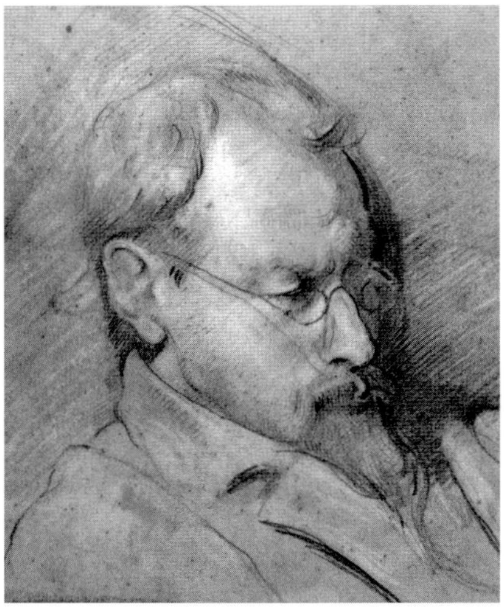

FIG. 35
William Crampton Gore
John Everett in Dorset
1900 / pencil / 16.5 x 17.2 cm
private collection

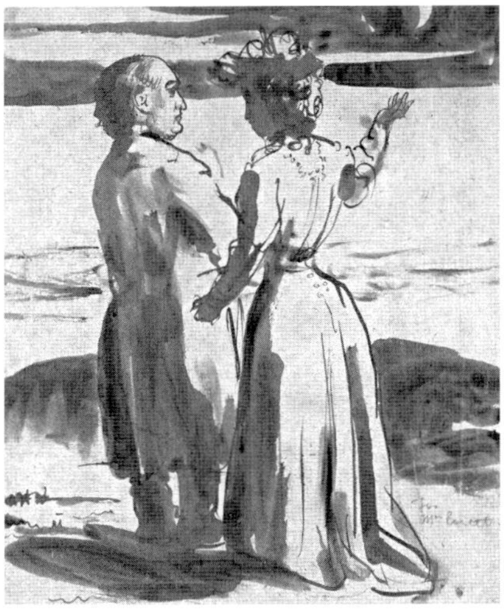

FIG. 36
Augustus John
Mrs Everett and Charles Conder at Swanage
1900 / pen and wash / 31 x 24 cm
A humorous sketch reversing the true sizes of Conder and Augusta Everett
© estate of Augustus John; courtesy Sotheby's

of John and Everett.[64] Finding Swanage 'quite untouched by modernism' he wrote to Rothenstein of the beauty of the area, and produced nine small Whistleresque scenes *en plein air.*[65] One freely painted oil panel, *Swanage*, faces beyond the coastguard station towards the Everett's first Swanage home at Peveril Point (fig. 37). Another *Swanage* (fig. 33) has a shimmering effect resembling Conder's paintings on silk, in which colours dissolve. It features a figure diving off the old stone pier at Swanage, close to Peveril Tower, to join a companion in the water. Indistinctly painted, several women standing on the pier seemingly merge with sky and sea. Several other Swanage paintings were influenced by the *fêtes galantes* which inspired Philip Wilson Steer – such as Conder's *The Embarkment* (Manchester City Art Gallery), exhibited at the New English in 1900. Rococo in style, Conder's oils fit John's description in a letter to Orpen from Peveril Tower: 'I am sweating over a decoration – Conder engaged on an ever more beautiful "Fête galante"'.[66]

For part of that summer of 1900, Everett was staying at Stokeford, near Wareham, with the Meades. Joined by the Swanage contingent and Slade painters, John Henry Titcomb, William Crampton Gore (fig. 35), Charles Julian Tharp and H.S. Chancellor, they visited the stunning location of Worbarrow Bay. Conder later wrote to Everett: 'I remember Warborough [sic] Bay with great pleasure it's a wonderful place.'[67] Everett had painted there before and a decade later returned to paint a series of powerful oil sketches (figs. 86–91). His oil sketch looking over Swanage Bay towards the Needles in the distance was probably painted in May 1901 (fig. 38). His vantage point is the Wellington Clock Tower, positioned on the edge of the garden of Peveril Tower and used by Everett as his living quarters (fig. 15).

64. Conder trained in NSW, Australia as a surveyor, where he met the painter Tom Roberts (born in Dorchester), known as Bulldog. Between 1882 and 1885, Conder was in Europe, where he admired the work of Jules Bastien-Lepage. Inspired by Roberts' paintings based on French realism and Impressionism, in 1888 Conder joined Roberts and Streeton at Eaglemount Camp near Heidelberg for the summer months over two years. By 1890 he was a member of the 'Naughty Nineties' and a friend of Aubrey Beardsley, Max Beerbohm and Toulouse-Lautrec. See Ursula Hoff, 'Charles Conder, Arthur Streeton and Tom Roberts', *Apollo*, 118ii, 1983, pp.508–12.
65. Cited in Ann Galbally, *Charles Conder: The Last Bohemian*, Melbourne: Miegunyah Press, Melbourne University Publishing, 2002, p.217. Everett's *Memoirs* noted that 'Conder's methods were interesting. He worked on a very absorbent, unprimed canvas. Without size or any preparations, started straight on the canvas', p.87.
66. John to Orpen, letter. Conder's painting, *Swanage Bay* (Tate), was lent by Charles H. Moore to the 'Twenty Years of British Art' exhibition held at the Whitechapel Art Gallery, 1910. Two entitled *Swanage Bay* were loaned to the Tate Gallery retrospective exhibition, 1927, one belonging to Morton H. Sands (no. 88) and the other to Geoffrey Blackwell (no. 93), who actively collected Slade pictures.
67. Letter from Charles Conder at the Hotel de Commerce, Cany, August 1900, to John Everett, private collection.

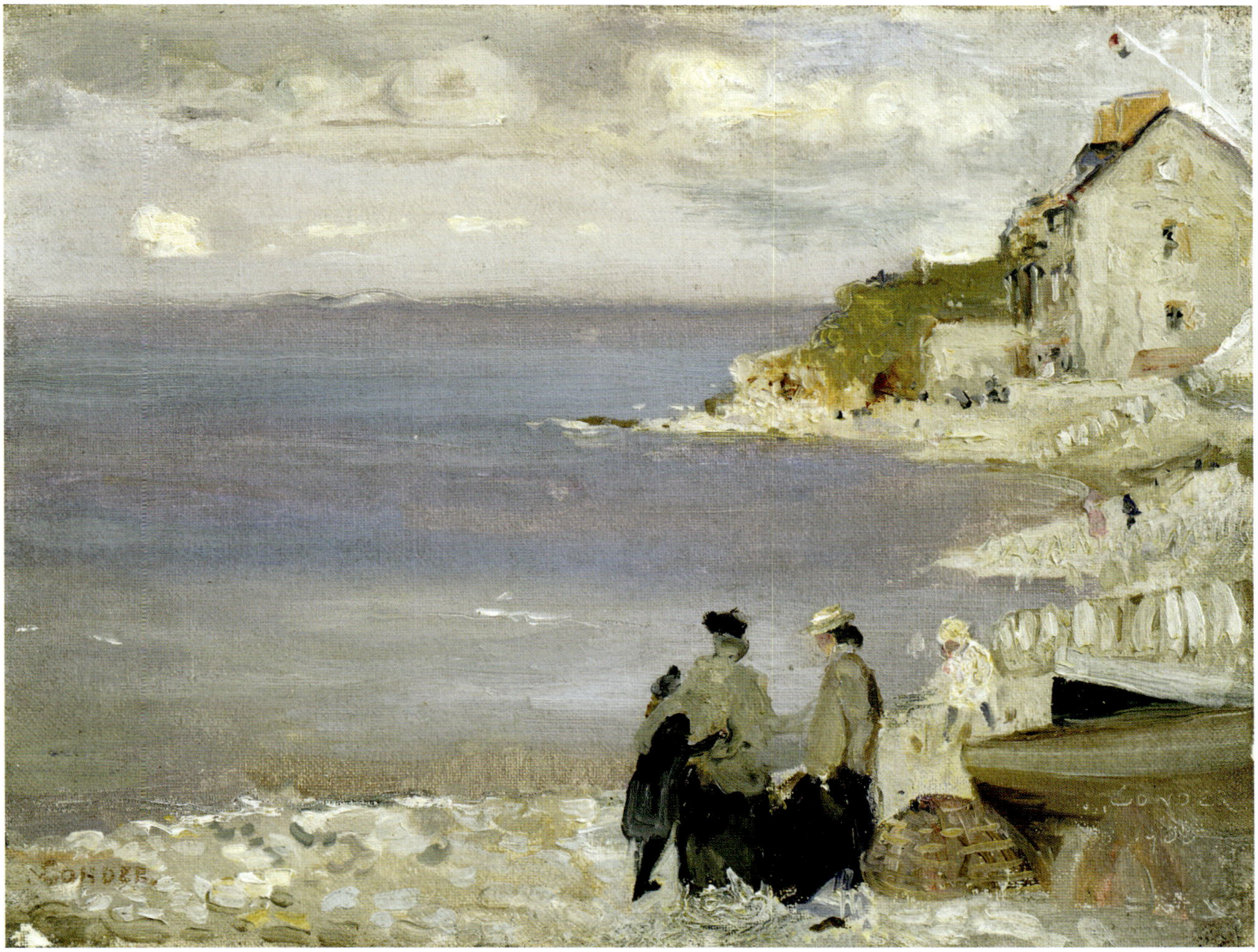

FIG. 37

Charles Conder / ***Swanage***

1900 / oil on canvas / 22.9 x 30.5 cm

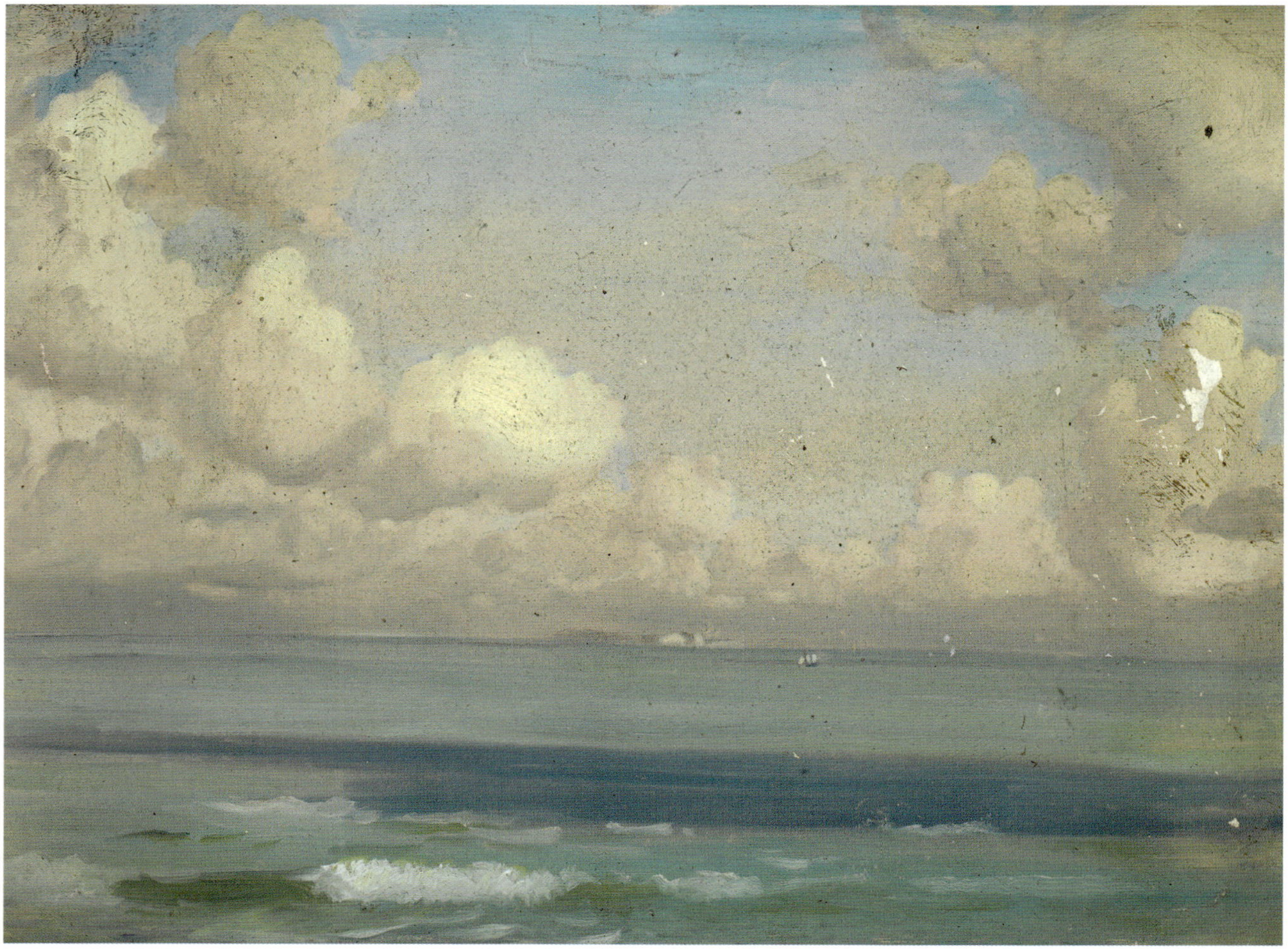

FIG. 38

John Everett / ***Swanage***

1900 / oil sketch on paper / 35.6 x 50.2 cm

The first decade of the twentieth century saw the fortunes of the New English fluctuate and by 1908 they had hit a low point, with the work of Everett's contemporary Ambrose McEvoy described as offering 'the art of the bottom drawer'.[68] *The Studio* began demanding more of British landscape painting than just the *plein air* work, which 'leaves the artist poorly equipped on the more poetic or imaginative side of his art'.[69] Artists were encouraged to seek other responses, like poetry, which, when combined with the personality of the artist, would satisfy these new demands. Herbert Edwin Pelham Hughes-Stanton, painting in Purbeck in 1905, was praised for being 'absolutely undisturbed by the fret and fume and unrest of an empirical age', and for his individual approach to nature, which 'add[ed] something worth possessing to the sum-total of the art of the country in which he lives'.[70] The *Art Journal* demanded more from landscape painters than work produced solely on instinct, praising Bertram Priestman, another Slade visitor to Dorset, for his landscapes, which rejected detail in favour of massiveness, simplicity and worthier aims 'borne of subtlety of knowledge' – effectively a bid towards a Modernist agenda.[71] The Sladites and Post-Impressionists of Bloomsbury were poised to play this out on the rolling downs and beaches of Purbeck.[72]

68. Martin T. Wood, 'The Pictures of Ambrose McEvoy', *The Studio*, vol. 42, 1908, p.96.
69. Marion Hepworth Dixon, 'The Landscape Paintings of Mr. H. Hughes-Stanton', *The Studio*, 1908, vol. 42, pp.269–79.
70. Ibid, p.270.
71. Frederick Wedmore, 'Bertram Priestman', *Art Journal*, 1907, pp.174–8.
72. See Kristina Huneault, 'The Painted Canvases of Helen McNicoll', *Art History*, vol. 27, no. 2, April 2004, pp. 212–49, Association of Art Historians, 2004, Oxford: Blackwell Publishing.

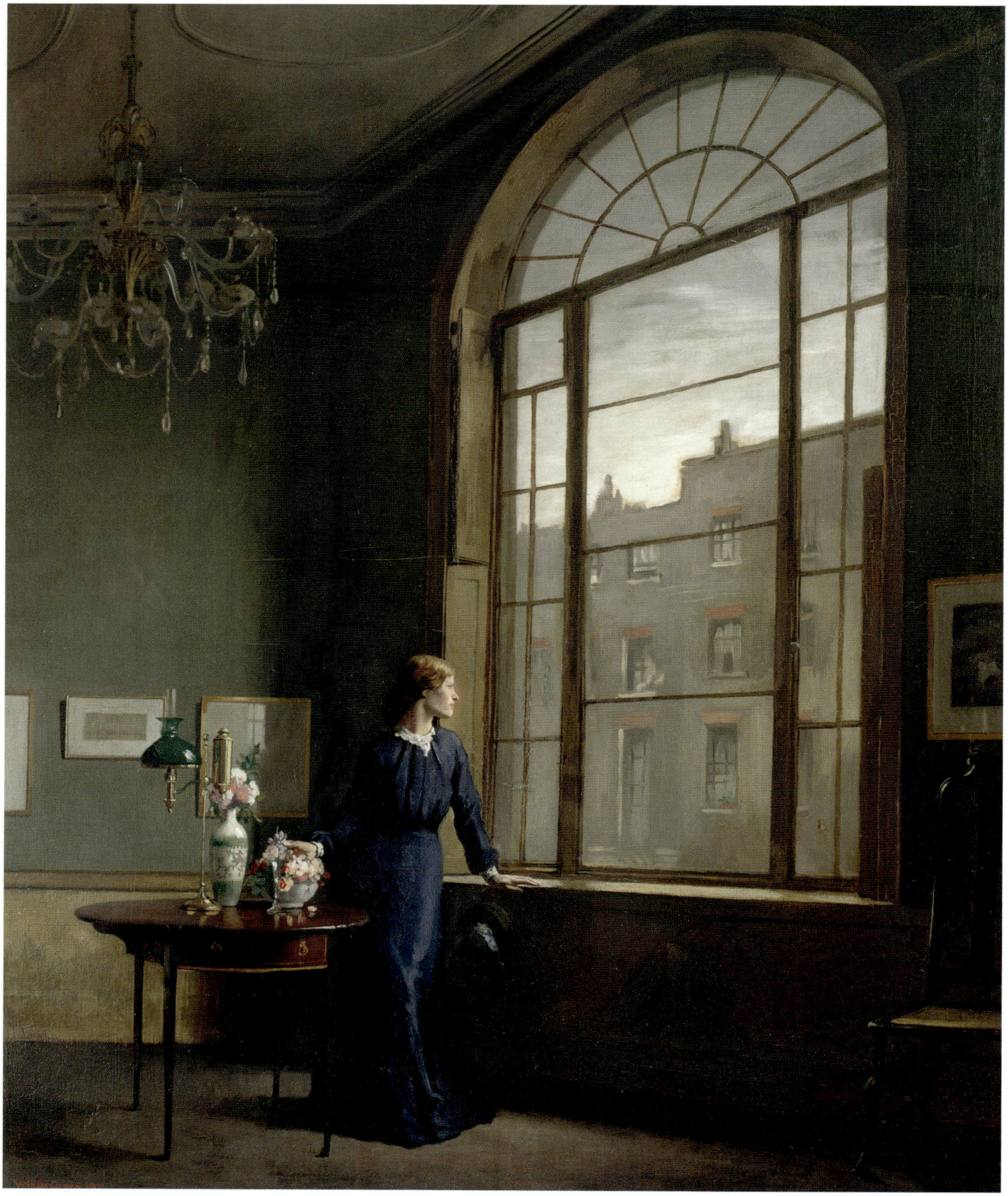

FIG. 39

William Orpen / ***Window in London Street***

1901 / oil on canvas / 103 x 87 cm

photo © National Gallery of Ireland

FOUR

ORPEN AND EVERETT

Orpen was the best company of any man I ever met[1]

William Orpen's arrival at the Slade, probably in May 1897, marked the beginning of a close friendship with Everett – who was also a distant relation.[2] Throughout the decade they corresponded regularly and a remarkable series of Orpen's illustrated letters to Everett survive, previously unpublished and undiscussed. This chapter draws largely on these extraordinary documents, to reconstruct the intimate friendship between Orpen, Everett and other members of the Slade circle. As discussed in the previous chapter, for some of the time at the Slade, Orpen made his home at the Newcomes, the Everetts' house in Fitzroy Street. Orpen's vigorous and gritty paintings of contemporary life, encouraged at the Slade, included references to his companionship with Everett, either using props from the Newcomes and Everett's studio or alluding to Everett's maritime interests. These details have been overlooked by previous scholars, unaware of the specific artistic milieu of the Everetts at Fitzroy Street, and deserve further exploration.

Before moving to Fitzroy Street, Orpen, living at Torrington Square, made sketches of Everett's 12-candle chandeliers to feature in the *Play Scene from 'Hamlet'*, 1899 (Houghton Hall), in which he conflated a history painting with contemporary figures in an interior.[3] They appeared in several Orpen interiors such as *The Mirror*, 1900 (fig. 42), reflected in the circular, black, wooden-framed concave mirror. Orpen also appears, working at his easel, in Everett's Fitzroy Street studio, surrounded by the props featured in his other paintings.[4] *The Mirror* focuses on Emily Scobel, a Slade model and Orpen's sometime mistress, seated in profile in the studio, below three of Everett's maritime sketches (of the *Iquique*), the same setting Orpen used in his portrait of Everett (fig. 49).[5] The chandeliers appear again in Orpen's *Window in London Street*, 1901 (fig. 39), featuring the distinctive window in Everett's studio, in *The Refugees*, 1901–5 (private collection), and in an illustrated letter showing Everett with a bottle of rum (fig. 40).[6]

TRAVELS IN EUROPE

Constant European travel was an important feature of British art in the first decade of the twentieth century, and in 1899 John, Orpen, Conder,

1. Everett, *Memoirs*, p.64.
2. Arnold, p.38; Everett, *Memoirs*, p.41. Arnold Orpen's arrival at the Slade could be taken as October, when he first signed the register. Everett suggested Orpen arrived in the summer term of 1897. I am indebted to Christopher Pearson of the Orpen Research Project, who reveals Orpen and Everett were fifth cousins twice removed.
3. Orpen's scene from *Hamlet* shows King Claudius watching a theatrical performance about the murder of a king (Act 3, Scene 2) and includes Orpen's contemporaries. The painting won the 1899 Slade prize for best composition. See *London: The Slade and UCL*, PCF catalogue, London, 2005, p.100.
4. His nod to Van Eyck's *Arnolfini Portrait*, National Gallery, shows how Orpen used the old masters as a reference point in his contemporary work.
5. Steer used Scobel as his model for his oil, *Convalescent*, 1898, Southampton City Art Gallery, 557, with Scobel seated in a bath chair.
6. Everett, *Memoirs*, Everett's studio faced London Street, later changed to Maple Street, p.39. Undated letter from William Orpen, Royal Hospital Road, Chelsea, S.W. to John Everett in Dorset (private collection).

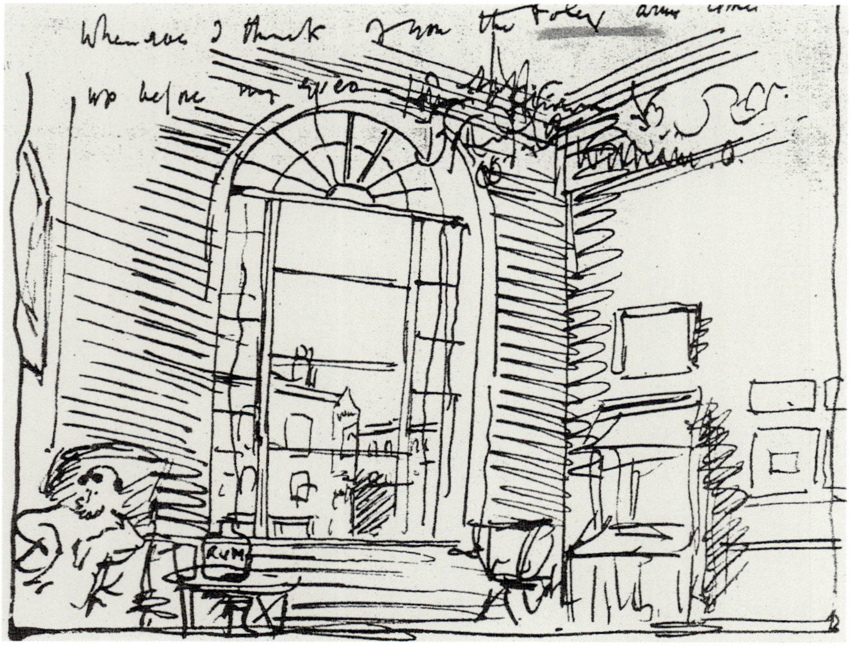

FIG. 40

William Orpen / *Everett's Room at 21 Fitzroy Street*

Sketch from a letter featuring Everett in his studio

private collection

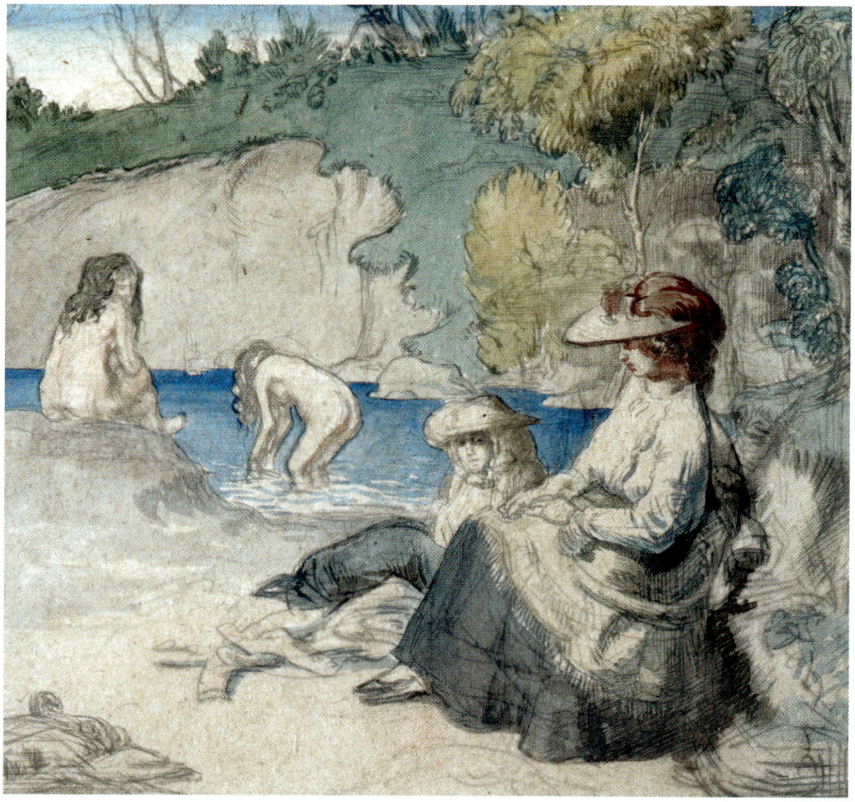

FIG. 41

William Orpen / *Noontide*

1899 / pencil and wash / 23 x 25 cm

private collection

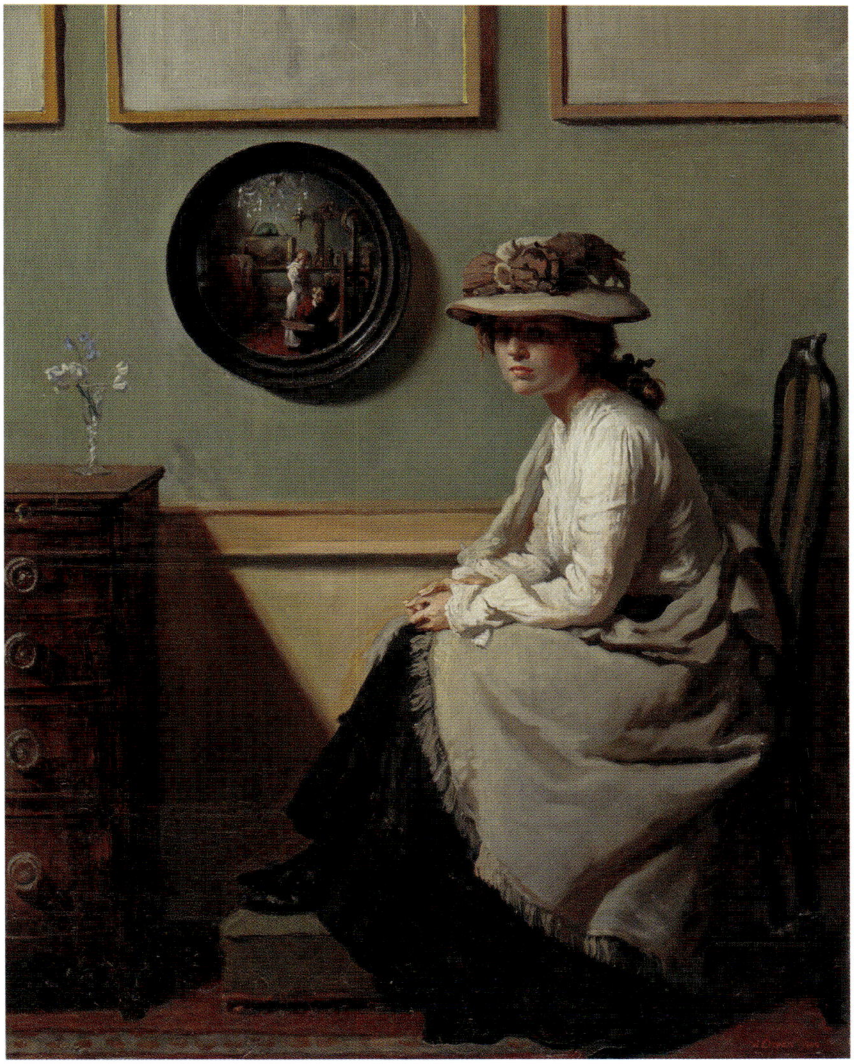

FIG. 42
William Orpen / ***The Mirror***
1900 / oil on canvas / 50.8 x 40.6 cm

William and Alice Rothenstein (née Knewstub), Alice's sister Grace and Albert Rothenstein were in Vattetot-sur-Mer in Normandy with Arthur Clifton, who ran the Carfax Gallery.[7] Both Rothenstein and Sickert were important influences on the younger Slade painters, who included Rothenstein's younger brother Albert (who changed his name to Rutherston in 1916). Orpen's drawing *Noontide* (fig. 41), given to Everett, relates to this Vattetot trip, with the seated figure in hat and shawl probably Alice and her sister Grace behind, whom Orpen later married.[8] Groundbreaking work was produced at Vattetot, such as Rothenstein's *The Doll's House* (Tate); he recalled 'that never had so many easels and paint-boxes been seen'.[9] Although Arnold's biography suggests Everett was in one of Orpen's Vattetot sketches, it was probably Arthur Clifton, since Everett was not present.[10]

The party travelled further afield to Etretat and Fécamp, and Orpen's sketch *The Bathers* (fig. 52), also owned by Everett, resulted from one such outing.

7. *Edwardian Opulence*, p.x.
8. Meynell, pp.177–85. The figure of one of the bathers reappears in Orpen's pen-and-wash study for *The Bathers*, 1900, Pyms Gallery, 'Lines from Nature and Memory', 23 November 2011–6 January 2012, cat. no. 6.
9. Rothenstein, p.347.
10. Everett, *Memoirs*, p.63. Arnold, p.59. See Orpen sketches in the Witt Library collection, private collection, negative number 909/30 (13). The error of identity was agreed in email communication with the author and Dr Samuel Shaw.

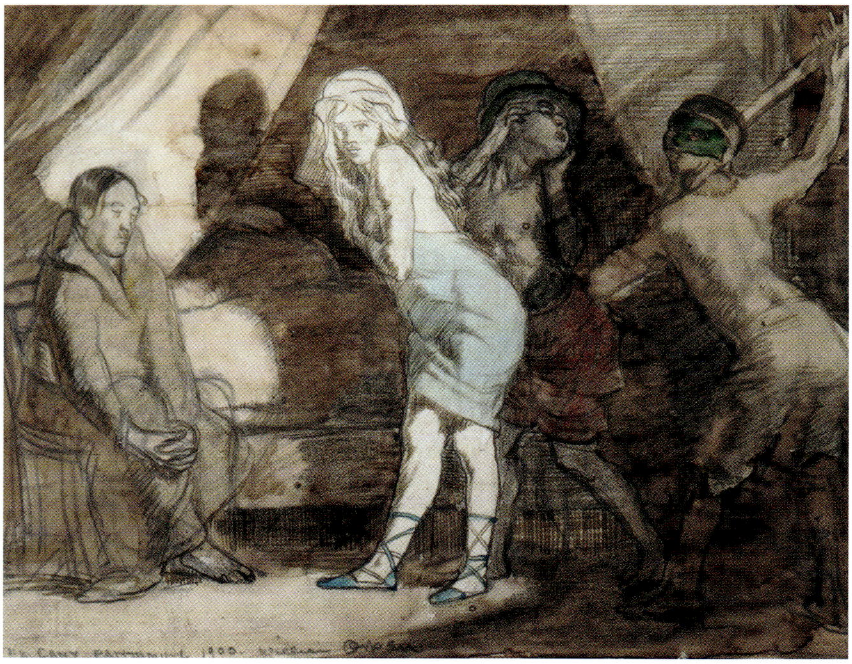

FIG. 43
William Orpen / ***The Cany Pantomime***
1900 / pencil and wash / 20 x 26.5 cm
private collection

The inscription on the drawing references the bohemian Conder, whose figures often hinted at eighteenth-century France, *fêtes galantes* and the work of Watteau. Arnold noted that he was the primary artistic and social influence on Orpen during the trip. The drawing is redolent with sexual possibilities, from the coquettish girls in bathing attire to the ogling, lascivious stance of the main figure on the left. The frothy hairstyles and frills on the girls' costumes evoke Conder's rococo figure paintings on silk. Orpen hints, too, at risk-taking by expressly locating the scene in front of the building marked Casino, echoed by the languid sunbathers, festive umbrellas and awnings, and the beach huts below La Terrasse du Casino.

Everett, meanwhile, spent that summer at Poole, painting the harbour and its shipping. Lodging close to the quay and church, he was fascinated by the trading activities of the sailing ships, finding the picturesque houses, warehouses and lanes eminently paintable. He kept up his Fitzroy Street studio and returned to the Slade for the autumn term, when Orpen, on returning from Vattetot in September 1899, rented Augusta's basement. John and Orpen hired models at 21 Fitzroy Street and Everett noted that they discarded a large number of their fifteen-minute Slade drawings by tearing them in three, which the unscrupulous Augusta retrieved, promptly stuck together and sold years later in Bond Street.[11]

Early in 1900 Everett began to sit to Orpen for his portrait (fig. 49). By July, Conder, Orpen, Albert Rothenstein and Scobel were in France staying at the Hotel dû Commerce, Cany in Normandy.[12] Normandy was the cradle of Impressionism and its proximity to Paris, together with burgeoning sea-side resorts like Dieppe, Honfleur, Le Havre, Deauville and Trouville along

11. Everett, *Memoirs*, p.138.
12. Now known as Cany-Barville, in Upper Normandy it lies slightly inland between Dieppe and Fécamp.

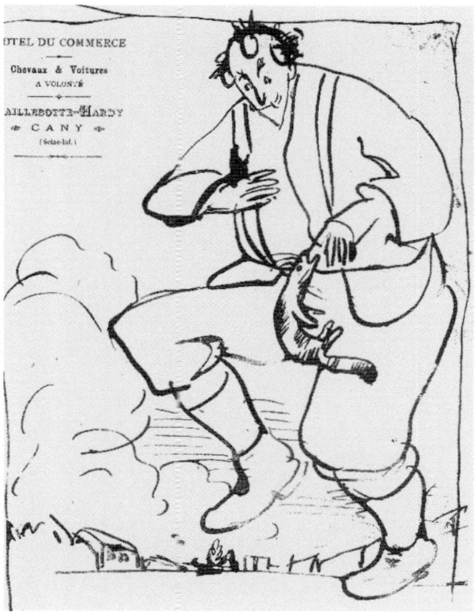

FIG. 44
William Orpen
Everett with a Cat, Cany
1900
private collection

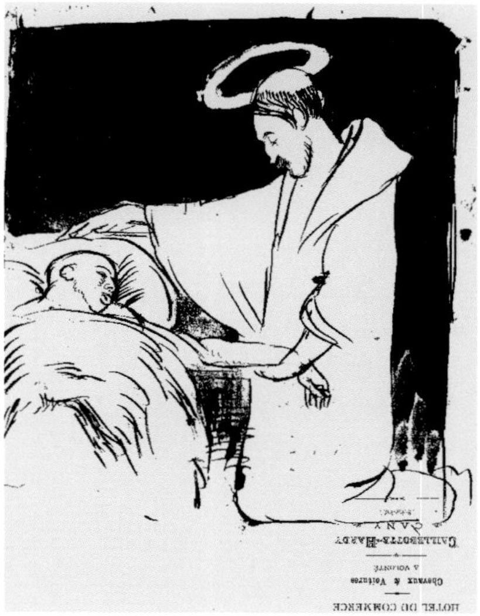

FIG. 45
William Orpen
Conder Kneeling Over Orpen
1901
private collection

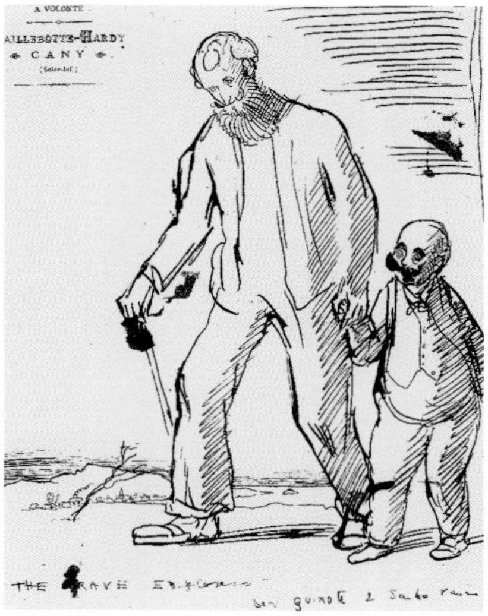

FIG. 46
William Orpen
The Brave Escapees
c.1900
private collection

its coast, saw artists visiting the region by train and producing an artistic legacy which influenced the young Slade painters. Orpen and Conder invited Everett to join them. He cycled down to Cany from Dieppe, arriving as Scobel was departing, having been propositioned by Conder.[13] Letters to Everett before his arrival suggested riotous goings-on there, implied by Orpen's wash-and-pencil sketch entitled *The Cany Pantomime* (fig. 43), given to Everett. The drawing shows a scene enacted in Orpen's hotel bedroom in front of a swathed, canopied four-poster bed. Conder is seated on the left in an overcoat and bare feet, with Scobel, barely draped, as she looks out of the picture space. To her left the figure bare to the waist in a top hat and loincloth is Albert Rothenstein. On the far right Orpen is partially clothed, in the guise of a masked satyr, wearing a beaded necklace and pantaloons, holding a musical instrument and adopting an exaggerated pose. None of the figures engage with each other, while Scobel and Orpen look in the direction of the viewer. We know from their Vattetot visit that they engaged in play-acting, as this title implies, perhaps also a pun on their heavy drinking and the confused relationships with Scobel.

At Cany, Everett and Conder sat in an orchard working side by side, as Conder produced paintings of women in picture hats from his imagination while Orpen painted and continued his humorous drawings (figs 44 and 45) of his companions.[14] His sensitive, three-quarter-length pastel sketch of Everett, made at Cany in early September (fig. 47), hints at their comfortable friendship. Everett wears the distinctive tweeds that defined him for Orpen. Laura Knight described Everett as striking in appearance, 'a typical Englishman; his pale blue eyes, fair skin, rough tweeds and thick boots singled him out astonishingly as he went his own way.'[15] Orpen's drawings exaggerated Everett's tweedy appearance and height to show him, at over six feet tall, towering over him: reinforcing their respective characteristics and his own nickname, 'ickle Orps'.

13. Everett, *Memoirs*, p.84.
14. See P.G. Konody and Sidney Dark, *Sir William Orpen: Artist and Man*, London: Seeley Service & Co. Ltd., 1932, p.28, 'Dear Albert. I fear we are all going the same road', for another of Orpen's allusions to their wild living.
15. Laura Knight, *Oil Paint and Grease Paint*, London: Macmillan, 1936, p.149.

After Albert Rothenstein left Cany on 10 September, followed shortly afterwards by Conder, Everett and Orpen cycled to Fécamp, Yport, Vattetot-sur-mer and Le Havre. With insufficient money to pay their final rent at Cany, they escaped and made for Paris by train, prompting Orpen's sketch of the two escapees in the guise of Don Quixote and Sancho Panza (fig. 46). They headed for the hotel Orpen and Augustus John had stayed in the previous year, but since Orpen couldn't find it, they missed John, who was then in France with Michel Salaman and Alice and William Rothenstein. Everett and Orpen visited the Louvre and the Palais du Luxembourg, but spent most of their week at the Paris Exhibition looking at paintings, where they bumped into fellow student Ambrose McEvoy at the Dome.[16] When Orpen and Everett left Paris, they were filled with admiration for the Barbizon School, with Orpen bemoaning Everett as a dull Parisian companion. Together with countless other artists Everett later studied in Paris ateliers, chiefly the Académie Julian, leading to distinctive loosely painted *en plein air* landscapes focusing on the effects of light. Many fellow students travelled to Europe and when in France some, like Orpen, sought out Walter Sickert at Dieppe. Orpen and Everett also headed for Dieppe to see him, but on finding Sickert was back in England, they remained in France until late October, before returning to the Slade.

WORK AT FITZROY STREET

Back in Fitzroy Street, the artists also used each other as models, leading to some fine early portraits by Orpen. Everett sat for his full-length portrait (fig. 49), completed that November, for which Orpen used a large canvas bought from Campin, the Slade porter, for one shilling. As it already contained a painting of a nude, Orpen primed it using burnt sienna and black and a covering of Hall's distemper, which meant the painting soon deteriorated as paint flaked off the canvas. Everett cautioned Orpen that painting over a dark ground would eventually lead to the portrait darkening. At this point the students were still influenced by Whistler, a visitor to the Slade with a studio close to 21 Fitzroy Street.[17] In portraying Everett as a gentleman from the 1860s, Orpen settled on a pose in the manner of Whistler's *Arrangement in Grey and Black, No. 2: Portrait of Carlyle*, 1872–3 (Kelvingrove Art Gallery and Museum). He seated Everett in profile against the wall of his studio, as in *The Mirror* (fig. 42). Everett recalled:

> Orpen got me a stock, I was in gaff topsail Hat, and Focle [sic] Door Coat. He painted it against the wall of my studio. I made him put in a telescope a blue backed chart, and some drawings of ships. He finished the portrait. It ended as a portrait of me when we came back from Cany. It was at the time, one of the best things he had done. As I foretold it went black ... Years later it started to flake off from the canvas. It's a fatal thing to paint on canvas prepared by artists' colour men, all they do is slap some Hall's distemper on the canvas, which never adhears [sic] to it and in time flakes off.[18]

Behind Everett are four of his drawings, with the lowest a recognizable profile of the *Iquique*.[19] Orpen worked on the Everett portrait intermittently throughout 1900 and wrote to him that Tonks and William Rothenstein thought it his best work to date.[20]

16. The *Exposition Universelle de 1900* in Paris ran from 15 April to 12 November.
17 Everett, *Memoirs*, p.85–6.
18. Everett, *Memoirs*, pp.80–81.
19. The drawings relate to Everett's first deep-sea sailing voyage between 1898 and 1899 to Australia on the *Iquique*. Immediately above Everett is *The Iquique at Cape Town*, 1898, a graphite and watercolour drawing, PAH4296, NMM.
20. Everett was given the telescope by his cousin, Lord Bantry. He purchased his Orpen portrait for £10, and it was loaned to various exhibitions before Everett bequeathed it to the National Portrait Gallery, who rejected it. The portrait was finally passed to the NMM.

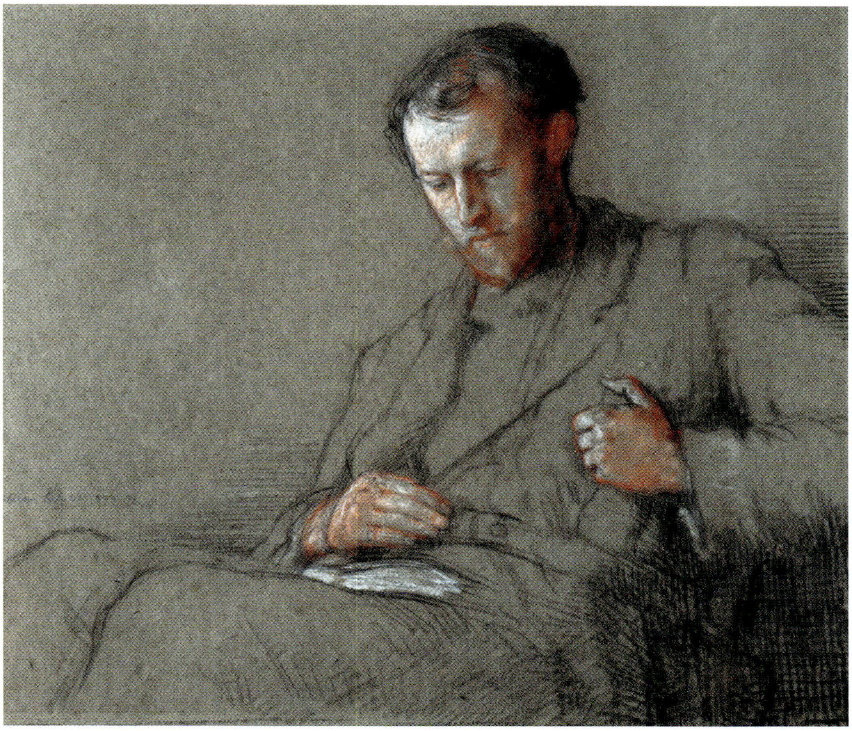

FIG. 47
William Orpen / *Herbert Everett*
1900 / charcoal and pastel drawing / 25.5 x 30.5 cm
private collection

Begun at the same time as Everett's portrait, Orpen completed his full-length portrait of Augustus John (fig. 48) first, and that summer exhibited it at the New English (118). It was one of the paintings that began to make his reputation. John sat for it in Orpen's basement studio with the four-poster bed, bought from Augusta, visible in the background. John claimed he was in a cast-off topcoat provided for the sittings by Conder.[21] Everett observed that Orpen worked with a simple palette, avoiding fugitive colours and matching tones with a palette knife. Orpen also produced a fine full-length self-portrait, *The Artist as a Young Man* (Glasgow Museums) there. At the New English winter show Orpen exhibited *Herbert Everett* (119), *The Mirror* (50) and a view of *Cany* (79). He also intended to paint a portrait of John Everett at sea, with Everett collaborating by painting the ship, to be jokingly called the *Everorpe*.[22]

ORPEN: THE PERSONAL MEETS THE FICTIONAL

Orpen's work at Fitzroy Street reflected his fascination with old master painting, Victorian literature and his life at the Newcomes. An important and startlingly original example is *A Mere Fracture: In the Newcomes, Fitzroy Street. The Fracture* (private collection) (fig. 50), which fuses personal connections with the fictional.[23] The scene takes an incident from Thackeray's *The Newcomes*, after James Binnie was thrown from Colonel Newcome's horse. Orpen's choice of this novel reflects how the Slade group saw themselves in relation to other artists and writers living in and around

21. John, p.41.
22. Orpen's paintings associated with Fitzroy Street included: *Grace Knewstub*, 1900, painted in Everett's rooms; *Augustus John*, (NPG) painted in the Newcome's basement, New English, 1900 s.(112); *Herbert Everett*, (NMM), New English, 1900 w. (119), painted at the Newcomes; *The Mirror* (Tate), painted in Everett's studio, New English 1900 w. (50); *The English Nude*, (Mildura Arts Centre), showing Emily Scobel in Orpen's basement room at Fitzroy Street, *c*.1900; *A Mere Fracture: In the Newcomes, Fitzroy Street. The Fracture* (private collection), New English, 1901, s. (57); *Window in London Street*, (National Gallery of Ireland), 1901, New English, w. (69); *Mrs. [Augusta] Everett on the Island of Patmos*, (Mildura Arts Centre), 1901; *Augusta Everett*, 1903, New English, w. (90); *The Refugees*, 1901–05; *The Valuers*, 1902, New English, s. (56); *John Staats Forbes* (art connoisseur and railway manager), 1900, New English, s. (97).
23. William Orpen *A Mere Fracture: In the Newcomes, Fitzroy Street. The Fracture*, Christie's, King Street, London, Irish Pictures Sale 5956, 22 May 1998, Lot 21.

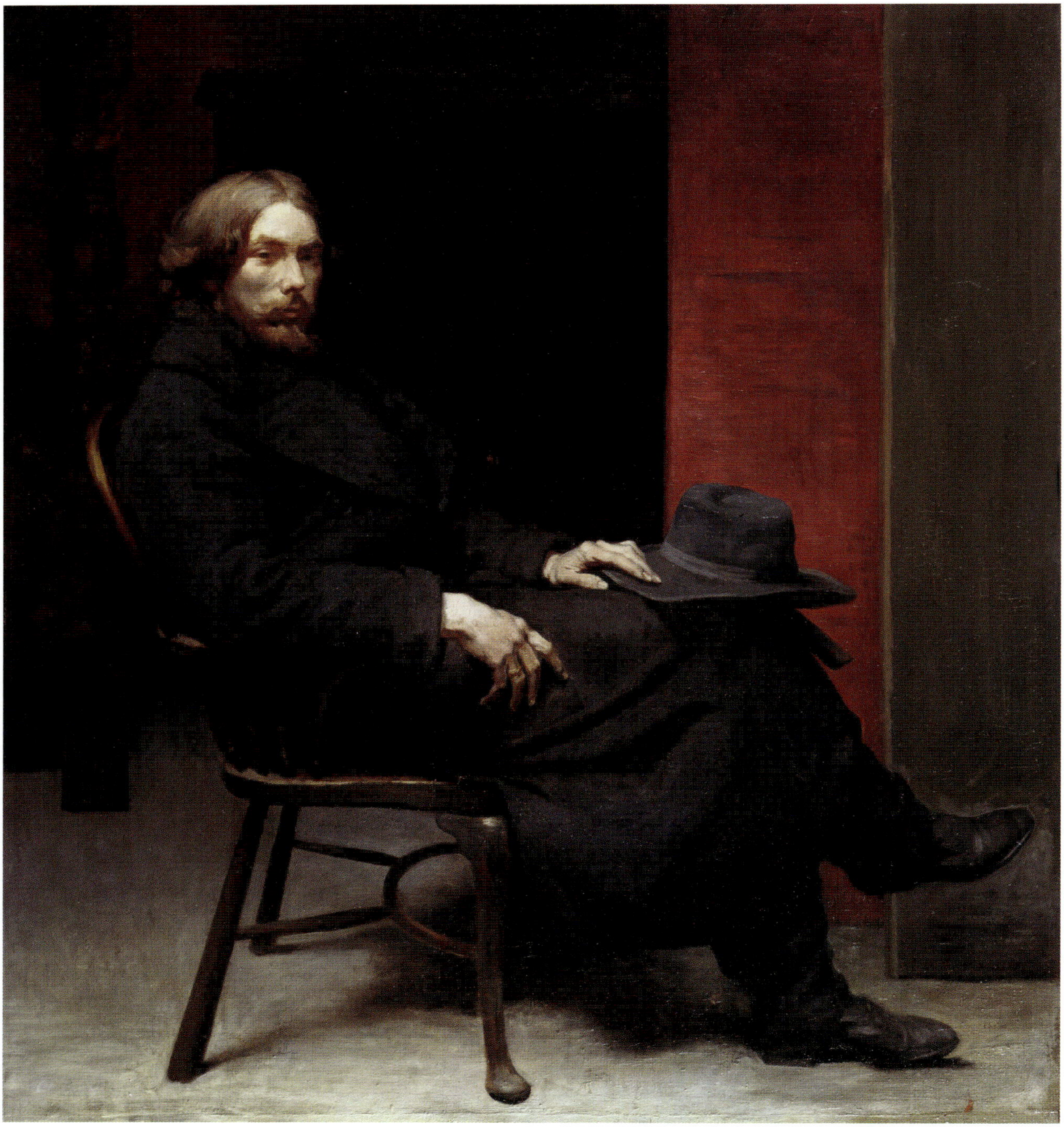

FIG. 48

William Orpen / ***Augustus John***

1900 / oil on canvas / 99.1 x 94 cm

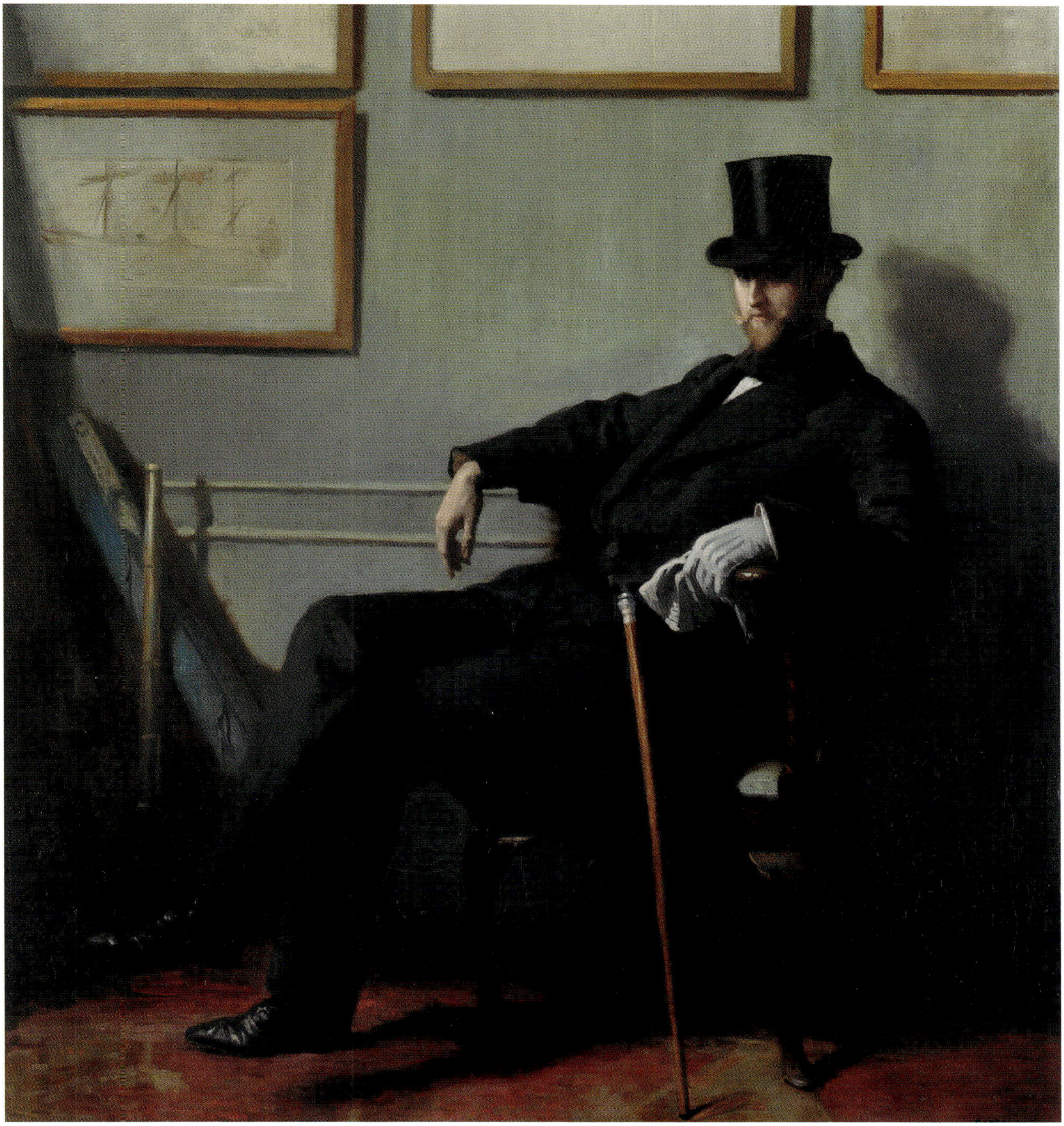

FIG. 49

William Orpen / ***Herbert Everett***

1900 / oil on canvas / 96.5 x 91.5 cm

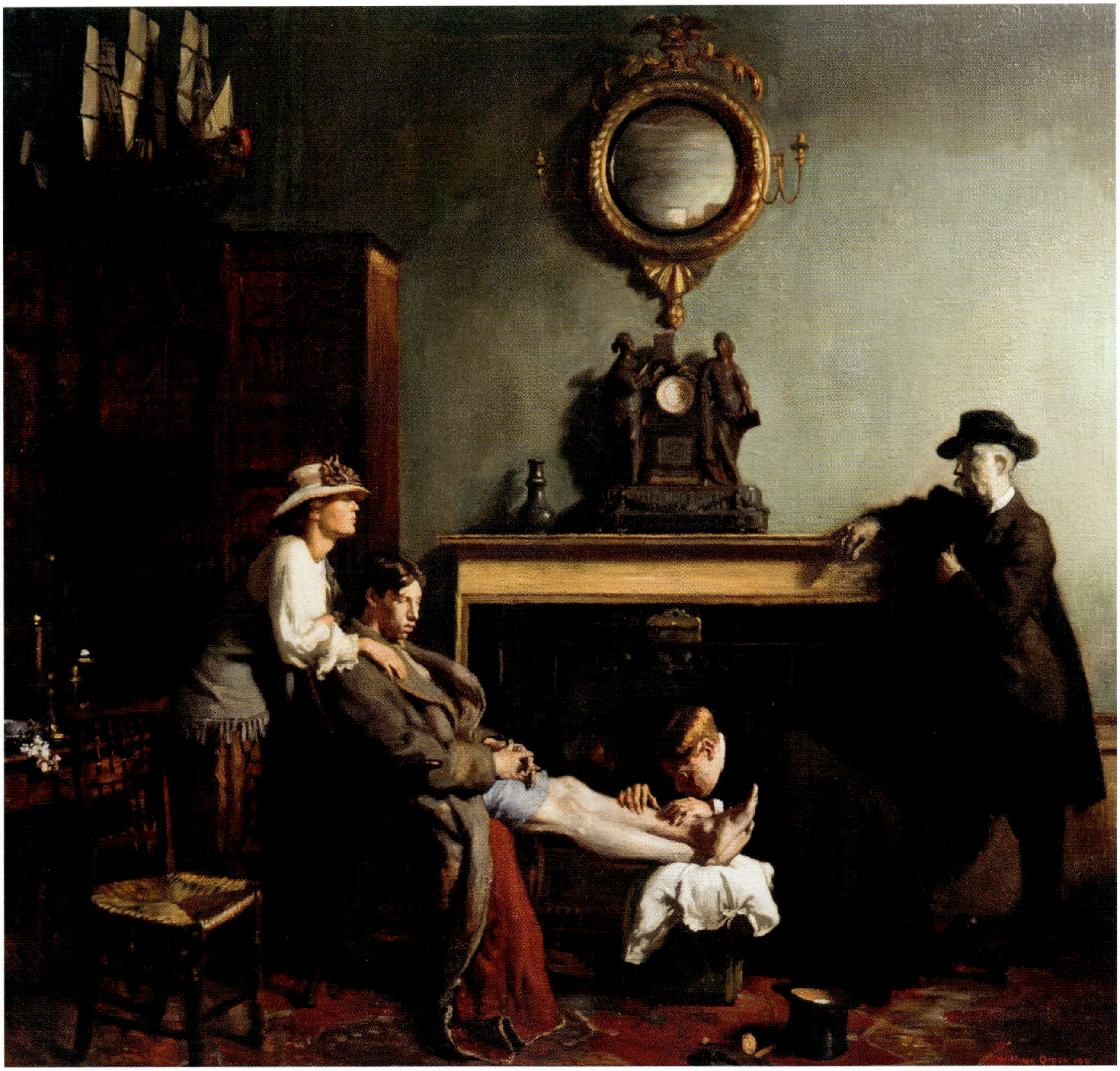

FIG. 50

William Orpen / *A Mere Fracture: In the Newcomes, Fitzroy Street, The Fracture*

1901 / oil on canvas / 93.8 x 99.1 cm

This scene from Thackeray's 'The Newcomes' was painted in Everett's rooms at 21 Fitzroy Street

photograph courtesy Pyms Gallery; private collection

Fitzroy Street. By 1901 Orpen was living in Everett's studio, which John described as 'littered with trophies from the tropics [that] bore witness to his extensive voyages'.[24] In June 1901 Orpen wrote to Everett about his new painting:

> I am doing a picture in your room called the "Local doctor" who is represented in the person of George Haywood Esq., who is the best model I have crossed for a long time. Mr. Cornelius Carr is the patient and Miss Evangelica Scobile [sic] is the fond wife. The painting of Haywood in it is I think amusing! When will you run up and see us oh Father of the Lizard.[25]

Carr was a fellow Slade student who admired Orpen's work, and George Haywood, born in Dorset, was the Everetts' handyman, who lived with his wife in the basement at Fitzroy Street close to Orpen. There, the couple kept an eye on the students and often fed them. According to William Crampton Gore (another student and friend of Everett's, who played the part of the kneeling doctor in *A Mere Fracture* and was renting Everett's room while he was in Cornwall), Orpen presented Haywood as a French physician and less formal than Gore's role. Scobel wears the same hat as in *The Mirror*, whilst a second mirror reflected in Everett's study within it has become the central point above the mantel and clock. The inclusion of Everett's model sailing ship also makes it clear that this is a painting centred around Orpen's time at Fitzroy Street. *The English Nude*, c.1900 (Dublin), with model Emily Scobel, was painted in the basement at Fitzroy Street, and Arnold has noted that Emily posed on the same four-poster bed featured in John's portrait (fig. 48).[26] Other of Orpen's Fitzroy Street paintings included several self-portraits and *The Refugees*, 1901–05, in which a supposed group of refugees peer anxiously out of the Fitzroy Street window at an angry crowd in the street. Portraits of this period also include *Grace Knewstub*, 1900, later his wife; his portrait of leading art collector *John Staats Forbes*; and *Mrs. [Augusta] Everett on the Island of Patmos* (fig. 25), c.1901.[27] Orpen's *The Valuers* of 1902, a social commentary in which a motley group of solicitors' agents puzzle over a picture, saw Haywood pose as a model.

Everett and Katherine were married in 1901 and set sail for Australia on their honeymoon voyage in 1902. Orpen wrote to Everett:

> I enclose you several drawings which I brought to the docks for you on Sat. but I forgot to leave them. I hope they will amuse you. I cannot tell you any news as I have turned into a recluse and see no one, except Stabb sometimes, as he sits to me. I have fought with all the Slade professors, as I sent no work to the show they had a few weeks back.[28]

The drawings were caricatures of Everett at sea and included such titles as *Rounding the Horn*; *Perfect Happiness for Mr. E.* (fig. 54); *Sighting a Homeward Bounder off the Rum Rocks* and *Goodbye Mr. E* (fig. 55).

The remarkable body of Orpen's highly personal drawings owned by Everett saw Orpen embed layers of meaning into them, illustrating their lives together (fig. 53). Some of the pen-and-wash drawings were inspired by literature, with Orpen drawing on a wide range of influences and personalizing his sketches when adapting scenes from *Don Quixote*, *Hamlet*, *The Fisherman and His Soul*, *Florentine Nights* or the *Arabian Nights*. Both

24. John, *Finishing Touches*, p.40. 'Sailing was his passion and the ocean the external setting for his top-heavy windjammers.'
25. Photocopy of letter in a private collection from William Orpen, Fitzroy Street, to John Everett, 1 June 1901.
26. Arnold, p.76.
27. Orpen painted a small portrait of Augusta, to settle a debt with her in 1903. The larger portrait, 1901, relates to an event from the 'Book of Revelations', in which John the Apostle received a vision of Jesus, in a cave on Patmos. Orpen impishly placed Augusta in this rôle, since to the amusement of the students, she loudly cited passage from 'Revelations' in the skeleton room at the Slade. Exhibited at the New English in 1901 it featured in an exhibition Augusta organized at her studio in Charlotte Street. Its ownership was the subject of dispute between Orpen, George Beresford and Augusta. Everett, *Memoirs*, p.133.
28. Everett, *Memoirs*, pp.78 and 107.

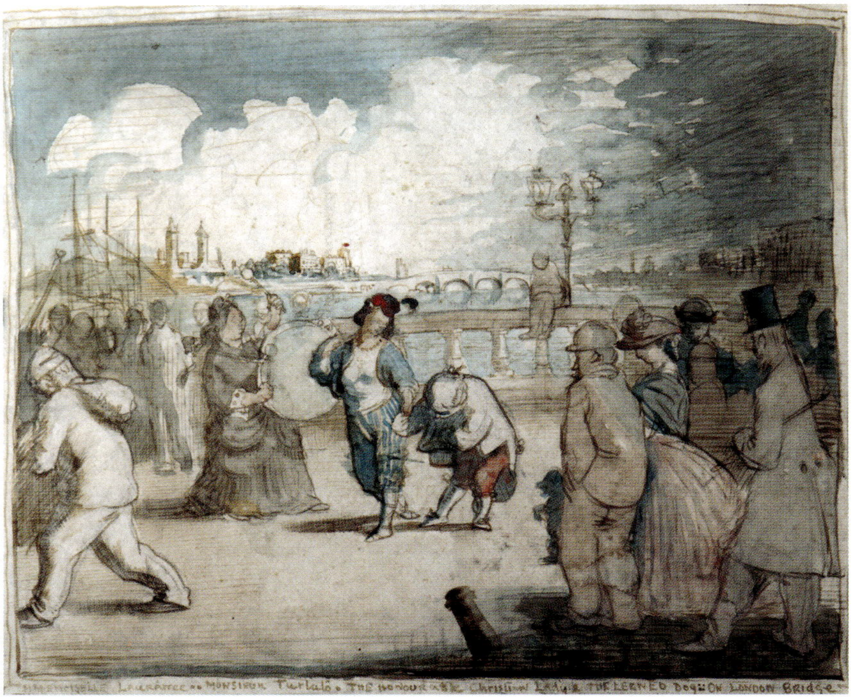

FIG. 51

William Orpen / ***Mademoiselle Laurance, Monsieur Turluto, The Honourable Christian Lady, and the Learned Dog on London Bridge***

c.1899 / pen and wash / 21 x 26 cm

private collection

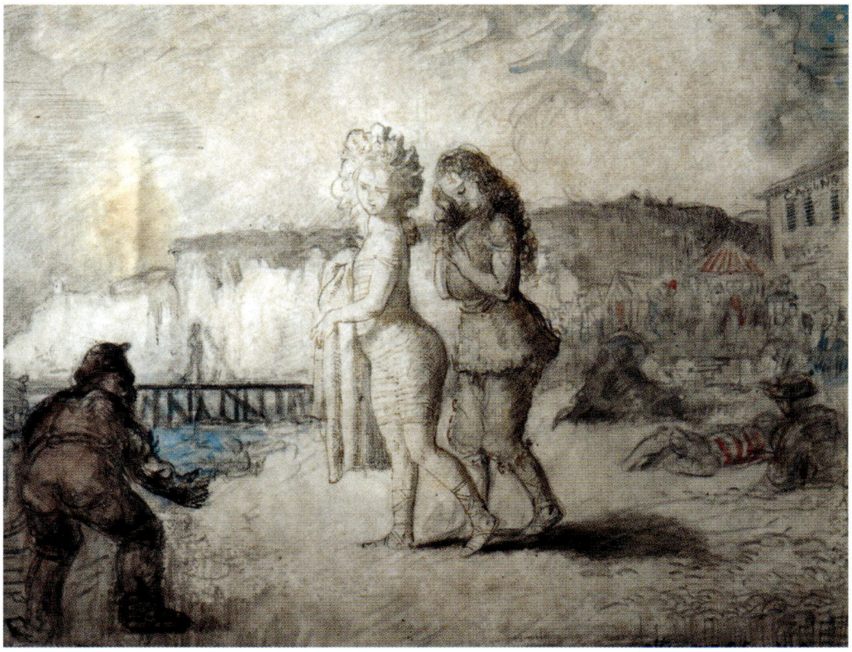

FIG. 52

William Orpen / ***The Bathers, Etretat after Mr C***[harles] ***C***[onder]

1899 / pen and wash / 20 x 26.5 cm

private collection

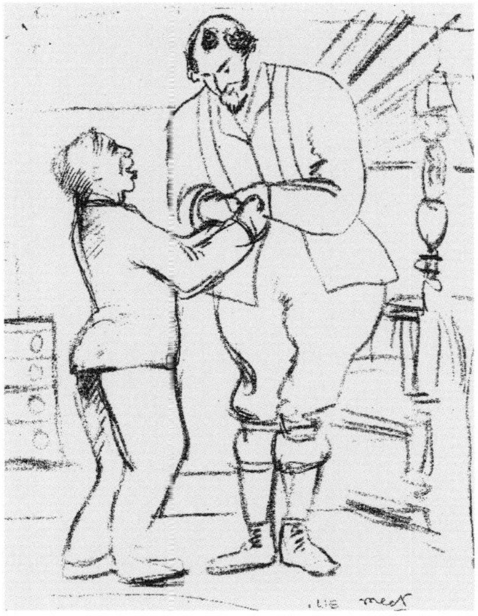

FIG. 53
William Orpen / *We Meet*
The first sketch of a triptych charting a visit to the Foley Arms, London, by Orpen and Everett
private collection

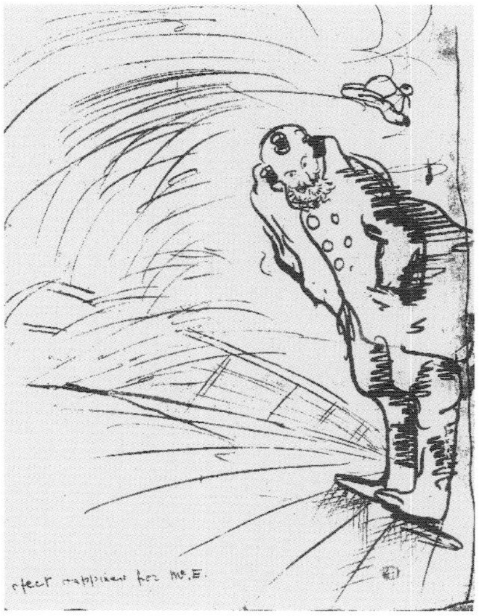

FIG. 54
William Orpen
Perfect Happiness for Mr. E.
1902
private collection

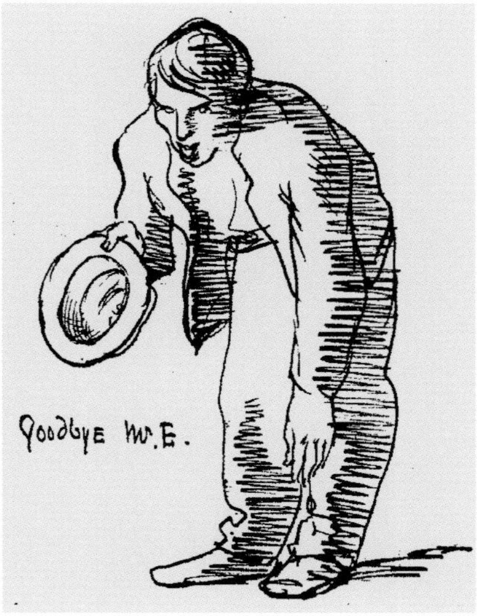

FIG. 55
William Orpen / *Goodbye Mr. E.*
1902
private collection

Augustus John and Orpen read Heinrich Heine's *Florentine Nights* and Orpen's *Mademoiselle Laurance, Monsieur Turluto, The Honourable Christian Lady, and the Learned Dog on London Bridge* (fig. 51) used characters from these tales.[29] The figure perched on the bridge is perhaps Orpen, with Madame Mère in widow's weeds playing the drum, almost certainly a reference to Augusta Everett, as the 'Honourable Christian Lady'.[30] In Heine's story the dog spells the name of the Duke of Wellington in alphabet letters, perhaps here a play on Everett's Peveril Tower, which once stood on the bridge as the Wellington Testimonial Clock Tower.[31]

Looking back on his work after Orpen's death, Henry Tonks sharply observed that 'with one exception (such as 'Homage à Manet') I did not feel he [Orpen] was at his best in portraits clever as he certainly was.'[32] These drawings demonstrate Tonks' assessment of Orpen that 'in an earlier period like Rowlandson he might have become an illustrator of the various humours of people.'[33] This chapter draws largely on these extraordinary unpublished documents, many of which contain drawings by Orpen, to reconstruct the close friendship which existed between Orpen, Everett and other members of the Slade circle. They are significant for a renewed understanding of Orpen, the Slade milieu and the positioning of Everett within this important group. As a gathering place for artists and their friends Augusta Everett's convivial house in Fitzroy Street became the subject of Orpen's most groundbreaking early works. The Everetts would continue to form a locus for Slade painters after their move to Dorset in 1903.

29. Heinrich Heine, Charles Godfrey Leland, trans., 'Florentine Nights, Second Night', *The Prose and Poetical Works of Heinrich Heine*, in twenty volumes, London: William Heinemann, 1906, pp.89–92. Heine's work ranged from romantic lyrics about the frustrations of love to sharp political satire. See John, *Finishing Touches*, p.40.
30. An early sketch showing Madame Mère is in a private collection; see the Witt Library, Neg. No. 909/19 (2).
31. Orpen's *Florentine Nights* drawings were exhibited at the Goupil Gallery in 1912, 'Drawings and Studies from Life, William Orpen, Gallery', Goupil, March 1912. *Mademoiselle Laurence, Monsieur Turluto, The Honourable Christian Lady, and the Learned Dog on London Bridge* (16); *Maximilian Finds Laurence on London Bridge* (20); *Mademoiselle Laurence* (28); *Market Place, Cany* (35); *Bathing* (37); *On the Beach* (45) and *Looking towards the Town, Cany* (53).
32. Letter from Henry Tonks, Priest's House, Sopley, Christchurch, Hampshire, to Healy at Knoedler, 6 June 1934, The Frank Simpson Archive, The Paul Mellon Centre for Studies in British Art (Filed under William Orpen).
33. Ibid.

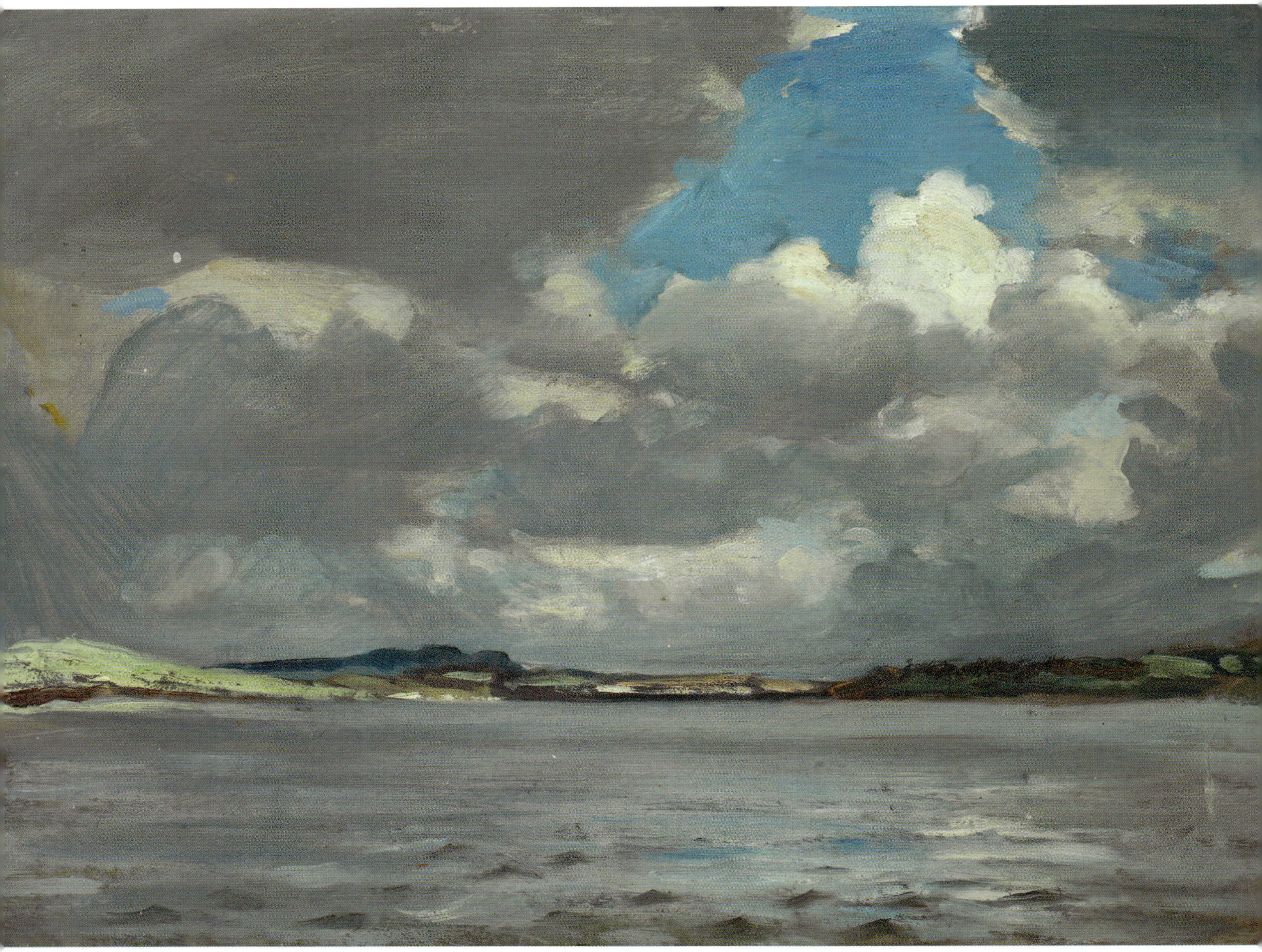

FIG. 56
John Everett / ***Poole Harbour***
c.1910 / oil sketch on paper / 35.5 x 50.7 cm

FIVE

RETURN OF THE NATIVE: EVERETT SETTLES IN DORSET

Slade marriages were obviously in the air when, in 1901, Augustus John married fellow student Ida Nettleship. At Swanage, Augusta loaned them a cottage in the grounds of Peveril Tower, for their honeymoon. Ambrose McEvoy was engaged to Slade student, Mary Edwards, rather than Gwen John as expected, and in early September, Orpen married Grace Knewstub in Ireland. A week later, to everyone's surprise, Everett married his half-cousin Katherine Herbert. That November, Everett held an exhibition at Baillie's Gallery in Notting Hill Gate, to which Augusta invited Thomas Hardy. He declined to go but wrote to Augusta: 'I had heard a faint report that your son was becoming a painter. I sincerely hope he may be a successful one ... If however I can influence anybody I will.'[1] Hardy went on to encourage Everett when he and Katherine returned to live permanently in Dorset in 1903. From then on Dorset became increasingly popular for painters from the Slade. In 1905 Henry Tonks spent the summer working close to the Everetts, using Katherine as the model for his important exhibition piece: *The Lost Path* (fig. 73). As a result, Dorset increasingly became an important subject within the oeuvre of the Slade painters and therefore arguably within modern British landscape painting itself.

The Everett's disastrous honeymoon voyage led Everett to conclude that women, sailing and painting did not mix. At Katherine's insistence, they let 21 Fitzroy Street to agents and gave up their London life, initially staying at the Priory in Wareham while looking for somewhere to rent in Purbeck. They were sent to a house at Holmebridge, near Wareham, to discover it already occupied by the painter William Wiehe Collins, whom Everett had first met in St Ives (fig. 57).[2] Their friendship was an example of the breadth of Everett's artistic contacts, since, aside from their mutual St Ives links, Collins' allegiance remained with the Royal Academy rather than the New English.

LIFE AT WOOL

By the following June, the Everetts were renting the fourteenth-century Woolbridge Manor at Wool, described by Hardy as a 'mouldy old habitation' where he set the drama of Angel Clare and Tess's wedding night, in *Tess of the D'Urbervilles*, 1892. With a railway station, Wool, a small village

1. Letter from Thomas Hardy, Max Gate, Dorchester, to Augusta Everett, 15 November 1901, DNHAS.
2. Collins painted landscapes, architectural subjects and naval scenes. He studied at Lambeth School of Art, attended the Académie Julian and exhibited at the RA and other London galleries from 1890. He was elected to the Royal Institute of Painters in Watercolours in 1898.

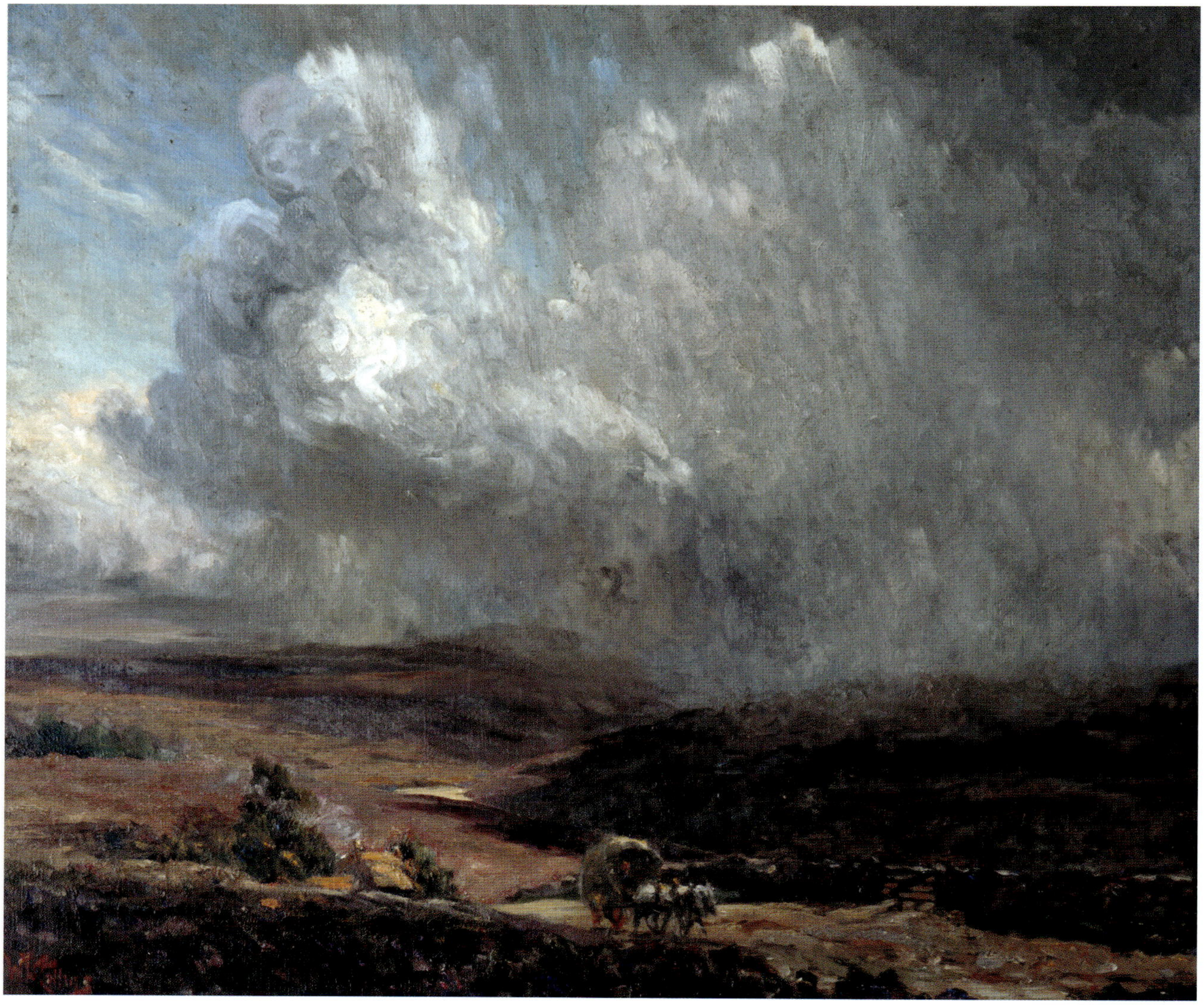

FIG. 57
William Collins / ***Arne Heath***
c.1903 / oil on canvas / 49.5 x 59 cm
private collection

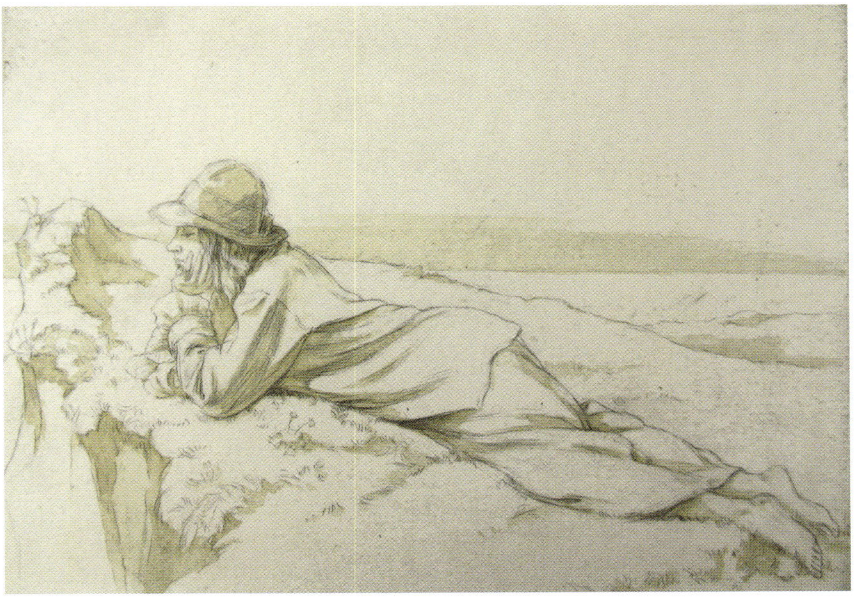

FIG. 58
John Everett / *Portrait of Katherine Everett watching from a cliff in Dorset*
c.1903 / pen and wash drawing

10 miles east of Dorchester and on the edge of Purbeck, was easily accessible from London on the main line to Weymouth. The Everetts bathed with friends in the river Frome, close to the house. They settled into Dorset life, with Katherine (fig. 58) serving on the local Parish Council and judging Sunday school competitions, and Everett painting. Everett recorded: '1903 was a terribly wet summer … the whole of the meadows were flooded, I only regretted I hadn't got a boat and a sail.'[3] Bathed in light, his oil sketch of the flooded meadows (fig. 60) focuses on its effects over water, quite different from his earlier muted palette. The distant landscape towards the Purbeck hills is loosely sketched, while in the foreground a few blades of grass rise above the floodwater. The sketch shows an important change in style and development in Everett's use of colour, revealing his growing fascination with the effects of the sun's rays on clouds and the surface of water, a theme he developed in his seascapes over the next 40 years.

Everett shared an exhibition in Dorchester in 1903 with Arthur Tomson from Wareham, Collins from West Holme and Bertha Newcombe. One of the earliest women students at the Slade, Newcombe lived at Arfleet Mill, Corfe Castle village, which she later rented to the Everetts.[4] Everett exhibited 39 Wool-related paintings and noted that when Hardy visited the exhibition he was disappointed that Everett had already sold his *Old Home of the Turbervilles*, 1903.[5] This supports the idea that Hardy was fascinated by, and actively encouraging, artists painting 'his' Wessex. Keen to see the painted portrait panels of two Turberville ancestors, in an upstairs wall of Woolbridge Manor, Thomas and Emma Hardy visited the Everetts at Woolbridge soon after they had moved in. Everett noted: 'Tom Hardy came to see me there, with the 1st Mrs Hardy in bloomers.'[6] As a result of the visit Hardy commissioned John Everett to produce a version of the two women.[7] He wrote to Everett:

3. Everett, *Memoirs*, p.82.
4. From a line of noted watercolour painters, Bertha Newcombe was the daughter of Samuel Prout Newcombe. Amongst the earliest women students to train at the Slade, in 1876 she exhibited with the New English, RA and other London galleries and, in 1903, was honorary secretary of the Whistler Memorial Fund. A socialist friend of the Webbs, Newcombe was an active campaigner for women's suffrage, yet developed a romantic fixation for George Bernard Shaw when he sat for his portrait. Bertha's illustrations appeared in *Cranford* and *Mill on the Floss*. Largely based in London, Everett's *Memoirs*, pp.104, 114, reveal she spent time in Dorset during the first decade of the century, and a visit to Emma Hardy invoked indignation when she implied that Mrs Hardy was a militant feminist, see Michael Millgate, *Thomas Hardy: A Biography Revisited*, Oxford: Oxford University Press, 2006, p.368.
5. Everett, *Memoirs*, p.104.
6. Everett, *Memoirs*, p.102.
7. Hardy described 'two life-size portraits on panels built into the masonry. As all visitors to the mansion are aware, these paintings represent women of middle age, of a date some two hundred years ago, whose lineaments once seen can never be forgotten. The long pointed features, narrow eye, and smirk of the one, so suggestive of merciless treachery; the bill-hook nose, large teeth, and bold eye of the other suggesting arrogance to the point of ferocity, haunt the beholder afterwards in his dreams' (*Tess*, chapter 34). In 1897 Hardy's sister Mary painted two small oils of the portraits, DNHAS 1962.200.1 and 2.

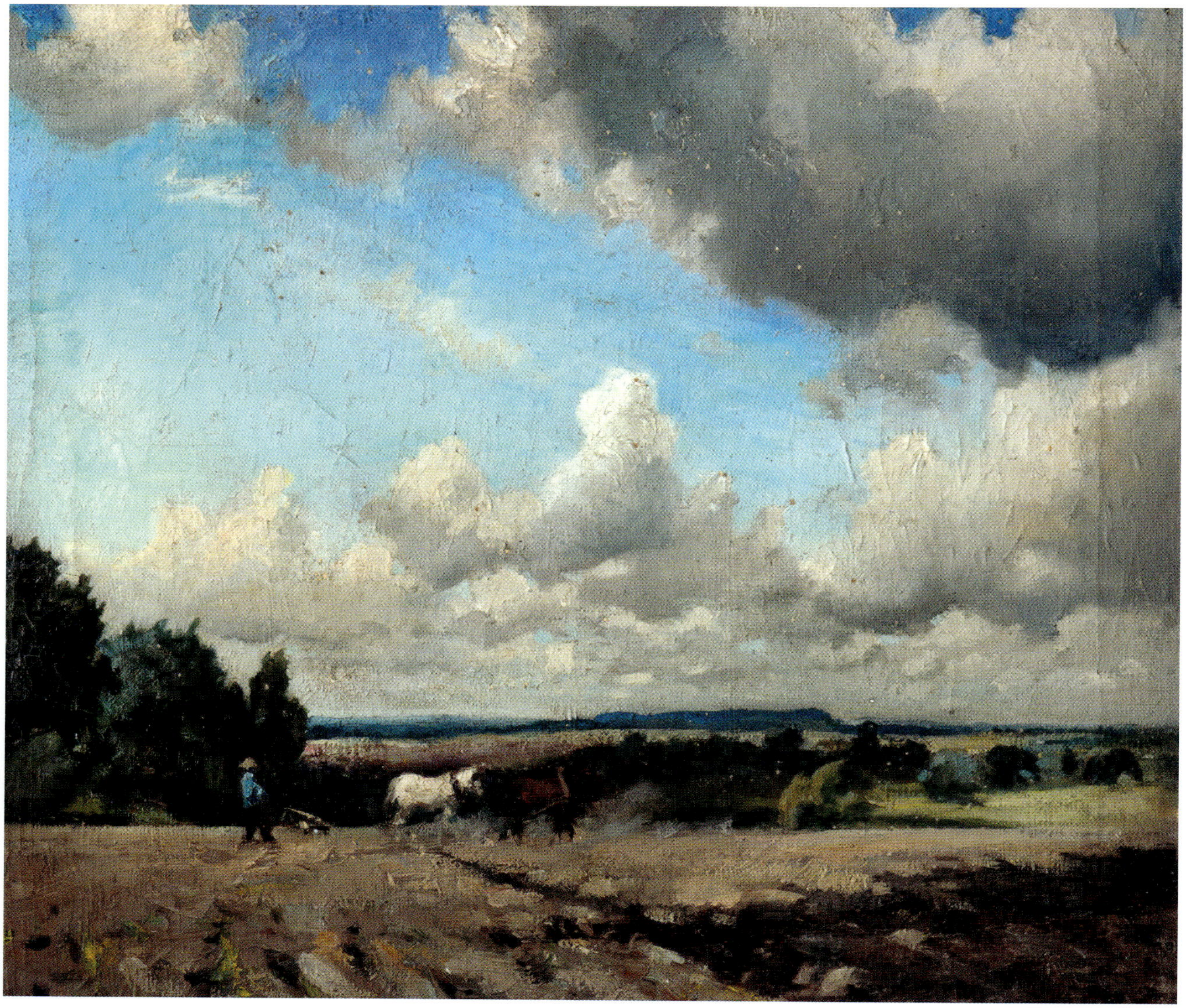

FIG. 59

John Everett / ***In Purbeck***

c.1905 / oil on canvas / 23.5 x 30 cm

private collection

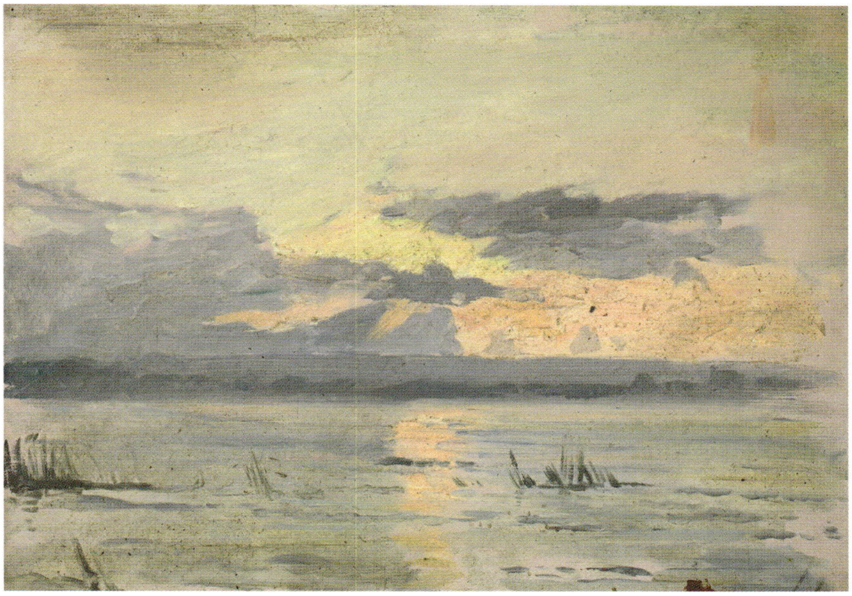

FIG. 60
John Everett / *Landscape near Wool, Dorset*
1903 / oil sketch on paper / 34.1 x 49.3 cm

> it is so kind of you to remember the portraits and I really value your reproductions of them apart from any interest in the portraits themselves. You have caught their expressions exactly, your drawings bring back to me the precise feeling with which the originals affected me when I first set eyes on them so many years ago, when they were much clearer than they are now.[8]

Collins also had Hardy's work in mind when he painted *Arne Heath* (fig. 57). After marriage he rented West Holme House, before moving to the Old Curetage in East Street, Corfe Castle. His dramatic portrayal of bleak moorland amidst a rain squall shows a covered horse-drawn carrier advancing over the sombre heath – the path it has traversed is picked out in the distance. The wispy smoke from a thatched cottage is visible in the fore-ground on the left. The focus of the painting is on the squall passing over the land, and evokes a Hardyesque scene:

> The face of the heath by its mere complexion added half an hour to evening; it could in like manner retard the dawn, sadden noon, anticipate the frowning of storms scarcely generated, and intensify the opacity of a moonless midnight to a cause of shaking and dread.[9]

Throughout this decade Everett also focused on painting the bleak nature of the heath, which could 'best be felt when it could not clearly be seen' (fig. 61).[10]

Everett was a keen sportsman and shortly after his arrival in Dorset in that wet summer of 1903, his preoccupation with cricket saw him take over the Wool Cricket Club.[11] He invited Slade colleagues, Charles Tharp and Spencer Gore, then staying at Old Cote Cottage, West Lulworth, with Wyndham Lewis, to play in the team. Though Lewis was not involved, Gore kept

8. Letter dated 17 November 1903, from Thomas Hardy, Max Gate, Dorchester to John Everett, Woolbridge Manor, private collection, acknowledging receipt of Everett's gouache drawings (DNHAS Hardy collection). For an illustration see Timothy O'Sullivan, *Thomas Hardy: An Illustrated Biography*, London: Macmillan London Ltd, 1975, p.133.
9. Thomas Hardy, Book One, 'The Three Women. A Face on Which Time Makes But Little Impression', *The Return of the Native*, London: Penguin, 1978, p.53.
10. Ibid.
11. Slater identified cricket as a feature of artists' colonies, demonstrating their integration with village life, p.85.

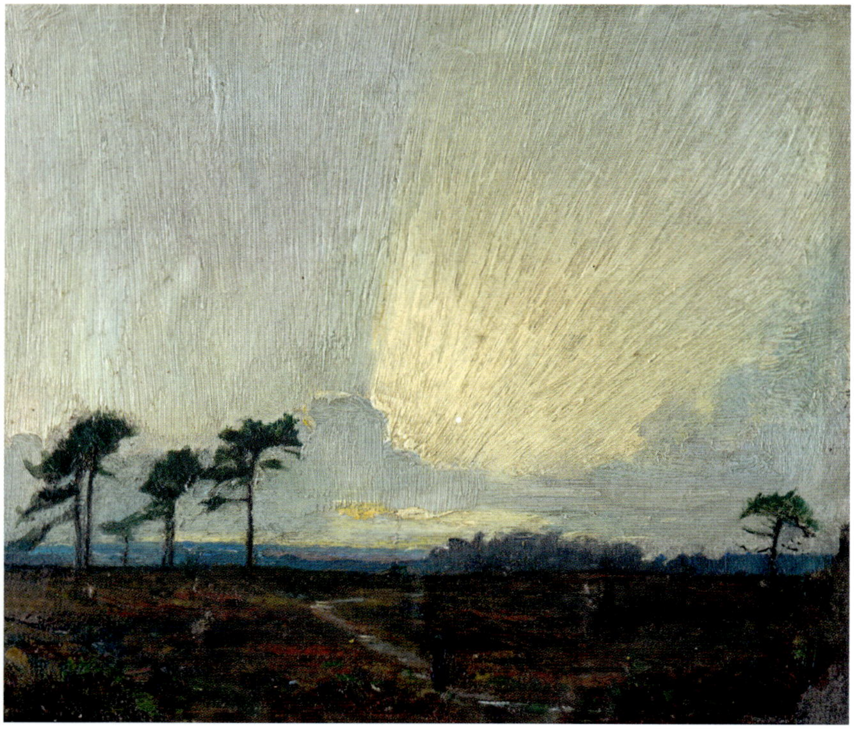

FIG. 61

John Everett / *Dorset Heath with Trees*

c.1905 / oil sketch on paper on card / 19 x 22 cm

private collection

wicket for Everett and found village cricket on the very rough pitch at Wool great fun.[12] An entry in one of Everett's sketchbooks lists Orpen batting at no. 11, but this is not sufficient evidence that Orpen was with Everett in Dorset.[13] Everett met up with Augustus John, also staying with Wyndham Lewis, and together they all visited fairs at Lulworth Castle and Woodbury. John returned to stay with the Everetts at Woolbridge the following year, for a fortnight. As he arrived without luggage the Everetts concluded he was in the midst of his fascination with gypsies, and Katherine described him as 'a fine and wild-looking figure with a great beard and a quantity of hair'. Everett took John all over Dorset, recalling that he was 'very taken with it'.[14]

FAMILY LIFE

The Everetts' first child, Henry, was born at Woolbridge Manor in December 1903, prompting a series of amusing sketches sent by Orpen (fig. 64). It was a place of increasing discomfort and damp, which they vacated by 1905 for 'Steinberg', a large house in Swanage. From here Everett pursued his *plein air* paintings of the Purbeck landscape (figs 59–61 and 67). About the time Henry was born, Everett bought an early Humber trailer motorbike (fig. 66) from his cousin, Lord Edward Churchill. On this he often escaped the constraints of increasing domesticity to live a solitary existence painting and sailing. Throughout his married life, Everett frequently undertook short sailing trips and rented cottages away from home to paint, sometimes living apart from his family for months at a time. This lifestyle echoes

12. Gore, who excelled in cricket at Harrow School,painted *The Cricket Match*, c.1909 (Wakefield Museums and Galleries).
13. Sketchbook, PAJ1347, NMM, Everett collection.
14. Everett, *Memoirs*, p.104.

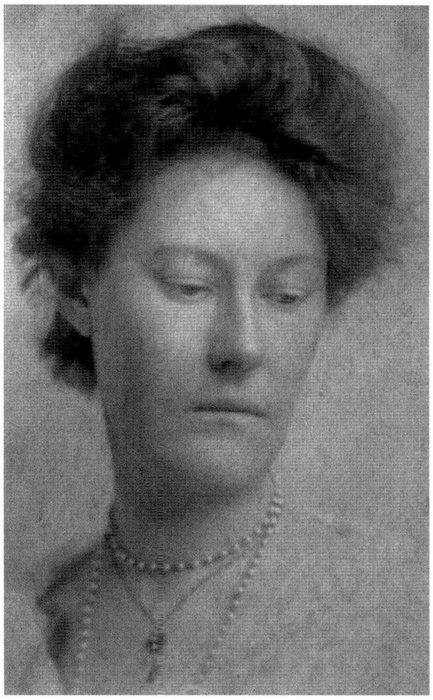

FIG. 62

Katherine Everett, c.1900

private collection

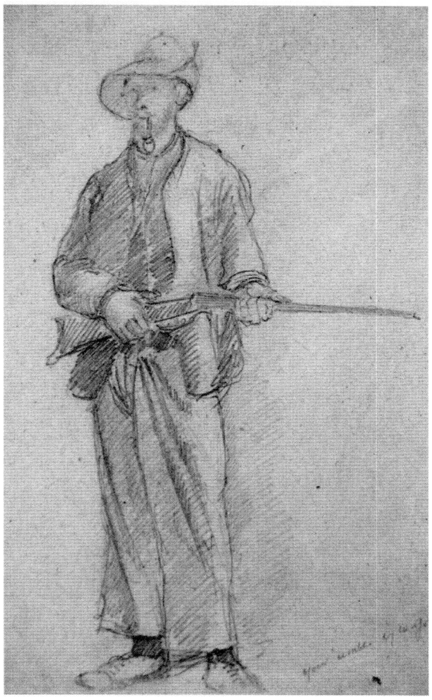

FIG. 63

William Crampton Gore

Your 'umble

1903 / pencil / 30.9 x 24.6 cm

A sketch of Everett holding a rifle with which to shoot the rats in their Dorset cottage

National Maritime Museum, Greenwich, London

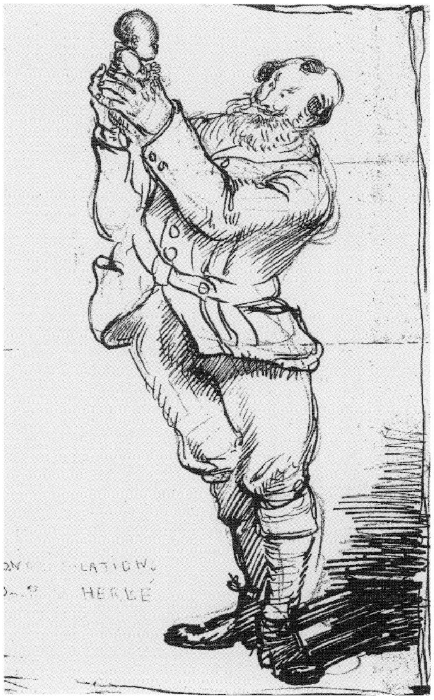

FIG. 64

William Orpen

Congratulations to Father Herbe

1903

In celebration of the birth of Everett's son Henry

private collection

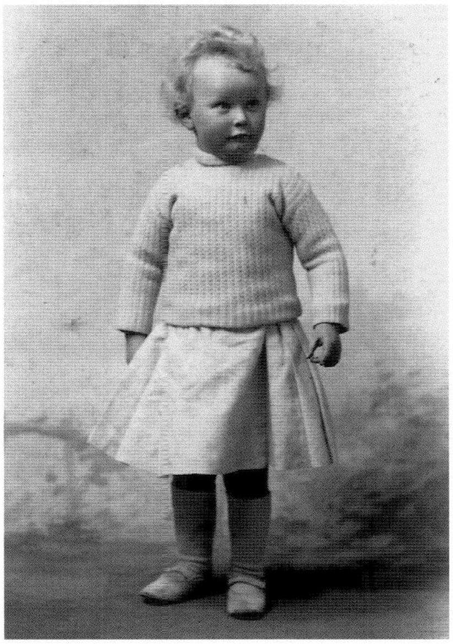

FIG. 65

Anthony Everett, aged 18 months

private collection

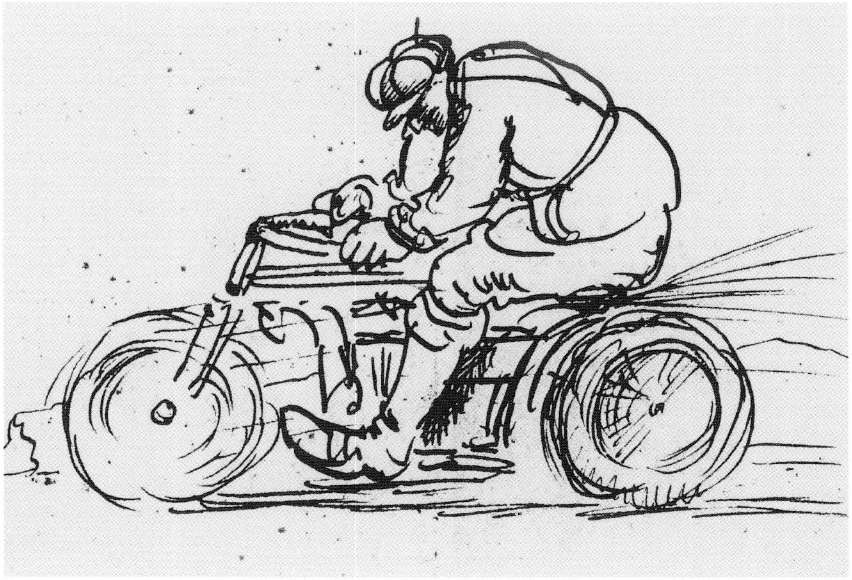

FIG. 66

William Orpen / *Everett on his Motorbike*

1903

private collection

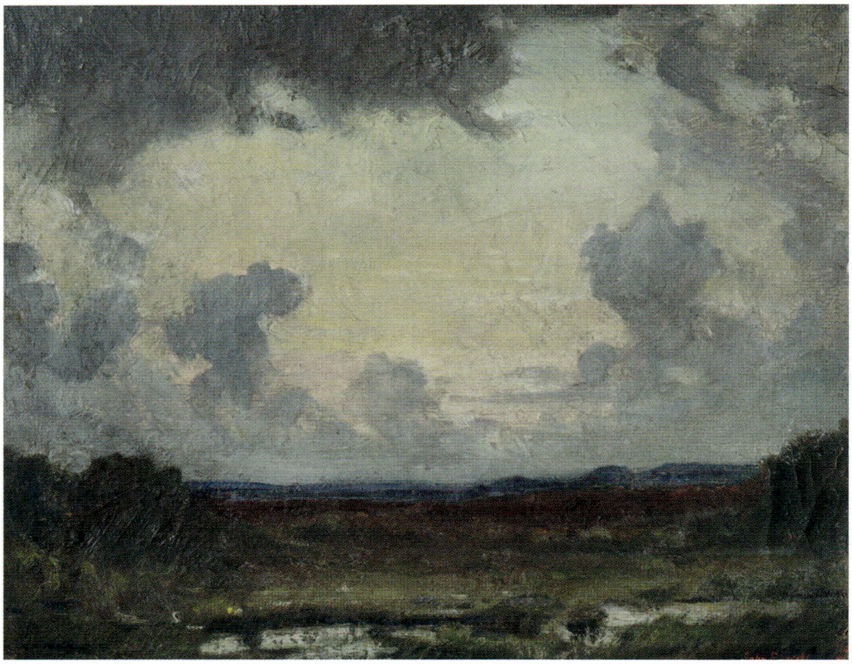

FIG. 67
John Everett / ***Purbeck Landscape***
c.1905 / oil on canvas / 35.5 x 38 cm
private collection

Augustus John's observation that the burdens of domesticity loomed ahead for the Slade women painters and were almost too heavy to bear. It is revealing that none of Katherine's art survives, as once domestic responsibilities took hold she experienced the common problem for women painters who married.

Everett first took a cottage at Hamside, opposite Brownsea Island, to use as a studio, often sleeping on the shore. He then moved to Newton Cottage at Ower on the Purbeck side of Poole Harbour near Corfe Castle, where Slade painters Charles Julian Tharp, Charles Stabb and William Crampton Gore joined Everett and Katherine to paint (fig. 63). In parallel with John's adoption of a gypsy lifestyle, they lived an isolated life of studied simplicity, baking their own bread and cooking with furze from the heath. When Stabb and Tharp were joined by William C. Coles, a master at Winchester School of Art (fig. 19), they moved on to Rollington Farm, Corfe Castle.[15]

In addition to Steinberg, the Everetts' modern and warmer house at Swanage, Everett rented a top-lit studio in Swanage where he took up gilding, carving and repairing his own frames. He left for Paris a couple of months later, to attend the commercially run atelier, the Académie Julian. Joined there by Katherine, their English cook, a nurse and baby Henry, life was very sociable, with Katherine recalling a visit to Rodin's studio. Back in Swanage by April 1906, Everett painted some landscapes at Holmebridge near Wareham. But when their second son, Anthony, was born at Steinberg (fig. 65), Everett again headed for Paris, studying at La Palette with William Crampton Gore and John Duncan Fergusson each morning and with Claudio Castelucho in the afternoon.[16]

15. William C. Coles was a landscape and marine painter who taught at Winchester School of Art and exhibited at the New English between 1881 and 1914.
16. Claudio Castelucho was a popular teacher among foreign artists like Everett studying in Paris. Professor at the Académie Colarossi, by 1905 he was amongst the first professors at the Académie de la Grande Chaumière in Paris, founded in 1902 by Alice Dannenberg and Martha Stettler. They refused to teach the strict academic rules of painting of the École des Beaux-Arts and kept their fees below the Académie Julian.

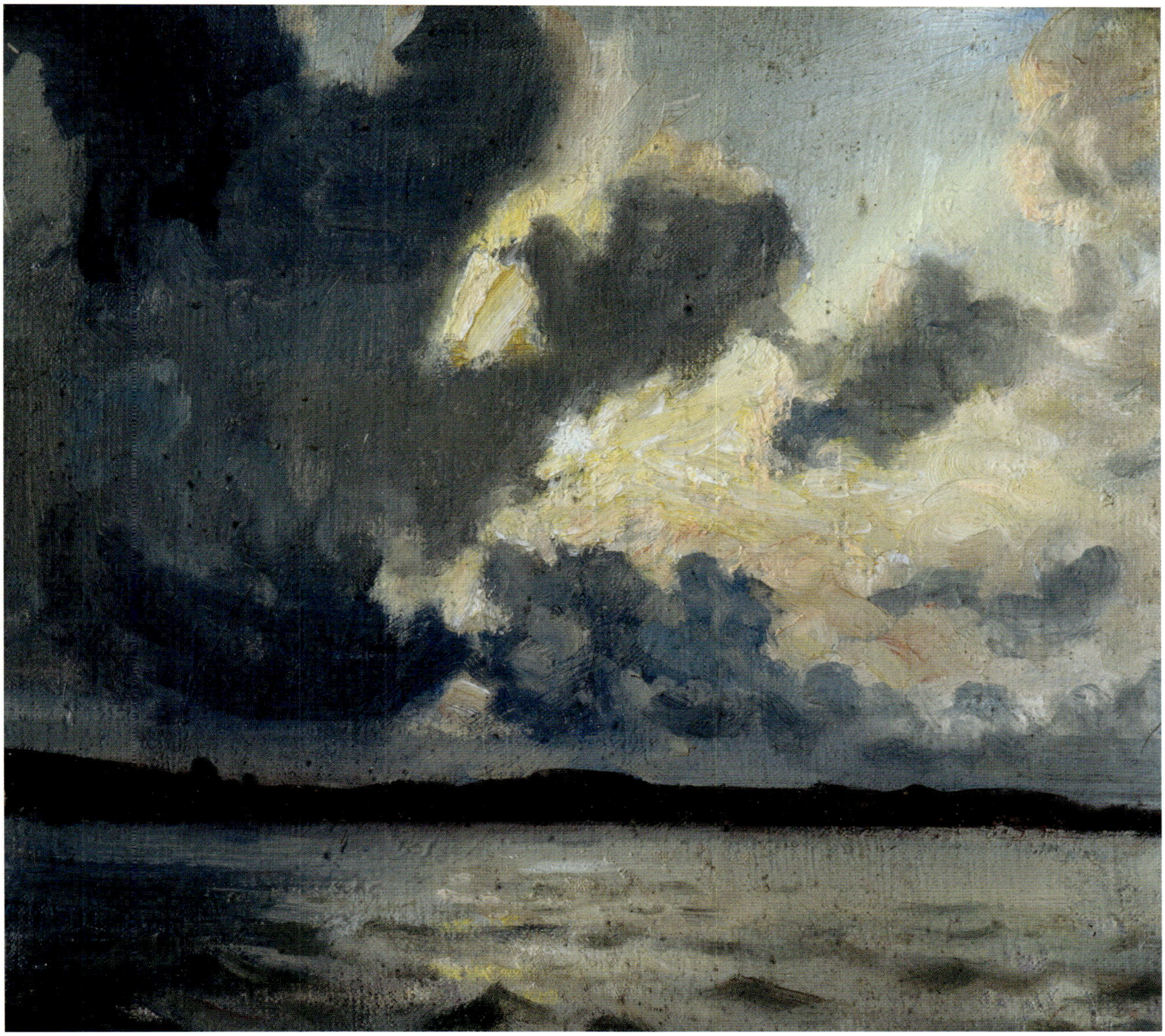

FIG. 68
John Everett / ***Clouds over the Sea***
c.1910 / oil sketch on board / 26 x 33 cm
private collection

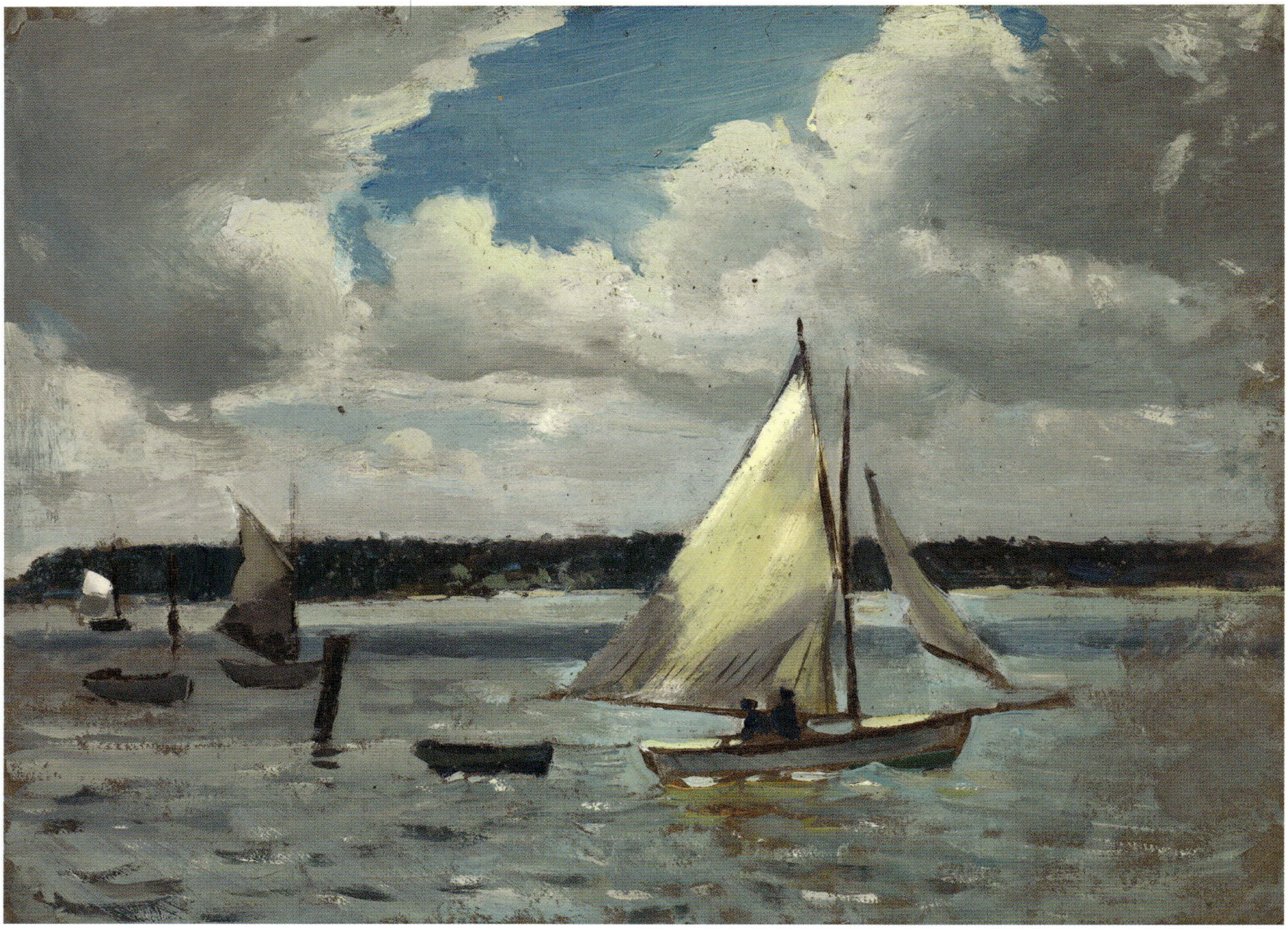

FIG. 69
John Everett / ***Poole Harbour***
c.1910 / oil sketch on paper / 25.4 x 35.5 cm

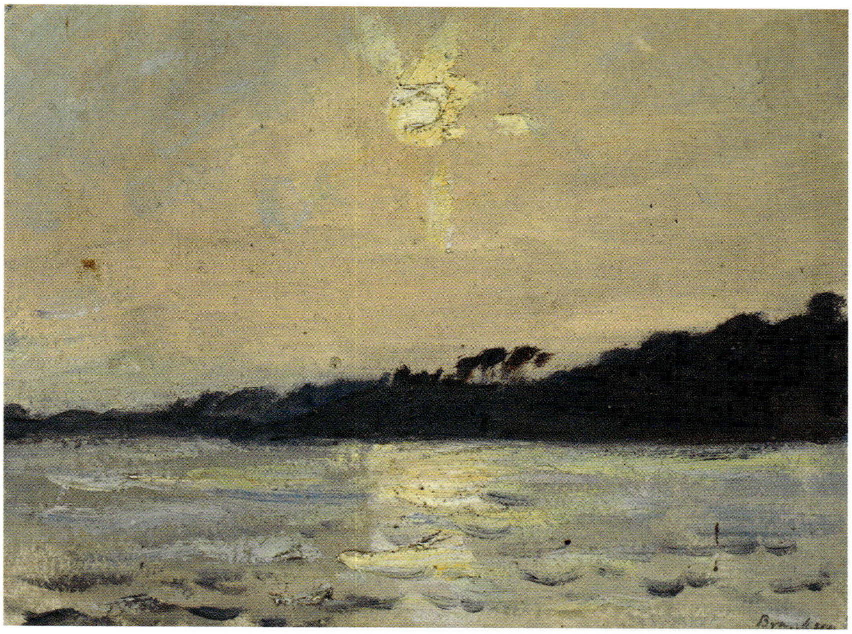

FIG. 70
John Everett / *Branksea Island*
c.1910 / oil on paper / 12.2 x 17.8 cm

THE ARTIST–SAILOR AND POOLE HARBOUR

Everett bought a 9-ton cutter, *Walrus*, 'from the landlord of the Shipwright's Arms, Poole'.[17] He adapted it as a floating studio and sailed it around Poole Harbour from spring to late autumn (fig. 69), where in 1907, he witnessed:

> a number of people coming down, back of Branksea [now Brownsea] Island, where you never saw a soul. I got the glasses on them. It was a man and some boys. They pitched some tents, made a camp, it was Baden Powell the start of the boy scouts.[18]

His oil sketch of Poole Harbour off Goathorn Point, with Brownsea Island on the left, reveals Everett to be both an artist and a sailor painting the locality. He produced many such oils on paper using a specially adapted easel, as well as associated sketchbooks. The oil sketch, taken from the low perspective of the *Walrus*, focuses on the landscape and the sky, whose fast-moving clouds occupy half the picture. Set against the backdrop of the island, Everett has placed a sailing boat in the foreground, similar to the 14-foot dinghy given to him by his cousin Edward Everett.

Amongst the largest of eight islands in Poole Harbour, at the time of this painting (fig. 70) Branksea Island was owned by rich industrialist Charles van Raalte, who bought it from Kenneth Robert Balfour in 1901.[19] Baden-Powell was at Branksea at the invitation of the van Raaltes. Everett's oil sketch, probably made close to Branksea, features another of the other small islands in the harbour, either Round or Long Island. Again painted from his boat, the focus is on the relationship between the sun, the clouds and the play of light on the surface of the water, and marks the way his seascapes developed. A further view of Poole Harbour (fig. 56) looks towards

17. Everett, *Memoirs*, p.115.
18. Everett, *Memoirs*, p.119.
19. The name of Branksea Island was changed to Brownsea in 1903 to avoid confusion, as the van Raaltes' London guests mistakenly alighted at Branksome Station, instead of continuing on to Poole. Rich from the jute and tobacco industry, the van Raaltes entertained on a grand scale with many European royal households visiting their island for house parties. In 1907 van Raalte allowed Baden-Powell to hold his boy-scout camp there, which marked the beginning of the Boy Scout movement witnessed by Everett. Van Raalte's wife Florence (née Clow) exhibited at the RA in 1884.

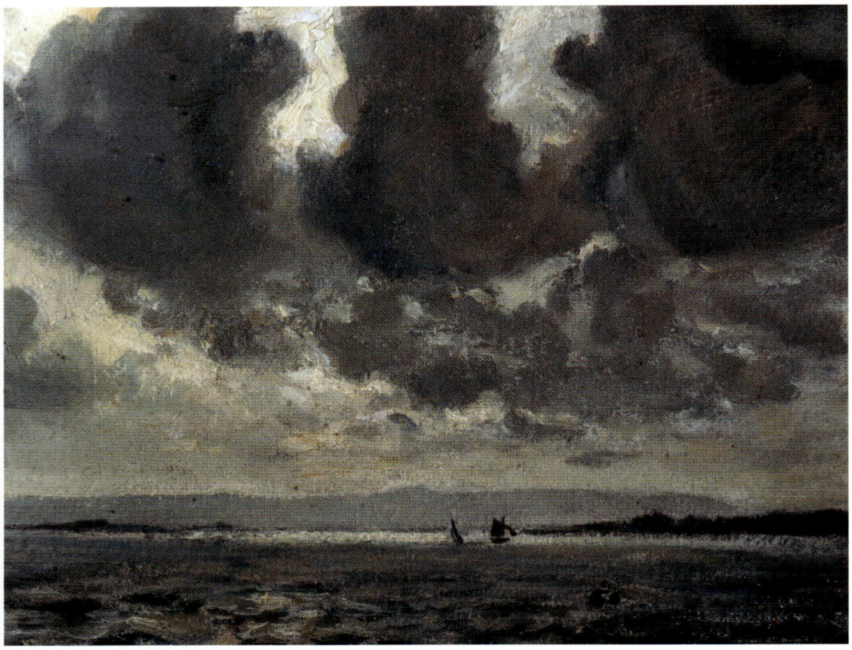

FIG. 71
John Everett / *Seascape and the Dorset coast*
c.1910 / oil sketch on board / 18 x 24 cm
Painted from Walrus looking south with Nine Barrow Down in the background, and towards Fitzworth on the right. The painting hung for some years at 11 Carlton House terrace, the home of Katherine Everett's relation, Lady Ardilaun
private collection

the mouth of the Frome.[20] Its low horizon suggests it was made from the *Walrus*. On the far left is Rough Point, with the raised ground of Fitzworth and Round Island on the right. The sky occupies two-thirds of the painting, with patches of bright light falling on the land to the left and centre. This landscape was very familiar to Everett, who spent each summer sailing boats up the inlets, producing paintings focusing on the landscape and the effects of light on the water and clouds (figs 68 and 71).

Everett had laid up his boat by October and rented a studio in Tite Street, Chelsea, for five weeks before renting Arfleet Mill, near Corfe Castle, from Bertha Newcombe. Filled with her paintings, Arfleet was a Tudor miller's house with an old working mill and a walled garden approached through a courtyard (figs 80 and 111). Everett used an old chapel in West Street, Corfe Castle, as his studio about the time Collins moved in to the Old Curetage there, and Henry Tonks was staying close by at Studland. Everett also found time to sail on the *Vendolian*, his first trip in a steamship, taking 10 days to sail from Cardiff to Marseilles and then on to Valencia, Burriana, Gibraltar, Genoa and Tarragona. Away for six weeks, Everett returned to Corfe Castle in March 1908. It was during this summer that Tonks and Steer made their important visit to Dorset, which is discussed in the next chapter.

20. See E.H.H. Archibald, *John Everett Marine Painter: A Memorial Exhibition*, 1964, exhibition catalogue, National Maritime Museum, no. 18, p.9.

SIX

PAINTING PURBECK

The new century saw painters turn towards the distinctive landscape features and wealth of subject matter that the Purbeck region of Dorset offered. During the first decade of the twentieth century the Everetts provided Slade painters with the companionship of fellow artists in Dorset combined with a wide range of potential subjects from which to produce paintings to exhibit in London. It is instructive to note that between 1905 and 1910 Slade tutors Steer, Tonks, Brown and Russell consciously selected Purbeck scenes to produce modern landscapes intended to promote and enhance their reputations in London and appeal to new patrons. Painters in Purbeck often concentrated on landscapes bearing evidence of previous civilizations and industry such as lime kilns or quarries. In marked contrast to the work of realist artists like George Clausen, this countryside was presented as a dispassionate space, largely emptied of agricultural workers. Lisa Tickner has suggested that artists like Augustus John would use this landscape for more personal and symbolic purposes to form the starting point – or backdrop – for more imaginary interpretations such as his *Lyric Fantasy*, 1913 (fig. 72), in which the Blue Pool near Wareham forms the setting for his highly personal tableau.[1] Henry Tonks also incorporated friends into his narrative Dorset work.

THE PURBECK LANDSCAPE

The chalk downs extending west from Lulworth Cove to Old Harry Rocks in the east form an ancient ridge of the Purbeck Hills, along which various Iron Age, Roman and Saxon sites, like Creech Barrow and Nine Barrow Down, remain. The art critic and painter Alfred Lys Baldry wrote of Purbeck as 'cut off from the rest of the county by the marshy lowland which extends from the upper waters of Poole Harbour to the neighbourhood of Dorchester'.[2] The area between Wareham and the mouth of Poole Harbour he described as an

> expanse of undulating moorland, intersected by marshy valleys, through which run small streams, and in which grow a few groups of trees; and this moorland reaches from the mud-flats of the estuary to the foot of the high range of the chalk downs which form a kind of rampart to the Isle of Purbeck itself.[3]

1. Tickner, 'Augustus John: Gypsies, Tramps and Lyric Fantasy', pp.49–79, and Holt, 'Seeking Classic Lands', pp.49–79.
2. A.L. Baldry, 'The Coast of Dorset', *Art Journal*, 1952, p.306.
3. Ibid, p.308.

At the village of Corfe Castle stand the remains of the medieval castle, which once guarded the main route through the surrounding hills, before it was damaged during the Civil War. Its dramatic ruins had long inspired artists and writers, including Hardy, who referred to it as Corvesgate Castle in his short novel, *The Hand of Ethelberta*, 1876. Surrounding Corfe, the strange, yet picturesque, scenery was desolate and crossed by few roads. Occasional farmhouses, cottages and clay pits evoked the primitive world of its ancient past, captured in the drama of Collins' *Arne Heath* (fig. 57). It was equally littered with the vestiges of a more recent industrial past, such as water-filled clay pits, lime kilns and the few remaining working stone quarries – forming dramatic, scarred scenes. Although the number of stone quarries on Purbeck's limestone plateau had declined, there were still working clay pits supplying clay to the potteries and chalk pits for lime kilns (figs 5, 82 and 109). These attracted *plein air* painters, who increasingly gravitated to the wild heath, moors and coast around Corfe Castle, Swanage and Studland, each with ancient traditions and customs apparently detached from encroaching modernity.

Holland, writing about Dorset at the turn of the century, viewed the pleasure resort of Swanage in Purbeck, as 'a small but growing modern watering place, with little or no history in the past save the more or less traditional battle fought in "Swanwic Bay" between Alfred and the Danes'.[4] The sandy bay, on an attractive peninsula, faced outwards towards the English Channel and Isle of Wight, rather than inwards to Poole Harbour. Within easy reach of popular sites such as Lulworth Cove and Kimmeridge Bay, by the beginning of the century Swanage had transformed from a working port shipping Purbeck stone to a pleasure resort. Special trains brought minor European royalty from nearby Bournemouth as well as less grand day-trippers, and at the height of its season holiday apartments were at a premium. Focusing on its old-world quaintness, Swanage actively promoted itself as a healthy resort (the average age at death for residents in 1896 was 81), offering outdoor activities and pastimes.[5] The landscape around Swanage contained remarkable geological features, prehistoric barrows and industrial interventions from quarrying. Combined with picturesque Napoleonic defences and Corfe's ruined castle, they presented a remarkably rich seam of subject matter for painters visiting Purbeck.

To the north-east of Swanage the small village of Studland rested between the mouth of Poole Harbour and the chalk cliffs forming one side of Swanage Bay, with a magnificent little bay of golden sand. Tucked away beneath the downs, by the beginning of the century Studland was becoming more élite as a holiday location for the leisured upper middle classes who, like Vanessa Bell, eschewed the more populist resorts of Bournemouth, Weymouth and Swanage. Sisters Vanessa Bell and Virginia Woolf (née Stephen) stayed at Studland at various times from 1909, with the Woolfs' last visit in January 1913.[6] In September 1911, Virginia wrote from Harmony Cottages, Studland, to Saxon Sydney-Turner, recounting a trip to Poole 'on a tug with two barges up to Wareham, which is one of the most lovely towns I have ever seen'.[7] Genteel pastimes included sea bathing, lawn tennis and cycling, with a golf course formed in 1892 between Corfe Castle and Studland. With only one hotel, by the time Bloomsbury arrived Studland had experienced 'an advancing tide' of small seaside villas and bungalows. Baldry lamented the rapid loss of its 'old worldliness', as by

4. Holland, 1906.
5. *Dorset County Chronicle*, 5 March 1896, p.6.
6. Virginia Stephen married the writer Leonard Woolf on 10 August 1912.
7. Nigel Nicolson and Joanne Trautmann, eds, *The Questions of Things Happening: The Letters of Virginia Woolf*, 1976, p.479.

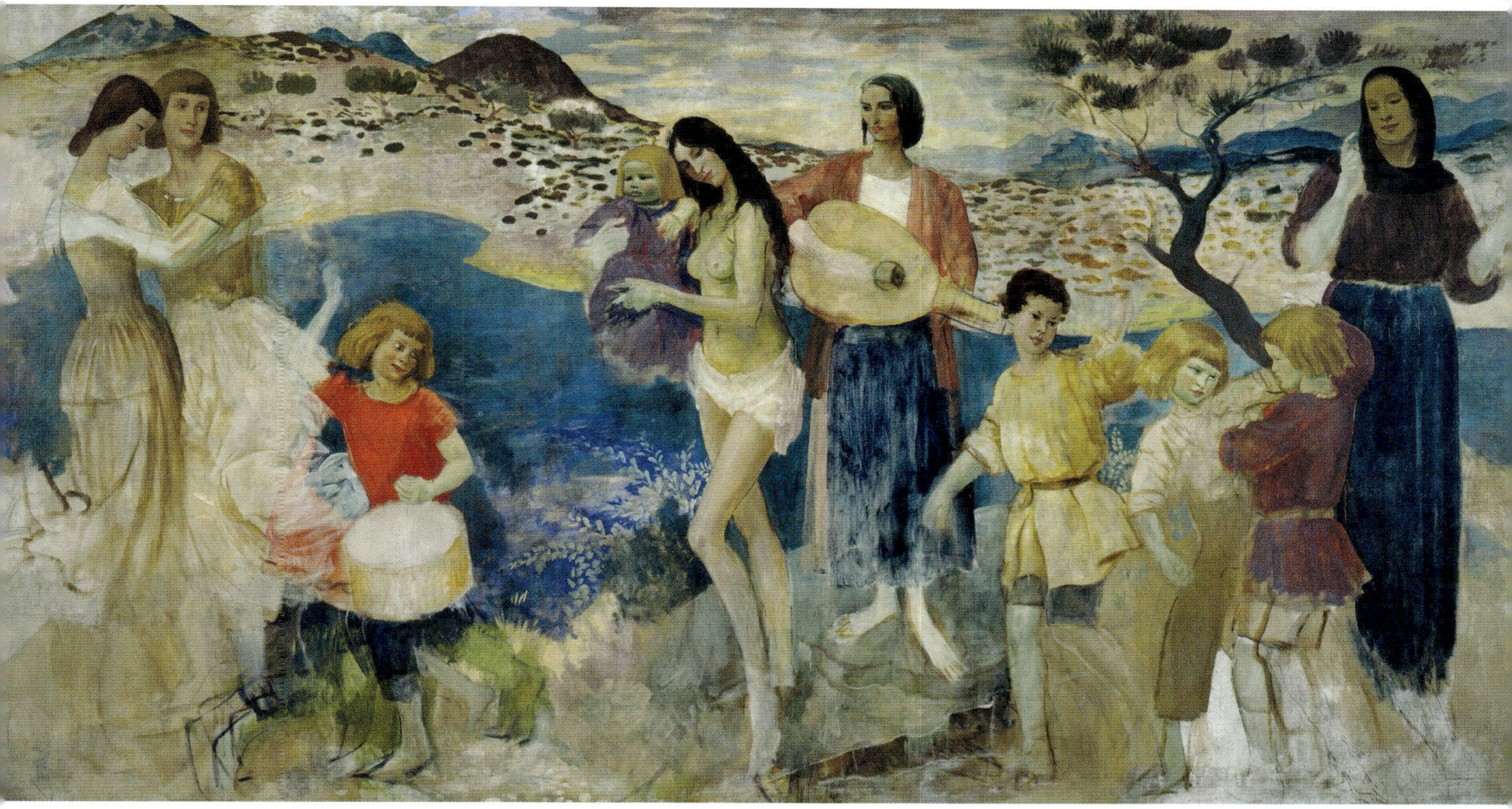

FIG. 72

Augustus John / ***Lyric Fantasy***

c.1913 / oil on canvas / 238 x 472 cm

the end of the decade, its beaches were accessible to all but the very poorest unable to afford to travel there.

Visiting Slade painters favoured the view towards the creeks and mudflats of Poole Harbour, a panorama, from the higher ridges of the Isle of Purbeck close to the golf course. It was specifically promoted by Baldry, as 'an artistic asset of which the value can hardly be too highly estimated'.[8] Painters such as Steer, Tonks, Russell, Everett and Friedenson all celebrated Purbeck's large skies.[9] Its entire coastline from Lulworth Cove, Durdle Door, Tyneham and Kimmeridge to Old Harry Rocks was dramatic, and thus lent itself as a subject to painters. Everett was very attracted to the area around Worbarrow Bay and returned many times to paint there (figs 85–91).[10] Exhibiting pictures of Studland, Corfe or Swanage in London had the effect of promoting the region, and artists feared this would attract visitors and tourists who neither valued nor understood its spirit and history. On his first trip to Corfe Castle in 1890 with Fred Brown and former Slade student Peter Moffat Lindner, Philip Wilson Steer sensed this would ultimately lead to the destruction of the highly valued peace and quiet of Purbeck.[11]

It was in this location that Slade tutors Steer, Tonks, Brown and Russell came to paint, tellingly selecting views for their modern landscapes to exhibit in London. In part their modernity depended on their choice of setting, and they all chose sites of former industry like lime kilns or quarries to present their unpopulated views.

HENRY TONKS

Henry Tonks made various visits to Dorset, sometimes staying in Dorchester with his childhood friend, the surgeon William Burrough Cosens. This close friendship surely accounts for his painting of Lulworth of 1890/1.[12] In 1905 Tonks was in Purbeck with Ronald Gray, a longstanding friend of both his and Steer's. There Gray painted *Summer Scene in a Garden with Figures*, 1905 (fig. 74) and showed *Chalk Cliff, Studland* at the summer exhibition of the New English in 1906.[13]

1905 was also the year Tonks produced his important work: *The Lost Path* (fig. 73). Four figures stand in a disused clay pit on a ridge between Corfe Castle and Studland above the Rempstone Estate. The location, now obscured by tree plantations, does not satisfactorily correspond with any estate maps, and most sandpits and quarries are now overgrown or have disappeared. However, his panorama takes in the patchwork of fields leading to the inlets of Poole Harbour with Poole's coastline beyond. Baldry applauded this as a setting for painters, admiring the

> magnificent views, inland over Poole Harbour, eastwards over Bournemouth Bay to the Isle of Wight, and westwards across the Isle of Purbeck, on which so many generations of worshippers of beautiful scenery have feasted their eyes.[14]

Tonks focused on the interaction in the foreground between the two women and local boy standing with his back to the viewer and pointing into the distance. The static narrative set in this landscape shows the boy, holding his rolled-up cap, leading the eye towards the panoramic vista

8. Baldry, p.310.
9. Cheston, p.25.
10. Letter from Augustus John, Cité Titian, Le Puy en Village, The Loire, 12 September 1900, to John Everett (private collection), about painting at Worbarrow, 'My dear Everett I was very disappointed at being unable to pay you a visit at Warborough [sic] Bay to see your work.'
11. Close in style to Whistler, Lindner created atmospheric landscapes with chromatic effects and exhibited Dorset paintings at the New English, between 1891 and 1905, such as *Swanage Bay, Dorset, Morning* (Aberdeen Art Gallery and Museums).
12. See *Kelly's Directory*, 1903, p.5; 1911, p.76. Physician and surgeon William Burrough Cosens lived at The Gables, Dorchester. He was author of *Your Servant The Doctor*, 1931. I am indebted to Sabina ffrench Blake for identifying the important Dorset connection between Tonks and Cosens.
13. MacColl, *Steer*, p.63. Gray was an engineer who studied painting in the evenings with Brown. At the beginning of the twentieth century he sometimes accompanied Steer on painting trips and later became Steer's artistic executor.
14. Baldry, p.309.

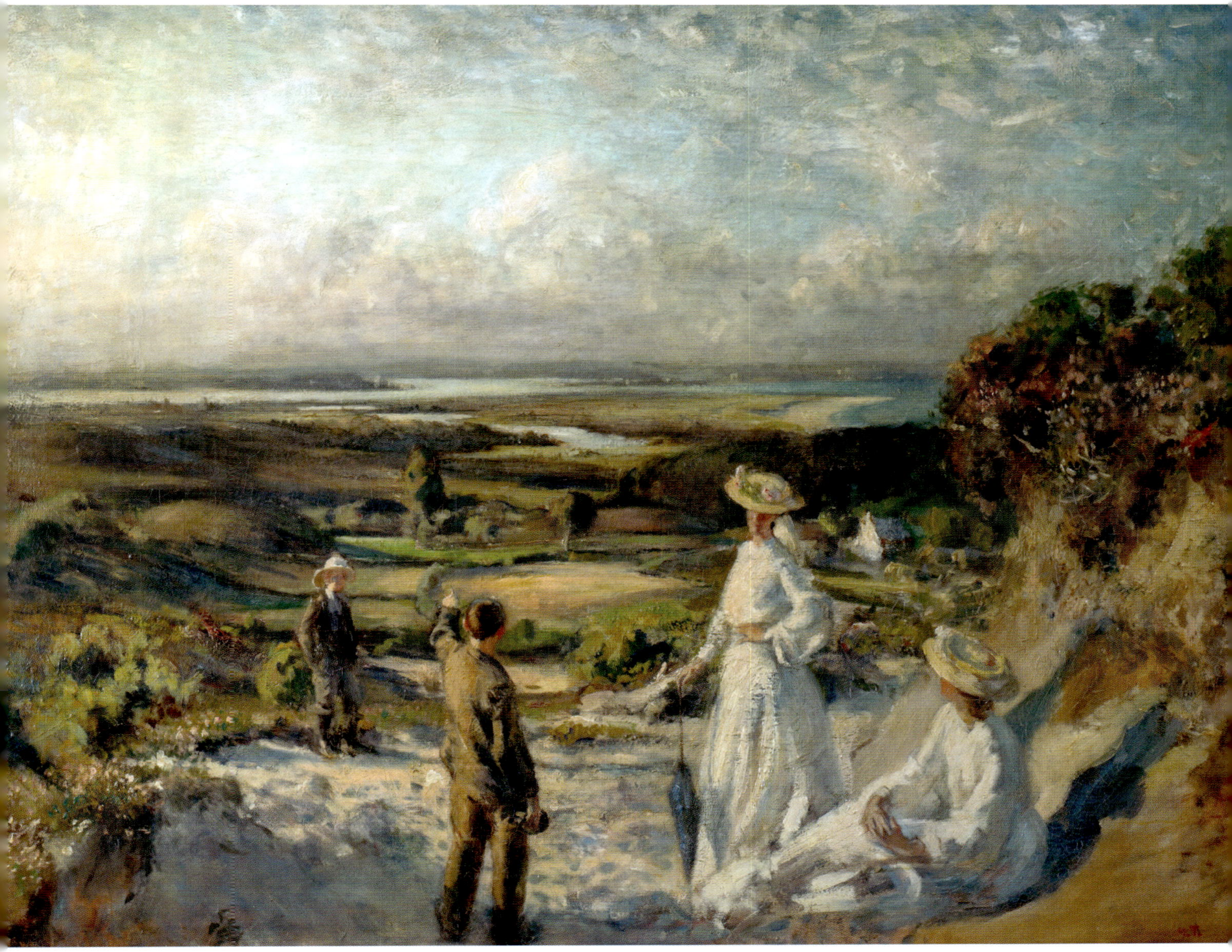

FIG. 73
Henry Tonks / ***The Lost Path***
1905 / oil on canvas / 60 x 94 cm
private collection

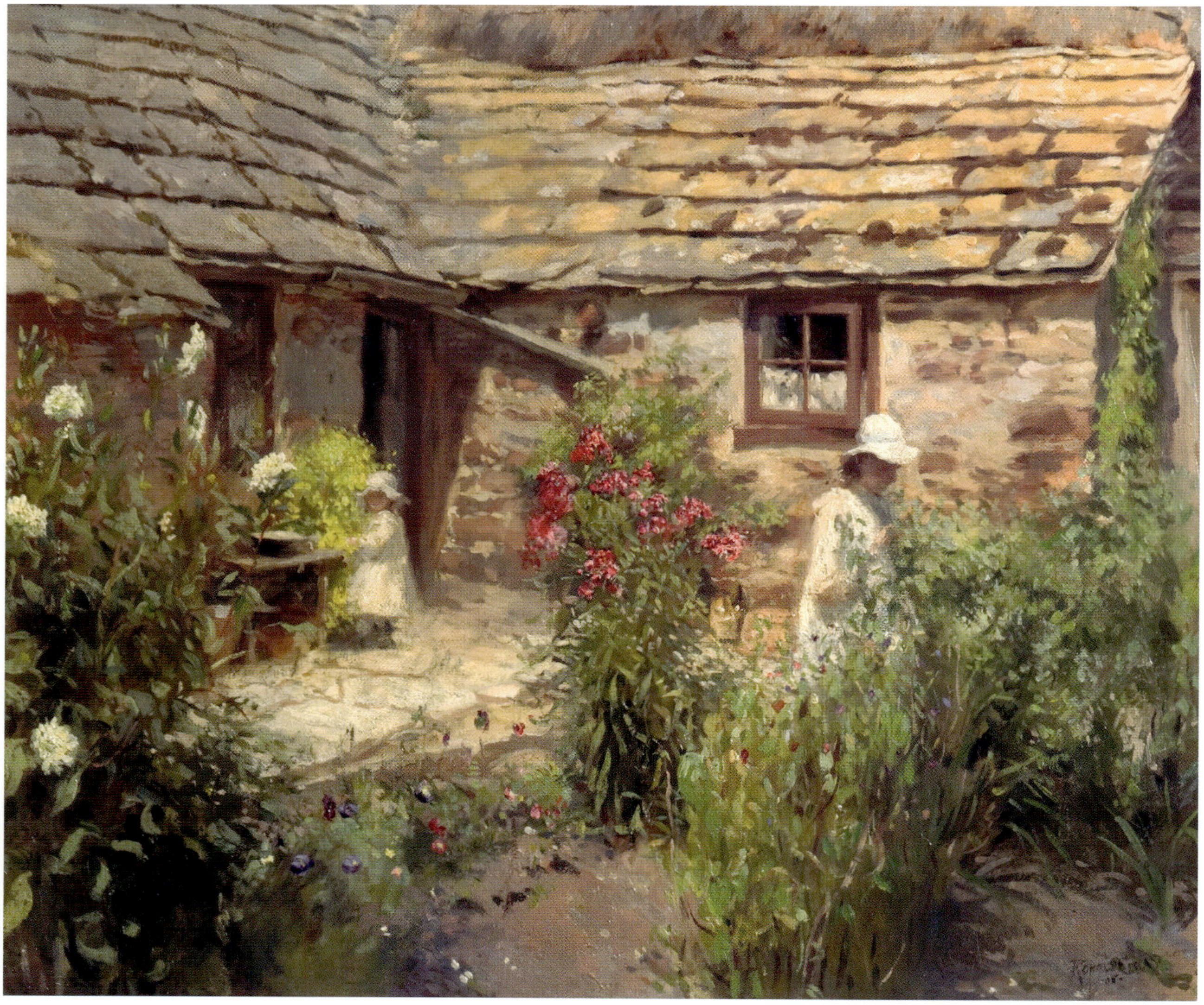

FIG. 74
Ronald Gray
Summer Scene in a Garden with Figures
1905 / oil on canvas / 49 x 59 cm
Bridport Museum Trust

from which the remaining group looks away. The jauntily dressed young man, perhaps an artist, faces the elegant women in their picture hats, dressed as appropriately for afternoon tea as for a country walk. The figure holding a parasol turns to the boy, a gesture which invites the viewer into the picture space. It is thought to be Katherine Everett. Since Everett's memoirs refer to Katherine sitting to Tonks, it is likely for this painting.[15]

Dorset offered Tonks freedom to experiment, since he intended *The Lost Path* to enhance his reputation and appeal to prospective buyers.[16] He vested considerable effort in terms of the ambition, scale and subject of the work, which marks a departure from his conversation pieces in enclosed interiors.[17] The critic Frank Rutter admired this Dorset picture as 'deliciously fresh and harmonious', declaring Tonks as a modern Zoffany, perhaps because of his skill at group portraiture. McConkey sees this as meaning that Tonks added anecdote to Steer's style of arcadian landscapes.[18] The figures in *The Lost Path* were regarded as compositional devices more suited to an interior setting; certainly its implicit anecdotal content was ignored by commentators who focused instead on the work as a landscape and admired Tonks's light effects. Art commentator Ernest G. Halton also observed:

> Mr. Henry Tonk's [sic] harmonious and attractive picture, 'The Lost Path', has much to interest the lover of English landscape. The figures in the foreground are not only well drawn, but they are also placed in the picture with due consideration for the balance of the composition. But the chief beauty of the work lies in the landcape, evidently painted in the neighbourhood of Poole Harbour, which is seen beyond, bathed in sunlight. The impression of distance is well conveyed, and the painting of the sky is especially good.[19]

The Lost Path was one of 50 paintings by New English and international artists included in Agnew's special exhibition 'Fifty Examples of the Independent Art of Today', held in February 1906. Rutter declared the exhibition a great victory for Steer, Tonks, Sickert, Rothenstein, Orpen and the New English, and in upholding the independence of these individual modern painters, art critics thought it the outcome of 20 years of modern artistic freedom.[20] Commenting on the show, *The Studio* observed:

> those who are seriously interested in the welfare of British art cannot fail to have noticed with gratification a growing appreciation during the last few years of the work of artists who are subject neither to conventionality nor officialism, who desire freedom of expression unfettered by any consideration beyond that demanded by the dignity of their art.[21]

Importantly, the exhibition generated a wider market for the artists. Tonks' painting was purchased from Agnew's by Judge William Evans, a patron of British artists, whom Tonks acknowledged as 'a true friend to painters'.[22] Evans admired Tonks' work and went on to buy his other major Dorset picture, *Summer*, 1908 (fig. 79).[23]

PHILIP WILSON STEER

The Everetts' importance in Slade circles effectively made them central to the production of a number of important British landscape paintings

15. The year Tonks held his first one-man show at the Carfax Gallery.
16. Frank Rutter, 'Round the Galleries', *Sunday Times*, 18 February 1906, p.11.
17. See Frank Rutter, *Sunday Times*, 2 December 1906, p.4, referring to Tonks' works exhibited at the winter New English of 1906, *The Town from Corfe Castle* (24) and *Poole Harbour* (28). *Woman Walking on the Sand*, watercolour, Cecil Higgins Art Gallery, Bedford, may feature Katherine Everett at Studland. See too *Woman in a White Dress with Others on a Beach*, coloured chalk, private collection; *The Beach*, watercolour, formerly Barbizon House; *Spring-time*, oil, c.1900, Birmingham Art Gallery. His other Dorset paintings exhibited at the New English included *In Lulworth*, 1891; *Resting among the Sand Hills*, 1904, private collection; *The Chalk Cliff* in the winter of 1905, possibly related to Dorset, *Poole Harbour*; three paintings of Corfe Castle and two of Wareham in 1906; *Summer*, 1903, Tate, and *Corfe Castle*, watercolour, Slade Collection.
18. McConkey, p.98, f.n.6, described Tonks' and Steer's landscape paintings of this period as 'garden England' pastorals. See Rutter, 'An English Painter: Henry Tonks', *The Times*, 11 October 1936, p.7.
19. Ernest G. Halton, 'Independent British Art at Messrs. Agnew's', *The Studio*, 1906, p.29, described Steer as intensely individual, p.26.
20. See Rutter, *Art in My Time*, 1933, p.127.
21. 'Independent British Art at Messrs. Agnew's', *The Studio*, 1906, p.18.
22. Letter from Henry Tonks to an important patron, Geoffrey Blackwell, 16 February 1918, Geoffrey Blackwell uncatalogued papers, Tate 2006.4, folder 17.
23. In addition to *The Lost Path* and *Summer*, Judge Evans owned Tonks' *The Bird Cage* and *The Strolling Players*, 1907, and a watercolour, *Scarborough*. A genial patron who did not follow established taste, Evans largely bought new work, amassing an eclectic collection of British art during the last 20 years of his life. After his death his collection was sold at the Goupil Gallery between May and June 1918, and Charles Aitken, Director of the National Gallery, noted in the accompanying catalogue that Evans bought 'Steer before he was Steer' and sought Tonks' pictures together with those of artists with rising reputations like Conder, John and Orpen. See Charles Aitken, 'Preface', *Catalogue of a Collection of Oil Paintings, Watercolours & Drawings Formed by the Late William Evans, Judge of the Mid-Wales County Court Circuit*, Goupil Gallery, William Marchant and Co., May–June, 1918, pp.7, 8. 'The Judge Evans Collection', *The Times*, 14 June 1918, p.9.

of this period. Their time at Arfleet Mill, close to Corfe Castle, formed a focal point for the many Slade painters attracted to the picturesque qualities of Corfe village and its castle. This confirmed art critic Alfred Yockney's observation that 'although most artists have nomadic tendencies there is usually a definite painting ground in mind for the chief adventure of the year.'[24]

For Steer, the summer of 1908 proved particularly productive. He initially rejected the Everetts' suggestion of Rollington Farm, very close to Arfleet, as a suitable place to stay, and without even visiting it, deemed the aspect too dull. Instead he decided to follow Tonks by seeking a studio and lodgings in Corfe, but when this proved unsuccessful the Everetts persuaded him to look at the setting of Rollington on the Rempstone Estate. Steer was so delighted at its remarkable views of Corfe, the castle and over to Poole Harbour, that he immediately settled there with Brown and Coles.[25] The tenant farmer's daughter initially tried to evict them when, much to Steer's amusement, she mistook Brown and Steer for their erstwhile students Stabb and Tharp, who had rented a cottage there in 1904 and kept the farmer awake all night playing the banjo.[26] After the Everetts smoothed things over, a shed on the farm was adapted with a top light to create a studio for Steer, within easy reach of dramatic scenery.

Thus Rollington was the locus for Steer's major paintings of Corfe Castle and Dorset, regarded as amongst his most important landscapes.[27] His *Moon Rising over the Downs* (fig. 75) was painted from the track leading up to the cut immediately behind Rollington farmhouse. It shows East Hill to the right and Nine Barrow Hill on the left, with the slash of creamy paint indicating the quarry used to extract chalk. Almost hidden, the rising moon of the title lends tranquillity and stillness to his scene of grazing cows seemingly suspended in time and space. Moonlit paintings were popular, offering opportunities for unusual lighting effects and evoking mystery, romance and stillness. Streaked with salmon-pink clouds and bathed in a golden glow, the sky takes up over half of Steer's painting, leading art critic Charles Holmes to suggest in *The Times* the painterly influence of Rembrandt and Daubigny.[28]

Over this summer of 1908 Steer painted some of his most mature and creative landscapes. He was working at Rollington at the same time that Tonks was based less than 2 miles away at Arfleet, painting *Summer* (fig. 79). Though Steer's earlier Swanage work offered a fresh, atmospheric, broad-brush approach, treating general features rather than detail, the Dorset work of 1908 marks a shift to a more intense and personal response to nature.[29] Despite the play of light and boldness, it is private, solitary and reflective, celebrating the old world order Steer admired, free from picnickers and modern intrusions. Often cited as the successor to Constable in his expression of the English countryside, Steer felt that a painting should be assessed primarily through the formal pictorial qualities of design, colour and organization. It has been suggested, therefore, that Steer provided a bridge between Constable and Bloomsbury artists interested in such qualities, such as Roger Fry (fig. 104 and 107), who, within a couple of years, came to challenge, through their Dorset work, the formal training the Slade stood for.

24. Alfred Yockney, 'An Artist's Holiday', *Art Journal*, 1910, p.240.
25. William C. Coles joined them, as he had done on previous Dorset painting expeditions.
26. Everett, *Memoirs*, p.116.
27. Katherine Everett suggested that Tonks, Steer and Brown also spent their subsequent summer at the farm, Katherine Everett, p.126, confirmed by Everett, who mentioned that Steer used *Walrus* over the summer of 1909, Everett, *Memoirs*, p.117.
28. Charles Holmes, 'Goupil Gallery of 1909', *The Times*, 22 April 1909.
29. See Steer, *Swanage Beach*, 1890, watercolour and graphite on paper, 26 x 36.1 cm, Courtauld Gallery.

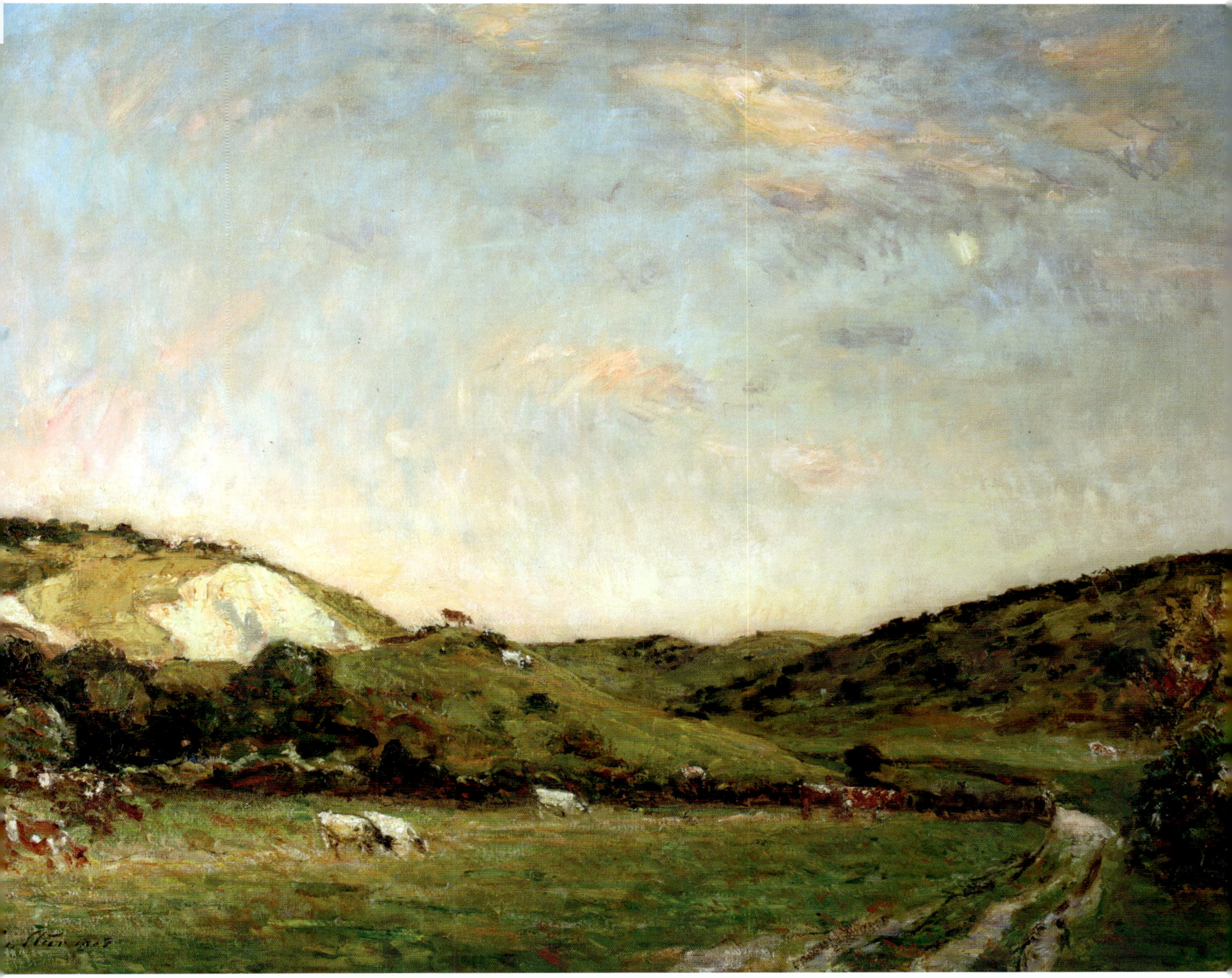

FIG. 75
Philip Wilson Steer / ***Moon Rising over the Downs***
1908 / oil on canvas / 75 x 100 cm
private collection

Although McColl suggested that in Dorset Steer led Coles and Brown 'over hill and dale till they wilted and cried for mercy', his account contradicts Steer's well-documented aversion to physical exertion, confirmed by his patron Geoffrey Blackwell.[30] Blackwell believed that, though not idle, Steer avoided physical activity and became increasingly lethargic, except when inspired to paint. Chronically bronchial, he could not paint in discomfort or draughts, and this tended to dictate his choice of subjects.[31]

The combined quality and accessibility of the spectacular views at Rollington Farm left Steer free to experiment. Everett observed in his memoirs that all three artists frequently painted the same subject, while on other occasions Everett noted that Brown and Coles stood and watched Steer at work. Steer reportedly struggled to capture views. Blackwell recalled that for Steer a painting had 'either "come off" or had not 'come off'" and that he sometimes deliberately brought canvases back from summer vacations lightly sketched in oils, which he then worked up in his studio over the winter.[32] Holt has noted how Steer pushed the boundaries and 'engaged and experimented with the intrinsic properties of paint, be it in oils or watercolour, while at the same time satisfying the growing market for grand panoramic vistas – timeless evocations of the native landscape'.[33]

Steer, in favouring panoramic vistas, was attracted to the spectacular views and dramatic ruins of Corfe Castle. His large painting *The Isle of Purbeck*, 1908, shows unfolding downs above Corfe Castle (fig. 76), demonstrating his innovation, experimentation and differing stylistic approaches over that summer and contrasting markedly in style and mood with *Moon Rising over the Downs* (fig. 75) and *The Lime-Kiln* (fig. 77), both 1908. The far-reaching view from the south slope of Nine Barrow Down looks west towards Flower's Barrow, Tyneham and Church Knowle, with Poole Harbour and Wareham Estuary in the far distance on the right. The misty ruins of the castle and village of Corfe are silhouetted in the gap of the Purbeck Hills. While the hatched brush strokes suggest the modern influence of Cézanne, the painting evokes the ancient landscape suspended in time, leaving the viewer with the sensation of hovering above the scene between the clouds and the fading blue of the distant unfolding hills.[34]

The painting was in Steer's 1909 Goupil exhibition, which Holmes felt 'ought to prove finally that in him England possesses a really great living master of landscape and figure painting'.[35] Regarding Steer as the modern successor to Constable, Holmes suggested that the subjects painted on a heroic scale prove Steer could 'stand comparison with the greatest names in English landscape'. *Isle of Purbeck* was purchased at the show by Geoffrey Blackwell, one of the few collectors of those contemporary British artists exhibiting at the New English. He was inspired to collect Steer after reading Holmes' laudatory account of the Goupil show of 1909 in *The Times*.[36] This exhibition led Blackwell to become the largest collector of Steer's work, as he eventually owned between 40 and 50 of his oil paintings and up to 100 watercolours.[37] In his notebook, Geoffrey Blackwell recalled: 'I first knew Steer in 1909 when he was 48 – from that date on he was one of my closest friends and I was much attached to him.' He later commented that Steer's oil paintings of this middle period 'show more fire and energy than those of later years'.[38] Interestingly, Holmes

30. McColl, pp.108–10.
31. T.G. Blackwell, 'Notes re P.W. Steer 1860–1942', 22 September 1942, Tate, Geoffrey Blackwell papers.
32. Ibid.
33. Holt, *Landscape and Modernity*, p.7.
34. Altogether Steer painted at least seven watercolours of the Corfe Castle area during the summer of 1908. Blackwell also owned *The Cliffs, Swanage*, 1890; *Poole Harbour*; *The Isle of Purbeck*; *Limekiln*, watercolour; and *Limekiln*, watercolour.
35. Charles Holmes, 'Goupil Gallery exhibition of 1909', *The Times*, 22 April 1909.
36. McConkey, p.75.
37. MacColl, p.51.
38. Blackwell.

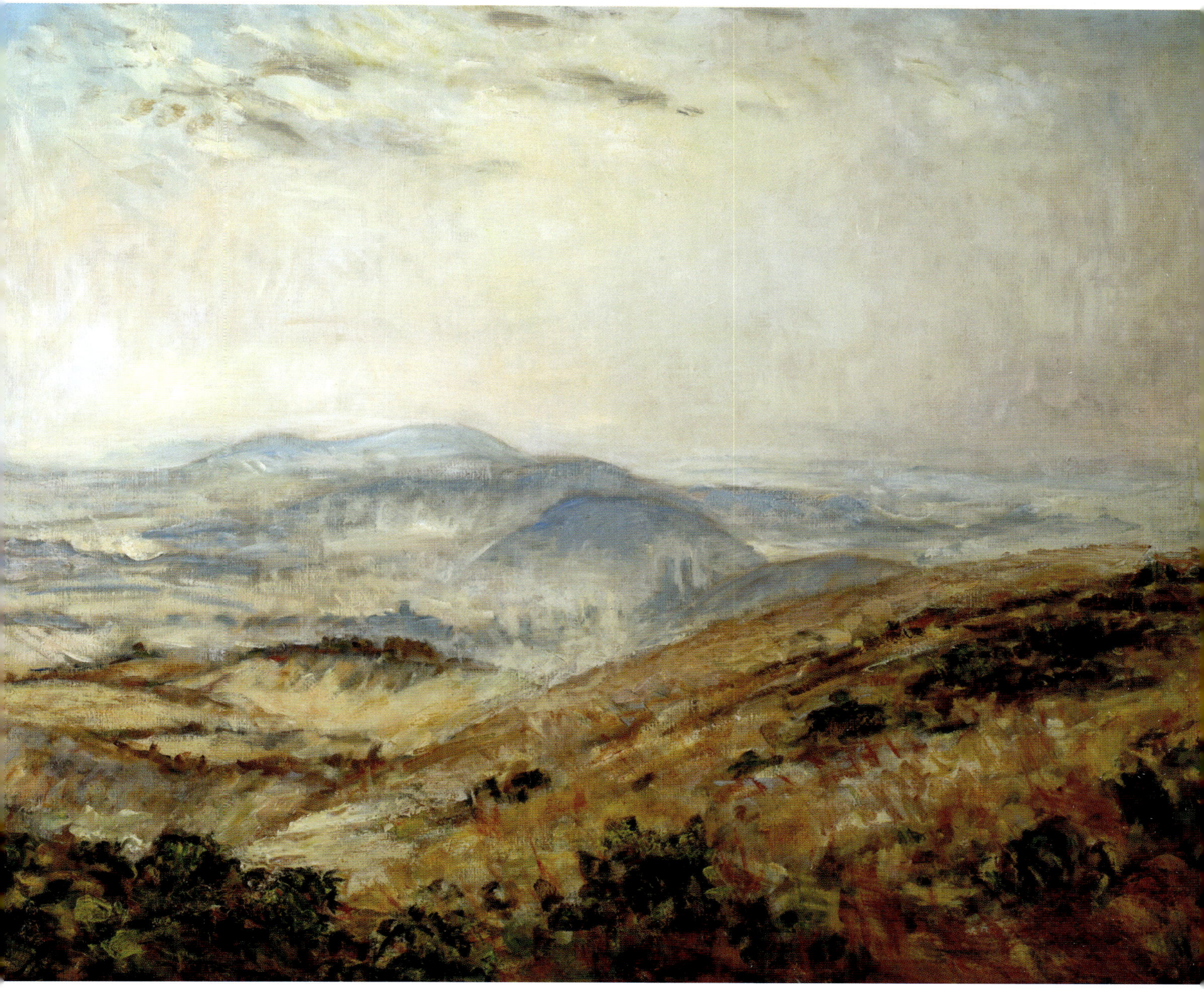

FIG. 76
Philip Wilson Steer / ***The Isle of Purbeck***
1908 / oil on canvas / 88 x 115 cm
private collection

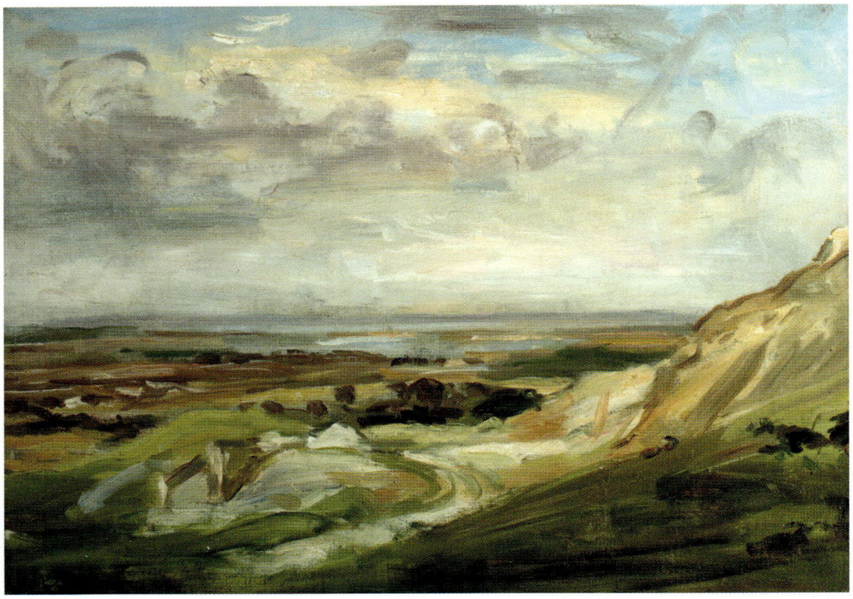

FIG. 77
Philip Wilson Steer / *The Lime-Kiln*
1908 / oil on canvas / 45 x 65 cm
private collection

considered another of Steer's Dorset canvases, *Corfe Castle and the Isle of Purbeck*, 1908, too powerful for most private houses, recommending that it 'would give permanent distinction to a public gallery'. The painting was indeed purchased for a gallery of modern art in Johannesburg, later the City of Johannesburg Art Gallery.[39]

Steer also produced a detailed, tightly constructed, and signed version of his lime kiln image, one of three of his paintings purchased from the Goupil show by Mrs Lionel Phillips (fig. 5), intent on forming a group of modern British landscapes for the Johannesburg gallery.[40] This version focused on the structure of the lime kiln, with a man and horse framed in the arched entrance, leading Holmes to commend it.[41] He queried Steer's judgement in also exhibiting less finished oil sketches, such as *The Lime-Kiln* of 1908 (fig. 77). This impressionistic, intuitive oil sketch was of the chalk ridge of Nine Barrow Down, close to Rollington, probably looking down towards the lime kiln above Rempstone Hall and over to Poole Harbour. The panoramic view is similar to Tonks' *The Lost Path*, 1905 (fig. 73), with Wareham Channel and Arne on the left and the inlets and islands of the harbour and shore on the right. Painted on the spot, the strong colours, bright palette and bold, thick brush strokes demonstrate Steer's interest in the play of light and lucid, free handling of paint, and again suggests the influence of Cézanne, whose work Steer had seen the previous year in Paris. Detail is eliminated in the loose handling of uninhibited and vigorous landscapes like this, to reveal Steer's instinctive qualities as a painter for whom 'nature was bathed in atmosphere' and who captured natural light and shadows by concentrating on colour rather than tone.[42] Hinting at its picturesqueness, timelessness and decay, Steer fused the industrial elements of lime kiln, path and scarring from chalk quarrying in the setting, to create a decaying scene.

39. MacColl, pp.181–2.
40. See MacColl, pp.181, 212, and Jillian Carman, *Uplifting the Colonial Philistine: Florence Philips and the Making of the Johannesburg Art Gallery*, Johannesburg: Wits University Press, 2006. *The Limekiln (Corfe)*, 1908, JAG Accession no. 371, donated by Mrs Lionel Phillips in 1909, having purchased it from the Goupil Gallery in 1909, for the proposed Johannesburg Art Gallery (JAG). Catalogued as no. 27 in the first JAG catalogue, 1910/11. *The Limekiln (Corfe)* was one of three oil paintings Mrs Lionel Phillips purchased for £350 from Goupil towards establishing a new modern art gallery in Johannesburg. The other two Steer paintings purchased from the same exhibition, donated by Phillips and not Sir Hugh Lane to JAG in 1909, were *Corfe Castle, Dorsetshire*, 1908 (£600), JAG Accession no. 372, and *A Balcony [Chelsea Window]* (£450), 1909, JAG Accession no. 373. These three Steer paintings were the first works ever acquired by JAG. As Mrs (later Lady) Phillips and Sir Hugh Lane worked closely together on the foundation of JAG between 1907 and 1910, there remains confusion over who donated works.
41. Ibid.
42. Exhibition catalogue, *Watercolours of P. Wilson Steer from the Blackwell Family Collection*, Williamson Art Gallery, 7 October–4 November 1944, nos 7, 28 and 35.

Steer's summer at Rollington Farm provided him with ample material to show in London the following year, when he exhibited several watercolours of lime kilns at the Goupil Gallery and New English.[43] Katherine Everett indicated that Steer, Coles and Brown were also back at Rollington in 1909.[44] Steer was a highly critically formative influence on fellow artists, and amongst those who acknowledged their debt to him was Australian Arthur Streeton, a longstanding friend of Charles Conder. Streeton came to England in 1897 and wrote to fellow painter Tom Roberts back in Australia:

> Steer is their great landscape painter. Steer, who is always amiable when I see him, does not like my work: well I'm competing with him – I've been down [to Chepstow] this summer painting his favourite subject and painting it in my own way, and I begin to feel I'm alright ... They'll have to accept me yet.[45]

VISITORS TO ARFLEET

In the summer of 1909 Streeton intentionally followed in Steer's footsteps with a cycling tour through Dorset with Tom Roberts, 'to look for subjects for the summer'.[46] Through Conder and Orpen, Everett first knew Streeton in London at the beginning of the century. Everett and Roberts were both natives of Dorchester, and although Roberts emigrated to Australia with his family seven years before Everett's birth, they shared people and places in common. It is therefore not surprising to find Roberts visiting the Everetts at Arfleet Mill with Streeton. The trip resulted in some of Streeton's most important oils, watercolours and lithographs of Corfe and Purbeck, with *Corfe Castle* exhibited at the New English that winter (cat. no. 81). While his watercolours bear the influence of Steer, one of his most distinctive paintings, *Everetts Old Mill, Corfe* [sic] (fig. 80), was of Arfleet mill yard, exhibited at the New English in 1910.[47]

The Everetts received a stream of visitors at their picturesque, rambling Tudor mill (figs 80 and 111) increasingly at risk of collapsing into the encroaching clay pits.[48] A keen gardener, Katherine claimed to have been so shocked at the conditions of Corfe villagers that she distributed seeds and lobbied in the press and at the House of Commons with a deputation of smallholders.[49] Ambrose McEvoy, Albert Rothenstein, Ronald Gray and Charles Stabb frequently spent evenings chatting and playing music with the Everetts, joined by others staying around Corfe, such as the water-colourist Alfred Rich.[50] The painters enjoyed excursions and walks, as in *The Lost Path* (fig. 73), and visiting neighbouring painters such as the Chestons, with whom the Everetts, Brown, Steer and Coles spent one Sunday (a day of rest for artists) in August 1908.[51]

Henry Tonks was staying at Corfe over the central summer of 1908, with Ronald Gray (his frequent companion on painting trips), while other Slade painters and tutors were in the immediate area.[52] Tonks had been in Italy the previous summer with John Singer Sargent and his sister, who expressed disappointment he was not joining them again.[53] That July Tonks began a painting of Katherine and her toddler son, Tony (fig. 65), in Arfleet's garden: *Summer*, 1908 (fig. 79).[54]

The completed work has the enclosed effect of a medieval tapestry with only

43. A chronological list of paintings is included in Bruce Laughton, *Philip Wilson Steer, 1860–1942*, Oxford: Clarendon Press, 1971. *Poole Harbour*, Goupil Gallery, 1909; *Storm Clouds, Poole Harbour*, Goupil Gallery, 1909 (now Leeds City Art Gallery); *Isle of Purbeck*, Goupil Gallery, 1909 (fig. 75); *Effect of Rain*, Goupil Gallery, 1909 (private collection); *The Limekiln* (related to Johannesburg painting, now National Gallery of Ottawa); *The Limekiln* (fig. 77); *Moon Rising over the Downs*, Goupil Gallery, 1909 (fig. 74); *Corfe Castle and the Isle of Purbeck* (Walker Art Gallery, Liverpool); *The Limekiln (Corfe)*, Goupil Gallery, 1909 (Johannesburg); *Corfe Castle and the Isle of Purbeck*, Goupil Gallery, 1909 (Johannesburg). Aside from the Goupil Gallery paintings exhibited in 1909, Steer exhibited Dorset work at the New English. In summer 1909, three watercolours, *The Lime-kiln* (318), *The Blue Pond* (319) and *Poole Harbour* (322). An oil of Corfe Castle (91) was exhibited in summer 1910, a further *Lime-Kiln* (24) in the winter exhibition and *Lime Kiln* (187) in the summer 1917.

44. Katherine Everett, p.126.

45. Letter from Arthur Streeton to Tom Roberts, 27 December 1902, quoted in Christopher Wray, *Arthur Streeton: Painter of Light*, Milton, Queensland: Jacaranda Wiley, 1993, p.99.

46. Letter from Arthur Streeton to Walter Withers, 25 May 1909, quoted in Ann Galbally and Anne Gray, eds, *Letters from Smike: The Letters of Arthur Streeton 1890–1943*, Melbourne: OUP, 1989, p.116. See too Geoffrey Smith, *Arthur Streeton 1867–1943*, exhibition catalogue, 1995–6, Melbourne: National Gallery of Victoria, 1995, p.150. Dorchester-born Tom Roberts returned to England in 1903 to complete his large commission, *The Opening of the First Parliament of the Commonwealth of Australia by H.R.H. The Duke of Cornwall and York (Later King George V), May 9, 1901* (Royal Collection, on loan to Government House, Canberra). Roberts remained in England until 1923, living in Hampstead Garden Suburb, before returning to Australia.

47. *Everett's Old Mill, Corfe*, Summer Exhibition, New English, London, June 1910, no. 284, private collection.

48. Landowner Douglas Ryder confirms Arfleet Mill was demolished by 1917.

49. Katherine Everett, p.122.

50. Rich painted a number of watercolours of the area, several of which were owned by Everett.

51. Letter from Miss M. Youngs, 26 October 1949, to R.H. Dolley Assistant Keeper of Oil Paintings, archive number NMM, 2405/4/49. Everett's companion Miss Youngs mentions a visit to Arfleet from William Orpen.

52. Ronald Gray was a fellow student from Westminster Art School days. He exhibited *Chalk Cliff, Studland* at the summer exhibition of the New English in 1906 (95).

53. Tonks joined them in Italy for the following two years and returned to Dorset in 1911, leading to more exhibited Dorset paintings of Wareham & Corfe at the New English (winter) 1913: *Near Wareham* (253), *Near Poole Harbour* (257), *Miss Katherine Ridley* (271) and perhaps *The Invalid*, summer 1914 (77). He was in Dorchester at the start of the First World War.

54. The Everetts lived at Arfleet Mill between 1907 and 1910. Everett rented a studio in an old chapel in West Street, Corfe Castle. W.W. Collins also moved to Corfe Castle to the Old Curetage at about the same time. The Everett's second son Tony was born at their Swanage house, Steinberg, in 1906.

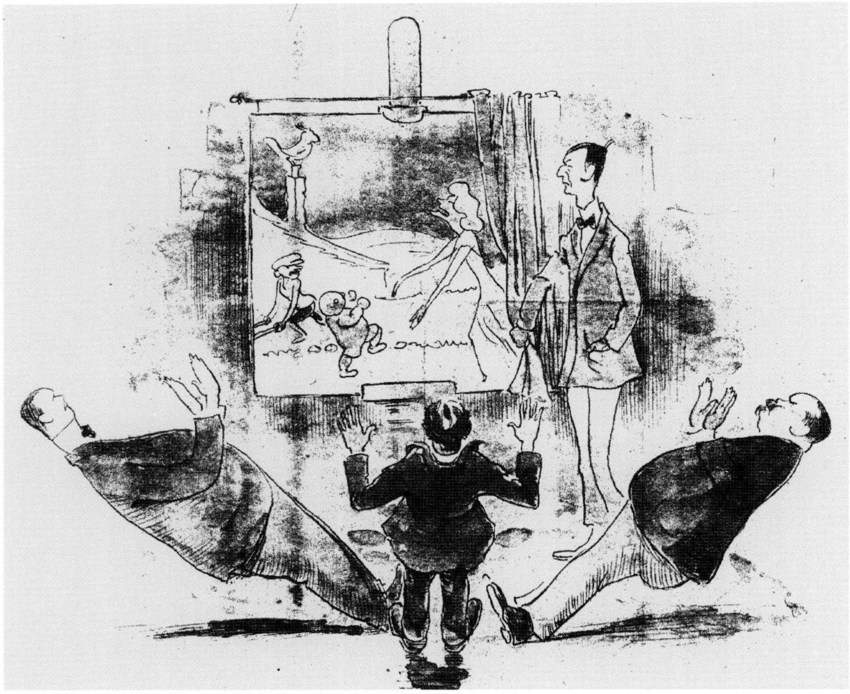

FIG. 78
Ronald Gray / *The Final Revelation*
1906
private collection

a small amount of sky and Creech Barrow visible in the distance. Katherine is shown tending a climbing rose, past its summer best, as her toddler son, Tony, totters with arms outstretched towards his rocking horse and a pet cockatoo.[55] A garden bench rests below the window on the range of buildings of the mill house. Katherine's autobiography gives a lively account of posing for the painting, having already modelled for a watercolour for Tonks at Studland and possibly for *The Lost Path* (fig. 73).[56]

Tonks worked on *Summer* until he returned to the Slade in October 1908, while also working in the mill on another painting, *Rustic Pageantry*, 1908 (Bradford Museums and Galleries), featuring a local girl having her hair braided. Begun in the Arfleet garden in July, over the ensuing months *Summer* had to be altered continually to reflect the changing plants from summer to autumn, presenting a fundamental problem for a painting nominally dedicated to a season. Comfortable producing intimate interiors and sensitive watercolours of landscapes, the difficulties of *plein air* painting with its constantly changing light and weather challenged Tonks. Charles Cheston recalled Tonks agonizing at the speed the plants grew and altered with the seasons, over which he had no control. He recalled 'a certain humour in the idea of our Professor direct from London, intent on seizing this fleeting florescence with Pre-Raphaelite fidelity, plus "natural effect"'.[57] The resulting painting was overworked, leading to Everett's observation that Tonks had never learned to paint, and his labouring on it for months led to technical problems.[58] Tonks' method of removing excess oil from canvas with paper (often newspaper) to revive overworked oil paintings – known as 'tonking' – was probably applied here. Tonks preferred not

55. Although a profile drawing in watercolour and charcoal, a similar child's rocking horse appears in Tonks' sketchbook; formerly owned by C.H. Collins Baker, Tonks' legatee, it has not been located at Tate.
56. Katherine Everett, pp.128–9.
57. Cheston, p.26.
58. Everett, *Memoirs*, p.87. A note in the Tate conservation file for *Summer* (N04565) indicates progressive cracking overall since 1931.

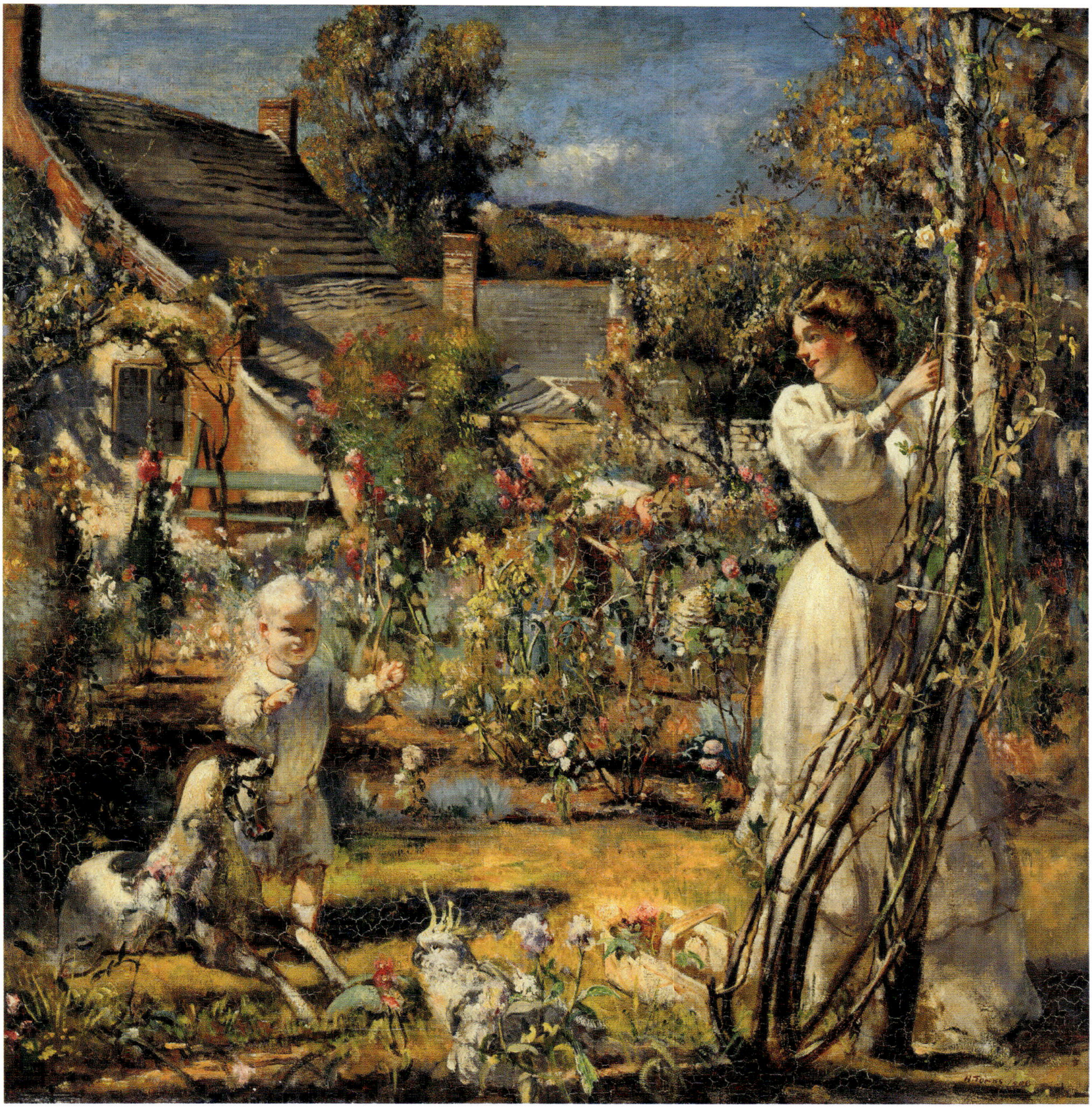

FIG. 79
Henry Tonks / ***Summer***
1908 / oil on canvas / 94 x 94 cm

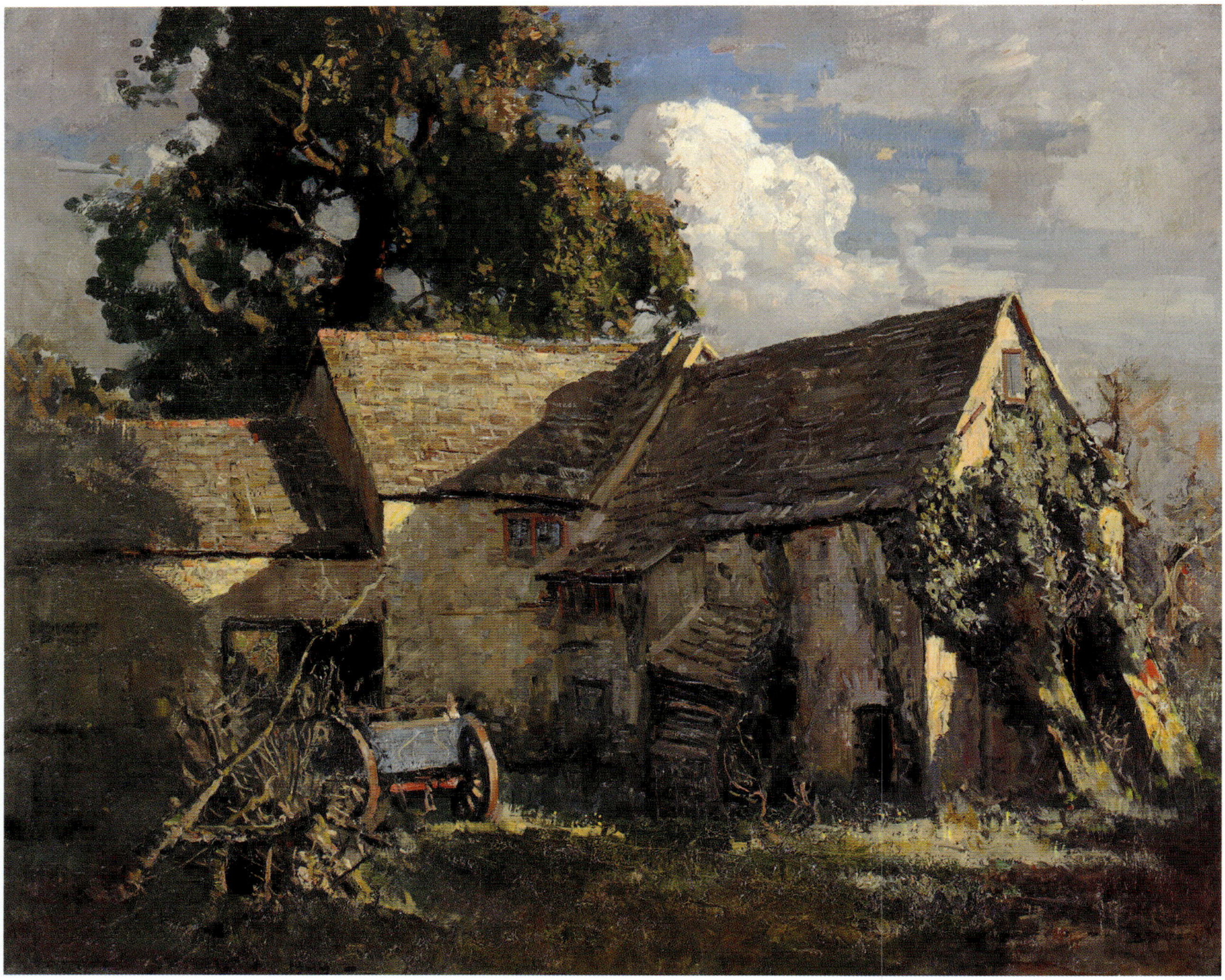

FIG. 80
Arthur Streeton / ***Everetts Old Mill, Corfe***
1909 / oil on canvas / 101.5 x 126.5 cm
private collection

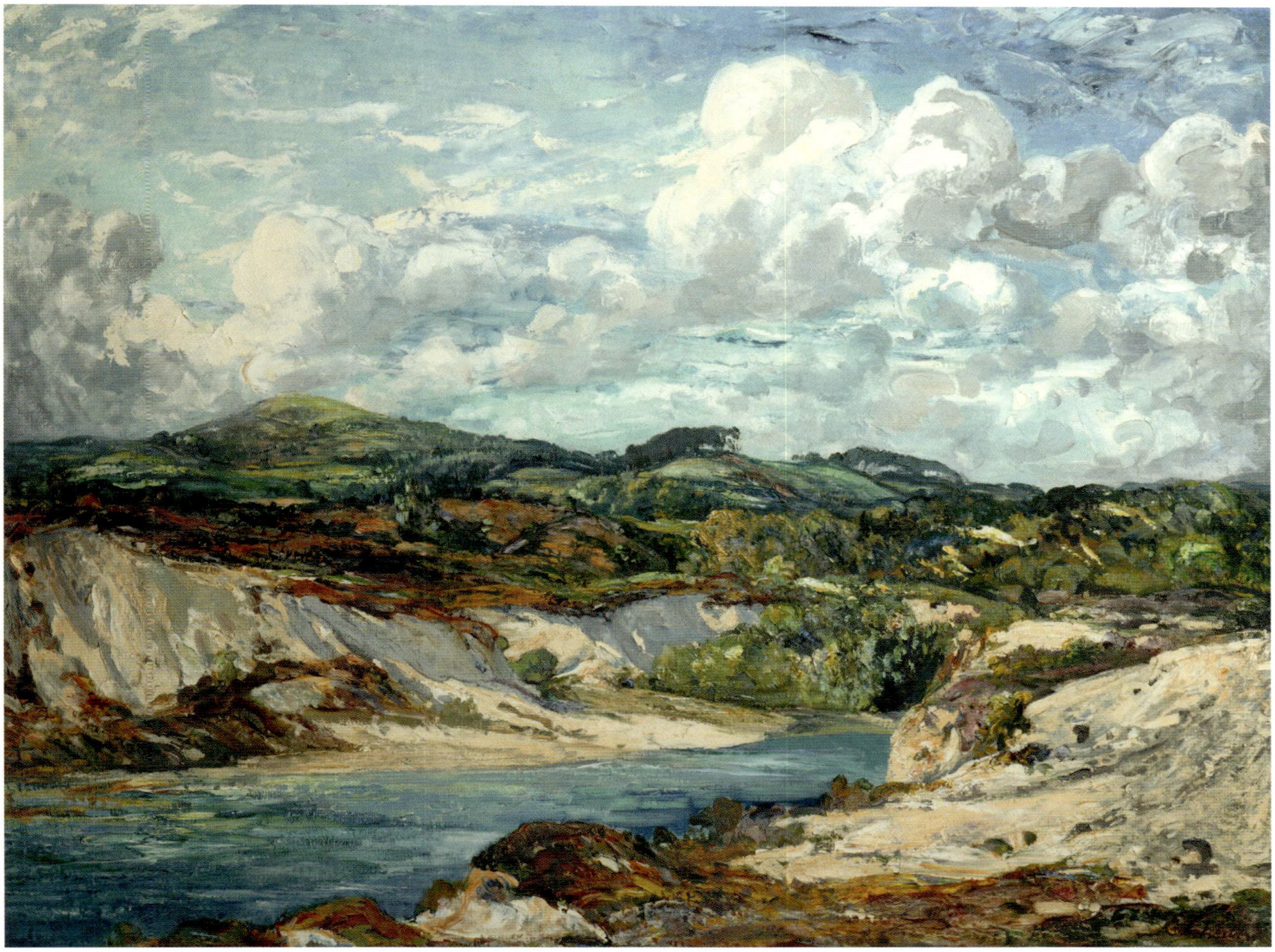

FIG. 81

Evelyn Cheston / ***Creech Barrow, Dorset***

1910 / oil on canvas / 84.4 x 110.5 cm

to show his paintings before they were completed, leading to Gray's gently lampooning cartoon of the unveiling of *Summer* (fig. 78) to an astonished audience of fellow Slade tutors, Steer, Russell and Brown.

OTHER SLADE VISITORS

Over this period former Slade students Evelyn and Charles Cheston were living at Studland. Evelyn met Cheston at a painting class organized by tutor Walter Russell in Richmond, Yorkshire in about 1902. Following their marriage they rented Hill Close, at Studland, a studio house built of Purbeck stone, designed by Charles Voysey and owned by playwright Alfred Sutro, also an acquaintance of Thomas Hardy. It overlooked the heath with panoramic views of Poole Harbour and across to the Isle of Wight.[59] There Cheston worked on a series of large landscapes including *September on the Sands*, 1906, and *Studland Bay*, 1909, described by Sickert as 'dreadnoughts'.[60] Evelyn's large painting, *Creech Barrow*, exhibited in 1910 (fig. 81), looks over the flooded, disused clay pit of Blue Pool towards the prehistoric barrow, a key landmark in the Purbeck hills, shown on the skyline on the left.[61] This painterly region between the Purbeck Hills and Wareham with its clay works and disused pits was off the beaten track and not easily approached. It became a popular haunt for artists including Augustus John (fig. 96), Derwent Lees (fig. 100), Steer, Collins and Harold Squire, attracted by the vivid blue and turquoise water caused by minerals in the ancient clay works.[62] Cheston's *Creech Barrow* was painted in July 1910 following a move to quarters at the hamlet of Furzebrook, close to Blue Pool.[63] The weather that summer was very unsettled, which Cheston demonstrates in her energetic, atmospheric work with disturbed sky, clouds and their shadows cast over the landscape. Cheston hints at the layered history embedded in this landscape, from ancient barrow burials to its more recent industrial past.

A combination of ill health and inclement weather saw Evelyn destroy her first attempt at this scene. She worked all summer on this second version, which she later enlarged by sewing on an extra strip of canvas. Though she painted landscapes *en plein air*, Evelyn completed them in her studio, where she found colour became even more precise. Mixing colours directly on the canvas, she scrubbed in sky or areas of tone with a stiff brush, which she then painted over.[64] Her primary focus was a painting viewed in its entirety rather than in detailed parts. Her husband claimed that, like Steer, Evelyn 'possessed a quick eye to detect good shape and design'.[65] Producing large canvases in all weathers was daunting for Evelyn, who was not only slight but in poor health, so Charles adapted a cycle trailer for her canvases and easels.[66] Though he also painted in Dorset, in a rare reversal of gender roles at this time, he acknowledged Evelyn's greater talent and devoted himself to her welfare.[67] Cheston's *Creech Barrow* was followed by *Blue Pool*, both praised at the New English exhibition of 1910 and admired by Lees.[68]

WALTER WESTLEY RUSSELL

Russell was the fourth Slade tutor to visit Purbeck during the Slade summer break. Following the example of Tonks, Brown and Steer, in 1909 he stayed with the Chestons, at Hill Close. He was almost certainly with them the

59. John Newman and Nikolaus Pevsner, *The Buildings of England, Dorset*, London: Penguin Books, 1972, p.405. Hill Close was designed by Charles Francis Annesley Voysey in 1896.

60. No. 80. *September on the Sands* at the New English's winter exhibition, 1906, and *Studland Bay* in 1909 winter. See Cheston, p.27.

61. The Celtic word *creech* means a mound or barrow. Blue Pool was a redundant clay pit filled with rainwater and part of the Furzebrook estate of 200 acres at the beginning of the century. The house, garden, heath, woods, cottages and farm were owned by the Pike family, who mined there for the ball clay, first supplied to Josiah Wedgwood in 1760. Some of the Furzebrook clay workings were filled-in, but Blue Pool and several others remained. Set in a deep clay bowl, surrounded by heath, woodland and gorse interlaced with sandy paths, it was dug in 1845. The pool's deep turquoise water was the main attraction, caused by the diffraction of light from minute clay particles suspended in the water, with the colours changing according to light and temperature conditions. At times the water even appeared emerald green.

62. McColl, p.168, Steer's watercolour of Blue Pool was owned by John Fothergill. In 1911 artist Harold Squire was living at Corfe Castle.

63. By 1911 they were back in London but returned to the area around Corfe and the Purbeck quarries for the summer, some of their resulting paintings appearing in the winter New English of that year.

64. Cheston, p.25. Cheston listed the colours Evelyn used, which included light red, rose madder, mars violet or purple madder, trans. golden ochre, yellow ochre, aureolin, trans. oxide of chromium, whites, mars orange, burnt golden ochre, ceruleum, burnt umber, cyanine or permanent blue and cobalt. Everett's list of oils for 1897 included flake white, rose madder, veronese green, lemon yellow, cobalt, light red, flake white, carmine, cinnabar, vermilion, aureolin and yellow ochre.

65. Ibid., p.41.

66. Ibid., p.28.

67. Both Katherine Everett and Augustus John lamented the toll domestic life took on female painters.

68. In 1908 Evelyn was elected a member of the New English. Her other Dorset paintings: *September on the Sands*, 1906, New English; *The Sands at Swanage*, New English, winter 1907; *Swanage Sands*, watercolour, 1909; *Under the Cliff*, New English, summer 1909; *Early Summer*, 1910; *Purbeck*, 1911, New English, winter; the Chestons continued to visit Dorset, see *Dorset Landscape with Quarry*, 1918, ink and pencil on paper, British Council. London-born Charles Cheston went on to exhibit widely, including shows at the Royal Academy, Goupil Gallery, Fine Art Society and New English. His first solo exhibition took place at Colnaghi's in 1929, the year Evelyn died. *The Studio*, 1908, vol. 42, p.223 refers to Cheston's *Swanage* at the New English.

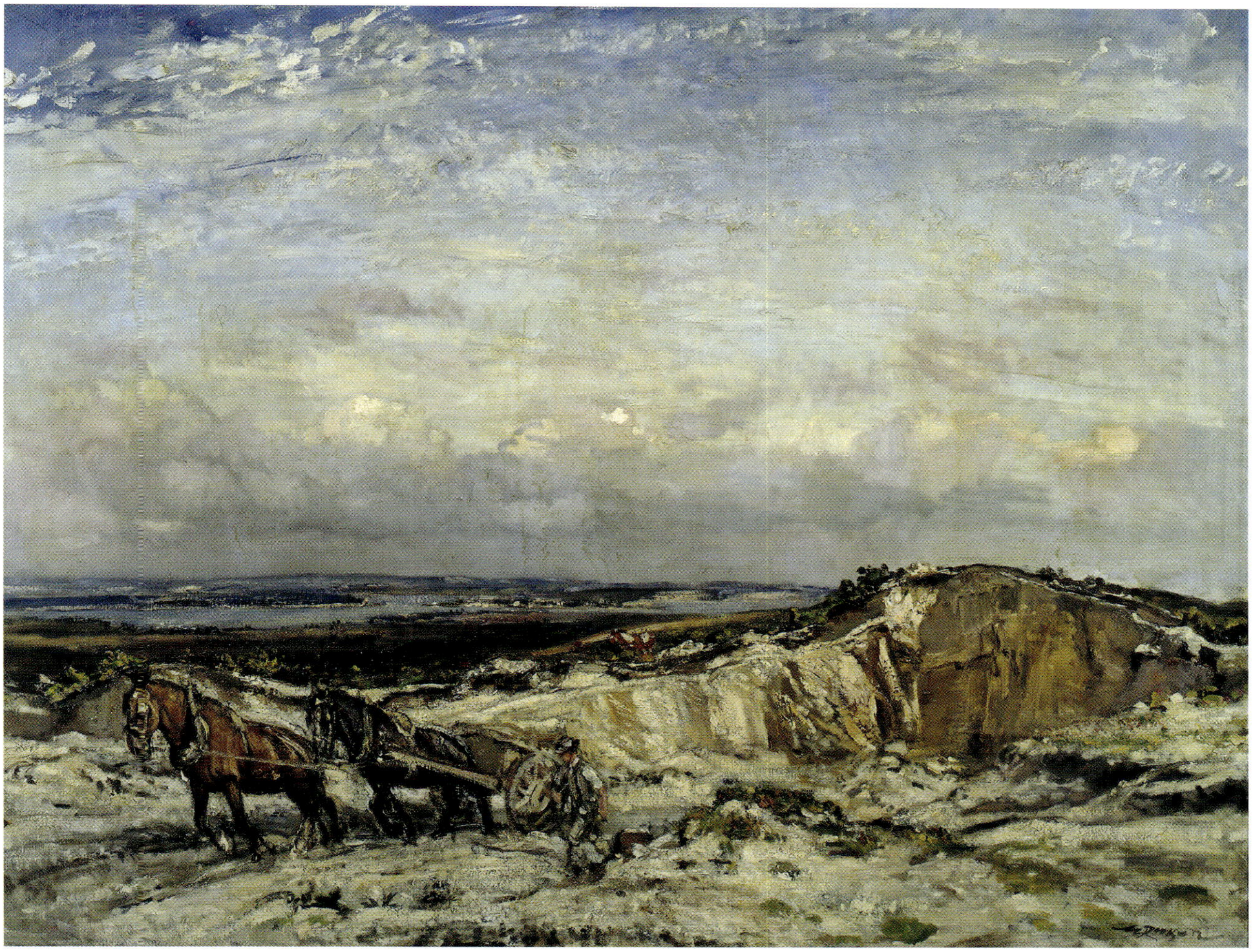

FIG. 82

Walter Westley Russell / ***Carting Sand***

1910 / oil on canvas / 86.4 x 111.8 cm

year before when Steer, Tonks and Brown were in Purbeck, since Russell exhibited *Studland Church*, 1909 (private collection) in the summer exhibition of the New English in 1909. His *Carting Sand*, 1910 (fig. 82) is essentially an industrial scene of the Purbeck peninsula, at Godlingston Heath below Kingswood. Two horses strain to pull a full cart of sand from the only sand pit in the area high enough to be dug out so deeply. The prominent rise in the land on the right had been cut in two from nineteenth-century mineral workings, creating a narrow defile through the hill known as 'Hill Cut in Two'. Like Tonks and Steer, Russell glories in the setting of Poole Harbour, with Goathorn on the far left, Brownsea Island in the middle distance and the mouth of the harbour towards Bournemouth on the right. The viewpoint is lower down than *The Lost Path*, and closer to Studland, where Russell was staying. The sky, flecked with layered clouds, takes up more than half the surface of the painting.

In April 1910, Russell followed Steer by holding his first one-man at the Goupil Gallery, which included his Dorset paintings. Interruptions in the landscape, such as the effects of quarrying, were explored by a number of artists at the New English during the decade. However, rather than being presented as industrial subjects or through the Hardy lens, they were treated as appealing painterly features enhancing the scene. This was true of Russell, Tonks, Steer and also Augustus John through his portrayal of the Blue Pool (fig. 96). In addition to *Carting Sand*, Russell exhibited two further oils, *The Rainbow* of 1910 and *The Sand Pit*, and three water-colours. That June Russell was the subject of an article in the *Studio* written by the Tonks admirer, Charles H. Collins Baker, who allied Russell closely to Tonks, Steer and their Slade/New English project. He claimed Russell followed Steer in emulating landscapes featuring limitless expanses of the blue distances of Chepstow and Poole, contributing 'an interpretation of wonderful and novel beauty'. Baker admired the lyric sentiment and grandeur of Russell's Dorset work, and as with critics of *The Lost Path*, made no comment about the central subject of *Carting Sand*, in this case an industrial process against a backdrop of stunning countryside. Instead he focused wholly on his depictions of landscape and nature. The following year Evelyn Cheston exhibited *Purbeck*, a large canvas of quarried landscape at the New English winter exhibition of 1911, echoing Cheston's observation that Russell painted 'so much so well that we saw our remaining subjects swept speedily into his net'.[69] This included several beach scenes at Studland and Sandbanks.[70]

During their time at Arfleet, Everett continued to disappear from home for months on end, leaving his wife to manage the household. In March 1909 he was staying with Henry Tonks in London, and met up with Augustus John and William Orpen. By May he was back in Dorset kitting out the *Walrus* at Goathorn, and in June joined Charles Stabb and Gerard Chowne at Hurstbourne Park to play cricket against the Artists' Cricket Club. Everett's self-portrait painted at Poole probably dates to this period (fig. 84). He joined the *Emma* barge, sailing from Goathorn to London with clay, and from London Everett went on to Dordrecht before heading for Cowes, leaving from the sand dunes by the Haven Hotel at Sandbanks, Poole, with his son Henry.[71] Everett also spent time sailing round Southampton, the Hamble and Lymington following the excitement in July 1909 when Blériot made his first flight across the English Channel, which Everett sketched.[72]

69. Cheston, p.26.
70. Russell's undated Dorset paintings include *Sandbanks* (Tullie House); *Studland Beach* (RA); *On the Sands* (Oldham); *The Bathing Huts*; *The Estuary Poole Harbour, Sotheby's*, London, 25 June 1980, Lot 19; *The Beach Huts*, also known as *Summer Pleasures*, Sotheby's, London, Victorian & Edwardian Art: Thursday, 12 July 2007, Lot 100; *A Panoramic View*, Christie's Interior Sale, 2570, 19–20 June 2012, New York, Lot 206; *Poole Harbour from Hamworthy Looking towards Wareham*, Phillips, London, 28 January 1986, Lot 56.
71. Everett, *Memoirs*, p.119.
72. Everett sketchbook, July 1909, PAJ1399, NMM.

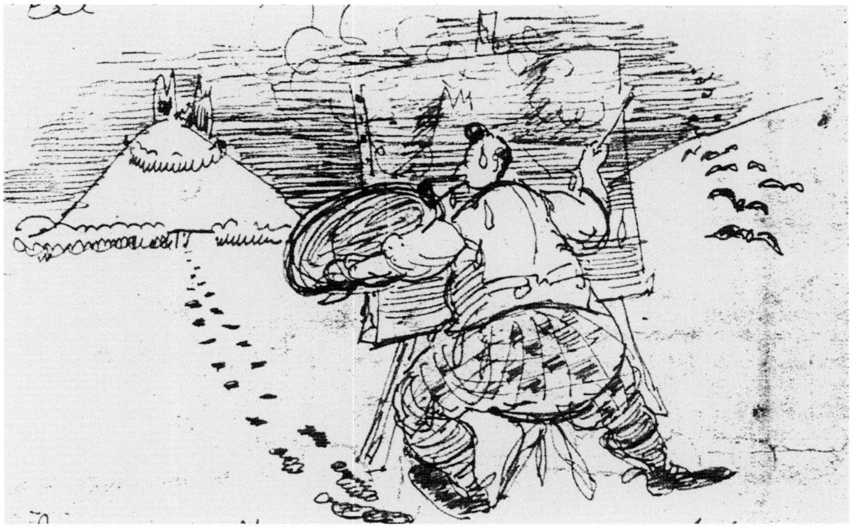

FIG. 83

Henry Tonks / ***John Everett painting at Arfleet***

1909

Tonks highlights the efforts involved in 'plein air' painting, in this case in the snow

private collection

EVERETT AT WORBARROW BAY

After laying up the *Walrus* for the winter, Everett rented Cliff Cabin at Worbarrow Bay, staying there for three months between December 1909 and March 1910. The 16-ft hut, owned by a Miss Middleton, was comfortably furnished with 'every sort of cooking thing and a library of French novels'.[73] It sat on the cliffs with magnificent views of Worbarrow Bay, a place Everett had long admired for its dramatic, painterly qualities.[74] Free from distractions, away from his family and 7 miles from the nearest shop at Corfe, he worked ceaselessly on seascape sketches and preparatory studies leading to his finished oil painting, *Gad Cliff, Worbarrow Bay*, 1910 (fig. 85), looking east towards Kimmeridge. This powerful evocation of cliff, sea and sky was taken from the little platform of flat stones that Everett constructed under Worbarrow Tout, a promontory at one end of the bay. From this low perspective he maximized the powerful effect of the stratified rocks, enforcing the dramatic scene with dark shadows against sunlit areas, swirling waves and a dark, vertical band of rain in the distance. Everett conveys the movement of the sea he understood well as a sailor, while the dramatic cloud formation captures the grandeur of the weather effects he studied closely.[75]

Closeted in his cabin on the cliff, Everett's sketch *The Great January Comet, Worbarrow Bay*, 1910 (fig. 86) records this unexpected phenomenon. He made a number of drawings, initially unsure as to whether this was an early sighting of Halley's comet, anticipated in May 1910, or the new, unpredicted comet Daylight, or Great January comet, first seen in Johannesburg. He shows the comet's tail lighting up the sky at night, to create a dramatic eyewitness account of its awe-inspiring nature. Everett frequently used his telescope – featured in his Orpen portrait in 1900 (fig. 49) – to study and paint objects in the far distance.

73. Everett, *Memoirs*, p.118.
74. Everett, *Memoirs*, p.92.
75. Everett sketchbook, PAJ1404, NMM.

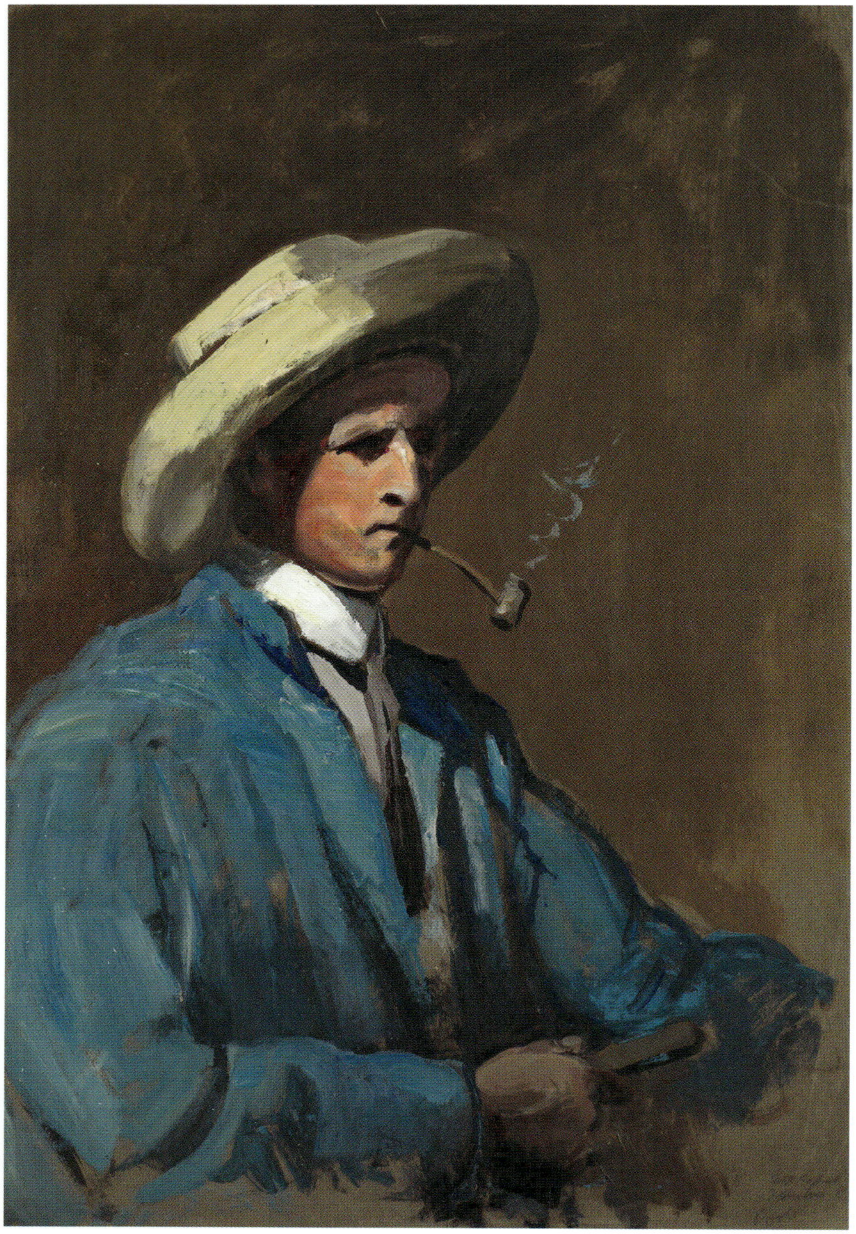

FIG. 84

John Everett / ***Self-Portrait, Poole***

1910 / oil on paper / 50.6 x 35.6 cm

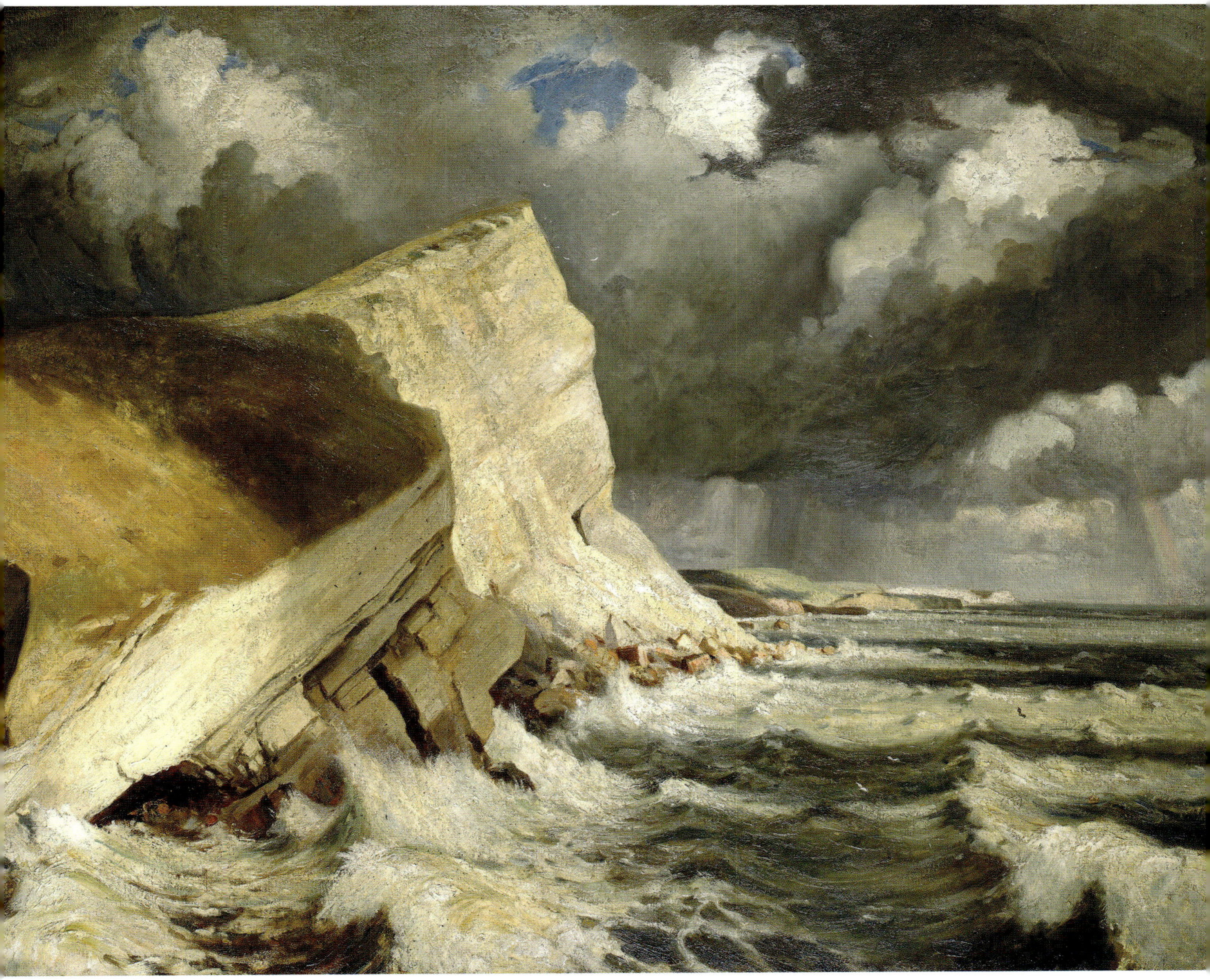

FIG. 85
John Everett / ***Gad Cliff, Worbarrow Bay***
1910 / oil on canvas / 97 x 130 cm

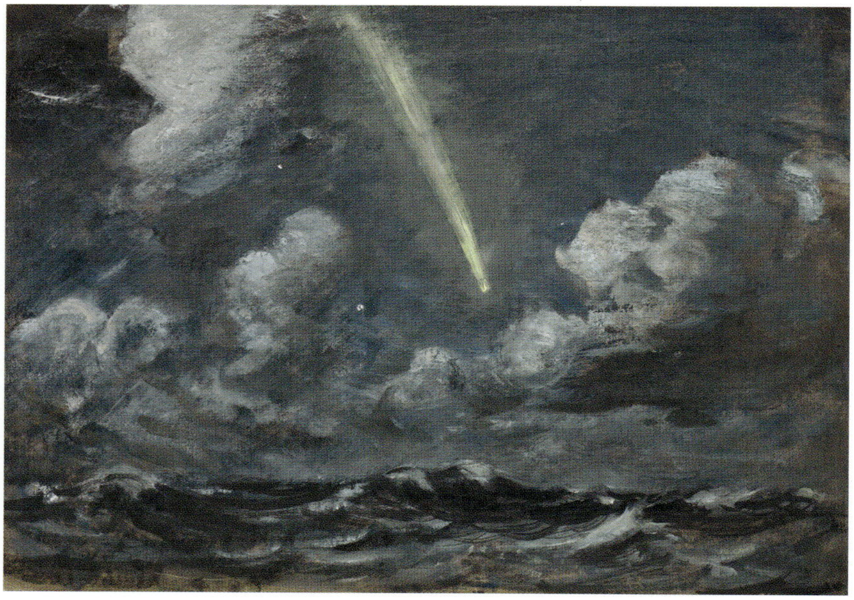

FIG. 86
John Everett / ***The Great January Comet, Worbarrow Bay***
1910 / oil sketch on paper / 35.9 x 50.8 cm

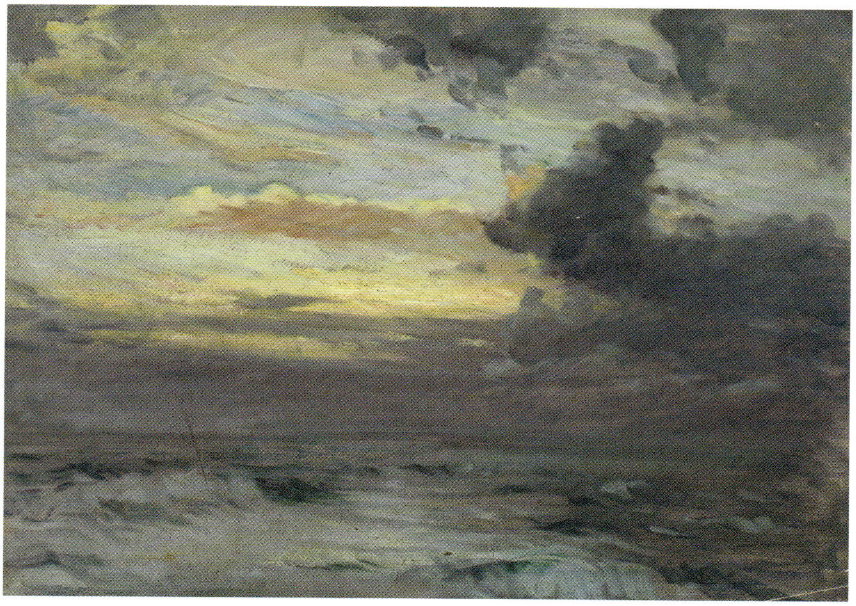

FIG. 87
John Everett / ***Worbarrow Bay***
1909–10 / oil sketch on paper / 34.1 x 49.3 cm

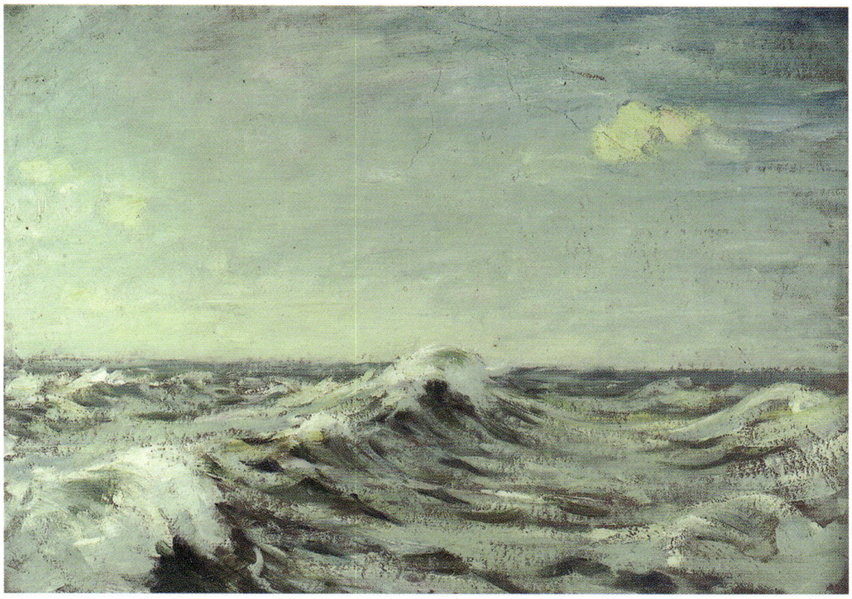

FIG. 88
John Everett / ***Worbarrow Bay***
1909–10 / oil sketch on paper / 35.2 x 50.9 cm

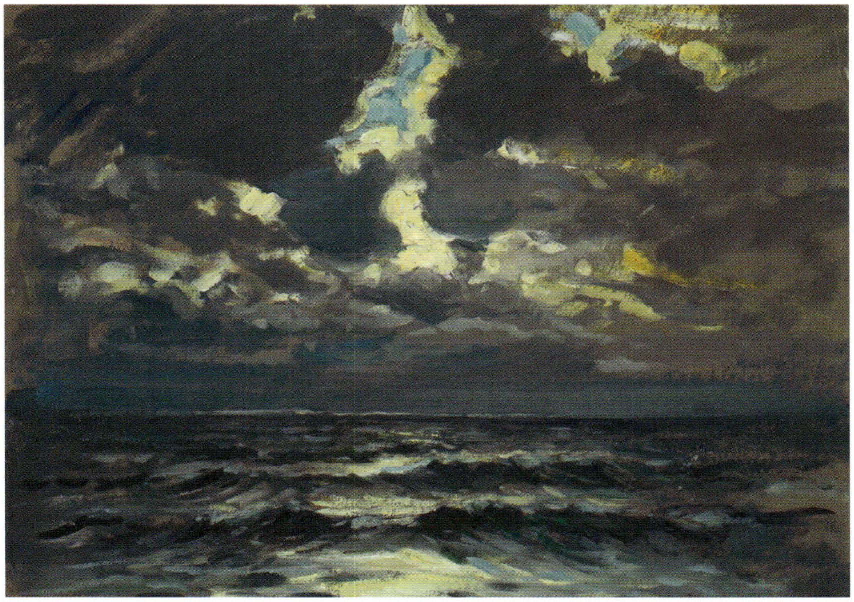

FIG. 89
John Everett / ***Worbarrow Bay, Christmas Day***
1909 / oil sketch on paper / 35.5 x 50.7 cm

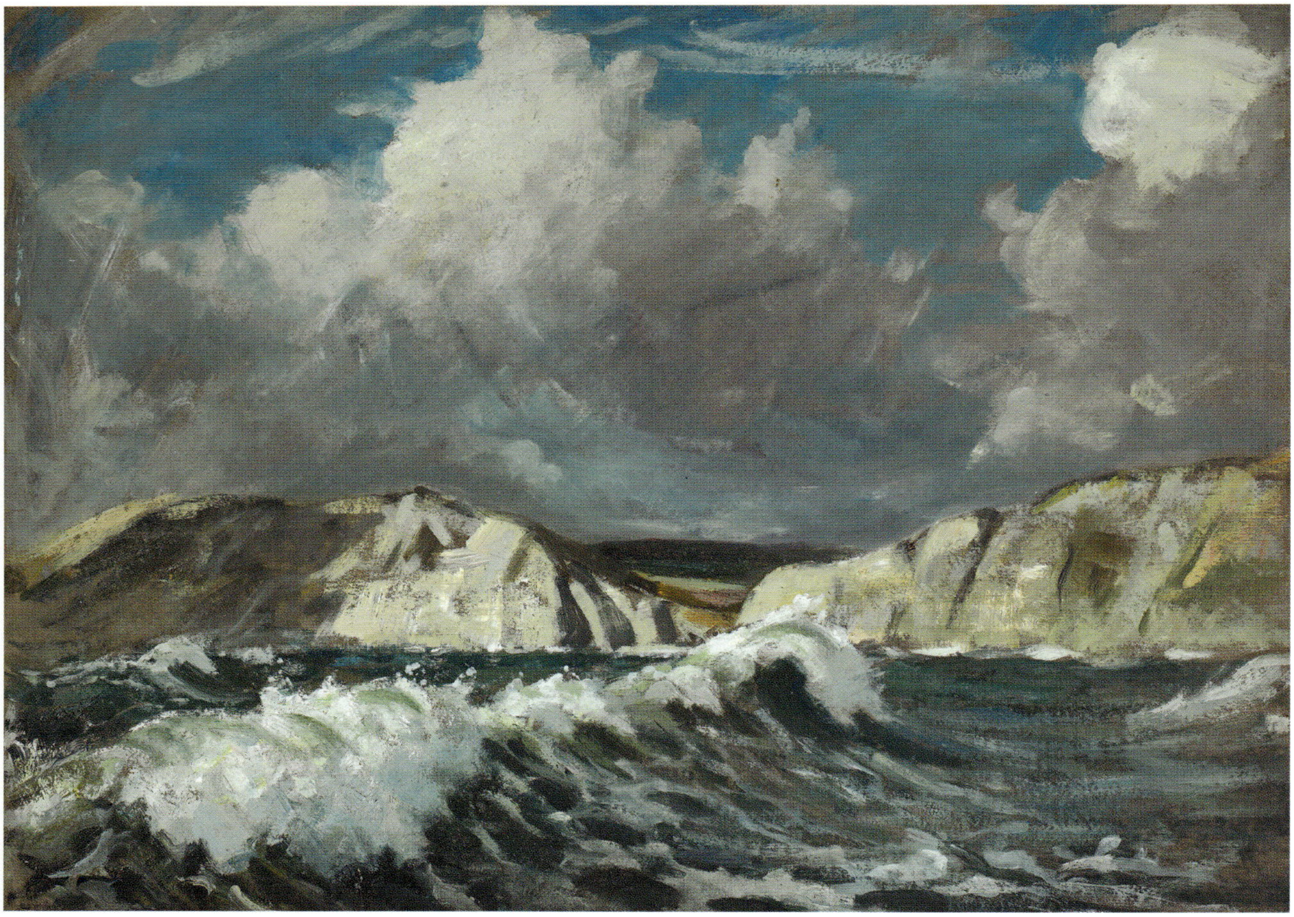

FIG. 90

John Everett / ***Worbarrow Bay***

1909-10 / oil sketch on paper / 35.5 x 50.7 cm

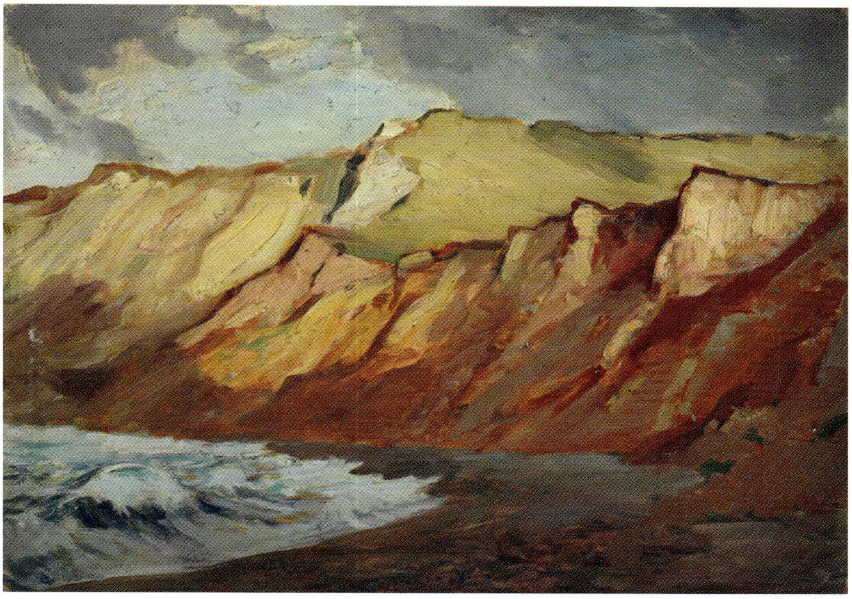

FIG. 91
John Everett / ***Worbarrow Bay***
1909–10 / oil sketch on paper / 35.3 x 50.5 cm

Influenced by Turner's seascapes, his St Ives experiences showed how to paint moving waves and the effects of light over water. He also studied cloud formations over the sea, as here, where the sky takes up two-thirds of the composition. Working rapidly, Everett skilfully captured the shifting effects of light on the surface of moving water, sometimes through a sequence of oil sketches showing the movement of a wave or cloud (figs 87 and 88). Taken low down on the horizon from the beach at Tyneham (fig. 90), Lulworth Cove is on the far left, with Mupe Rocks, Arish Mell Gap and Worbarrow Tout on the far right. Everett has concentrated on waves breaking close to shore and light falling on the cliffs beyond. Baldry considered this stretch of coastline relatively inaccessible, with 'nothing to be seen but a wall of rock which forms the base of a long range of hills running parallel to the sea'.[76]

Everett's atmospheric sea sketches often focused on light shining through the clouds and reflected on the sea. Devoid of boats or narrative content, one particular sketch (fig. 89) is solely concerned with the effect of light, while the sketch from the shore at Worbarrow Bay (fig. 91) focuses on the ancient earthwork of Flower's Barrow on the right, with Worbarrow Tout behind, and unusually focuses on light falling on the steep cliffs. Importantly, it was at Worbarrow that Everett evolved the habit of painting numerous small oil sketches recording varying sea states and cloud conditions, which was a hallmark of his later maritime work.

HARRY VAN DER WEYDEN

Other Slade painters inspired by the Purbeck coast, and known to Everett, included John Hodgson Lobley and American-born Harry van der Weyden,

76. Baldry, p.309.

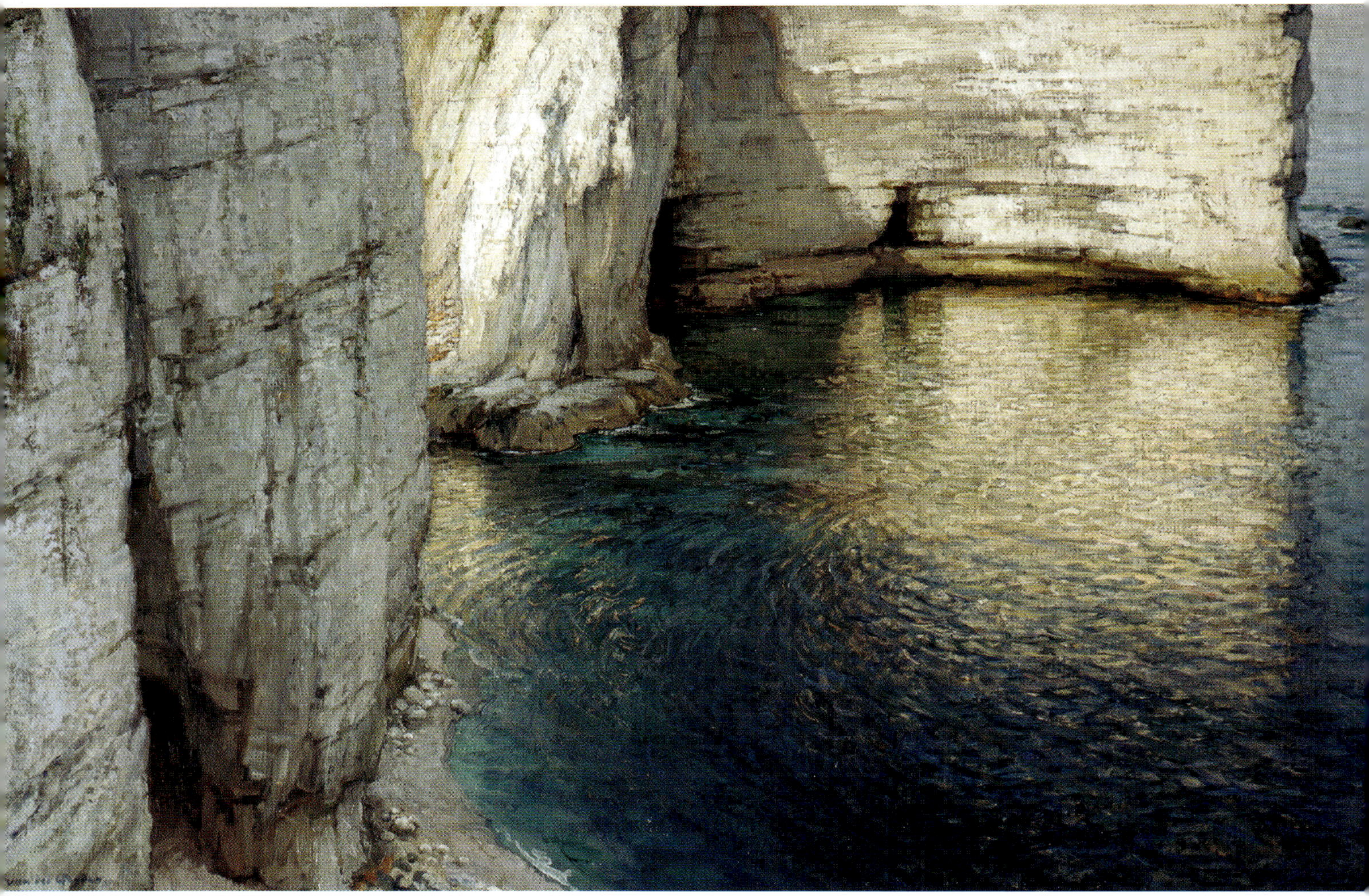

FIG. 92

Harry van der Weyden / ***Cliff End, Studland***

1909–10 / oil on paper on board / 35.5 x 57.1 cm

photograph reproduced with kind permission of the RUSSELL-COTES ART GALLERY & MUSEUM, BOURNEMOUTH

who was in Dorset towards the end of the first decade of the twentieth century.[77] A prolific painter, admired for his innovative coastal and night scenes, van der Weyden was born in Boston, Massachusetts of American parents of English descent on his mother's side. He considered himself British as his family came to England in 1871, and though London remained his base, much of his work was done in France. He studied at the Slade with Brown, and at the Académie Julian in 1890–91 and 1895.[78] Like Everett, van der Weyden was often regarded as a marine painter who knew the coast of Dorset well, as in later years he sailed there with Major General Harold Bamfield on his ketch yacht *Diantha*.[79] Taken from an unusual viewpoint, possibly an adjacent chalk outcrop, van der Weyden's serene treatment of the chalk stacks known as Old Harry Rocks – *Cliff End, Studland* (fig. 92), – shimmers with golden sunlight against the deep blue and turquoise sea. The sparkling reflective surface of the sea, and the translucent qualities of its shallows, eloquently conveys the moment the sun catches the cliffs. The use of chiaroscuro makes a strong contrast with the dark area in the foreground. He has focused on the reflection of the sky and cliff in the water, complicated by the colour of the water, even below the surface. Van der Weyden's highly detailed painting engenders a sense of awe at the transcendent power of nature, creating an acutely observed atmospheric and powerful composition with the subtle tone values of the sea and stratification of the chalk formation. *The Studio* admired the work for its 'composition, decoration and harmonious colour', remarking on a striking, varied tonal palette which showed van der Weyden at his best.[80]

The years 1908 to 1910 therefore witnessed major painting activity in Purbeck as Steer, Tonks and Russell all responded to this dramatic and stark landscape by producing some well-received modern landscape paintings. As these were exhibited in London, it led to more artists seeking to visit the area – such as Gerald Moira, whose *Goathorn Clay Pit* of 1913 was exhibited at the Goupil Gallery.[81] Yet the British art world was about to be challenged by Fry's Post-Impressionist exhibitions of 1910 and 1912, when once more Dorset was the site for experimentation. This challenge was suggested by Vanessa Bell in 1910 when she described the Purbeck landscape as 'like a Steer' – Bell was already alive to these Slade modern landscapes, yet her Post-Impressionist circle would take modernity much further in their expressions of nature.[82]

77. Most of van der Weyden's paintings are in private collections. His Dorset oils include: *Ballard Down*, exhibited RA1930; *Cliffs – Old Harry, Swanage*, 1929; *Swanage: Pinnacle Rock near Old Harry Point, Studland, Dorset*. Lobley's undated oil painting *Poole Harbour from Creech Barrow, Dorset*, is in the collection of Poole Museum Service, PCF20A.
78. After his marriage in 1893, van der Weyden lived at Montreuil-sur-Mer near Étaples on the Normandy coast until World War I, when it became the British GHQ, with Étaples a major transit point and storage depot for the British. During the war van der Weyden was a camouflage officer with the Royal Engineers, and was granted British naturalization in 1919.
79. Letter from Harry van der Weyden to the curator of the Russell-Cotes Art Gallery and Museum, Norman Silvester, 29 April 1936, written from 26a West End Lane, NW6, in picture file, Accession number 701, Russell-Cotes Art Gallery and Museum. The painting was exhibited in the 'Prominent Living Artists' exhibition at the Russell-Cotes in 1936 and purchased by Norman Silvester for the collection in May 1936 for £21. See Norman L. Silvester, 'Harry Van Der Weyden', *Bulletin of the Russell-Cotes Art Gallery and Museum*, vol. XV, September 1936, p.35.
80. Herbert, B. Grimsditch, 'Mr Harry Van Der Weyden', *The Studio*, vol. 94, 1927, pp.10–16.
81. 'Goupil Gallery Salon', *The Studio*, 1914, p.225.
82. Vanessa Bell to Virginia Woolf, 3 October 1910, Berg Collection, NYPL. Letter cited in Tickner, p.133, fn.60.

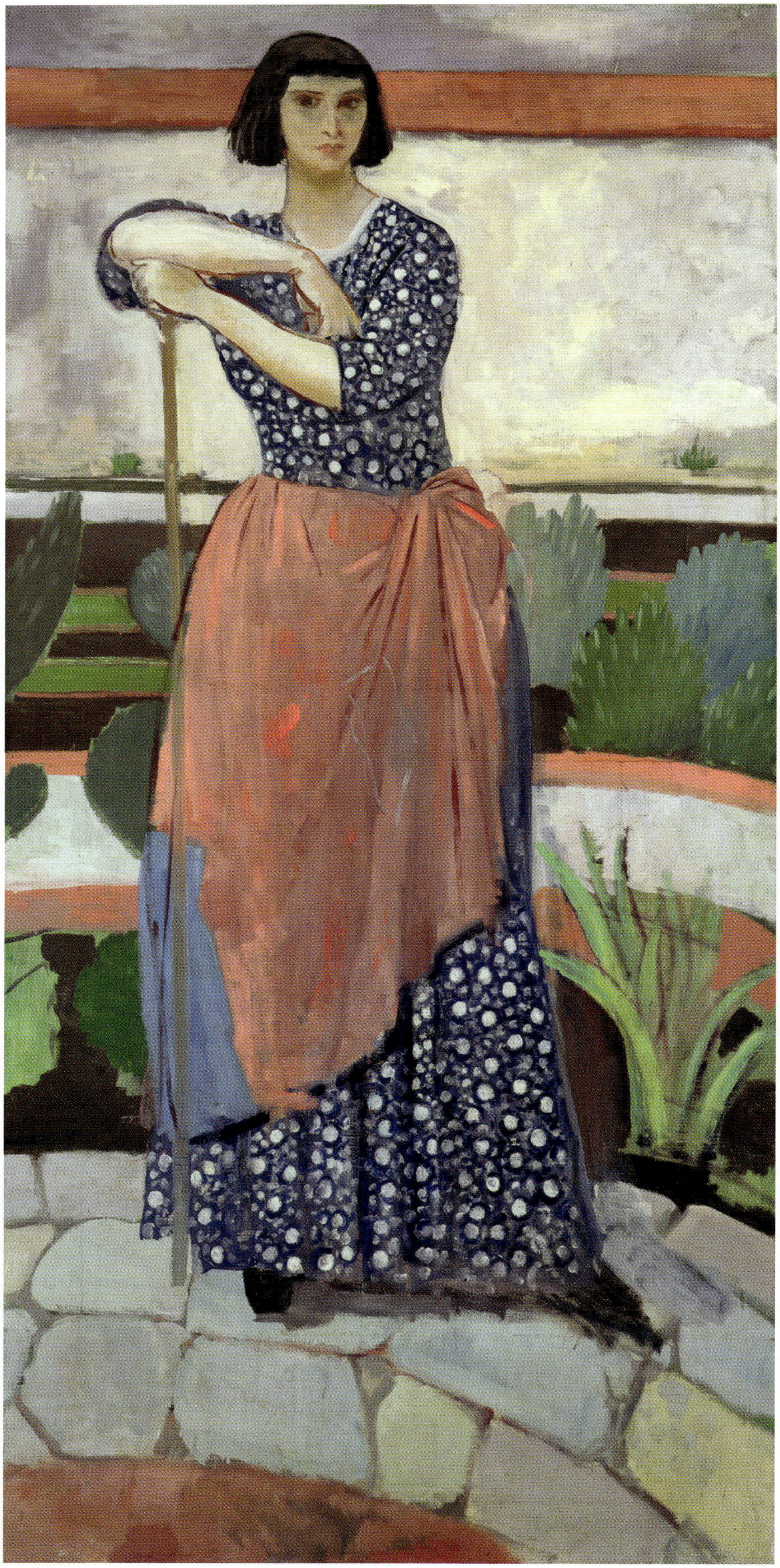

FIG. 93
Augustus John
Dorelia McNeill in the Garden at Alderney
1911 / oil on canvas / 201 x 101.6 cm

SEVEN

FROM ALDERNEY MANOR TO BLOOMSBURY

The connecting circle of painters linked to Purbeck through the Everetts saw the Slade group visiting Dorset and producing landscapes for the New English and other exhibitions in London. When, after a visit from Studland to Corfe, Vanessa Bell wrote her letter to Virginia in which she characterized the countryside as a Steer painting and imagined it peopled with 'Sladites',[1] she explicitly made the link between Slade students, tutors and the appeal of the Purbeck countryside, identifying herself with them. Her suggestion that the Corfe landscape was indistinguishable from Steer's Purbeck paintings reveals both the recognized status of his work and his pre-eminence among those 'disciples' who congregated close by during the summer months. As arguably the principal British landscape artist of the early century, Steer was a magnet for past students and painters. However, in the years leading up to the First World War, the Dorset landscape would become the subject of radical new approaches to painting, from Augustus John's lyrical mode to Vanessa Bell's equally personal experiments with formalism.

AUGUSTUS JOHN AT ALDERNEY MANOR

By 1911 the Everetts were forced to leave Arfleet Mill. They bought three acres of land at Broadstone, close to Wimborne and Poole (owned by Lady Wimborne, who lived at Canford Manor), and built four houses there between 1911 and 1914.[2] Their first home, Prospect, had a panoramic view over Poole Harbour, on the opposite side of the bay from Corfe. It was in the same year that Augustus John enlisted Everett's help to find a suitable home for his large family, writing:

> we think of taking a house in the country and Dorset seems to me the most attractive county. Tonks advised me to write to you and ask you if you knew of any house available. It will have to be pretty large for my family. I would be greatly obliged to you if you would be so kind as to let me know of anything you know of.[3]

The Everetts again turned to Lady Wimborne, who, delighted at the prospect of a distinguished artist living on the estate (by now John's reputation as the leading draughtsman in England was well established), suggested Alderney Manor on the Ringwood Road, outside Parkstone. Three miles

1. 'The whole country was like a Steer and so was the day. I expected to see many Sladites perched on the surrounding hills like myself, but luckily the season was too late for them and all have disappeared', Vanessa Bell to Virginia Woolf, 3 October 1910, Berg Collection, NYPL. Letter cited in Tickner, p.133, fn.60.
2. Lady Cornelia Henrietta Maria Spencer-Churchill was the daughter of Sir John Winston Spencer-Churchill, 7th Duke of Marlborough. She married Ivor Bertie Guest, 1st Baron Wimborne of Canford Magna in 1868. The mother of the 7th Duke, Lady Jane Stewart, daughter of Admiral George Stewart, 8th Earl of Galloway, was related to the Everetts.
3. Letter dated 1 February 1911 from Augustus John from 153 Church Street, Chelsea to John Everett, private collection. John, *Chiaroscuro*, p.104 wrongly gives the date of the move from Chelsea to Alderney Manor as 1909.

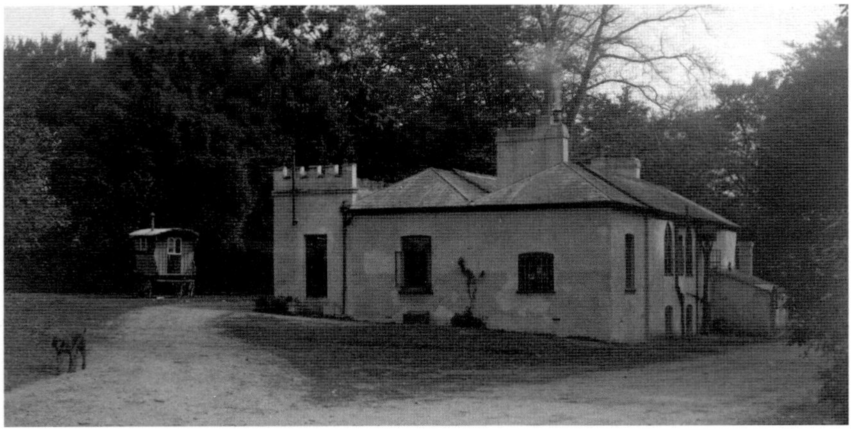

FIG. 94
Alderney Manor, 1926, showing the gypsy caravan in the grounds sometimes used to house their guests

over the heath from Prospect, Everett described Alderney as 'a big queer-looking castellated bungalow with 60 acres of ground, mostly fir woods'.[4] The house, for which John paid £50 annual rent, came with a walled garden, a cottage (fig. 94), which on arrival John described as neglected, and stables which he converted into his studio.[5] Whilst the house was prepared, John and his family stayed with the Everetts at Prospect, recorded in a series of evocative photographs (fig. 95) showing Dorelia and John at ease with the Everetts and their two sons.[6]

In 1911 Augustus John's unconventional household consisted of the five sons by his wife, Ida (who had died in childbirth in 1907), and two children by his mistress Dorelia McNeill, who by then had assumed responsibility for managing the household, with her sister Edie. John was enjoying considerable professional success.[7] In 1901 he became acting Professor at the art school in Liverpool, was elected to the New English in 1903 and began exhibiting in London at the Carfax and Chenil Galleries. From 1903 to 1907 he was involved in the Chelsea Art School with Orpen, undertook portrait commissions and met important patrons such as Hugh Lane (a distant relative of Orpen) and John Quinn. He was keen to settle his family, though he continued to travel in Britain and Europe as it suited him, and his arrival in Dorset marked a more stable phase for his family. This is reflected in the spontaneous work John produced at Alderney Manor: brightly coloured, powerful, reductive paintings of his family in the Dorset countryside, which remain some of his most important works.

The 1910 French Post-Impressionist show in London belatedly introduced the Parisian modernism of Cézanne, Gauguin and Van Gogh to an English audience, to whom it appeared radical, and had a major impact on young artists. Following this significant exhibition, John was developing his highly personal free and expressive style of painting figures in the Dorset landscape. John's biographer Michael Holroyd noted that whilst at Alderney he worked on numerous drawings and brightly coloured panel paintings of Dorelia (figs 93, 96, 98 and 99) and the children alone or in groups (fig. 97).[8] *Dorelia McNeill in the Garden at Alderney* (fig. 93) was

4. Everett, *Memoirs*, p.120.
5. Letter from Jean Hornak Montesfield, Freshwater Bay, Isle of Wight to Vivien White, c/o Dr J.C.White, Faculty of Medicine, University of Malaya, Kuala Lumpur, January 1974, private collection. Ibid., John described restoring the neglected garden to 'luxuriance'. Jeanett (Jean) Hellen Hornak and Nancy (Nancie) McNeill Newman were the daughters of Dorelia McNeill's sister, Jessie Slade, and spent much of their childhood at Alderney. Jessie was married to Edgar Slade, who trained at the Slade, which was founded through a bequest from his uncle Felix.
6. Everett, *Memoirs*, p.120.
7. Augustus John married Ida Nettleship in 1901 and they had five children: David Anthony Honore Nettleship, Caspar, Robin, Edwin and Henry. Dorelia McNeill, who managed the household following Ida's death, was his mistress and gave him a further four children – Pyramus, Romilly, Elizabeth Ann (Poppet) and Vivien – at Alderney Manor before the family moved to Fryern Court, Fordingbridge, Hampshire in 1927, where Augustus died on 31 October 1961.
8. Holroyd, 1996, p.369. This included portraits of the many visitors to Alderney and figure studies for his large decorative groups, *Forza e Amore*, *The Mumpers* and *Lyric Fantasy*.

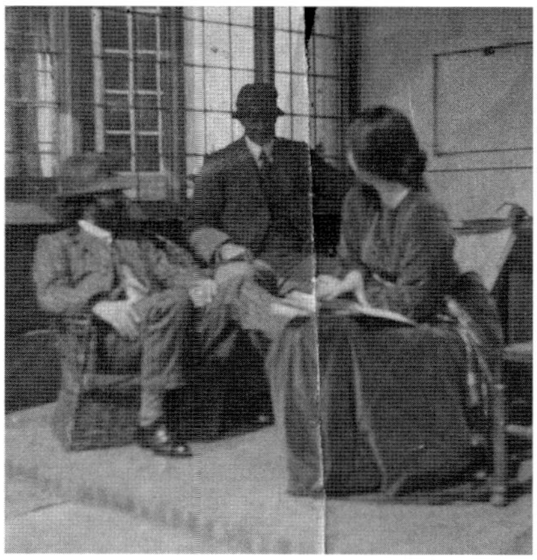

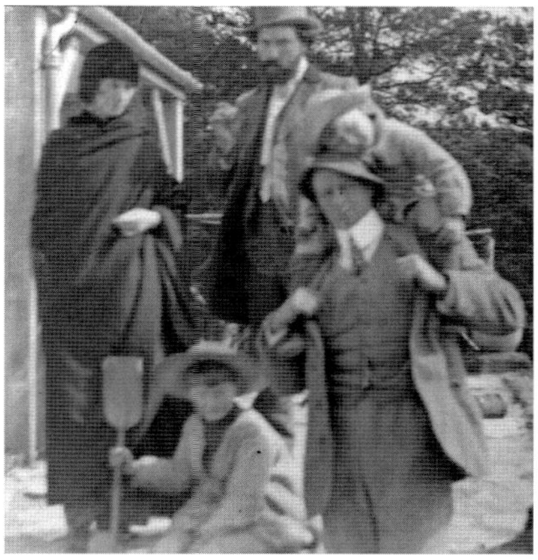

FIG. 95
Prospect, Brocdstone, 1911: [top] Augustus John, John Everett and Dorelia McNeill in the garden room; [above] McNeill, John and Everett, with Everett's sons Henry and Tony

painted the year they arrived and celebrates sunny optimism and hope for the stability that Alderney Manor could offer the family.

The low-built pink house with gothic windows was described as:

> that absolutely unique castellated house with its strange little rooms each end at the front. The very special smell it had as you entered the house of burning log fires, beeswax and honey.[9]

Largely self-sufficient, they acquired cows, saddleback pigs, donkeys, New Forest ponies, carthorses, cats, dogs, bees and a dovecote, from which the doves escaped. Children and visitors had the run of the grounds, and sometimes free-roaming animals raided Dorelia's kitchen garden, described by her niece as the

> secret walled-in garden which always seemed to be sunny and filled with the hum of bees and the scent of lavender while we lazed around the pond having picnic teas and absurd conversations.[10]

As John's most important model and inspiration, Dorelia dominates the highly stylized, full-length portrait (fig. 93), perhaps his first Dorset *plein air* painting. Standing in the walled garden, Dorelia wears a blue-and-white spotted dress and a swathe of pink-and-blue material for an apron, and rests on her hoe as she stares out of the picture. John has flattened the perspective and sharpened the background with chalky-dry, even areas of vivid colour.[11]

John's monumental painting defines the importance of Dorelia in the unconventional domestic set-up. Jean Slade, Dorelia's niece, who stayed at Alderney Manor as a child, noted that:

> the figure of Dodo, as Dorelia was called, is so mysteriously beautiful and unusual that she is very hard to describe. She presided over everything looking serene, wise and ageless; surrounded by children; always making everything about her look unusual and romantic and always doing things with inimitable gracefulness. The whole family dressed by Dodo and Edie had the appearance of a mixture of gypsy, Spanish, French and Indian. Dodo managed to find the most unusual prints to make clothes with – some were like Provencal prints, some like Indian. The furniture and pottery and carpets she found for the house are only just being appreciated now and I suppose the whole Romantic Bohemian and colourful set-up was far in advance of its time.[12]

In *Washing Day* (fig. 98), Dorelia wears characteristically loose clothing – of the sort seen in the informal photograph of Dorelia and John at Prospect taken by Katherine Everett – to carry out an archetypically 'dutiful' feminine role of washing clothes in the garden. Though simplified and reductive they are at the same time monumental and often, as here, richly coloured. Surrounded by nature, female domestic activity is the subject of the painting, representing a shift from the more totemic *Dorelia McNeill in the Garden at Alderney* to a softer narrative.[13]

In Dorset John produced some of his finest paintings involving his family and it is clear that the relative calm of Alderney was of great importance to him. Jean Slade remembered him as

9. Letter from Nancie Newman, Montesfield, Freshwater Bay, Isle of Wight to Vivien White, January 1974, private collection.
10. Nancie Newman.
11. A sketch plan by Everett details the apple-tree planting in the walled garden at Alderney. Everett Sketchbook, 1910–11, PAJ1430, NMM.
12. Jean Hornak.
13. See Tate archive ibid. The date of the painting is unclear and while Augustus John confirmed 1912 in a letter to the Tate, when he sold it to American collector John Quinn, following his 1916 exhibition at the Chenil Gallery, he described it as 'quite a recent thing'.

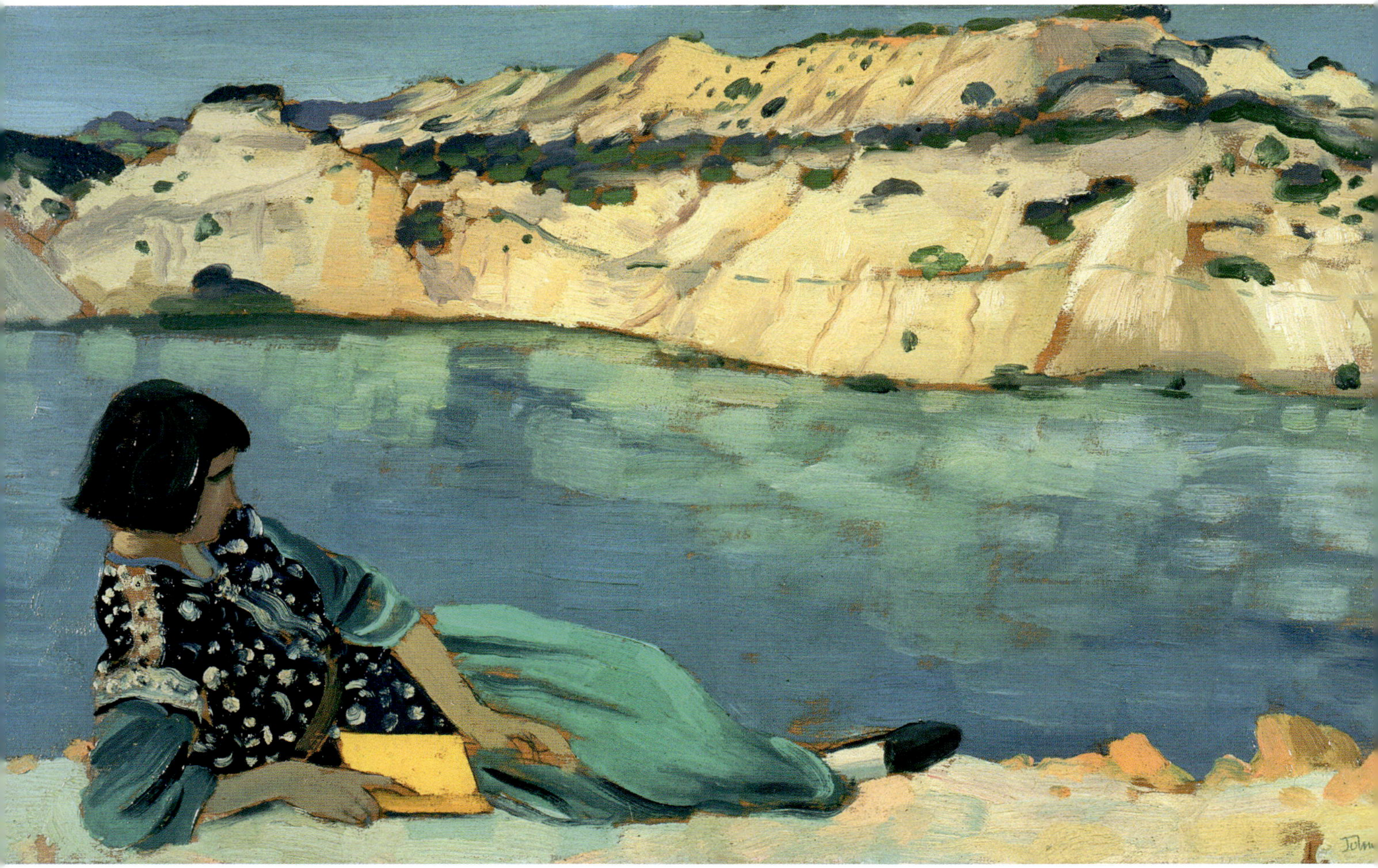

FIG. 96

Augustus John / ***The Blue Pool***

1911 / oil on panel / 30.2 x 50.5 cm

> someone keeping himself in the background – not remote but preoccupied, always looking. When he did notice one it was with a penetrating stare which was a bit disconcerting – or with a look of pleased amusement. He liked to have a lot of children to watch when he felt like it and said they were 'gorgeous things to have around … He had a very pleasant voice and could be witty in a very dry restrained way.[14]

John took part in afternoon jazz sessions and presided over countless parties, bonfires and trips to local pubs, particularly *The Shoulder of Mutton*, where he drank with the local gypsies. John's pleasure in his children is apparent through his large number of canvases featuring them.

Not all John's Dorset paintings focused on Alderney. His series of small oil panels of Canford Heath often featured Dorelia (fig. 99). Shown in profile seated on the heath, she wears a similar dress to *The Blue Pool*, a headscarf and blue shawl, with her features in shadow, as she appears to be either sewing or knitting. John's loosely painted and boldly coloured image leaves the underpainting exposed to outline the form and demonstrates his almost symbolic positioning of a woman at work in the Dorset landscape.

Set in a deep clay bowl between Wareham and Corfe, the Blue Pool at Furzebrook was formed when digging its valuable clays had ceased and the pit filled with water. Held in suspension, the fine clay diffracted light to produce a spectrum of constantly varying shades of green or turquoise. This resulted in the vivid greenish blue to cerulean hues which attracted artists to paint at the relatively inaccessible location. John's *The Blue Pool*, 1911 (fig. 96) was produced the year he moved his family to Dorset.[15] The exceptional blue of the pool dictated the vivid palette, adopting the glowing quality of light of the South of France. A reclining Dorelia frames the landscape in the foreground. In an exercise of varying lengths of horizontal bands of colour, John has flattened the perspective and application of paint, virtually reducing the landscape to geometric slashes. Holroyd argues that this was the point at which John was considered the most avant-garde artist in the country, and certainly his reductive, idealized landscape is an outstanding Modernist essay.[16]

A smaller version of *The Blue Pool* (Fitzwilliam) shows Dorelia standing by the pool, and a further signed version, *The Shores of the Blue Pool, Dorset*, was in John's Christies's sale after his death.[17] Blue Pool was also the location for his mythical *Lyric Fantasy* (fig. 72), begun the same year.[18] Set against the backdrop of Blue Pool, this large, unfinished picture is a fantasy of the children and women of central importance in John's adult life, in surreal Dorset surroundings. In this ambitious composition he evoked various artistic influences to seek a classical, idealized setting of his family and friends within the Dorset landscape. The figures on the far left are two of John's lovers, Nora Brownsword and Euphemia Lamb, with his son by Dorelia, Pyramus, playing the drums. In the centre, an unidentified female figure holds Poppet, John's first daughter by Dorelia, who stands to the right. The figure on the far right, in shadow, represents his dead wife Ida, with her children Edwin, Romilly and Caspar in the foreground.

Dressed in handmade clothes, the children helped with chores, ran wild over the heathland and woods and bathed in the lake.[19] John made numerous studies of the family in and around Alderney – for example, *David and*

14. Jean Hornak.
15. The painting was in the collection of Sir James Murray (1850–1932), a collector and chairman of Aberdeen Art Gallery, where his collection was exhibited in 1925. He sent 10 Johns to the Murray Christie's sale of April 1927, selling *Blue Pool* to Aberdeen Art Gallery for 600 guineas and *An Hour at Swanage* for 480 guineas to W.W. Sampson for the James Guthrie Orchar Art Gallery at Beach House, Broughty Ferry.
16. Holroyd, p.334 McConkey, p.75, presented John as adopting a new decorative approach to landscape.
17. *Catalogue of the Drawings and Paintings from the Studio of the Late Augustus John*, Christie's, 20 July 1962, no. 130.
18. It was one of the murals commissioned in 1909 by old master dealer and distant relative of Orpen, Hugh Lane, to decorate the hall of his Chelsea house. John designed the composition using his own family and friends as models. The commission was not completed before Lane was drowned in the *Lusitania* in 1915.
19. See Romilly John, *The Seventh Child: A Retrospect*, London: William Heinemann Ltd, 1932, for further descriptions of life at Alderney.

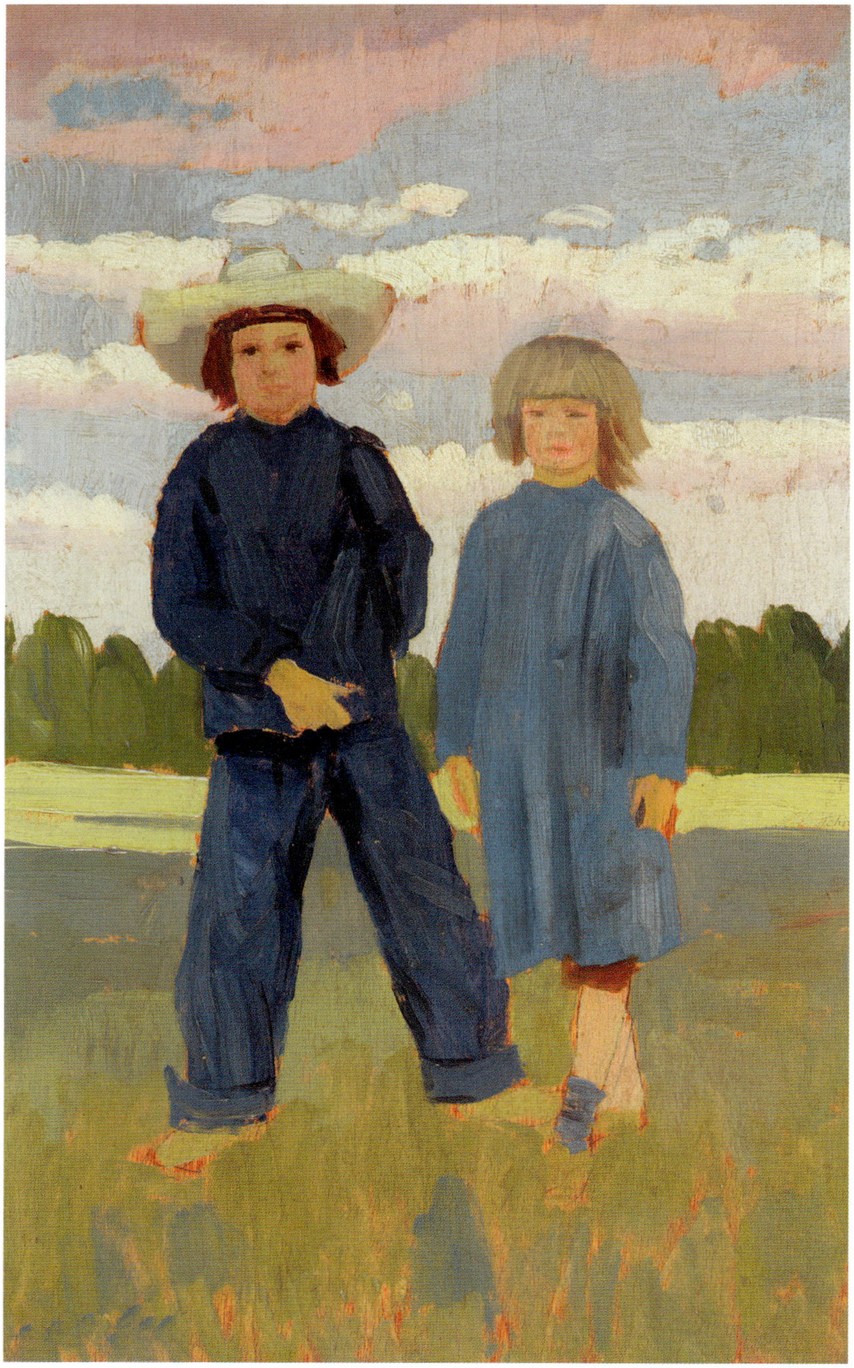

FIG. 97

Augustus John / ***David and Caspar at Alderney***

1912 / oil on panel / 53 x 35.1 cm

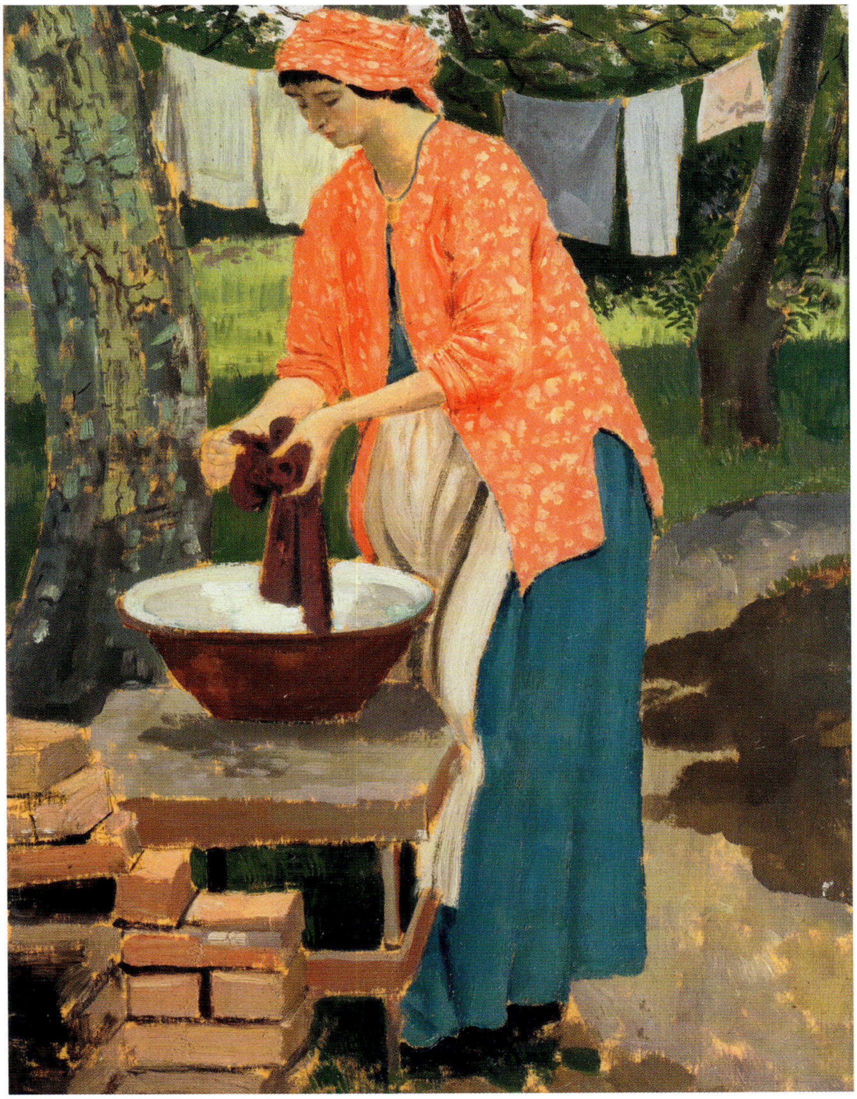

FIG. 98

Augustus John / ***Washing Day***

c.1915 / oil and pencil on panel / 40.6 x 30.2 cm

Caspar at Alderney (fig. 97).[20] The identity of the sitters in John's painting is puzzling. David and Caspar were the oldest of John's five sons by Ida, with Caspar just one year younger than David. He would have been 9 when he sat for the portrait, which seems to show a far younger boy with fair hair. As Caspar was also dark-haired, it is possible that the names of the sitters have been confused or perhaps wrongly named at some point. It is more likely that the portrait is of David with either Romilly or Edwin, or perhaps Caspar with either Romilly or Edwin.[21] The ambiguity underlines the way in which John used his family as models for experimenting with colour and form, rather than being strictly interested in the specifics of portraiture.

Alderney Manor was home to countless visitors, members of their extended families and fellow painters. Derwent Lees, a Tasmanian who enrolled at the Slade in 1905, where Tonks invited him to join the teaching staff, remained

20. Other examples include *Edith and Caspar in Dorset*, 1911 (private collection) and *An Hour at Ower* (Fitzwilliam Museum).
21. This proposal was suggested by Rebecca John, daughter of Caspar John, in an email discussion with the author. David later became a musician and postman (fig. 105), while Caspar rose to become an Admiral of the Fleet and served as First Sea Lord from 1960 to 1963. See 'Sir Caspar John', *Oxford Dictionary of National Biography*.

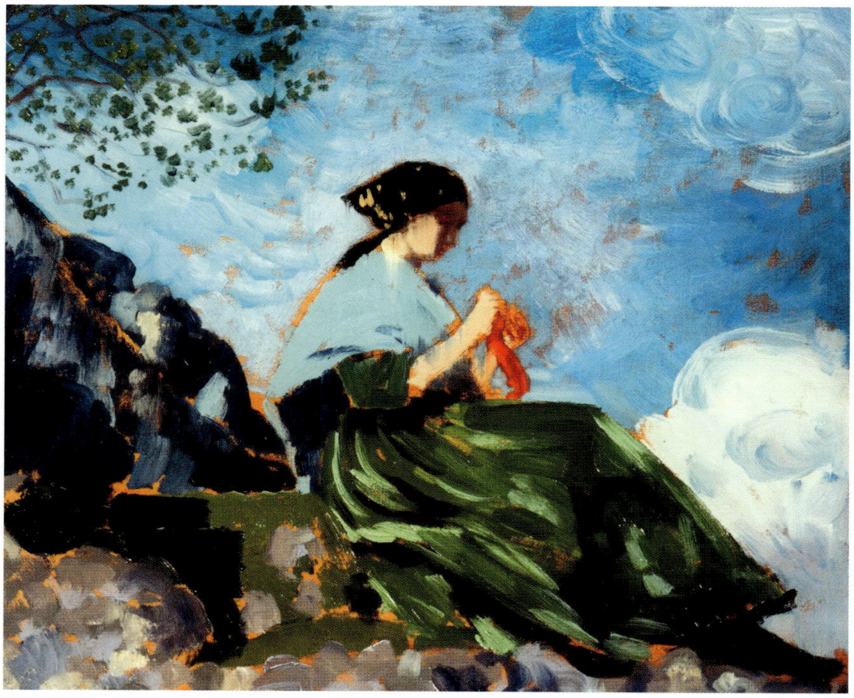

FIG. 99

Augustus John / *On Canford Heath*

c.1913 / oil on board / 31.8 x 39.4 cm

there from 1908 to 1918.[22] This link led to Lees joining Augustus John and J.D. Innes on painting trips in Wales between 1910 and 1912, echoing Everett's absences from family life. In 1912 he spent several weeks at Collioure, where Henri Matisse and André Derain produced their most radical Fauvist canvases, reflected in Lees' *Blue Pool* (fig. 100). His broadly painted imitative landscape, evoking the south of France rather than Dorset and emptied of people, adopts diagonal brushwork, while the thickly applied strong colours suggest Augustus John's panel paintings.[23] Lees' wife Lyndra modelled for John and so Lee's *Blue Pool* may have resulted from seeing John's versions.[24] Other Slade visitors included Henry Lamb, who was infatuated with Dorelia and would return to Dorset after the First World War, living close by at Poole.[25] By 1914, Nora Summers (née Munro) was another frequent visitor. She had attended Bristol School of Art before enrolling at the Slade from 1907 to 1910 and also befriended Innes and Lees and sat for John, Lamb and Russell. After Nora married fellow student, Gerald, they spent the summer of 1914 in a caravan near Creech, in Purbeck, where they painted with Lees. Nora exhibited at the New English Art Club and occasionally the Walker Art Gallery, Liverpool.

BLOOMSBURY IN DORSET

> On or about December 1910, human character changed.[26]

It is instructive that, while in Dorset, Augustus John, Vanessa Bell and Roger Fry were all pushing forward the boundaries of landscape painting.

22. Chaplin, 6:38–6:60.
23. Lees' life was cut short by psychiatric illness and he spent the last decade of his life in an asylum.
24. See B of Plate 1. Randolph Schwabe, 'Reminiscences of Fellow Students', *The Burlington Magazine for Connoisseurs*, vol. 82, no. 478 (January 1943), pp.6–9. A smaller version by Lees was owned by Fairlie Harmar.
25. Lamb was previously at Corfe with Lytton Strachey in 1911. See Miranda Seymour, *Ottoline Morrell: Life on a Grand Scale*, London: Sceptre, 1998, p.175.
26. 'On or about December 1910, human character changed. I am not saying that one went out, as one might into a garden, and there saw that a rose had flowered, or that a hen had laid an egg. The change was not sudden and definite like that. But a change there was, nevertheless; and, since one must be arbitrary, let us date it about the year 1910.' Virginia Woolf, *Mr Bennett and Mrs Brown*, 1924, London: Hogarth Press, 1924, from a paper read to the Heretics, Cambridge, on 18 May 1924.

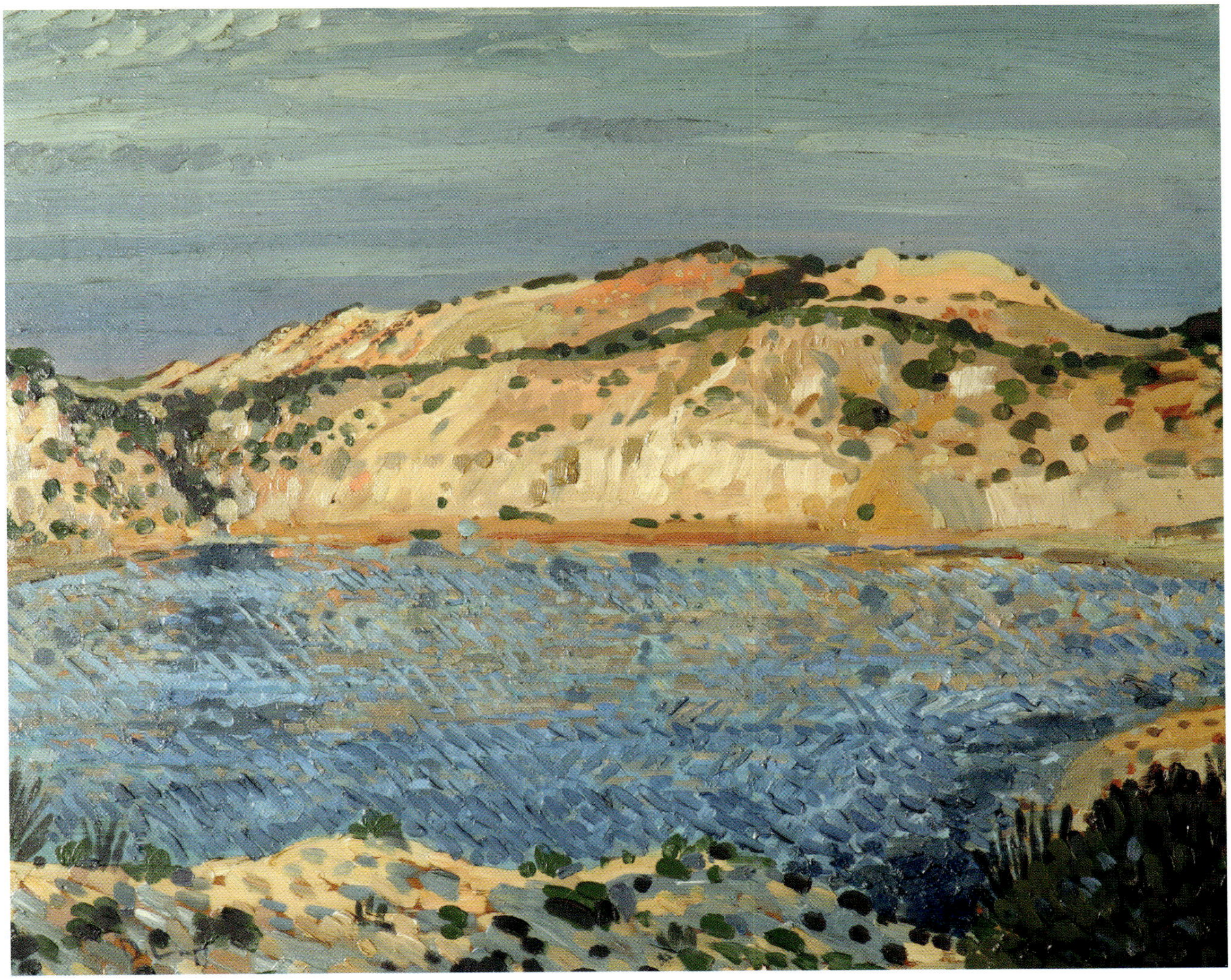

FIG. 100
Derwent Lees / ***Blue Pool***
1911 / oil on panel / 40 x 50.7 cm

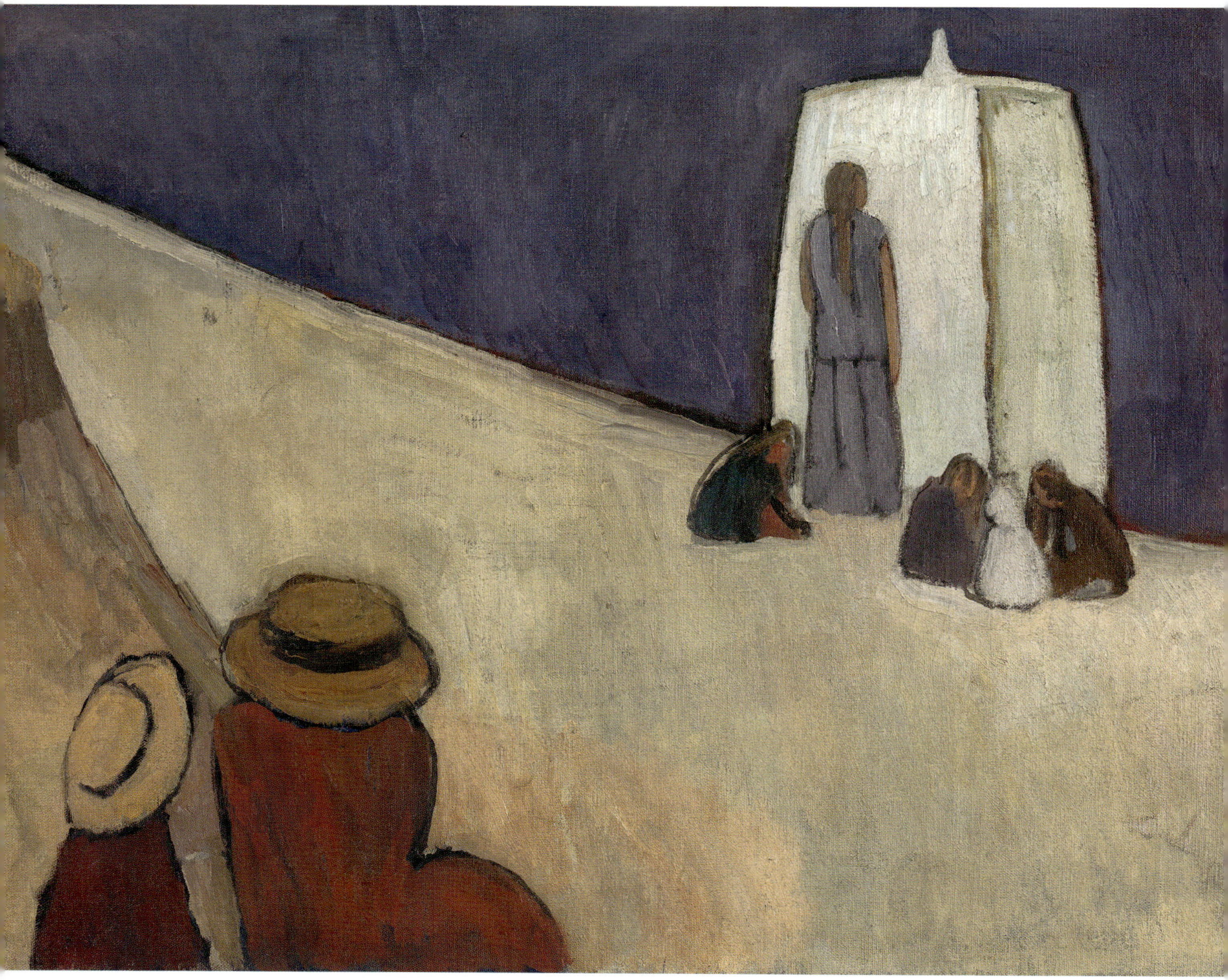

FIG. 101
Vanessa Bell / ***Studland Beach***
1911 / oil on canvas / 76.2 x 101.6 cm

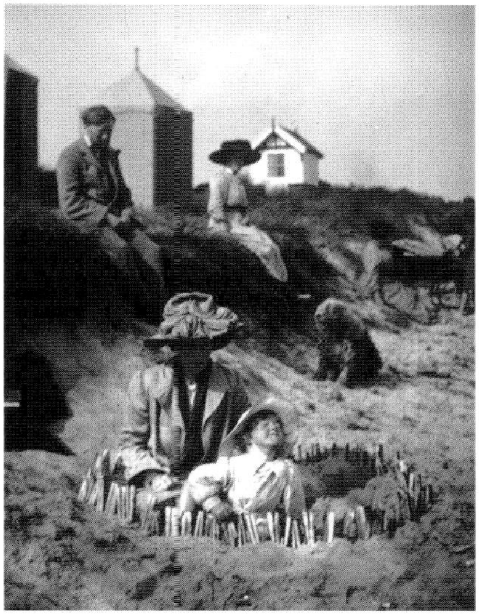

FIG. 102

Vanessa Bell with her son Julian

photograph of Vanessa Bell and her son Julian on the beach at Studland, Dorset, with Clive Bell and Mabel Selwood, their maid, in the background, 1910; black and white negative; © Tate, London 2014, from the albums of Vanessa Bell

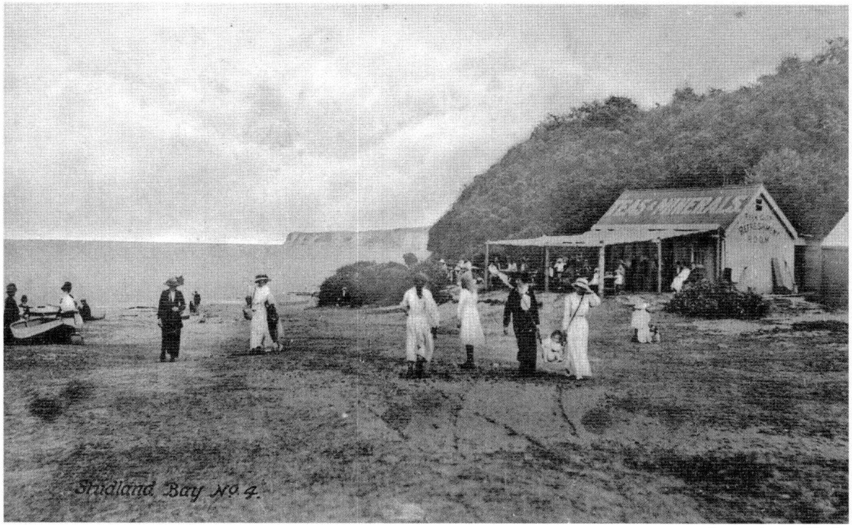

FIG. 103

Studland Beach looking towards Middle Beach with Fern Glen tea room, c.1912

private collection

Tensions between Modernism and modernity had emerged during the 1890s, and by 1911 were played out on the sands of Studland. The atmospheric, empathetic Slade and New English responses to Purbeck, discussed in chapter six, differed markedly from the Modernist, reductive work of Fry and Bell, who were more concerned with shape, form and blocks of colour, pushing towards abstraction.[27] The artistic core of the Bloomsbury Group centred around two prominent sisters, the writer and essayist Virginia Woolf and the painter and designer Vanessa Bell, who with Roger Fry discovered Dorset just as the Everetts moved to Broadstone.[28]

Fry and Bell's paintings differed from Augustus John's which, though owing something to the Post-Impressionists by adopting bright colours and simplified form, leaned towards a Symbolist concentration on monumental figures, often overtly personal, set in the landscape. Lisa Tickner's excellent essay, *Vanessa Bell*, discusses Bell's *Studland Beach* (fig. 101) in detail and suggests the development of the beach as a place of recreation and as a Modernist space lacking the Arcadian connotations of landscape.[29] She presents the case for Bell's painting *Studland Beach* being a Modernist work imbued with personal meaning, a tight distillation of experiences and sensations and links to the past, positing it as the visual equivalent of her sister's *To the Lighthouse*, one of Woolf's most experimental works in which the characters are based around her parents and siblings. References to the sea appear throughout the novel, which deals with the passage of time and the awareness that the world around the characters is transient.

In his attempt to break with the recent past, Roger Fry argued that landscape painting could no longer be endorsed through the New English emphasis on the 'expression of nature', but, inspired by Cézanne, should be centred on discovering those significant values of design independent of what might actually be represented in the work.[30] Writing about significant form, Vanessa's husband, Clive Bell, argued that the form of an artwork,

27. The period between 1910 and 1914 was significant for the circulation of European, especially French, paintings in England and for resulting developments in British art. Organized by Bloomsbury Group member Roger Fry, 'Manet and the Post-Impressionists' opened late in 1910, and was seen by many critics to be the first major show of modern art in London, featuring works by over 200 continental artists, including Cézanne, Gauguin, Manet and Picasso. Greeted with indignation by some critics, but celebrated for its radical break with Victorian convention, Fry's show importantly encouraged a rich debate about the value of modern art in the London press.

28. Peter Stansky, *On or About December 10: Early Bloomsbury and Its Intimate World*, Cambridge, MA, and London: Harvard, 1997, p.17. Stansky's is the clearest account of the incident, pp.17–46. See too 'Bunga-Bunga', 'When the Royal Navy was Hoaxed in Portland Harbour', *The Dorset Year Book*, 1991, pp.93–5. Woolf came to Dorset on 7 February 1910 when she was involved in a prank described by the writer Pete Stansky 'as the most significant event in Virginia Woolf's external life'. She was amongst the Bloomsbury party with Duncan Grant, ringleader Horace Cole, Anthony Buxton, Adrian Stephen and Guy Ridley, who played a practical joke on the British Navy's most potent, powerful symbol, HMS *Dreadnought*, anchored in Portland Harbour. They darkened their skin colour, dressed up in long caftans, placed turbans on their heads and glued on fake beards to appear as Abyssinian princes (fig. 111). Received with full ceremonial pomp, they inspected the fleet and were given a private tour of the flagship. Adrian and Virginia even shook hands with their cousin, William Fisher, chief staff officer on the ship, who failed to see through their disguises. After a few hours, Adrian declared the state visit over and the party returned to catch the train from Weymouth. Ever the attention-seeker, Cole thought the incident 'shriekingly funny', and went to the press without telling the others; within a few days the hoax was headline news.

29. Tickner, pp.117–42.

30. Dissatisfied with Impressionism, Fry resigned from the jury of the New English in 1908. See Virginia Woolf, 'The Post-Impressionists', *Roger Fry: A Biography*, London: Hogarth Press, 1940.

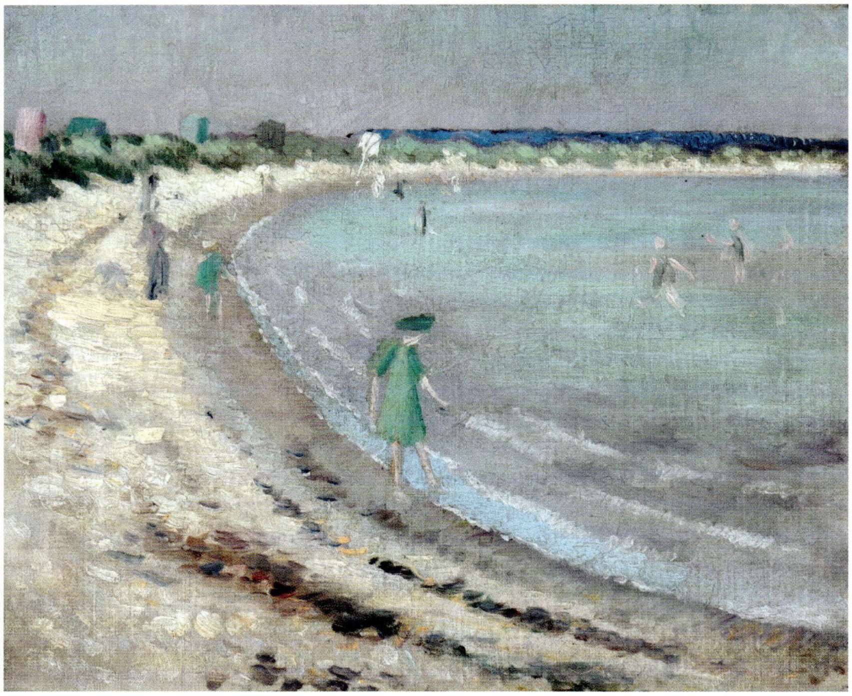

FIG. 104
Roger Fry / *Studland Beach* (recto)
1911 / oil on board / 27 x 33.5 cm
The Bloomsbury Workshop, London

or forms within an artwork, might be expressive, even when divorced from a recognizable reality, a debate largely supported by Fry but which Tonks hotly denied.[31] Writing a scathing attack on Fry in a letter to patron Geoffrey Blackwell, Tonks drew the battle lines and concluded that 'he resembles certain not first-rate French painters.'[32] Fry was in Dorset when the influence of his two Post-Impressionist exhibitions was at its height. Tonks considered the second Post-Impressionist exhibition of 1912 'a mistake, anyone dallying with post impressionism would dally no more if Fry was their only inducement'.[33] Nonetheless it is significant that Purbeck provided subjects for Fry and Bell to attempt radical paintings.

In his small, intimate painting, *Studland*, of 1911 (fig. 104), Fry applied blocks of distinct colour to capture the familiar view of the sweep of Middle beach, with its dunes, beach huts and figures paddling at the water's edge. Probably painted on the spot, distinctive patches of violet and vivid green indicate the distant hills and huts, with a young girl in the foreground. Mirroring several of Bell's lesser known oils of *Studland Bay*, the picture is ambivalent, the girl in the green dress almost hesitant at the water's edge, while the distant hills appear dark and forbidding.[34] Fry's use of colour and sparsely detailed figures creates an unreality in which they seem almost suspended in time and space. The incongruous photograph of Fry (fig. 105) painting on Studland beach shows him dressed in tweeds, hat and sturdy shoes, using a portable easel to paint amidst the familiar seaside detritus of a discarded child's shoe, bucket and newspaper anchored with a towel. Fry's painting verso (fig. 106) also shows Middle beach, but includes buildings in profile and a tree in the foreground.

31. Chaplin, 6:67, p.151; Clive Bell, 'Preface', *Art*, London: Chatto and Windus, 1914, p.6, in which he claimed to have 'tried to develop a complete theory of visual art'.
32. Letter from Henry Tonks, Vale Studio, 6 January 1912, to Geoffrey Blackwell, Blackwell papers, Tate 2006.4, folder 17.
33. Ibid.
34. Sotheby's, London, 22 November 1995, lot 20, Vanessa Bell, *Figure on the Beach Studland Bay*, 1910–11, Tickner, p.118, fig. 86.

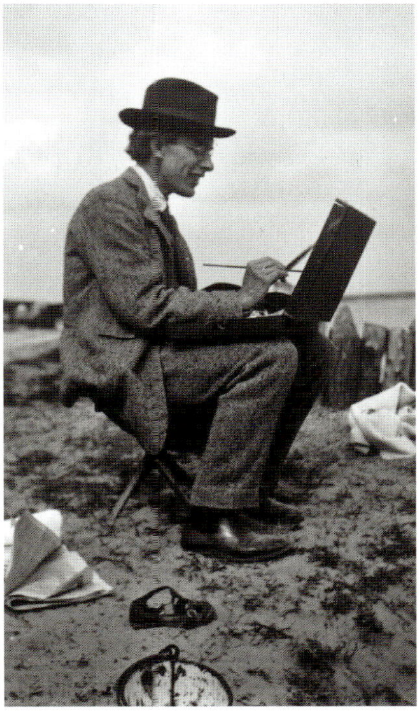

FIG. 105

Roger Fry, Studland Bay, 1911

photograph of Roger Fry painting by the sea at Studland; Bay, Dorset, 1911; black and white negative; © Tate, London 2014

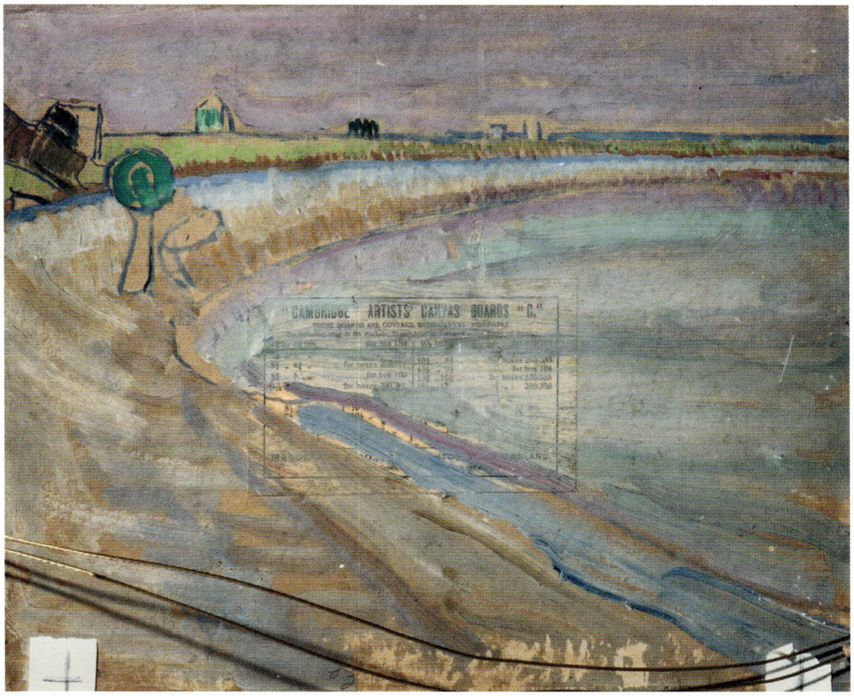

FIG. 106

Roger Fry / ***Studland Beach*** (verso)

1911 / oil on board / 27 x 33.5 cm

The Bloomsbury Workshop, London

Attracted by the beauty and restorative qualities it offered for Virginia, Vanessa and Clive Bell visited Studland from 1909. Fry was there with his sister Joan in September 1911 after his first Post-Impressionist exhibition, when they rented a cramped house in Studland close to the Bells.[35] Fry and Vanessa, lovers at this point, produced a number of paintings of Studland, often featuring its distinctive beach huts (see figs 101, 102, 104 and 107). Fry's stylized, rather than naturalistic, Dorset paintings reveal him working in a spatially simplified Post-Impressionist idiom, perhaps in homage to works like Matisse's important *Dance* of 1910 (Hermitage Museum), in which he makes prominent the outlines of shapes.[36] Fry's *Studland Bay, Dorset* (fig. 107) also suggests these influences. Highly stylized, it focuses on the strong shapes of clouds, cliffs and sea, showing them as blocks of colour while creating a decorative cloisonné effect with dark outlines. The two figures walking hand in hand on the winding path suggest energy and movement, and may represent Clive Bell with his son Julian. The beach of the title is painted as a thin strip with the beach huts, with the chalk cliffs in the distance leading from the enveloping heights on the right to Old Harry Rocks. Fry created a dynamic rhythmic mosaic of shapes that is nevertheless recognizable in terms of subject and place. The simplified boats, clouds and figures suggest a child's picture book, and a contemporary account hinted that, overall, Fry's strong sense of design and subject resembled a seaside poster.[37] The motionless sea sharply contrasts with Everett's Worbarrow *plein air* series of 1910 (figs 85–91) and was probably produced in a studio. In promoting modernity Fry wanted his art to separate interpretations of the landscape from the mundane, famously arguing that artists should not seek to imitate form but create it, which amounted

35. See R. Fry and D. McCarthy, 'Manet and the Post-Impressionists', London, Grafton Gallery, 8 November 1910–15 January 1911.
36. Frances Spalding, *Roger Fry: Art and Life*, Norwich: Black Dog Books, 1999, p.140.
37. Tickner cites Robert Ross, 'Mr Fry's Paintings', *Morning Post*, 4 January 1912, p.4, who described another Studland painting by Fry as resembling a railway poster with which Post-Impressionism has 'much in common', fn.20, p.125. See too Roger Fry, *Near Studland*, Witt Library.

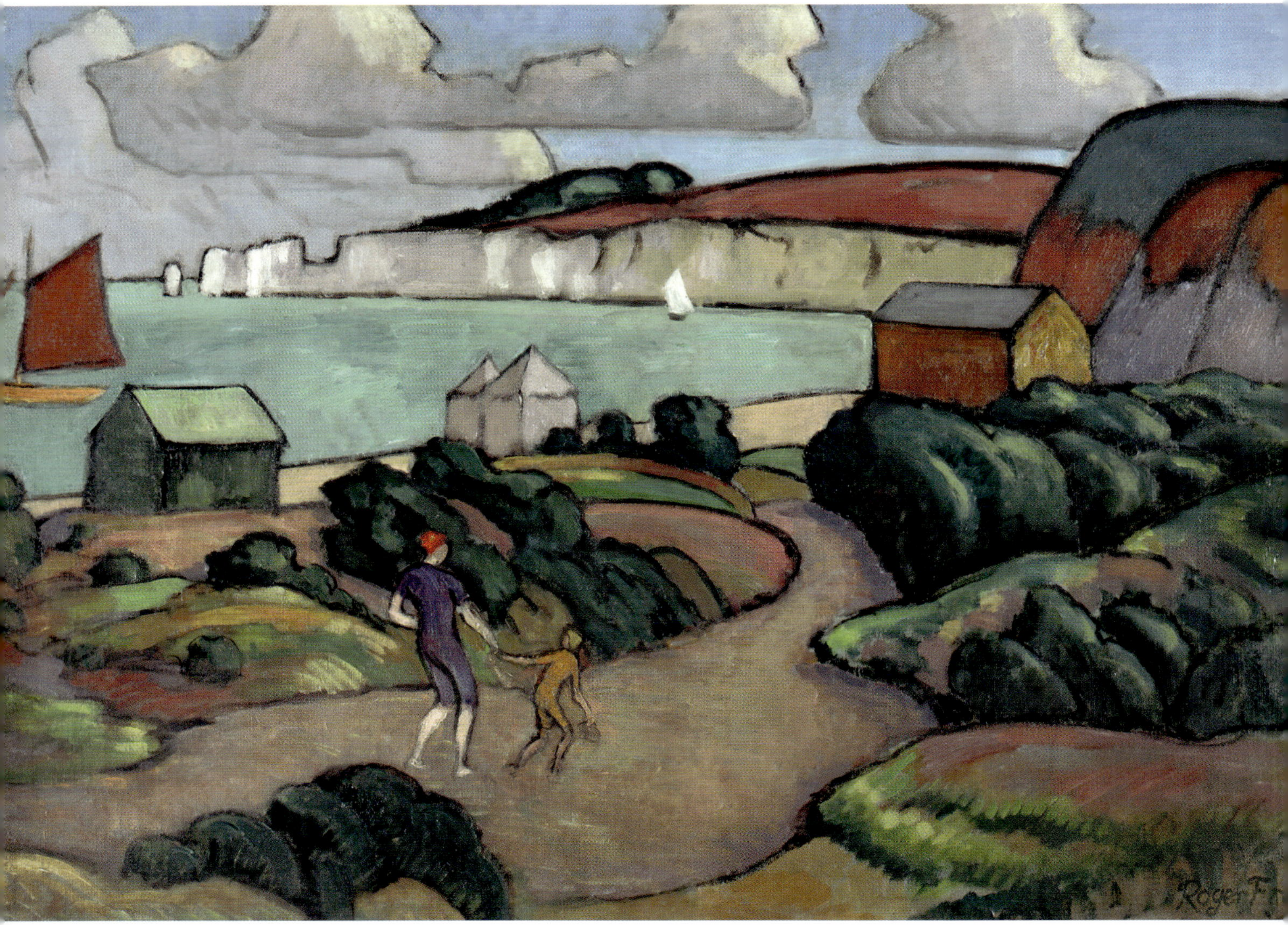

FIG. 107
Roger Fry / ***Studland Bay, Dorset***
1911 / oil on canvas / 62 x 90 cm

to a repudiation of what the Slade and New English painters stood for. Fry returned to Dorset periodically after establishing the Omega Workshop in London in 1913, producing Modernist designs by artists like Duncan Grant and Bell. As some designs were produced by Carter and Co. (later Poole Pottery), then experimenting with new glazes and colours, Fry was a regular visitor to the Poole pottery.

Vanessa Bell produced at least five oil paintings of Studland between 1909 and 1913. *Studland Beach* (fig. 101), dating to the second half of 1912, was a studio work showing the influence of Matisse. Here she has rejected descriptive detail and form to severely simplify the scene, and has reduced it to a few essential components of figures in outline, tent, sea/sky and sand. This radical work, painted in rich colours, represents a stylistic development from Bell's previous Studland Beach paintings by flattening the figures and reducing them to simple form as blocks of colour with dark outlines, as in Fry's painting (fig. 107). Tickner suggests that its monumentality and pervasive melancholy, certainly the figures, with no faces showing, appear isolated within a horizon-free space anchored in reality only by the dunes on the left and Studland tent at the waterline. Without a base and shown virtually floating, the looming tent generates uncertainty, even foreboding – reinforced by the standing figure apparently denied any obvious entrance to it.[38] Although the beach appears unpopulated, in April that year Studland had so many visitors it broke all records.[39] There was also a small, thriving café on the beach that Bell was facing away from (fig. 103).

Over the period during which 'Bloomsbury' visited, Studland was thought 'the favourite "rest place" of a whole host of notables – the musical, literary, artistic and social'.[40] It is instructive to position the works discussed in this chapter under the umbrella of a specific geographic location. Comparison with the Slade tutors' modern landscapes revealed in chapter six clearly demonstrates the influence of the Post-Impressionist exhibitions on modern painters working in the county. Bloomsbury continued to attract visitors to the Studland area, along with others settling in the region, including Everett's relative, Alexander Hillier Berens, who, with Louis Churchill, established the workshops of the Studland Art Industries.[41] Holroyd, considered the number of painters visiting Alderney Manor too numerous to list, with artists like the Lees and the Summers producing their own paintings of the Dorset landscape. Some, like Lamb, returned to live in Dorset in the early 1920s following their shocking experiences in the First World War.

38. Tickner, p.124.
39. *Dorset County Chronicle*, 20 April 1911.
40. Clive Holland, *The Gossipy Guide to Swanage and District*, C. Arthur Pearson, London, 1900, p.4.
41. See V&A collections w.25-1977http://collections.vam.ac.uk/item/O370966/letter-box-berens-alex

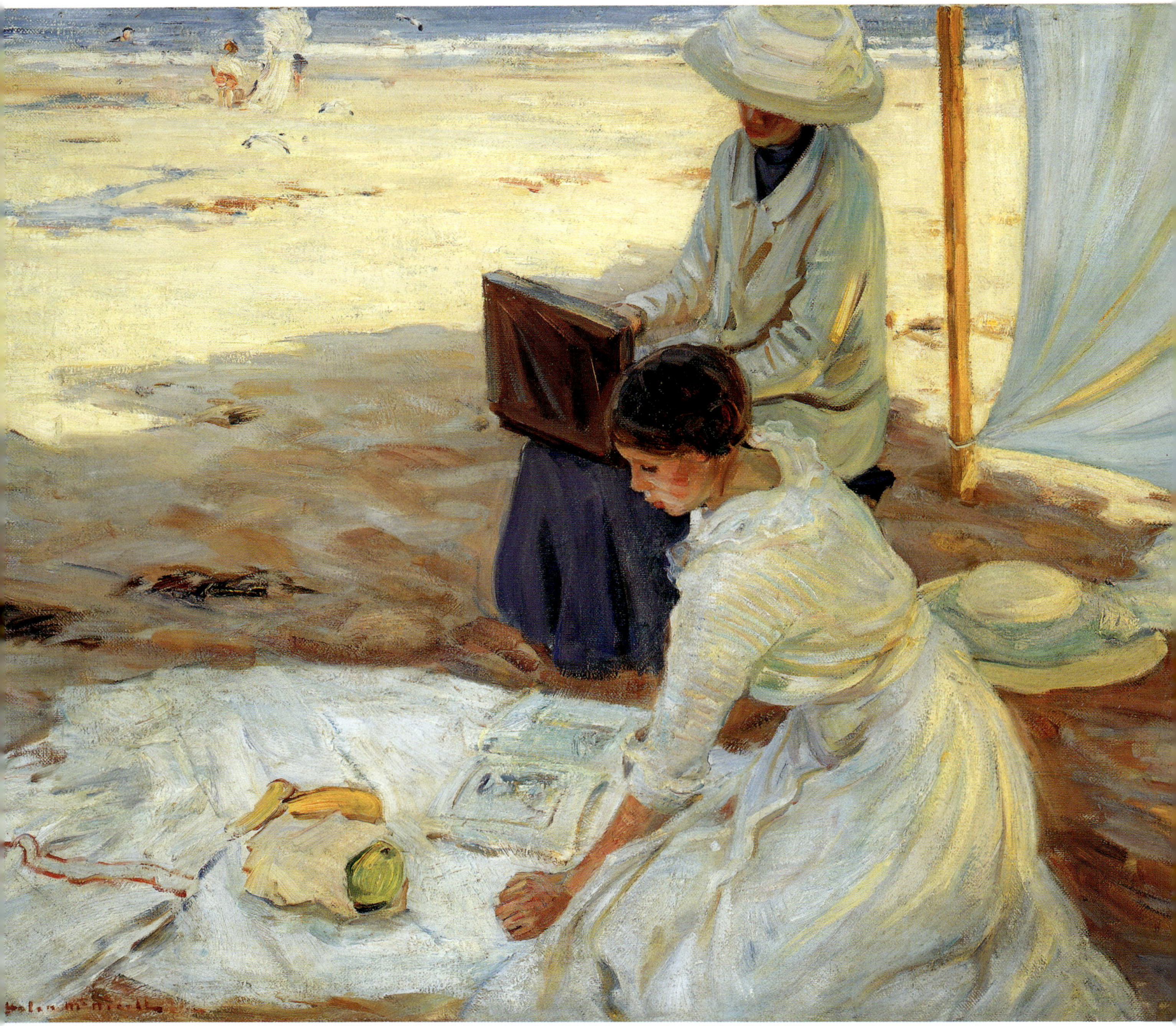

FIG. 108

Helen McNicoll / ***Under the Shadow of the Tent***

1914 / oil on canvas / 82 x 102 cm

EIGHT

THE END OF AN ERA

While Bloomsbury experimented with Modernism at Studland, other painters on the beaches of Purbeck continued to paint impressionistic works. Canadian-born Helen Galloway McNicoll was at the Slade between 1902 and 1904. After a short spell in Paris she spent some time at St Ives, studying with Algernon Talmage. There she met Dorothea Sharp, the British painter, with whom she formed a lifelong bond, travelling together, sharing studios and posing for each other. In the tradition of Berthe Morisot and Mary Cassatt, McNicoll's *plein air* work was restrained but flooded with the effects of sunlight. McNicoll and Sharp focused primarily on painting women and children in outdoor settings. For periods between 1910, 1913 and 1915, they settled at Swanage, where McNicoll painted the Impressionist landscapes, figure studies, seashore scenes and intimate subjects for which she is now best known.[1] Her Swanage beach scene, *Under the Shadow of the Tent* (fig. 108), contrasts markedly with Bell's *Studland Beach*, painted a couple of years earlier. With its references to Steer's Walberswick beach scenes of 1890, McNicoll's luminous picture uses light and shade to convey the women reading and painting, with the artist, thought to be Dorothea, under the shade of an awning. Reminiscent of Studland tents, the awning affords a degree of privacy from the public space of the beach – perhaps acting as a metaphor for the role of a female painter in Edwardian Britain. Already distanced from society through profound deafness from childhood, McNicoll sadly died at the age of 36 in Swanage, of diabetic complications.[2]

The Everetts remained in the Broadstone area and built their next home, Broadstone House. Grander and larger than Prospect, it was in the style of Edwin Lutyens, with twelve bedrooms, three bathrooms, two 'motor houses', a carpenter's shop, a tennis court and an orchard. Gertrude Jekyll advised on the garden, with its spectacular views over Poole Harbour towards Purbeck and the Isle of Wight, ideal for a landscape painter.[3] Katherine Everett also built a further two houses close by. Despite this show of affluence, comfort and domesticity, by 1917 the Everett marriage had irretrievably collapsed; Katherine was left to bring up their two sons and never saw Everett again. At the outbreak of war Everett hurried back to London and immersed himself in a world of clubs and artists, concluding: 'the country is deadly dull, the people utterly stupid.'

1. I am indebted to Bob Field for this information.
2. See Canadian Dictionary of Biography, www.biographi.ca/en/bio/mcnicoll_helen_galloway_14E.html, vol. XIV (1911–20); Kristina Huneault, 'Impressions of Difference: The Painted Canvases of Helen McNicoll', *Art History*, vol. 27, no. 2, Association of Art Historians, Oxford: Blackwell Publishing, 2004, pp.212–49.
3. Following their separation, Katherine was gardener-companion to Gertrude Jekyll's cousin Nelly Baring, at Burley in the New Forest.

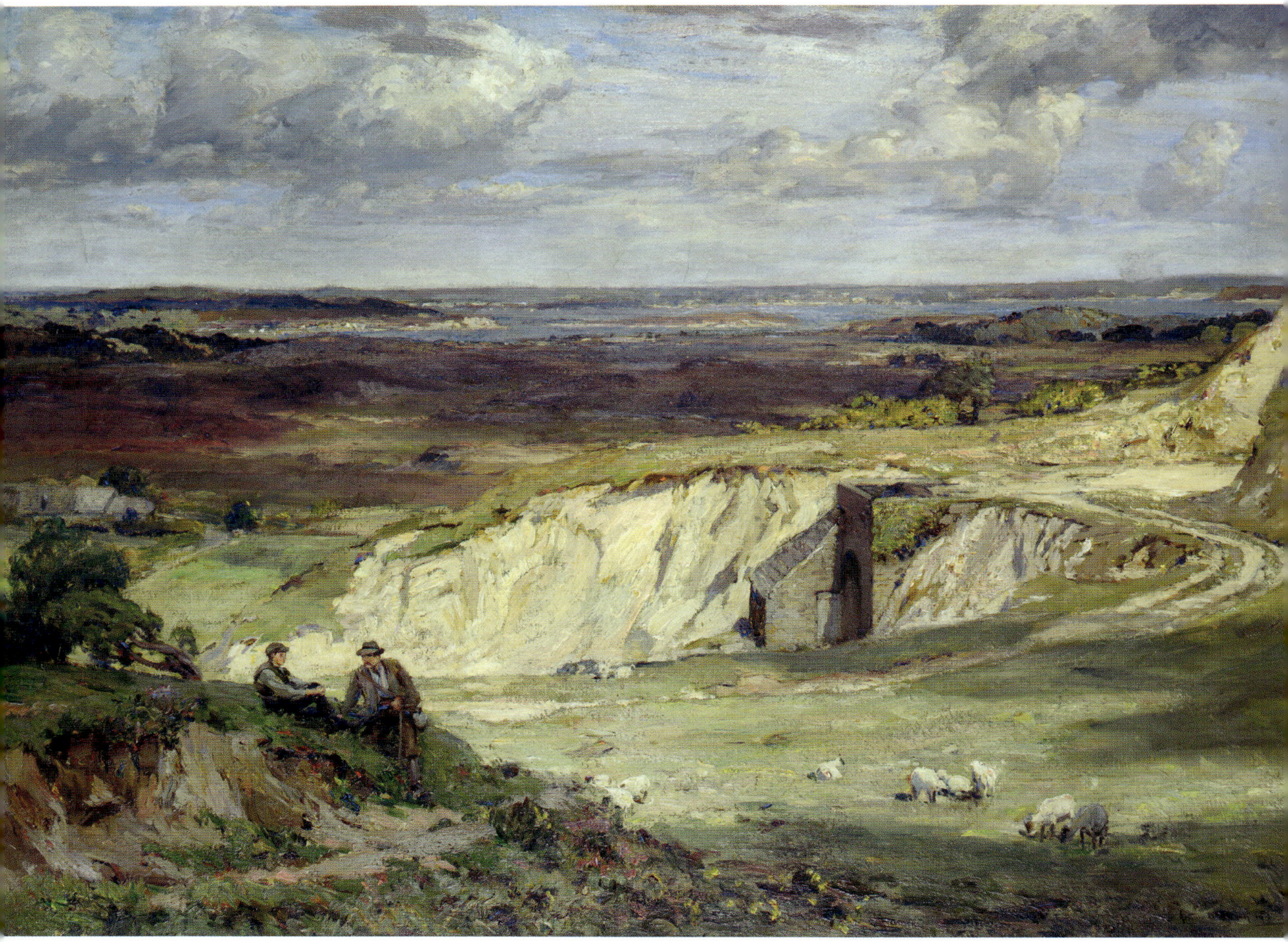

FIG. 109

Arthur Friedenson / ***Cloud Shadows, Isle of Purbeck***

1915 / oil on canvas / 82 x 120.5 cm

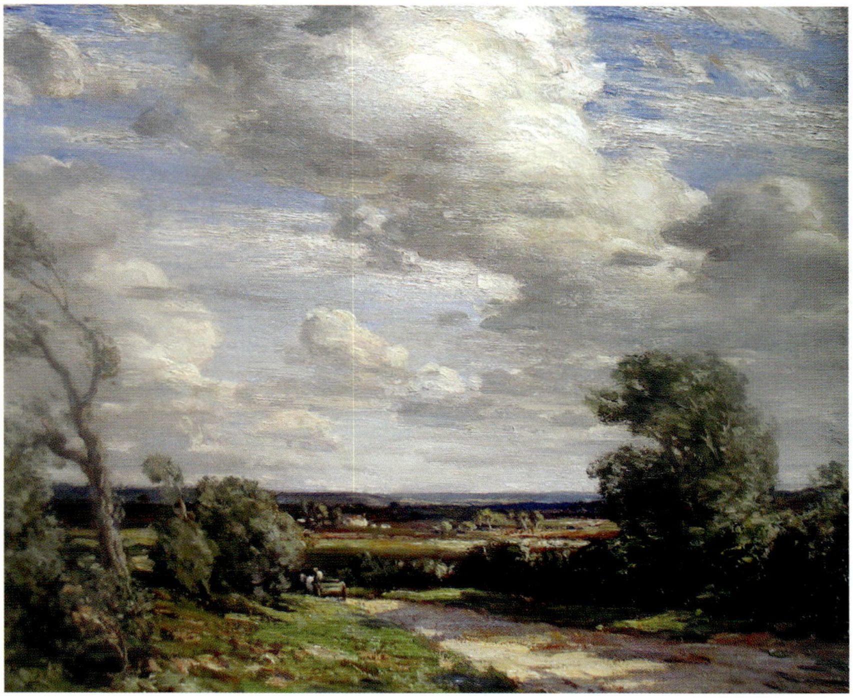

FIG. 110
Arthur Friedenson / *A Breezy Morning Near Wareham*
1914 / oil on canvas / 49.5 x 60.9 cm

FRIEDENSON, RICH AND HAMILTON HAY

Arthur Friedenson arrived in Dorset in 1910 from Staithes, where he was part of its artist colony. Friedenson was a regular exhibitor at the Royal Academy from the age of 17 and showed a number of Dorset subjects between 1911 and 1938. He was in Staithes from 1892 until 1908, joining artists Laura and Harold Knight, Rowland Hill and Robert and Isa Jobling. The Staithes Group had begun to disintegrate by 1907, as many were drawn south in search of fresh horizons – and, tellingly, Friedenson chose Dorset. The year he arrived in Purbeck he submitted two related paintings to the winter exhibition of the New English, where he would have seen other Dorset subjects.[4] This perhaps encouraged him to settle; he was to find enough subject matter to spend the rest of his life living close to Wareham (fig. 110). Everett befriended Friedenson soon after his arrival, and his memoirs indicate they exhibited together in Dorset.

Friedenson's *Cloud Shadows, Isle of Purbeck* (fig. 109) features the same setting as Steer's *Lime-Kiln* (fig. 77), but extends the panorama to show the view above Kingswood, including Greenlands Farm and Clotten Cottage on the Rempstone Estate. In the foreground, sheep are grazing, while the two men sitting in shadow on the outcrop on the left are distinguished by their clothes: a worker on the left, and the leisured gentleman to the right. Behind them the whitened, scarred face of the chalk quarry and lime kiln – both bathed in light – dominate the picture. Beyond, in the middle distance, the dark heath gives way to the unfolding panorama of Brownsea Island on the right, Furzey Island in the centre and the Arne Peninsula on

4. I am indebted to the work of Rosamund Jordan of the T.B. & R. Jordan Gallery, for all the information on Arthur Friedenson. See too Peter Phillips, *The Staithes Group*, Phillips and Sons Exhibition catalogue, Nottingham, 1993, p.46.

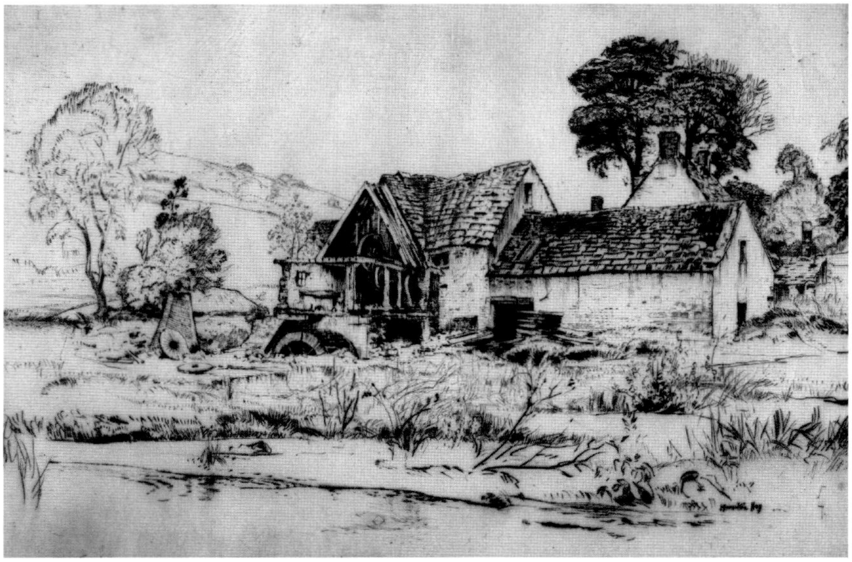

FIG. 111
James Hamilton Hay / *View of Arfleet Mill*
1914 / drypoint on paper

the left. Friedenson exhibited this major work at the Royal Academy in 1915. Despite the industrial elements of the scene he makes it clear that the play of light highlighting the landscape is his primary point of focus. As the title suggests, the painting confirms *The Times*' opinion of Friedenson as 'a follower of Constable', by focusing on the ever-changing light, tones and colours on the land formed by clouds scudding across the sky.[5] Friedenson had exhibited a related theme, *A Dorset Sand Quarry* at the RA in 1912, also shown in an exhibition of modern art in Liverpool the following year, and painted many scenes close to his home at Redcliff, Wareham.

The watercolourist Alfred Rich, also at the Slade during Everett's time, was working in Dorset at the time of Friedenson's arrival. It is unsurprising that Rich was at Corfe in 1909 so soon after Steer, as he often painted landscapes visited by Steer, such as Ludlow and Richmond. Steer's summer rambles, in turn, saw him following in the footsteps of Turner, an artist he greatly admired.[6] Rich visited the Everetts at Arfleet, and exhibited two Corfe subjects at the New English in 1910. Older than most of the group, he sat on the Slade-dominated Selecting Jury of the New English and was in the photograph of its selecting jury of 1904 (fig. 20). As Rich appeared in Orpen's 1909 oil caricature, *The Selecting Jury of the New English Art Club* (National Portrait Gallery), with MacColl, Brown, McEvoy, Orpen, Sickert, Steer, John, Tonks and Rothenstein, he would have heard where artists were heading for summer painting trips.[7] Rich admired Orpen and sat for his *The Sketcher*, 1910, *The Model* (Tate), 1911, and also for Tonks in 1917 (National Portrait Gallery).[8]

Also in Dorset just before the First World War was a New English artist from Liverpool: James Hamilton Hay. Like Everett and McNicoll, he studied under Talmage and focused on landscape painting but was also a printmaker. Based in Chelsea, he was in Dorset towards the end of his

5. 'A Landscape Exhibition', *The Times*, 5 January 1914, p.10.
6. McColl confirmed that Steer felt Turner to be 'a safe lead' over places to visit, such as Corfe, p.80.
7. Email correspondence with Alexander Rich, a descendant. Rich was a key source of biographical data for MacColl's 1945 biography of Steer.
8. 'Watercolour-Painting', in *Connoisseur*, vol. 50, 1918, suggests Rich was admired as 'the most scholarly of all living exponents of water-colour painting, his work showing a thorough knowledge of the tradition of the old English school combined with a modern directness of technique', p.57.

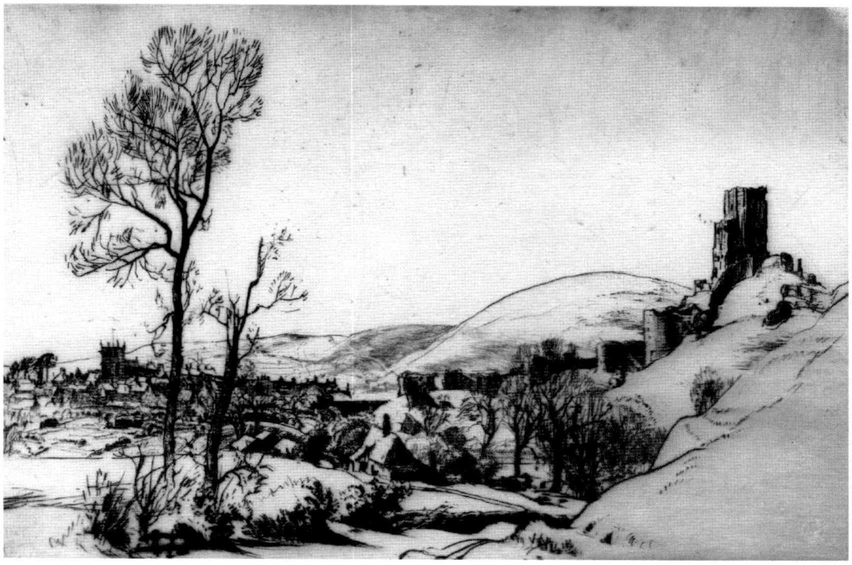

FIG. 112
James Hamilton Hay / *Corfe Village*
1914 / drypoint on paper

life in 1913 when he produced a series of etchings of Corfe Castle and the now derelict mill at Arfleet (figs 111 and 112), abandoned by the Everetts. His may be the last record before it fell into the clay pits and vanished from view. Hay's highly detailed drypoint also captures the drama and setting of the castle and the village of Corfe nestling in the Purbeck Hills.

INTO A POST-WAR WORLD

Slade painters and New English exhibitors of a more Modernist caste continued to visit during and after the First World War, such as Charles Ginner, Lucien Pissarro, Mark Gertler, Gilbert Spencer, Henry Lamb, Gwen Raverat, Richard Eurich, Cedric Morris and Gerald and Nora Summers. Another Slade group would settle during and after the war, many through connections made during this earlier period. Better known, they include Paul Nash, with his seaside surrealism based on Swanage and the famous Shell Guide to *Dorset*, Henry Lamb, Lucien Pissarro and Richard Eurich.[9] In 1915, William Rothenstein worked on a commission at Moreton House near Dorchester, to paint the portrait of Sir Ernest Debenham. He recalled Debenham was 'full of projects for the improvement of his villagers and of new methods of farming which startled the conservative natives'.[10] A scheme involving a new village hall there saw John Nash and Dora Carrington staying near Briantspuddle in 1916, to work with MacDonald Gill towards a set of murals, never executed.[11] After the war Francis Newbery, founder of the Rennie Macintosh-designed Glasgow School of Art, and the painter Frances Hodgkins, settled at Corfe. The Spencer Watsons moved to Dunshay Manor in Purbeck having visited Studland before the war. A successful portrait painter, Spencer Watson brought London artists, like Gerald Kelly, to Dorset to paint, and they exhibited at local art clubs and societies.[12] In East Dorset, local art societies gained

9. Although in Hampshire, Bournemouth also played host to London painters. Sargent visited Robert Louis Stevenson in 1885 to paint his portrait. See New English Art Club, Summer Exhibition, Dudley Gallery, April 1887, no. 84, *Robt. Louis Stevenson and Mrs. Stevenson*. A sketch. Aubrey Beardsley moved to Boscombe in mid-August, 1896. Leslie Ward moved to Bournemouth in childhood and trained at the Drummond Road Art School in Bournemouth under Arthur Lister Lobley and the RA School, where he exhibited from 1915 to 1959. Lucy Kemp Welch, involved with Herkomer's school, also lived and painted in the Bournemouth area.
10. William Rothenstein, *Men and Memories: Recollections of William Rothenstein, 1900–1922*, New York: Coward-McCann, Inc., 1932, p.290.
11. Sue Taylor, *The Bladen Estate Centenary Exhibition: A Celebration of Debenham's Vision 1914–1952*, exhibition booklet, Briantspuddle Village Hall, August 2014.
12. They were part of a larger circle including Kerrison Preston, Bournemouth lawyer and collector of Victorian paintings, and art historian Archibald George Blomefield Russell from Swanage, both authorities on William Blake. See too Ilay Cooper, *Purbeck Arcadia: Dunshay Manor and the Spencer Watsons*, Wimborne: Dovecote Press, 2015, p.152.

in importance, and by the 1920s Bournemouth Art College, Poole Art School and the Poole and East Dorset Art Society (formed in 1924) continued the wealth of paintings and artists working in the county.

The purpose of this book has been to reclaim the importance of Dorset, and Purbeck in particular, in the story of British landscape painting at a moment when landscape itself was at the forefront of modern British art; from the Impressionism of Steer and Tonks, to the colourism and lyricism of Augustus John and the Post-Impressionism of the Bloomsbury painters Vanessa Bell and Roger Fry. Central to this narrative has been the life and work of John Everett, together with his wife Katherine. Recovery of the personal and professional networks around the Everetts has thrown important new detail on the life, interaction and work of the circle of Slade painters which included Orpen and John. Everett was instrumental in persuading artists to visit Purbeck, providing figures such as Steer and Tonks with the subject matter for some of their most important mature works.

PURBECK'S UNIQUE LEGACY

Through the Dorset paintings discussed here we can chart the evolution of British approaches to landscape in the first decades of the twentieth century, from the *plein air* explosion of the late 1800s, which continued into the 1920s through the work of Whitehead and Friedenson, to Bloomsbury's return to the studio. Littered with evidence of past and recent industrial activity, the Purbeck landscape offered heathland, medieval water meadows, barrows, pools in disused clay pits, chalk and lime pits, dramatic coastline and beaches. Its relative remoteness, close by burgeoning Bournemouth, compelled artistic experimentation. Redefining the emergence of landscape painting in the early twentieth century within a specific geographic context has offered a different way to comprehend a group of painters who appear stylistically diverse. Furthermore, by understanding Purbeck in this period as a form of artists' colony, it has enabled the recovery of the careers of a number of overlooked artists who, aside from Everett, include: Evelyn Cheston, Harry van der Weyden, Arthur Friedenson and Helen McNicoll – painters who deserved to be considered within the wider narrative of British landscape painting in this period up to the First World War. The relative accessibility of Purbeck from London for Edwardian painters ensured that its unique landscape combination offered them an irresistible appeal, which went beyond Hardy's rolling images of a timeless Dorset to something far more spectacular and painterly.

BIBLIOGRAPHY

Adams, Steven, and Anna Gruetzner Robins, eds, *Gendering Landscape Art*, Manchester: Manchester University Press and Rutgers University Press, 2000

Anderson, Margaret Steele, *The Study of Modern Painting*, New York: The Century, 1914

Arnold, Bruce, *Orpen: Mirror to an Age*, London: Jonathan Cape, 1981

Baedeker, Karl, *Great Britain: Handbook for Travellers*, London: T. Fisher Unwin, 1910

Baldry, A.L.,'The Coast of Dorset', *Art Journal*, 1907

Behlmer, George K., 'The Gypsy Problem in Victorian England', *Victorian Studies*, vol. 28, nno. 2 (Winter, 1985), pp.231–53, Indiana University Press

Bell, Clive, *Art*, London: Chatto & Windus, 1914

Carman, Jillian, *Uplifting the Colonial Philistine: Florence Philips and the Making of the Johannesburg Art Gallery*, Johannesburg: Wits University Press, 2006

Cecil, David, *Some Dorset Country Houses, A Personal Selection*, Wimborne: The Dovecote Press, 1985

Chambers, Emma, 'Slade School Influences on the Camden Town Group 1896–1910', Helena Bonett, Ysanne Holt, Jennifer Mundy, eds, *The Camden Town Group in Context*, Tate Research Publication, May 2012, www.tate.org.uk/art/research-public ations/camden-town-group/emma-chambers-slade-school-influences-on-the-camden-town-group-1896-1910-r1104373 (accessed 20 August 2015).

Cheston, Charles, *Evelyn Cheston Member of the New English Art Club, 1908–1929*, London: Faber & Faber Ltd, 1931

Christian, Jessica, *Wyn George, Traveller and Artist.* Wimborne Minster: The Dovecote Press, 2013

Clausen, George, *Six Lectures on Painting. Delivered to the Students of the Royal Academy of Arts in London, January 1904*, London: Methuen, 1904

Cooper, Ilay, *Purbeck Revealed*, Bath: Pembroke Publishing, 2004

Cooper, Ilay, *Purbeck Arcadia: Dunshay Manor and the Spencer Watsons*, Wimborne: Dovecote Press, 2015

Corbett, David Peters, *The Modernity of English Art, 1914–30*, Trowbridge: Redwood Books, 1997

Corbett, D.P., Y. Holt and F. Russell, eds, *The Geographies of Englishness*, New Haven and London: Yale, 2002

Davies, Peter, *Art in Poole and Dorset*, Poole: Poole Historic Trust, 1987

Dixon, Marion Hepworth, 'The Landscape Paintings of Mr. H. Hughes-Stanton', *The Studio*, vol. 42, 1908

Dutta, Shanta, *Ambivalence in Hardy: A Study of His Attitude to Women*, Basingstoke: Macmillan; New York: St Martin's Press, 2000

East, Alfred, *The Art of Landscape Painting in Oil Colour*, London: Cassell & Co., 1906

Everett, Katherine, *Bricks and Flowers: Memoirs of Katherine Everett*, London: Constable, 1949

Farr, Dennis, *English Art, 1870–1940*, Oxford: University Press, 1978, 1984

Forster, E.M., *Howard's End*, London: Arnold, 1910

Fothergill, John, *James Dickson Innes*, London: Faber & Faber, 1946, pp.7–11

Fothergill, John, 'The Principles of Teaching Drawing at the Slade School', in *The Slade: A Collection of Drawings and Some Pictures Done by Past and Present Students of the London Slade School of Art, 1893–1907*, London: Slade School, 1907, John Fothergill, ed.

Fry, R., and D. McCarthy, *Manet and the Post-Impressionists*, London, Grafton Gallery, 8 November 1910–15 January 1911, London: Ballantyne and Company Ltd

Galbally, Ann, *Charles Conder: The Last Bohemian*, Melbourne: Miegunyah Press, Melbourne University Publishing, 2002

Galbally, Ann, and Anne Gray, eds, *Letters from Smike: The Letters of Arthur Streeton 1890–1943*, Melbourne: OUP, 1989, p.116

Garnett, David, *The Sailor's Return*, London: Harmondsworth, Penguin, 1978

Gathorne-Hardy, R., ed., *Ottoline: The Early Memoirs of Ottoline Morrell*, London: Faber, 1963

Gaunt, William, *A Concise History of English Painting*, London: Thames & Hudson, 1976

Grimsditch, Herbert, B., 'Mr Harry Van Der Weyden', *The Studio*, vol. 94, 1927

Haggard, Henry Rider, *Rural England. Being an Account of Agricultural and Social Researches Carried Out in 1901 and 1902*, vols. 1 and 2, London: Longmans, Green and Co., 1902, revised version 1906

Haines, F.H., 'Frederick Whitehead', *The Dorset Yearbook*, The Society of Dorset Men, 1938

Hardy, Thomas, *Tess of the d'Urbervilles: A pure woman*, London: James R. Osgood, 1892

Hardy, Thomas, *The Return of the Native*, London: Penguin, 1978

Harper, Charles G., *The Dorset Coast*, London: Chapman & Hall, 1905

Harrison, Charles, *English Art and Modernism, 1900–1939*, London: Allen Lane, 1981

Hattersley, Roy, *The Edwardians*, London: Abacus, 2004, revised 2006

Heath, Sydney, *The Heart of Wessex*, London: Blackie and Son Limited, 1910

Heinrich Heine, trans. Charles Godfrey Leland, 'Florentine Nights, Second Night', *The Prose and Poetical Works of Heinrich Heine*, 20 volumes, London: William Heinemann, 1906

Hissey, James John, *An English Holiday with Car and Camera*, London: Macmillan & Co. Ltd, 1908

Hoff, Ursula, 'Charles Conder, Arthur Streeton and Tom Roberts', *Apollo*, 1983

Holland, Clive (pseudonym for Hankinson, Charles James), *The Gossipy Guide to Swanage and District*, London: C.A. Pearson, 1900

Holland, Clive (pseudonym for Hankinson, Charles James), 'The Work of Frederick Whitehead, a Painter of Thomas Hardy's "Wessex"', *The Studio*, vol. xxxii, no. 135, June 1904

Holland, Clive (pseudonym for Hankinson, Charles James), *Wessex*. London: Adam & Charles Black, 1906

Holroyd, Michael, *Augustus John*, London: Pimlico, 2011

Holt, Ysanne, *Philip Wilson Steer*, Bridgend: Seren, 1992

Holt, Ysanne, 'Nature and Nostalgia, Philip Wilson Steer and the Edwardian Landscape', *Oxford Art Journal*, vol. 19, no. 2, 1996

Holt, Ysanne, *British Artists and the Modernist Landscape*, Aldershot: Ashgate Publishing, 2003

Hone, Joseph, *The Life of Henry Tonks*, London: Heinemann Press, 1939

Hopkins, Robert Thurston, *Thomas Hardy's Dorset*, New York: Appleton, 1922

Huneault, Kristina, 'The Painted Canvases of Helen McNicoll', *Art History*, vol. 27, no. 2., 2004

Hynes, Samuel, *The Edwardian Turn of Mind*, London: Pimlico, 1991

Ironside, Robin, *Wilson Steer*, British Artists Series, ed. John Rothenstein, London: Phaidon, 1943

John, A., *Chiaroscuro: Fragments of an Autobiography*, London: Jonathan Cape, 1952

John, A., *Finishing Touches*, London: Jonathan Cape, 1964

John, Romilly, *The Seventh Child: A Retrospect*, London: William Heinemann Ltd, 1932

Johnson, Jane, *Works Exhibited at the Royal Society of British Artists, 1824–1893 and the New English Art Club, 1888–1917*, Suffolk: Antique Collectors' Club Ltd, 1975

Johnson, Jane, and Anna Gruetzner Robins, *The Dictionary of British Artists 1880–1940*, Suffolk: Antique Collectors Club, 1976

King, James, 'Bloomsbury in Dorset: Manufacturing Modernisms at Poole Pottery 1914–1939', *Interpreting Ceramics*, no. 15, 2013

Knight, Laura, *Oil Paint and Grease Paint*, Macmillan: London, 1936

Konody, P.G., and Sidney Dark, *Sir William Orpen: Artist and Man*, London: Seeley Service & Co., 1932

Lambert, Andrew D., Robert J. Blyth, Jan Rüger, eds, *The Dreadnought and the Edwardian Age*, Aldershot: Ashgate Publishing, 2011

Laperrière, C. Baile de, ed., *The New English Art Club Exhibitors 1886–2001*, 4 vols, Calne: Hilmarton, 2002

Laughton, Bruce, 'Steer and French Painting', *Apollo*, vol. 91, 1970

Laughton, Bruce, *Philip Wilson Steer, 1860–1942*, Oxford: Clarendon Press, 1971

Lea, Hermann, *Thomas Hardy's Wessex*, London: Macmillan and Co. Ltd, 1913

Light, Vivienne, *Circles and Tangents: Art in the shadow of Cranborne Chase*, Frome: Canterton Books, 2011, 2012

Luckyj, Natalie, 'McNicoll, Helen Galloway', *Dictionary of Canadian Biography*, vol. 14, University of Toronto/Université Laval, 2003

MacColl, Dugald Sutherland, *Life, Work and Setting of Philip Wilson Steer*, London: Faber, 1945

MacColl, Dugald Sutherland, *Nineteenth-Century Art*, Glasgow: James Maclehose and Sons, *c.*1902

McConkey, Kenneth, *Memory and Desire: Painting Britain and Ireland at the Turn of the Twentieth Century*, Aldershot: Ashgate Publishing, 2004

McConkey, Kenneth, *The New English: A History of the New English Art Club*, London: Royal Academy of Arts, 2006

McKenzie, Tessa, *The Art Schools of London*, London: Chapman and Hall, 1895

Marlborough, Andrew, 'Harry van der Weyden: Forgotten Boy Wonder', unpublished essay, Southampton Institute, 2003

Masterman, C.F.G., *The Condition of England*, London: Methuen, 1909

Mate, Chas. H., and Chas. Riddle, *Bournemouth: 1810–1910. The History of a Modern Health and Pleasure Resort*, Bournemouth: Messrs. W. Mate & Sons Ltd, 1910

Mate, W., *Dorsetshire Illustrated 1900*, W. Mate and Sons, Illustrated Guides, reprint by Chantry Press, Dewsbury, 1986

Meates, Joyce, *Goathorn, Studland, Dorset: A Forgotten Clayworking Community*, Swanage: Purbeck View Publishing, 2013

Meynell, Wilfrid, 'William Orpen', *The Artist*, August 1901, vol. XXXI, no. 260.

Millgate, Michael, *Thomas Hardy: A Biography Revisited*, Oxford: Oxford University Press, 2006

Morrell, Ottoline, *Ottoline: The Early Memoirs of Lady Ottoline Morrell*, ed. Robert Gathorne-Hardy, London: Faber, 1963

Morris, Edward, *French Art in Nineteenth-century Britain*, New Haven and London: Yale University Press, 2005

Newman, John, and Nikolaus Pevsner, *The Buildings of England, Dorset*, London: Penguin Books, 1972

Nunn, Pamela Gerrish, *Victorian Women Artists*, London: Women's Press, 1987

O'Day, Alan, ed., *The Edwardian Age: Conflict and Stability, 1900–1914*, London: Macmillan, 1979

O'Sullivan, Timothy, *Thomas Hardy: An Illustrated Biography*, London: Macmillan, 1975

Pankhurst, Estelle Sylvia, *The Suffragette: The History of the Women's Militant Suffrage Movement, 1905–1910*, New York: Sturgis and Walton, 1911

Panton, Jane. *Fresh Leaves and Green Pastures*, London: Eveleigh Nash, 1909

Peters, John, David Couling and Michael Ridley, eds, *Bournemouth Then and Now*, Blandford Press, Poole, 1978

Public Catalogue Foundation catalogues, *London: The Slade and UCL*, PCF catalogue, London, 2005

Purdy, Richard Little, and Michael Millgate, eds, *The Collected Letters of Thomas Hardy*, vol. 2, Oxford: Clarendon Press, 1980

Ricketts, Charles, 'Puvis de Chavannes: A Chapter from "Modern Painters"', *The Burlington Magazine*, vol. XIII, 1908

Roe, Sue, *Gwen John: A Life*, London: Chatto & Windus, 2002

Rothenstein, John, *Modern English Painters: Sickert to Smith*, London: Eyre and Spottiswoode, 1952

Rothenstein, William, *Men and Memories: A History of Arts 1872–1922*, London: Faber and Faber, 1931, 1932

Ruskin, John, *The Art of England*, Orpington: George Allen, 1884

Rutherston, Albert, 'From Orpen and Gore to the Camden Town Group', *The Burlington Magazine*, vol. 83, no. 485, 1943

Rutter, Frank, *Art in My Time*, London: Rich & Cowan, 1933

Saywell, David, and Jacob Simon, eds, *Complete Illustrated catalogue / National Portrait Gallery*, London: National Portrait Gallery, Unicorn Press, *c.*2004

Saxleby, F. Outwin, *A Thomas Hardy Dictionary*, London: Kegan Paul, 1911

Schwabe, Randolph, 'Three Teachers: Brown, Tonks and Steer', *The Burlington Magazine*, vol. 82 (June 1943), pp. 141–6

Schwabe, Randolph, 'Reminiscences of Fellow Students', *The Burlington Magazine*, vol. 82, no. 478, 1943

Seymour, Miranda, *Ottoline Morrell: Life on a Grand Scale*, London: Sceptre, 1998

Sherren, Wilkinson, *The Wessex of Romance*, London: new and revised edition, Francis Griffiths, 1908

Shone, Richard, *The Art of Bloomsbury*, London: Tate, 1999

Silvester, Norman L., 'Harry Van Der Weyden', *Bulletin of the Russell-Cotes Art Gallery and Museum*, vol. XV, September 1936

Slater, Robert, 'Artists' Colonies in Staithes and Runswick Bay, *c.*1880–1914', unpublished doctoral thesis submitted for the degree of Doctor of Philosophy, University of Leicester, March 2010

Smith, Sidney Ure, ed., 'The Art of Arthur Streeton', *Art in Australia*, Sydney, 1929

Speight, Robert, *William Rothenstein: The Portrait of an Artist in His Time*, London: Eyre and Spottiswoode, 1962

Stansky, Peter, *On or About December 10: Early Bloomsbury and Its Intimate World*, Cambridge, MA, and London: Harvard, 1997

Stephenson, Andrew, 'Introduction: Edwardian Art and Its Legacies', *Visual Culture in Britain*, vol. 14, no. 1, 2013

Stoyan, Ronald, *Atlas of Great Comets*, Cambridge: Cambridge University Press, 2015

Swaine, Hume, *An Artist's Rambles Round About Swanage*, London: Hume Swaine, 1893, reproduced Weymouth: Gallant Publications, 1989

Symons, Arthur, 'The New English Art Club', *The Saturday Review*, 1 December 1906

Taylor, Brandon, *Art for the Nation: Exhibitions and the London Public 1747–2001*, Manchester: Manchester University Press, 1999

Thornton, Alfred Henry Robinson, *Fifty Years of the New English Art Club, 1886–1935*, London: Curwen Press, 1935

Tickner, Lisa, *Modern Life and Modern Subjects: British Art in the Early Twentieth Century*, New Haven and London: Yale University Press, 2000

Tillyard, Stella, *The Impact of Modernism: The Visual Arts in Edwardian England*, London: Routledge, 1987

Tomson, Arthur, 'Dorchester', *The Art Journal*, 1901

Tovey, David, *Pioneers of St Ives Art at Home and Abroad, 1889–1914*, Tewkesbury: Wilson Books, 2008

Treves, Frederick, *Highways and Byways in Dorset*, London: Macmillan and Co. Ltd, 1906

Trumble, Angus, and Andrea Wolk Rager, eds, *Edwardian Opulence: British Art at the Dawn of the Twentieth Century*, New Haven: Yale University Press, 2013

Watkins, Nicholas, 'Augustus John and the Everetts', *Apollo*, 1974, pp.188–93.

Wedmore, Frederick, 'Bertram Priestman', *Art Journal*, 1907

Wedmore, Frederick, *Some of the Moderns*, London: Virtue & Co., 1909

West, Vita Sackville, *The Edwardians*, London: Hogarth Press, 1930

Whybrow, Marion, *St Ives, 1893–1993: Portrait of an Art Colony*, Suffolk: ACC Art Books, 1994

Wilkes, James, *A Fractured Landscape of Modernity: Culture and Conflict in the Isle of Purbeck*, Basingstoke: Palgrave Macmillan, 2014

Windle, Bertram C.A., *The Wessex of Thomas Hardy*, London: John Lane, 1906

Wood, Martin T., 'The Pictures of Ambrose McEvoy', *The Studio*, vol. 42, 1908

Woolf, Virginia, *The Letters*, vol. 1: 'The Flight of the Mind', 1888–1912, ed. Nigel Nicolson, London: Chatto & Windus, 1975

Woolf, Virginia, *The Letters*, vol. 2: 'The Questions of Things Happening', 1912–1922, ed. Nigel Nicolson with Joanne Trautmann, London: Chatto & Windus, 1976

Woolf, Virginia, 'Mr. Bennett and Mrs Brown', 1924, The Essays of Virginia Woolf, vol. 3, ed. Andrew McNellie, London: Hogarth Press, 1988 [421], London: Hogarth Press, 1924. (A paper read to the Heretics, Cambridge, on 18 May 1924)

Woolf, Virginia, *Roger Fry: A Biography*, Hogarth Press, London, 1940

Wray, Christopher, *Arthur Streeton: Painter of Light*, Queensland: Jacaranda Wiley, 1993

Yarker, Gwen, *A Victorian's View of Dorset: The Life and Watercolours of Henry Joseph Moule, 1825–1904*, Dorchester: Henry Ling Ltd, 1997

EXHIBITION CATALOGUES

Arthur Friedenson and the Staithes Group, Marlow (Philips and Sons), 1976
Arthur Streeton 1867–1943, Geoffrey Smith, Melbourne (National Gallery of Victoria), 1995–6
The Bladen Estate Centenary Exhibition: A Celebration of Debenham's Vision, 1914–1952, Sue Taylor, Briantspuddle (Briantspuddle Village Hall), 2014
The Bloomsbury Group Artists, Tony Bradshaw, Sherborne (Sherborne House), 2002
Catalogue of a Collection of Oil Paintings, Watercolours & Drawings Formed by the Late William Evans, Judge of the mid-Wales County Court Circuit, London (Goupil Gallery, William Marchant & Co.), 1918
Catalogue of an Exhibition of Paintings by P. Wilson Steer, London (The Goupil Gallery, William Marchant & Co.), 1909
Formed Catalogue of the Drawings and Paintings from the Studio of the late Augustus John, 20 July 1962, London (Christie's), 1962
Commemorative Exhibition of Works by Late Members. Winter Exhibition, 52nd year, 7 January to 11 March 1933, London (Royal Academy), 1933
The Edwardians: Secrets and Desires, Anne Gray, ed., Edinburgh (National Gallery of Scotland), 2004
Edwardians and After, Mary Anne Stevens, London (Royal Academy of Arts), 1988
An Exhibition of Paintings by Modern Masters, London (Leicester Gallery), 1931
Frederick Whitehead – Dorset Landscapes, Dorchester (Dorset County Museum), 1988.
Gwen John and Augustus John, David Fraser Jenkins and Chris Stephens, eds, London (Tate), 2004
Henry Tonks and the 'Art of Pure Drawing', L. Morris, ed., Norwich (Sch. A. Mus.), 1985
Impressionism in Britain, Kenneth McConkey with Anna Gruetzner Robins, London (Barbican), 1995
John Everett Marine Painter: A Memorial Exhibition, E.H.H. Archibald, London (National Maritime Museum), 1964
John Quinn, 1870–1925, Collection of Paintings, Water Colors, Drawings & Sculpture, Forbes Watson, New York (The Art Center), 1926
Lines from Nature and Memory, London (Pyms Gallery), 23 November 2011–6 January 2012
Manet and the Post-Impressionists, R. Fry and D. McCarthy, London (Grafton Gallery), 8 November 1910–15 January 1911
Memorial Exhibition of the Works of Philip Wilson Steer, OM, 1860–1942, London (Tate), 1943
P.W. Steer 1860–1942, London (Tate), 1942
Philip Wilson Steer, 1860–1942, Paintings and Watercolours, Cambridge (Fitzwilliam Museum, Arts Council of Great Britain), 1986
Watercolours of P. Wilson Steer from the Blackwell Family Collection, Birkenhead (Williamson Art Gallery), 1944
Wessex, London (Dickinson & Foster), 1895
William Orpen: Early Work, London (Pyms Gallery), 1981

BOOKS OF REFERENCE

Calendars, University College, London
Dictionary of British Artists 1880–1940, J. Johnson and A. Gruetzner [sic], eds, Suffolk: Antique Collectors' Club, 1976
The Dictionary of British Women Artists, Sara Gray, Oxford: Casemate Publishers, 2009
Dictionary of Canadian Biography
The Dorset Year Book, 1991
The Eton College Register, 1871–1880
Kelly's Directory, Dorchester, 1903
The New English Art Club Exhibitors, 1886–2001, de Laperriere, Charles Baile, ed., Calne: Hilmarton Manor Press, 2002
Oxford Dictionary of National Biography
Proceedings of the Dorset Natural History and Antiquarian Field Club, Dorchester: Dorset County Chronicle, vols xix–xxxv, 1898–1914

UNPUBLISHED MATERIAL

Private collections
Augustus John family letters
Geoffrey Blackwell papers
Everett, John, *Wicked Devils, Wicked Devils*, unpublished manuscript, 1945
Everett family papers
Rempstone Estate Papers

Hyman Kreitman Research Centre, Tate Britain
Private papers of Geoffrey Blackwell
New English Art Club Archive
Picture Files

Paul Mellon Centre for British Art
Frank Simpson Archive

National Maritime Museum
John Everett Collection

University College of London Special Collections (Slade Archive)
in Chaplin, Stephen, Report by Slade School of Art Archivist 1990–97, 'A Slade School Reader 1868–1975, a compendium of documents in UCL', vol. 2, 1868–1930, *Slade archive MSS ADD400 (A623, A631)*, 19 March 1998
Signing-in Books, 1895–1900

NEWSPAPERS AND PERIODICALS

Apollo
Art History
Art Journal
The Artist
Burlington Magazine
Connoisseur
Dorset County Chronicle
Harper's New Monthly Magazine
Interpreting Ceramics
The Listener
The Saturday Review
The Studio
Sunday Times
The Times
Victorian Studies
Visual Culture in Britain

INDEX

Numbers in **bold** are illustrations

ACKNOWLEDGEMENTS

By the late nineteenth century, many landscape painters from Britain, Europe and America had visited the West Country, inspired by Cornwall's Newlyn and St Ives and Dorset's Frome valley and Purbeck. Many West Country painters trained at London's Slade School of Fine Art and exhibited landscapes at the New English Art Club. So it is apt to hold an exhibition of Wessex paintings at Bristol's Royal West of England Academy in Clifton. Provincial centres like Bristol, with its lively art academy, provided an important artistic training, operating in parallel with the Slade. Henry Tonks, Roger Fry and both Titcomb brothers attended Clifton College, with Augustus John close by. I am truly grateful to director Alison Bevan and the RWA trustees for embracing this project with curator Gemma Brace. The RWA team has seen the project come to fruition with charm, enthusiasm and professionalism, and I thank them all.

The Paul Mellon Centre for British Art has generously supported the project by funding my research curatorship and publication. Mark Hallett, Martin Postle, Mary Peskett Smith and the Advisory Panel have been very understanding and encouraging. Through a joint partnership with the RWA, the National Maritime Museum generously covered the costs of the conservation, reframing and image reproduction of their loans. My Caird Research Fellowship at NMM enabled the complete assessment of its collection of John Everett's work. The exhibition would not have been possible without the generosity and support of the trustees of the Foyle Foundation, to whom I extend my personal thanks, as well as to the Anthony Pitt-Rivers Trust Fund. Carlyle Membership awarded by the London Library also proved invaluable.

Sue Hayward, at whose instigation I embarked on the project, and Rebecca Sitch have given support, friendship and encouragement, and I extend to them my heartfelt thanks. I am grateful to Sabina ffrench Blake for her guidance, sharing discoveries and our days exploring Purbeck. Sue, Sabina, Carolyn Holmes, Eliza Oxley, Roger Peers and Jonny Yarker all read my various drafts and made perceptive, helpful comments. I am indebted to Rebecca, who juggled reviewing the book with coping with lively toddler, Joseph.

Will and Caroline Everett answered my endless queries with humour and enthusiasm. Helen and Jonathan Barnes have been keenly supportive throughout and, together with Barbara and John Crowell, produced much invaluable material. I have enjoyed getting to know them and am very sad that Barbara died before the project she did so much to encourage was completed. Fine art photographer Dave Penman has, as ever, been a pleasure to work with. Kenneth McConkey has given long-distance advice and practical help, as has Ysanne Holt. A special thanks goes to Julius White for both his kindness and generosity over the use of images. Finally, deep appreciation goes to my husband Tim.

I am very grateful to all the following for their support, enthusiasm and time:

Carlotta Barrow; Sue Beckett; Hugh Belsey; Mark Bond; Richard and Susie Bond; Tony and Frances Bradshaw; Jo and Joff Crichton; Jessica Christian; Jill Cook; Ilay Cooper; Jeremy Drax; Anthony du Boulay; Peter Duffell; Robert Field; Sarah Foot; Alison Fraser; Patrick Frazer; Henrietta Garnett; Charlotte Gerard; Rose Goad; Pauline Gyles; Bryony Hartley; Andrew Hawkes; Richard Heathcote; Felicity Hedger; Caroline Hirst; Alan Hobart of Pyms Gallery; Jane Hylton; Helen Ivaldi; Anthony Jaggard; Lianne Jarrett; Rebecca John; Tom and Rosamund Jordan; Helen Kennett; Hester Kirkham; Tim Knox; Dominic Lee; Margarette Lincoln; Rupert Maas; Lara Manningham-Buller; Belinda Matthews; Jon Murden; Virginia Nicholson; Richard Ormond; Christopher Pearson; Roger Peers; Richard Pikesley; Jeff Pilkington; Roger Quarm; Christine Rew; Alexander Rich; James Russell; Douglas and Sarah Ryder; Hilly and James Ryder; Sam Shaw; Mike and Joseph Sitch; Denis Smale; Doreen Smith; Geoffrey Smith, Chairman, Sotheby's, Australia; Michael Smith; Dan and Jenny Thompson; Lisa Tickner; David Tovey; Philip Trevelyan; Robert Upstone; Will Vaughan; Duncan Walker; Giles Waterfield; Annabel Watt; Janet Watts; Ian West; George Wickham; Toby Wiggins; Mary-Kay Wilmers; Barnaby Wright; Sophia Wright; and the generous people who prefer to remain anonymous.

INSTITUTIONS

UCL special collections/Slade School of Art: Liv Mills, Mandy Wise. London Library. Tate Archive: Lisa Cole; Adrian Glew; Anna Golodnitsky; Jane Kennedy; Maxine Miller; David Thompson. National Portrait Gallery: Emma Butterfield; Paul Cox; Juliet French; Imogen Lyons; David McNeff; Ruth Slaney. Paul Mellon Centre: Charlotte Brunskill; Emma Floyd; Mark Hallett; Martin Postle; Mary Peskett Smith. NMM: Jon Astbury and team; Robert Blyth; Geraldine Charles; Birthe Christensen and her team of conservators; Lizelle de Jager; Kevin Fewster; Sarah Kmosena; Philippa Mackenzie; Nigel Rigby; Christine Ryder.

With gratitude to all the private lenders and lending institutions for their generosity: Aberdeen Art Gallery & Museum; British Museum; DNHAS (Dorset County Museum); The Fitzwilliam Museum; Government Art Collection; The Higgins Art Gallery & Museum; T.B. & R. Jordan Gallery; Manchester Art Gallery; National Portrait Gallery; New English Art Club; Rochdale Art Gallery; Royal Academy; National Maritime Museum, Greenwich; Russell-Cotes Art Gallery and Museum; Worcester City Art Gallery & Museum; Williamson Art Gallery & Museum.

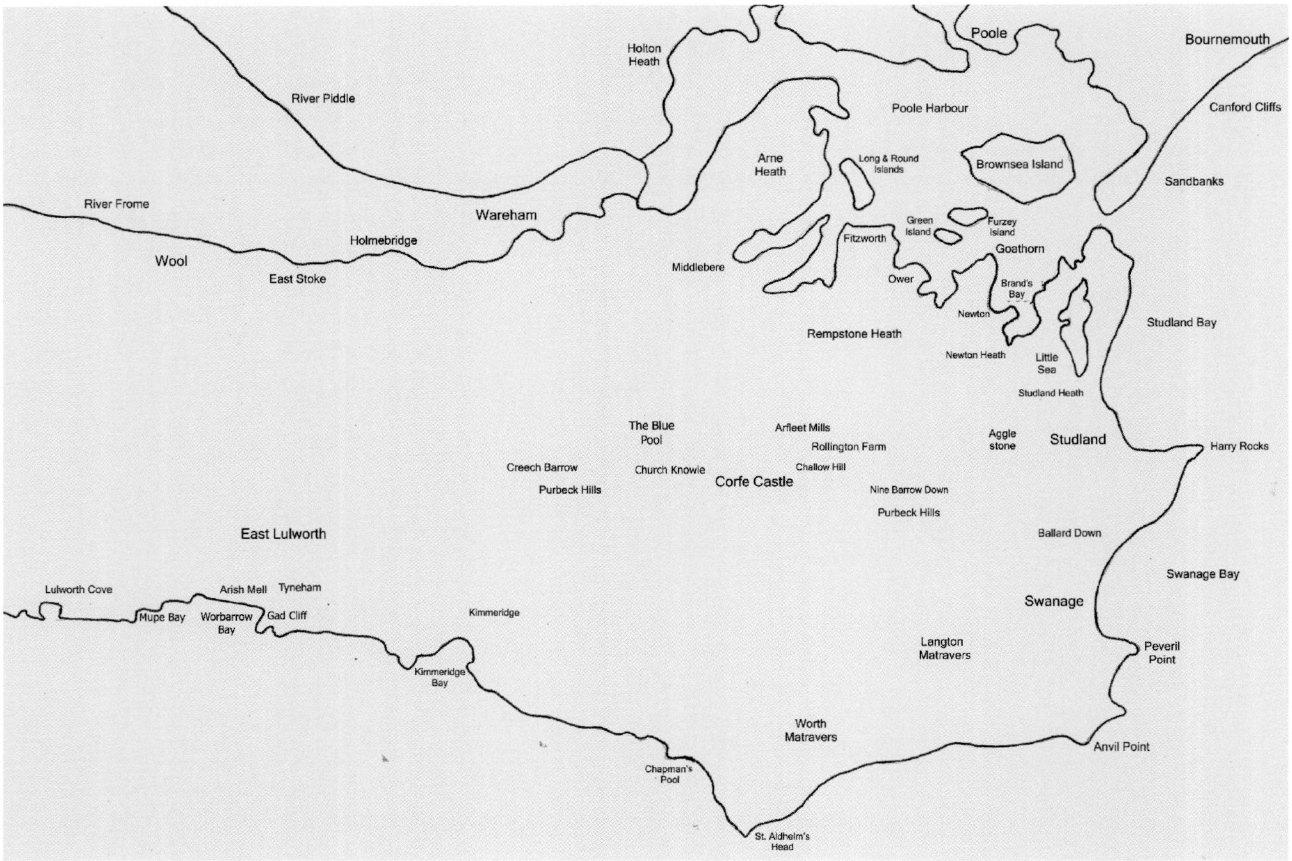

FIG. 113

Map of Purback

courtesy the author

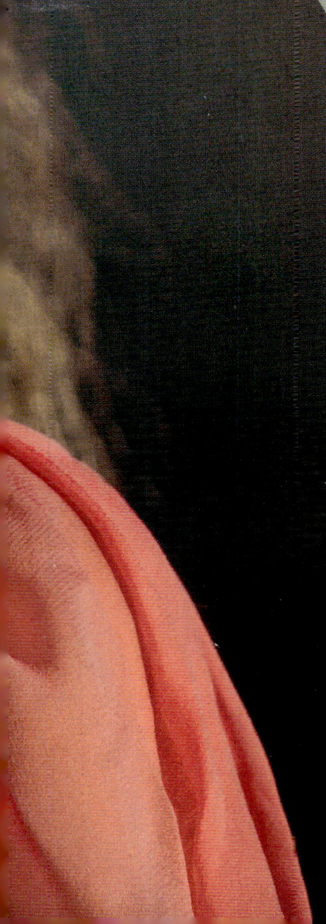

Welcome

You don't need to be religious to be spiritual. Inside this book is a deep, personal journey to finding your very own, individual spirituality. It is a pathway that can be travelled by followers of all faiths as well as those who don't follow a religion at all. Spiritual practice isn't one-size-fits-all and it doesn't need to be defined by prescribed structures of worship or belief in deities. Join us on a voyage of self discovery, where all that is required of you is an open mind and an open heart. Within these pages you will discover a guide to finding and embracing your inner light, which can be dipped in and out of at your own pace to awaken your spiritual self. Learn how simple rituals and practices such as meditation, visualisation and manifestation can help you achieve personal enlightenment and enrich your everyday life. Become a master at staying calm in stressful situations. Put an end to the tossing and turning and achieve better sleep. Level up your emotional intelligence. And, most importantly, learn more about yourself, your inner workings, and distinctive attributes. Find the confidence to love and accept yourself, embracing your own unique gifts and blossoming into who you were always meant to be.

Contents

54

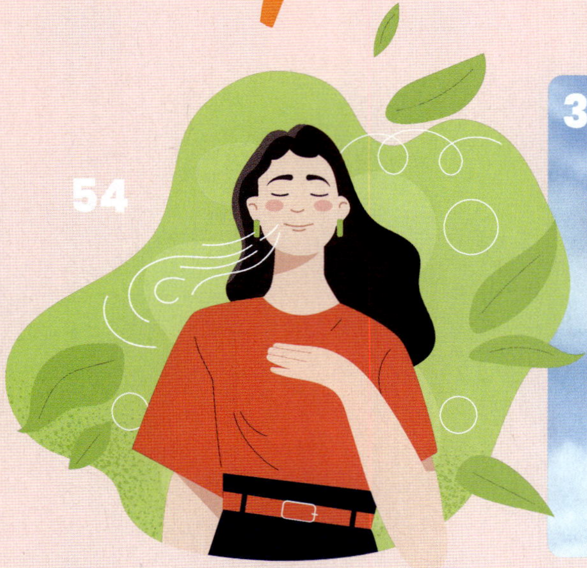

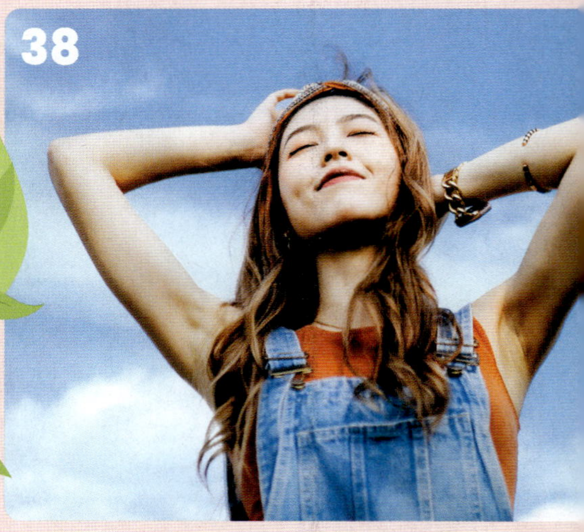

38

Mind

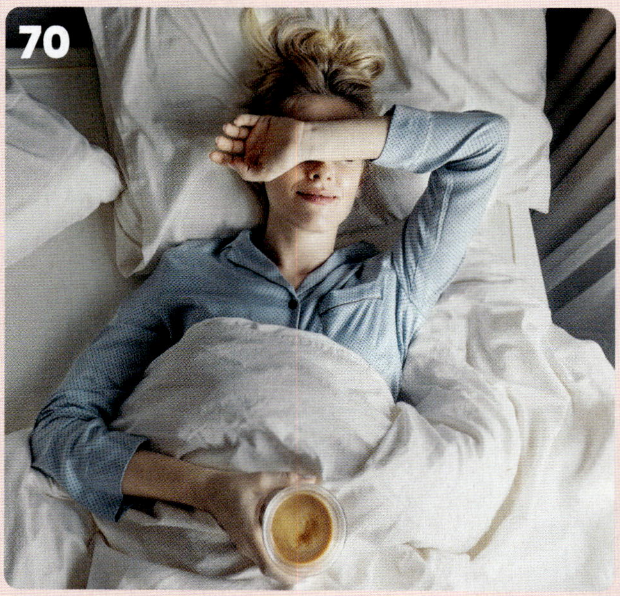

70

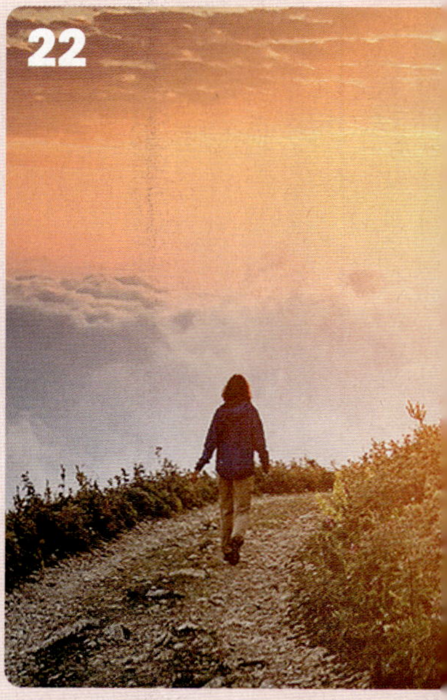

22

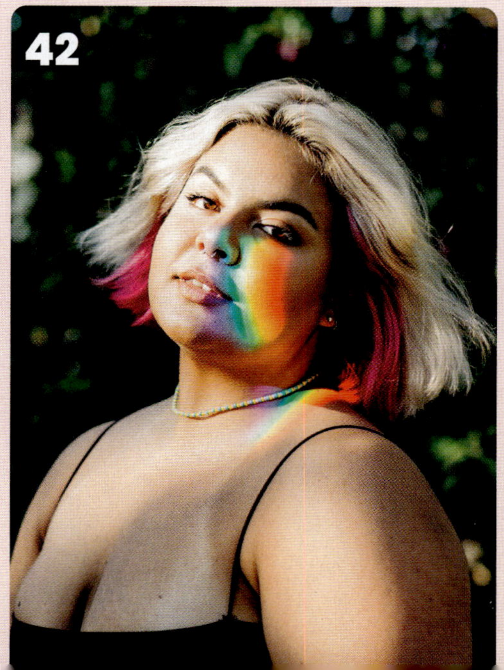

42

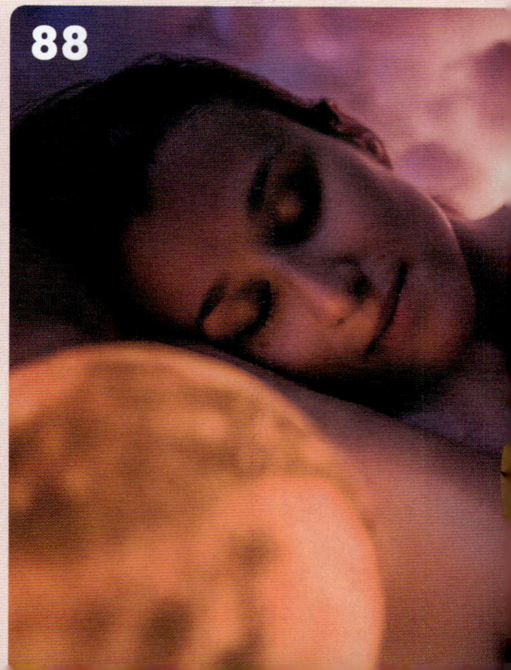

88

Body

92

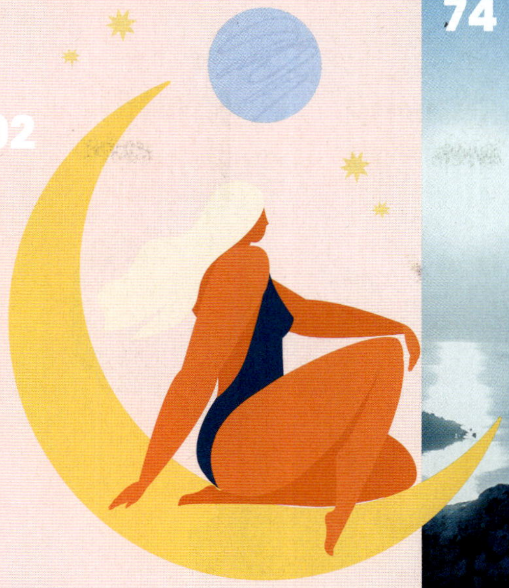

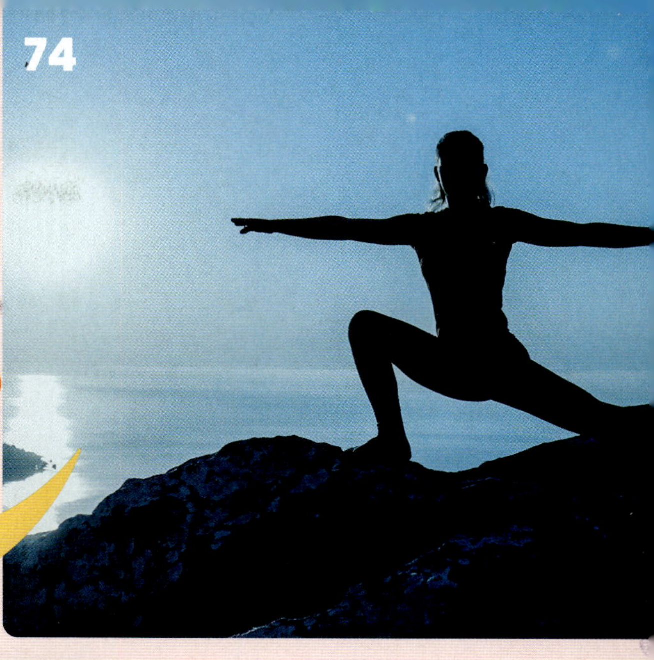

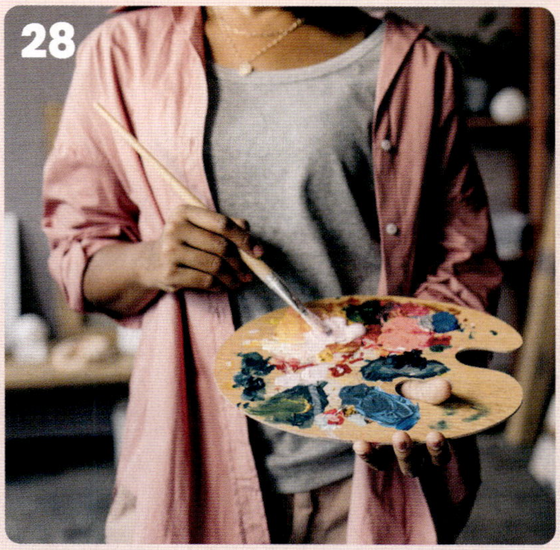

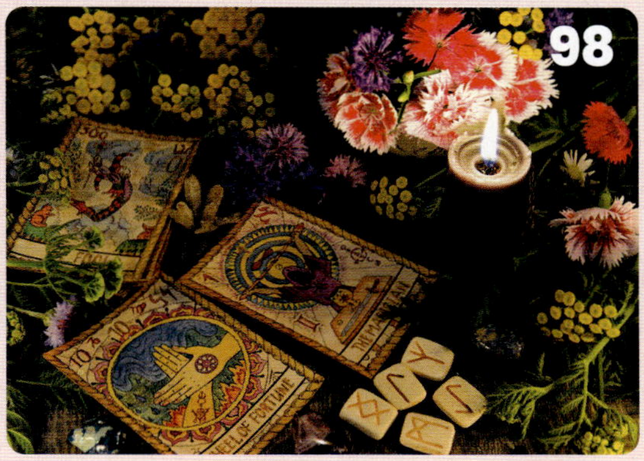

110

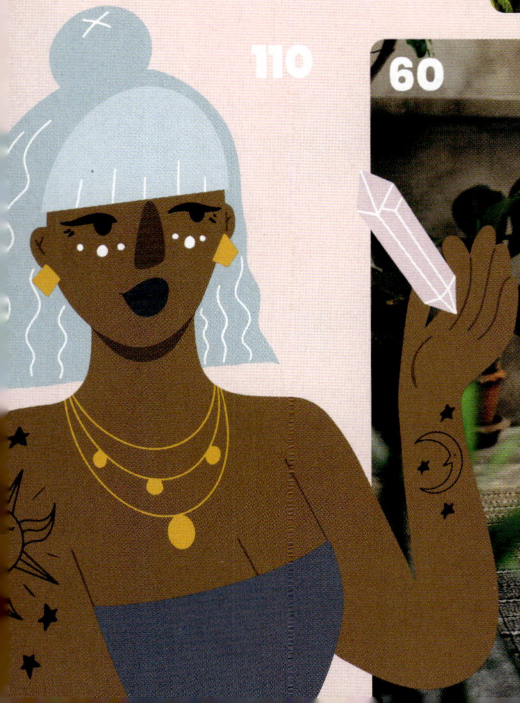

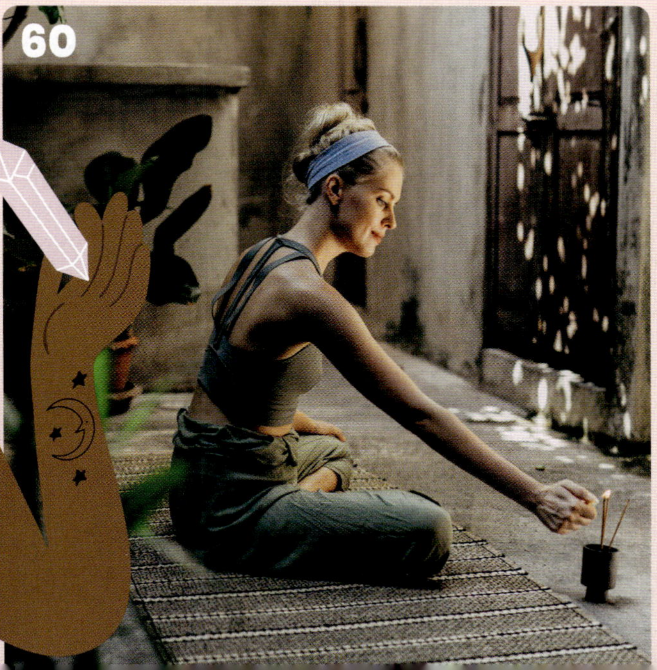

Spirit

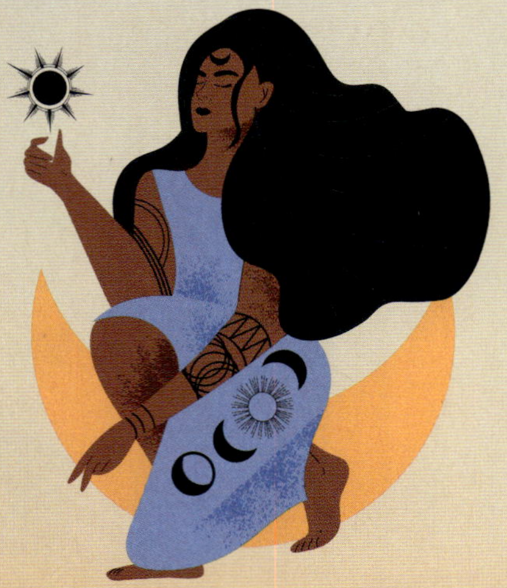

Spirituality & YOU

IN A FAST-MOVING WORLD IT CAN BE HARD TO TAKE TIME OUT FOR YOU, BUT WHEN YOU DO, YOU'LL FIND THE REWARDS ARE ENDLESS

WORDS: CATHERINE CURZON

When you think of spirituality, it may conjure up ideas of organised religion and a host of deities. However, spiritual practice need not be defined by any particular religion, nor by any prescribed structure of worship. Spiritual practice is individual to each person and will provide them with a unique path to understanding themselves and the world around them; in short, you can achieve enlightenment at your own pace, by working on facets of yourself, as and when you are ready to.

You are made up of three facets, the mind, body and spirit. Taken together they are what makes you the unique person you are and, just as you can develop your stamina or knowledge, you can use meditation to develop each of these elements too. In fact, by spending time meditating away from the hustle and bustle of modern life, you will experience a type of enrichment and reward that will be unlike any you have known before; by nurturing yourself, your spirituality will flourish and your understanding of yourself will deepen. When you nurture what makes you uniquely you, you will see yourself and the world around you in a whole new light.

> “You are made up of three facets, the mind, body and spirit”

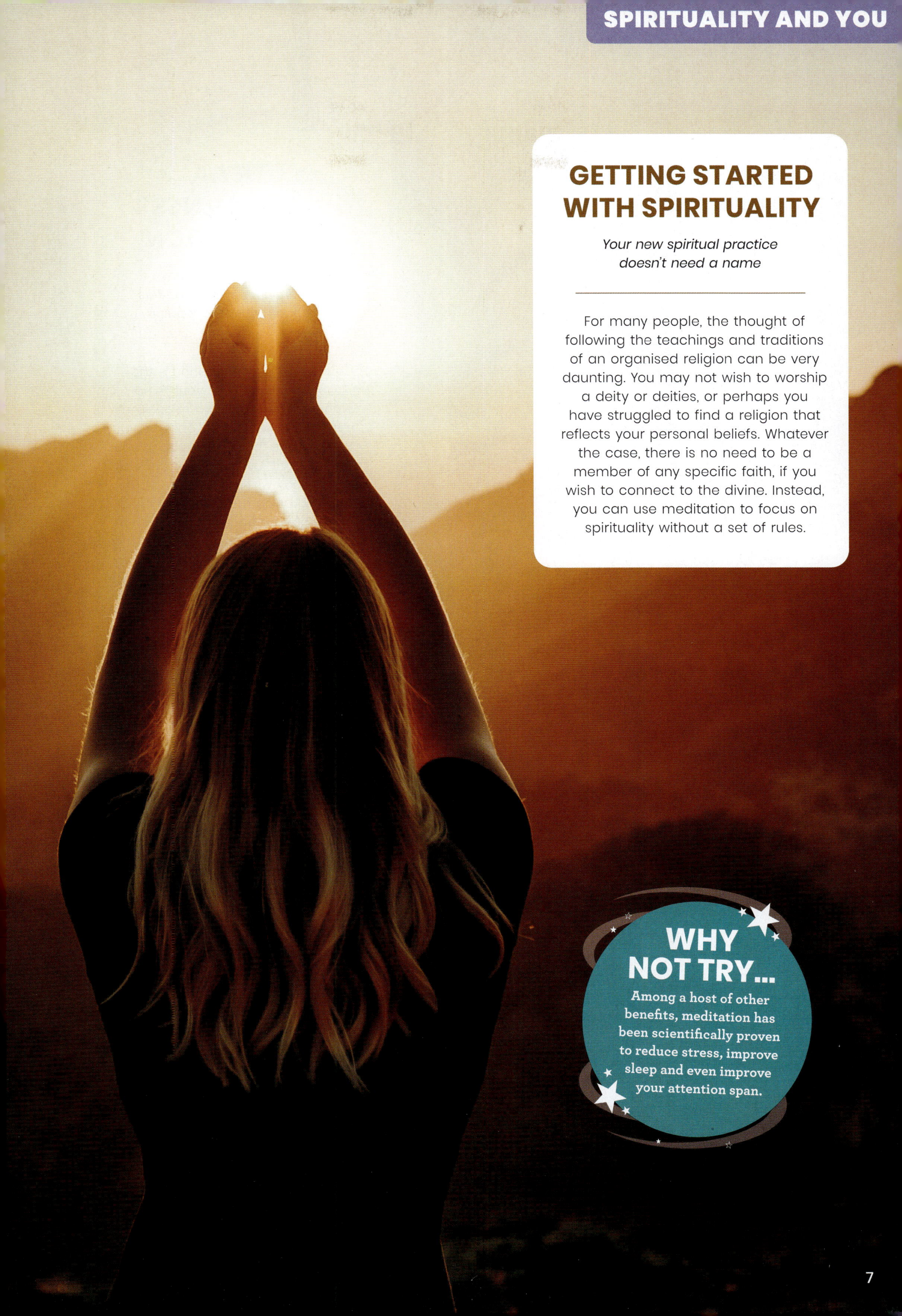

GETTING STARTED WITH SPIRITUALITY

Your new spiritual practice doesn't need a name

For many people, the thought of following the teachings and traditions of an organised religion can be very daunting. You may not wish to worship a deity or deities, or perhaps you have struggled to find a religion that reflects your personal beliefs. Whatever the case, there is no need to be a member of any specific faith, if you wish to connect to the divine. Instead, you can use meditation to focus on spirituality without a set of rules.

WHY NOT TRY...

Among a host of other benefits, meditation has been scientifically proven to reduce stress, improve sleep and even improve your attention span.

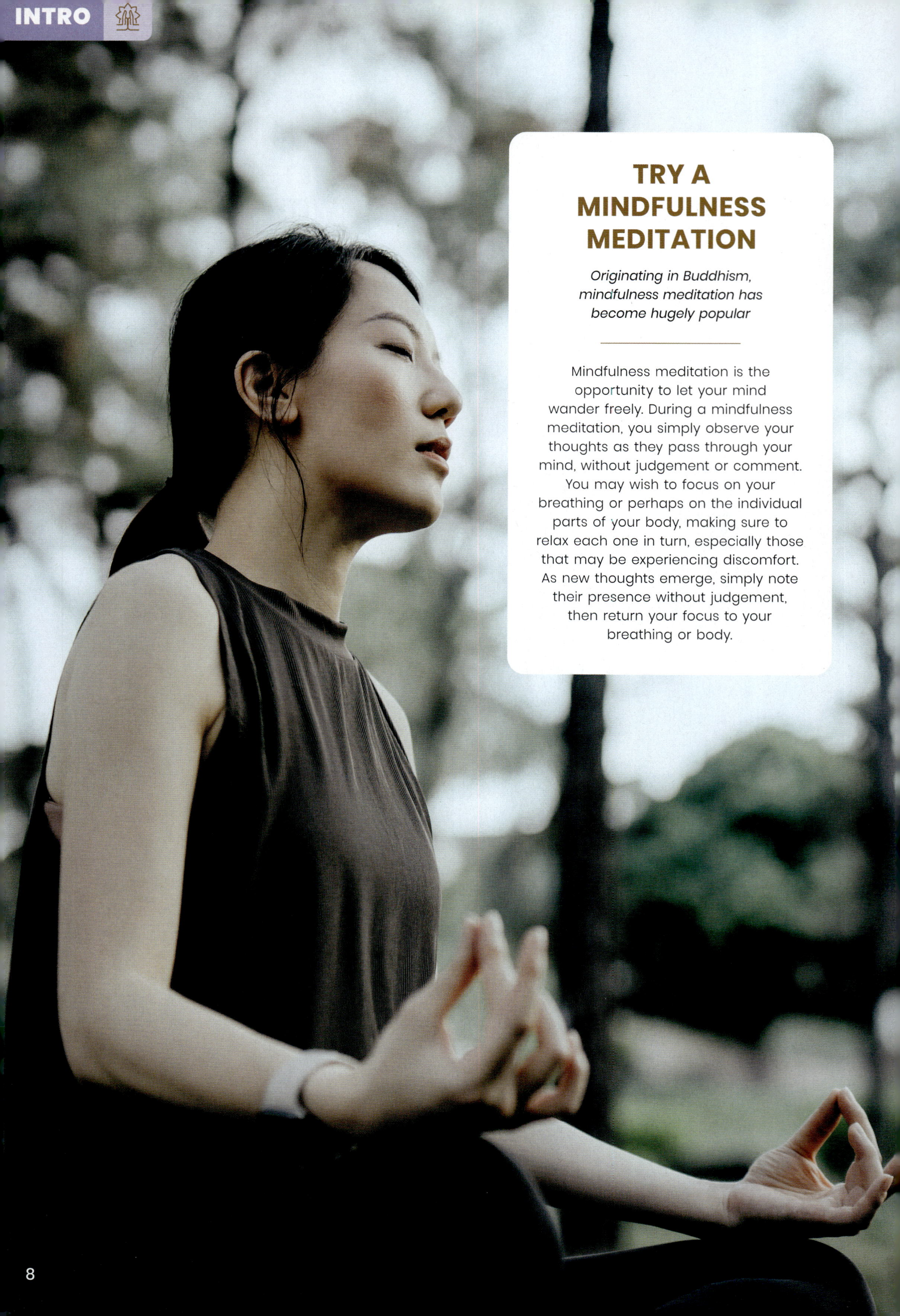

TRY A MINDFULNESS MEDITATION

Originating in Buddhism, mindfulness meditation has become hugely popular

Mindfulness meditation is the opportunity to let your mind wander freely. During a mindfulness meditation, you simply observe your thoughts as they pass through your mind, without judgement or comment. You may wish to focus on your breathing or perhaps on the individual parts of your body, making sure to relax each one in turn, especially those that may be experiencing discomfort. As new thoughts emerge, simply note their presence without judgement, then return your focus to your breathing or body.

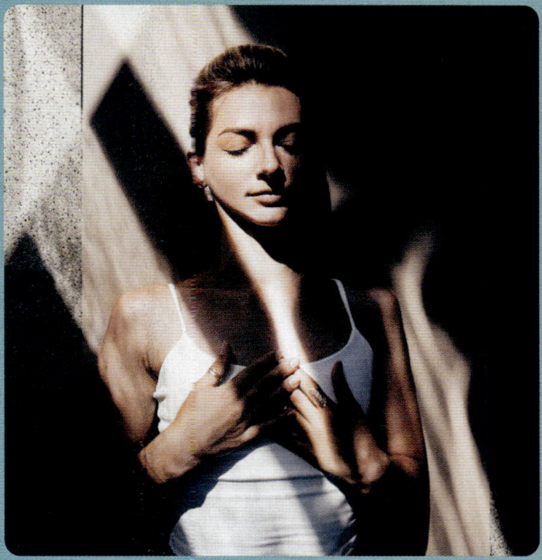

TRY A VISUALISATION MEDITATION

Find peaceful calm in the positivity of visualisation

Visualisation meditation offers the chance to find a deep sense of relaxation as you visualise images and scenes that carry positive connotations. For instance, if you are experiencing stress and anxiety and long for the countryside, but simply can't get there, visualisation meditation will help you to envision that place you long for and reap the benefits.

Once you are settled and have started your meditation, simply visualise a place in which you feel a sense of contentment and calm. This may be a real place that you know well or remember from the past, or a place of your own imagining, where you can design each aspect. Once you have a clear image of the place, bring in your other senses, perhaps hearing birdsong or the sound of a gentle stream; it may be that you can smell the flowers around you or the ocean scent. This is your haven, for as long as you wish.

“Visualise a place in which you feel a sense of contentment and calm”

PRACTICE a Loving Kindness MEDITATION

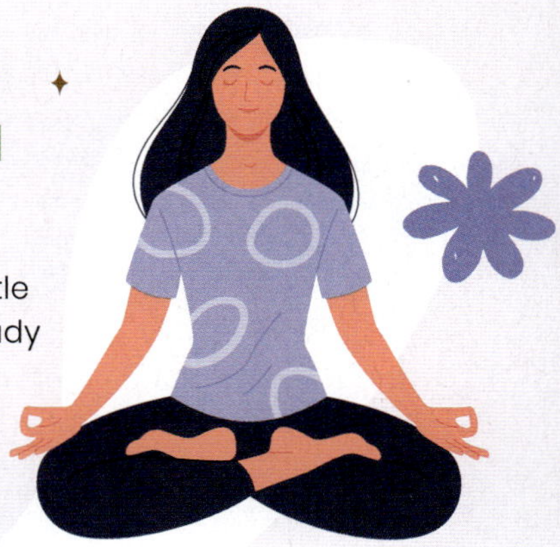

1 BEGIN YOUR MEDITATION

Once you're in your favourite meditation position, let yourself settle into a state of calm, ready to spread some love.

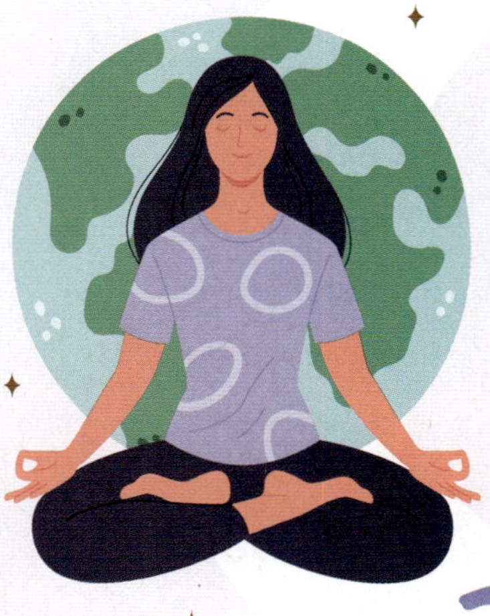

2 SHARE THE LOVE

Focus on wishing love and kindness to yourself, followed by your loved ones, friends, town and so on, slowly widening the feeling to encompass all living things.

3 END THE MEDITATION

As you prepare to end the meditation, work back through the circle from all living beings to yourself, wishing love and kindness all the way.

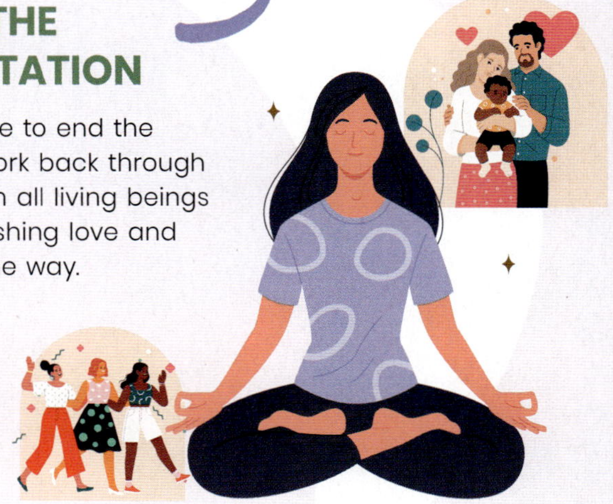

MOVEMENT MEDITATION

You don't have to be sitting still to practice meditation

Whether you prefer yoga or tai chi, or even or to get out in the garden or for a walk in nature, movement meditation is an active practice where your very movement will guide you to connect with your body. You will be aware of yourself and your presence in each moment, no longer simply going through the motions, but making a deep connection with your physical self and your spirituality.

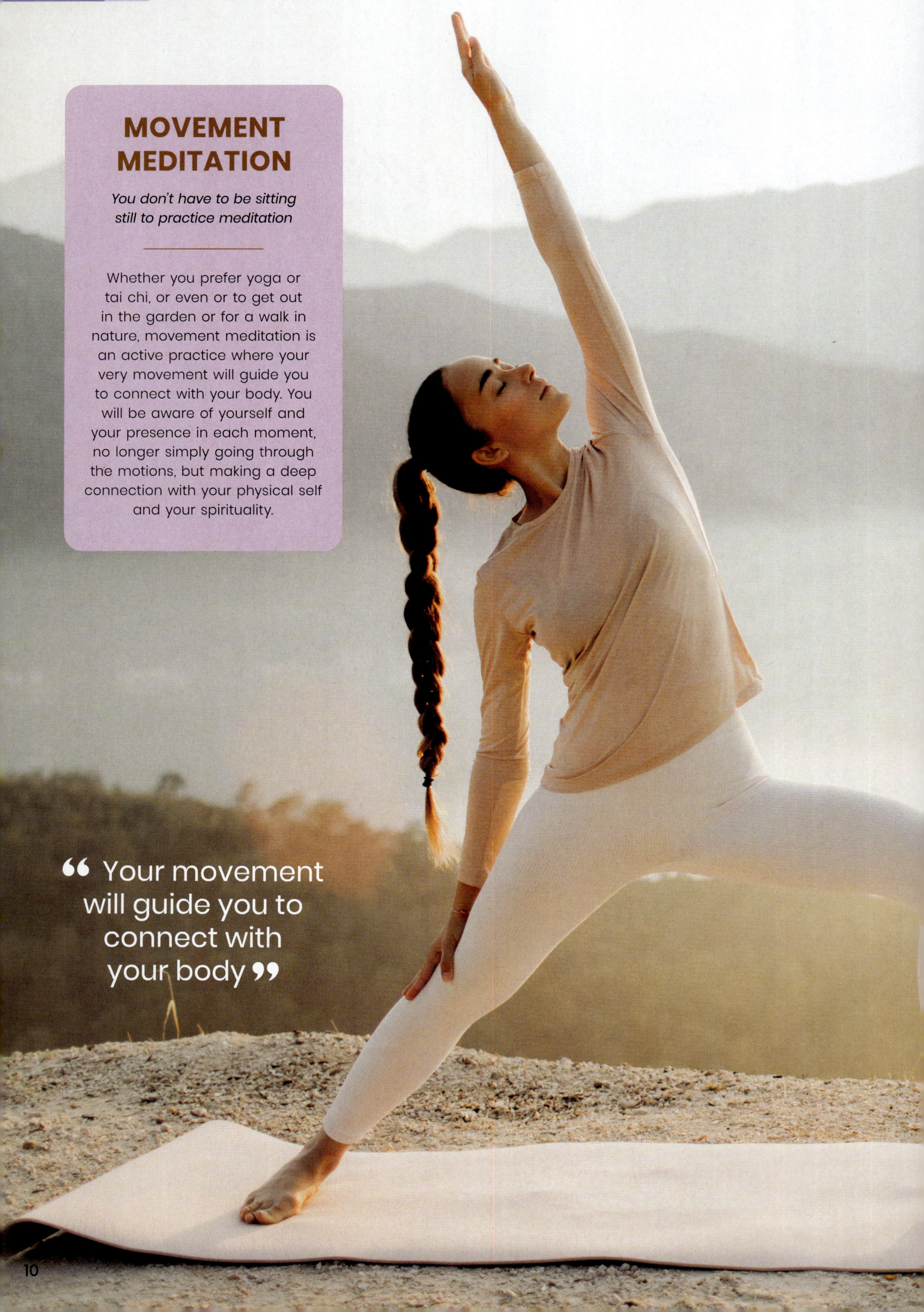

"Your movement will guide you to connect with your body"

BODY SCAN

Also known as progressive relaxation, this can soothe tension, aches and pains

If you feel tension in your body as you sit to meditate, body scan meditation (also known as progressive relaxation) is an excellent way to address those issues. As you meditate, focus on any part of your body that you wish or, if you have no preference, simply on your feet, and slowly tighten the muscles in them. Then focus on relaxing those muscles and the sense of release and looseness that brings. As you move up through your body, repeat this on each muscle group in turn, allowing your whole body to unwind from the stress and tension that has been holding it tight. If you experience pain, don't feel angry, but acknowledge your discomfort and continue without judging yourself or your body. This is an excellent meditation to practice if you are experiencing tension and stress in the evening and are concerned that it may keep you from falling asleep.

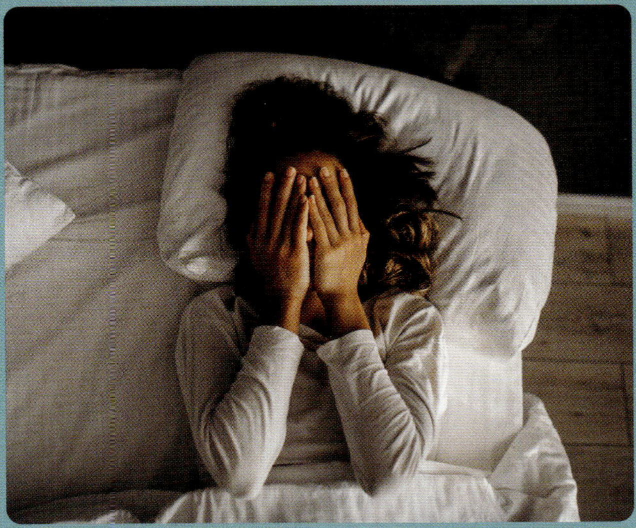

TRY A FOCUSED MEDITATION

Focusing on a sound or rhythm can clear your mind of other things

1 CHOOSE YOUR FOCUS

Whether you want to listen to a gong being struck, watch a candle flame or perhaps count your breaths, choose the focus for your meditation.

2 HOLD YOUR FOCUS

As you meditate, maintain your focus on whatever you have selected. Whilst this sounds easy, it can be deeply challenging.

3 DON'T BE HARD ON YOURSELF

Keeping focus without letting your mind wander can be hard. Don't judge yourself, but simply note wandering thoughts, then return to your focus.

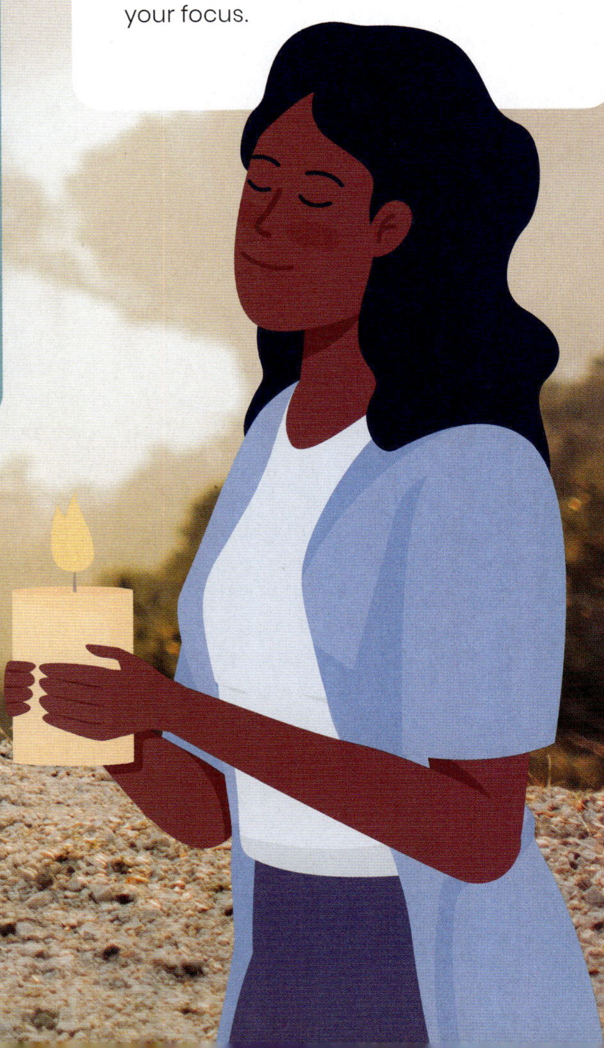

SPIRITUAL MEDITATION

Each spiritual tradition and religion has its own spiritual meditations

Spiritual meditation is familiar to each follower of a religious faith or other spiritual practice. If you wish to connect to a higher power or learn more about a particular faith and its deities, spiritual meditation will form part of that practice. When in the form of prayer or another practice, it will offer an opportunity for spiritual growth and connection to the divine.

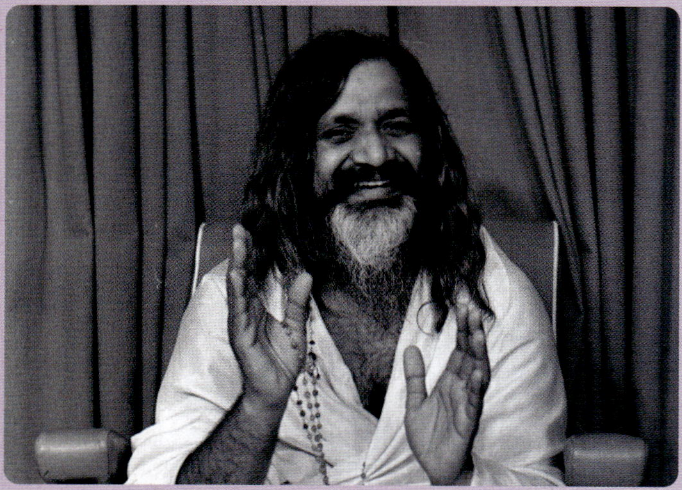

TRANSCENDENTAL MEDITATION

Known to its followers as TM, Transcendental Meditation is rarely self-taught

Transcendental meditation was founded by Maharishi Mahesh Yogi in the 1950s, based on the teachings of monk Brahmananda Saraswati. Whilst many other forms of meditation can be self-taught or learned in a more casual manner, it is recommended that that anyone who wishes to learn TM should approach a certified practitioner. TM is a meditation that involves the silent repetition of a mantra and is practiced twice each day for around 20 minutes. Whilst TM was initially promoted as a religious movement and famously became popular with superstars such as the Beatles, today it is promoted as a secular activity to reduce stress, promote increased awareness and develop a higher state of consciousness. The mantra, a meaningless sound which is unique to you and never revealed to others, is intended to help quiet the mind until it reaches a point of silence and utter peace.

TRY A MANTRA MEDITATION

A mantra is a specific focus sound that attunes you to the universe

1 CHOOSE YOUR MANTRA

Choose the phrase, word or sound on which you'd like to focus as you clear your mind. The most popular is "om".

2 CHANT YOUR MANTRA

As your meditate, chant your mantra as quietly or loudly as you wish. Your spiritual awareness will deepen as you focus only on the mantra.

3 NOTICE YOUR BODY

Notice the change in your body as you chant. Hear and feel the sound as it vibrates deep within you, connecting you to your deeper consciousness.

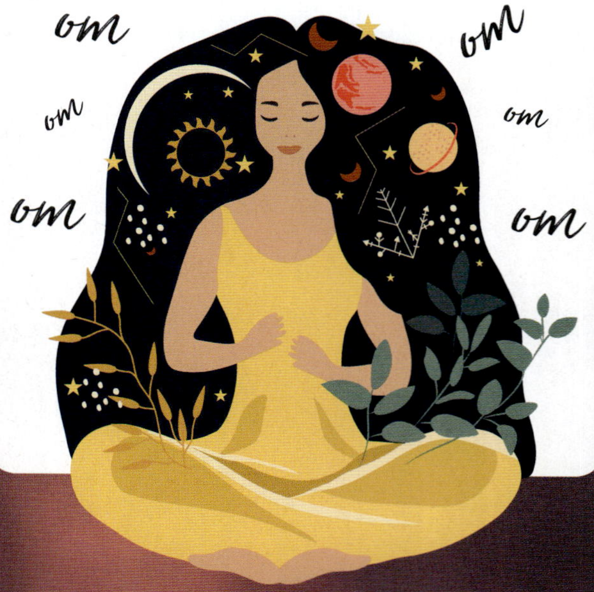

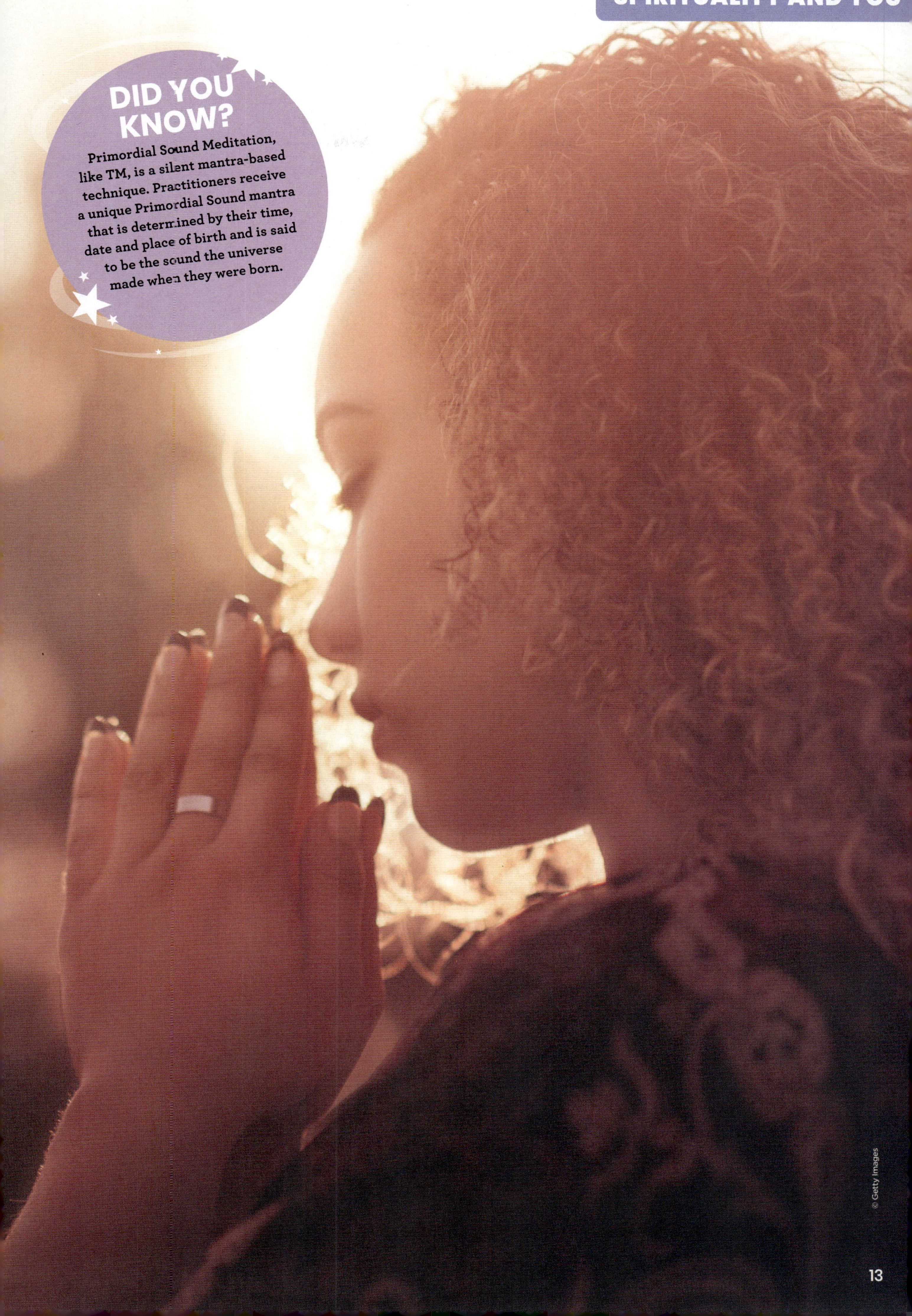

DID YOU KNOW?

Primordial Sound Meditation, like TM, is a silent mantra-based technique. Practitioners receive a unique Primordial Sound mantra that is determined by their time, date and place of birth and is said to be the sound the universe made when they were born.

Mind

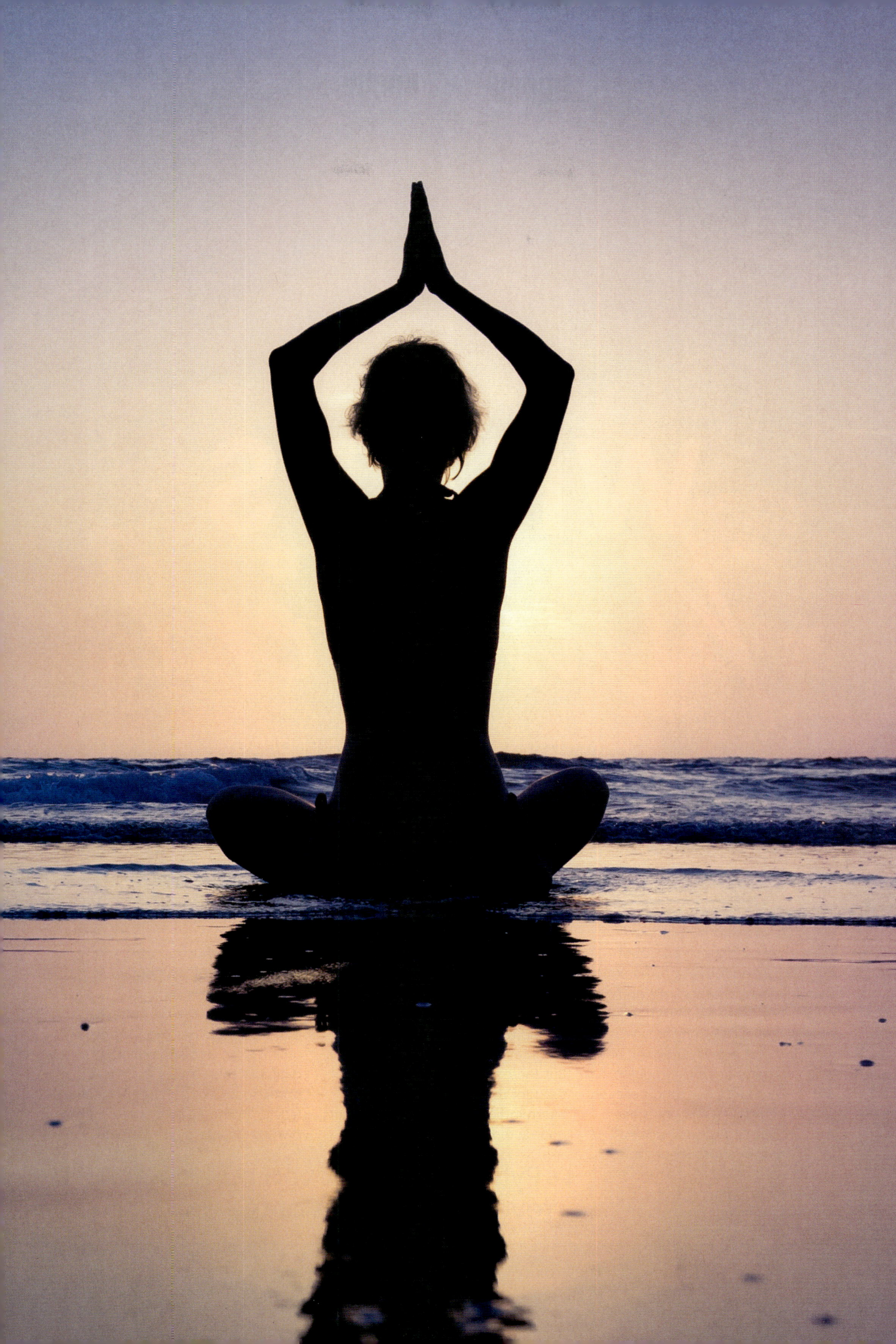

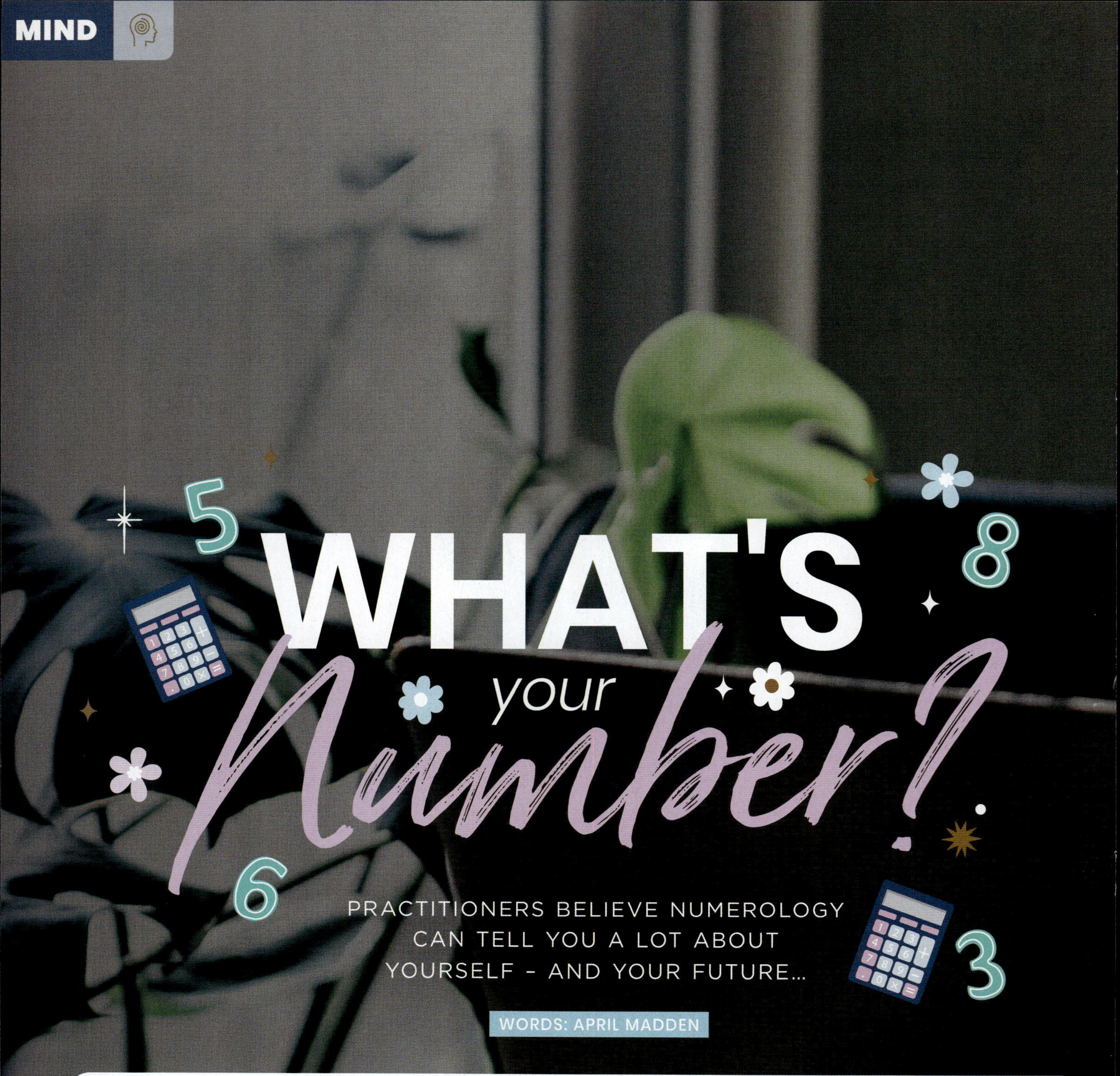

WHAT'S *your* Number?

PRACTITIONERS BELIEVE NUMEROLOGY CAN TELL YOU A LOT ABOUT YOURSELF – AND YOUR FUTURE...

WORDS: APRIL MADDEN

Remember back when your maths teacher was droning on about Pythagoras? It turns out the legendary mathematician had a lot more going for him than just triangles. In fact Pythagoras was something of a mystical guru: he was a vegetarian, experimented with communal living, and believed in the harmony of the universe. The ancient Greek geek was so fascinated by numbers because he believed they could reveal the secrets of the universe.

Today some of his theories underpin the study of numerology, which says you can reveal the path your life will take and even your destiny through a few simple sums. How? Let's get started with an easy one – your birthday. Add up the day, month and year and you'll reveal your Life Path number. But there's more. Pythagoras thought that everything was interrelated. He thought that letters connected with numbers. If you add up the numbers connected to the letters in your name it'll reveal your Destiny Number, and with it the traits that will help you to achieve your goals.

Most of the time we add the numbers together over and over until we are left with a single digit, but there are a couple of exceptions: 11 and 22 are known as Master Numbers and stand on their own as double digit numbers.

> "Pythagoras believed numbers could reveal the secrets of the universe"

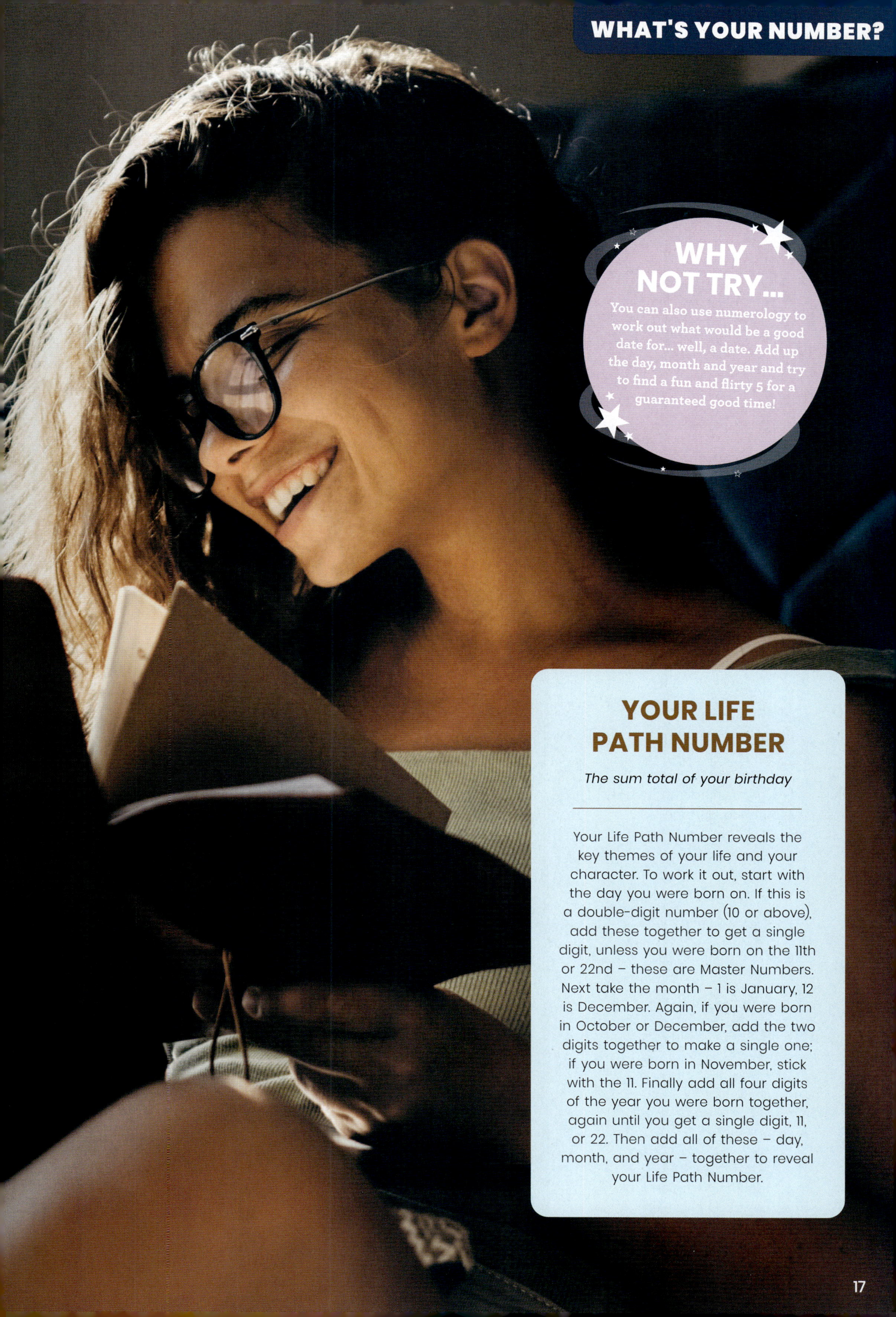

WHY NOT TRY...

You can also use numerology to work out what would be a good date for... well, a date. Add up the day, month and year and try to find a fun and flirty 5 for a guaranteed good time!

YOUR LIFE PATH NUMBER

The sum total of your birthday

Your Life Path Number reveals the key themes of your life and your character. To work it out, start with the day you were born on. If this is a double-digit number (10 or above), add these together to get a single digit, unless you were born on the 11th or 22nd – these are Master Numbers. Next take the month – 1 is January, 12 is December. Again, if you were born in October or December, add the two digits together to make a single one; if you were born in November, stick with the 11. Finally add all four digits of the year you were born together, again until you get a single digit, 11, or 22. Then add all of these – day, month, and year – together to reveal your Life Path Number.

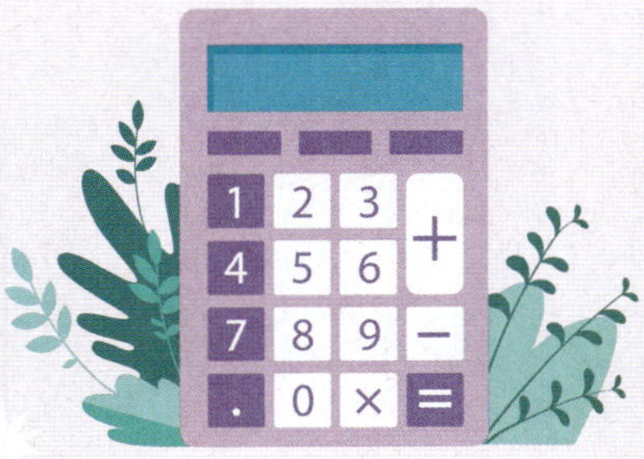

NUMBER *Meanings*

ONE
Independent, pioneering, active, a leader

TWO
Balanced, egalitarian, empathetic, sensitive, harmonious

THREE
Creative, communicative, innovative, escapist, connective

FOUR
Solid, practical, grounded, hard-working, responsible

FIVE
Spontaneous, vivacious, brave, free-thinking

SIX
Supportive, gentle, straightforward, empathetic, nurturing

SEVEN
Clever, perfectionist, analytical, detail-oriented

EIGHT
Magnetic, ambitious, successful, a leader

NINE
Wise, spiritual, experienced, an old soul

ELEVEN
Intuitive, psychic, hyper-aware, a healer

TWENTY TWO
Dynamic, industrious, dependable, transformative, creative

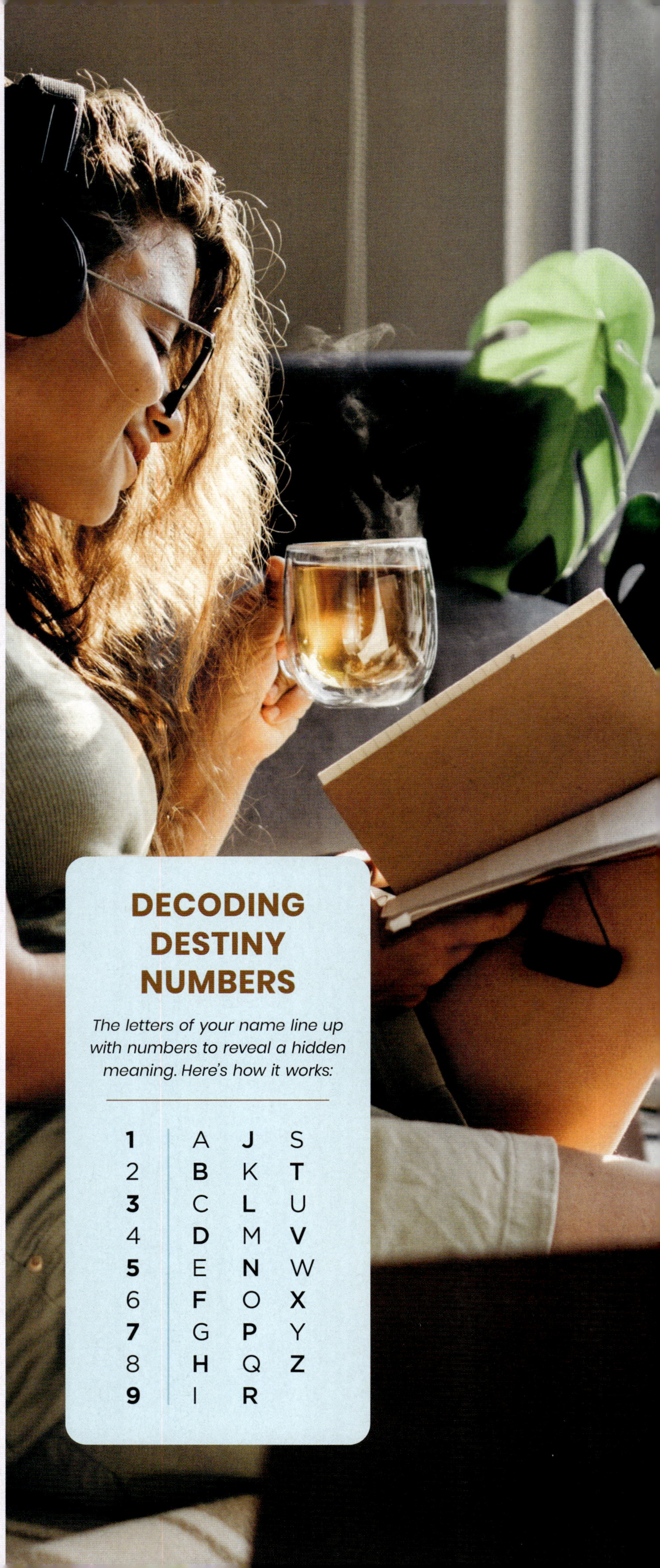

DECODING DESTINY NUMBERS

The letters of your name line up with numbers to reveal a hidden meaning. Here's how it works:

1	A	J	S
2	B	K	T
3	C	L	U
4	D	M	V
5	E	N	W
6	F	O	X
7	G	P	Y
8	H	Q	Z
9	I	R	

> “Reveal the path your life will take through a few simple sums”

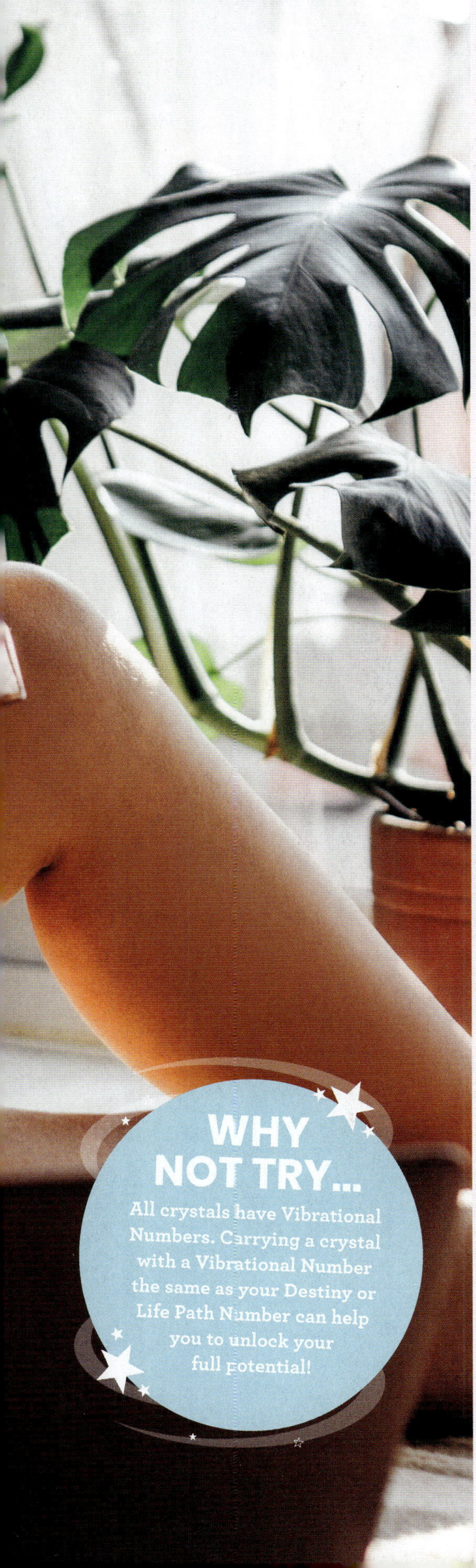

MATHS *Homework*

How to discover your destiny with numbers

1 DO THE SUMS

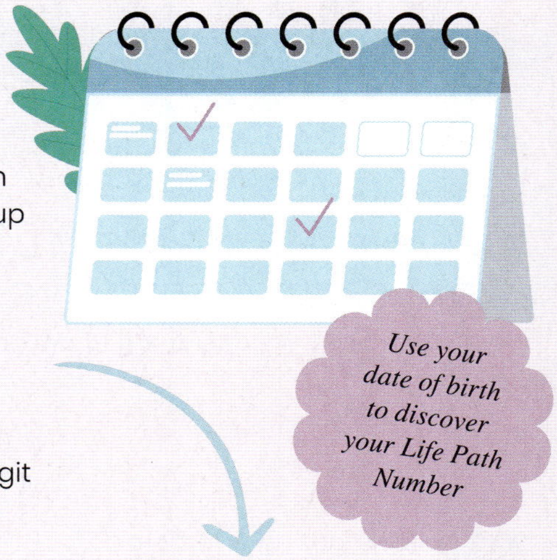

Grace's date of birth is 15th May 1994. To find her Life Path number, we start by adding up 1+5 to make 6. May is month number 5. Then we add the year together: 1+9+9+4. This makes 23, so we add 2+3 to make 5. Finally we add all the numbers together: 6+5+5 makes 16. This is still a two-digit number, so we add 1+6 and reveal that Grace's Life Path Number is 7.

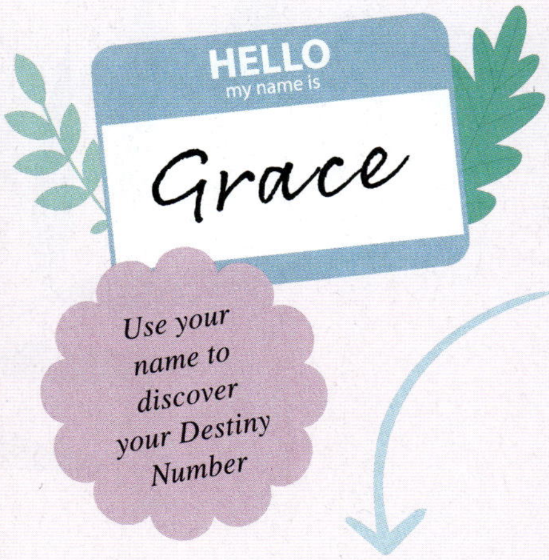

2 SHOW YOUR WORKING OUT

To find your Destiny Number, first you need to work out the root number of each of your names. Grace's full name is Grace Lily Rose. GRACE becomes 7+9+1+3+5, which is 25. That turns into 2+5, making her first name a 7. We repeat the process for her middle name (LILY, 3+9+3+7; 22, a Master Number) and surname (ROSE, 9+6+1+5=21, 2+1=3).

© Getty Images

3 ADD IT UP

Finally we add together all of the root numbers: 7+22+3. That gives us 32, so we add the 3 and 2 together, and reveal that Grace's Destiny Number is a 5. As a Life Path 7 Grace is very methodical and detail-oriented, but her Destiny Number 5 is telling her to loosen up, laugh and live a little!

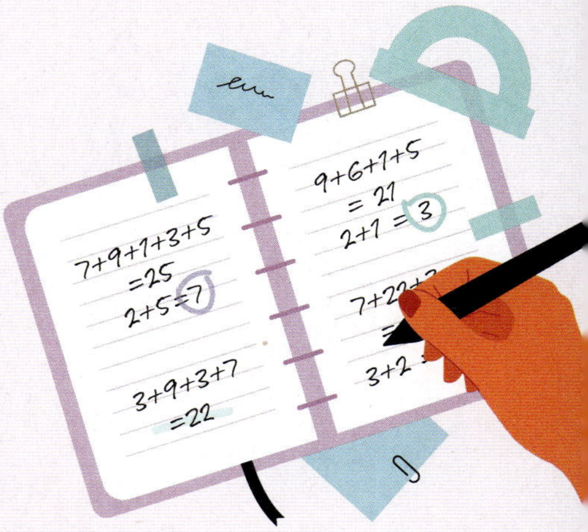

WHY NOT TRY...

All crystals have Vibrational Numbers. Carrying a crystal with a Vibrational Number the same as your Destiny or Life Path Number can help you to unlock your full potential!

IGNITE your Intuition

A FLAME GAZING RITUAL CAN NOT ONLY BE A WONDERFUL MEDITATIVE EXPERIENCE, BUT IT CAN HELP AWAKEN YOUR INNER WISDOM

WORDS: ALICE PATTILLO

Flame gazing can be a wonderful way to find stillness. A dancing flame has a hypnotic effect on the mind, something yogis have known for centuries. Known as 'tratak sadhana' in yoga, candle gazing is a focus meditation. This is a type of meditation that involves focusing, or gazing, on an object or sensation, and can bring your awareness to the present moment. This can not only help to calm the mind, but to tap into the third eye chakra, increasing psychic ability, intuition and spiritual awareness.

In order to meditate and help awaken your third eye, just follow these simple steps:

WARNING!

Stop if your eyes water or feel tired. Avoid if you have ever experienced migraines, seizures (including epilepsy), mental health issues or eye disorders now or in the past.

DID YOU KNOW?

Flame gazing not only promotes mindfulness, but can aid in tapping into your psychic abilities too.

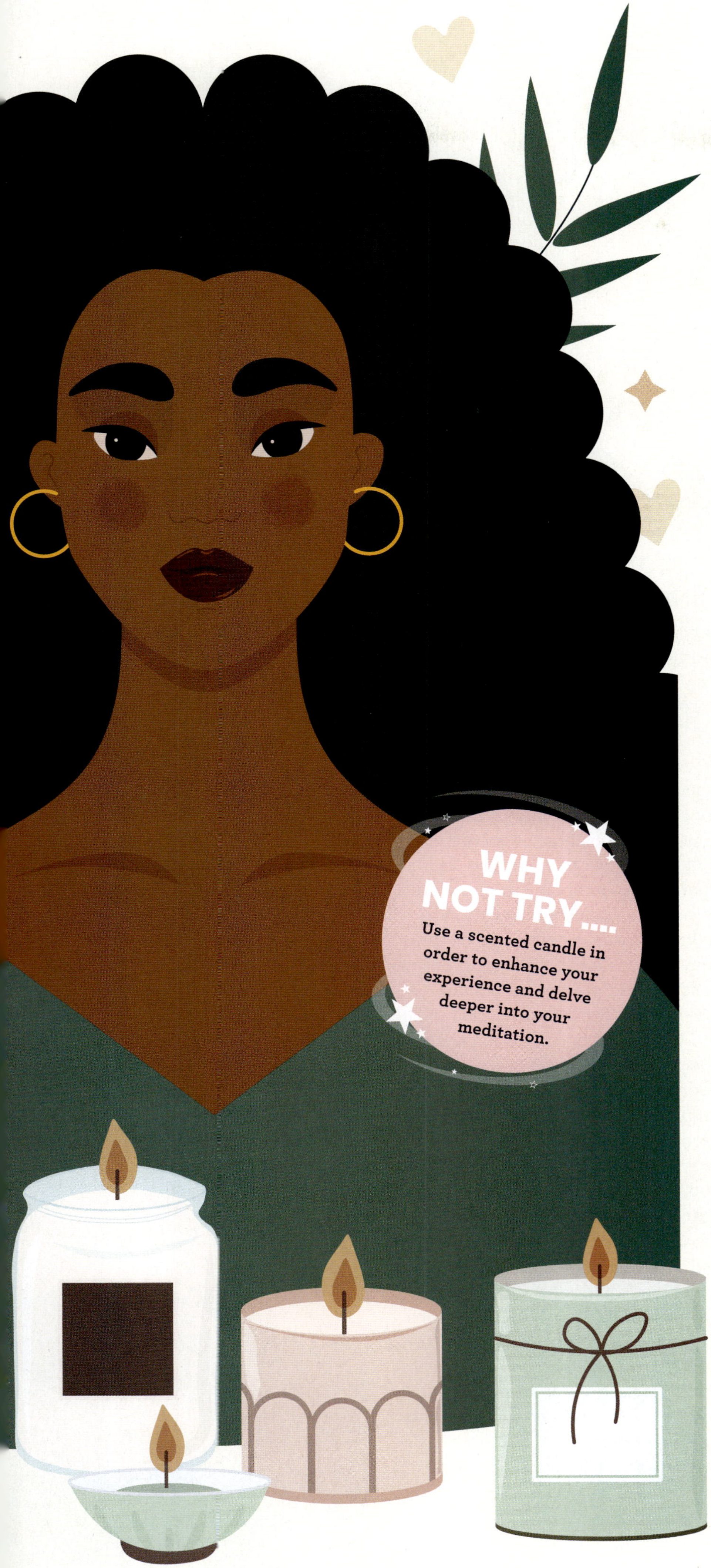

1 Pick your candle. It can be large or small, but pick one with only one wick. You might choose a scented one in order to enhance your experience. Sandalwood, jasmine, lavender, rose, patchouli and sage are all great for both grounding, calming and tapping into your third eye chakra.

2 Light your candle. Be careful not to burn yourself! Then place it on a non-flammable surface.

3 Set a timer for five minutes and sit down in front of your candle, making sure you can gaze at the flame comfortably. You might want to place it on a coffee table and sit cross-legged or place it on a dining table and sit in a chair to ensure it is at eye level.

4 Now relax your shoulders and gaze softly at the candle, focusing all of your attention on watching the flame.

5 Notice thoughts come into your mind and simply imagine pushing them away, regaining focus on the flame.

6 You may want to use a mantra while you flame gaze to focus your attention further on the present. Try a simple "Om", the yogic mantra for opening the third eye. Mantras are like a personal spell, so why not try simply repeating "I am magic, I am wisdom", or come up with your own!

7 Once your timer goes off, blow out your flame! Never leave your candle unattended when lit.

8 Repeat this ritual, increasing the length of your meditation by a few minutes each time until you can successfully meditate for half an hour.

Flames have also been used as a scrying tool for divination. As you gaze at your flame, does anything come immediately to mind? Do you see any shapes within the flame that can be interpreted as signs or messages? Look deeper and you might find answers to some of life's most burning questions!

FIND *your* HAPPY *place*

DIDN'T THINK MEDITATION WAS FOR YOU? YOU MIGHT THINK AGAIN ONCE YOU'VE TRIED ONE OF THE MANY NEW WAYS TO FIND YOUR INNER ZEN...

WORDS: LOUISE PYNE

For many of us, it's taken a global pandemic to wake up to the need to take better care of our mental well-being. As we get to grips with this new world of social distancing, constantly changing quarantine rules, while simultaneously navigating the challenges of working from home, we have become forced to try and approach life in a new way.

Of course, there are days when demands pile up and things feel utterly overwhelming – there always have been after all. We end up slowly sinking to the bottom of the ocean instead of seamlessly riding the wave. These new-found situations we find ourselves in have also brought with them a rollercoaster of emotions.

One minute we're feeling revved up and motivated to stick to our usual schedules; the next our lives feel thrown out of course and we're struck battling lows of anxiety, panic and frustration.

During the height of the UK lockdown, there was a 95% increase in Google searches for 'self-care' techniques as the nation strived to carve out a sense of zen. "When the world outside us has felt so out of control we have been looking for inner peace and balance and ways to manage stress and anxiety. Also, in times of such uncertainty, people naturally look for something to believe in, something greater, an anchor," explains meditation expert, author and founder of online resource *Lunar Living*, Kirsty Gallagher.

So it comes as no real surprise that caring for the mind has suddenly become a top priority. In fact mindfulness app Headspace reported a 70% increase in its live meditation classes throughout lockdown earlier this year as we desperately tried to evoke our body's relaxation response when things felt beyond our control.

Meditation is nothing new. Humans have been paying attention to the breath and practising self-awareness for centuries, and for many years researchers have been exploring the benefits of mediation on both our physical well-being and our minds

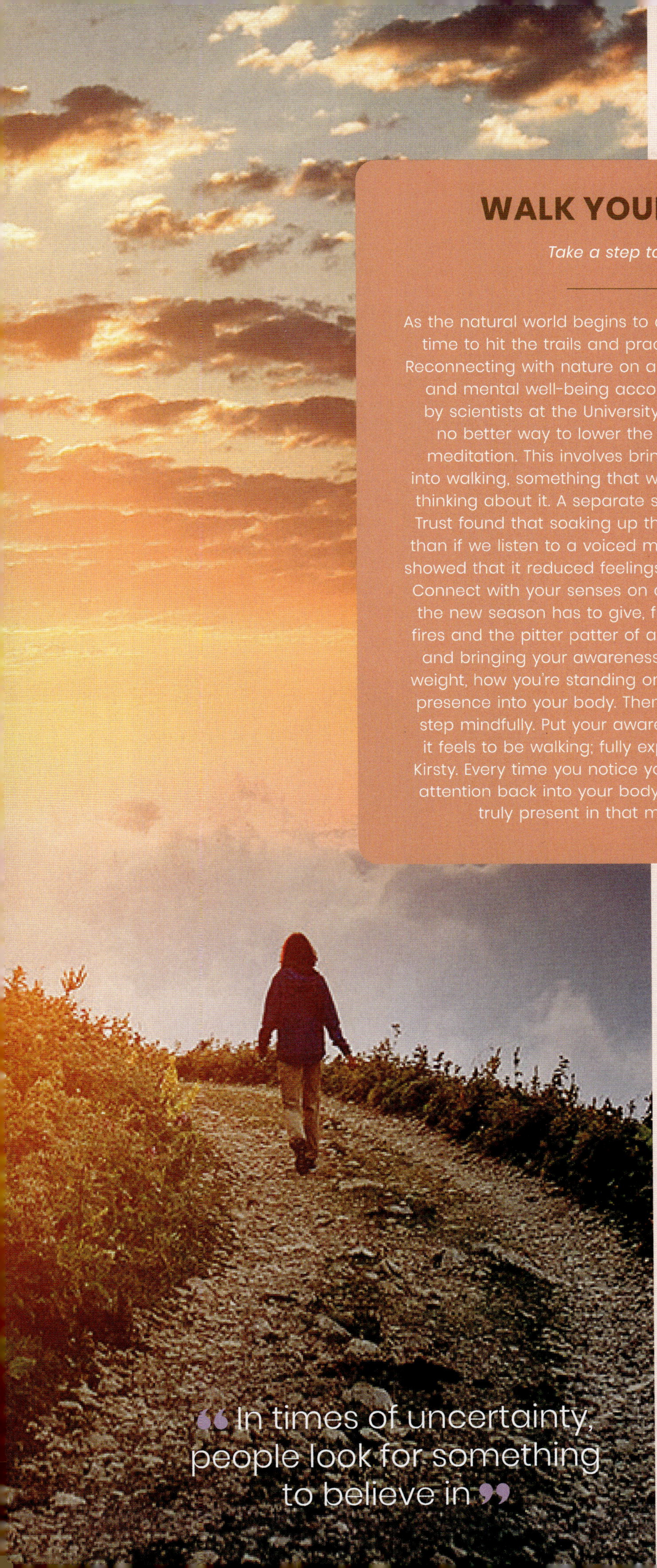

WALK YOUR WAY TO ZEN

Take a step towards inner peace

As the natural world begins to change colour, autumn is the perfect time to hit the trails and practice being present in the moment. Reconnecting with nature on a weekly basis helps to boost physical and mental well-being according to a recent study conducted by scientists at the University of Plymouth, and there's probably no better way to lower the stress scales than with a walking meditation. This involves bringing full presence and awareness into walking, something that we do all day every day without even thinking about it. A separate study commissioned by the National Trust found that soaking up the sounds of nature relaxes us more than if we listen to a voiced meditation app, and results from tests showed that it reduced feelings of stress and anxiety by over a fifth. Connect with your senses on a mindful level to experience all that the new season has to give, from the crunching leaves, crackling fires and the pitter patter of a rainy day. 'Begin by simply standing and bringing your awareness into your body, where you feel the weight, how you're standing on the earth, bring full awareness and presence into your body. Then begin to walk slowly and feel each step mindfully. Put your awareness fully and completely into how it feels to be walking: fully experience the act of walking,' shares Kirsty. Every time you notice your mind wandering, stop, bring your attention back into your body and begin walking again. Try to be truly present in that moment in the act of walking.

with the body of scientific evidence steadily growing. The list of benefits is pretty impressive. Slowing down racing thoughts has been shown to slash the risk of depression (or help treat it if you're already struggling with your mental health), by altering the release of mood-altering cytokines (inflammatory chemicals that are thought to lead to the development of chronic depression). It's also been shown to improve focus and attention, and help to beat insomnia. "Meditation has been shown to reduce stress and anxiety, enhance self-awareness and increases the ability to self-regulate emotions. It helps you to get to know yourself, process what you are going through in life and puts some space between learned behaviours and knee jerk reactions," explains Kirsty. But if traditional methods of meditation don't appeal, there's crop of meditation techniques which promise a chill fix.

> "In times of uncertainty, people look for something to believe in"

BOOST SLEEP with Beditation

Add a mindful ritual to your bedtime routine

With the pressure of stacked up work and family commitments, it can be a challenge to quieten a chattering mind after a busy day so that you drift off into a blissful sleep. As many as 16 million of us suffer from poor sleep with a third confessing to insomnia according to one study by Aviva insurance.

Sleep has a huge impact on long-term physical and mental well-being, and while how much we need per night varies from person to person, around seven to eight hours is the recommended amount.

A study published in *JAMA Internal Medicine journal* which compared two groups of adults with sleeping troubles found that practising a mindful meditation program was more effective at improving insomnia, than a sleep education class that taught ways to improve sleep habits. Furthermore, if your goal is to improve sleep, practising meditation before hitting the hay (a technique called beditation) could possibly improve snoozing time more effectively than meditating during the day. "Beditation is the act of consciously releasing your day helping you to de-stress, relax and let go ready for a good night's sleep," says Kirsty.

The great thing is that you can practice beditation from the comfort of your bed. "Close your eyes and take a few long, slow deep breaths. Take a mental scan of your physical body and also how you feel energetically, mentally and emotionally. Notice anywhere that you feel tightness or as though you are gripping or holding on. This could be physical or emotional tension." She goes on to add that with each long slow deep breath, simply let go. "Feel as though you are processing and releasing your day ready for a restful sleep. Stay here for as long as you need, simply exhaling and letting go until you feel a sense of becoming more relaxed and present."

MEDITATE TO MUSIC

Soothe your soul with sound

If sitting in silence doesn't do it, try a sound bath. This ancient therapy uses the sound of crystal singing bowls and chimes to ignite a relaxed, meditative state. Music makes us feel good, so it's no wonder that 88% of us turn to music when we need a boost. Sound baths work by altering the theta and delta brain waves which trigger healing and relaxation. All you have to do is lie back, get comfy and listen. Advocates maintain that the repetitive sounds and frequencies vibrate through your body creating a sense of peace.

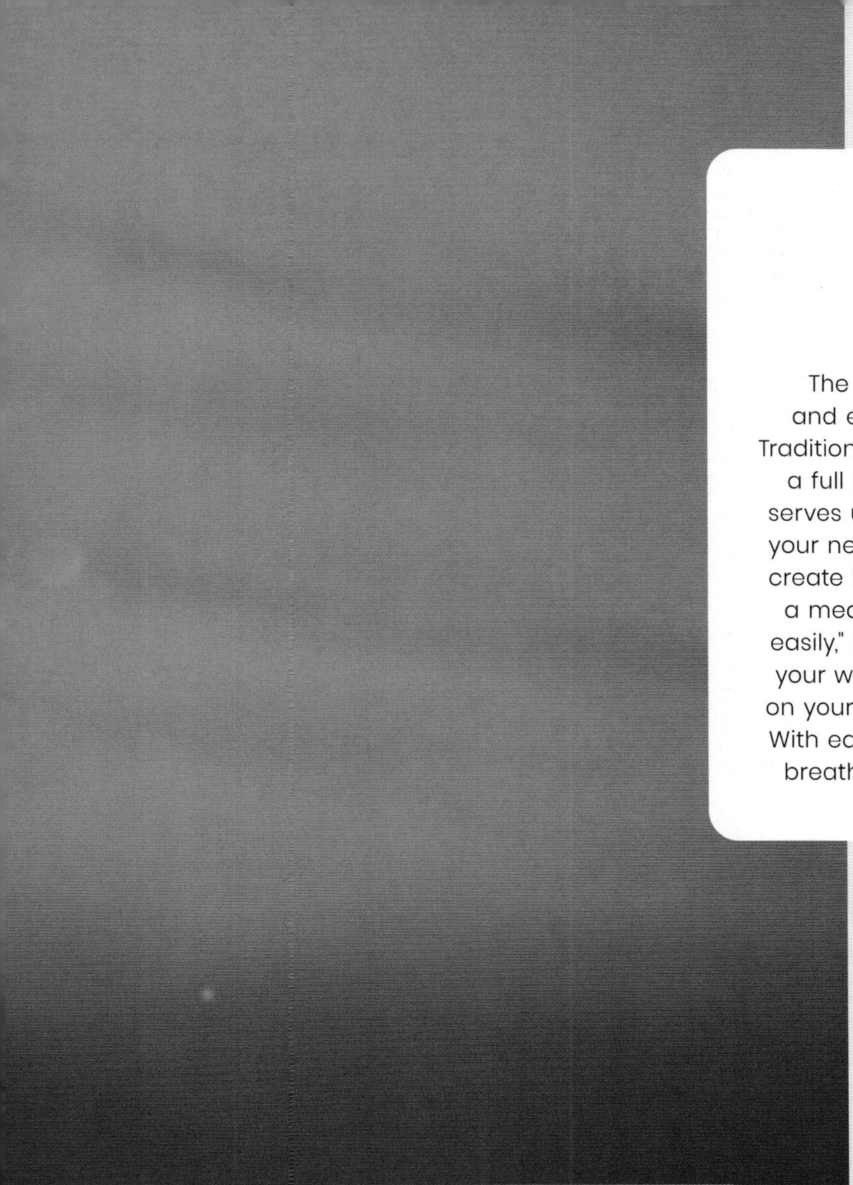

GAZE AT THE MOON

Manifest a little moon magic

The lunar cycle is thought to affect our moods and energy and we can tune into it for guidance. Traditionally, a new moon amplifies manifestation while a full moon cleanses and releases what no longer serves us. "On the night of a new moon make a list of your new moon intentions and what you would like to create in your life over the next lunar cycle. Then take a meditation where you visualise all of this coming easily," Kirsty explains. "Make a list of all that stands in your way and all you would like to let go of. Then lay on your back and begin to breathe slowly and deeply. With each deep exhale, feel as though you are gently breathing away anything that you no longer need."

HARNESS THE POWER OF CRYSTALS

Find inner stillness with support from semi-precious stones

Crystals have been used for thousands of years to support emotional well-being. "Rose quartz will help amplify love, compassion and acceptance. Citrine will help with abundance and happiness. Amythest will help bring calm, or something like black tourmaline will help you to feel grounded and protected," says Kirsty. "As you meditate with your crystal it will emit these vibrations to you so that you can more easily begin to tune in to these things in yourself." They can also help amplify intentions and provide a 'touchstone' through a meditation practice. "So, you can program your chosen crystal with what you would like to bring more of into your life and each time you sit and meditate with your crystal it will bring your back to your intention," she adds.

MEDITATION TIPS for Newbies

Power up by powering down

1 MAKE A SCHEDULE

Try to set a meditation goal for two weeks or a whole month. Even if you feel like you won't have time, once you see the benefits you're likely to want to find the time to practice. Allocating roughly the same time for your practice each day will help with consistency.

2 KEEP A JOURNAL

Scribble down how you feel before and after each session. Even jotting down a short sentence or two will help you to keep track of how the sessions are helping you. and observe your local birds.

3 SET AN INTENTION

Not to be confused with a goal, an intention is something you want to align within your life such as a purpose or attitude you'd like to commit to. Before each practice set a specific intention to help focus your mind and heart. It could be to 'release fear' or 'to practice being kinder to yourself and to others', anything that is connected to your values and life principles.

Finding PEACE in a CHAOTIC World

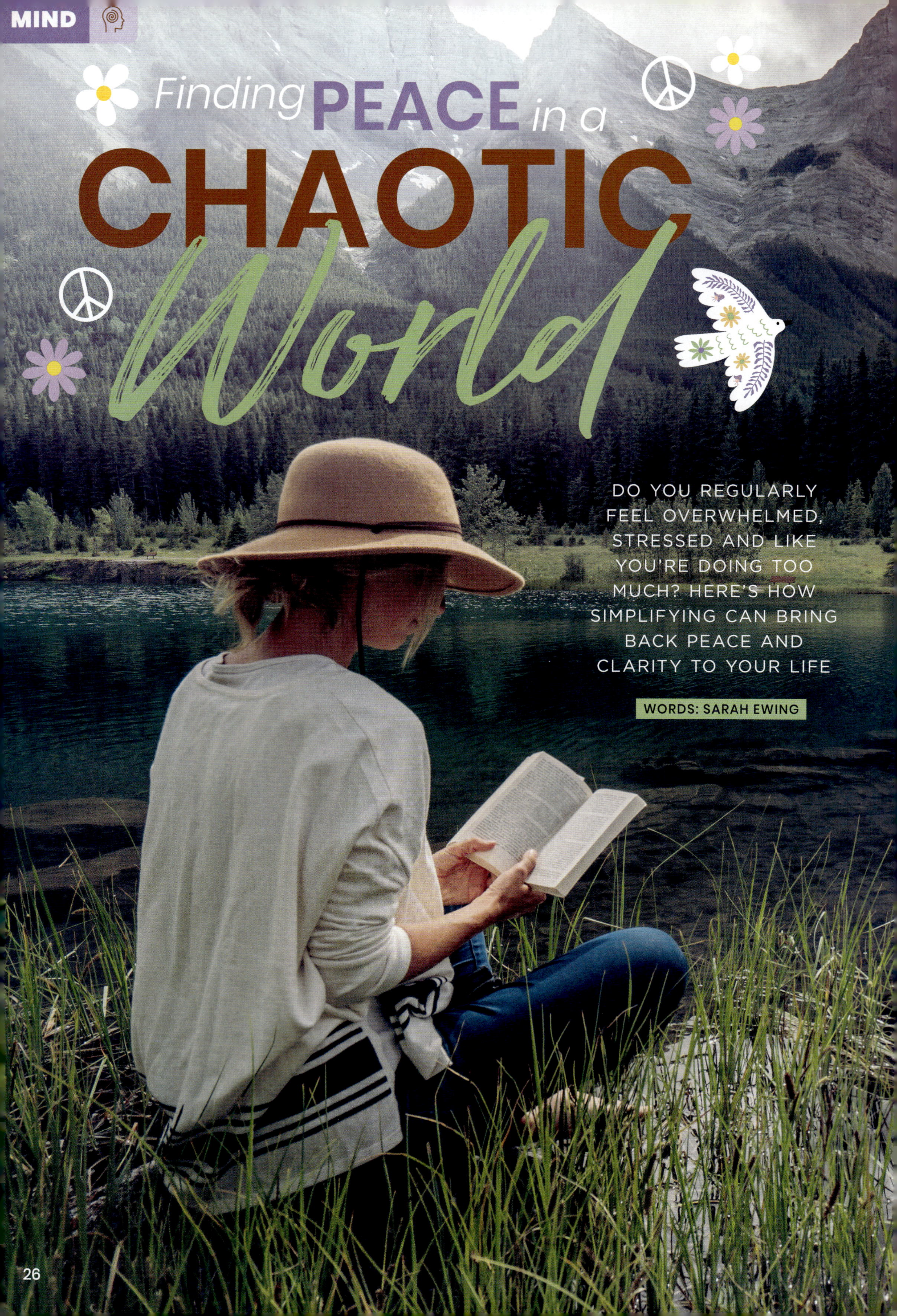

DO YOU REGULARLY FEEL OVERWHELMED, STRESSED AND LIKE YOU'RE DOING TOO MUCH? HERE'S HOW SIMPLIFYING CAN BRING BACK PEACE AND CLARITY TO YOUR LIFE

WORDS: SARAH EWING

We've all had periods where we feel life is getting on top of us, that we're struggling to keep up. Whether it's health, work, money or family, there are so many demands on you and the stress can get too much. Do you feel the joy is being sucked out of life? Here's how simplifying your life can help you get back on track and feel happier.

1 WHAT'S YOUR "WHY"?

Simplifying is all about finding what really matters to you. Decluttering is a part of it, but for permanent change, you need to change your mindset. Several recent studies have shown a link between depression and physical and mental clutter I started simplifying my life after several tough years of family ill health and bereavement, relationship problems and job stress. I felt like I had become derailed and wanted to get back on track.

ACTION What is your main goal in life or what would you like to make a priority? Use that to underpin your simplifying journey.

2 LESS DECISION FATIGUE

To cut the overwhelm, you simply need to have less stuff. Your day will run much more smoothly if your wardrobe is pared down to things you really love and your house isn't filled to the brim. Giving yourself that white space will be a relief.

ACTION Ask yourself: do I really need this? Will I use it again? If it's redundant or outdated, you don't get brownie points for keeping something longer than necessary.

3 APPRECIATE THE SIMPLE THINGS

When your life is so busy and full, it's impossible to slow down and appreciate the smaller things. We're so accustomed to busy is better, that it's almost sacrilegious to unbusy your schedule. And too much of a good thing makes it lose its allure. Once you have got rid of the unimportant things in your life and are focusing on your priorities, you can enjoy (often free) things.

ACTION Listen to the morning birds with a good cup of coffee. Learn to make your favourite cocktail at home.

4 BECOME A CONSCIOUS CONSUMER

Hands up who's bought things they don't really need on a whim? We all need to treat ourselves once in a while, but really think about whether it's essential and what your motivation is. By thinking more carefully about what you're purchasing, you'll only bring new things into your house that will get used.

ACTION For any purchase over £50, give yourself a cooling off period before buying it, say seven to 30 days. Often, you'll forget all about it or realise you can get by without it. If it doesn't, it clarifies your determination that you need it.

5 HELP OTHERS WITH YOUR REMORSE

One of the hardest things when you pare back your belongings is the feeling of guilt, whether it's about wasted time or money. But to counteract this, think about all the good causes you'll be helping when you purge and the pleasure the recipients will get from them.

ACTION As a family, decide on a charity that you would like to donate your items to or for extra motivation, get each member to choose a cause that's important to them. Many do pick-ups direct from your home. I donated my stuff to three charities – Cats Protection, Borders Pet Rescue and homeless charity Streetwork.

6 TIDY HOUSE, TIDY MIND

Once you're in the full swing of purging and are able to see more white space, you really will notice a sense of peace return. Your home will be less stressful, you'll enjoy it more and that, in turn, will carry over into your life outside. I found it much easier to cope with my job stress and family health issues, knowing that my home was a calm sanctuary. I also knew the calmer I was, the more able I was to distinguish between minor irritations and things that really mattered.

ACTION If something is bothering you, ask yourself: Is it really an issue or am I just overwhelmed? Will it help if I say or do something or will I make it worse and waste my time? Learning to bite your tongue is very hard but will save you a lot of unnecessary hassle.

7 VALUE EXPERIENCES OVER THINGS

Having something to show for your money is a big motivation when you work hard, but when you think about your priorities in life, no one ever looks back and thinks "I need more stuff". Spend your time and money doing something to create memories and connect with friends and family.

ACTION Cool off the online shopping and message a friend to make a coffee date. Have a themed pot-luck dinner party.

8 DON'T SAVE THINGS FOR SUNDAY BEST

It's natural to want to keep your nice things nice, but having things and not enjoying them is a waste of money. If you wait for the ideal time to use something or do something, you'll always put it off.

ACTION Try wearing dressing up this weekend. Use that gift certificate to get a nice haircut and go out to dinner.

9 STREAMLINE YOUR KITCHEN

You've had a long day, you're tired, you're hungry. Cook a meal from scratch? No thanks, that's the last thing you probably want to do. Start meal planning and bulk-cooking. You'll save time and money. Also, anything out on your kitchen counter has to be used daily or several times a week. Otherwise, put it away.

ACTION Invest in a slow cooker, start saving recipes from Pinterest or purchase a good cookbook.

10 DITCH THE ANXIETY AND OVERTHINKING

This is one of the hardest things to tackle in your simplifying journey. Once you've cleared all the crap from your life, it can leave you feeling exposed and vulnerable initially because you're not hiding behind the busyness of life or mountains of clutter. But by this stage, you'll realise that it's not stuff you need to feel good about yourself. You'll build your self-esteem from a better foundation.

ACTION Perform one simple act of kindness each day for a confidence boost. Read *Rising Strong* by Brené Brown and *Creating Space To Thrive* by Courtney Kenney.

Creativity MATTERS

YOU MAY NOT ALWAYS FEEL LIKE IT BUT, AS HUMANS, WE ALL HAVE GREAT CAPACITY FOR CREATIVITY. PRACTISE MINDFULNESS AND STOP PRE-JUDGING YOURSELF FOR NOT BEING A 'CREATIVE TYPE'

WORDS: REBECCA LEWRY-GRAY

Getting creative and messy is a great way to keep our minds open and active. Art can also have a calming effect on a person; you can spend time focusing on one task being fully immersed in the moment – so much so, you might very well lose track of time! When creating, keep yourself grounded in your activity by breathing and taking note of the sensations you're experiencing. Remind yourself that this is "me time" and if you do find your mind wander back to day-to-day worries, gently and kindly bring yourself back to the task at hand.

Art can also give us great joy. Many psychologists believe that being creative is just as important as food, exercise and meditation due to the positive effects it has on our mental and physical health. While we might not view it as equally as important as nutrition or other basic physical human needs, exercising our creative muscles is a key part of human wellness.

There are so many ways to tap in to our creative impulses. And getting creative doesn't have to be an expensive hobby either! Consider what it is that you want out of your creative activities: are you looking to gift to those you love; are you wishing to surround yourself with meaningful beauty; or are you simply hoping for a mindful practice to help nourish your own soul?

1 MUSIC

Whether you consider yourself a musician or not, music and music-making has amazing therapeutic benefits. In mindfulness practice, we work on not worrying about the future or the past, and instead focus on the here and now. Negative self-talk regarding 'talent' can be controlled when mindfully making music. Perfection isn't the goal here. Work on non-judgementally enjoying the sensations and the process of music. If making music holds no interest for you, try to practise mindfully enjoying music – choose something you haven't listened to a lot and pay attention to what emerges in your head.

2 CANDLE MAKING

Try to include different essential oils in making your candle; work with your favourite scents, or those that bring back special memories. When melting your wax, you can build a ritual, setting a mindful intention while mixing, or verbalising goals while you set your wick. The uses of candles in meditation are numerous too – an extra layer is added if you are the one who made the candle! Candle meditation is a simple technique in which you focus your attention on an eye-level flame and focus and control your breathing. There is something hypnotic in the flame of a candle and it can greatly assist in calming your mind.

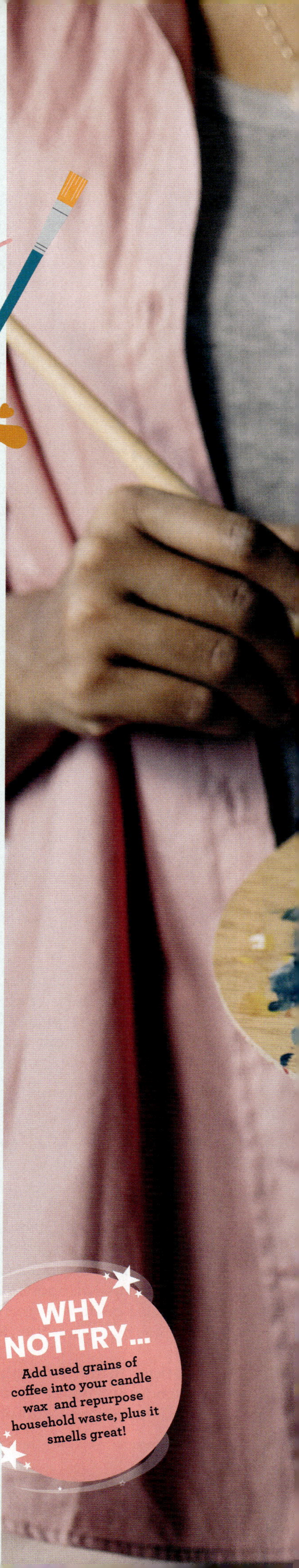

WHY NOT TRY...

Add used grains of coffee into your candle wax and repurpose household waste, plus it smells great!

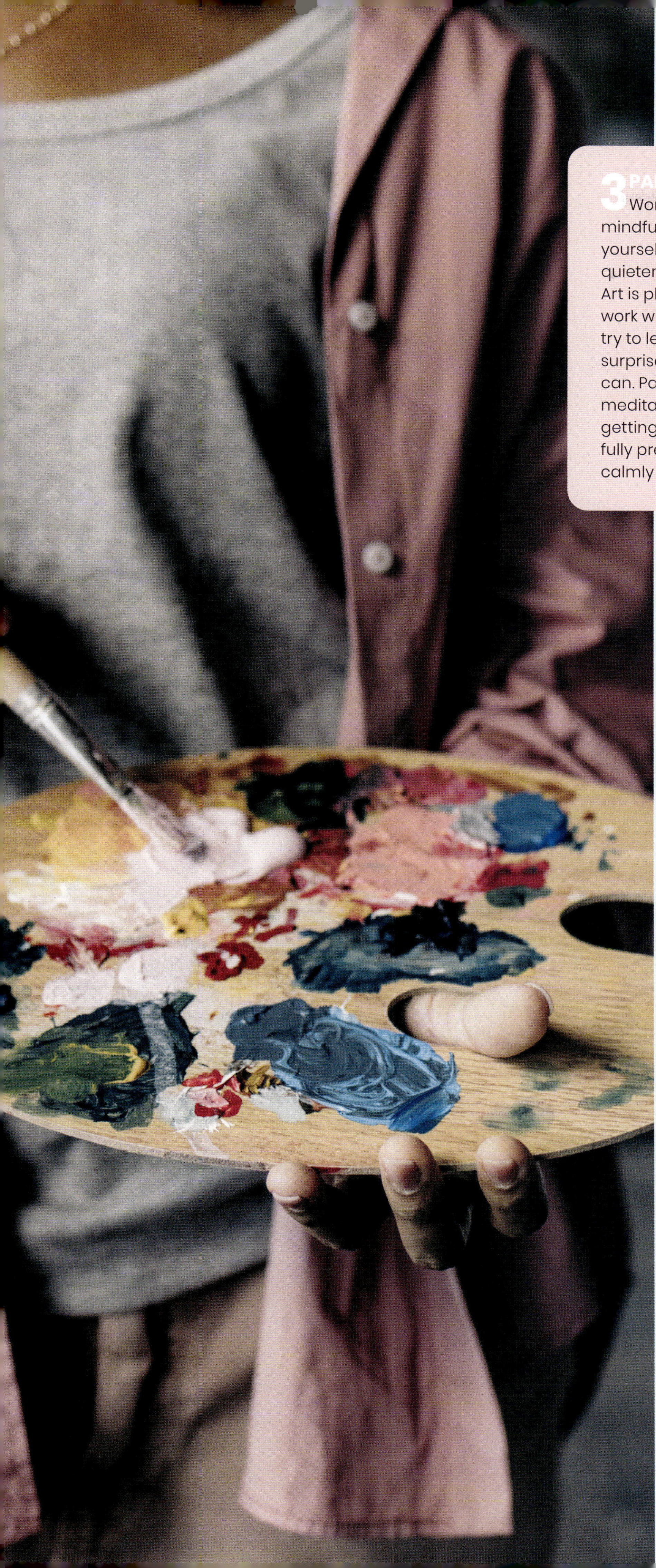

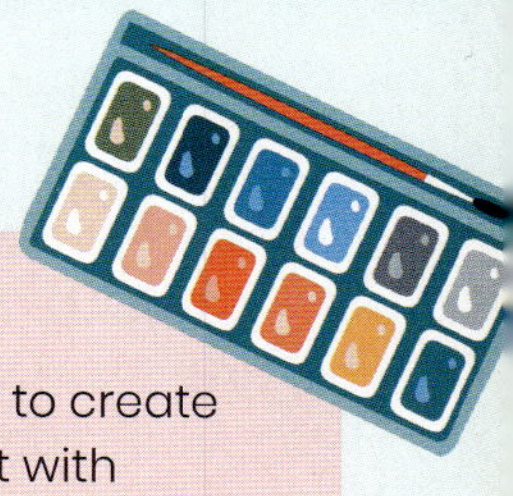

3 PAINTING

Working with paint is a great way to create mindfully. Take a moment to connect with yourself: let go of your pre-judgements and quieten that noisy negative voice in your head. Art is play and you should allow yourself to work without an end goal. If you are an artist, try to let your established style go for a bit – surprise yourself by painting as freely as you can. Painting usually encourages a mindful meditative state, but if you do find yourself getting side tracked or pulled away from being fully present, take a breath and kindly and calmly bring yourself back to your task at hand.

4 SCRAPBOOKING

Scrapbooking is a great 'entry-level' way to get into mindful journaling, especially if you're a visual person. You can chose any format of book (large or small) and use any kind of material you have to hand. Many people enjoy the work of combining papers, tapes and stamps to create reflection spaces in the scrapbook. Other people might prefer to use photographs to inspire ideas. As with all mindfulness practice, it's very much an individual process and yours alone – nobody else needs to peek inside. The cutting, arranging and sticking involved in scrapbooking requires care and focus – try to give your full attention to the activity you're doing and shake yourself out of auto-pilot if you feel it creeping in! To keep costs low, scrapbooking can be done online, but many prefer to stay analogue – you can't beat the feeling of laying out pages with your hands.

5 CLAY

Clay is the perfect mix of earth and water, and connecting with these two elements makes for an incredible mindful activity. You don't need to rush out and buy a potter's wheel or a kiln; there are many accessible ways for people to get their hands dirty and re-centre themselves. Connect what your eyes are seeing with what your hands are making; take note of the temperature and texture of the clay and how that changes as you manipulate it. Whether your ceramic works are meant to be enjoyed or used, simply take pleasure in the fact that you made them.

6 COLOURING BOOKS

In bookshops, supermarkets and stationery stores, it's impossible to ignore the wonderful range of adult colouring books. They help you to slow down, have fun and be creative away from a screen, and the complex designs are great for a focused creative meditation. The brilliant thing about their popularity is that there will likely be a colouring book out there that is tailored to your interests.

7 KNITTING AND CROCHET

Many long-time knitters and crocheters talk about the feeling of 'flow' that they get from creating with wool. That flow shows you're 'in the zone', and everything around you (time, distractions and so on) ceases to matter. The kind of repetitive action that occurs in crochet and knitting triggers our calm chemical – there are schemes in prisons around the world to get inmates knitting. More advanced knitting and crochet patterns include detailed instructions and a whole new language to learn that requires focus. You can be so occupied that you have no time for pervasive worries to bubble up. The physical act of creating an item out of wool is amazing for self-esteem; be proud of your pieces (no matter how wonky they may be to start!). Notice yourself improve and enjoy the process of productivity.

8 CREATIVE WRITING

You can use mindfulness to work through creative blocks and work on your self-compassion when it comes to your creative output. To begin mindful creative writing, you can start with observing the world, without letting your thoughts get away from you. Work on focusing on sights, smells and sounds that are in that very moment you are in. Remember to focus on your breath when starting mindful creative writing; don't judge the thoughts that pop into your head – notice them and calmly and kindly return to the task at hand. You can use free writing to unload, and work on not editing yourself.

9 MAKE CLOTHES

Clothes can cause a myriad of anxiety: you might feel guilt that you haven't worn something 'enough', or you may feel paralysed by the decision of what to wear in the morning. Take stock of what you own, identify what you might be missing, and try your hand at making it yourself! There are lots of easy-to-follow patterns in fabric stores and all over the internet. The pride of being able to say 'I made this' is undeniable. You're also consuming more ethically (you know exactly who made your clothes), as well as customising your wardrobe to be truly individual.

10 NEEDLEWORK

Needlework is a creative project that has had a resurgence in recent years. Much like knitting and crochet, the slowness of the task and repetitive movements help you focus on your hand work. There is no need to learn complicated techniques – keep it simple and don't get stressed if your thread knots!

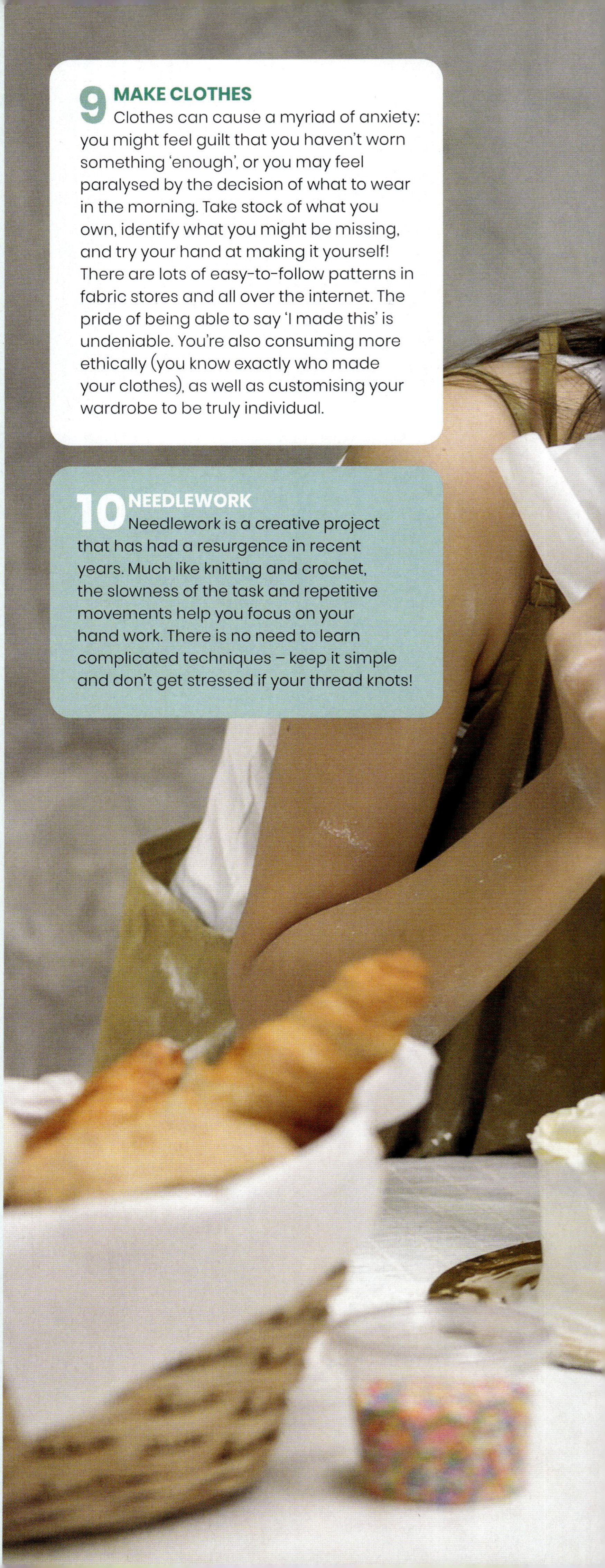

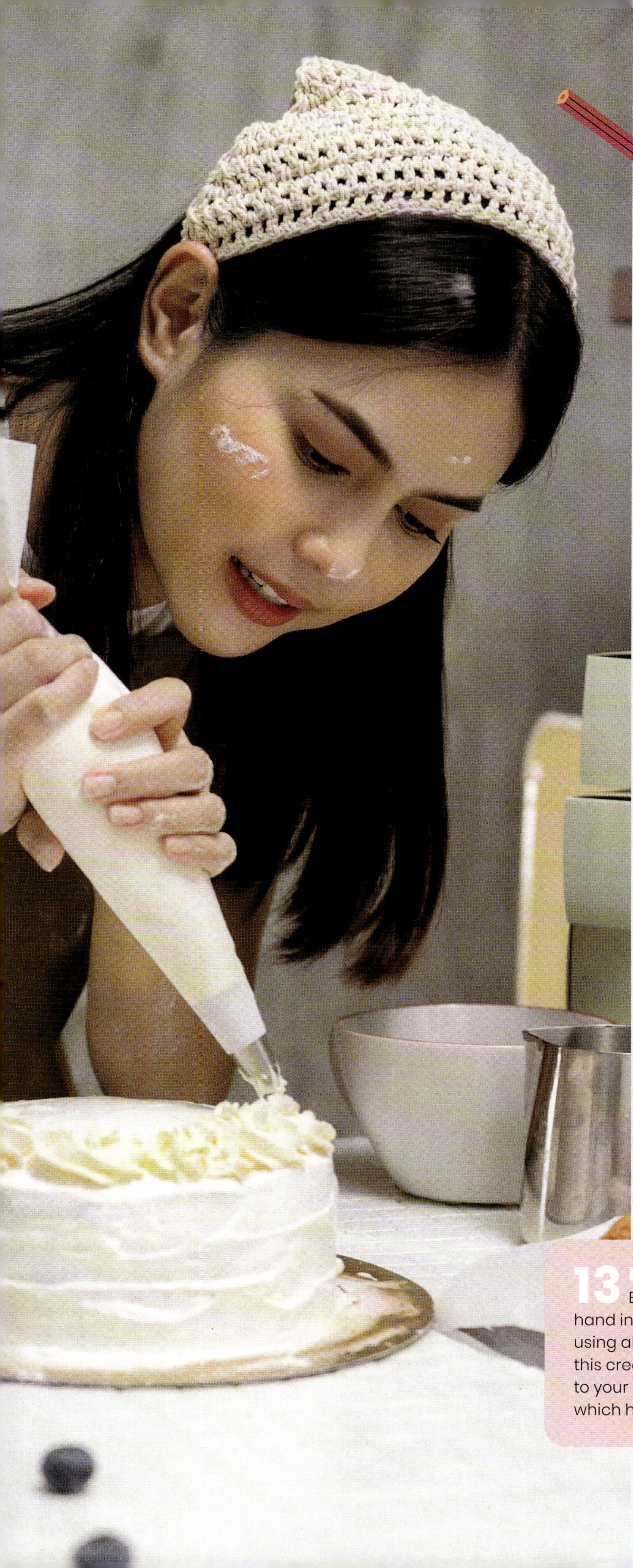

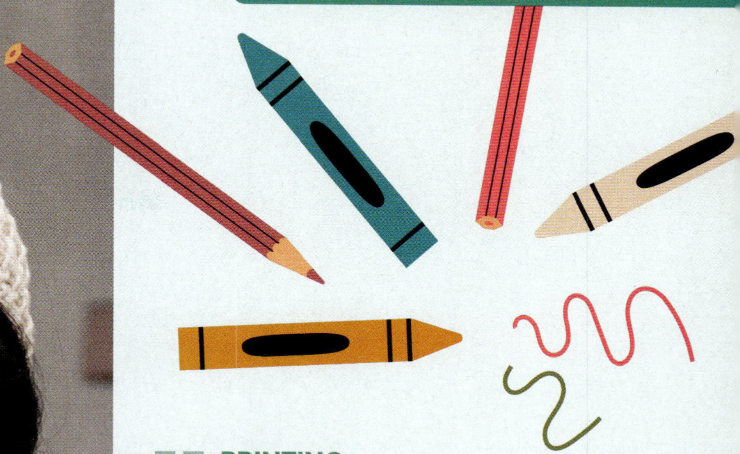

11 PRINTING

Art is good for you. It might be easy to assume that art and creativity have a purely aesthetic impact on our mental health. While it is true that they do have this impact, the creation of art can also help our creative thinking and improve our productivity. Print making is a great creative practice to experiment with, as there are so many ways to make a mark and change the way it is transferred. It might sound simple but potato printing is simple and effective for creating patterns. Making drawings on pieces of styrofoam to then transfer with paint is also rewarding and cheap.

12 DRAWING

As small children, so many of us enjoyed drawing. Take a moment to consider if and when that stopped for you. Being creative is a great way to keep our minds open and active. We're constantly learning news things in life, but sometimes you can get stuck in one way of thinking, which is detrimental to your overall wellness. By trying something new or unexpected in the name of art and creativity, we engage different learning styles. In adopting more patterns of wellness, we're breaking out of the everyday auto-pilot routines, and nowhere can you do that more easily than in art. Sketching, drawing and putting pen to paper is a great way of letting your mind take a break; you can fully consume yourself in the task of drawing. Enjoy the smells, feeling and gradual revelation of your work as it develops. Use drawing prompts if you really don't know where to start.

13 BAKE

Baking and mindfulness in the kitchen go hand in hand. Unlike so much else on this list, you're using almost all of your senses while working on this creative hobby. You also need to pay attention to your recipe and your quantities of ingredients, which helps to quiet your internal voice.

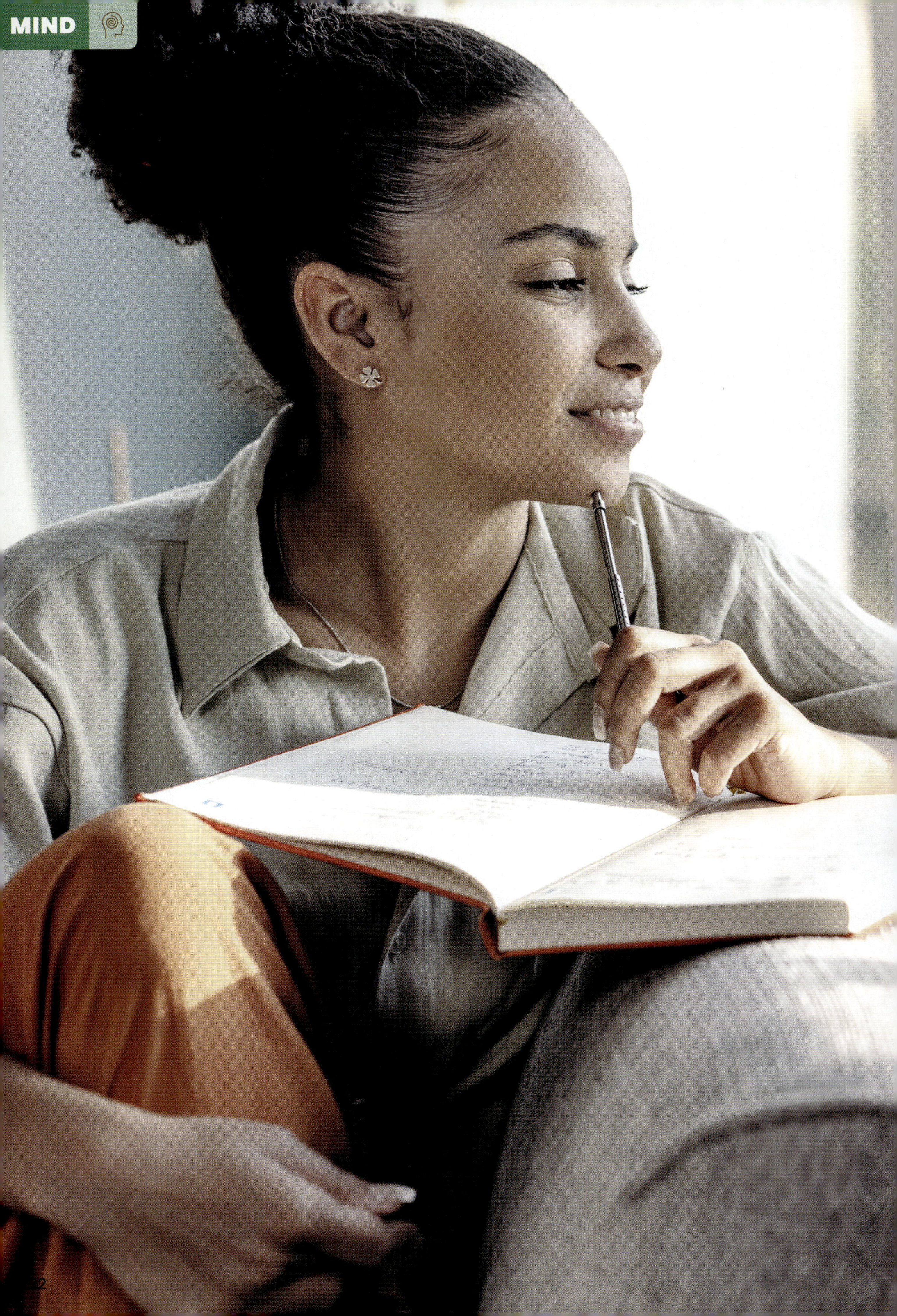

Put PEN to Paper

WE CAN SOMETIMES STRUGGLE TO ARTICULATE WHAT IT IS THAT IS REALLY BOTHERING US ABOUT A SITUATION, BUT BY GIVING OURSELVES SPACE AND TIME TO PRACTISE JOURNALING WE CAN OFTEN HIT THAT PAINFUL NERVE

WORDS: REBECCA LEWRY

If you find mindfulness a tricky habit to develop, give journaling a try. In short you're writing down your thoughts and feelings in a mindful fashion, keeping an eye on your emotions and triggers. We can use journaling to reflect on our behaviours and solve anything that keeps reoccurring.

WHY JOURNAL?

Journaling is on a par with meditation as it taps into that deep part of your psyche that may ordinarily be drowned out by the noisier distractions in your head. You're giving yourself a quiet moment to 'be' and look inwards.

SO MANY USES!

We can use journaling as a management tool for the stresses that modern life throws at us. Journals can be used to manage your workload and organise your racing thoughts and anxiety-inducing 'to dos', as well as calm yourself by dispassionately analysing your day. Journaling isn't just the preserve of teenagers in their bedrooms!

Journaling also trains your brain by using both hemispheres at the same time; the creative right side and rational left side.

There are also so many different styles of journaling practice to try, so don't feel constrained to one – or if one type doesn't 'stick' start a new blank page and try again! Check out some of the options on the following pages.

> "Journaling is on par with meditation as it taps into that deep part of your psyche that may ordinarily be drowned out"

1 GRATITUDE JOURNAL

Gratitude journaling is a way of reflecting and taking stock of what you're thankful for in your life. These things can be life changing or minuscule in detail but it's important as you are essentially rewiring your viewpoint, by looking at your life in a positive way. If we think hard on the people and events in our life that we are grateful for, we may find ourselves becoming less materialistic – we're realising that the things we usually value (materially) aren't what make the world go around! Allow the gratitude you practise in your journal to spill into your life.

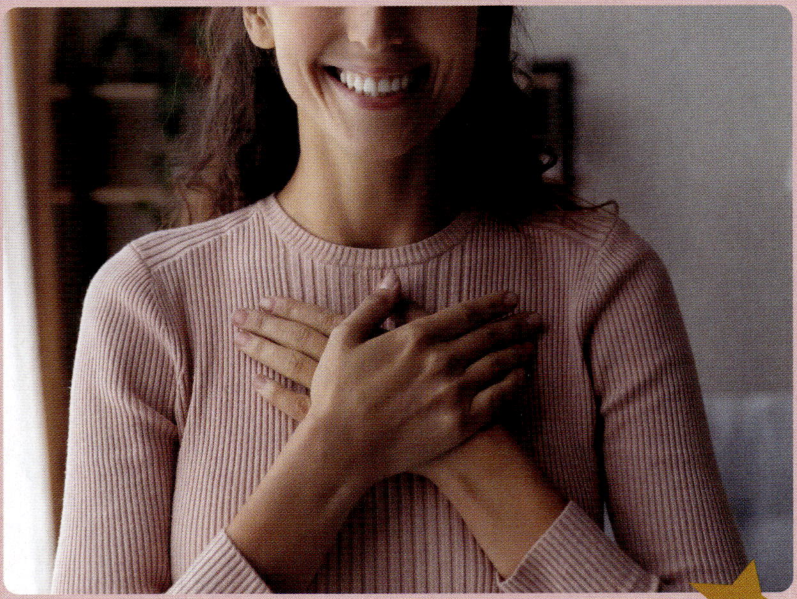

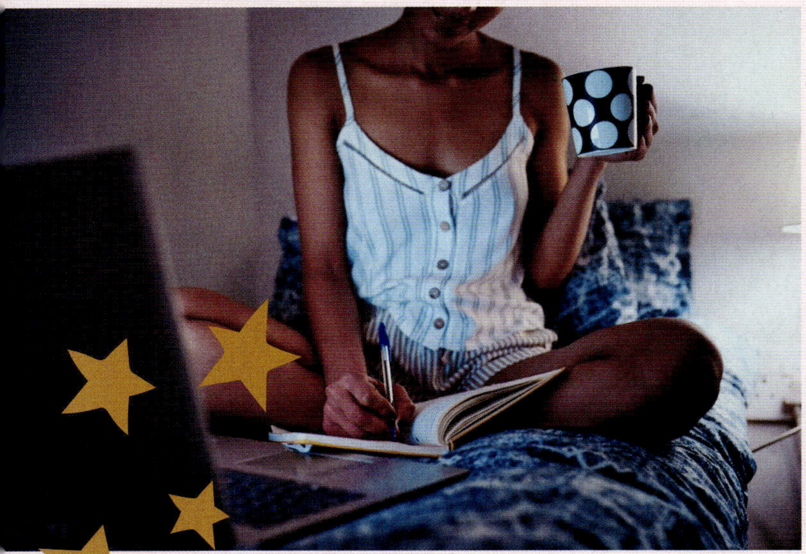

2 PROMPTED JOURNALS

If the idea of a blank page fills you with dread, help is at hand. Journaling has become really popular over recent years, and for many people prompted journals are a great place to start. These journals guide you through the process and can keep you accountable and focused. The wide range of prompted journals also cater for many specific types and kinds of journal-ers – from teens to people looking to be more mindful. There is no standard prompted journal, as the 'right' choice for you may not be the same for everyone. Keep in mind what you want to get out of journaling when looking for a prompted journal. Take a look at reviews to check the tone and commitment level before you buy.

3 DREAM JOURNAL

Dreaming is a little like unconscious mindfulness, our brains process our past in a subjective way, filing it all away. Annoyingly, we often forget our dreams as soon as we wake. Writing a dream journal can help improve our dream memory skills and you may find that after a period of dream journaling your dream memory becomes stronger. Try to write your dreams down as soon as you wake up to catch all the details. You can then use a dream dictionary to find reoccurring themes or try to work out your own personal meanings.

4 POSITIVITY JOURNAL

Try to use your journaling time to reflect on the positive things in your life. When we drill down we can find that under the surface there is a lot to be happy about. When things go wrong in life it is important to look for the silver linings. There is no point in practising positivity in your writing if you still expect everything to go wrong when you wake every morning! Remember, use the power of positive thinking; like attracts like!

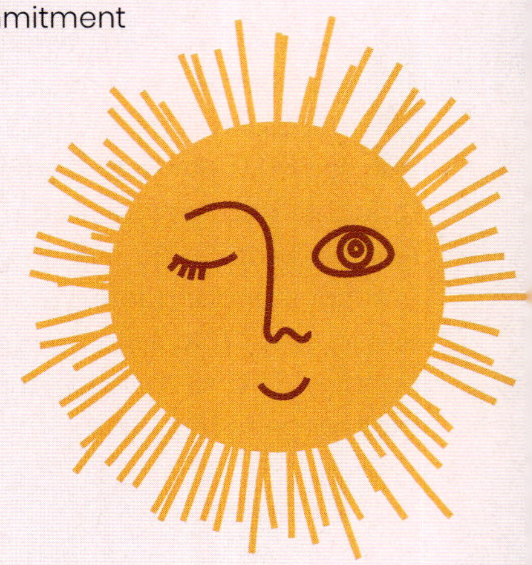

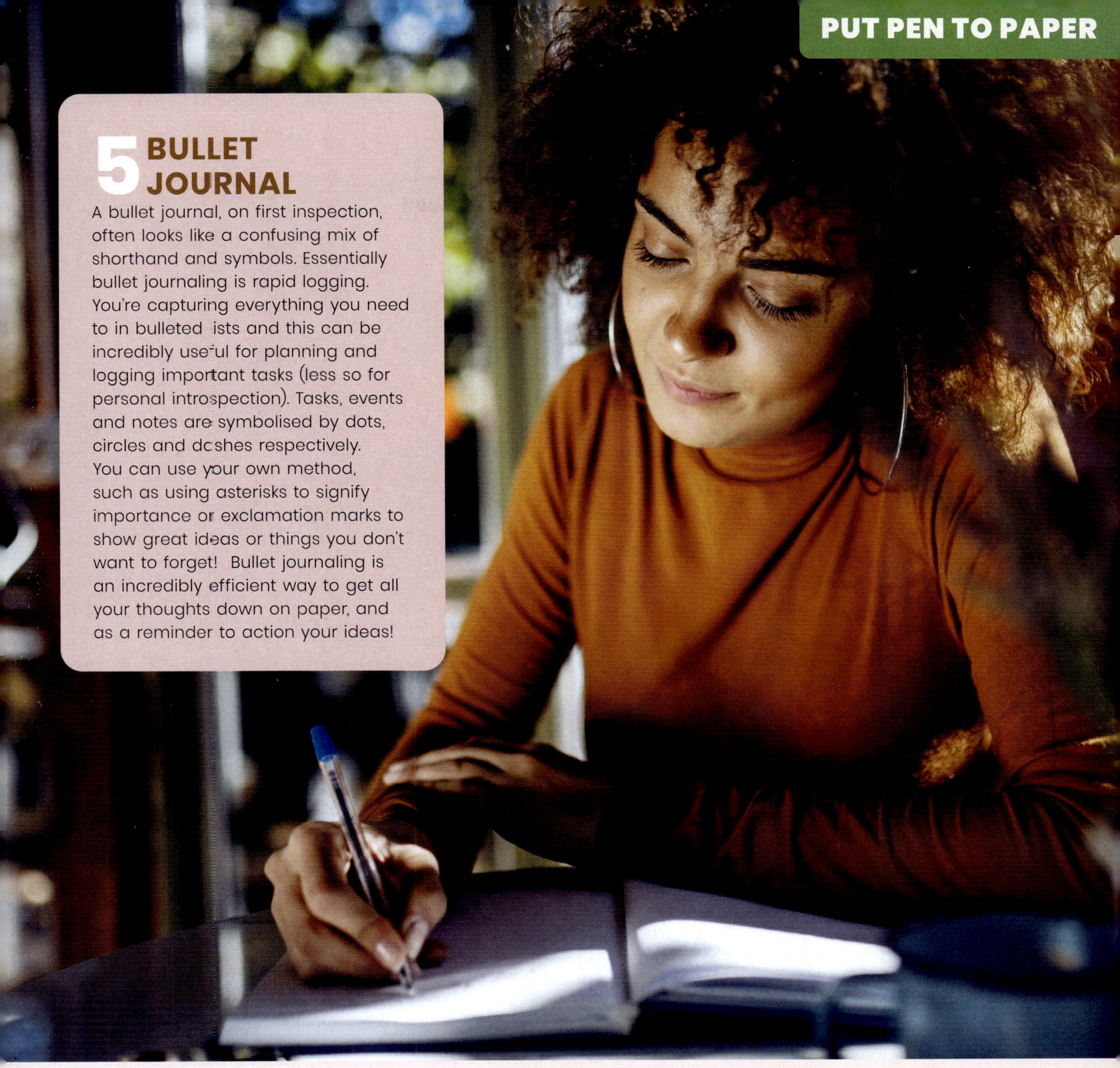

5 BULLET JOURNAL

A bullet journal, on first inspection, often looks like a confusing mix of shorthand and symbols. Essentially bullet journaling is rapid logging. You're capturing everything you need to in bulleted lists and this can be incredibly useful for planning and logging important tasks (less so for personal introspection). Tasks, events and notes are symbolised by dots, circles and dashes respectively. You can use your own method, such as using asterisks to signify importance or exclamation marks to show great ideas or things you don't want to forget! Bullet journaling is an incredibly efficient way to get all your thoughts down on paper, and as a reminder to action your ideas!

6 ART JOURNAL

Journaling doesn't have to take the form of a handwriting-heavy tome. If you are a visual person or a creative one at that, an art journal may be the best way for you to begin your journaling journey. Try to include your sketches, experiments and your reflections on how a task turned out – whether this is a piece of art or a day-to-day task. Play with your journal, often we can articulate ourselves better through mark making and art than through words. It's important to get pen (or pencil/crayon/paint) to paper and make that first mark and not get too hung up on perfection – this journal is just for you, you don't have to let anyone else in.

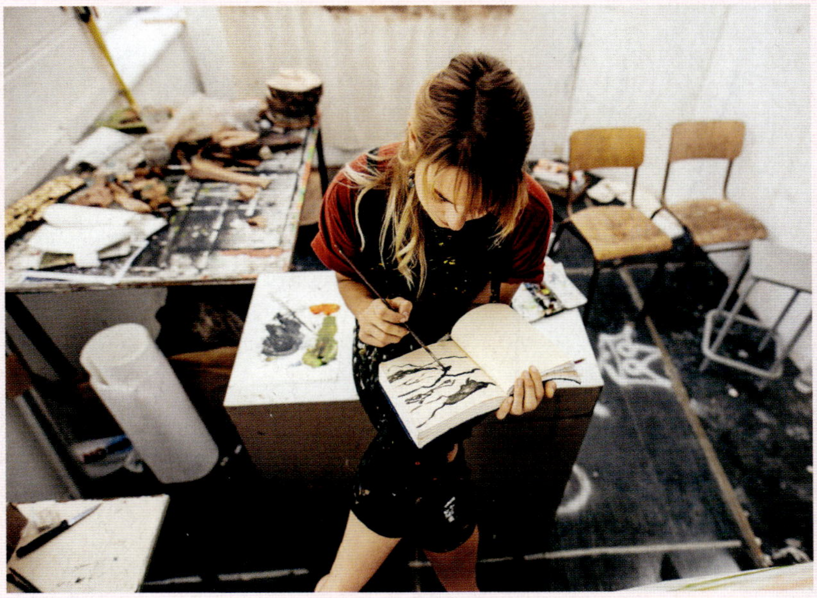

7 FREE WRITING

Spill your thoughts out onto your page. Free writing is quite different to the other types of journaling on this list. While journals such as dream journals, bullet journals and planning journals work due to their structure, free writing is more free (the clue is in the name)! Think of it like a brain dump or stream of consciousness writing. Try not to edit yourself and you may find you're getting into the nitty gritty of what you're really concerned about. Use this kind of journaling consciously, instead of feeling like it's yet another thing to do on your list of jobs, enjoy the task. Focus on your 'why' of journaling and keep yourself in the present moment while writing.

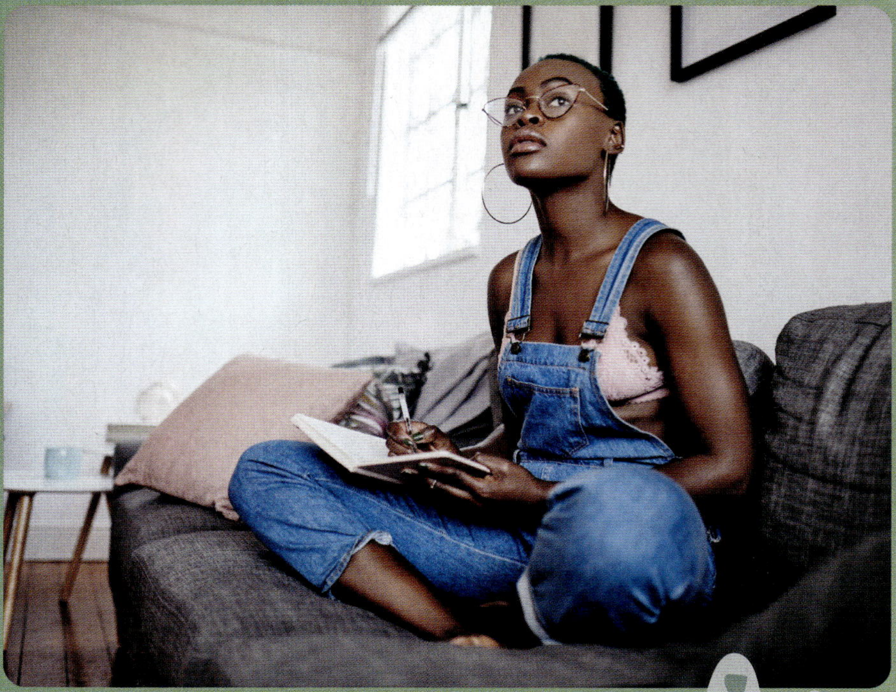

8 PLANNING JOURNAL

Whether you consider yourself a 'planner' or not, a planning journal is a great investment in your mental health. Everyone can miss things off the to-do list or fail to hit a deadline. You can use planning journals for short to medium-term planning in home life as well as work. In short, this kind of journal can help you develop the habit of planning – and can assist in goal setting too. If you find your day gets eaten up by constantly checking emails and addressing things as they come in, you can find security in organising your day hour-by-hour to ensure your tasks are completed.

9 SPIRITUAL JOURNALS

If you are a spiritual or religious person you can use a journal to help you explore this more fully. You can use this kind of journal to carve out time in your day for this kind of focus and track your growth. Pick a daily reflection and work on it in your journal.

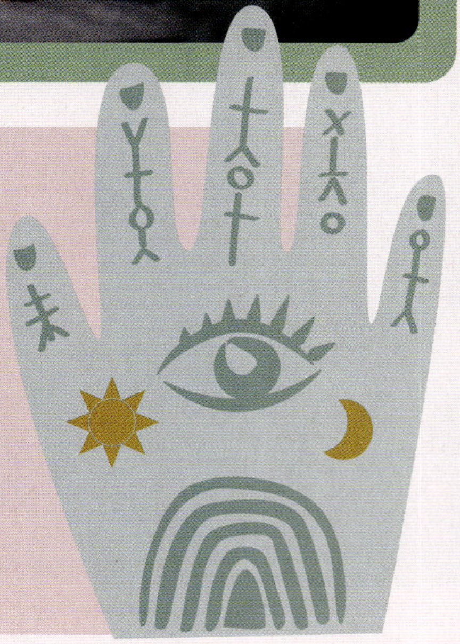

10 TIME CAPSULE

Journaling can have a finite timeline. You may wish to journal about a very specific part of your life; whether positive or negative. You may also wish to journal about current events – we live in interesting times and by including clippings and collages you can create a full picture of what life is like.

11 FAMILY JOURNAL

Family journaling is essentially sharing your journal and writing with other members of your family. You take turns writing in the journal, talking about things you may struggle to address in person. Do this mindfully, keeping an eye on your intentions – you're not looking to start a fight. You and your family members are opening yourselves up to each other and perspectives can change, depending on the viewpoint of others. Family journals can be very interesting with children, who may struggle to express themselves eloquently. When you focus your writing with other people you're practising empathy, which can only be a good thing.

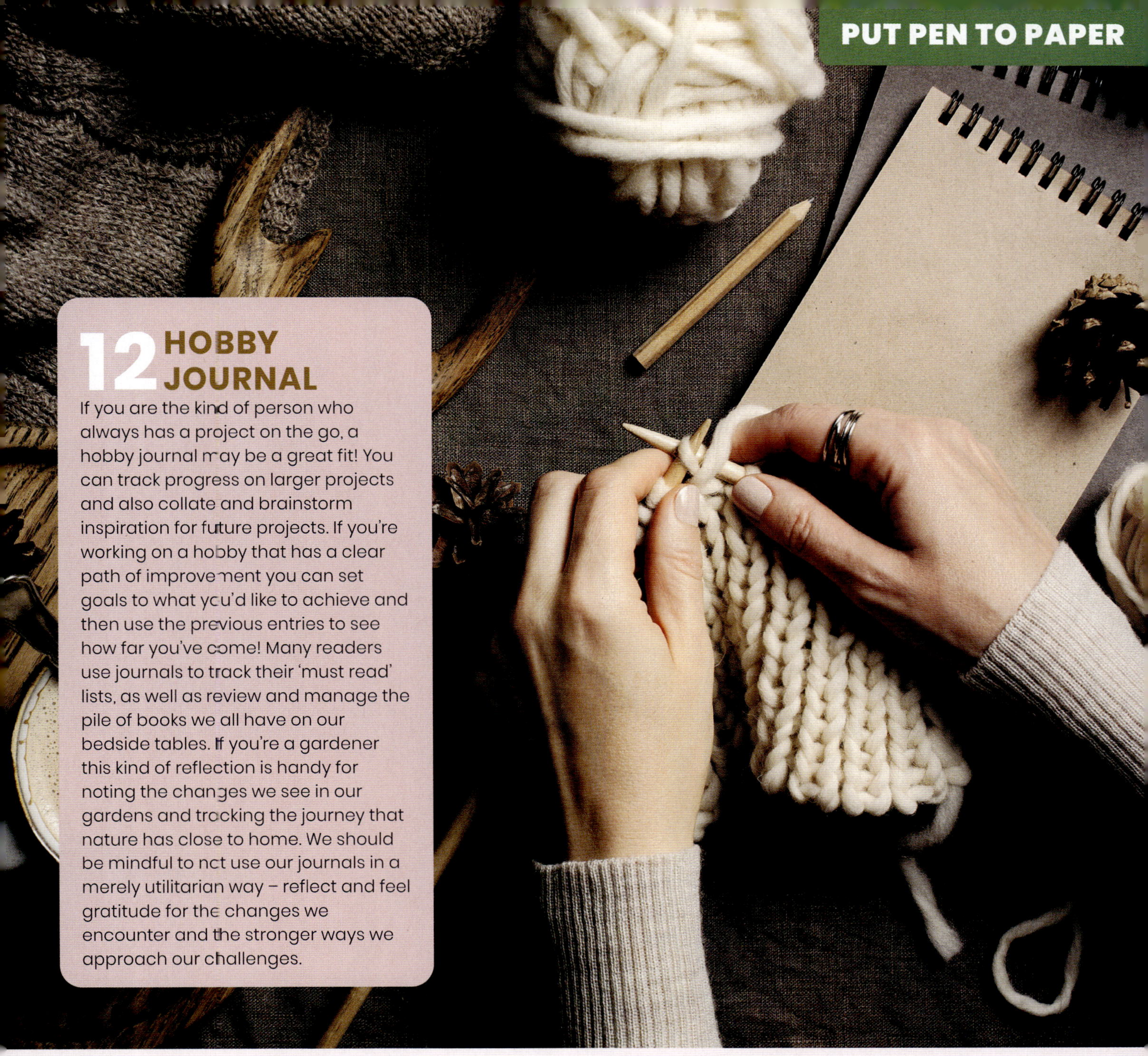

12 HOBBY JOURNAL

If you are the kind of person who always has a project on the go, a hobby journal may be a great fit! You can track progress on larger projects and also collate and brainstorm inspiration for future projects. If you're working on a hobby that has a clear path of improvement you can set goals to what you'd like to achieve and then use the previous entries to see how far you've come! Many readers use journals to track their 'must read' lists, as well as review and manage the pile of books we all have on our bedside tables. If you're a gardener this kind of reflection is handy for noting the changes we see in our gardens and tracking the journey that nature has close to home. We should be mindful to not use our journals in a merely utilitarian way – reflect and feel gratitude for the changes we encounter and the stronger ways we approach our challenges.

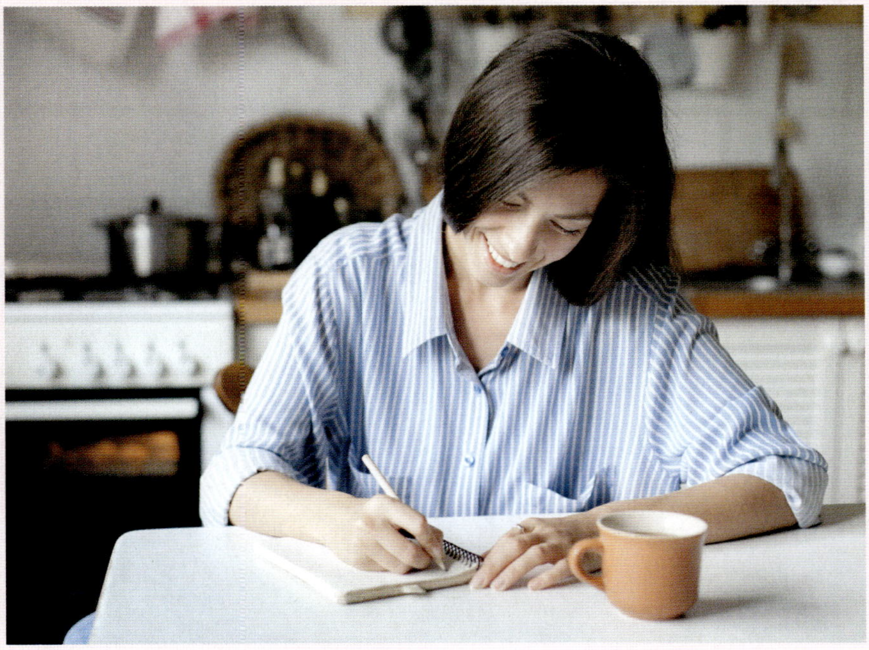

13 QUICK JOURNAL

If you feel like regularly journaling is too much of a time sink for you, give quick journaling a try. It's simple, write one sentence a day (that's it!). While this may sound simple, it's an incredibly interesting exercise as you are editing your memories of your day and working out what is truly important – what is valuable to record and reflect on? Keep this habit for as long as you can and you may find the routine sticks and you extend your entries. Your journal may evolve and change during your time writing – there's no rule to say you must stick to one type.

BLUE SKY *Thinking*

THE SKY IS THE REALM OF AIR AND ITS CELESTIAL DEPTHS ARE BRIMMING WITH MAGIC

WORDS: POPPY-JAY ST PALMER

ASTROLOGICAL TRANSITS

What are they and how do they work?

When reading your horoscope, you may have seen that a planet is 'in transit', but what does that actually mean? Astrological transits involve interpreting ongoing movement of the planets as they move across the horoscope, and are one of the biggest indicators of future trends and developments in horoscopic astrology. Perhaps the most important transit is the 'planetary return', during which the transiting planet returns to the same point in the sky it was at during a person's birth – the planet has completed a whole circuit of the sky, meaning a new cycle of someone's life is beginning. Some returns are less common than others. For example, the Jupiter return happens once every 12 or so years, whereas the Saturn return happens every 30 years. Each planetary return brings with different meanings that could become significant to a person's life.

WHY NOT TRY...

Pick a patch of sky that you can see every day from a window and observe it at different times and in different weather. How does the cloud cover change it? What stars can you see there at night?

WHY NOT TRY...

If you want more success when wishing on stars, try looking up the date of the next meteor shower and getting out of the city and into nature. Once you've picked your observation spot, layer up, get some snacks ready and enjoy.

20 20 20

Switch things up on office days

Bring the healing power of the sky into your working life by using the 20 20 20 rule: every 20 minutes, give your eyes a break from looking at a screen by looking at something 20 feet away for 20 seconds. But instead of focusing on other office equipment, look out of the window at the open sky. It's not only good for eye strain but also for your wellbeing and creativity levels.

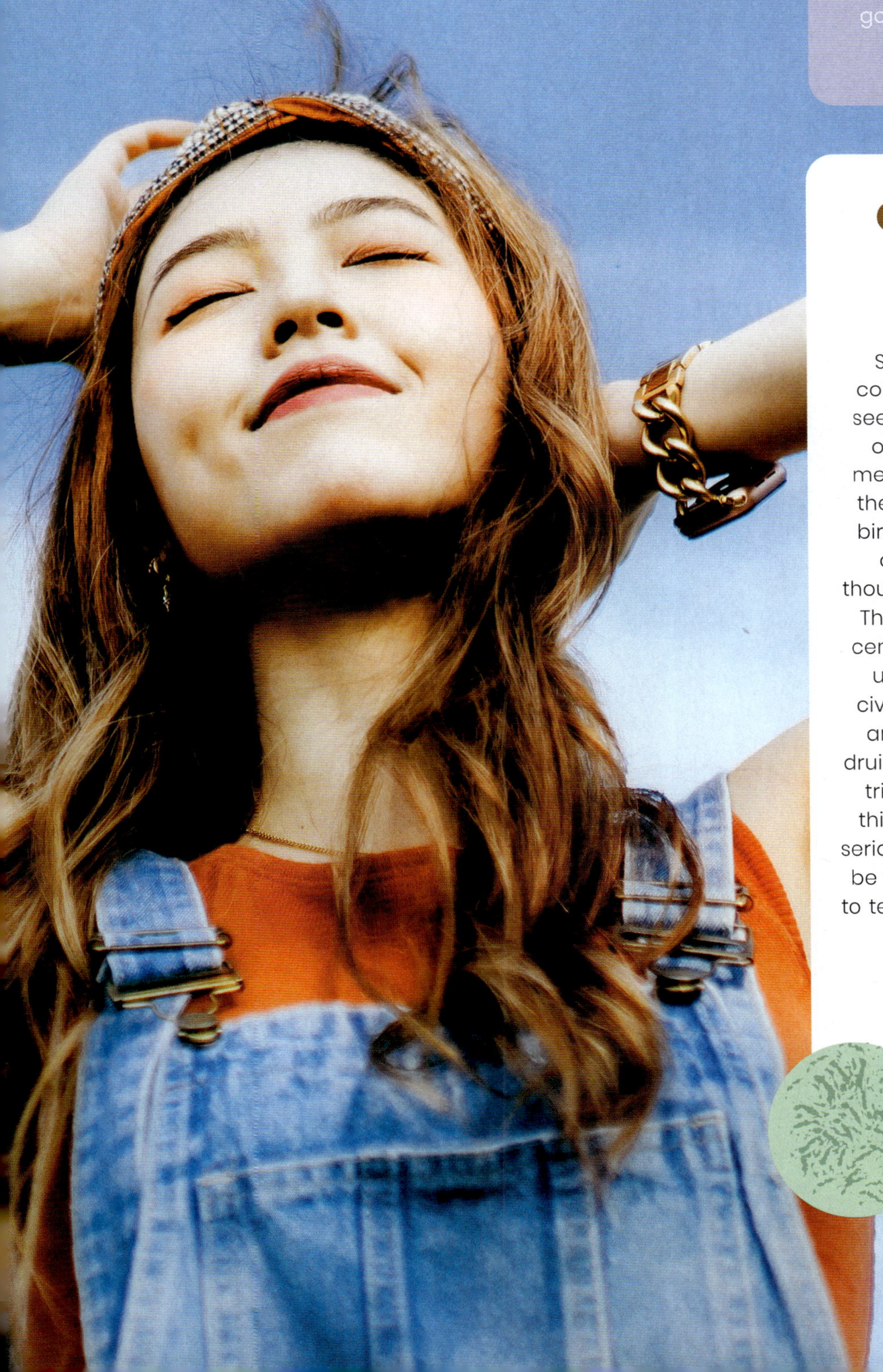

ORNITHOMANCY

A little birdy told me...

Some people watch birds to feel connected to nature. Others do it to see the future. From the Greek words ornis meaning 'bird' and manteia meaning 'divination', ornithomancy is the practice of reading omens from birds and their actions. As creatures of the sky, birds have long been thought to be spiritual communicators. The divining method has existed for centuries, and is known to have been used by a number of groups and civilisations, from the ancient Greeks and Romans to the Celts and their druids, and Indigenous North American tribes. Ornithomancy is still used to this day, though perhaps a little less seriously in most cases. You might even be familiar with a certain rhyme used to tell the future from magpie sightings:

One for sorrow,
Two for joy,
Three for a girl,
Four for a boy,
Five for silver,
Six for gold,
Seven for a secret,
Never to be told.

STAR LIGHT *Star bright*

How making wishes on shooting stars became a modern tradition

Human beings have long sought celestial intervention through the tradition of wishing on stars. In ancient Greek times, astronomer Ptolemy presented the theory that shooting stars crossed gaps between cosmic spheres from when the gods parted them so they could spy on mortals. Later on, Christians liked to think they represented rising or falling souls or angels. Modern urban light pollution has caused shooting star sightings to become rarer, and made the act of wishing upon them feel more magical.

THE CLOCK STRIKES LUCKY

Planetary hours uses the planets' positions to be in the right place at the right time

Astrology and time have always been deeply linked. Much of the thinking and calculation behind the relationship between the two is complex, but those with a more basic knowledge can take meaning from time through the concept of planetary hours. Each of the seven classical planets – which include Saturn, Jupiter, Mars, the Sun, Venus, Mercury and the Moon – are believed to rule over each day, and even various parts of the day. Their positions can change outcomes of events, meaning there are therefore more favourable times to do certain things. It takes 'being in the right place at the right time' literally. Once you start studying the planets and learning the types of magic associated with each planet, calculating auspicious times becomes easy. Use this online calculator to get started: **lunarium.co.uk/planets/hours/**

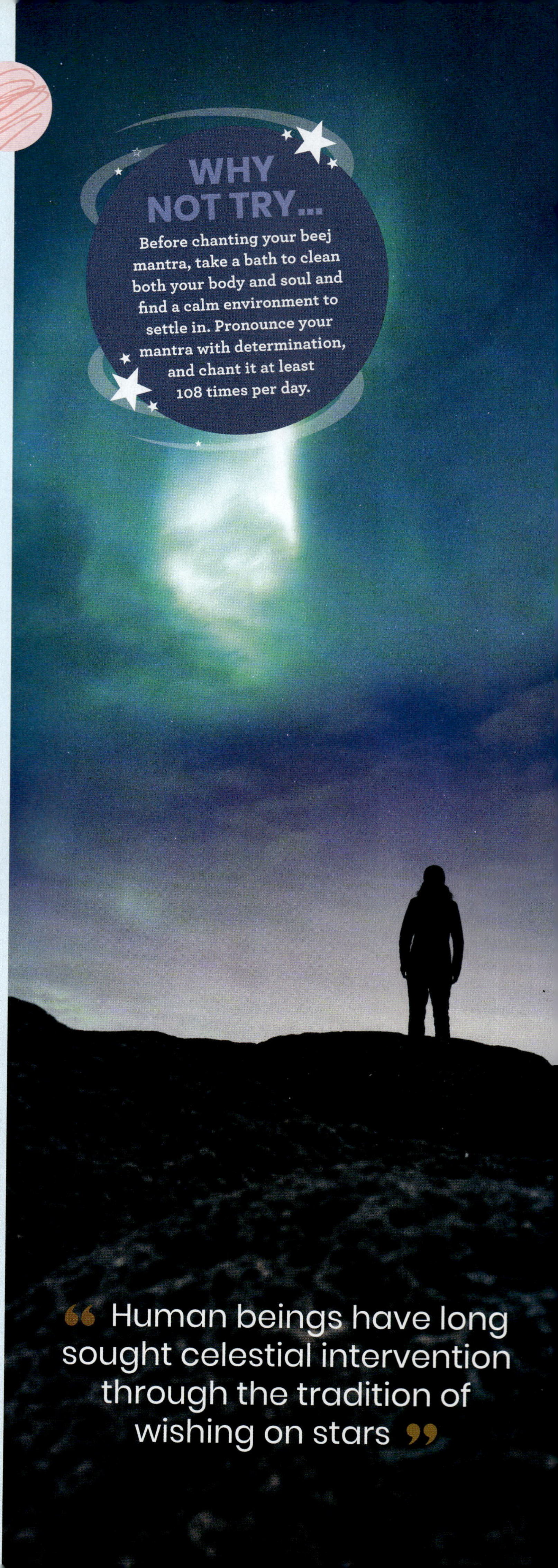

WHY NOT TRY...

Before chanting your beej mantra, take a bath to clean both your body and soul and find a calm environment to settle in. Pronounce your mantra with determination, and chant it at least 108 times per day.

"Human beings have long sought celestial intervention through the tradition of wishing on stars"

FIND YOUR NAKSHATRA

The ancient traditions of Vedic astrology

Astrology uses different methods and traditions around the world. In Vedic astrology (or Hindu astrology), the zodiac is divided into 27 or 28 lunar constellations known as Nakshatras, with each Nakshatra covering 13.20 degrees. Vedic astrology contains the rich spiritual myths of Indian culture: as such, all 27 Nakshatras are the deity Daksha's daughters, and the Moon is married to each of them. The Moon spends almost one day in each constellation, which are divided according to their many attributes around caste, sex, deity, species and more. Each Nakshatra also has a powerful sound associated with it, known as a beej mantra, which are thought to have been born from the sound waves that were made during the creation of the universe. Chanting the beej mantra connected to your birth Nakshatra bestows good health and longevity. Calculate your Nakshatra and beej mantra here: **prokerala.com/astrology/nakshatra-finder/**

CLOUD AND CLEAR

Tap into your creative mind with a spot of cloud gazing

Cloud gazing – the tradition of staring up at the clouds and seeing what shapes you can find – is a fantastic way of taking time out to tap into your imagination. Whether you're lying out on a picnic blanket with a friend or simply taking a couple of minutes out of your busy day to look up, cloud gazing offers opportunities to feel connected to nature, relieve stress and get your creative juices flowing.

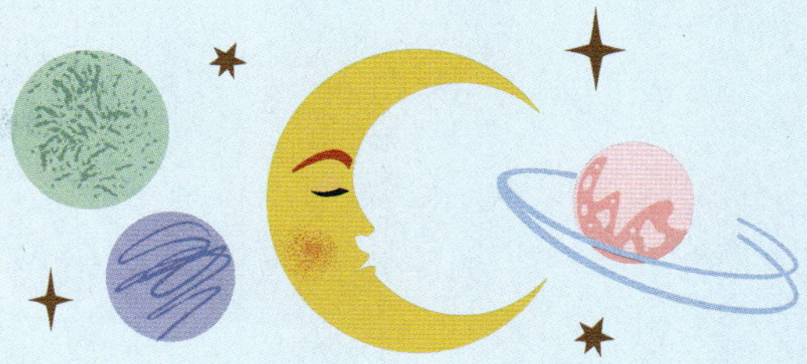

DRAWING DOWN the Moon

This Wiccan rite allows practitioners to connect with their goddess

Wiccan magic makes use of the power of the night sky in many different ways; one of the most popular is the ritual known as Drawing Down the Moon. This beautiful rite involves the practitioner, usually a coven's High Priestess, invoking the goddess directly into themselves and entering a trancelike state. The goddess, symbolised by the moon, then speaks through them.

There are many different ways to draw down the moon, depending on the practitioner's needs and spiritual customs. One thing that many practitioners agree on is the thrum of energy that passes through their body as well as their mind and spirit when they invoke the goddess in this rite. For that reason, it's usually practised only by High Priestesses who have invested a lot of time, thought and meditation in their spiritual training – and many still say the sensation takes them by surprise the first time they perform this ritual!

The name of the ritual comes from the name given to an ancient Greek vase that shows the moon and two women who appear to be worshipping it; Roman poetry also alludes to "Thessalian witches [who] pull down the bright moon". But the modern ritual that is practised today originated from Gardnerian Wicca – the original branch of this modern witchcraft-based religion – in the 1950s, and uses the words of, or based upon, one of the two Charge of the Goddess incantations created by High Priestess Doreen Valiente after her own initiation into the craft. These were influenced by earlier rituals by famous occultist Aleister Crowley.

Could COLOUR be the Cure?

DISCOVER HOW IMMERSING YOURSELF IN THE RIGHT TONES CAN WORK WONDERS FOR YOUR WELLBEING

WORDS: FAYE M SMITH

Do you feel more confident when wearing purple or more positive after walking in green spaces? It could be that colour is having a much bigger effect on your wellbeing then you realise.

"Colour is a quintessential part of life," says colour specialist Mark Wentworth (colourforlife.com). "Each colour creates a different physical and emotional response and, as we have evolved as a species, so has our understanding of the depths and intricacies of human emotion and behaviour."

But how we respond to the effects of certain hues, whether positively or negatively, can be very personal – there isn't a one-colour-fits-all when it comes to colour therapy. "On one level, colour is instinctual, and on another it connects us to our own personal memories and experiences," explains Wentworth. "Most people love something, such as sky blue, as it has an overall calming effect, maybe it reminds us of summer holidays and times of carefree daydreaming, and yet for some it's depressing, cold and detached." Hertfordshire University fashion psychologist Professor Karen Pine, working with Comfort UK, agrees: "We may love or hate the colour of our old school uniform, for example, depending on whether we have strong positive or negative memories of school."

With such personal responses to colour, there might be some trial and error when finding what hue is right for you before you begin reaping the benefits. "Be brave, experiment," says Wentworth. "Learn to understand your own colour language and how it reflects the highs and lows of your life story. Love your colours and watch your life transform." Read on to shine a light on your own colour language...

> "Each colour creates a different physical and emotional response"

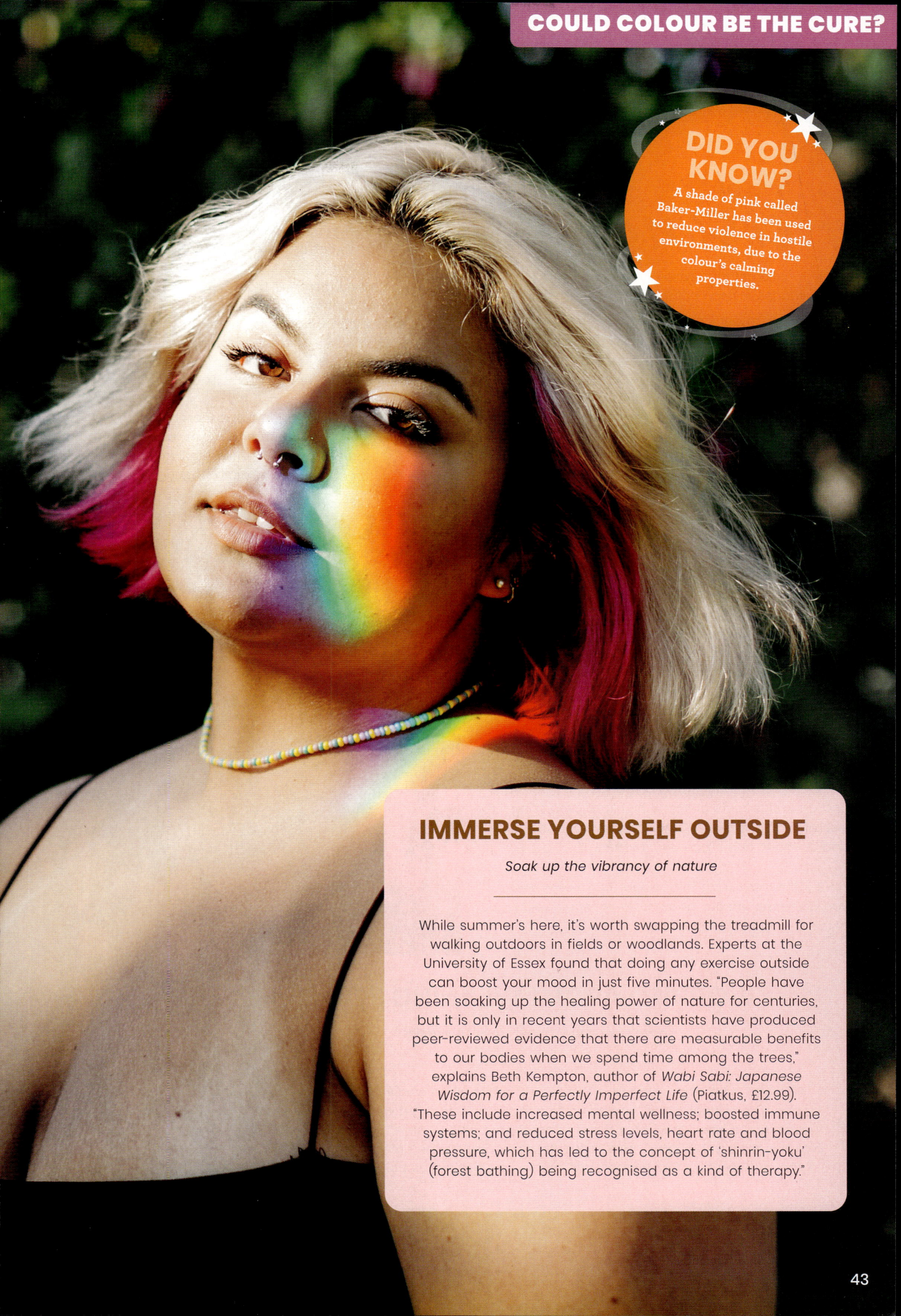

DID YOU KNOW?

A shade of pink called Baker-Miller has been used to reduce violence in hostile environments, due to the colour's calming properties.

IMMERSE YOURSELF OUTSIDE

Soak up the vibrancy of nature

While summer's here, it's worth swapping the treadmill for walking outdoors in fields or woodlands. Experts at the University of Essex found that doing any exercise outside can boost your mood in just five minutes. "People have been soaking up the healing power of nature for centuries, but it is only in recent years that scientists have produced peer-reviewed evidence that there are measurable benefits to our bodies when we spend time among the trees," explains Beth Kempton, author of *Wabi Sabi: Japanese Wisdom for a Perfectly Imperfect Life* (Piatkus, £12.99). "These include increased mental wellness; boosted immune systems; and reduced stress levels, heart rate and blood pressure, which has led to the concept of 'shinrin-yoku' (forest bathing) being recognised as a kind of therapy."

A WARDROBE of Personality

Forget this season's most stylish shades, instead opt for feel good fashion

Whether you're dedicated to fashion or not, the colour of your clothing can have a significant impact on your mental health. You don't have to go head to toe, just a pop of colour will work, which is good news, as 34%* of women are scared to change the way they look. "Dressing for how you feel promotes an overall confidence and authenticity, which creates a positive approach from other people," says Wentworth. "If you have a goal, you can booby-trap your wardrobe with colour to attract what you want." He suggests the following...

YELLOW is sunshine, brightness and fun. There'll never be a dull moment when you're wearing yellow.

PURPLE says "I am my own person and I'll stand out from the crowd". Wearing it inspires creativity and commands respect.

BLUE conveys trust and openness. We'd probably sit down and share our hopes and dreams with someone wearing blue, as blue overall tends to make us feel safe, whatever the shade.

GREEN brings freshness and the impression that everything will happen in its own good time. When we wear green, we offer a level-headed approach to life.

BLACK is sophistication and elegance – it adds style and class due to its ability to highlight everything else around it. It makes other colours appear bolder and stronger, and it conveys mystery.

Love a PATTERN?

You'll still benefit from the colours, but mixing them can dilute the effects, as intricate or repetitive detailing can pull focus.

BLONDES REALLY DO HAVE MORE FUN

Try a new tone on your tresses

Feel more positive after a trip to the salon? You're not alone. A study by Nottingham Trent University and Clairol found that women who dyed their hair blonde had increased levels of confidence. It's thought that a strong and bold hair colour is similar to what we had as children, and therefore exudes a feeling of youthfulness. "Colouring your hair may seem like an art to most people, but there is actually a lot of science behind it," says Dr Mark Sergeant, who led the research. "Not only were their confidence and mood levels elevated, but many reported feeling more attractive and sexually exciting."

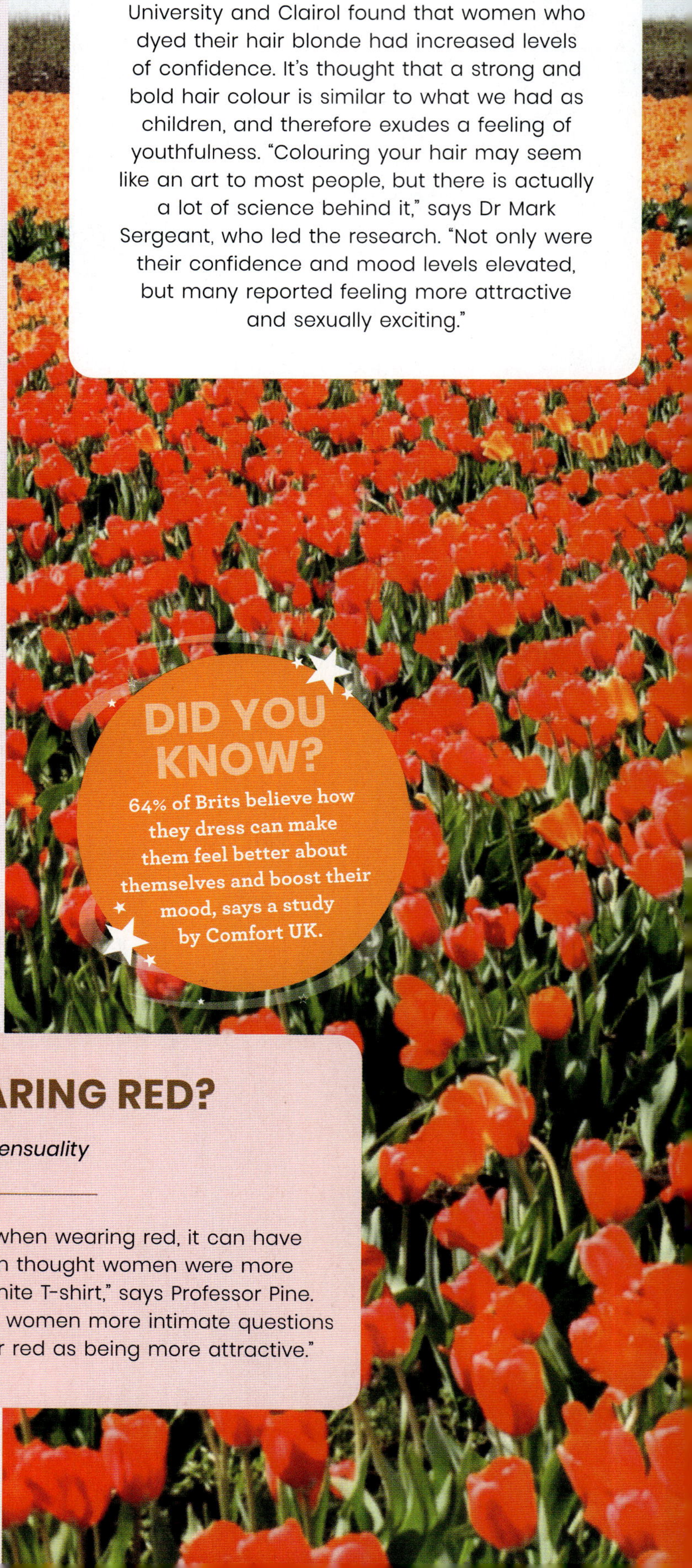

DID YOU KNOW?

64% of Brits believe how they dress can make them feel better about themselves and boost their mood, says a study by Comfort UK.

WORRIED ABOUT WEARING RED?

Those sexy scarlet hues ooze sensuality

Although a lot of people talk about feeling brave when wearing red, it can have negative connotations. "According to a study, men thought women were more interested in sex if they wore a red rather than a white T-shirt," says Professor Pine. "Evolutionary psychologists have shown that men ask women more intimate questions if they are wearing red. Women rate men who wear red as being more attractive."

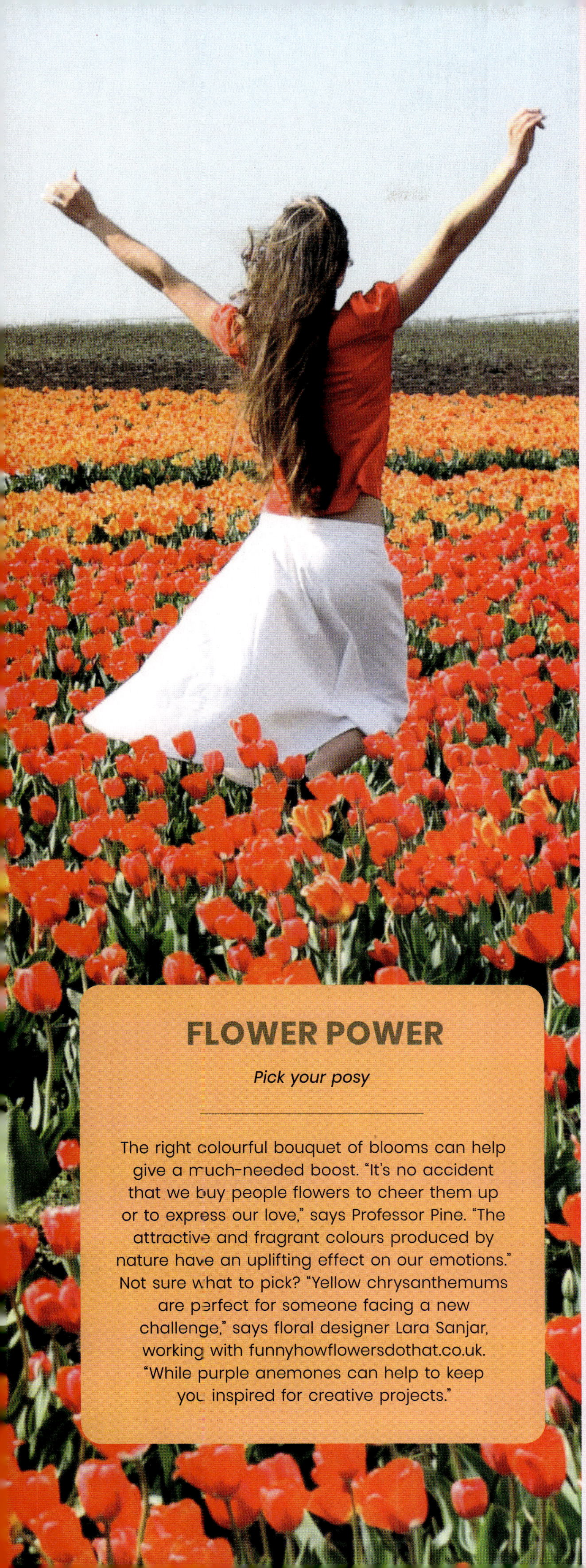

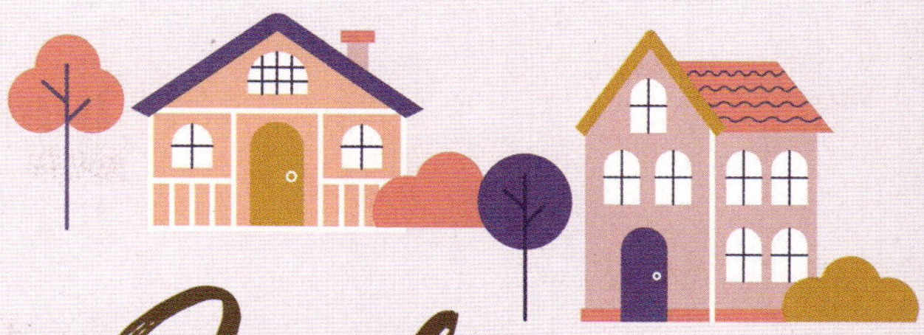

Colour in the HOME

Forget impressions, your pad is for expression

When it comes to the walls or decorations at home, following the trends can be a bad idea. "We should be wary of doing so when painting in our homes," says Professor Pine. "Our environment is an expression of our individuality – it needs to resonate with our emotions and provide a haven to return to. We will feel more at home in a colour scheme that chimes with our personality than one dictated by a trend." Don't have the same taste as your partner? "Choosing colours can be a minefield for couples so agree at the start that you may need to compromise," says expert Georgina Burnett, from homeimprovementmonth.co.uk. "If you like orange and he/she isn't keen, maybe this needs to be an accent colour in the room, against something more neutral like grey."

KITCHEN OVERHAUL?

Had the same set of crockery for years? The colour of your plates could affect how you eat...

- If you're caring for someone with health issues, avoid serving food on white plates. "They are the worst colour for hospitals," says professor of experimental psychology Dr Charles Spence. "With dementia or visual problems, there may not be enough of a contrast between the food and the white plate, so you want the food to stand out against a coloured plate."
- Don't want to add extra spice? University of Valencia scientists found that those who ate from a white plate found food 13% more flavourful.
- Researchers from the University of Oxford have discovered that if you eat from a red plate, you will eat less. "What you serve food on turns out to have more of an impact on our taste and flavour perception than any of us realise," says Dr Spence. "You end up eating a little bit less because red on a plate seems to trigger some sort of avoidance signal."

FLOWER POWER

Pick your posy

The right colourful bouquet of blooms can help give a much-needed boost. "It's no accident that we buy people flowers to cheer them up or to express our love," says Professor Pine. "The attractive and fragrant colours produced by nature have an uplifting effect on our emotions." Not sure what to pick? "Yellow chrysanthemums are perfect for someone facing a new challenge," says floral designer Lara Sanjar, working with funnyhowflowersdothat.co.uk. "While purple anemones can help to keep you inspired for creative projects."

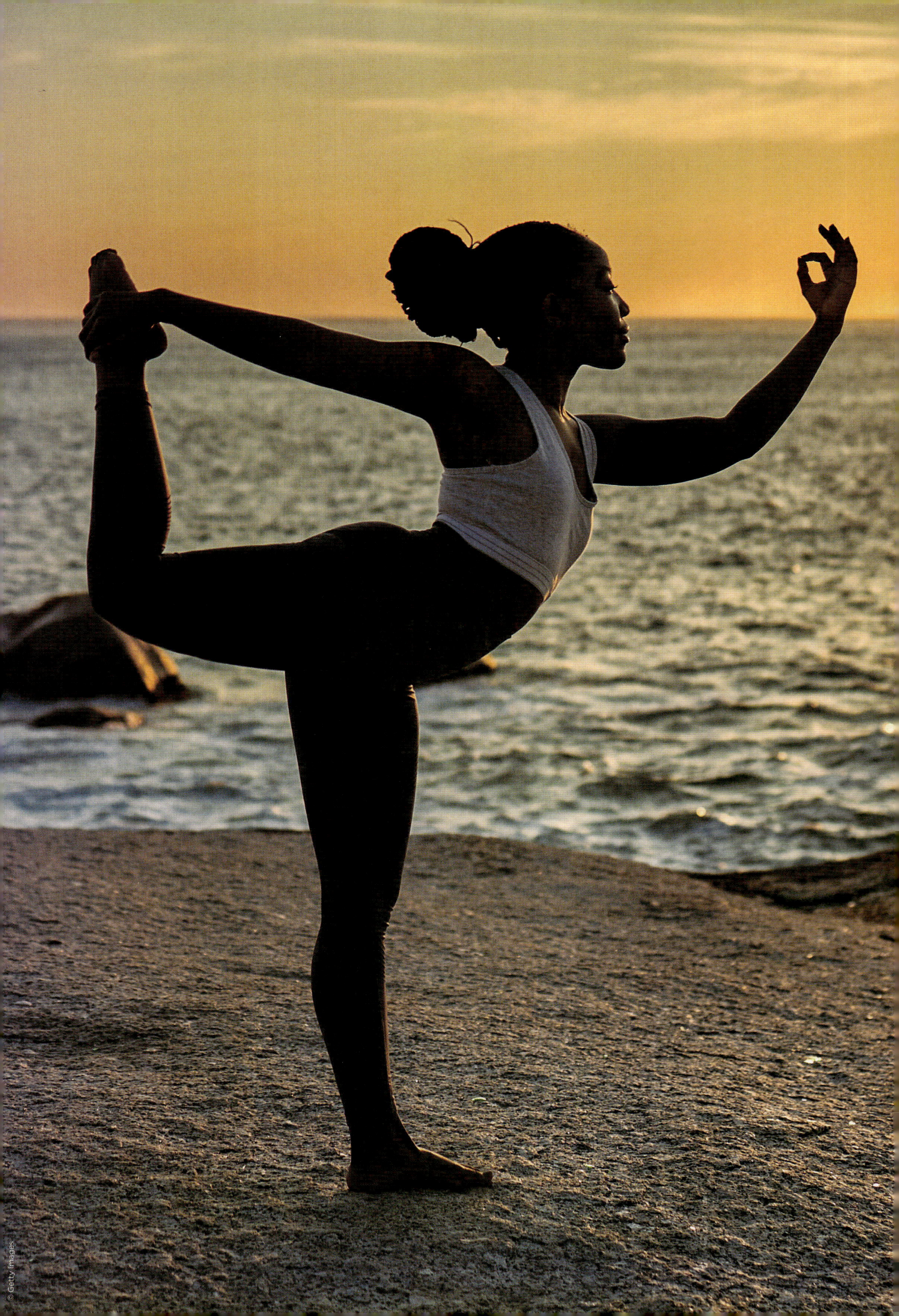

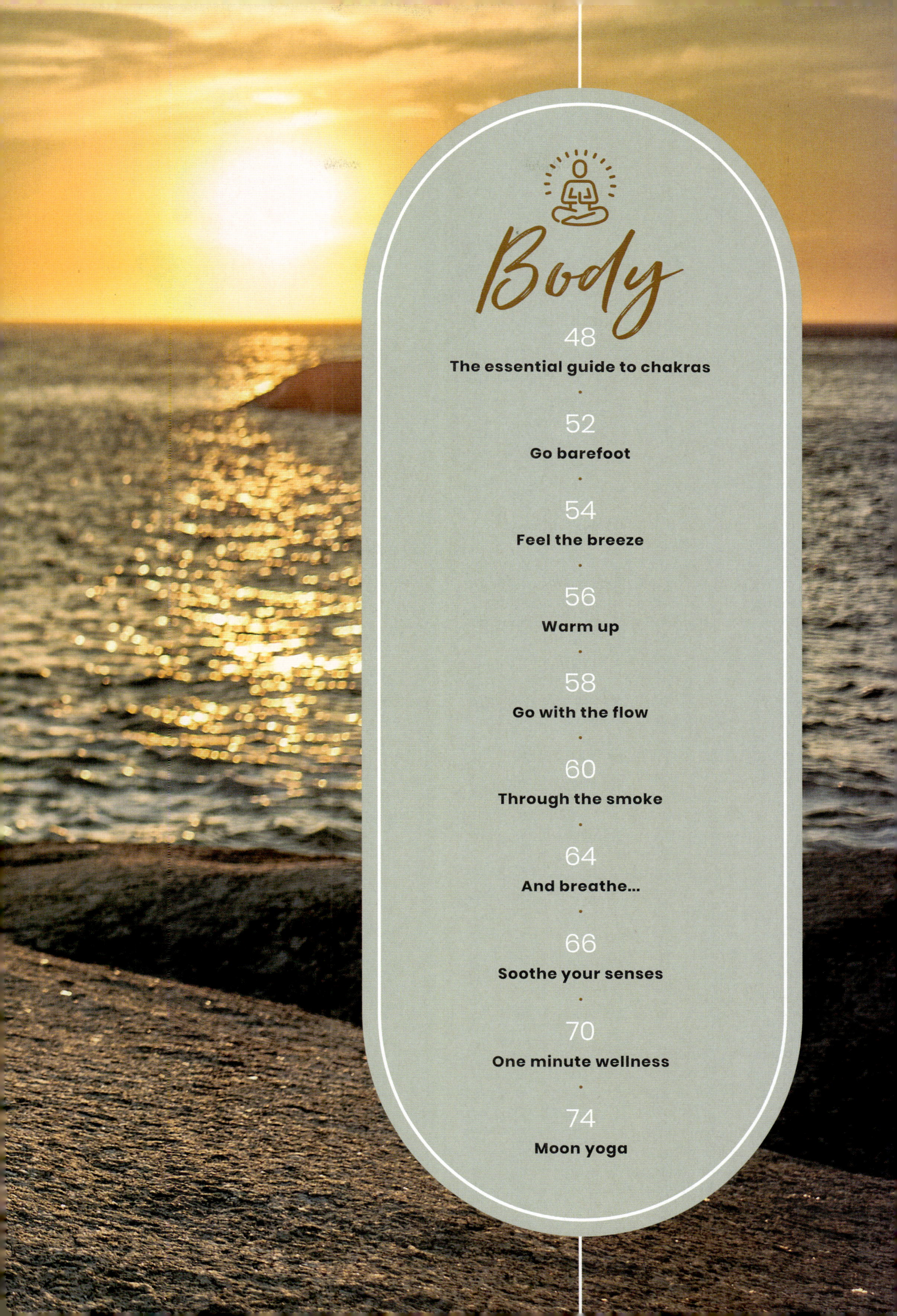

Body

THE ESSENTIAL GUIDE TO Chakras

EVERYTHING YOU NEED TO KNOW ABOUT THE BODY'S ENERGY CENTRES AND WHAT TO DO WHEN THEY BECOME DISCONNECTED

WORDS: STEVE WRIGHT

First written about over 4,000 years ago in ancient India, chakras are energy centres located within certain areas of the body that serve as connecting points between its thousands of energy channels, They both draw in and expend energy, helping you to feel healthy and function properly. There are seven main chakras located within the body: the crown; brow; throat; heart; solar plexus; sacral and base of the spine.

Healing crystals are closely associated with chakras and placing a relevant crystal at a chakra location is an easy way to help the body to balance each energy centre. This technique is known as 'laying of stones'.

IS YOUR CHAKRA OUT OF BALANCE?

When one of your chakras is blocked or out of balance, you may feel unbalanced and disconnected. Check whether this is the case by using a crystal pendulum, which picks up on the energy produced by each chakra. To perform this test, you'll need to enlist the help of a friend. Then, lie down on your back and have your friend hold the pendulum between their thumb and forefinger just a few inches above your body at each chakra site, keeping their hand as still as possible. Notice how the pendulum swings and note the direction and size of the swing for each location to discover the health of each of your chakras:

. **Clockwise** The chakra is open, energy is in balance and flowing freely.
. **Counterclockwise** The chakra is closed, energy is restricted and out of balance.
. **Straight line** The chakra is partially open or closed, signifying an energy imbalance and/or partial blockage.
. **Elliptical swinging** An imbalance on either side, meaning that while energy is flowing, it's unbalanced on one or both sides and could be overactive.
. **No movement** The chakra is completely blocked, no energy is flowing through.

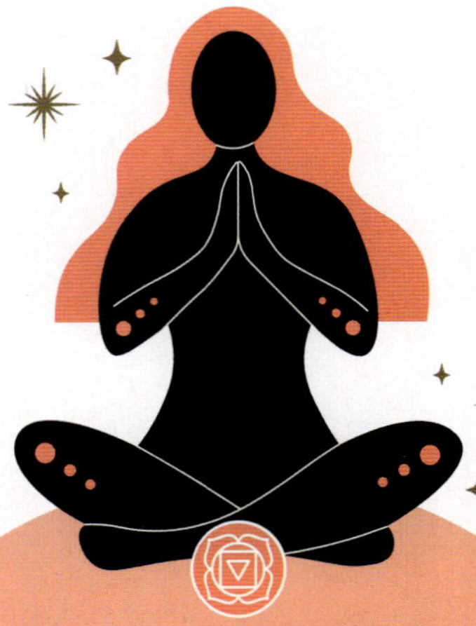

ROOT

Muladhara

Four Petal Lotus

LOCATION
Base of the spine

ELEMENT
Earth

CRYSTALS
Ruby, hematite, red jasper, garnet, smoky quartz, black tourmaline, obsidian

KEY WORDS
Balance, stability, grounding, security, energy

ASSOCIATED PHYSIOLOGY:
Sexual development & function, sex hormones, legs & lower body, pelvis

BALANCED:
Anchored and grounded in reality. Self-confident and focused, organised and action-driven, full of energy, fit and active.

UNBALANCED:
Difficulty sleeping, bowel issues, incontinence, weight gain and loss, fatigue, weakened immunity, leg, foot and hip pain, pelvic pain, lower back issues. Aggressive, angry or irritable. Anxiety and depression. Disorganised, disconnected, and lacking in focus. Low self-esteem and confidence. Stress and feeling trapped.

HOW TO ALIGN
Try simple yoga poses that activate the legs. Earth or ground yourself with crystals or by physically feeling the ground between your toes. Fill your home with nature – get hold of some plants and rocks! Eat healthy. Walk, run, hike in nature. Try some gardening.

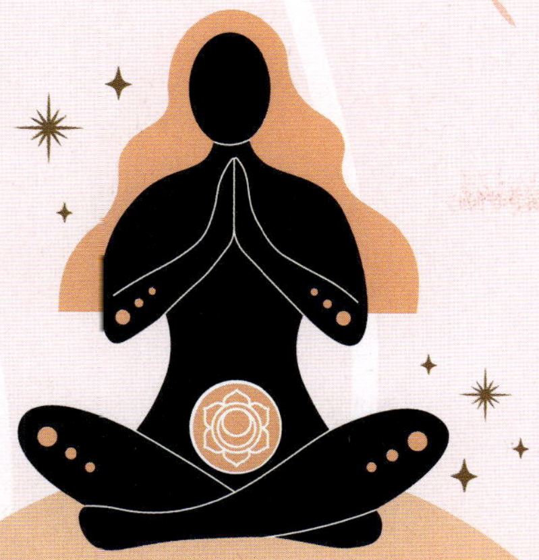

SACRAL

Svadhishthana

Six Petal Lotus

LOCATION
Below the navel

ELEMENT
Water

CRYSTALS
Carnelian, orange calcite, peach moonstone, amber, citrine

KEY WORDS
Sexuality, sensuality, creativity, emotion, fantasy, feminine energy

ASSOCIATED PHYSIOLOGY:
Kidney, bladder, reproductive organs & genitals

BALANCED:
Constantly have new ideas, in tune with your own desire and pleasures, fluidity of expression, particularly in regards to wants and needs in relationships.

UNBALANCED:
Anaemia, lower back pain, spleen and kidney issues, joint problems, hypoglycaemia, water retention, menstruation problems, erectile dysfunction and reproductive health issues. Conflict, thriving on drama and experiencing unhealthy relationships. Lacking creativity, fatigue, insecure, detached and have a low or unusually high libido.

HOW TO ALIGN
Eat a range of orange foods. Stretch your hips. Tap into your creativity by trying writing, drawing, acting, photography, sculpture, dance or anything that gets those juices flowing.

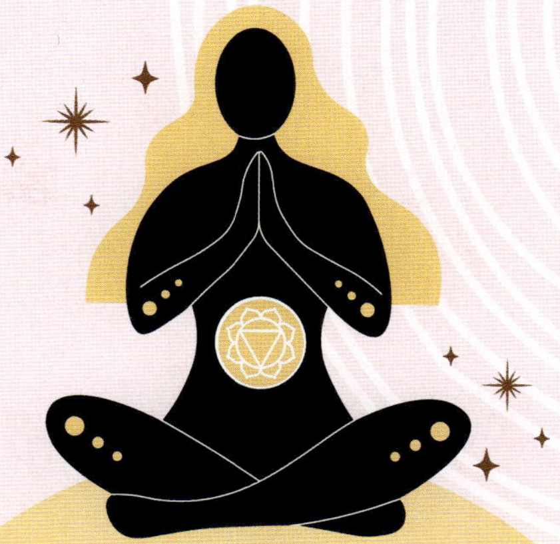

SOLAR PLEXUS

Manipura

Ten Petal Lotus

LOCATION
Upper abdomen

ELEMENT
Fire

CRYSTALS
Yellow calcite, lemon quartz, pyrite, tiger's eye

KEY WORDS
Ambition, power, confidence, personality, intellect, strength, joy

ASSOCIATED PHYSIOLOGY:
Metabolism & digestion

BALANCED:
Happy, powerful, confident and organised. Strong willpower, sense of self and ambition (a real fire in your belly!), the confidence to trust your gut instinct.

UNBALANCED:
Insecure and/or lack self-esteem. Overly critical, stubborn or controlling, lack a sense of purpose. Too controlling and dominating. Anxiety, stomach pain, intestinal contraction, abdominal pain, IBS and digestive issues.

HOW TO ALIGN
Spend time in the sun and whisper positive affirmations to yourself. Try heat-building yoga poses that engage your abs, weight training and boxing or martial arts to improve your sense of inner power.

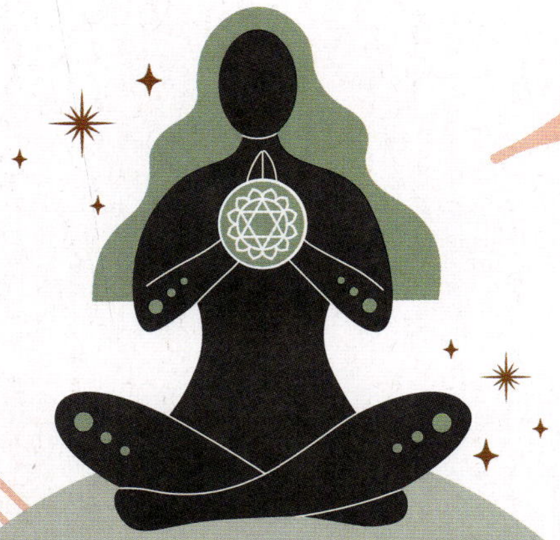

HEART

Anahata

Twelve Petal Lotus

LOCATION
Centre of the chest

ELEMENT
Air

CRYSTALS
Chrysoprase, jade, rose quartz, rhodochrosite, bloodstone, malachite, ruby in fuchsite

KEY WORDS
Love, compassion, emotional balance, calmness, serenity

ASSOCIATED PHYSIOLOGY:
Immune system, heart & blood

BALANCED:
Loved and loving

UNBALANCED:
Colds, flu, heart and lung issues, high/low blood pressure, poor circulation, asthma, breathing difficulties. Codependent, needy, distant, jealous, self-critical. Shy, lonely, anxious or depressed. Lack of forgiveness and empathy.

HOW TO ALIGN
Try performing a 'loving-kindness' meditation. Increase your intake of green vegetables and take lots of walks in nature. Generate a love for the environment and seek out sustainable lifestyle choices. Hug more. Be kind to yourself. Take time to practise self-care.

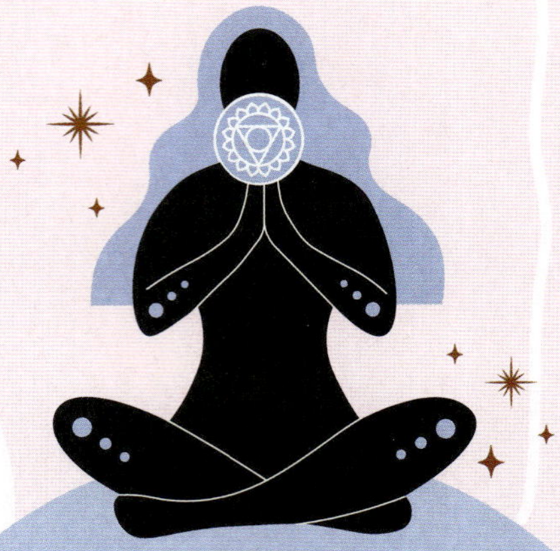

THROAT

Vishuddha

Sixteen Petal Lotus

LOCATION
Above the collarbone

ELEMENT
Ether

CRYSTALS
Sodalite, turquoise, aquamarine, kyanite, amazonite, larimar, blue apatite, blue lace agate

KEY WORDS
Communication, expression, guidance, inner truth

ASSOCIATED PHYSIOLOGY:
Thyroid, body temperature

BALANCED:
Express yourself freely and easily

UNBALANCED:
Sore throat, mouth ulcers, gum disease, tonsillitis and thyroid issues. Argumentative, too loud or too quiet, ignorant, offensive, unassertive and dishonest. Hesitation in expressing emotions or voicing opinions, overly opinionated, lacking vocabulary, often being misunderstood.

HOW TO ALIGN
Wear blue crystal pendants and necklaces. Try some neck stretches and yogic breathing exercises (Lion's Breath is a particularly good one). Get in the habit of expressing yourself more through personal style or actions. Give journalling a go and sing your heart out.

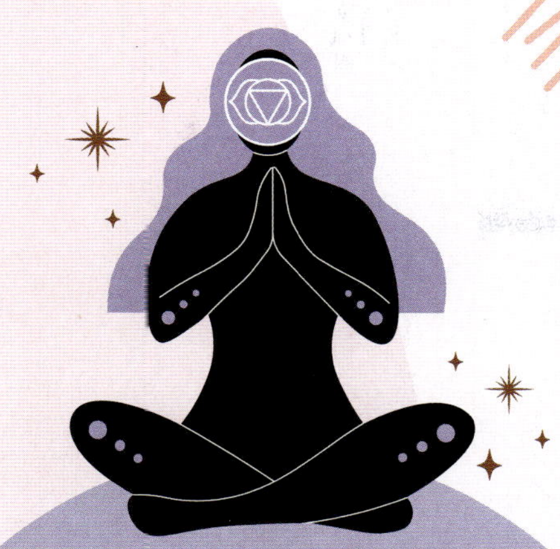

THIRD EYE

Ajna

Two Petal Lotus

LOCATION
Between the eyes/brow

ELEMENT
Light

CRYSTALS
Amethyst, sugilite, blue sapphire, labradorite, lolite, lapis lazuli, fluorite

KEY WORDS
Spiritual awareness, intuition, psychic power, focus, mental clarity

ASSOCIATED PHYSIOLOGY:
Hormones, pituitary & pineal glands, brain & eyes

BALANCED:
Calm, meaningful dreams, intuitive, plans ahead, perceptive.

UNBALANCED:
Eye problems, headaches, migraines, insomnia, brain disorders. Overwhelming emotions, disassociation or hallucinations. Impatience or negative thoughts. Lack of imagination, poor vision and memory, obsessions, unable to visualise, fixed mindset.

HOW TO ALIGN
Meditate while holding a crystal to your brow. Try some inverted yoga poses, such as Plough Pose. Enhance your diet by eating purple foods, such as grapes and blackberries. Tap into your intuition and give it a workout with some visualisation and manifestation exercises.

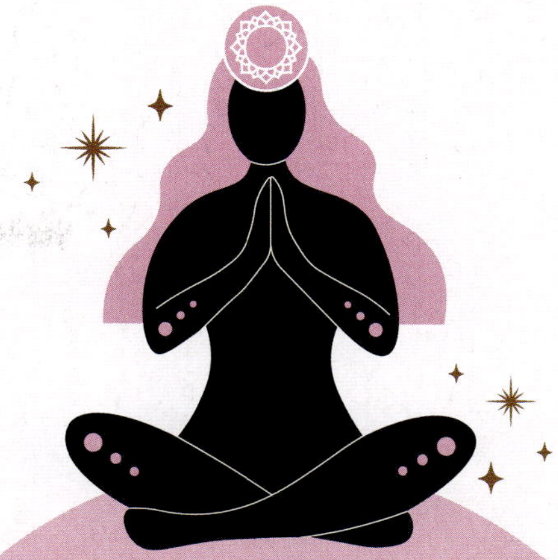

CROWN

Sahasrara

Thousand Petal Lotus

LOCATION
Top of the head and several inches above

ELEMENT
Spirit

CRYSTALS
Amethyst, lepidolite, clear quartz, diamond, rainbow moonstone

KEY WORDS
Consciousness, enlightenment, unity, peace, transcendence

ASSOCIATED PHYSIOLOGY:
Biological cycles

BALANCED:
Spiritually content, feels at one with the universe. Forgives, shows compassion and empathy and is altruistic.

UNBALANCED:
Poor coordination, chronic headaches, exhaustion. Cynicism or apathy, addicted to spirituality, self-destructive tendencies, megalomania and hubris. Lack of direction and goals, desire to oversleep.

HOW TO ALIGN
Use associated crystals to help unlock this gateway to the soul. Try meditation and energy-shaking exercises such as cardio and yoga. Cut down on your intake of sugars and processed foods. Focus on rest and achieving a good amount of sleep – set up a healthy sleep routine. Avoid toxic relationships.

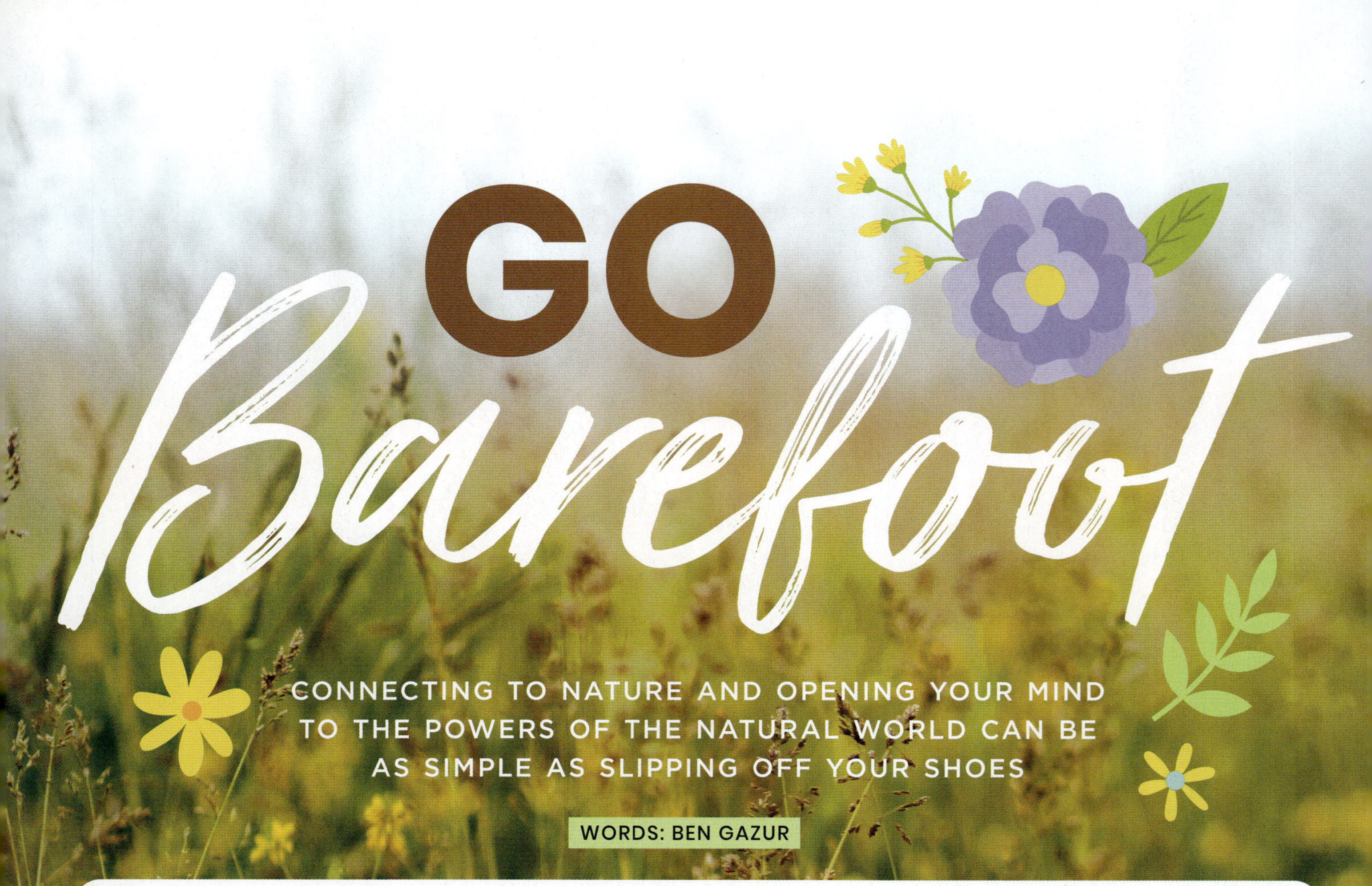

GO *Barefoot*

CONNECTING TO NATURE AND OPENING YOUR MIND TO THE POWERS OF THE NATURAL WORLD CAN BE AS SIMPLE AS SLIPPING OFF YOUR SHOES

WORDS: BEN GAZUR

Study after study has shown that spending time in nature is good for our mental health. Just a few hours among plants reduces anxiety and stress, as well as improving your mood. One of the easiest ways you get a natural boost is to kick off your shoes and socks and stand barefoot on the grass. As well as the proven benefits of being in nature, you will be transported back to your childhood, when running about with bare feet was a mark of your freedom from worry.

Going barefoot offers wonderful new vistas for mindfulness. The nerves on our feet are incredibly sensitive and wearing shoes can dull us to a whole world beneath us. Allowing ourselves to feel the grass, earth, or sand creates a feeling of connection to the world that might otherwise be lacking. Some practitioners refer to going barefoot as earthing or grounding because of the link that forms between the person and the Earth.

To begin your meditation, find a spot outdoors where you can focus without too many distractions. Make sure the ground is free from rubbish (particularly broken glass), dog mess and any particularly pointy pebbles. Take off your shoes and socks so that there is nothing coming between you and the ground. Plant your feet a comfortable distance apart and parallel to each other. Flex your toes and bring each one down to the ground in turn. Notice the sensations that well up from this contact. For those who are unable to stand, another approach is to lay on the ground and allow your fingertips to explore the earth under you. Place your fingertips firmly down and sense the connection they form.

Now breath deeply. As you open your lungs imagine that you are pulling energy from the Earth. Feel it travelling up through your exposed skin in contact with the ground and upwards until it suffuses your entire body. As you exhale, picture the energy emerging from you like a plume. Repeat this three times then relax and clear your mind.

If you cannot go to a quiet space outdoors, then houseplants offer the convenience of connecting with nature in your own home. Make sure your plant is a not a skin-irritating species. Sit comfortably in front of it. Notice as much detail as you can. Then close your eyes and allow your fingers to wander over the leaves and stalks. What do you notice that your eyes may have missed? Now try the breathing exercise above as you focus on the connection you have made with your plant.

> “Going barefoot offers wonderful new vistas for mindfulness”

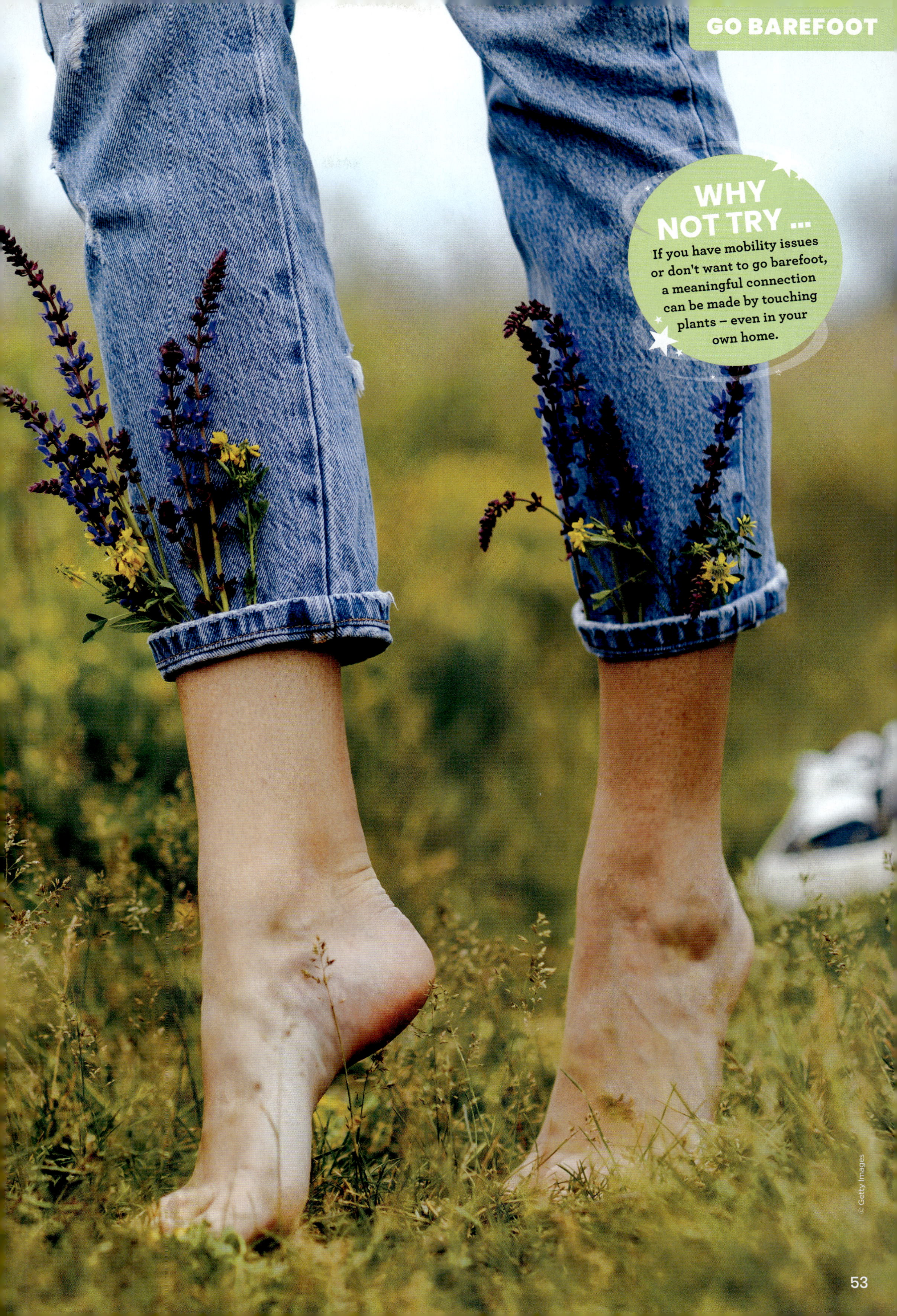

WHY NOT TRY ...

If you have mobility issues or don't want to go barefoot, a meaningful connection can be made by touching plants – even in your own home.

© Getty Images

FEEL *the* breeze

CONNECTING WITH THE AIR ELEMENT CAN INVIGORATE YOUR MIND, BODY AND SOUL, LEAVING YOU WEIGHTLESS AND INSPIRED

WORDS: ALICE PATTILLO

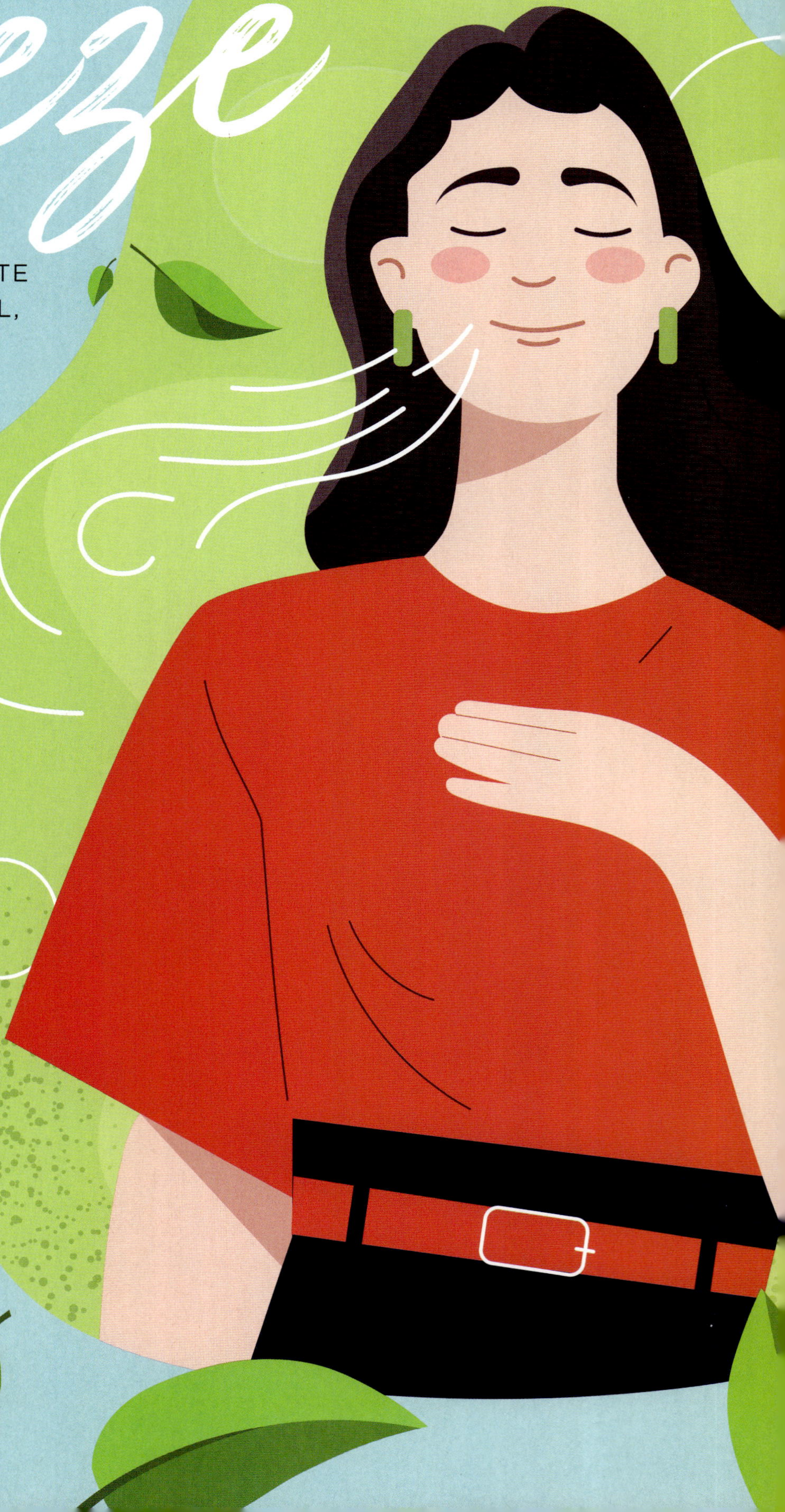

WHY NOT TRY ...

Embracing the air element can be as simple as taking a stroll on the beach and watching the effects of the breeze: the waves on the shore and the movement of the clouds upon the horizon.

WHY NOT TRY ...

Open a window and let the air element inside! Stagnant air can feel stifling.

Connecting with the air element is essential to unlocking your creativity, tapping into your own mind and reaching your full potential. The air is pure energy – in fact, we utilise it through wind farms to power our homes and businesses. It is associated with the throat and third eye chakras. It is the element of spirit and divination and higher consciousness, new ideas, curiosity, communication, speaking our truths, sensory perception and awareness, flexibility and transcendence. If you feel trapped in old patterns, are too focused on the past and are struggling to let go, are resisting change and find yourself fixating on material things, the air can help to set you free. Likewise, if you feel like you are struggling to be understood, to take action and make decisions or finding it difficult to sleep thanks to a busy mind, you may need to tap into the air element. The air is movement, clarification, open-mindedness and lightheartedness. It's cleansing and flowing and always moving forward.

One way to connect with the air is to literally connect with it. Feel the breeze on your face and embrace the fresh life-giving air. Go for a brisk walk, dance in the wind, pay attention to your breathing and practise breath work.

To connect further with the air element, try this simple meditation exercise designed to release the weight off your shoulders and leave you feeling invigorated and renewed, inspiring your creativity and freeing your mind.

First, get outside! If that's not possible, simply open your window and let the air inside. Try and pick a day when you can see the trees moving, when the wind is blowing firmly, but not too harshly so that you can really feel the breeze on your face or the fresh air entering your home. If that's not possible, try releasing the stagnant air within your space by plugging in an electric fan.

Secondly, get comfortable. If you are outside, you might want to lie down and look at the sky. If you are looking out the window or using a fan, take a seat and watch wherever the air is blowing from.

Next, if you can get or see outside, take a look at the clouds. Notice how they move. That's the air! Notice the movement in the trees, pay attention to their dance. If you are using a fan, watch the effects of the air's movement within your room.

Now, close your eyes. Breathe in through your nose and feel the air fill up your chest and expand your stomach. Exhale. Now breathe in again and focus on the top of your head. Can you feel the air? Slowly scan down your body, with every exhale move to a different part of your body. From your forehead to your nose, ears, and lips. Inhale and notice your neck, your shoulders, down each arm to your fingertips. Keep breathing as you pay attention to your chest, your torso, your pelvis and down each leg to your feet. Notice the sensations on your skin. Can you feel the breeze? Take your time and feel the air surrounding you, filling you up and imagine you are weightless. Allow yourself to let go of all that which does not serve you. Let it disperse into the air, the wind blowing it away.

> "The air element is essential to unlocking your creativity"

WARM *Up*

FOCUS YOUR MEDITATION PRACTICE BY HARNESSING THE ELEMENTAL POWER OF FIRE, TO CREATE A POWERFUL ENERGY FILLED WITH PASSION AND STRENGTH

WORDS: CATHERINE CURZON

The fire element is connected to the sun, the giver of life. It can be intense and filled with energy, passion and emotion, lighting the way and nurturing us with its warmth. Fire knows no boundaries, and by bringing it into your meditation, you can harness its power to bring fresh courage and strength to your own life. Yet fire that's uncontrolled can rage and cause destruction, so it's important you know how to work with it, rather than fear its strength. It's inevitable that we will all face obstacles as we move through life, but once you have that fire within you, you'll feel ready to cope with anything.

When it comes to bringing the fire element into your meditation, you'll envision the warmth and illumination of the flames in your centre, where you hold the core of your power. There are many ways to connect to the element during meditation, but however you choose to do so, you can be sure that it'll nurture your passions and give you fresh impetus to take on the world. By working with the element of fire during your meditations, you'll learn how to make fire work for you and ensure that the flames neither burn out of control, nor smoulder away to ash.

Once you're comfortable in your meditation, you can truly focus on welcoming the fire element. As you breathe deeply, picture a flame deep in your heart; it might be small or a raging fire. This inner fire is yours to command, and you shouldn't fear it; give it permission to spark and grow, so that it fills you. Really feel the fire's warmth as it spreads from your heart to every part of your body, letting it burn through any blocks that stand in its way. Bask in its glow and let its heat and light penetrate every cell, illuminating the places deepest within you where your passions and dreams reside. Really envision tvgniting the passion and fire that you already carry in yourself. By harnessing the power of fire, you will truly free your own inner power, and overcome any obstacle that might stand in your way.

> “Fire knows no boundaries – bring it into your meditation to harness its power for courage and strength”

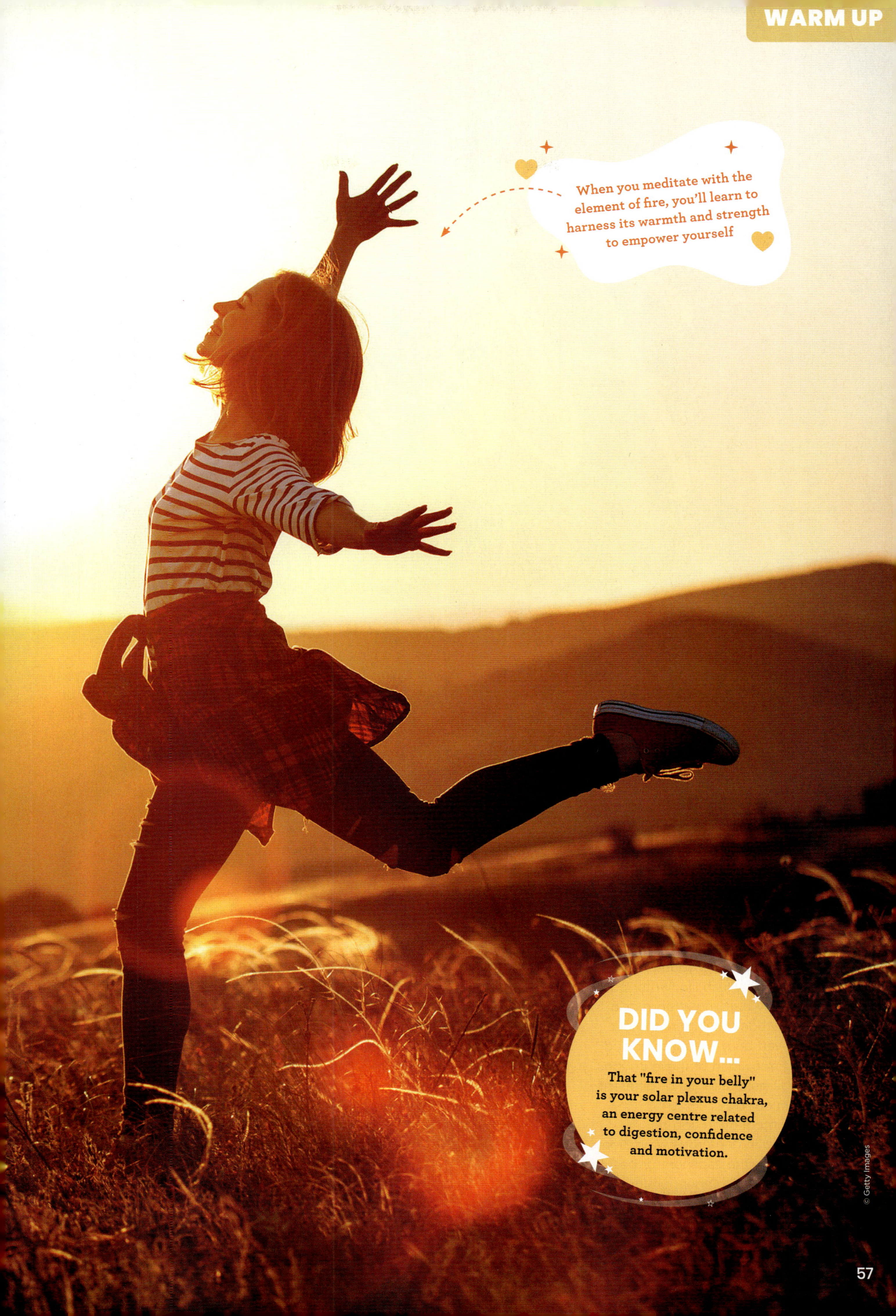

When you meditate with the element of fire, you'll learn to harness its warmth and strength to empower yourself

DID YOU KNOW...

That "fire in your belly" is your solar plexus chakra, an energy centre related to digestion, confidence and motivation.

GO WITH the Flow

WATER IS A POTENT IMAGE FOR MEDITATION AND CAN BE EMPLOYED AT ANY TIME TO HELP CLEAR THE MIND OF TROUBLES AND THOUGHTS

WORDS: BEN GAZUR

Water has long been used in many religions as a means of cleansing oneself and bringing us to a state of purity. During meditation we can use the image of water for a similar purpose. The unending flow of water allows us to wash away many of the blockages in our mind and reveal what truly matters.

The beauty of water is that it comes in many forms. We can picture a still mountain lake that reflects nothing but the clear sky. We might think of a country pond surrounded by lush life. Water can be a gently burbling stream or a relentless tide moving in and out. It can even be a weightless cloud floating free. Each of these images might be helpful for us at different points in our life.

Water meditation can be performed in numerous ways. Some like to sit on the seashore or beside a body of water. Others prefer to submerge themselves in water while they meditate. Still others find even a comfortable bath is sufficient to connect with water. In truth, you can focus your mind on a cup of water or simply use your imagination.

However you connect with water, it is important to be free of distractions that might pull your mind out of focus. Get comfortable however feels best to you. Prepare yourself by noticing your thoughts. If one comes to your mind then allow it to flow away like water without making any lasting impression. Using the image of water, begin a breathing process. Inhale deeply and hold for several seconds before allowing the breath to slowly exhale. Repeat this until you no longer need to focus on your actions. Without effort, bring the image of water you want into being. Notice the state of the water and the situation around it. Feel the flow of the water and its relation to your emotional being.

Once the water is held in your mind, imagine submerging yourself into it. If the water is flowing, think of how its energy is entering you before being carried gently away. If the water is still then feel the perfect connection between your form and the liquid. Dissolve the boundaries between yourself and the water.

When you feel perfectly relaxed begin to focus again on your breathing. Bring your mind back into your body by making note of the sensations you are feeling. Let the image of water go as you gently end the meditation.

“The unending flow of water allows us to wash away many of the blockages in our mind”

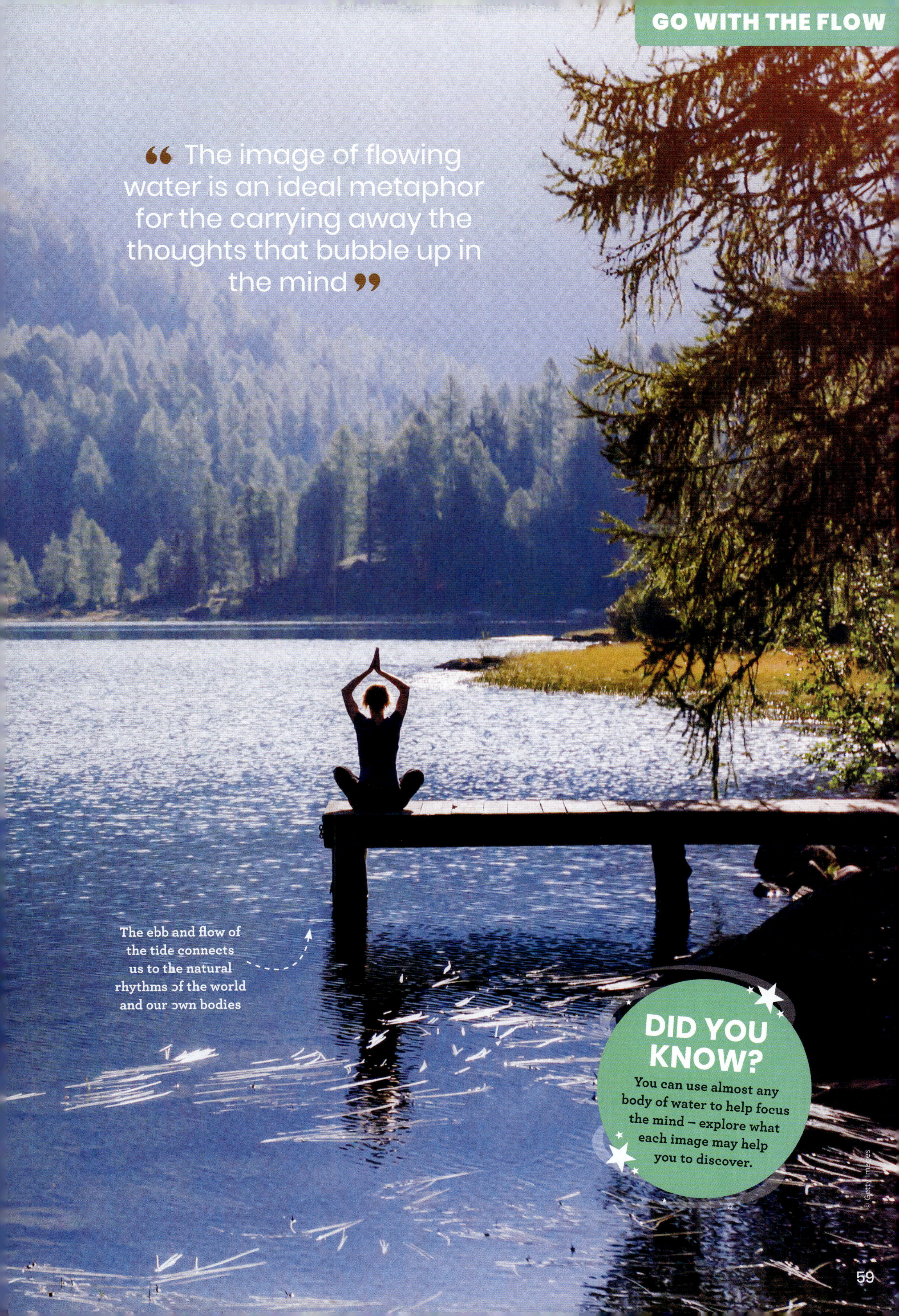

> “The image of flowing water is an ideal metaphor for the carrying away the thoughts that bubble up in the mind”

The ebb and flow of the tide connects us to the natural rhythms of the world and our own bodies

DID YOU KNOW?

You can use almost any body of water to help focus the mind – explore what each image may help you to discover.

THROUGH the Smoke

SMOKE IS A VISIBLE MANIFESTATION OF AIR, UTILISED IN GLOBAL SPIRITUAL PRACTICES FOR CENTURIES

WORDS: ALICE PATTILLO

The use of smoke in ritual and magic dates back to the ancient world. Resins, woods, herbs and spices have all been burned as incense for therapeutic and religious reasons, and many are still used across every continent and within every religion. Some substances are said to heal or to cleanse and purify a space, while others can help you to enter a hypnotic state, foretell the future or meditate. Some are even used as an aphrodisiac. What all cultures seem to have in common though, is that incense and aromatic smoke can bring about a higher state of consciousness and connection with the spirit realm, connecting us to the air element and the crown chakra.

Smoke, like mist in mythology, is often perceived as an ethereal barrier between worlds. In the Viking world, the smoke that arose from cremated remains was said to carry the spirit of the dead to Valhalla, while, in Australia, Aboriginal Australians perform smoking ceremonies during each milestone of a person's life in order to seal their spirit to their mortal body. Essential oils imported from China and India were burned by ancient Egyptian priests to treat mental health issues such as depression, mania and anxiety, as well as to commune with and appease deities. The Babylonians burned cedar branches for aromatic divination during religious ceremonies and the Greek oracles burned laurel leaves to facilitate visions.

Myrrh and frankincense were infamously gifted to the baby Jesus, and many Catholic churches continue to burn incense during Mass to this day. In the East, joss sticks are an integral part of Buddhism. Tibetan monks use incense in order to meditate, while joss papers and the burning of effigies to appease spirits is common across China during the Hungry Ghost festival. Meanwhile, Indigenous Americans smudge spaces and people with dry plants, woods and herbs such as red cedar, white sage, palo santo and even tobacco. This sacred smoke is used for spiritual and healing cleansing rituals.

So whether you are seeking a deeper level of meditation, to tap into your intuitive crown chakra, banish negative vibes or purify your home environment, smoke can be the perfect tool for cleansing both your soul and your space.

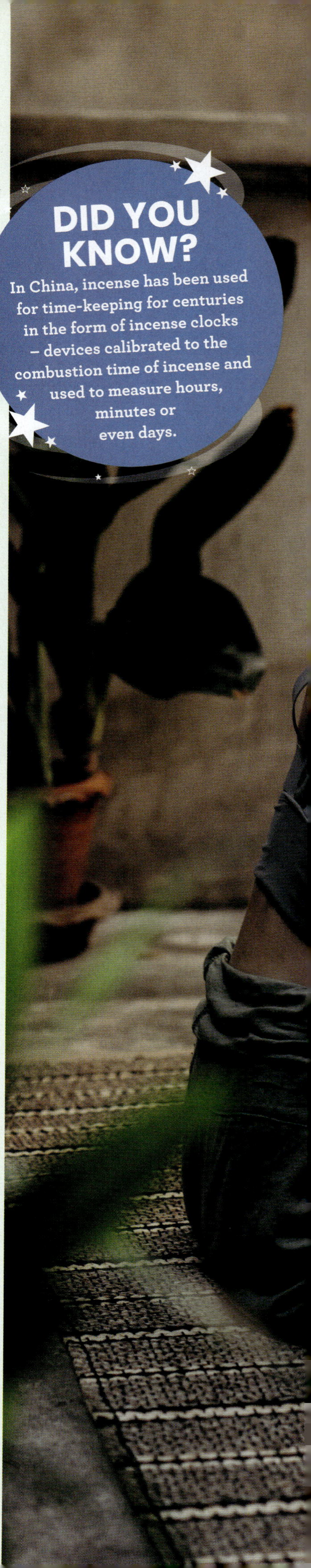

DID YOU KNOW?

In China, incense has been used for time-keeping for centuries in the form of incense clocks – devices calibrated to the combustion time of incense and used to measure hours, minutes or even days.

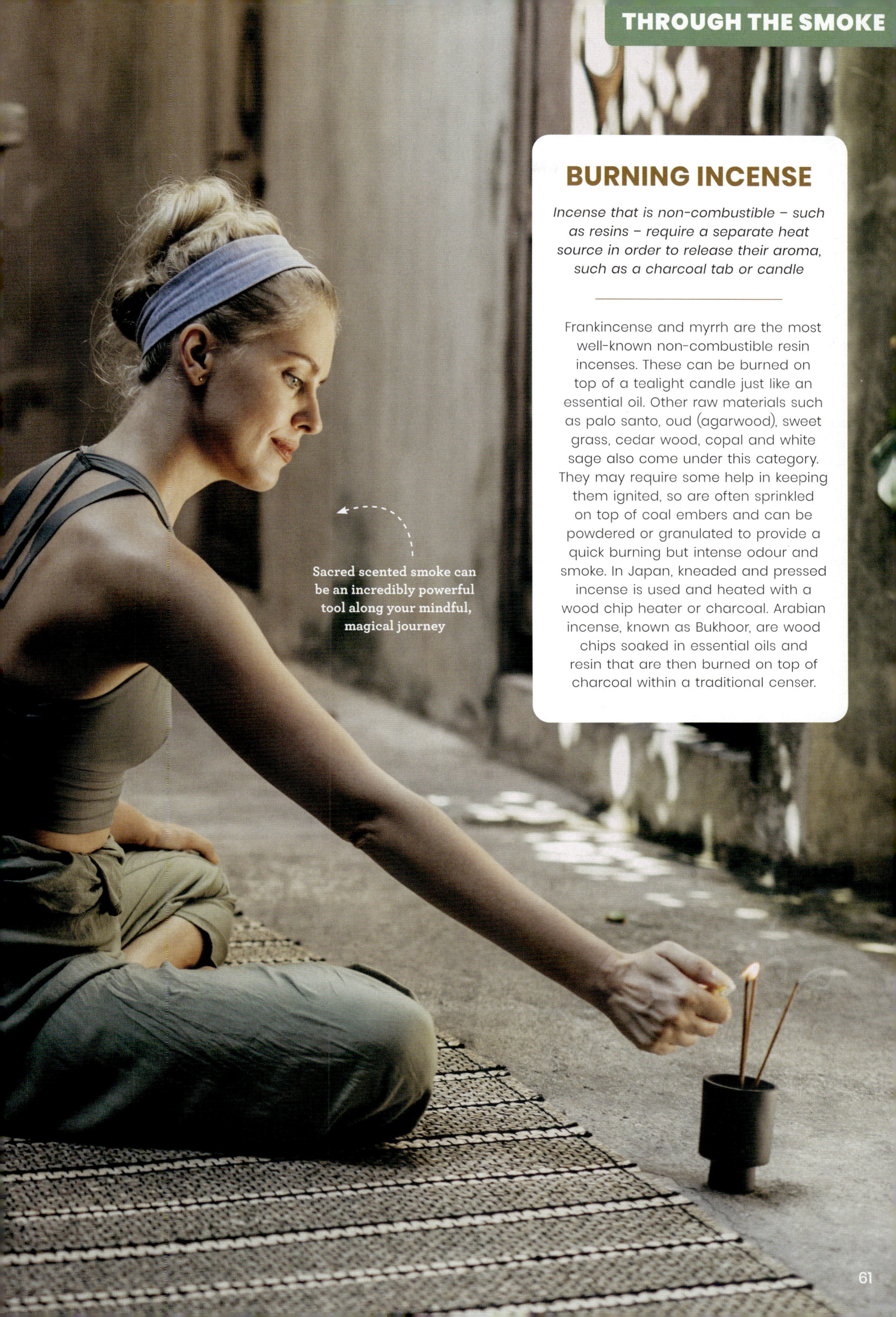

Sacred scented smoke can be an incredibly powerful tool along your mindful, magical journey

BURNING INCENSE

Incense that is non-combustible – such as resins – require a separate heat source in order to release their aroma, such as a charcoal tab or candle

Frankincense and myrrh are the most well-known non-combustible resin incenses. These can be burned on top of a tealight candle just like an essential oil. Other raw materials such as palo santo, oud (agarwood), sweet grass, cedar wood, copal and white sage also come under this category. They may require some help in keeping them ignited, so are often sprinkled on top of coal embers and can be powdered or granulated to provide a quick burning but intense odour and smoke. In Japan, kneaded and pressed incense is used and heated with a wood chip heater or charcoal. Arabian incense, known as Bukhoor, are wood chips soaked in essential oils and resin that are then burned on top of charcoal within a traditional censer.

FRAGRANT *Pharmaceuticals*

Essential oils are known for their purifying and therapeutic properties

Essential oils, also known as volatile oils, are the oils contained within plants used in aromatherapy. They can be extracted through expression, the use of solvents or through distillation. Expression is the oldest form of essential oil extraction and includes cold-pressing. Many essential oils have scientifically proven purifying properties such as antiviral, antifungal, antibacterial, antiinflammatory, digestive, sedative and diuretic. The Vedas, ancient Indian texts that form the basis of yoga philosophy and Ayurvedic medicine, mention incense and its therapeutic properties. In the 4th century BCE, Greek physician Hippocrates – the father of medicine – recognised that burning aromatic substances could offer protection against disease. In fact, plant extracts have formed the basis of modern medicine. Pure essential oils can be applied to the skin topically or inhaled, and are contained within high-quality incense resins and sticks. When you inhale essential oil vapours, the molecules are absorbed via the olfactory system, which is connected to the limbic system in the brain. Depending on the oil used, this can produce therapeutic effects, such as relaxation, lowering blood pressure, improving memory, reducing stress and depression, stimulating appetite, energising and balancing hormones.

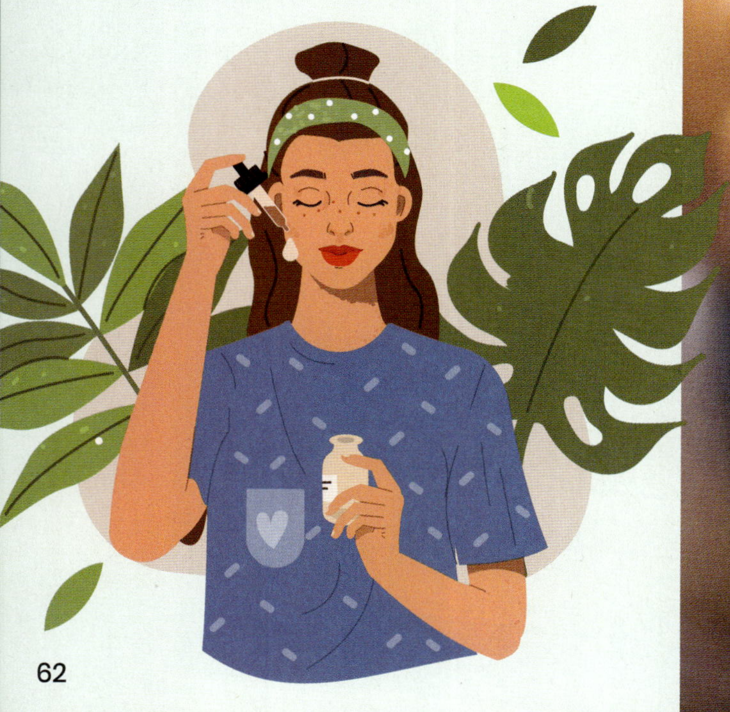

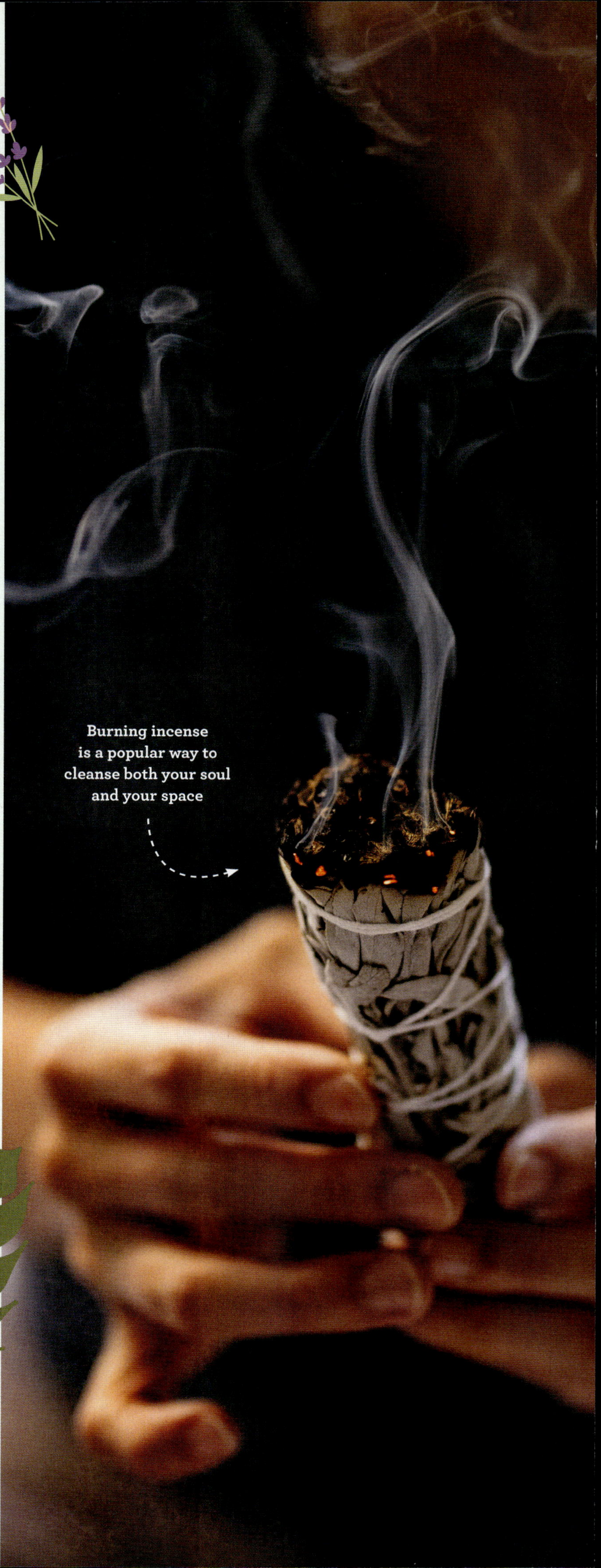

Burning incense is a popular way to cleanse both your soul and your space

CLEANSE your SPACE with incense

1 CHOOSE YOUR INCENSE

This should be an incense stick, a bunch of dried herbs or scented wood. Native American white sage and palo santo have been illegally over-harvested and are endangered. Instead, we recommend creating your own out of dried herbs native to your country. Try lavender, rosemary, cedar, common sage, oregano or thyme. Other incense scents to consider include sandlewood, peppermint, eucalyptus and lemongrass.

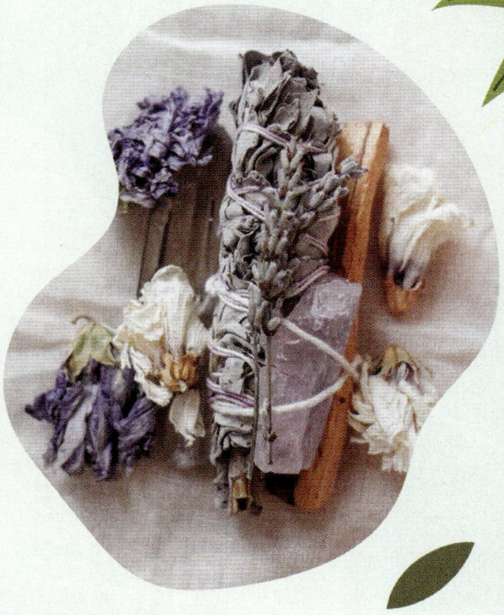

2 LIGHT IT UP

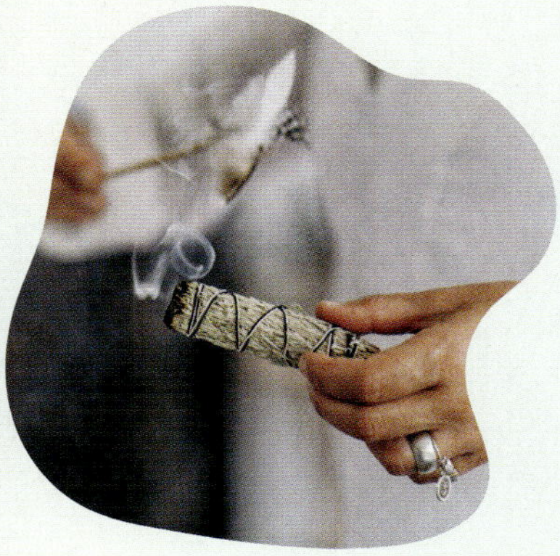

Light your stick of incense, herbs or wood and let the flame burn for a few seconds to ensure it is properly lit, then gently blow on the flame to extinguish it, leaving a red glowing ember and a distinctive stream of aromatic smoke. Make sure to keep a flame-proof dish beneath it to catch any ashes, and open your windows.

3 BANISH THE BLUES

Starting in the corner of your room, move around clockwise wafting the incense smoke from the floor to the ceiling. Use a fan, feather or your other hand to direct the smoke. Make sure to waft the smoke in each corner and direct it into each corner of any windows. Visualise casting all negativity and stagnant energy out of your home and it being carried away with the smoke through your open windows!

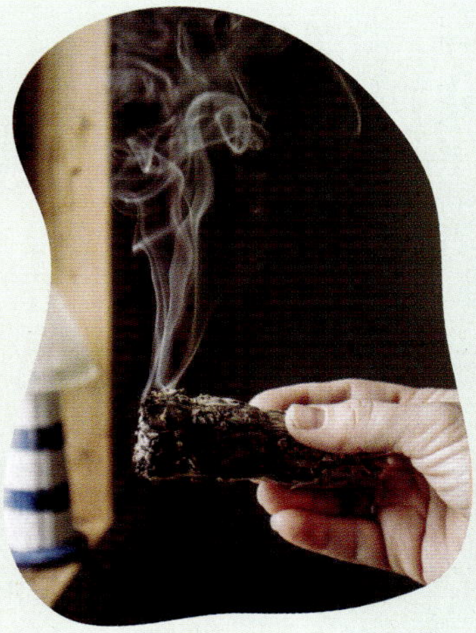

© Getty Images

DID YOU KNOW?

Some varieties of Tibetan and Chinese bamboo incense sticks and cones can all be burned directly without the need for charcoal.

DIRECT-BURNING INCENSE

Incense sticks and cones are the most common forms of combustible incense, and require little preparation but the process can result in some scent notes being lost

Combustible incense is available in most scents, from classic fragrances such as sandalwood and lavender to synthetic novelty perfumes such as sour apples. Direct-burning incense is made from a moldable mix of finely ground or liquid incense with an odourless binding agent. Types include cones, coils, papers and incense sticks. Incense sticks are most commonly available in two types: one with a core stick, and one without. Those with a core stick (often made of bamboo, but some use sandalwood), are the most common form available in the West and are often referred to as joss sticks. Those without a core are solid, thicker and denser, often contain a higher concentration of essential oils and are usually sold as Tibetan or Japanese incense. Coils are another form of stick, available with or without cores, and shaped for longer-lasting burn times, while cones are a solid form that burn faster.

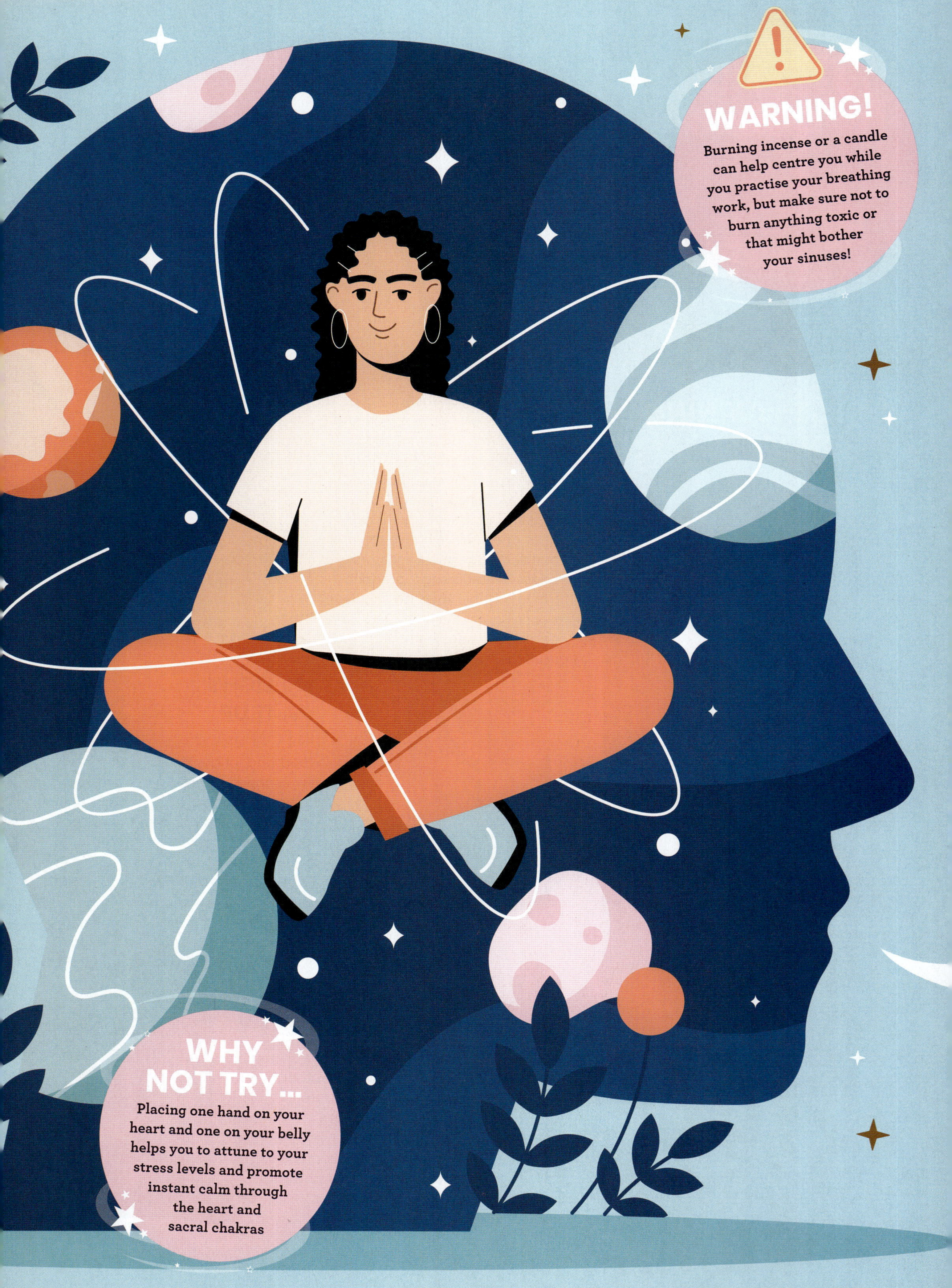

WARNING!

Burning incense or a candle can help centre you while you practise your breathing work, but make sure not to burn anything toxic or that might bother your sinuses!

WHY NOT TRY...

Placing one hand on your heart and one on your belly helps you to attune to your stress levels and promote instant calm through the heart and sacral chakras

AND *Breathe...*

SIMPLE BREATHWORK CAN BE AN INVALUABLE TOOL TOWARDS FINDING A MINDFUL MOMENT

WORDS: ALICE PATTILLO

Meditation is a magical skill. Whether you are in the midst of a tough time, or simply need to focus, finding a moment of calm is a useful tool to have in your back pocket. But for many of us, the idea of clearing our minds just isn't a viable option, so how can we find that mindful moment? The answer is simple: through breathing.

In yoga, breathwork is essential and forms the basis of every posture. Yogic breathwork is called pranayama, and it forms a mindful connection between your body and mind. It can also promote relaxation, reduce blood pressure, increase lung capacity and improve brain function. There are many breathing techniques in yoga, but the most basic yogic breathwork, also called belly breathing, is easy to master and can be put into practice anywhere, at any time, as a quick way to find inner peace. Just follow these few steps!

1 Find somewhere quiet and peaceful and stand or sit, maintaining good posture so that your airways are clear. You might want to light a candle or incense and sit cross-legged, propping yourself up on a cushion for some comfort.

2 Place one hand on your belly, one on your heart and close your eyes.

3 Scan your body for any tension. Remember to relax your shoulders away from your ears.

4 Close your mouth and take a deep breath through your nose. Try and count to ten as you inhale.

5 Feel the air fill your belly. Take a moment here and notice how your hand rises as your stomach fills.

6 Constrict your throat, as if you are going to breathe the air out of your mouth in order to steam up a mirror – but don't! Keep your mouth closed and slowly release the air back out through your nostrils, counting to ten again. This exhale should feel powerful and controlled.

7 Take a moment here to notice how you feel and then repeat the process.

8 Take time each day to quietly find focus and calm through breathwork and note your feelings on paper. Start by doing this eight to ten times and increase the number of breaths each time you practise.

Once you've got the hang of it, you can try gazing at the flame of your candle at the same time and/or quietly repeat a mantra. A mantra is a sacred chant and can be a word, syllable or verse spoken out loud or repeated in your mind and can be seen as a personal spell used to boost your self-esteem. Used with yogic breathwork, you'll be meditating – and manifesting – in no time!

> "In yoga, breathwork is essential and forms the basis of every posture"

SOOTHE your Senses

WATER IS ASSOCIATED WITH SOOTHING AND HEALING, SO WHY NOT DIP A TOE (AND THE REST!) INTO THIS POOL OF WONDERFULLY WATERY IDEAS?

WORDS: POPPY-JAY ST PALMER

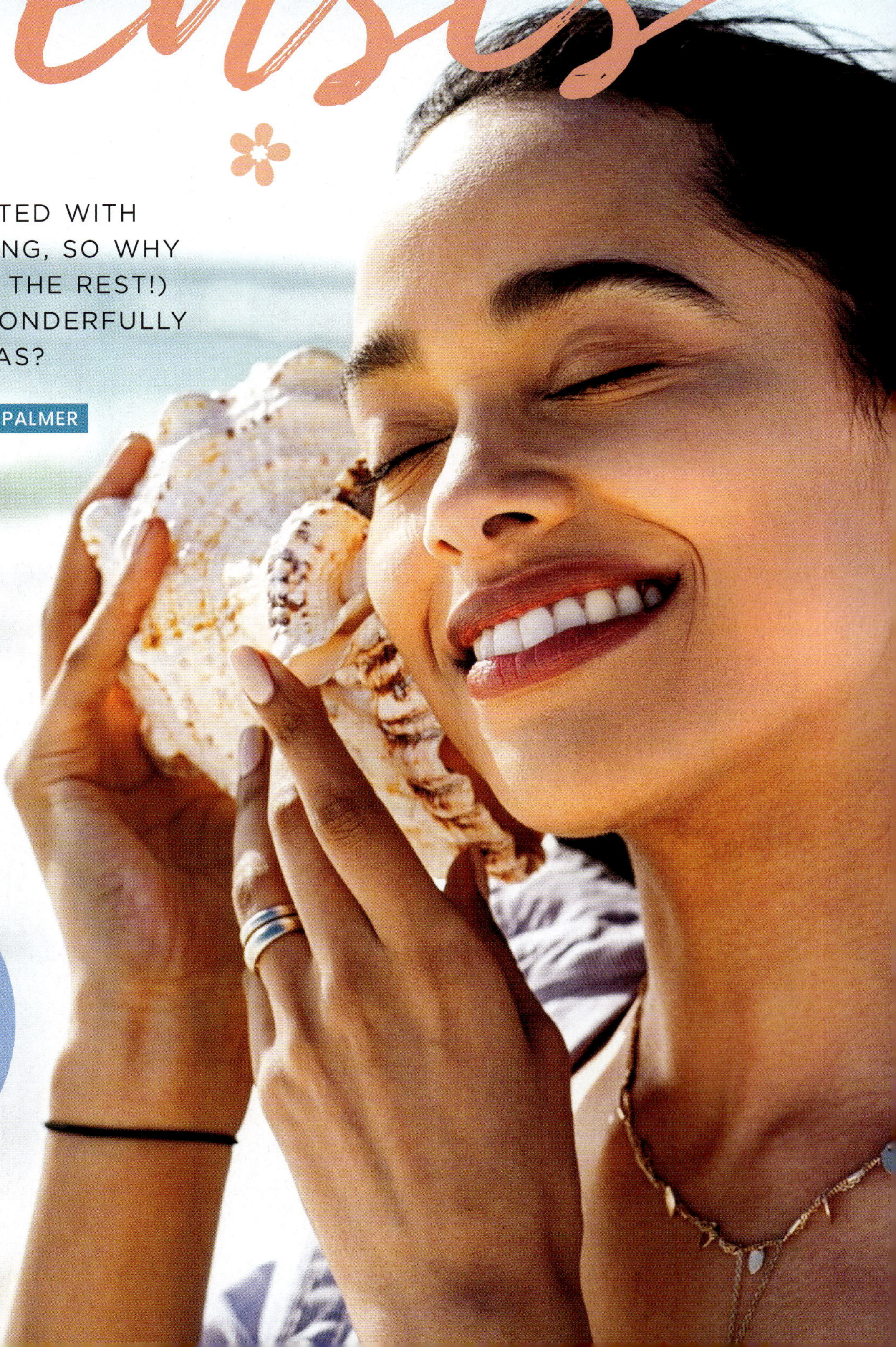

WHY NOT TRY...

Try performing rituals while standing in bodies of water to utilise its powerfully magical properties. Just make sure to stay safe and only do it in shallow water!

Transfer your intent to the shell by warming it in your hands and blowing on it

SEASHELLS BY THE SEASHORE

Release things that no longer serve you with this healing seashell ritual

In elemental witchcraft, water is often thought to be the most essential of the four classical elements. Its healing and life-sustaining qualities mean that it's often used in spells and rituals. The following spell can be performed as a way of letting go of things that no longer serve you.

Head to a beach or other body of water and walk along the shore until you find a shell that speaks to you. It could be because of its shape, colour, size or even location. Next, pick up the shell and hold it in your hands. While holding the shell, close your eyes and start to visualise the emotion, person or event that you wish to release. Charge the shell with your intent before blowing on it and placing it on the shore near the water so it can be washed back out to sea.

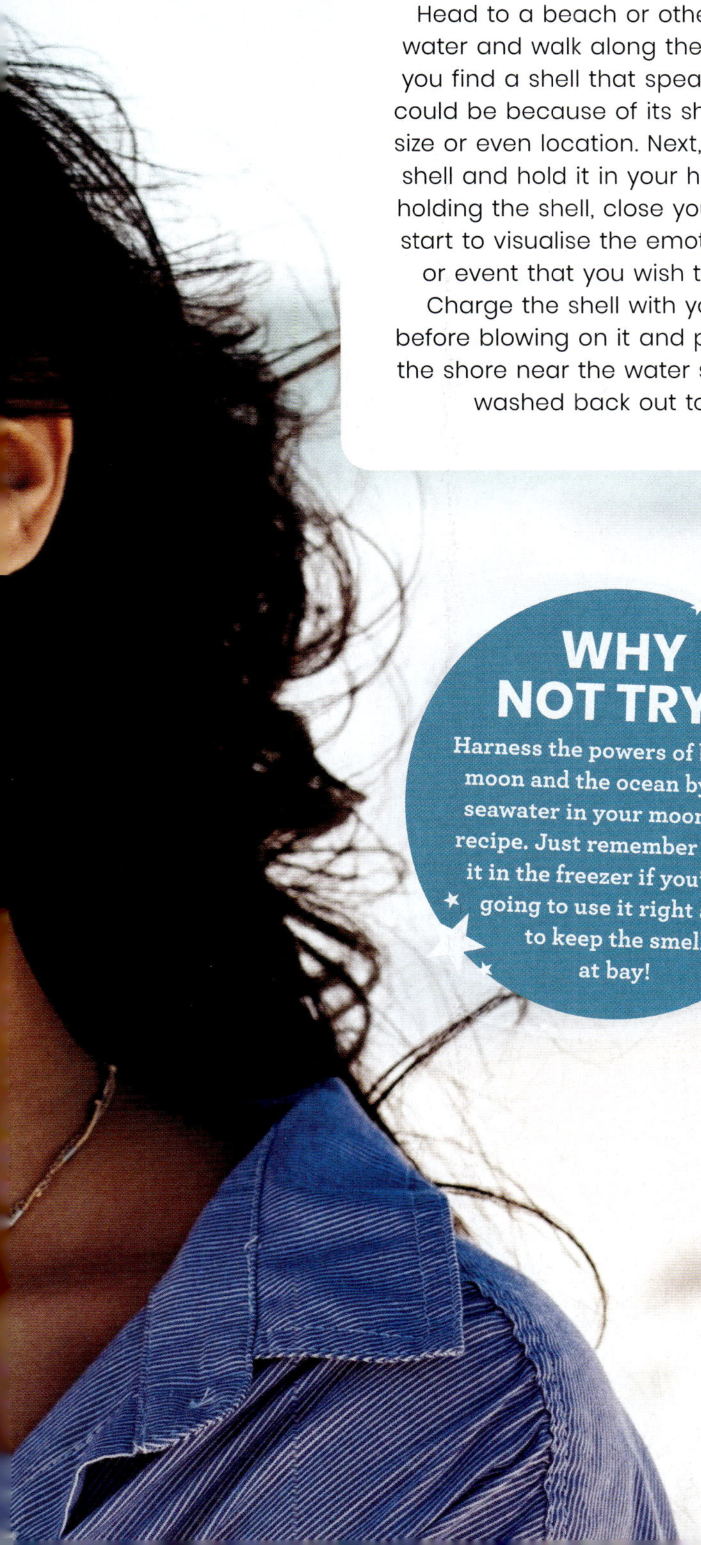

WHY NOT TRY...

Harness the powers of both the moon and the ocean by using seawater in your moon water recipe. Just remember to keep it in the freezer if you're not going to use it right away to keep the smell at bay!

WATER OF LIFE

The chemical properties of H20 make it a powerful and unique substance

Water is considered to be a magically powerful substance because it is vital to life on Earth. All living things need water to survive, from vegetation to creatures great and small. With molecules made up of two positively changed hydrogen atoms and one negatively charged oxygen atom, water's chemical properties are unique. The opposing charges mean that water molecules stick together, as well as interact with the charged elements of other molecules. It can break apart and dissolve almost anything, making it a 'universal solvent'.

THE BLUE MIND

The connection between water and the human mind is a powerful thing

As well as sustaining all life on Earth, water can have an incredible effect on the human mind. Many people use their vacations to flock to lakes, rivers and oceans thanks to the way brains behave near water. And it's not just all in your head, so to speak: behavioural and neurophysiological research has proven that being around water can reduce levels of stress and anxiety, lower heart and breathing rates, boost creativity and generally help you sustain elevated levels of happiness. People have been reaping the benefits of water therapy since at least the classical age of ancient Greece.

The human-water connection is so powerful that the peaceful ebb and flow of waves can actually activate your parasympathetic nervous system, which is responsible for helping you relax and feel more at ease. So next time you need to de-stress try listening to the ocean, going for a wild swim or even running a bath.

The POWER of MOON *Water*

Combine the energies of water and the moon to create an even more powerful substance

Both water and the moon are powerful tools when it comes to magic, so combining the two can create even more energy. The practice of making moon water, or water that has had time to sit under the light of the full moon, has been present in witchcraft since at least the 1800s. Although a full moon can make moon water more powerful, the good news is it can be made during any moon phase, so you don't have to wait a month to create your own. However, you should avoid making moon water during a lunar eclipse. In witchcraft, eclipses are dark and should be used to release energy rather than harness it.

First, fill a container with water (fresh rainwater is preferable) and cover with a lid to keep the water clean. Next, place the container somewhere exposed to direct moonlight like a patio or windowsill. Say a prayer or affirmation over the jar to set an intention for the ritual. Optionally, you could also place crystals like selenite, quartz and moonstone on the lid to give it an extra boost. Leave the jar to sit in moonlight overnight, and the moon water will be ready to use the next morning.

Moon water can be used however you choose. Many people add it to cleaning solutions, use it to water their plants, take full moon baths in it, and use it to recharge their crystals. Label the jar clearly if you're keeping it in the fridge for further use!

TAKE A DIP ON THE WILD SIDE

Wild swimming and cold water therapy has been proven to improve both mental and physical health

Gone are the days of sports centre swimming pools; wild swimming is making a comeback. As well as being far more scenic, swimming in ponds, lakes and the sea can also have fantastic health benefits through cold water therapy. Many people find wild swimming to be good for their mental health, especially the nature aspect of it, but it has also been proven to work wonders for your physical health. Research has found that swimming in water less than 15 °C in five-minute intervals can help increase metabolism. Other benefits include reduced muscle soreness and body pain, improved circulation, a boost in brain function, a dip in blood pressure and cholesterol, and healthier skin and hair.

In terms of mental health, it can help to manage anxiety, stress and depression, increase energy levels, release endorphins, inspire feelings of achievement, and even bring a sense of community if you're lucky enough to meet other wild swimmers out for a dip. Just make sure you swim safely!

WASH YOUR HANDS OF IT

Banish negative energy with this easy hand-cleansing ritual you can perform at home

Many people find submerging themselves in bodies of water to be immensely healing. But if jumping into the sea isn't for you, performing hand-cleansing rituals might sound more appealing. Bring the ocean to you by decorating an altar with seashells, candles and a bowl of salt or seawater. Pour water into a large bowl before adding things like essential oils, shells, crystals and flower petals. Wash your hands in the bowl and imagine any negative feelings you may have melting away.

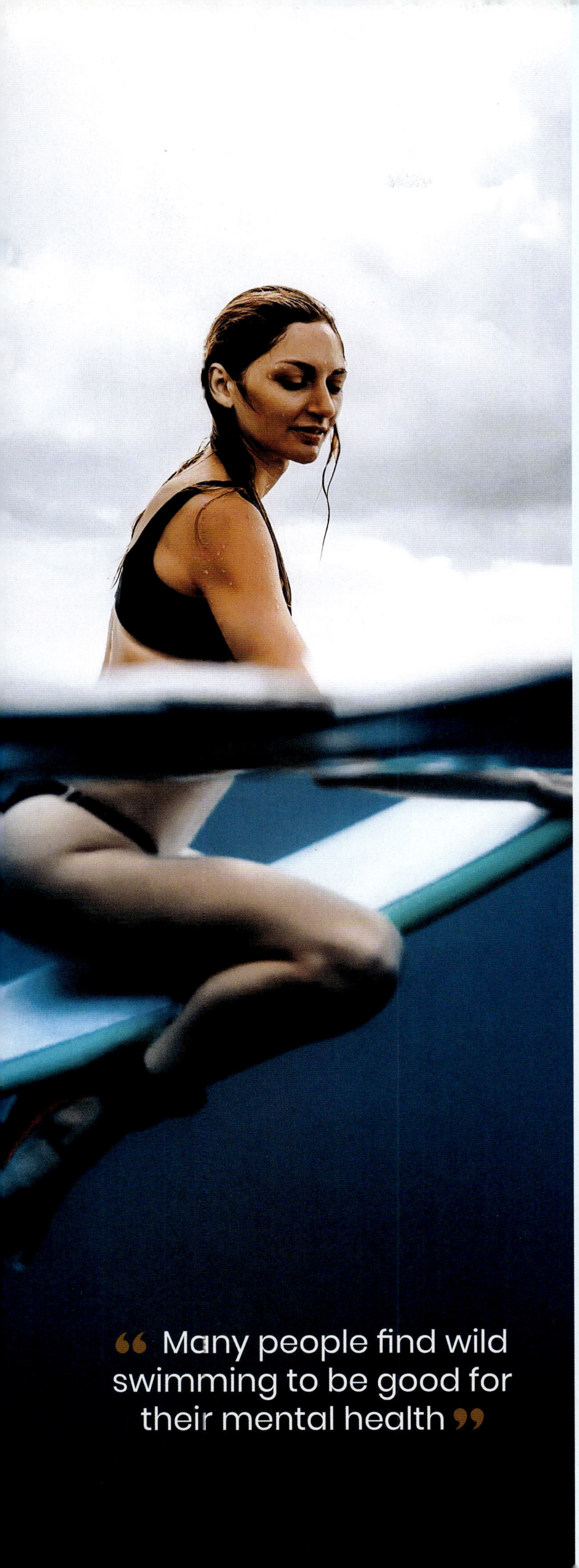

WATER *Wellness*

How drinking water positively affects your physical health

The human body is around 60 per cent water, so staying hydrated is integral to feeling well. Drinking water can maximise physical performance (athletes can lose up to 10 per cent of their water weight in sweat); significantly affect brain function and energy levels; help prevent and treat headaches (a common symptom of dehydration); relieve constipation; help treat kidney stones; and prevent hangovers (alcohol makes you lose more water than you take in).

SEA MAGIC

Harness the power of the ocean to unleash the sea witch within

Witches that feel an affinity with the ocean might wish to bring out their inner sea witch and harness its powers. Here are a few ways you can do just that.

Build a sea witch altar: If you don't live near the ocean, you can still continue the connection by building a special altar from things you've collected from the seashore. These can be anything from shells and sand to fishing nets, rope, pieces of driftwood and even jars of sea water from a special beach.

Make an ocean potion: Capture the power of the ocean by creating a special ocean-inspired spell oil to use. Start by trying two drops each of lemongrass, rosemary, lavender and spearmint steeped in carrier oil, and use it to anoint yourself or your tools.

Utilise ocean sounds: Create a soothing nautical atmosphere in your sacred spaces by playing natural ocean sounds over a speaker when you perform your rituals.

"Many people find wild swimming to be good for their mental health"

One MINUTE Wellness

BOOST YOUR HEALTH WHEN YOU'RE SHORT ON TIME WITH THESE 60-SECOND TIPS

WORDS: ALI HORSFALL

MINI MEDITATION

Reset your mindset and let go of stress – fast – with a guided meditation. Headspace subscriptions start from £5.99 per month, headspace.com.

EAT AN APPLE

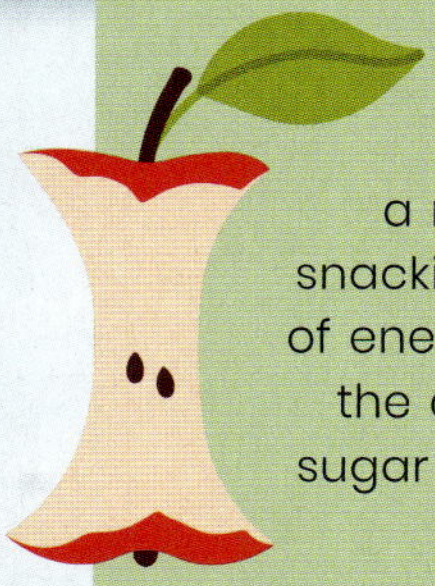

Apples are low in calories, packed with vitamin C, and encourage the growth of healthy bacteria in the bowel to keep the gut healthy. So, why not reach for one in that mid-afternoon slump? 'As a rich source of fibre, known as pectin, snacking on an apple offers a slow release of energy to keep us feeling fuller later into the day and avoids that spike in blood sugar levels from sugary alternatives,' says nutritionist Rhiannon Lambert.

SWITCH OFF THE NEWS

Binge-reading bad news can spike anxiety levels, according to studies. Too much negative media can also cause headaches, tummy troubles, muscle tension and may mess up your sleep patterns. 'Limit your intake to a quick scan of the headlines, or spend just once a day catching up – and look out for positive news stories, too, because these will help lift your mood,' says psychologist Dr Meg Arroll.*

FILL UP YOUR WATER BOTTLE

Staying hydrated supports your body's ability to eliminate toxins and waste materials, which is vital for a strong immune system and a healthy body. Not drinking enough can cause headaches and tiredness, too. 'Aim for 1.5 to 2 litres of water every day and if you're craving something warm, reach for herbal teas', advises Jane Clarke, dietician and founder of Nourish. Avoid too many caffeinated drinks, as they can dehydrate you.

THROW IN SOME GARLIC

Garlic has potent antiviral properties that can help boost your body's immunity – giving you a greater chance when it comes to fighting off bugs and illness. It's also known to reduce blood pressure. Aim for a clove or two a day in your meals or take a supplement, such as **Odourless Garlic (myprotein.com).**

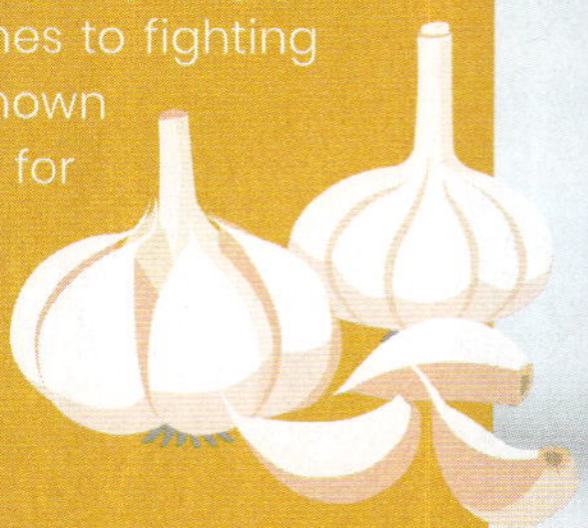

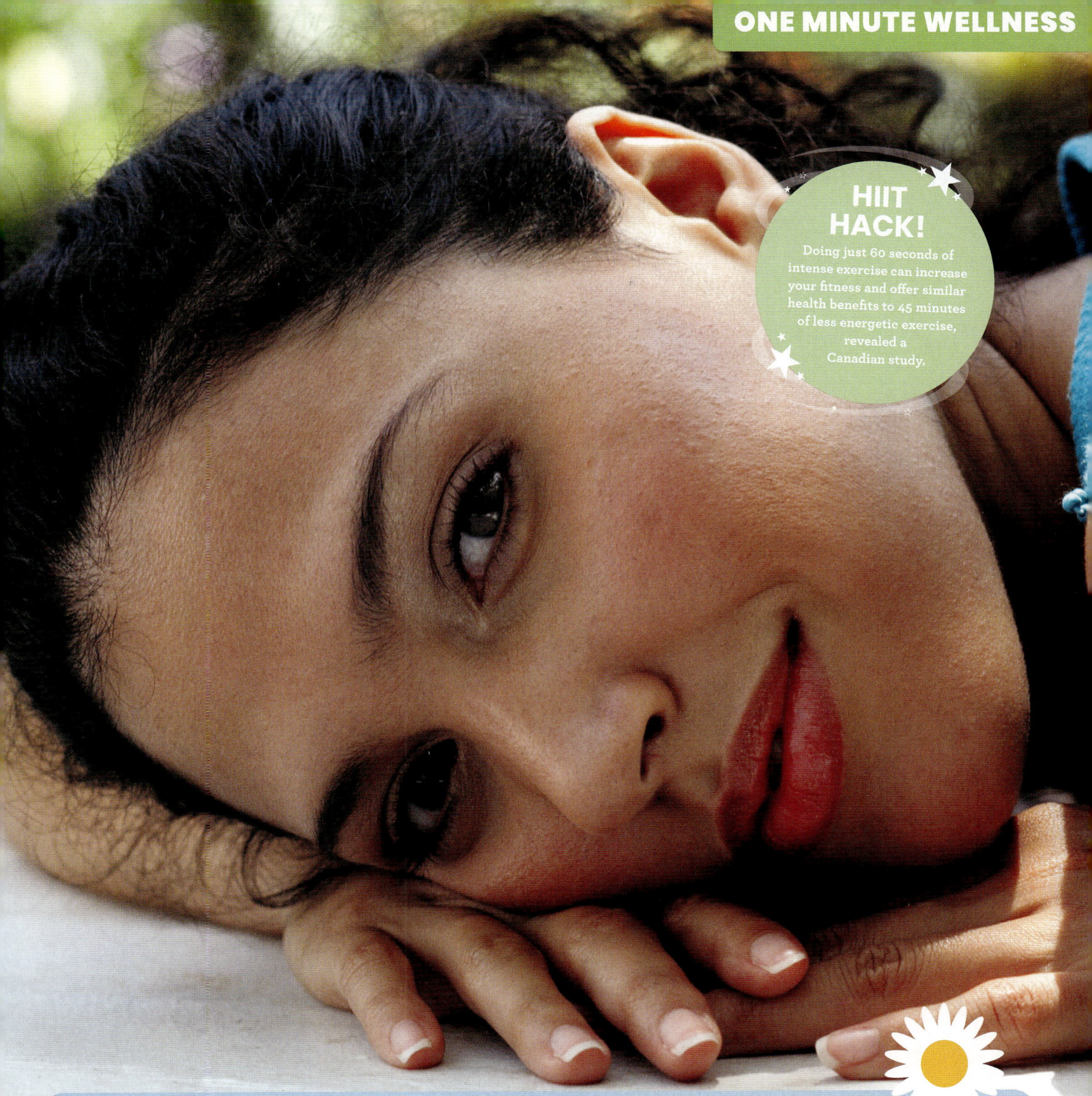

HIIT HACK!

Doing just 60 seconds of intense exercise can increase your fitness and offer similar health benefits to 45 minutes of less energetic exercise, revealed a Canadian study.

FIND YOUR PRESSURE POINTS

*Acupressure is an ancient alternative therapy that sends signals to the body to aid healing. Here, acupuncturist Renata Nunes** reveals the points to press that can improve wellness. Apply pressure for 30-40 seconds at a time.*

- The Yin Tang acupoint is located between the eyebrows. This is one of the main points that will soothe and relieve anxiety when stimulated.
- Gently press the CV17 acupoint to calm the heart and deepen the breath. You'll find it in the centre of the chest, between the nipples.
- On the forearm, the Pericardium 6 acupoint is roughly three fingers below the wrist, between the tendons. It's a good point to press if you have nausea, also to calm the mind and reduce anxiety.
- If you're tired, apply some pressure to the Stomach 36 acupoint to increase energy. It's a hand's length below the kneecap, on the outside of the tibia bone.

HAVE A CHAT

Connecting with others has never been so important. In fact, studies show that friendships in midlife and beyond increase our happiness levels, maintain cognitive functioning and help physical health. Can't get together with your friends right now? Hook up by video call to enjoy that face-to-face experience.

EMBRACE ESSENTIAL OILS

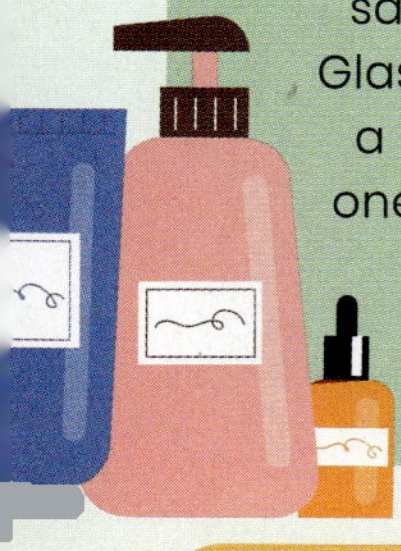

Orange aromatherapy oil has been proven to be uplifting and tranquillising: it alters our mood and boosts motivation, relaxation and clarity, says certified health coach Suzy Glaskie of Peppermint Wellness. 'Put a drop of orange essential oil on one palm, rub your hands together and inhale deeply for 60 seconds to get the benefits.'

STEP AWAY FROM YOUR SCREEN

Computer vision syndrome (CVC), caused by staring at digital screens for too long, is a condition becoming increasingly common in the UK. Eye strain can be reduced by following the simple 20-20-20 rule: take a screen break every 20 minutes and focus on something 20 feet away for 20 seconds. 'Visual fatigue can also be helped by using special lenses, designed to stop the eyes from working so hard in order to reduce and prevent eye strain,' says eye-health expert Dr. Andy Hepworth.

TWEAK YOUR SLEEP

Four million menopausal women in the UK are affected by poor sleep, and a recent survey revealed that women with sleep problems experienced almost twice the number of menopause symptoms compared to those who sleep well – proving the importance of quality shut-eye. 'Sleeplessness tends to magnify the negative effects of hormonal changes, which can worsen a range of symptoms,' says sleep expert Dr Sophie Bostock. Before bed, use **Health & Her Natural Sleep Aid and Sleep Balm. (amazon.co.uk).**

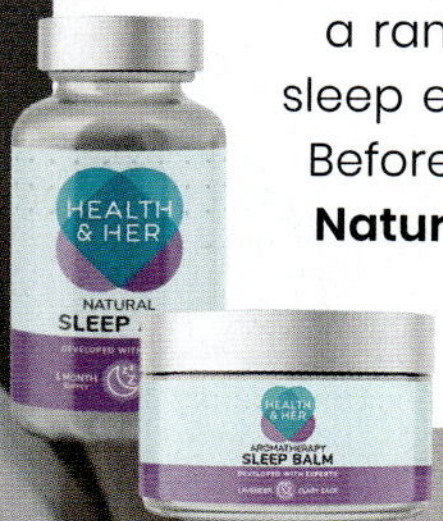

WASH YOUR HANDS

You know the drill, but doing it is so important to stay well. Wash hands regularly with soap and water, for at least 20 seconds. To moisturise them, slather on Green People's Manuka and Lemon Tea Tree hand cream (greenpeople.co.uk).

> “Sleeplessness tends to magnify the negative effects of hormonal changes, which can worsen a range of symptoms”

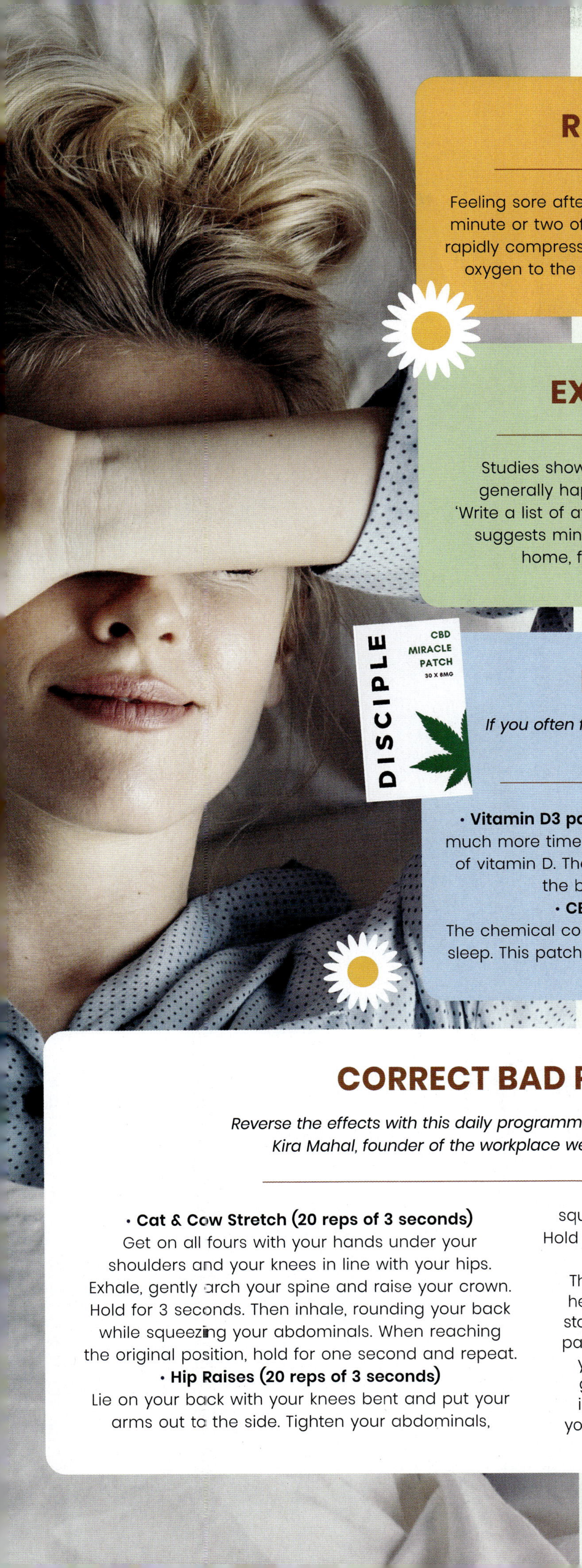

RECOVER QUICKER

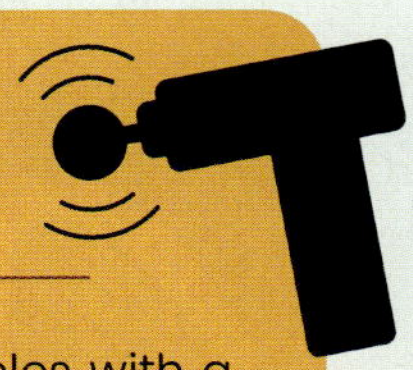

Feeling sore after a workout? Relieve your aching muscles with a minute or two of percussive therapy. Self-massage guns work by rapidly compressing soft tissue to stimulate blood flow, increasing oxygen to the muscle. **Liv Essential Theragun, theragun.com.**

EXPRESS GRATITUDE

Studies show that those who regularly express thanks are generally happier and less likely to experience depression. 'Write a list of at least three things that you're grateful for today, suggests mindset coach Alexis Jane. 'This could be a warm home, food in the fridge, or freedom of speech.'

POP ON A PATCH

If you often forget to take a supplement, then a health patch may be for you. Here are two to try...

• **Vitamin D3 patches, villwellness.com** With lots of us spending much more time indoors, it's crucial we still get adequate amounts of vitamin D. These deliver the vitamins through the skin and into the bloodstream to ensure high absorption.

• **CBD Miracle Patch,disciplelondon.com**
The chemical compound CBD can help with stress, anxiety and aid sleep. This patch releases 8mg of full-spectrum CBD over 24 hours.

CORRECT BAD POSTURE

Reverse the effects with this daily programme of 60-second stretches by PT Kira Mahal, founder of the workplace wellness provider Reset LDN.

• **Cat & Cow Stretch (20 reps of 3 seconds)**
Get on all fours with your hands under your shoulders and your knees in line with your hips. Exhale, gently arch your spine and raise your crown. Hold for 3 seconds. Then inhale, rounding your back while squeezing your abdominals. When reaching the original position, hold for one second and repeat.

• **Hip Raises (20 reps of 3 seconds)**
Lie on your back with your knees bent and put your arms out to the side. Tighten your abdominals, squeeze your glutes and raise your hips upwards. Hold for three seconds, lower back down and repeat.

• **Half Cobra (15 reps of increasing time)**
This releases tension in the lower back and can help reverse a slouched posture. Lie flat on your stomach with forearms touching the ground and palms facing down. Slowly lift the chest and prop yourself onto elbows. Hold for 15 seconds and gently lie back down. Every two or three reps, increase the time held by five seconds – until you're holding the pose for a total of 30 seconds.

Moon YOGA

BOTH THE SUN AND THE MOON ARE IMPORTANT ASPECTS IN YOGIC TRADITION, WHERE WE, AS TWOFOLD BEINGS, REPRESENT THE UNION BETWEEN THESE FUNDAMENTAL ENERGIES

WORDS: ALICE PATTILLO

Yoga isn't just a series of exercises, it's a way of life that dates back to ancient India. Derived from the Sanskrit word "yuj" meaning "yoke" or union, the exercises we perform and call yoga in the West are simply the physical disciplines taught within this deeply spiritual system that aims to promote a way of life free of suffering and in harmony with the higher powers. To achieve this peace of mind, body and spirit, you must adhere to a set of rules or disciplines called the eight limbs. These include Asana (the yoga postures) and Pranayama (breathing exercises), which focus on harnessing Prana, the universal life force.

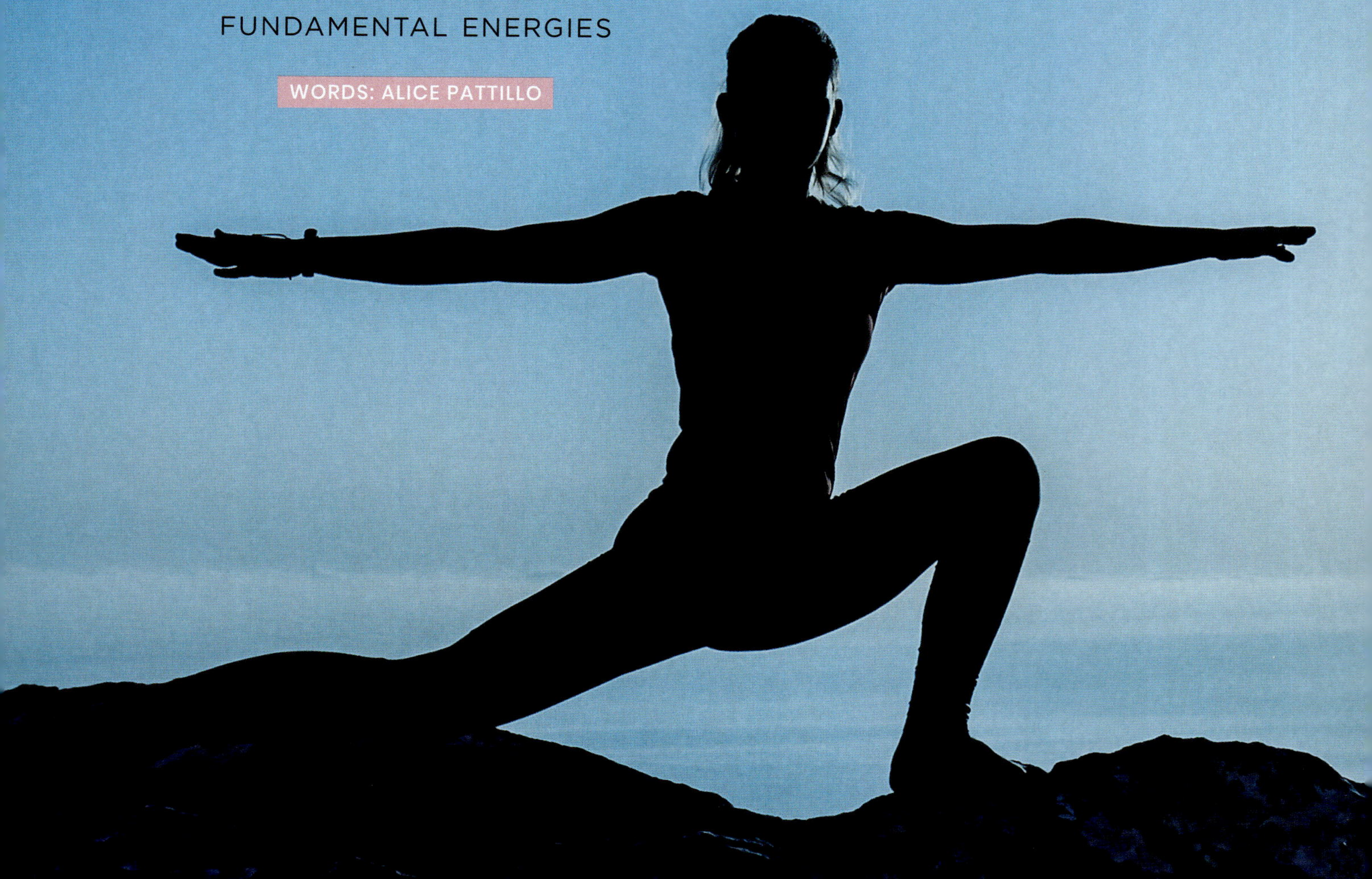

"This deeply spiritual system aims to promote a way of life free of suffering and in harmony with the higher powers"

In the West, the Asanas (postures) are taught in sequences as Hatha Yoga (or Vinyasa), and offer an effective exercise class that can aid in increasing flexibility, toning and strengthening muscles, improving circulation and cardiovascular health, reducing high blood pressure, stimulating metabolism and promoting fat loss, enhancing general fitness and athletic performance, and reducing stress and anxiety. You may already know a few yoga poses, as they are often used during stretches and cool-down routines in exercise classes, but a yoga flow is a powerful cardiovascular exercise in its own right and promotes a peace of mind unlike any other gym class, so why not add it into your self-care routine? Try a few postures in the morning to wake your body up or a few Moon Salutations after work to balance your mind.

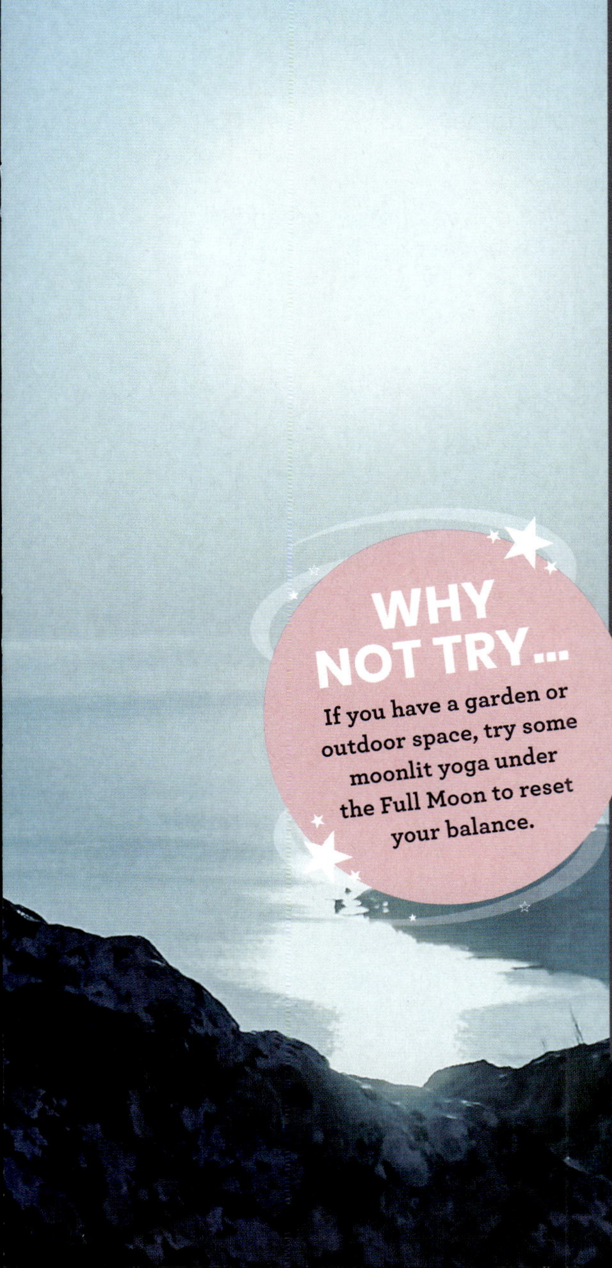

WHY NOT TRY...

If you have a garden or outdoor space, try some moonlit yoga under the Full Moon to reset your balance.

MOON PHASE PRACTICE

NEW MOON

Rejuvenation · Intention setting

POSES AND SEQUENCES FOR RESTORATION

Try back bends such as Bridge, Cat, Cow, Sphinx and Crescent Moon to improve spinal flexibility.

WAXING CRESCENT

Manifestation · Growth

POSES AND SEQUENCES FOR BALANCING

Build balance, strength and focus with standing and core poses such as Side Plank, Tree Pose and Half Moon.

FIRST QUARTER

Action · Energy

POSES AND SEQUENCES FOR BUILDING HEAT

Try fast and dynamic sequences designed to energise and awaken your body.

WAXING GIBBOUS

Rooting · Regenerating

POSES AND SEQUENCES FOR CENTERING

Prepare for the effects of the Full Moon with a sequence that incorporates inversions for strength and to reverse blood flow such as Forward Fold and Downward Facing Dog.

FULL MOON

Grounding · Resetting

POSES AND SEQUENCES FOR GROUNDING

The perfect time to meditate with yogic breathing. Try a deep stretching sequence of poses followed by recharging with Corpse Pose.

WANING GIBBOUS

Presence · Gratitude

POSES AND SEQUENCES FOR HEART OPENING

Try chest openers like Upward-Facing Dog and Bow Pose to increase your openness to self-love and acceptance.

LAST QUARTER

Forgiveness · Reflection

POSES AND SEQUENCES FOR OPENING AND RELEASING

Try grounding hip openers such as Crescent Lunge and Goddess Pose to release tight hips and emotional blockages.

WANING CRESCENT

Letting go · Restoration

POSES AND SEQUENCES FOR DETOXING

Try forward bends and twists such as forward fold, head to knee pose and Half Lord of the Fishes to aid digestion and calm the mind.

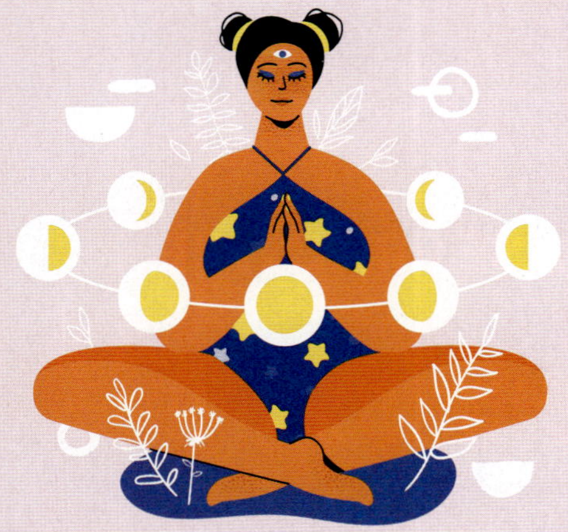

The Moon in YOGA

The word Hatha is derived from Ha (Sun) and Tha (Moon). The aim of Hatha yoga, therefore, balances the two energies – solar and lunar. The Sun is masculine energy, the energy of your body, the day, light, Yang in Chinese philosophy. The Moon is feminine energy, the energy of your subconscious mind, your emotions, the night, darkness and Yin in Chinese philosophy. According to yogi master BK Iyengar, "the energy of the Sun never fades, whereas the Moon fades every month and again from fading comes to fullness."

The Moon and Sun are both honoured in yoga. The Moon is connected to the emotional, sensory mind and is deeply associated with introspection and how we perceive ourselves. The Moon represents purity and therefore has a cleansing and purifying effect on our body. In Ashtanga yoga, a form of Hatha yoga, the New Moon and Full Moons are observed with rest – a day off from performing physical poses. It is believed that on the day of the New Moon our bodies feel the effects of gravity the strongest and therefore feel very heavy and inflexible. In contrast, on the day of the Full Moon, we are at our least grounded, creating physical instability. You too might choose to honour the Moon cycle by abstaining from practice on these days, but you may also want to try a gentle, slow restorative flow or Yin Yoga, where each pose is held for a long period of time.

It's not just the Full and New Moons that hold different energies. As we know, each phase of the Moon's cycle holds a different energy and therefore you may want to use this knowledge to inform your yoga practice.

SAGE ADVICE

Before you start...

- It is important that you seek medical advice before taking on any new exercise routine.
- We recommend that you attend a few in-person yoga classes before attempting any of the poses yourself to avoid injury and ensure you are performing the postures correctly and engaging the correct muscles.
- Always take your time and don't force yourself into postures. No two bodies are the same and your flexibility and balance can change from day to day. Yoga is about listening to your body, not looking good. There is no room on the mat for your ego!
- Always remember to keep a slight bend in your knees, scoop your pelvis up and in towards your spine to protect your back and relax your shoulders and jaw to prevent strain.
- Follow the breathing prompts to ensure you are inhaling and exhaling deeply and regularly in order to fuel your practise. Never hold your breath during yoga!
- For more yoga, try *Yoga With Adriene* on *YouTube* for free classes. If you are willing to pay, apps like *Down Dog, Daily Yoga, Glo Yoga, Alo Moves* and *Asana Rebel* will help you level up your practise or help you stick to a daily routine. If you like a variety, *Peloton* even offers yoga and Pilates classes with some killer soundtracks.

YOGIC BREATH

Banish negative energy with this easy hand-cleansing ritual you can perform at home

Yogic breathing (Pranayama) is a core element to yoga and can prove a vital skill for meditation and mindfulness. During physical yoga practice, it is most common to enlist Ocean Breath (Ujjayi). In order to do this you must inhale deeply through your nose and then constrict the back of your throat while breathing out, again through your nose. You can develop the breathing method by starting off by simply imagining you are fogging a bathroom mirror with your breath and breathe out through your mouth to recreate this act. Once you feel confident to do so, close your mouth and using the same technique, breathe out through your nose. Eventually, you are aiming to constrict your throat while inhaling too!

MOON Salutation

(CHANDRA NAMASKAR)

Soothing, cooling and balancing

Time to Practise: Evening, summertime, or anytime you are feeling exhausted, anxious, overstimulated and overwhelmed.

Originally conceived as an evening sequence, the Moon Salutation is the Yin equivalent of the Sun Salutation practised in most yoga classes. The Sun Salutation is traditionally more invigorating, designed to build heat and energy, while the Moon Salutation is designed to soothe, cool, calm and unwind after a long day. However, both can be used interchangeably depending on what you require from your practise. They both strengthen and stretch your entire body, aid circulation and digestion, boost your immune system and still the mind, but the Moon Salutation is particularly useful as a full body de-stresser when you are struggling with anxiety or drained and overwhelmed.

STEP 1
MOUNTAIN POSE
(Tadasana)

Stand with your feet parallel, hip width apart. Spread your toes and ensure your weight is evenly distributed throughout your feet. Relax your shoulders, lift through the legs and lengthen through your spine. Engage your glutes and draw your naval in towards your spine to engage your pelvic floor and abdominal muscles while ensuring your pelvis remains neutral – it helps to keep a slight bend in your knees. Straighten your arms beside you and open your hands wide and face your palms towards the front.

STEP 2
EXTENDED MOUNTAIN POSE

Inhale and turn your palms inwards, extend your arms outwards and sweep them up high above you in one swift circular motion. Ensure your feet remain grounded as you reach as high as you can, lifting your waist away from your hips to stretch and lengthen through your entire spine, ensuring you draw your shoulders away from your ears. Exhale and bring your palms together overhead bending ever so slightly backwards ensuring you feel no pressure on your lower back, and then return to centre on an inhale.

STEP 3
STANDING CRESCENT MOON POSE
(Indudalasana)

Clasp your fingers together leaving only your forefingers outstretched and pointed towards the sky. Exhale and gently bend lean towards the right. Ensure your hips remain still, engaging your core and your glutes. You should feel a stretch in the left side of your torso. Stay here through another few breaths. As you inhale, bring yourself back to centre, pause and then exhale to repeat the same bend towards the left, feeling a stretch in the right of your torso. Stay here for as many breaths as you stayed for on the right. Inhale and return to the centre.

STEP 4
GODDESS POSE
(Utkata Konasana)

As you exhale, step your feet wide apart. Your toes should be pointing slightly outwards from centre – at approximately 11 and 1. Bend your knees and aim to lower your body parallel to the ground, your knees at 90 degrees, stacked over your ankles. Don't force yourself – you may not be able to come down that low; that's okay! Just ensure you are still engaging your core and glutes. Your body should not be leaning forward or backwards – envision a string keeping you upright. If you start to tip forward, don't squat so far down. As you lower, bring your upper arms down to become level with your shoulders. Your forearms should be perpendicular to your upper arms, with your palms facing forward, hands open. Ensure that your knees are facing outwards and you can feel a deep stretch in your inner thighs. Stay here for a few breaths.

STEP 5
FIVE POINTED STAR POSE
(Utthita Tadasana)

Inhale, and pivot your feet parallel. Straighten your legs while maintaining a slight bend in your knees and draw your chest up as you straighten your

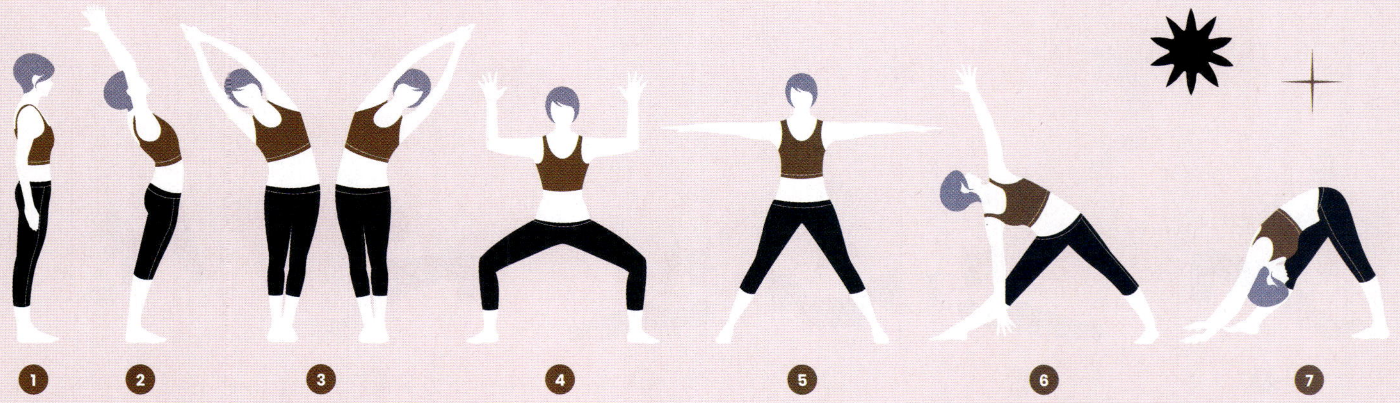

arms outwards into a T-shape. Stay here for a few breaths.

STEP 6
EXTENDED TRIANGLE POSE
(Trikonasana)

Pivot your right foot towards the front of the mat and your left foot to 45 degrees. Exhale, reach your right arm towards the front of the mat and shift your torso with it, keeping your hips still. Hinge from the hip joint towards the right leg and reach your right arm towards the floor. You may need a block here, or you might be able to touch the ground with your finger tips or simply place your hand on your shin. Lift up from the waist, engage your abs and glutes and reach your left hand to the sky, palm facing left. Do not let your head drop or your waist relax towards the floor! Inhale, twist your chest forward and gaze up past your right fingertips towards the sky.

MODIFICATION Use a block or even the wall to support you! Don't look up towards the sky if you feel off balance – keep your gaze towards the front but try and lift your chest as you reach!

STEP 7
PYRAMID POSE
(Parsvottanasana)

Exhale, untwist your chest and turn your torso towards the right. Reach your left arm back down towards the mat. Pivot your hips towards the front of the mat, keeping them square and level. Now hinge forward from your hip joint and release your body towards the mat, reaching towards the right knee with your head and stretching the spine long. Inhale and interlink your hands behind your back - you might want to try your palms together (Anjali Mudra) if this is possible for you. Stay here for a few breaths, stretching further forward and downward as you exhale and pull the naval in towards your spine.

MODIFICATION If you are less flexible, only go half way down. Straighten your spine and keep your back flat, parallel to the floor. Use two blocks either side of your right leg and rest your hands to keep your stable.

STEP 8
LOW CRESCENT LUNGE POSE
(Anjaneyasana)

Inhale as you lift as you bend your back knee and rest it down onto the floor while moving your gaze forwards, shifting your body towards the front of the mat and into a low lunge position. Exhale. As you move forward into the pose, engage your glutes and abs and shift your hips forward to stretch your back leg out. Inhale and sweep your hands up above your head, palms facing each other. Lift your chest upwards as you gently lean backwards into a backbend. Feel the stretch in your leg, hips and back as you breathe, ensuring you tighten the abdominal muscles and glutes to protect the spine.

MODIFICATION Enlist blocks if you are struggling to reach the ground with your hands and place a pillow or towel under your knee for support.

STEP 9
SIDE LUNGE POSE
(Skandasana)

Inhale and turn your body to the left, and straighten your back leg, shifting your weight over to the right. Exhale and rest your left heel on the floor and sit on your right toes. Place your hands on the floor in front of you for balance or your palms together if you feel stable. Ensure you keep your chest up and spine straight, feeling the stretch in your hips and legs and maintaining your balance.

MODIFICATION You can use blocks for support if you cannot reach the ground with your fingertips on your own, simply place beneath your hands.

STEP 10
GARLAND POSE
(Malasana)

With your hands on the mat to guide you, shift your body back to the centre and bend your back leg, bringing it in towards your body. Exhale and place both feet on the floor and press your elbows inside the thighs to open your hips and find stability. Stretch your spine and lift your chest connecting to your breath.

MODIFICATION Swap this pose for Goddess Pose if this is too deep of a stretch!

STEP 11
SIDE LUNGE POSE
(Skandasana)

Now shift your weight to your left leg and repeat Side Lunge Pose on the other side, stretching out your right leg and balancing on your left foot.

STEP 12
LOW CRESCENT LUNGE POSE
(Anjaneyasana)

Inhale and shift your body towards the back of your mat and repeat Low Crescent Lunge Pose with your left leg bent and right leg stretched out behind you.

STEP 13
PYRAMID POSE
(Parsvottanasana)

Exhale and engage your glutes and abs to lift yourself up and straighten your legs. Inhale and try and raise your body while still facing the left in one fluid motion. Exhale and stretch out your torso either leaving your arms stretched out in front of you or clasped behind your back to repeat Pyramid Pose on the other side.

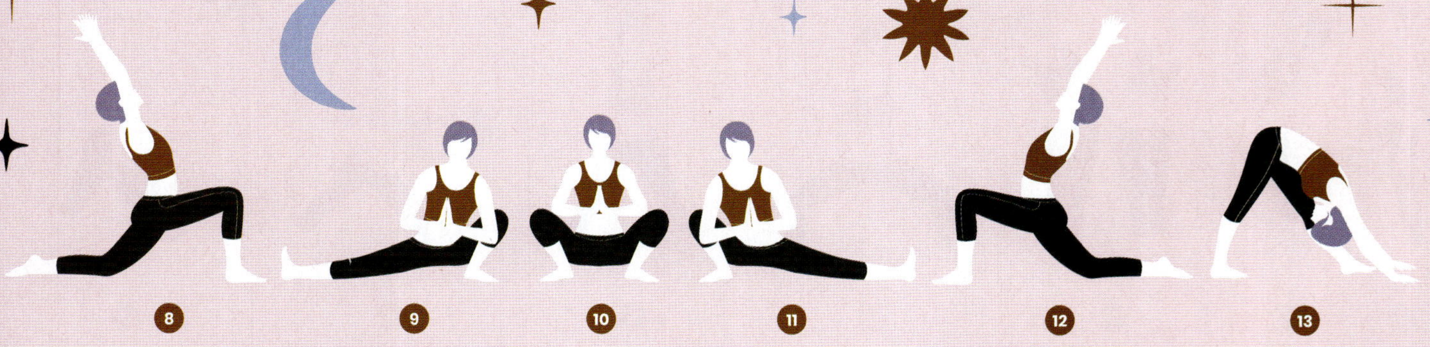

STEP 14
EXTENDED TRIANGLE POSE
(Trikonasana)

Carefully release your arms from Pyramid Pose and keep a soft bend in the knee, draw your naval in towards your spine and lift your torso. Exhale and reach your left arm forward and your right arm behind you, shifting your weight towards your left arm and hinging at the waist to move back into Extended Triangle Pose. Reach to the sky with your right arm, twist your body and gaze towards your fingers.

STEP 15
FIVE POINTED STAR POSE
(Utthita Tadasana)

Inhale and slowly lift your torso back up to standing. Pivot your left foot so that it is parallel with your right and your body is facing the side of the mat. Move into Five Pointed Star Pose, elongating your spine and drawing up through your legs, extending your arms ensuring your feet are grounded.

STEP 16
GODDESS POSE
(Utkata Konasana)

Inhale and move back into a wide-legged squat for Goddess Pose. Inhale and raise your arms, bending at the elbows, opening your fingers and straightening your spine.

STEP 17
STANDING CRESCENT MOON POSE
(Indudalasana)

Inhale and engage your legs, drawing up through your knees and glutes, ground yourself through your feet to raise yourself back up. Bring your feet back into a natural hip-width apart and raise your arms to the sky, pressing your palms together overhead. Repeat step 3 on either side.

HALF MOON POSE

Feel like challenging yourself? Try adding this balancing pose during the Waxing Crescent or First Quarter phase of the moon

Feel like challenging yourself? Try adding this balancing pose during the Waxing Crescent or First Quarter phase of the moon

Good for:

. Improving balance, stability and focus
. Stress and anxiety relief
. Improving digestion
. Stretching your hips and back
. Easing menstural cramps
. Aiding circulation
. Strengthening lower body
. Do not try if... You have any leg, hip, shoulders or back injuries or issues – seek medical advice!

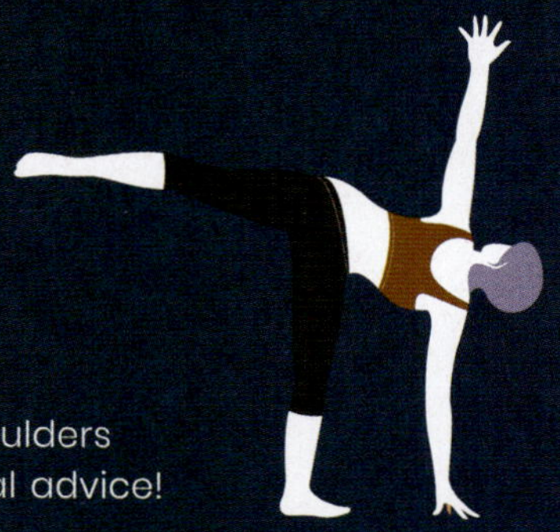

From Five Pointed Star Pose you might want to try moving into Half Moon Pose. With your feet wide and legs straight with a soft bend in the knee, step your left foot in a little and pivot your right front towards the front of your mat. Place your left hand on your hip and keep your right arm outstretched. Inhale, bend your right knee and shift your weight into your right leg as you lift your back leg off the ground. Reach for the ground or a block to stabilise you. Inhale and rotate your chest and pelvis to the left, extend your left arm up as you look down to the ground and try to lift your left leg higher, so it is level with your hip and parallel to the ground. Flex your left foot and extend through the ball of your right foot. Now gaze up at your left hand. Repeat on the other side (after the second Five Pointed Star Pose in this sequence).

MODIFICATION: Use a block under your right hand to support you, keep your left hand on your hip and maintain your gaze towards the floor.

STEP 18
EXTENDED MOUNTAIN POSE
(Tadasana)

Once you are back to centre don't release your hands. Keep your palms together and as you exhale, slowly draw your palms down from above your head to your heart. Repeat all steps again three or four times and finish by lying on your back with your legs outstretched. Place one hand on your belly and one on your heart in Corpse Pose (Savasana). Stay here for up to 10 minutes.

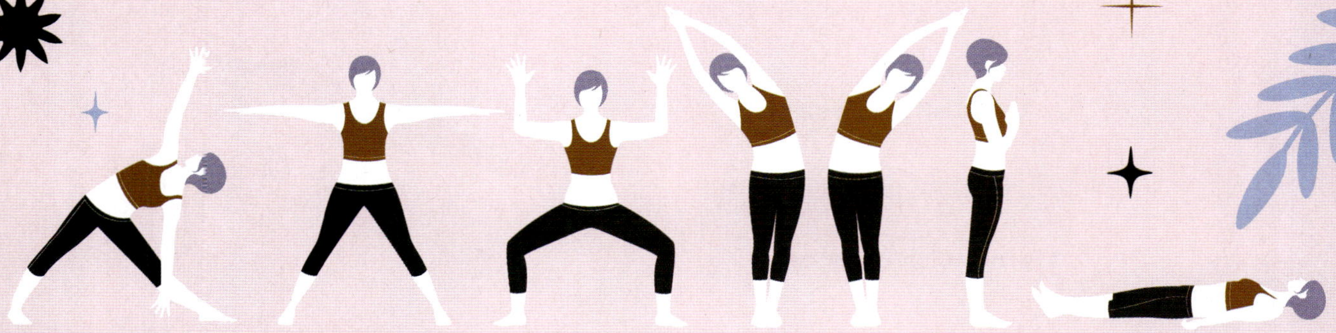

14 15 16 17 18

Spirit

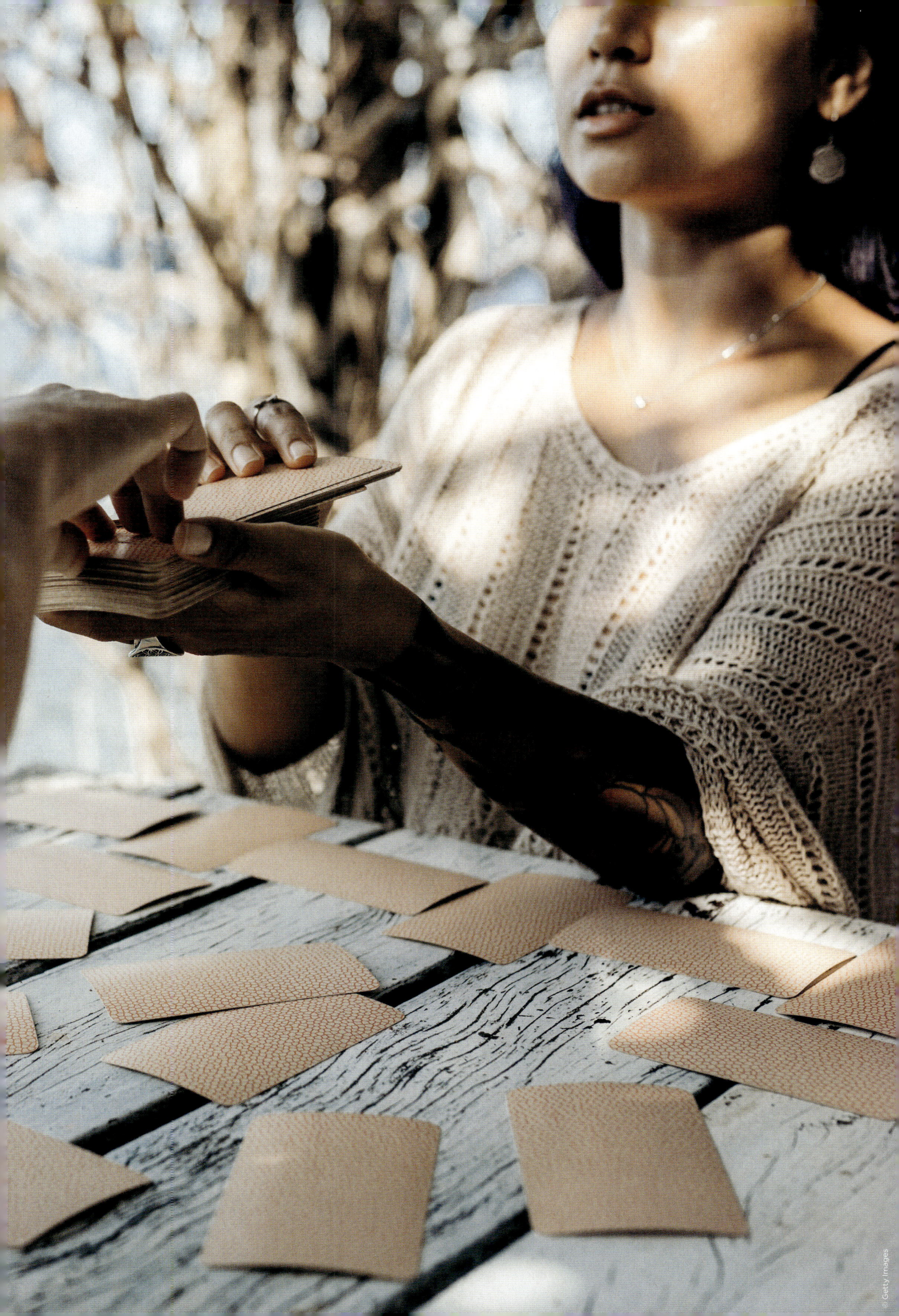

The SPIRIT of MINDFUL *magic*

DISCOVER HOW CONNECTING WITH THE FOUR TRADITIONAL MAGICAL ELEMENTS OF EARTH, AIR, FIRE AND WATER CAN LEAD YOU TO AN UNDERSTANDING OF THE MYSTICAL FIFTH

WORDS: APRIL MADDEN

For centuries, there has been an idea that magic is divided into four schools, governed by the four traditional elements of the ancient world – earth, air, fire, and water. This ancient idea was popularised again in the 16th century by a doctor called Paracelsus. Back when he was practising medicine, astrology and alchemy were a big part of the discipline, and Paracelsus drew his healing philosophies from stars and spells as much as he did from science. While we know today that physical and mental illnesses should always be treated by a healthcare professional, many of us find that complementary therapies, such as meditation to connect with the four traditional elements, can help us to feel grounded, blow away our cares, energise our passions, and soothe our troubles.

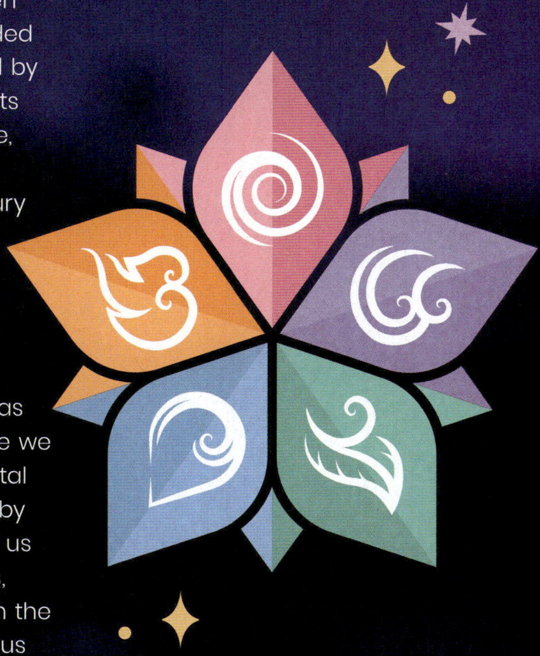

But did you know that there's a fifth magical element? Spirit, also known as akasha or aether, is the guiding force of the universe. When we learn to connect with the four physical elements, we are moving closer to the spirit that guides them. When we practise magic mindfully, and mindfulness magically, we open ourselves to a powerful connection with this universal life force and invite awareness, empathy and wisdom into our everyday lives.

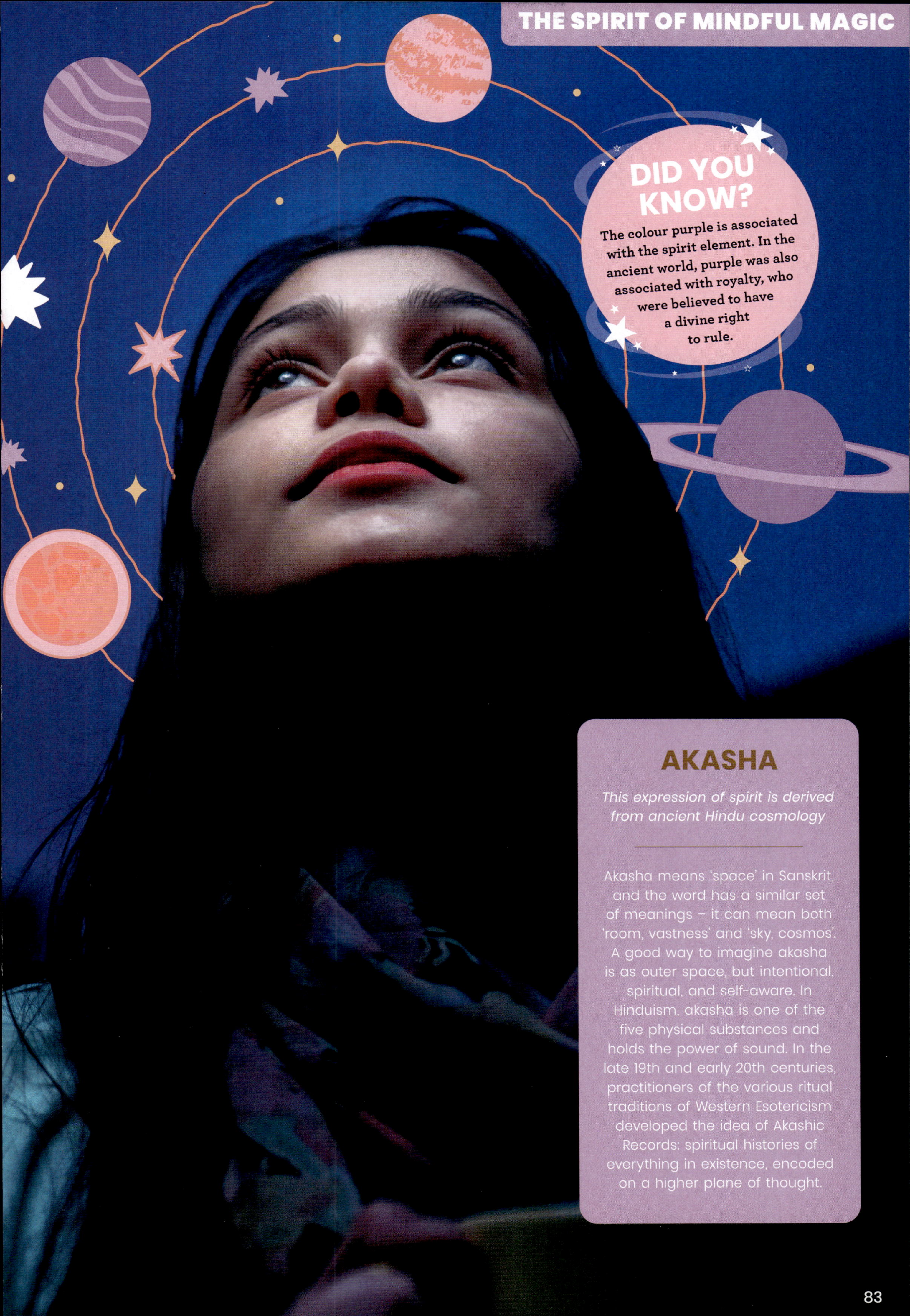

DID YOU KNOW?

The colour purple is associated with the spirit element. In the ancient world, purple was also associated with royalty, who were believed to have a divine right to rule.

AKASHA

This expression of spirit is derived from ancient Hindu cosmology

---

Akasha means 'space' in Sanskrit, and the word has a similar set of meanings – it can mean both 'room, vastness' and 'sky, cosmos'. A good way to imagine akasha is as outer space, but intentional, spiritual, and self-aware. In Hinduism, akasha is one of the five physical substances and holds the power of sound. In the late 19th and early 20th centuries, practitioners of the various ritual traditions of Western Esotericism developed the idea of Akashic Records: spiritual histories of everything in existence, encoded on a higher plane of thought.

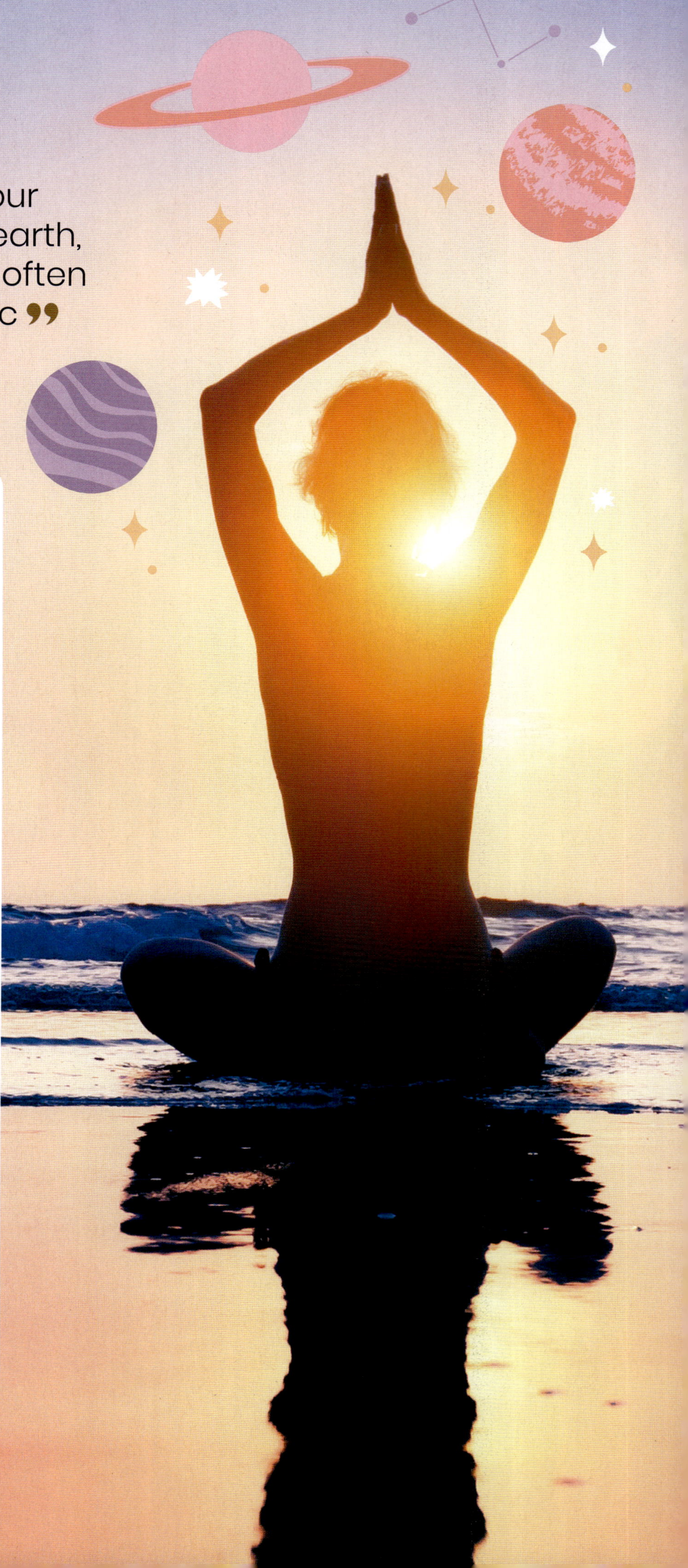

> "The use of the four physical elements – earth, air, fire and water – is often called natural magic"

GET INTO THE SPIRIT OF THINGS

Spirit can be invoked by considering space and time, and the connections between all things

In traditional Western occultism, spirit is considered to be higher in status than the four physical elements, while in some more modern magical systems, it's equal to them. Either way, spirit still permeates and interacts with the other four, and can be thought of as providing the connections between them. Water, air and the fiery sun allow earth to produce trees and plants; warmth acting on wet earth allows air to draw up clouds. You can imagine spirit as the energy that powers these transformative interactions. Spirit is also associated with the depths of space. Starlight takes centuries to reach us – even sunlight takes eight minutes to travel to Earth. This interrelation of physical space and conceptual time is the province of spirit. In some ceremonial magic traditions, the use of the four physical elements is referred to as natural magic, while the use of the spirit element is called high magic.

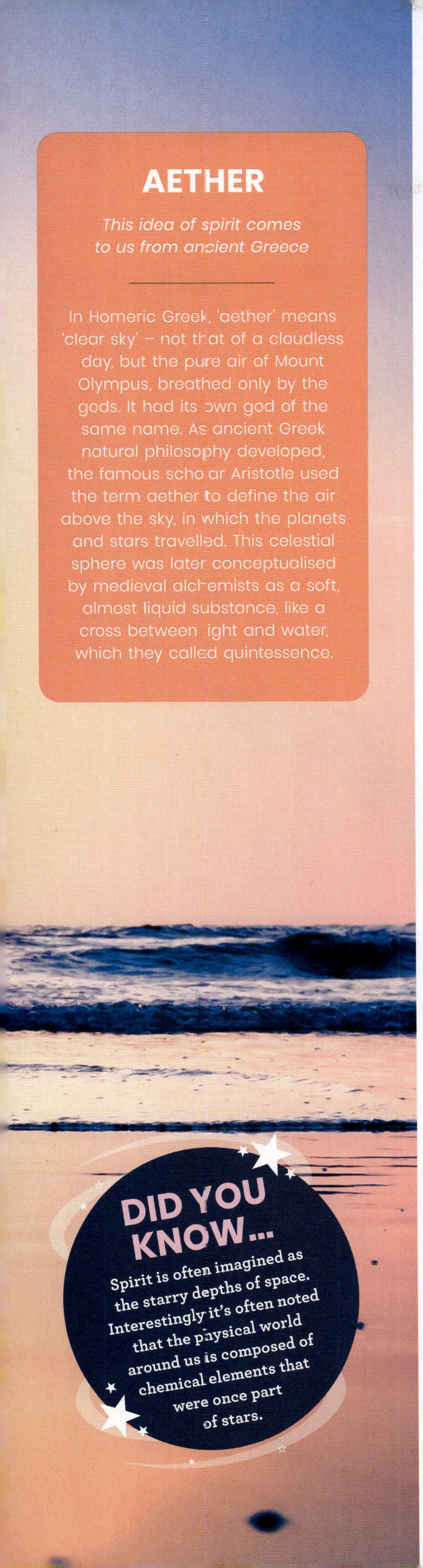

AETHER

This idea of spirit comes to us from ancient Greece

In Homeric Greek, 'aether' means 'clear sky' – not that of a cloudless day, but the pure air of Mount Olympus, breathed only by the gods. It had its own god of the same name. As ancient Greek natural philosophy developed, the famous scholar Aristotle used the term aether to define the air above the sky, in which the planets and stars travelled. This celestial sphere was later conceptualised by medieval alchemists as a soft, almost liquid substance, like a cross between light and water, which they called quintessence.

DID YOU KNOW...

Spirit is often imagined as the starry depths of space. Interestingly it's often noted that the physical world around us is composed of chemical elements that were once part of stars.

CONNECT with *Spirit*

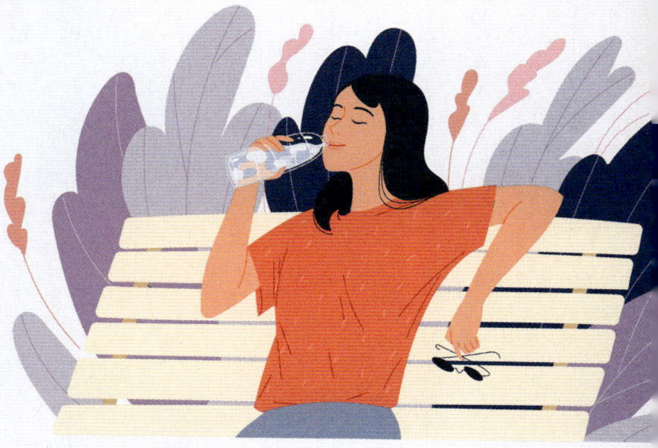

1 TAKE SOME QUIET TIME

Stop during your busy day and sit quietly for a few minutes, letting your awareness drift outwards into the world around you.

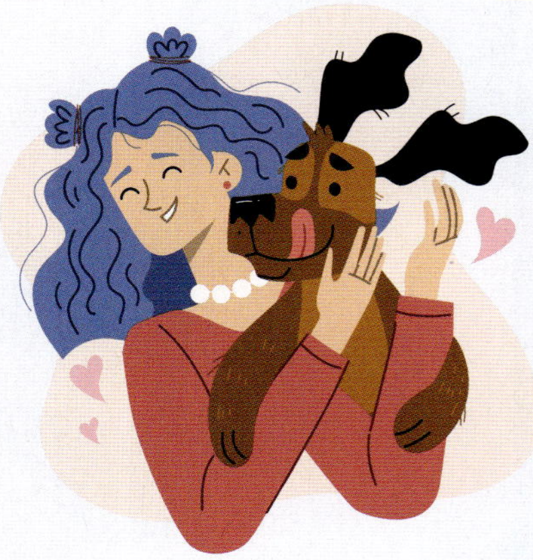

2 CONNECT WITH CREATURES

If you have a pet, sit with them for a while and contemplate the connection of love and life between you. If you don't, open a window or go outside and observe your local birds.

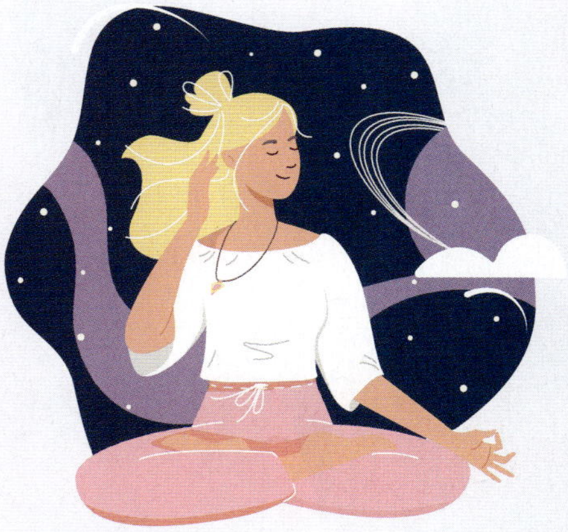

3 TRY A RITUAL

What makes you feel connected to the spiritual? This might be meditation, spellwork, or visiting a sacred space or building and participating in worship.

> "The physical world around us is composed of chemical elements that were once part of stars"

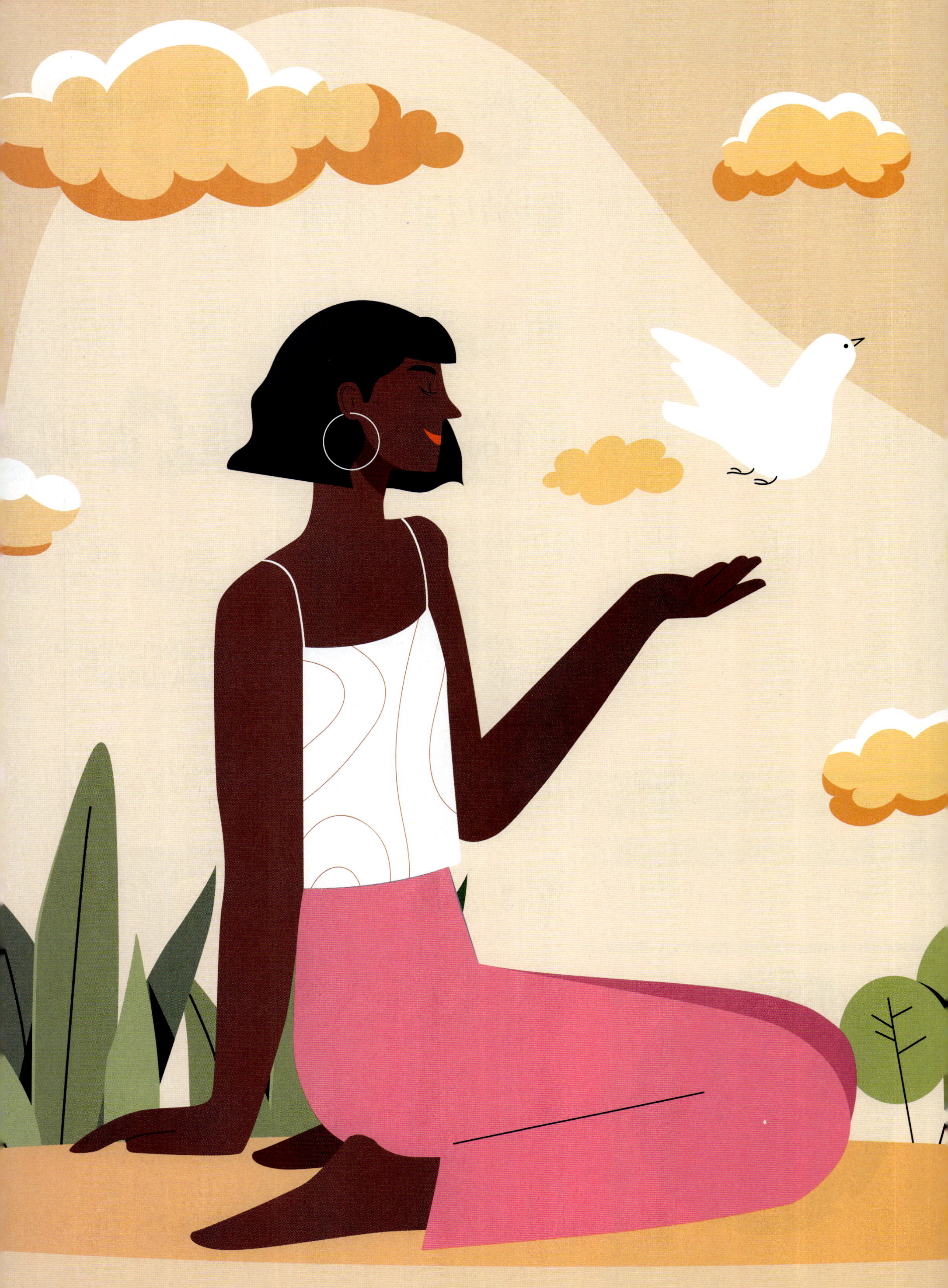

The Power of MANIFESTATION

WITH A LITTLE PRACTICE, YOU CAN HARNESS THE POWER OF MANIFESTATION AND MAKE YOUR LIFE EXACTLY WHAT YOU WANT IT TO BE

WORDS: CATHERINE CURZON

Manifesting is a powerful tool that can allow you to bring something into your physical reality through the power of your focused energy and meditation. Though it won't make a Ferrari appear in your driveway overnight, you can work on manifesting a goal such as a new job by visualising and focusing your inner strength to help make it happen. It's easy to feel daunted when we think of the life we want, but the secret to manifesting is to not only believe it is possible, but to visualise that new reality.

Before you begin your manifestation meditation, choose a specific thing that you want to manifest and set a believable timescale. Be sure that it is something that you truly want and that it is something that will benefit not only you, but others too – this is why we focus on things like a new job, not a Ferrari!

Prepare yourself for meditation by sitting in a comfortable, quiet space, where you won't be interrupted for as long as you wish to meditate. You may want to light candles or have music playing.

As you focus on your breathing and relax your body, imagine a warm light entering your body from the bottom of your feet. The light moves slowly up through your limbs, warming you and filling you with energy as it continues up through your torso, filling your arms and flooding your body with new possibilities and endless opportunity. When this light reaches your heart, notice how you are open to the future and all the possibilities and new discoveries yet to be experienced.

> "You can work on manifesting a goal such as a new job by visualising and focusing"

As the light enters your head and your entire being is filled with its warmth and power, acknowledge to yourself the thing that you wish to manifest. Visualise yourself taking the steps to achieve this desire and the moment when it is yours. Notice all the details, from the people present with you to the sounds you hear and the colours you see; all the small details that are part of achieving your goal. Let this experience be imprinted on your heart, cradled in the golden light, and embrace the future yet to come.

Let your focus return slowly to the floor beneath your feet and the sounds of the world around you. Tell yourself that you believe your dreams will come true, repeating this mantra before you open your eyes.

By repeating this meditation regularly, you'll manifest your desire more strongly every time, helping turn it into a reality. You truly can achieve your dreams, with focus, energy and the power you hold within yourself.

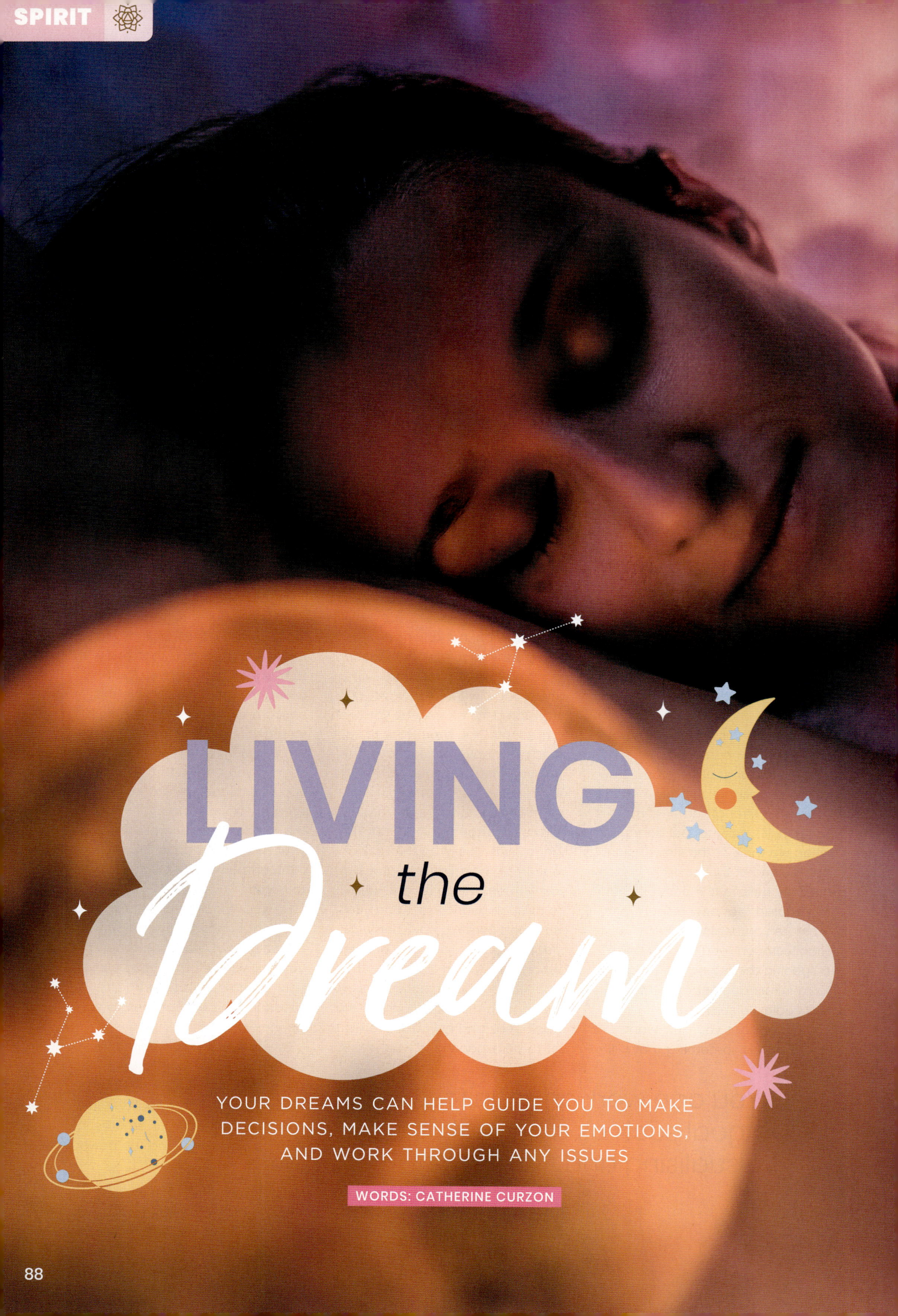

LIVING the Dream

YOUR DREAMS CAN HELP GUIDE YOU TO MAKE DECISIONS, MAKE SENSE OF YOUR EMOTIONS, AND WORK THROUGH ANY ISSUES

WORDS: CATHERINE CURZON

WHY NOT TRY...

If nightmares are troubling you, practicing good sleep hygiene could change your night for the better. Before you go to bed, wind down by reading a relaxing book or taking a hot bath. Once you're settled in your bed, practice some deep breathing as you let yourself drift off into a mellow sleep.

THE IMPORTANCE OF DREAMS

Everyone dreams, but did you know that our dreams can carry messages of great significance?

Throughout history, dreams have fascinated and sometimes frightened us, as we seek to understand not only why we receive these messages from our subconscious as we sleep, but what our dreams might mean. When we dream, we process our emotions from the day just passed, working through our experiences and anxieties and preparing to face tomorrow. Yet our dreams can do so much more than that. Originating from deep within our subconscious with no input from our waking mind, they offer a window into our very deepest selves, from our most heartfelt wishes to our deepest fears, not to mention hints as to what the future might hold. By learning how to interpret the symbolism of our dreams, we can better understand not just ourselves, but the path we are taking through the world. Our dreams offer a wealth of significance and guidance, we just need to learn how to interpret it.

SLEEP HYGIENE

Good habits make for good sleep!

Sleep hygiene is vital to a refreshing sleep. Listen to your body when it's tired, go to bed; set a routine for your body clock by getting up at the same time every day, even weekends. Your sleeping environment is important so make sure the temperature is comfortable, and the room is dark and quiet; if you need them, use a sleep mask or earplugs. Get the best mattress and pillows that you can afford and reserve your bed for sleep and for intimacy: if you watch TV or play video games, it will lose its association with sleep and rest. Don't be tempted to scroll on your phone before bed, as the blue light from its screen will inhabit your body's production of melatonin, which is vital to sleep. Instead, keep things mellow, relaxed and free of stress. Lastly, if you can't sleep, don't force it: get up and do something relaxing until sleep comes naturally.

REM AND DEEP SLEEP

With rapid eye movement sleep, our dreams begin

REM (rapid eye movement) sleep comes about 90 minutes after we drift off and is the period in which we dream our most vivid dreams. Though muscle movement is limited, our brain is highly active and functioning at levels similar to waking. REM sleep is also vital in emotional wellbeing as it helps the mind process and suppress distressing experiences. Though you can dream in other sleep stages, none are as vivid as those that occur during REM sleep.

DREAMING *of* Animals

Each animal has its own unique dream meaning

Animals that you encounter in your dream each have their own interpretation; once you learn what they signify, you'll gain an insight into your subconscious

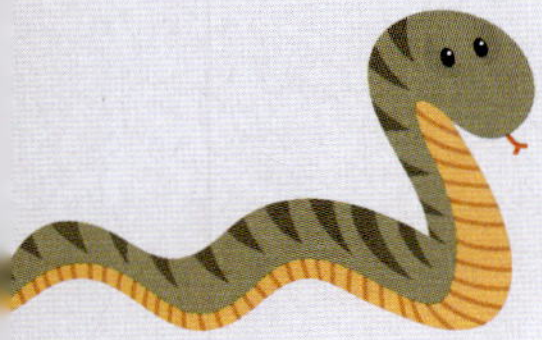

If you dream of a **SNAKE**, it's time to shed bad habits and open yourself up to a new beginning; the watchword here is renewal.

Dreams of **DOGS** encourage you to cherish and nurture the loyal companions you have. A dog is man's best friend, after all.

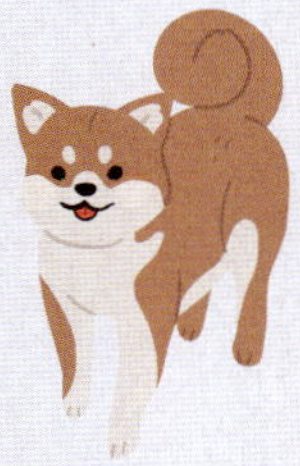

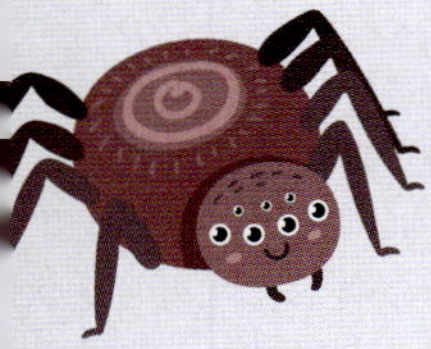

While encountering a **SPIDER** in a dream might be a nightmare for some, these misunderstood creatures are actually letting you know that your destiny is yours to weave, just as the spider weaves its web. Your future is yours to create.

Should a **CAT** visit you, your subconscious is telling you to trust your instincts. Symbolic of wisdom and independence, the cat in your dreams is a sign that you know what's best for you.

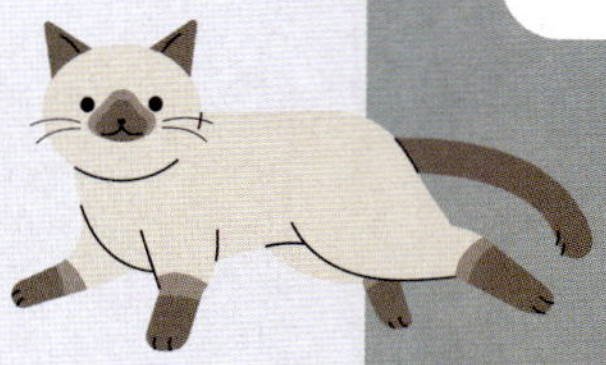

DREAMING OF PLACES

Dreaming of a particular place may be symbolic of your psychological or spiritual needs

If you often find yourself dreaming of unfamiliar places, this can be a great opportunity for self-reflection and analysis. After all, your own subconscious has created a whole location, whether a landscape or building, that you have never seen before, and everything that has gone into its creation has come from deep within you. It may be that you yearn to travel and experience new horizons, or that you feel trapped by a situation in your life. When you dream of a familiar place, however, you may find that it has changed subtly or even dramatically from the reality of the physical world. In this case, the dream environment may signify a few different things. Firstly, it suggests that you are open to change and happy to embrace it. You can also take it as a reassuring sign that you can work through and grow with any changes or challenges that might be waiting around the corner.

CHRONOTYPES

Discovering your chronotype may transform your sleep

Some scientists believe that everyone has a sleep chronotype (or sleep animal), which is related to their circadian rhythm and determines their ideal sleep schedule in relation to their body's production of melatonin. Some people really are morning people, while others function best when they understand that their body likes to sleep and wake at different times. Lions wake early and get most done in the morning, but need to be in bed by 10pm. Bears are the 'work hard, play hard' type; they can do a 9 to 5 and then party until 11. Wolves are the 'night owl' type, getting up at 8am makes them most productive in the afternoon, and they're awake into the wee hours. Dolphins wake early, go to sleep late, and are light sleepers; their sleep is often disrupted and fragmented so they really need to prioritise peace and quiet. Whether you're a Bear, Lion, Wolf, or Dolphin, tapping into your natural schedule will help you understand exactly when your body needs to sleep in order to reap the most rewards for your health and wellbeing.

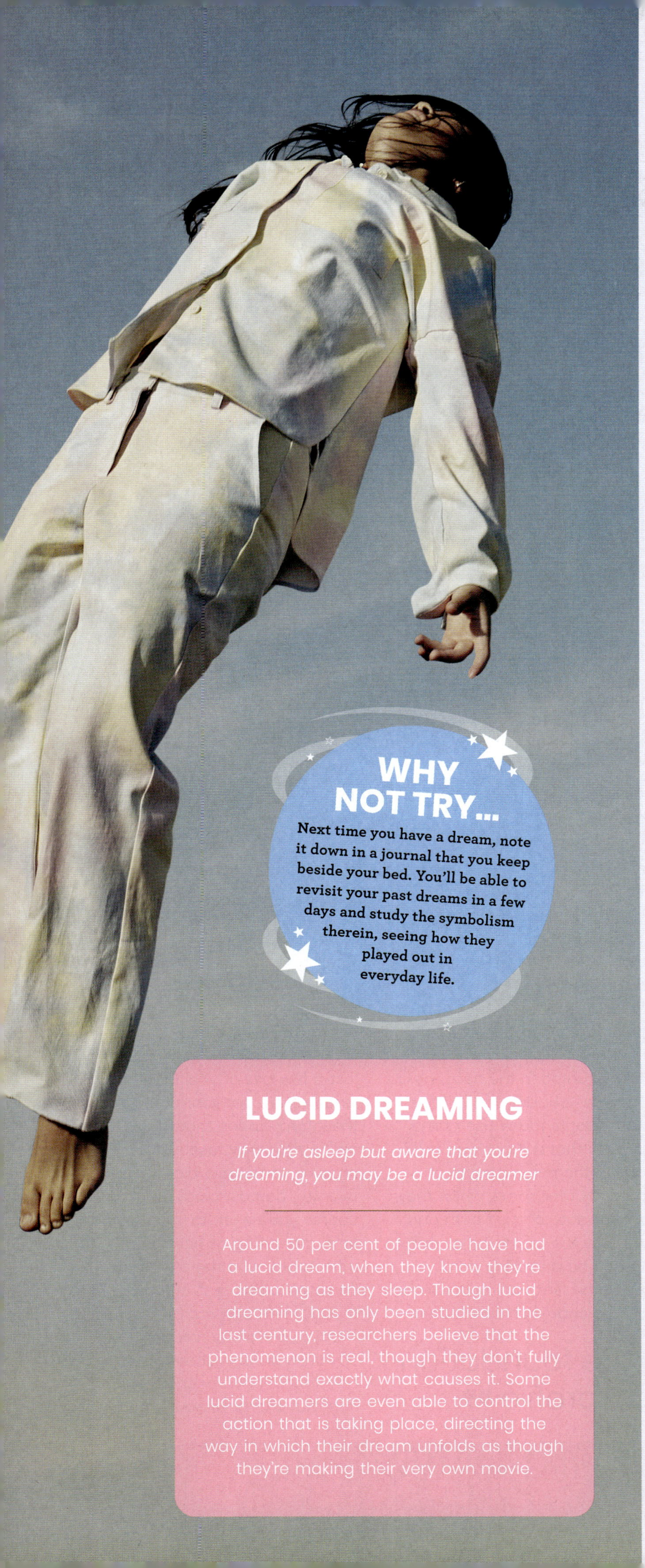

DREAMING of *Flying*

If you dream of flying, you could be harnessing your inner power

Dreams of flying are very common and symbolise freedom and empowerment; perhaps you feel held back in your waking life and want to escape. This dream tells you that you have the strength within you to do so.

However, dreams of flying can have other meanings too. Just as you look down from on high in your dream, it may be that you need to take a step back from a situation to get a different perspective on it. If you're in need for some self-reflection, dreaming of flying suggests that you are searching for the higher meaning in your life and have some soul-searching to do.

A dream of flying can feel liberating and thrilling, but if that dream suddenly turns into one of falling, it can be a frightening experience and may even wake you. However, this is simply your subconscious urging you to look at your life and identify an element in which you feel as though you have lost control. By acting on the symbolism of your dream, you can turn the fear of falling into the opportunity to identify and deal with a vulnerable element of your life, empowering yourself to move forward.

Dreams of flying have been present across cultures for centuries, sometimes simply through the air like a bird, sometimes in a vehicle. If you experience this dream, your subconscious is urging you to examine your situation and look for those mundane or troublesome elements that you may wish to rise above, like a bird soaring through the clouds.

WHY NOT TRY...

Next time you have a dream, note it down in a journal that you keep beside your bed. You'll be able to revisit your past dreams in a few days and study the symbolism therein, seeing how they played out in everyday life.

LUCID DREAMING

If you're asleep but aware that you're dreaming, you may be a lucid dreamer

Around 50 per cent of people have had a lucid dream, when they know they're dreaming as they sleep. Though lucid dreaming has only been studied in the last century, researchers believe that the phenomenon is real, though they don't fully understand exactly what causes it. Some lucid dreamers are even able to control the action that is taking place, directing the way in which their dream unfolds as though they're making their very own movie.

REACH for the Stars

CHANCES ARE, AT SOME POINT YOU'VE READ YOUR DAILY HOROSCOPE. BUT THERE'S FAR MORE TO YOUR PERSONAL ASTROLOGY THAN 12 FAMOUS SIGNS

WORDS:CATHERINE CURZON

If your experience of astrology and your horoscope has been a bitesize look at your daily or annual destiny, the first time you come across a natal or birth chart it may seem like an impenetrable tangle of symbols, circles and criss-crossing lines. The good news is, all of those symbols, circles and criss-crossing lines have a purpose and, taken together, will tell the story of the person you are and your path through life.

Learning to understand your birth chart is both an exciting and revealing adventure to embark on. It will provide you with a great deal of reward and insight into the person you are and the experiences you will have, both positive and challenging.

Your natal chart is the foundation of your astrological profile. It is calculated using the exact time, date and location of your birth, and it is basically a snapshot of where the planets – including the Sun and the Moon – were situated in the heavens as you made your debut on Earth.

Most people today use online resources that will draw up their chart for them in a couple of minutes but for some, whilst they know the date of their birth and most likely the location, the exact time can be a sticking point. Happily, this isn't vital and a fairly accurate chart can be created without the need for a precise time of birth.

> "Your natal chart is the foundation of your astrological profile"

Interpreting your natal chart seems confusing at first glance, and drawing up your own chart is not for the beginner! Luckily, there are plenty of trustworthy and accurate online resources that will draw up your chart for you with just a few bits of vital information. Once you've got your chart and the interpretation that reputable online astrology resources usually provide, you'll have plenty to pore over (try cafeastrology.com). Of course you'll want to spent some time marvelling at how well it reflects you and there will definitely be some areas that merit further thought and consideration.

Online astrology resources are obviously a very recent thing, yet astrologers have been drawing up natal charts without electronic

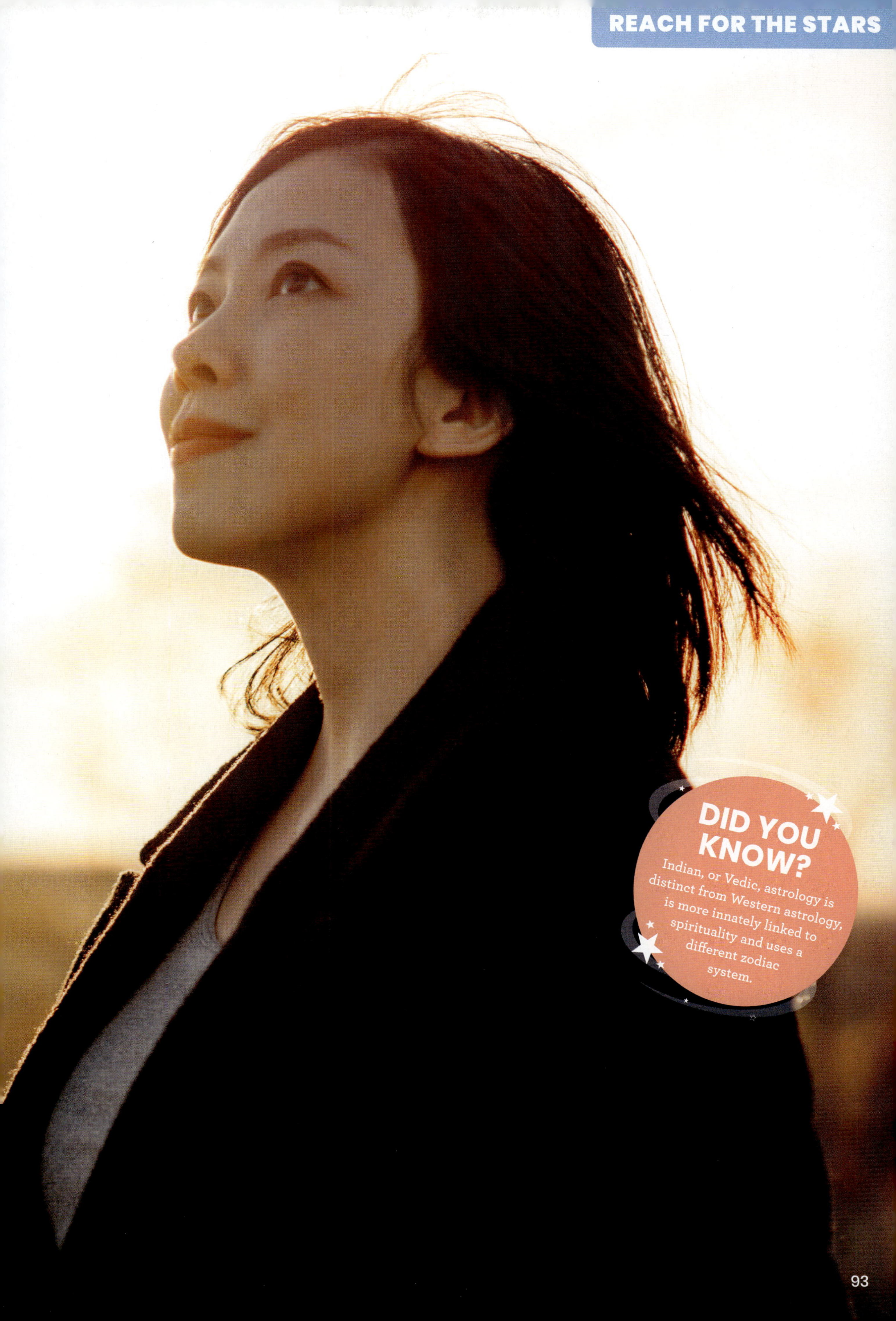

DID YOU KNOW?

Indian, or Vedic, astrology is distinct from Western astrology, is more innately linked to spirituality and uses a different zodiac system.

Natal Chart

TAKE A LOOK AT THIS EXAMPLE CHART. YOURS WILL BE UNIQUE TO YOU AND THE DATE AND TIME OF YOUR BIRTH

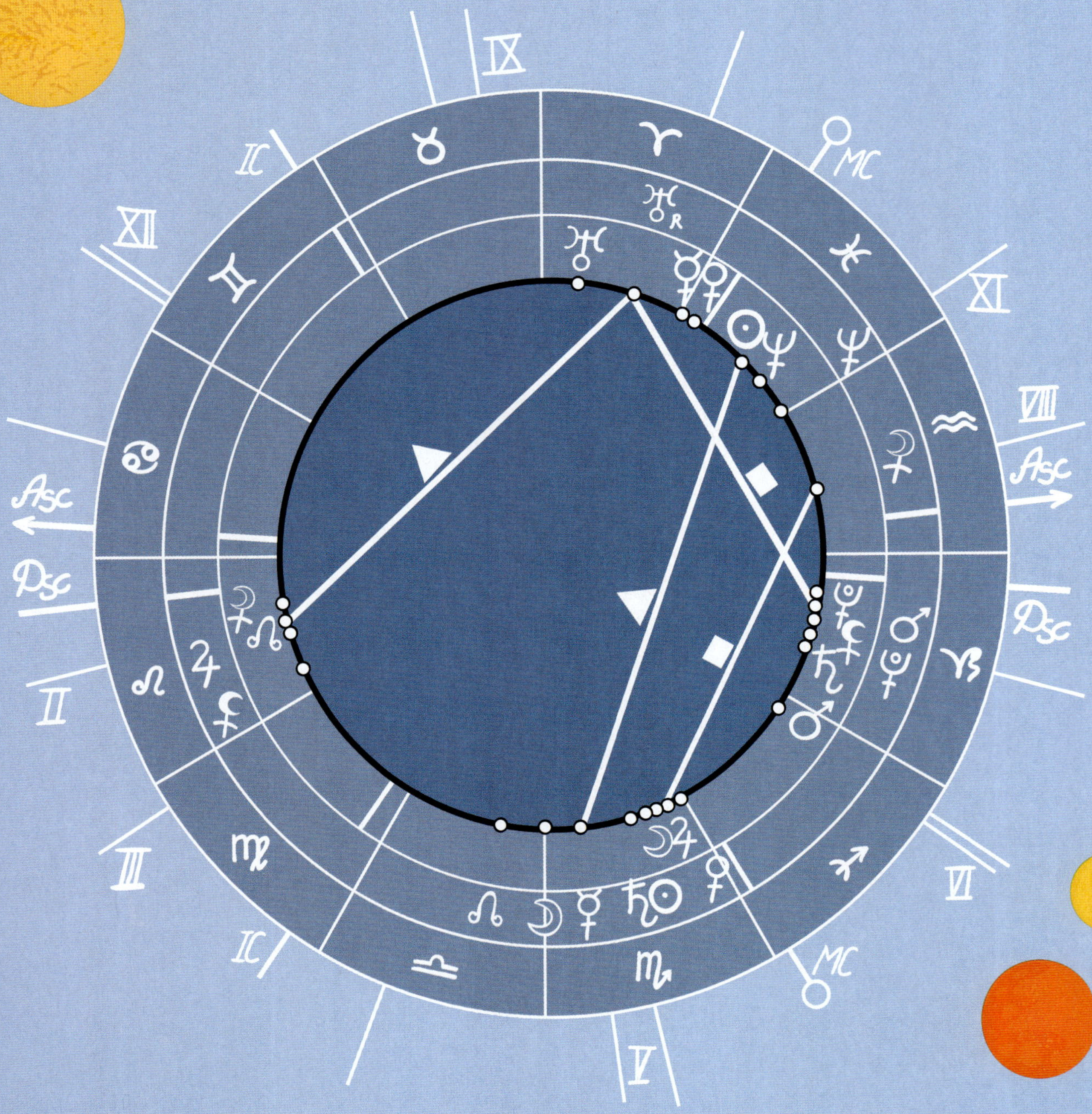

1 YOUR SUN SIGN By identifying the Sun symbol and which sign it sits in on your chart, you can find your Sun sign. This is your daily horoscope sign.

2 THE HOUSES The wheel is divided into 12 houses. Your first house is at your rising sign, then they go round the circle anti-clockwise.

3 THE PLANETS Where the planets are in the heavens both individually and in relation to each other is key in astrology.

4 RISING SIGN Located at nine o'clock, this is the sign of the zodiac that is glimmering on the eastern horizon at the exact time of your birth.

5 THE ASPECTS The lines and shapes in the centre of your chart are aspects, which show the relationships between the planets in your chart.

6 THE ANGLES The angles divide the wheel vertically and horizontally. They represent the horizon, ascendant and descendant, and midheaven.

Your natal chart is your own personal snapshot of the heavens at the moment of your birth, and it's filled with insight.

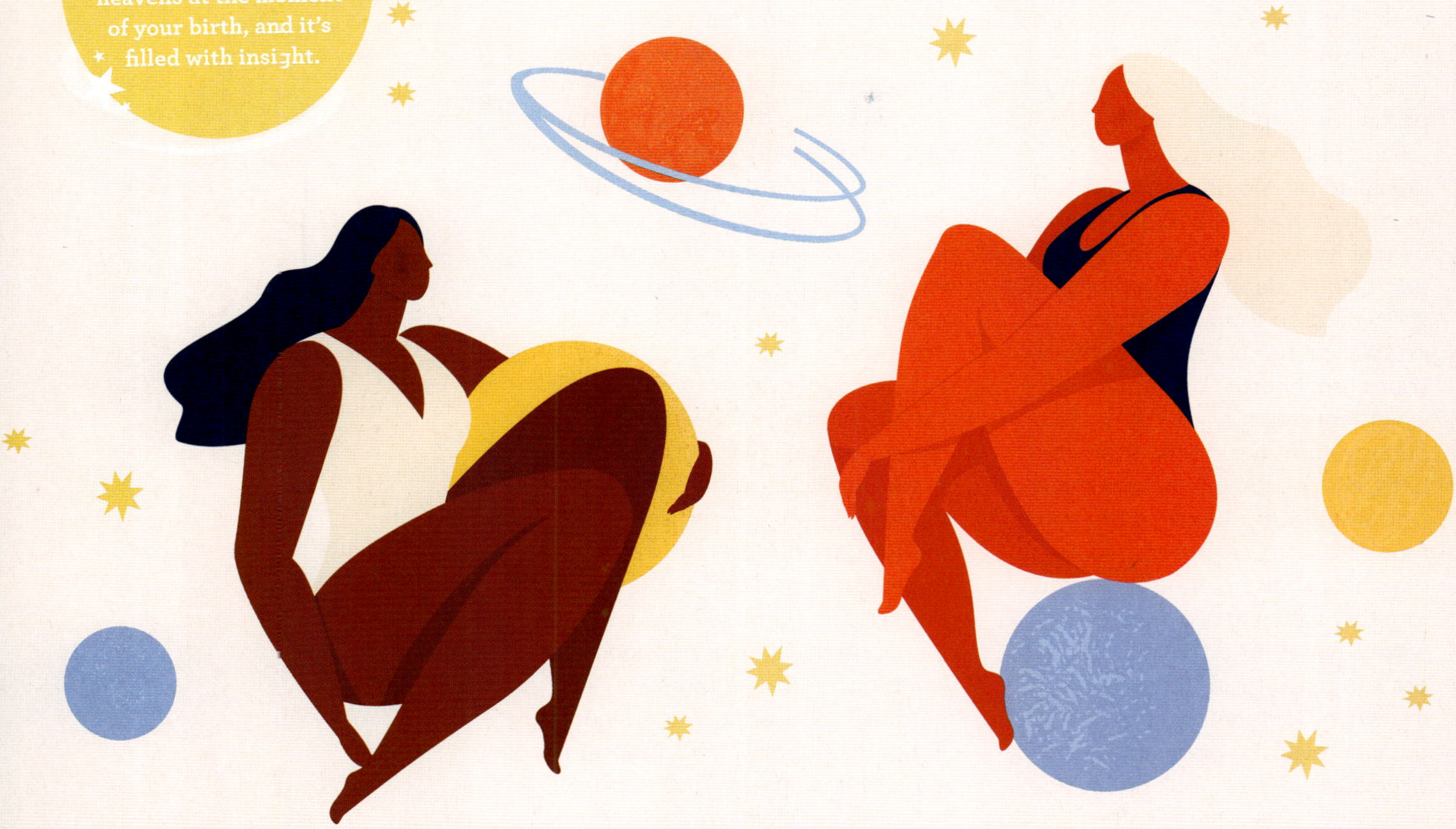

assistance for literally millennia. Whilst it's certainly possible to draw up your own chart using a template or even from scratch, this definitely isn't something for the novice. Instead, let an online resource do this for you and use the outcome to learn how to read and interpret a chart and the insights it contains. Then as your confidence grows, you'll be able to widen your skills and abilities.

Whether you use an online astrological site to create your chart or have an astrologer draw one up for you, you'll likely receive guidance on how to interpret the information it contains and how to take it further. It's a fascinating journey into the self and one that will introduce you to a number of new concepts that will hopefully offer fresh insight into your life and experiences.

As you interpret your chart you'll encounter the all-important 'Big Three', which will introduce you to your Sun sign – you might know it as your star sign – your Moon sign and your rising signs. This trio of signs reflects the essence of the person you are, both in terms of your personality, your fundamental character and the most intimate, deepest part of your inner self. You'll identify where these are on your chart by means of the symbols that represent the planets and where they sit on the chart.

Moving through the chart you will be able to track each of the 12 houses, starting with the first that sits at the nine o'clock position, with your rising sign. Every house has its own associated sign of the zodiac, so everybody has all 12 signs in their wheel. Once you understand what each house rules and how it relates to the horoscope sign which occupies it, and the planets which may or may not sit in it, you'll be able to deepen your understanding of some very specific parts of your destiny and path. By the way, not everyone has

"Learning to understand your birth chart is an exciting and revealing adventure and one that will provide you with a great deal of insight"

a planet in every house, so if you see empty houses on your chart there's no need to panic. An empty house simply means that the area that house represents doesn't have a particular emphasis in your life.

Each of the planets can be identified on the horoscope wheel that encompasses your natal chart by a simple symbol. As you study your chart, you'll identify each planet and see where on the wheel it sits and in which of the 12 houses. Because your natal chart is a snapshot of which constellations the planets were occupying at the moment of your birth, it is unique to you and those who were born at exactly the same time and date. For some people the chart shows planets clustered together with some constellations empty, whilst for others the planets are scattered far and wide across the wheel. Neither is right nor wrong, but wherever the planets are, they will influence your personality, experiences and interrelations. Just as we don't exist in isolation, whilst the positions of the individual planets is important, where they sit in relation to one another and their relationships, whether in support or opposition, are vital components in your chart.

The relationships between the planets is shown on your chart by the aspects, the lines you'll see in its centre. Each aspects has its own name and meaning and as you learn to identify and interpret them, you'll soon be able to apply them to yourself or those you might be working on charts for. You'll be able to identify areas of tension and harmony and though you might not always be able to do much about them, understanding that everything happens for a reason might well offer new ways of seeing areas of conflict or challenges in your life. Though we can't change everything, we can change how we react to adversity and turn obstacles into acceptance and personal growth.

Moving through the wheel you'll notice two lines that cut through it on the vertical and horizontal. These angles determine your ascendant and descendant and the imum coeli and midheaven. Each of these has its own specific purpose in your life and offers one more layer of nuance for you to consider. The more you learn, the more you'll want to keep learning and understanding and as you factor in the four elements you'll soon see the subtle relationships between not only the planets, but the different aspects of your chart. Likewise, as you cover aspects of astrology including cusps, progressions, eclipses and transits, you'll shine a light on areas of understanding that will offer rich and deep rewards both in terms of understanding your own chart and your wider relationships, reactions and experiences too.

Astrology really is a discipline that rewards carefully study and reflection,

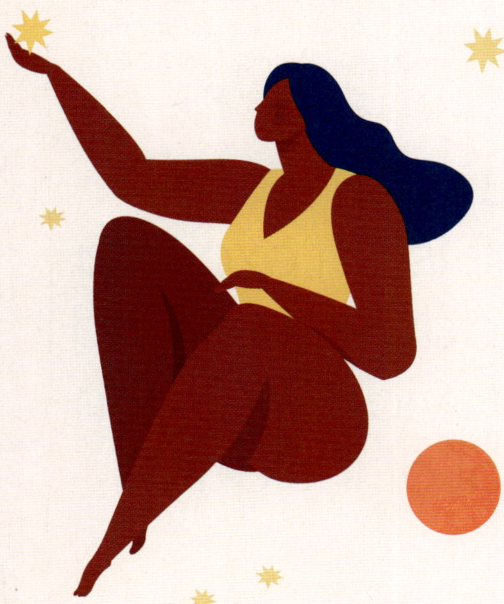

"It's a fascinating and insightful journey that will introduce you to concepts that will lend a new illumination to your life and experiences"

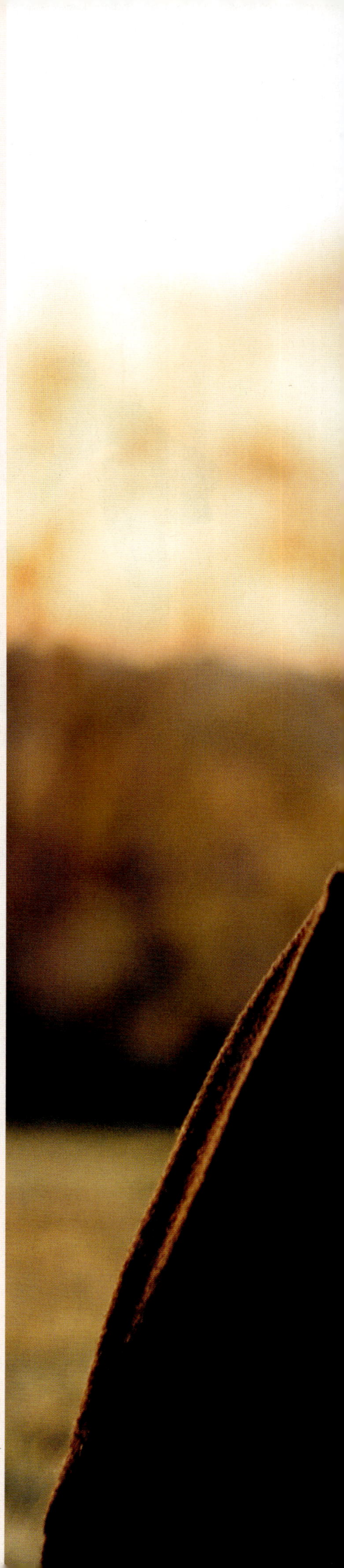

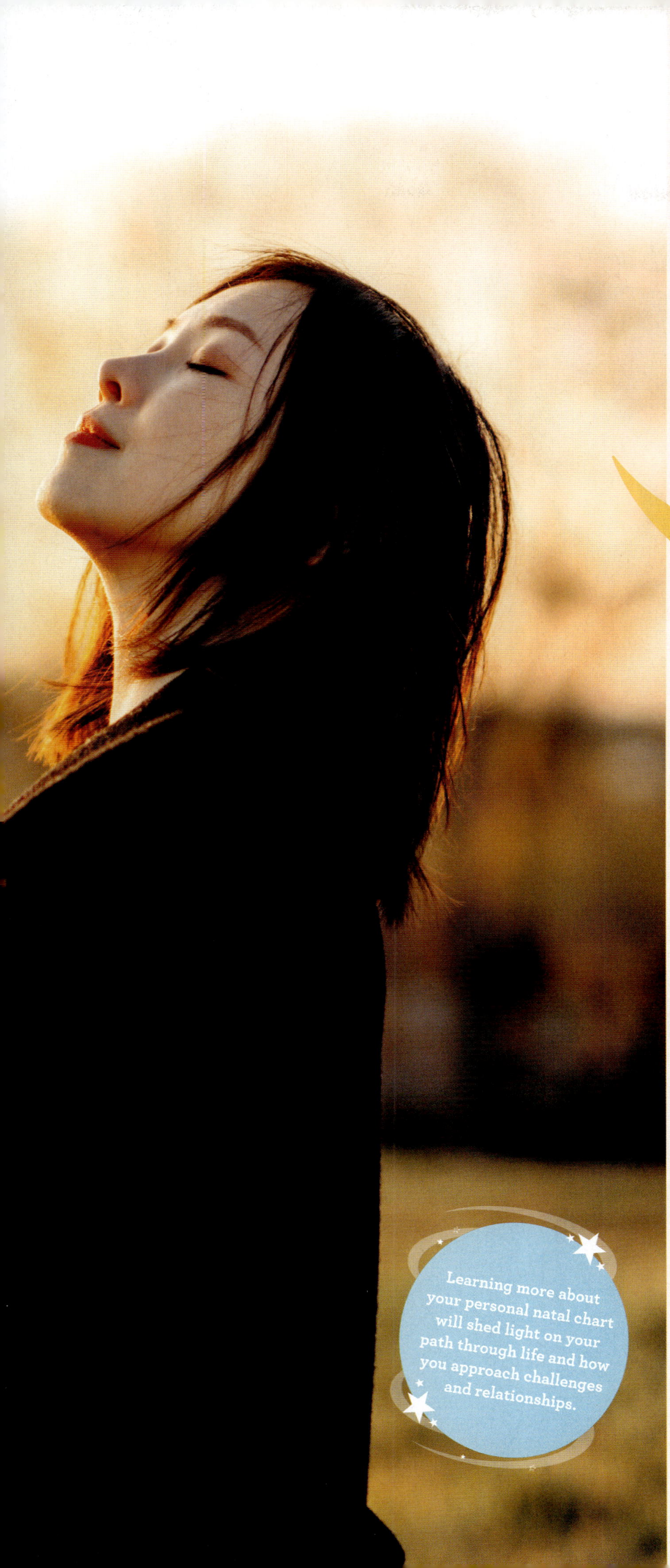

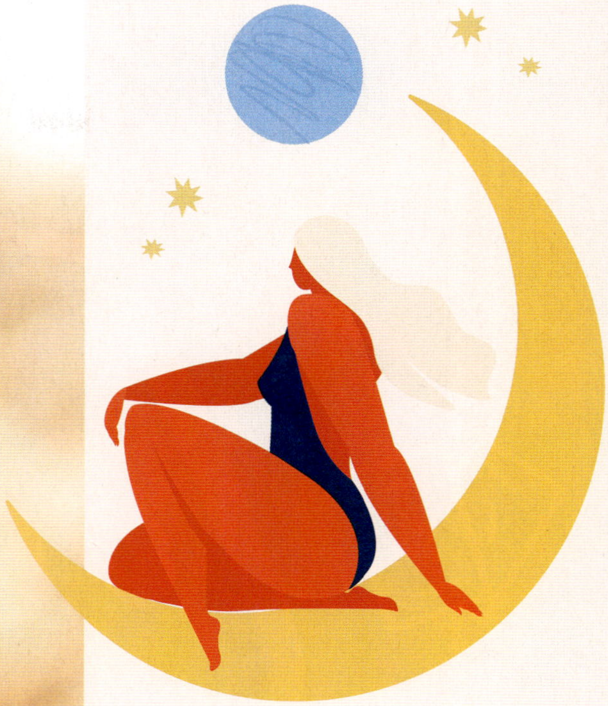

Learning more about your personal natal chart will shed light on your path through life and how you approach challenges and relationships.

and reading your birth chart is a perfect and personal way to start. Analysing your natal chart can be as basic or as in depth as you want to make it, and taking it step-by-step, if you're new to the art of astrology, is a great way to progress at a manageable pace. Move too fast and you might get lost or completely overwhelmed, but taking it slowly and steadily is a great way not only to be sure you understand everything, but also to fully consider and reflect on the insights your personal chart contains. The stars can reveal a lot given the chance!

Your natal chart is your personal key to understanding what the stars mean for you and your life, far beyond a few hundred words in a magazine or website that reveals your daily horoscope. As you better understand how the heavens looked at the moment of your birth and how the planets relate to one another and yourself, you'll open up a whole new understanding of your own personality, from the face you show to the world to your most deep and intimate places. The celestial landscape will illuminate your path through life, the relationships you make along the way and the challenges and achievements that have shaped you.

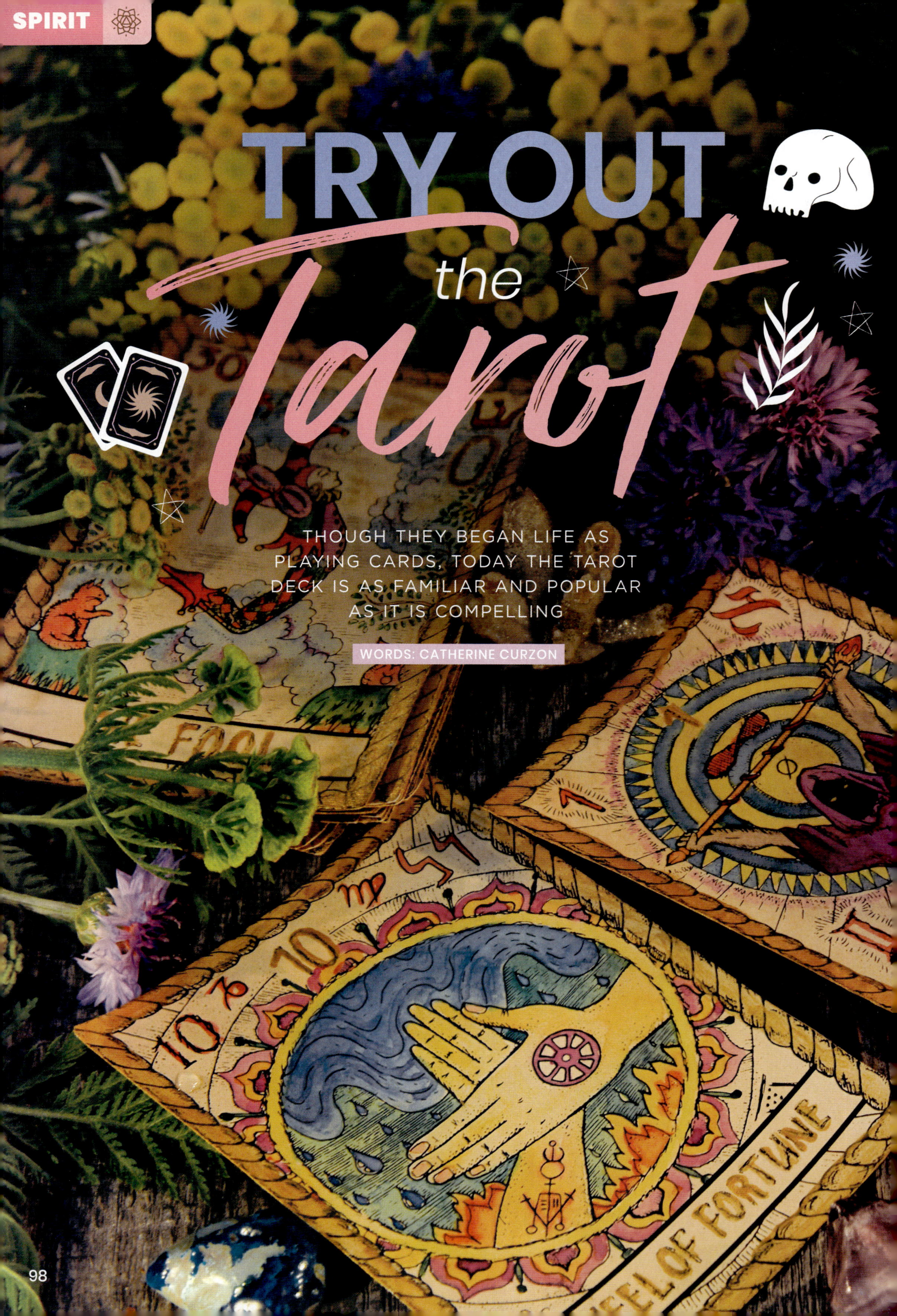

TRY OUT *the* Tarot

THOUGH THEY BEGAN LIFE AS PLAYING CARDS, TODAY THE TAROT DECK IS AS FAMILIAR AND POPULAR AS IT IS COMPELLING

WORDS: CATHERINE CURZON

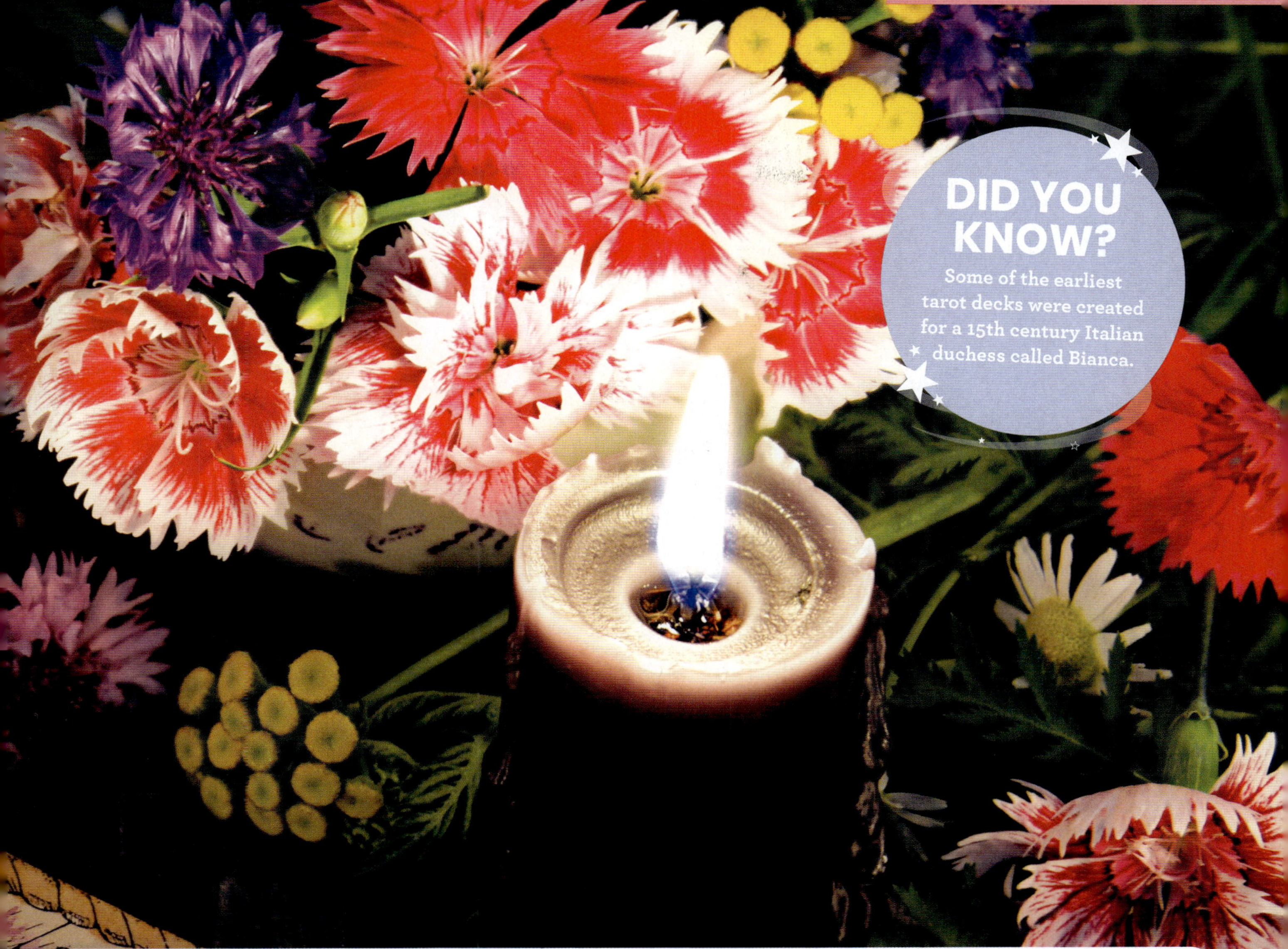

DID YOU KNOW?

Some of the earliest tarot decks were created for a 15th century Italian duchess called Bianca.

The tarot deck is one of the most instantly recognisable and popular divination tools around. It's also one of the easiest to pick up, even as a novice, and taking the time to learn to interpret the tarot cards will offer rich rewards.

The exact origin of tarot is cloudy, but it began as a card game rather than a divination method. Despite tall stories of ancient Egyptian magic, the craze of using tarot for fortune-telling developed in 18th century France and flourished from there, until the major and minor arcana were firmly established in the public consciousness as mysterious tools for revealing the future. Whether you choose the ever-popular Rider-Waite deck or plump for another of the innumerable decks on the market, the 78 cards of the tarot are filled with symbolism, meaning and insight.

Although learning the meanings of nearly 80 cards might seem like a daunting task, it doesn't have to be. Rather than try to learn what they mean by rote, the best way to get to grips with the tarot is to use it. The illustrations on the cards themselves will help you to understand their most basic meanings as you begin to practice, and as you get to know the cards better you'll begin to develop a deeper understanding of their individual meanings. You'll use your intuition to think about and interpret the relationship between multiple cards in a reading, regardless of the layout (or spread) you use to ask a question or seek guidance.

When it comes to tarot, the sky really is the limit. Many tarot readers like to draw out a card each morning and decipher what this means is in store for the day ahead. Some will pull a card from their tarot deck in the evening instead, and use it to reflect on the day they've just had in relation to its meaning. You can ask the cards for insight into your career, love life or simply your day-to-day existence. Tarot cards won't tell you that a future is set in stone, so don't worry about those Hollywood films where the Death card is a portent of disaster: they're much more nuanced than that. The more you work with them, the more you'll appreciate not only the insight they can offer, but also your own intuition and the self-reflection that will guide you through life.

The MAJOR Arcana

THE TAROT'S TRUMP CARDS ARE SYMBOLIC ARCHETYPES AND DIVINATORY DEVICES THAT CONTAIN MYSTICAL MEANINGS AND EXPRESS A PHILOSOPHICAL JOURNEY WHEN LAID OUT SEQUENTIALLY

WORDS: ALICE PATTILLO

The Major Arcana are the named and numbered trump cards in a pack of traditional tarot cards. These cards always overpower the other cards in both impact and outcome and indicate important events. In the Rider-Waite deck there are 22 cards in the Major Arcana, all numbered in Roman numerals except that of the Fool, who is given the number zero. In other decks, the Fool is often un-numbered completely or placed after the trump cards. When reading tarot, the Major Arcana trump all other cards pulled, and should be interpreted as the most significant. Their importance also increases as you follow the sequence from I to XXI.

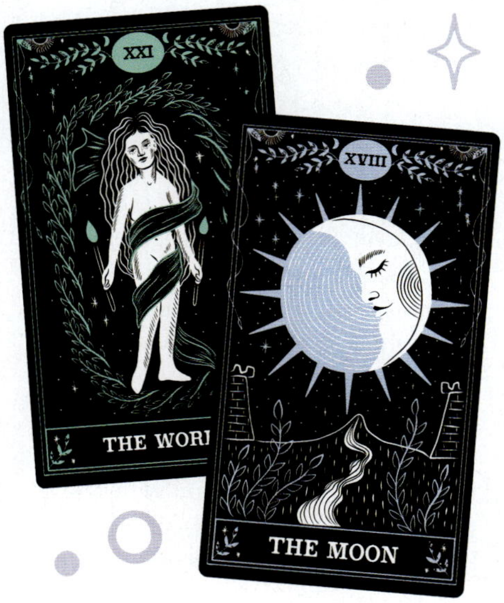

THE ORDER OF THE MAJOR ARCANA

In the Rider-Waite tarot, the trump cards are: The Fool (0), The Magician (I), The High Priestess (II), The Empress (III), The Emperor (IV), The Hierophant (V), The Lovers (VI) , The Chariot (VII), Strength (VIII), The Hermit (IX), The Wheel Of Fortune (X), Justice (XI), The Hanged Man (XII), Death (XIII), Temperance (XIV), The Devil (XV), The Tower (XVI), The Star (XVII), The Moon (XVII), The Sun (XIX), Judgement (XX) and The World (XXI).

In older decks such as the Tarot de Marseilles, Court de Géblin and Etteilla's Tarot, the Strength and Justice cards are the other way around. These were altered by the Hermetic Order of the Golden Dawn (of which Rider-Waite creators A.E. Waite and Pamela Colman Smith were members) in accordance with the order of their astrological correspondences. These are as follows: Air (The Fool), Mercury, the Moon, Venus, Aries, Taurus, Gemini, Cancer, Leo, Virgo, Jupiter, Libra, Water, Scorpio, Sagittarius, Capricorn, Mars, Aquarius, Pisces, the Sun, Fire, and Saturn.

THE FOOL'S JOURNEY

The Major Arcana can be read as an allegory, dubbed 'The Fool's Journey', believed to represent the stages of life and an initiatory sequence of events that establishes a human's path of spiritual ascension, or self-discovery, and the challenges we face along this path. Each trump card represents an archetype, challenge, obstacle, lesson or reward along life's path, and they can all be compiled into three groups of seven cards, each representing a different stage of life that forces a person to grow. The

> "With each repetition of the journey, The Fool reaches a new, higher level of understanding and consciousness"

Fool, who does not have a Roman numeral assigned to it, represents the everyday human, who journeys through each of the trump cards in order. However, the fool never ends the journey, repeating it over and over and growing each time, interacting with each card on a higher spiritual level and with more self-awareness each time.

STAGE ONE

The first act begins with the Fool card, representing the basic human archetype, a simple, innocent soul who is open and ready to begin their first part of their spiritual ascent, through personal lessons and growth. Cards I to VII represent various aspects of day-to-day life and the social realm, asking questions about identity and relationships with others and the wants and needs of humanity. The Magician and High Priestess represent both conscious and unconscious awareness, willpower, unrealised potential and intuition. The Emperor and the Empress are the mother and father archetypes, and our introduction to nature and sensuality, and structure and authority. The Hierophant is the world of conforming, organised belief systems and education. The Lovers are sexual awakening, relationships and values, and finally, the Chariot is maturation, the sense of a strong identity and the confidence, occasional arrogance, of youth.

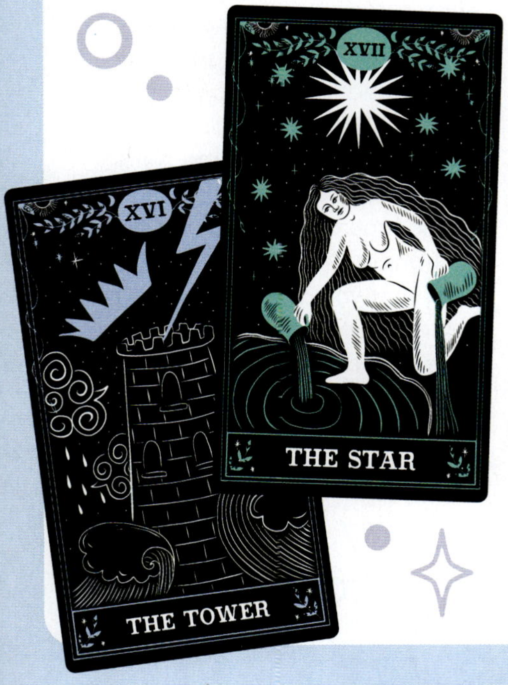

STAGE TWO

The second act of ascension is where the Fool begins to look further afield and learn about time, morality and virtue – or the will of humanity. Strength offers the quiet courage to continue despite setbacks, patience and tolerance. The Hermit forces the Fool to look inwards, to ask why and search for a deeper truth and to seek solitude, following their own path. The Wheel Of Fortune is a symbol of the mysterious yet harmonious universe, pushing the Fool to recognise their part in this world, embrace change and to act towards their destiny and purpose. Justice is the act of taking responsibility for your actions, and a time of big decisions, while the Hanged Man forces The Fool to let go, to be open and vulnerable and surrender to their experiences, embracing obstacles to fulfil their goal. Death is the changes the Fool makes to themselves, ending things that no longer serve them in order to transition into a more fulfilling way of life – often interpreted as the death of the ego – and Temperance is the balance that the Fool has found since embracing themselves: stable, centred and harmonious.

STAGE THREE

The third act begins with the bad (the Devil) and ends with the good (the World). It is the final ascent towards a higher spiritual power, reason, absolute understanding and godliness. After finding a level of fulfilment in life, the Devil represents the material seductions that may lead us off our path, or things that the Fool may still be holding on to that are preventing him from achieving true enlightenment. The Tower frees the Fool from the grasp of the Devil with sudden painful change, release and revelation. Following this monumental shift, the Star offers hope and inspiration once again. The peace after the storm. The Moon is a time to rest and prepare, another time of reflection and once again shedding anything holding the Fool back, perhaps aspects of the Jungian "shadow self" or fears and anxieties that once again need to be addressed. The Sun symbolises the victory over those shadows, the Fool's inner light, pure radiance and joy. Judgement is the Fool's readiness to ascend into a higher level of consciousness, having finally understood their purpose, free of ego. Finally, the World is the end of the cycle, yet also a new beginning. the Fool is accomplished, fulfilled and ready to re-enter the world with a new level of understanding. With each repetition of the journey, The Fool reaches a new, higher level of understanding and consciousness.

The MINOR Arcana

THE CARDS OF THE MINOR ARCANA FORM THE BULK OF THE TAROT DECK, AND ARE CENTRAL TO GUIDING QUERENTS THROUGH THEIR JOURNEY TO UNDERSTANDING

WORDS: CATHERINE CURZON

The 56 cards of the Minor Arcana are the foundation of any tarot deck and form the vast bulk of its contents. Whilst an understanding of the cards of the Major Arcana is vital, the nuances of the Minor Arcana cannot be overlooked if one is to work with the cards to their full potential.

Just like a deck of playing cards, a tarot deck has four suits. However, whilst playing cards are instantly recognisable as the hearts, diamonds, clubs and spades, the suits of tarot can vary depending on the deck and the geographical territory from which it originated. Today, most readers recognise the suits that were used in the immensely popular Rider-Waite deck, those of Pentacles, Wands, Swords and Cups. Other popular decks do make substitutions though, so in the influential Tarot of Marseilles readers will find not Pentacles but Coins, and Clubs in the place of Wands. Likewise, when Aleister Crowley designed his esoteric Book of Thoth, he replaced Pentacles with Disks. Despite the nomenclature though, the elemental significance and meanings of the suits are, as a rule, retained.

The Minor Arcana are, essentially, the minutiae of life. They reflect our daily journey, whether it is remarkable or more mundane, and they are able to uniquely reflect even the most seemingly insignificant day-to-day situations that may be having an impact on us. Perhaps most significantly, the cards of the Minor Arcana can signify a more transitory situation than those reflected by the Major Arcana. Whilst they do not necessarily speak of matters that may seem enormously significant though, every stitch in the tapestry of life has an impact on the overall pattern. By listening to and interpreting the messages communicated by the Minor Arcana during a reading, a querant might be able to make even a small change to a minor situation and change the wider picture to a degree that might seem surprising.

Despite its name, there is nothing minor about the Minor Arcana when it comes to its place in the tarot deck. Without a thorough understanding of these cards and what the suits themselves stand for, a wealth of significance and nuance will be lost from any tarot reading. Read in concert with the Major Arcana, they are important building blocks in the process of understanding the tarot.

> “The cards of the Minor Arcana can signify a more transitory situation than the Major Arcana”

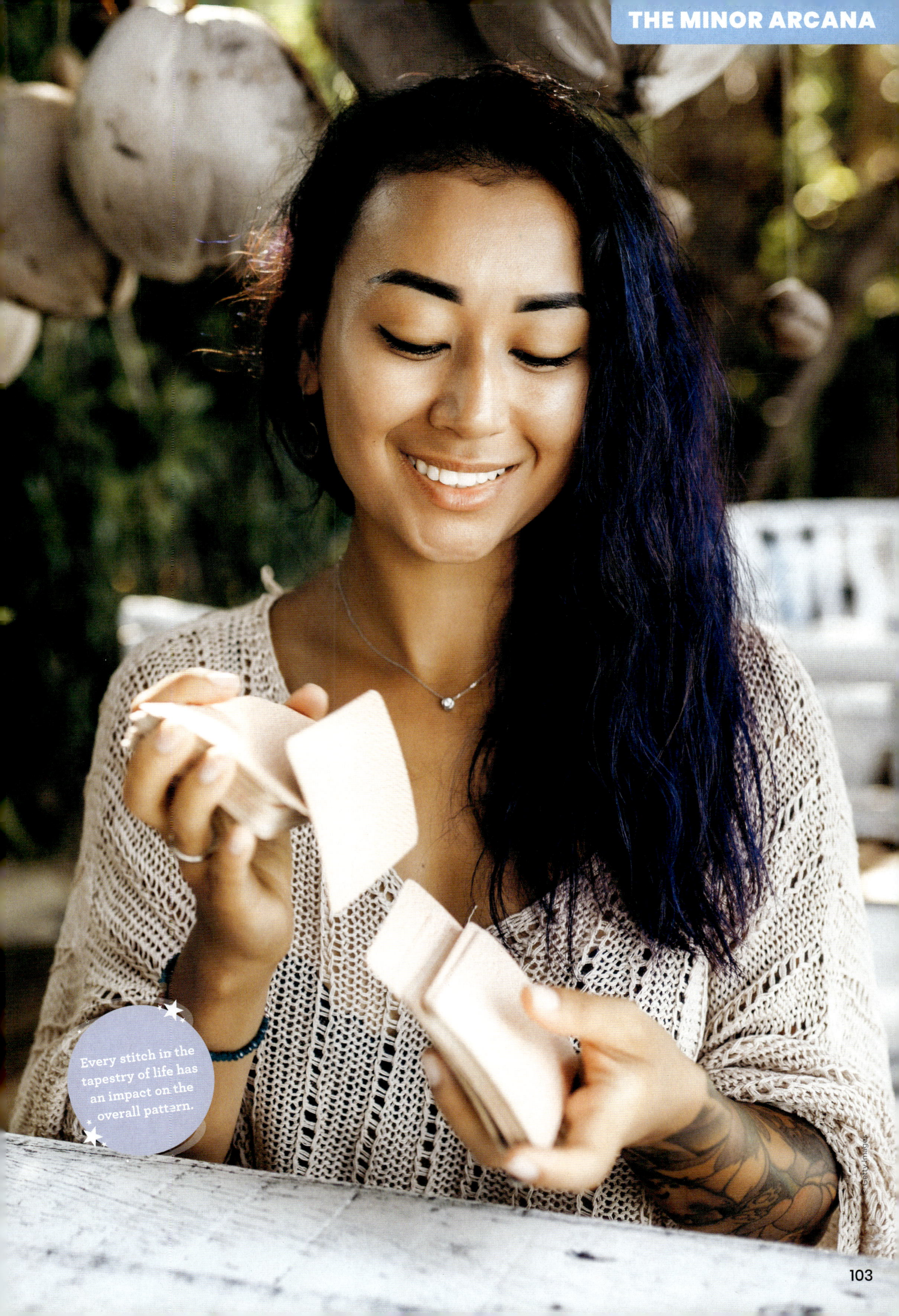
Every stitch in the tapestry of life has an impact on the overall pattern.

Pulling a Three CARD SPREAD

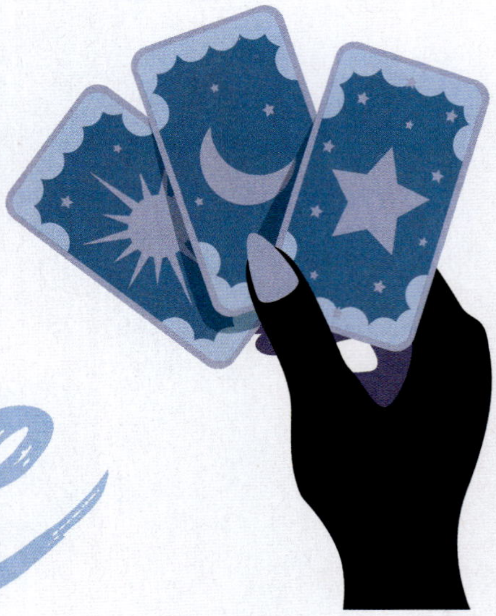

THE CARDS OF THE MINOR ARCANA FORM THE BULK OF THE TAROT DECK, AND ARE CENTRAL TO GUIDING QUERENTS THROUGH THEIR JOURNEY TO UNDERSTANDING

WORDS: ALICE PATTILLO

A three-card spread is a popular layout for beginners, or those seeking more in-depth advice in a hurry. This spread offers insight into the progression of a given situation, and is more often than not used in a past/present/future layout format. However, you can pretty much nominate each card in the layout with whatever label you so choose. For example, a situation/action/outcome spread.

There are two ways to create a three-card spread. The first way is to separate your pack into three equal piles and turn the top card of each pile upwards. The second way is to shuffle your cards and select three cards from the main pile, lay them out next to each other and turn each one to face upwards, one after the other. It doesn't matter which technique you use, just do what feels right for you. Of course, as with all tarot spreads, it is important to focus on your question or situation as you shuffle the cards!

INTERPRETING YOUR CARDS

The most common reading of a three-card spread is past/present/future or basis of the matter-near future-outcome. In this reading, the first card represents what has already come to pass, or the events and circumstances that have led up to where you are now. The second card represents the present situation you are in and how you feel about it, or perhaps a new direction or condition that will soon come into fruition. The third card is the outcome or future, representing the end result or resolve of the situation. This spread is very useful for financial matters, issues concerning your career path or other difficult decisions and situations that may be occurring in your life.

For example, you lay out a spread of past/present/future for a question regarding financial matters and turn the cards Ace of Pentacles/the Devil/the Sun. Card one is an Ace, representing fresh

> "The most common reading of a three-card spread is to look at the past (card 1), the present (card 2) and the future (card 3)"

CARD 1

The first card could represent the past, a specific situation, your own needs, where you are or the mind, depending on your question

CARD 3

The third card could represent the future, the outcome of a given situation or relationship, where your potential lies or the spirit, depending on your question

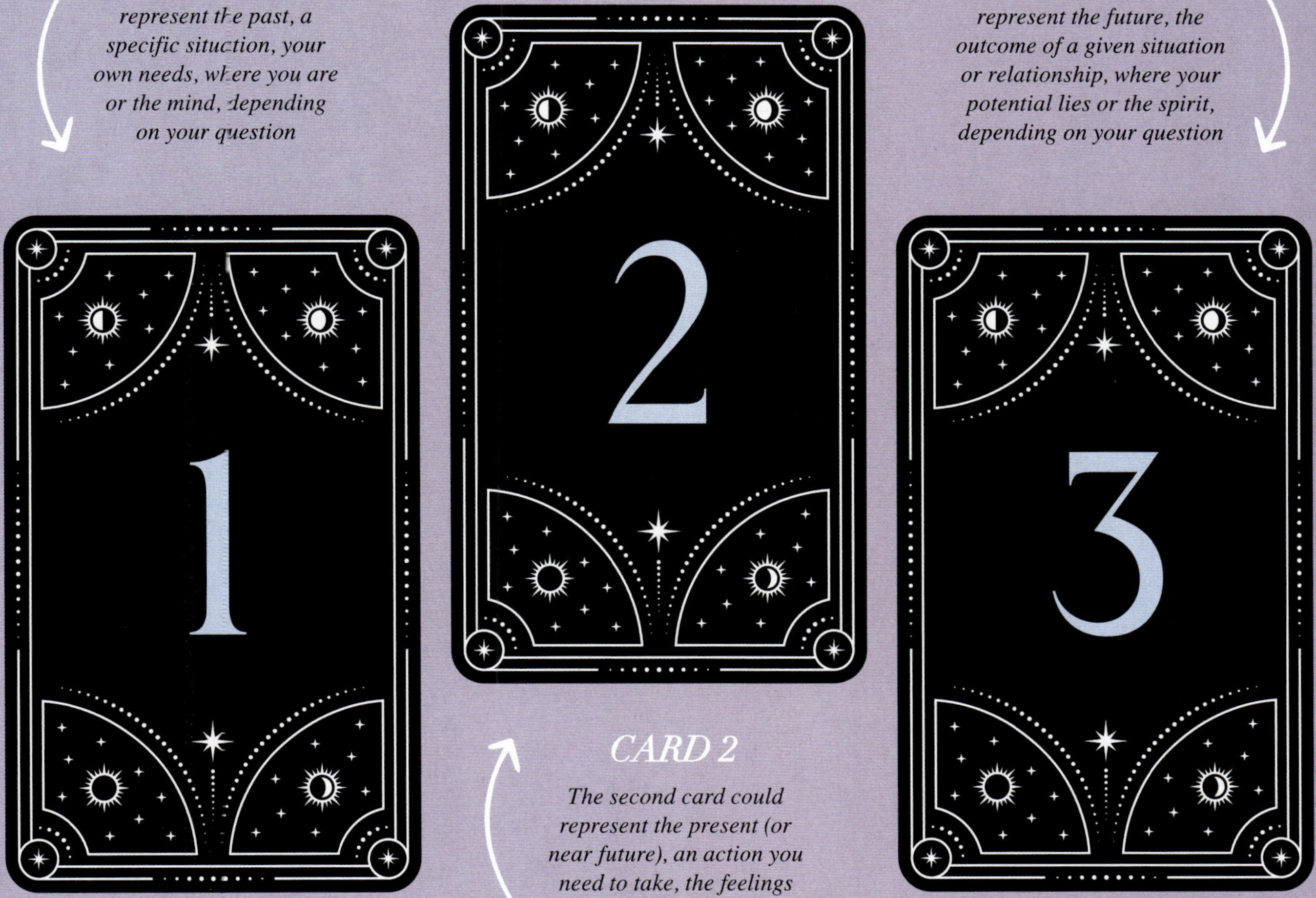

CARD 2

The second card could represent the present (or near future), an action you need to take, the feelings of another, where you are headed or the body (physical self), depending on your question

starts. The basis of the matter is new investments or money that you have invested that was held up but recently received. Card two is the Devil, a Major Arcana card that always signifies an important event. You are stuck in a negative cycle of events and are struggling to see clearly and perceive the whole picture. You may have been seduced by the material world and made a mistake with your finances; unexpected losses and major financial difficulties have plagued you, but you will soon receive another opportunity to make more money, just use discretion from here on out. Card three is the future outcome, in this case, it is the Sun. The Sun's focus is on people and society, achievement and accomplishment, indicating that your financial situation will be sorted. New money will come in and the anguish that has plagued you will finally be rewarded.

ROMANCE AND SELF LOVE

For matters of the heart, you may wish to use a different three-card spread, for example a you/them/relationship outcome spread or spread that looks at relationship positives/relationship negatives/where the relationship is headed. The three-card spread can also be used for self discovery and personal growth. You may want to delve into the cards to help bring up unconscious thoughts and feelings, and learn where you may need to head or aspects of yourself that need working on. For example, where you stand in terms of your mind/body/spirit, where you are/where you are headed now/where your potential lies.

CARD 1

The first card gives insight into the current state of affairs, including aspects of it that you may not be aware of

CARD 2

The factors which are influencing the area you wish to examine are revealed by this card, including your motivations and desires

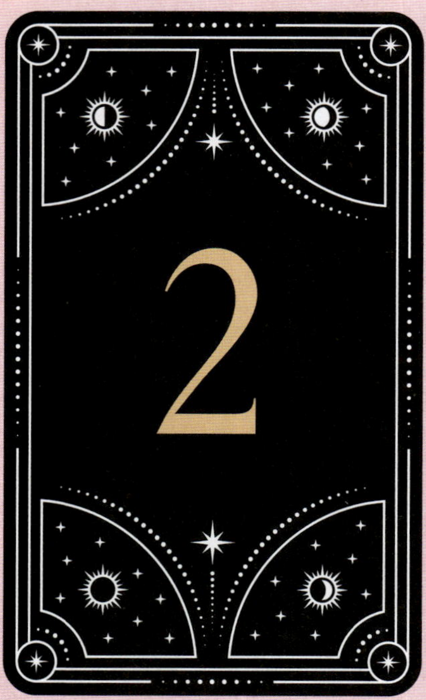

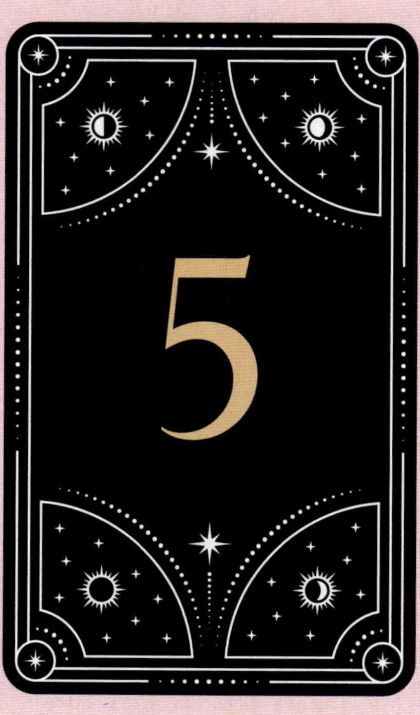

CARD 3

The third card displays the challenges that you are facing in this part of your life and ones which may occur in the future

CARD 4

This card predicts how things will turn out for you in this area in the long run

CARD 5

The fifth card sits at the heart of the spread and reveals the theme of the entire reading, with its meaning influenced by the surrounding cards

The FIVE CARD Rectangle

WHEN YOU HAVE A QUESTION RELATED TO AN AREA OF YOUR LIFE, FROM LOVE TO YOUR CAREER, THE FIVE-CARD RECTANGLE CAN HELP UNTANGLE THE SITUATION

WORDS: BEN GAZUR

Five-card tarot spreads allow for greater insight than simpler, smaller spreads. By increasing the number of cards more can be gleaned for the questioner. The five-card rectangle has many uses. It can be used to answer specific questions about an aspect of your life or analyse the general situation.

The last card to be pulled in the five-card rectangle is sometimes known as the theme card. This fifth card sits at the heart of the spread and its meaning will also be at the heart of the questions you wish to have answered. When used to help understand a relationship this card represents the querent themselves. Indeed the fifth card in the rectangle will usually be closely related to the querent as invariably we tend to have the strongest influence on our own lives.

The first card relates to the present situation of the questioner. Are they in a positive or negative place in this moment? Just as the present is influenced by the past so this card will also point to past factors that may still be at work.

The second card looks more generally at things which may be beyond your control and how they are causing your situation to be in flux. These may be the intentions of other people or their actions, or simply the state of the world and your place in it.

When looking at what challenges are in wait for the querent it is the third card which has the most to say. If you have asked a specific question then this is the card that might point to the biggest obstacles that lay before you. Remember, these difficulties can be ones which we cause ourselves.

When attempting to understand what the final outcome will be for the area under scrutiny the fourth card points the way. This card must be understood in relation to the others which have been pulled. If the answer appears to be negative this could be a warning that you must pursue a different tactic to achieve your goals. Acting in the same way as always will rarely lead to change. A positive card in this place can be guiding a person to remain on the course they are already charting – and a reminder not to lose focus.

> "The five-card rectangle has many uses – to answer specific questions or analyse the general situation you find yourself in"

The *Celtic* CROSS

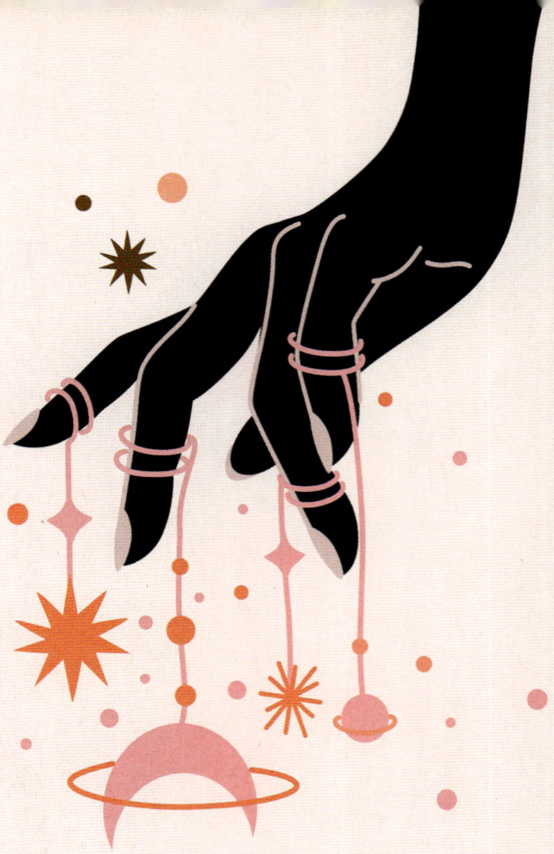

THIS COMPLEX SPREAD MIGHT SEEM INTIMIDATING AT FIRST, BUT ONCE MASTERED IT OFFERS PROFOUND INSIGHT INTO THE SUBCONSCIOUS

WORDS: BEN GAZUR

This tarot spread gets its name from the central cross and pillar of Celtic crosses that are found in Ireland dating back to at least the 9th century. The first recorded mention of the Celtic cross spread comes from 1911 in Arthur Edward Waite's *The Pictorial Key to the Tarot*. He describes it as "an ancient Celtic method of divination" and suggests that it is best used by those with clearly defined questions.

The cards of the Celtic cross can be read one-by-one as they are drawn as well as in relation to each other. The cross is formed from the first six cards that are drawn. These represent the present situation and all the factors that have lead to the current state of affairs. At the heart of the cross is a smaller cross formed by cards one and two. These cards are central to the question being asked – they refer to the questioner and the challenges they will face.

Cards three and five are sometimes called the Above and Below cards, echoing the infamous occult phase "as above, so below." These cards represent the conscious and subconscious mind. Here, the relationship between the two will tell a questioner if they are at war with themselves. They may offer ideas on how to bring your conscious goals into agreement with your unconscious desires.

The pillar is created by the four final cards laid out in a vertical line. These offer further insights and give the querent the background they need to judge the meaning of the other cards.

The Subconscious (card three) may be hard to understand. By looking to Hopes and Fears (card nine) in the pillar, a querent can get a better understanding of what it is telling them. Our hopes and fears often spring from our subconscious, so by looking at both cards in tandem it can be easier to interpret each card individually and see how best to move forward.

The Future card (card five) can best be viewed in relation to card ten – the Outcome. Are they both positive? Then this means that the querent is on the right path, and acting in a way that will lead to the best possible result. When the Future card is negative but the Outcome card is positive the tarot is indicating that if the querent makes some active changes they will be able to reach the best outcome. When this mismatch between the two cards exists then all cards should be looked at carefully to fully examine what aspects might be contributing to the unhappy outcome, and what could be changed.

Card eight is the External Factors card. These are often larger things outside of the querent's control. If they are negative then it can mean that they are simply something that must be accepted and overcome before a situation can be fully resolved.

FUTURE
This card presents the many possibilities which are open to the querent to give guidance about waat options they may choose

PRESENT
This card reveals the current state of affairs in the querent's life as well as their state of mind

PAST
This card represents the paths and actions which have led to the situations a person is facing at this moment

CHALLENGE
This card uncovers the most pressing problems facing the querent which, if resolved, would improve their life

SUBCONSCIOUS
The ideas, desires, and hopes bubbling away underneath a person's mind with be revealed by this card

THE CROSS

THE PILLAR

OUTCOME
The final result of the current situation is revealed here – though it may be changed if the querent changes their actions

HOPES AND FEARS
This card deals with the twin factors of hope and fear within the querent to show how they may influence the outcome

NEAR FUTURE
Those things which will happen soon, and are already taking shape, are found in this card

EXTERNAL FACTORS
The people and energies which will shape the outcome of the question at hand are shown in this card

INTERNAL FACTORS
This card represents the person asking the question and their state of mind. What is your view of your ability to change your life?

LIVING with Crystals

PEOPLE ARE OFTEN UNSURE AS TO HOW THEY MIGHT INCORPORATE CRYSTALS INTO THEIR LIVES, BUT ONCE YOU START YOU'LL WONDER HOW YOU EVER MANAGED TO LIVE WITHOUT THEM!

WORDS: JOANNA ELPHICK

Einstein famously stated that "everything is energy and that's all there is to it", but what happens when that energy becomes blocked or, even more worryingly, turns negative? Those who have discovered the energetic potency of crystals know exactly what to do and with a few handy hints, you too can harness the power of crystals. It's hard to imagine how a geometrically regular formed lump of homogeneous solid substance could change a life for the better but millions of people the world over have found that they do, simply by allowing them to assist in their flow of energy.

SO, HOW DO YOU BRING CRYSTALS INTO YOUR LIFE?

The answer is 'through daily rituals' and the good news is that it's incredibly easy to do. We all carry out little rituals day in day out, whether consciously or unconsciously, but these repeating behavioural patterns can easily take on magical significance if they are completed with crystals.

Find yourself flustered at work or easily distracted by the noisy telephone conversations on the neighbouring work station? By decluttering your desk and adding a piece of fluorite you can promote clarity and enhance your productivity. If you need a little pick-me-up, place some citrine by the front door and every time you leave the house, make sure you pop that joyous yellow crystal in your pocket for a happy and fun-filled day.

CRYSTALS EVERYWHERE!

Every aspect of your life can be improved by turning your daily activities into beautiful miniature crystal-infused ceremonies.

> "With a few handy hints, you too can harness the awesome power of crystals"

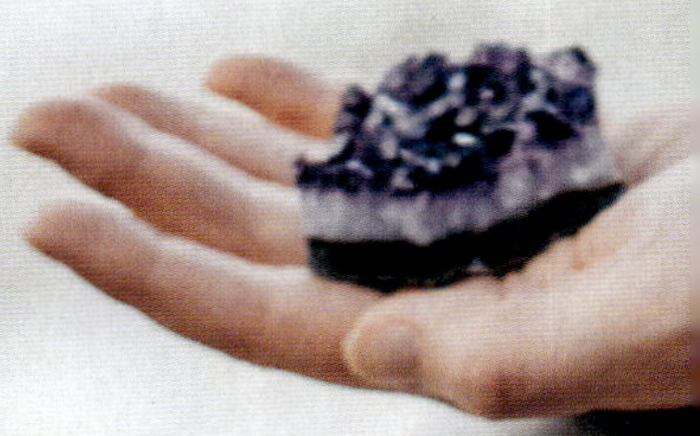

TIME TO GROUND

Find your focus by planting your feet firmly in the ground

Before you begin your daily crystal rituals, it's important that you take the time to ground yourself. Ideally you want to let your head float in the clouds while keeping your feet firmly planted on planet Earth! By grounding yourself you will be more focused, centred, and present in the here and now. When searching for an appropriate grounding crystal it's always best to look at those of a red, black or brown hue. Once you have chosen the perfect crystal, clasp it in your left hand and concentrate on the feel of it against your palm. As you breathe deeply, repeat the affirmation 'I am here, I am rooted and connected to the Earth, I am grounded'. Wear a smoky quartz against your skin to remain grounded all day long.

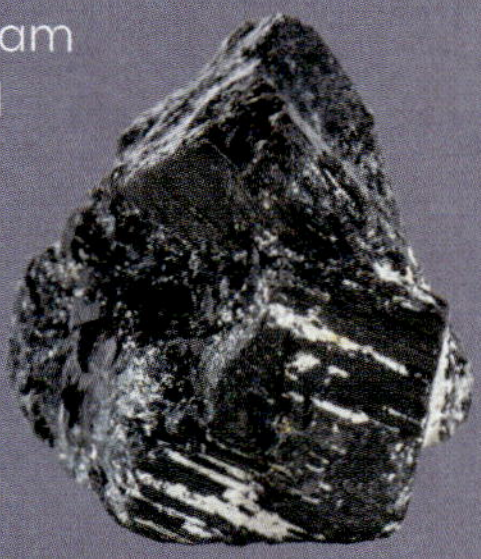

Also known as schorl, black tourmaline is the perfect crystal to ground yourself with – its strong energy can easily dispel negative vibrations

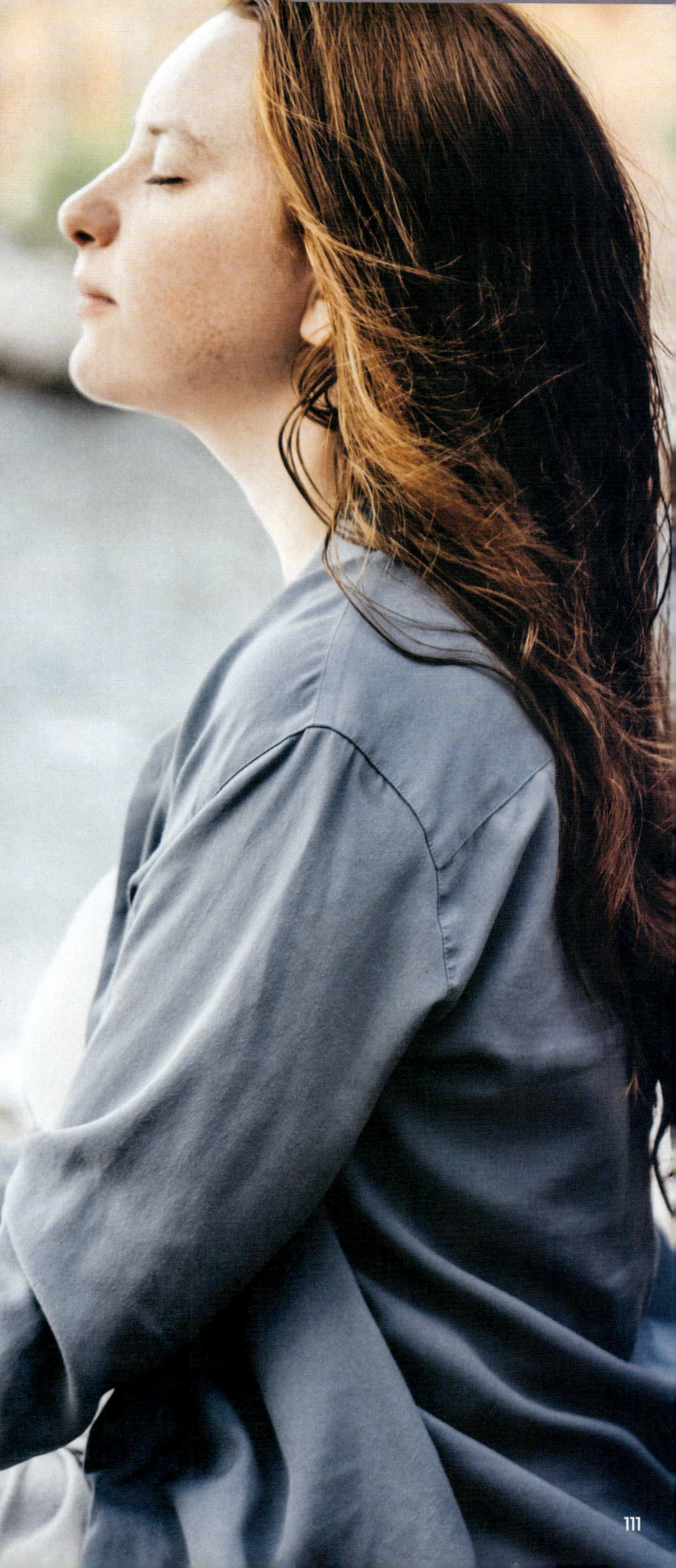

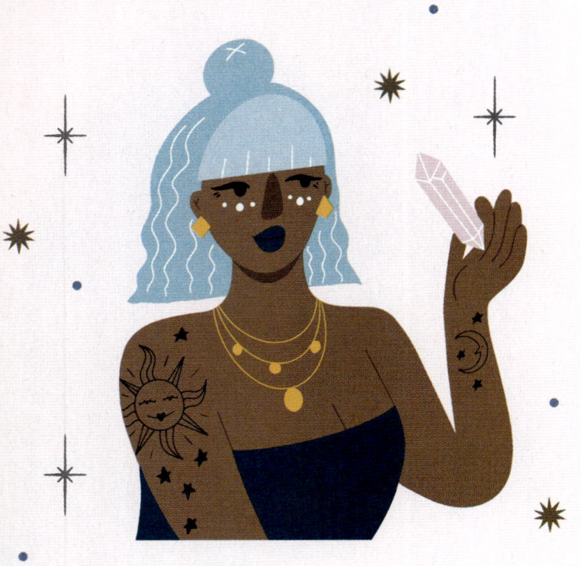

Meditating with CRYSTALS

Whether you are seeking spiritual enlightenment, wishing to harness Earth's natural powers or simply looking for some peace and tranquillity, meditation can help you achieve your goals. It could be argued that all you need to reach the threshold of inner peace is you and your ability to calm those ever-intrusive thoughts, but many people have discovered a way to enhance their meditation experience by incorporating crystals into their ritual. It is particularly useful for those who have never meditated before and need that extra boost to help them concentrate, not to mention the fact that everything is more beautiful and magical when crystals are involved!

While in a relaxed state, most people find that they are far more open to the world around them. The universe is a web of pulsing energy and as you drift into a meditative state you will become aware of this connectedness. Crystals act as a focal point, enabling you to pierce through the noise of everyday life. The right crystal can support your desires and help you to hear your inner voice. The power of the Earth will be amplified and, when you become more adept at quietening your thoughts, you may be fortunate enough to hear the 'voice' of your crystal. In this way you can let go of the unnecessary hubbub inside your brain and focus on what is truly important.

EVERYDAY RITUALS

How to invite the power of crystals into your everyday routines

• If you already do yoga then you know the calming benefits, but why not enhance the experience by incorporating crystals into your exercise regime? Place a beautiful amethyst on your yoga mat as you perform your relaxing movements. By adding crystals into your yoga ritual you will find that it amplifies the soothing aura.

• Everybody knows the importance of drinking enough water but by creating gem water you can turn a bland drink into an effortless crystal ritual. Simply pop some black tourmaline into a pitcher of fresh spring water and leave it in the fridge overnight. In the morning, take out the crystal and sip your elixir all day long to keep those negative energies at bay.

• Sometimes we need a confidence boost to get us ready to face the day. By warming an aragonite star cluster in your hand as you choose what you want to wear, the positive energy will infuse throughout your body and make it feel fabulous.

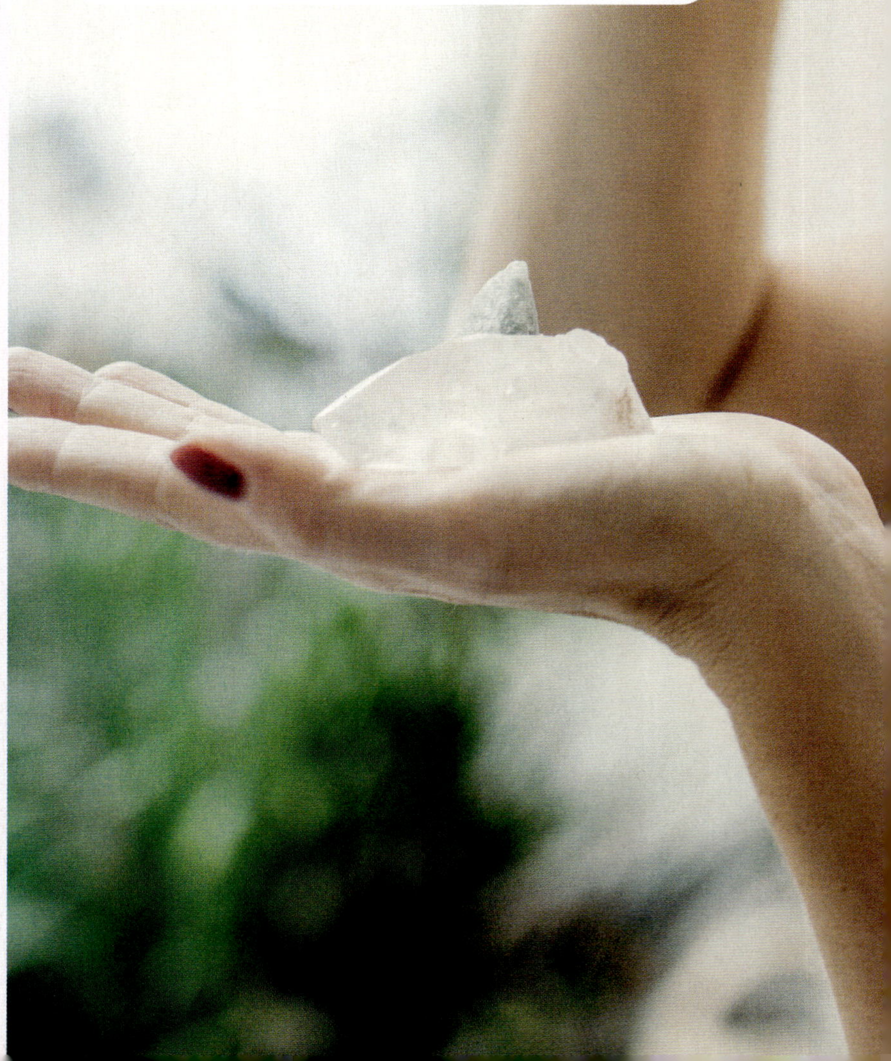

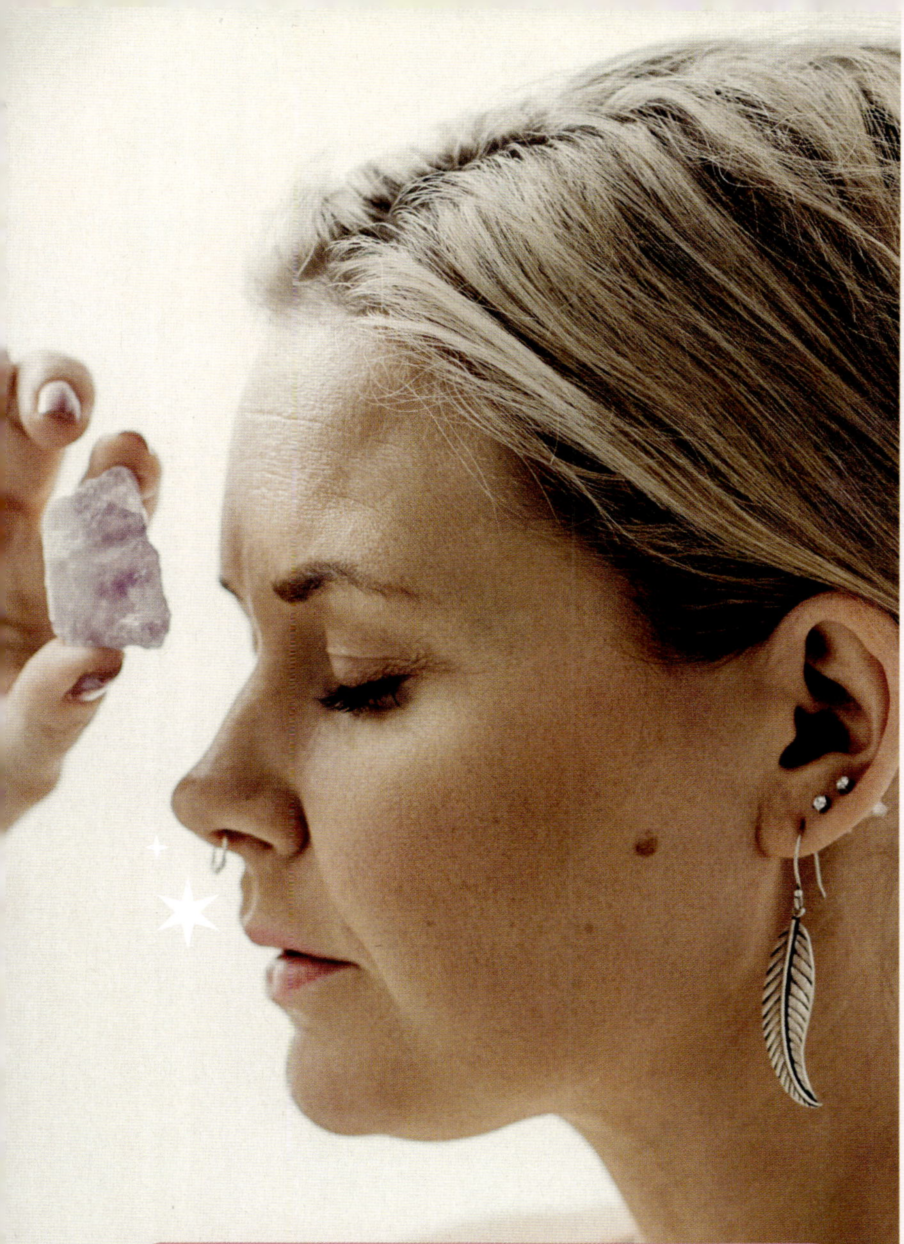

CHOOSING THE RIGHT CRYSTAL

Each gemstone has a unique set of properties that can be utilised for healing

Take time to pick the perfect crystal for your meditative needs since every crystal packs a different punch. Aventurine and smoky quartz will promote a sense of peace while also decreasing stress. Amethyst will heighten your intuition. Need pepping up? Focus on some selenite or citrine. If you're suffering from a broken heart or on the lookout for a new love then incorporate rose quartz into your meditation session. Make sure that you have chosen the crystal that aligns with your needs. If you are unsure, hover your hand over your collection and let the crystal choose you.

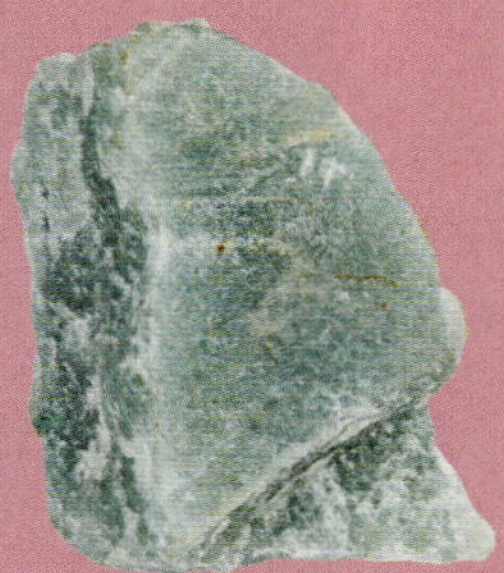

The delicate mint green aventurine will bring you inner peace

Try this simple exercise to meditate with crystals:

1 Choose an appropriate crystal. This will depend on your reasons for meditating. You should always ask your crystal for permission to work with it. You may initially feel self-conscious about this step but when you start connecting with your crystal, you will soon realise that it has a life of its own.

2 Cleanse your crystal, making sure that any residual energy from previous usage has been removed.

3 Find a quiet location where you can sit upon the ground and connect with the Earth.

4 Turn off your phone and make sure that no one will disturb you. This is YOUR time.

5 Allow your eyes to drift shut.

6 Think about your breathing and monitor it as you breathe in and out, in and out…

7 Clasp your crystal in your hand and gaze into its soul with your mind. Imagine you are looking into its very core, even though your eyes are shut.

8 Focus on your intentions but be receptive to the messages emanating from your crystal too.

9 When you are ready, reconnect with your breathing and gently open your eyes.

10 Don't forget to thank your crystal for sharing its energy with you.

CRYSTAL SPIRITS

Once you have become adept at meditating with crystals you may be able to connect with the spirit that lies within its heart. Each crystal has a personality and, with practice and perseverance, you can learn to hear the messages locked inside. Here is the best way to bond with your crystal spirit:

. Follow the basic steps to calm your inner voices.
. Now imagine that you are staring into the crystal.
. Push your way through the surface and start walking towards its centre.
. Imagine a door right at the heart.
. Focus until the door begins to open.
. Whoever steps through the door will be the crystal spirit.
. Make its acquaintance and know your crystal's true nature.

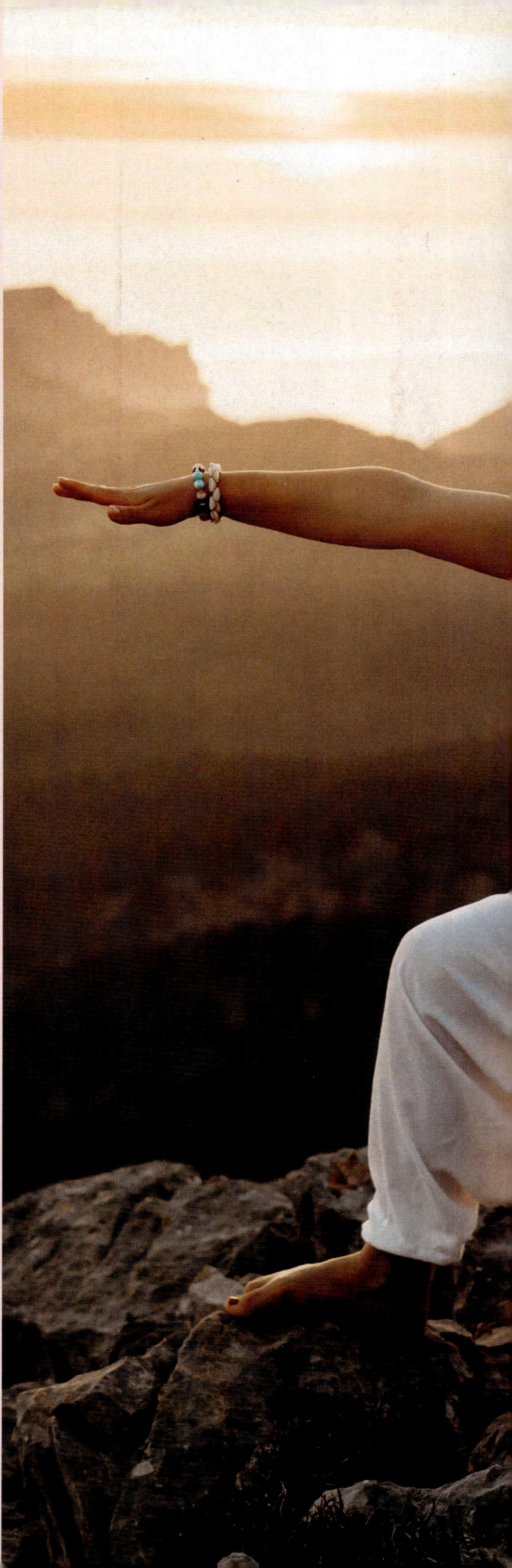

Spirituality & YOU

Future PLC Quay House, The Ambury, Bath, BA1 1UA

Bookazine Editorial
Editors **Alice Pattillo & April Madden**
Art Editor **Madelene King**
Head of Art & Design **Greg Whitaker**
Editorial Director **Jon White**
Managing Director **Grainne McKenna**

Cover Images
Getty Images

Photography
All copyrights and trademarks are recognised and respected

Advertising
Media packs are available on request
Commercial Director **Clare Dove**

International
Head of Print Licensing **Rachel Shaw**
licensing@futurenet.com
www.futurecontenthub.com

Circulation
Head of Newstrade **Tim Mathers**

Production
Head of Production **Mark Constance**
Production Project Manager **Matthew Eglinton**
Advertising Production Manager **Joanne Crosby**
Digital Editions Controller **Jason Hudson**
Production Managers **Keely Miller, Nola Cokely, Vivienne Calvert, Fran Twentyman**

Printed in the UK

Distributed by Marketforce – www.marketforce.co.uk
For enquiries, please email: mfcommunications@futurenet.com

Spirituality & You First Edition (LBZ6973)

FUTURE

Connectors.
Creators.
Experience Makers.

Future plc is a public company quoted on the London Stock Exchange (symbol: FUTR)
www.futureplc.com

Chief Executive Officer **Jon Steinberg**
Non-Executive Chairman **Richard Huntingford**
Chief Financial Officer **Sharjeel Suleman**

Tel +44 (0)1225 442 244

Widely Recycled

ipso. For press freedom with responsibility